A Talent
for Trouble

A Talent for Trouble

THE LIFE OF HOLLYWOOD'S MOST ACCLAIMED DIRECTOR,

William Wyler

JAN HERMAN

G. P. PUTNAM'S SONS

NEW YORK

G. P. PUTNAM'S SONS
Publishers Since 1838
200 Madison Avenue
New York, NY 10016

Library of Congress Cataloging-in-Publication Data
Herman, Jan, date.
      A talent for trouble : the life of Hollywood's most
acclaimed director, William Wyler / by Jan Herman.
            p.   cm.
      Includes bibliographical references and index.
      ISBN 0-399-14012-3 (acid-free paper)
      1. Wyler, William, 1902–1981.   I. Title.
PN1998.3.W95H47   1996
791.43'0233'092—dc20   95-22432 CIP

Book design by Julie Duquet
Photographs of William Wyler courtesy of the Wyler family

Printed in the United States of America
10   9   8   7   6   5   4   3   2   1

This book is printed on acid-free paper. ∞

For Janet
and Olivia

CONTENTS

No wreaths please—
especially no hothouse flowers.
Some common memento is better . . .

—William Carlos Williams

Prologue: Swing Gang

ONE DAY IN THE LATE SEVENTIES, Steven Spielberg took a solitary walk along the surf in Malibu looking for a particular house. When he found it, he knocked and hoped he wasn't presuming. The director he wanted to meet didn't know him personally and wasn't expecting him.

William Wyler came to the door. He recognized Spielberg at a glance. "Come on in," he said, not missing a beat. "Let's talk movies."

The disarming welcome made Hollywood's newest wunderkind feel as though he had arrived by special invitation. Years later, when asked why of all directors he had sought out William Wyler, Spielberg replied, "He was the best director on the beach. I sat there with everything but a microphone in my hand and asked him all the questions I possibly could."

Wyler's rise from youthful obscurity to master filmmaker has long been one of Hollywood's best-kept secrets. It is the paradoxical story of a maverick who had the force of personality and artistic genius to withstand the dictatorial embrace of the most ruggedly self-aggrandizing moguls and who yet became the quintessential director of Hollywood's Golden Age.

Regarded with only slight exaggeration as a man who couldn't make a flop, Wyler was an establishment star despite a lifelong talent for trouble that had Carl Laemmle, Sam Goldwyn, Louis B. Mayer, and Jack Warner gnashing their teeth. He was also the love of Bette Davis's life, Laurence Olivier's mentor, John Huston's best friend, Audrey Hepburn's discoverer, and Barbra Streisand's father figure.

Wyler arrived in Hollywood when he was nineteen years old and the movie colony was still an open-air circus on the outskirts of Los Angeles. His first picture, a silent Western filmed less than two weeks after he turned twenty-three, launched a directing career that has had few, if any, equals. It ranged from *Jezebel* and *Wuthering Heights* in the thirties to *The Little Foxes* and *The Best Years of Our Lives* in the forties, from *Roman Holiday* and *Ben-Hur* in the fifties to *The Collector* and *Funny Girl* in the sixties.

No Hollywood director had wider scope or better taste. None had a more intuitive approach to the subtleties of acting performances or went to the extremes he did to shape them. Wyler was, in the words of his confidante and frequent collaborator Lillian Hellman, "the greatest of all American directors." His pictures not only resonate with poetry and humor, they offer psychological maturity and sophisticated treatment of character more typical of literature than movies.

They have also won twice the number of Academy Awards as any other director's: thirty-eight. Similarly, the hundred and twenty-seven nominations they earned—half of them in the best picture, director, and acting categories—are not even remotely approached by Spielberg's, Billy Wilder's, or John Ford's, their closest competition. Wyler guided more actors to Academy Awards than anyone: thirteen, out of thirty-five nominations. And he himself won three Oscars, in addition to Hollywood's most prestigious prizes—the Irving G. Thalberg Award, the D. W. Griffith Award, and the American Film Institute Life Achievement Award.

Wyler used to say he started his directing career as an "assistant errand boy." It was no exaggeration. In 1922, at Universal Pictures' sprawling studio in the San Fernando Valley, he began on the swing gang sweeping sets at night. A quarter of a century later, the University of Southern California invited him to give the commencement address to the graduating class of its School of Cinema-Television. Wyler, who spoke three languages but never graduated from high school, called up his friend Robert Parrish, an Oscar-winning film editor, and asked him to lunch.

"I've just been offered what I think is an honor," Wyler said, "and I need your advice."

At Musso & Frank, the Hollywood hangout, they each ordered a Bloody Mary.

"Didn't you go to USC?" Wyler wanted to know.

Parrish, who'd recently become a director, said he had.

"What'll I say?" Wyler asked. "These kids are thirty years younger than I am."

"Tell 'em what it's like to direct Bette Davis, Humphrey Bogart and Laurence Olivier. Tell 'em what it's like to win Academy Awards. Tell 'em what it's like to argue with Sam Goldwyn."

Wyler grinned and sipped his Bloody Mary.

"That's all there is to it?"

"That's just bullshit to fill in the time," Parrish said. "After that you ask if they have any questions. They'll ask you about the change from silents to sound, who's the best cameraman you ever worked with, the best cutter, the best producer, the best writer. Then one of them will ask you the key question."

"What's that?"

"How do you become a director?"

Thirty minutes after Wyler took the podium at the commencement, Parrish remembers, a newly minted graduate stood up at the back of the auditorium and asked precisely that. The audience broke into loud applause.

"I've known many directors in my day," Wyler said, "some good, some bad, and lots in between. But I don't know of any who became directors in exactly the same way. Ernst Lubitsch, John Ford, Lewis Milestone, Jean Renoir, and others are great directors. I don't think any of them became great by following the same rules."

Then he launched into a streamlined version of events surrounding his arrival in America—all of it entertaining and most of it approximate. Like many of the film colony's early immigrants, he was born in Europe. When he got to his experience on the swing gang and how he made it up the Hollywood ladder, the audience was hanging on his words.

"Part of my job," he explained, "was to sweep the street in front of the cutting department. As I was doing this one night, I saw a man standing outside leaning against the building. He was the head of the cutting department, and he had an unlit cigarette in his mouth. He said, 'Got a match?' I said yes, because I smoked too. He lit his cigarette and offered me one. I lit mine and leaned against the building with him. After a while, he said, 'We can't smoke inside because we work with nitrate film and it's highly inflammable.' He thanked me for the match. I thanked him for the cigarette. And we went our separate ways."

The next time Wyler was on the night shift, he sneaked into the head cutter's room and set up a long-distance smoking arrangement.

"I got a piece of copper tubing from the machine shop, put an ivory cigarette holder on each end and ran it from the cutting bench, through the window, to the outside. I went out and lit a cigarette and put it in the cigarette holder on the end of the copper tube. Then I ran inside to the head cutter's bench and sucked until the smoke came through. It worked. You could now smoke in the cutting room and not blow up the studio."

When the head cutter discovered the setup, he sent for Wyler and offered him a job as an apprentice in the cutting department.

"I jumped at the chance. I liked the work, I learned fast, I kept the copper tube supplied with cigarettes and I was soon promoted to assistant cutter. Before I knew it, I was invited to address the graduating class."

Today, despite his extraordinary accomplishments, Wyler is hidden from view, almost as invisible as the cigarette from the cutter's bench. Even in Hollywood—where his work is admired by later filmmakers as different from each other as Clint Eastwood and Mike Nichols and where his reputation still flourishes among knowledgeable insiders—Wyler has been relegated to the distant past. His pictures, which were touchstones for an entire generation of moviegoers, are often mentioned and seen. But the man himself—gutsy, beguiling, unpretentious—is little known. This book, I hope, will change that.

—JAN HERMAN
August 1995

1

THE NAME SHOULD BE WILLI

IN THE ALSATIAN CITY OF MUL-
house on July 1, 1902—a Tuesday—Willy was born at home and immediately upset his parents' expectations, a habit he would perfect later on.
Melanie and Leopold Wyler were so eager to have a girl, after the birth
of a son not quite two years before, that the name "Camill" had already
been written on their second son's birth certificate in bold calligraphic
letters. Leopold went the following Thursday to the birth registry at
City Hall and had the name crossed out. He inserted a clause to read:
"Instead of 'Camill,' the name should be: Willi."

Years later, Wyler was dubbed William at Universal Pictures. "In Alsace," a studio executive noted, "Willy is a perfectly dignified and up-
standing name. In America, it is colloquial, diminutive and utterly
unimposing." Wyler went along with them for screen credits from the
time he began directing in the summer of 1925, when he turned out his
first six Westerns in six weeks. But he never legally changed his name,
and friends always called him Willy.

His older brother Robert had been born on September 25, 1900, at 8
rue de Metz, where Melanie and Leopold first lived in Mulhouse. By
the time Willy came along, they'd moved to larger quarters at 15 rue de

Zurich. Theirs was a block-long street lined on both sides by row houses with sloping roofs of black slate and alternating facades of gray stone and striped brickwork. The family had a second-floor apartment with high, shuttered windows, a small balcony where you could listen to the sounds of the Rhône Canal just two streets away, and a maid's room tucked beneath an ornamental spire on the fourth floor. The Wylers, who were Jewish, shared the building with a Protestant family below them and a Catholic family above them. This was a surprising ecumenical arrangement, because relations between Catholics and Jews were among the worst between any two groups in Alsace. Leopold's haberdashery was within ten minutes' walk. The central train station was even closer. At the far end of the street lay the rue de Bâle, a main thoroughfare leading out of the city toward Basel just over the Swiss border twenty miles to the south.

Willy's gender notwithstanding, Melanie took pleasure in dressing up her younger son as a girl on special occasions. A childhood photograph of Willy shows him gotten up as a three-year-old Empress Josephine in an exquisite white dress with layers of petticoats. A stylish ribbon and bow set off his shoulder-length curls, and an open fan is held with a certain delicacy in his tiny hand. If Willy resented his mother's fussing, there is no indication in the grave expression of his pudgy face. He gazes alertly but obediently at the camera. Robert stands next to him, a five-year-old Napoleon in a brass-buttoned uniform and three-cornered hat. He has a pair of campaign medals pinned to his chest and a sword with a tasseled handle at his waist. Apparently, no detail was too small to claim their mother's attention.

All the Wyler relatives knew of Melanie's "flair for the theatrical." Dora Picard, who lived in Basel and was two years younger than her cousin Willy, remembers it well. Throughout Dora's childhood she was invited to her aunt's "evenings at home." They were essentially children's costume parties presented with a refinement that gave them the ambience of kiddie soirees. "We would have dinner first," Picard recalls. "Then we would have a little play or a little concert. I remember Willy would get out his violin. Melanie loved to arrange these 'evenings.' She was very kind." Leopold rarely participated. He seemed to the young Dora a remote presence.

Leopold Wyler had come to Mulhouse from Switzerland on March 4, 1896. He was a small man with a stiff manner, a neatly clipped moustache and an owlish face. His steady, prosaic qualities served him well as a wholesale merchant of textiles and clothing. He opened a haberdashery shop on the choice downtown corner of rue du Sauvage and

Passage Central. Wyler offered merchandise equal to the best in Basel, where his brother, Armand, had an exclusive lingerie shop near the banks of the Rhine.

Leopold was born on March 19, 1864, in the Swiss village of Endingen, several miles from southern Germany. His father, Judas Wyler, and his mother, Rachel Dreyfus, had been married—hastily, it would seem—just six weeks before his birth. Various Wyler families had lived in the Jewish quarter of the village dating back before 1800.

Just how Leopold met Willy's mother, Melanie Auerbach, is a mystery. Possibly, theirs was an arranged marriage. They wed in Stuttgart on October 12, 1899. He was thirty-five years old, she twenty-one. The gap in ages aside, their temperaments could not have been more different. Melanie, full-figured and fair-skinned, had a magnetic personality. Unlike Leopold, who was silent but quick to anger, she had unusual warmth. Her blue eyes communicated lively intelligence as well as humor. By all accounts, she was attractive, outgoing and dynamic. When Melanie entered a room, everyone knew it.

"She was a poet," Poumy Moreuil, a cousin on the Wyler side of the family, recalls. "She was extraordinary. Leopold was ordinary. She had imagination, charm, joie de vivre. Willy took after her."

This was not only a family impression. The New York playwright Ruth Goetz met Wyler's mother in 1948 during a stay in Hollywood to collaborate on *The Heiress* with him. "She was one of the most cultivated women I ever met," Goetz recalls. "She had obviously been educated in a very good school. Her French was exquisite, much better than Willy's—and his was already excellent. She had read every bloody thing you could imagine. She knew Proust extremely well. She knew all the twentieth-century French literature. You could see that Willy was very much the son of a cultivated Central European woman."

Born in Stuttgart on June 8, 1878, Melanie came from a sprawling, middle-class family of assimilated German Jews. Relatives lived in Munich and in small towns from one end of Bavaria to the other. Many were highly educated, even locally prominent. Melanie's uncle Bertold Auerbach, who lived in nearby Freiburg, had an especially imposing history of literary and intellectual attainment. A Spinoza scholar, he was also the celebrated author of the early nineteenth-century *Black Forest Village Stories*.

Dora Picard believes Melanie's imagination spurred Willy's own, even when he went in for adolescent antics that would not have pleased his mother. She recalls that when Willy was sixteen, he once arrived at her home wearing a long, blond wig and asked to borrow a dress as well as a bonnet. "Willy looked like a floozie," Picard recounted. "It was very funny. This was something out of the ordinary. Of course, he wanted me to dress as a boy. So I did. I put on his clothes." They went to a local street carnival, where they sat for a photograph with her sister and one of Willy's boyhood friends. It shows Willy with his hands held primly in his lap while the faint smugness of a Gioconda smile plays on his lips.

Willy did not excel in school. Perhaps to avoid comparison with his older brother at Le Petit Lycée on the rue Jacques Preiss, he simply did not apply himself. Willy's sharp intelligence was apparent, but he always had a knack for getting into trouble. "I don't know why," Wyler once said, recalling his youth. "I wasn't consciously rebelling. I think I was just showing off. Other kids would laugh and say, 'Oh, that Willy! He's a terrific cutup!' That would make me feel important." A close childhood friend, Edmond Cahen, remembered a very young Willy eating a goldfish on a dare. Another friend, Paul Jacob, recalled Willy going out of his way to test the ice on a pond in the Parc du Tivoli and falling in.

When Willy learned to swim the breaststroke for the first time at age ten, someone dared him to cross the river that flows through the center of Mulhouse and becomes a canal near the school he attended. He plunged into the water where the canal was narrowest and struggled to the other bank. He didn't get home until long past dark, however, causing a panic in the neighborhood. When he finally showed up, his clothes still wet, Melanie nearly collapsed with relief.

Willy's mother was always being terrified by him, especially by his love of heights. While preparing dinner one day, she looked up from the kitchen counter to see his head bobbing in the second-story window. Willy had scaled the outside wall of the building. But his escapades at a favorite childhood haunt, the deeply wooded zoo overlooking the town from a small mountain beyond the train station, were the most hair-raising stunts of all.

"The zoo was very important to Willy because it had a bear pit," said Talli Wyler, recalling a story about her husband that became legend in the Wyler family. "As a little kid he would go to the bear pit and walk around it on top of the railings that fenced it off. He'd sort of teeter there. He apparently did this many times, not just once. But one time his cap fell in and it was torn to pieces by the bear. Someone rushed home and told his mother. When he got home, she was furious. She absolutely adored Willy, but he was driving her to distraction. She told his father: 'Beat him! Beat him! Beat him!' She just couldn't stand what this kid was doing to her."

In fact, the great heartache of those years for Melanie turned out not to be Willy but rather her third son, Gaston, through no fault of his own. Within months after his birth on September 27, 1907, it became clear that he suffered from some form of mental retardation. Gaston lived with Leopold and Melanie on and off, and sometimes with his brothers, until his death at forty-one.

WHEN WILLY WAS SEVEN-AND-A-HALF YEARS OLD, HIS FATHER came home one evening in November 1909 with startling news. It had happened a few doors from his shop. The band at the elegant Hotel Central, which was the favorite billet of the town's German officers, had played "The Marseillaise," the French national anthem. The Kaiser's song "Heil Dir im Sieger-Kranz" had, in the meantime, been greeted by boos.

The Kaiser, on hearing of the incident, was furious. His top military commanders had long considered Alsace-Lorraine, lying between France and Germany, to be the most strategically vulnerable of the Reichland territories. Even in 1910, four decades after its annexation to the Reich following the French defeat in the Franco-Prussian war, Alsace-Lorraine had more German soldiers stationed there than any other region of the German empire: roughly ninety thousand troops. That came to a sixth of the entire German Army and virtually equalled the population of Mulhouse.

To Willy's taciturn, middle-aged father—who spoke German and preferred with good reason to keep his politics to himself—the incident did not augur well. He heard rumors that the hotel band had been bribed to play "The Marseillaise." The next day, a German general placed the hotel off limits to all army personnel but had to rescind the order several weeks later because his officers missed their comforts. The Hôtel Central provided luxurious accommodations, after all. Its grand salon could serve two hundred and fifty guests. With billiard rooms, newspapers delivered from the capitals of Europe and a private fleet of carriages going to and from the train station, the hotel lent life in the provinces the sort of cosmopolitan atmosphere deemed suitable for the morale of the aristocratic officer corps.

What came to be called "the Mulhouse affair" sounds today like a scene out of *Casablanca*. The Kaiser's favorite newspaper, *Correspondenz Wedekind*, described all of Alsace as "a wasp's nest of anti-German agitation." But the confrontation had more significance as a symbol of pro-French sentiment than as any realistic threat to the authorities. Other confrontations were more serious. Gravest of all was "the Saverne affair," despite similar comic operetta trappings. A German lieutenant insulted his Alsatian recruits with an ethnic slur. Testy exchanges resulted between military patrols and civilians on the village streets of Saverne, culminating in a wave of ludicrous arrests. A baker's apprentice was detained for laughing at German officers, a bank clerk for suspicion of laughing. Boys scarcely older than Willy were threatened with arrest.

Seen from Leopold Wyler's point of view, the greatest irony in all of this came down to the fact that the Alsatians were distrusted on both sides: by France no less than Germany. He had not forgotten the explosion of hatred that erupted just before he arrived in Mulhouse. Captain Alfred Dreyfus—born and raised in Mulhouse and the first Jewish officer to serve on the General Staff of the French Army—had been falsely accused and convicted of spying for Germany. After Dreyfus's release from Devils Island a decade later, in 1905, the hatred he engendered was still pervasive. Anti-Alsatian feeling among the French had been exceeded only by their rabid anti-Semitism. Mulhouse, like many cities across France, had a virulent group of anti-Semites dedicated to memorializing the French colonel who forged the documents used to convict Dreyfus.

Even within the small Jewish community, where political loyalties were subject to doubt, all sorts of animosities ran deeply. Of the twenty-three hundred Jews who lived in Mulhouse in 1910, a significant number had come from Germany after the Franco-Prussian war, seeking refuge from officially sanctioned anti-Semitism within the Reich. In Alsace-Lorraine, where Jews had been emancipated under the republican laws of France, anti-Semitism at least had no legal standing—even if it was socially approved. The German-Jewish immigrants replaced many of the native Alsatian Jews who had departed in fear of the German takeover. The cultural, linguistic and economic divisions between the Jews who remained and the new immigrants triggered bitter internecine clashes.

The Wyler family spoke German at home, principally because of Leopold. But Melanie pressed the boys to converse in French as much as their fluency would allow. Her Francophilia echoed prevailing sentiment and widespread practice. Cultural resistance to the official "Germanization" of Alsace was common, including opposition to linguistic regulation in the schools. Middle-class families who could afford it— Jews and non-Jews alike—routinely provided their children with French lessons after school. The upper stratum of the Alsatian Jewish community also had a long tradition of sending its sons and daughters to boarding schools outside the annexed provinces for total immersion in a French education.

For all Leopold's success in business, Melanie came to believe that Mulhouse held little promise for their two older sons. She wrote to relatives of her fears. "We always had detailed letters," Picard recalled. "We hoped maybe she was mistaken." At first it seemed so, "the affair" at the Hotel Central notwithstanding. By 1911 a new constitution for Alsace-Lorraine appeared to signal major political reform. But two years later the German authorities tried to suppress French-language newspapers and reimposed a ban on any organization believed to have "anti-German tendencies." Within months, Melanie prevailed upon Leopold to send Robert and Willy to school in French-speaking Switzerland.

Leopold's Swiss birth conferred automatic Swiss citizenship on his sons. The plan was for Robert, not yet fourteen years old, to go first. He would be followed by eleven-year-old Willy. In the winter of 1914, the Wylers left Mulhouse to stay with relatives in Endingen, while Melanie sought a school. And on May 20, 1914—two and a half months before Germany declared war on France—Robert was enrolled at the Institut Bloch, an expensive boarding school in Lausanne for Jewish boys of various European nationalities.

Robert lived there for the next five years, according to the Lausanne city archives, along with two dozen other boys who found themselves similarly cut off from their families by the outbreak of World War I. Willy, who had returned to Mulhouse with his parents, was forced to spend the war at home. But even with the eventual defeat of Germany and the restoration of Alsace to France, Melanie would remain convinced that Willy's future lay elsewhere. In the meantime, life on rue de Zurich shed its usual routine and took on the quality of a bizarre dream.

2

A Kid's Point of View

Less than a week after German troops invaded Belgium on August 3, 1914, the French took Mulhouse without firing a shot. An assault force had been detached from the French First Army for the liberation of the city. Accompanied by the cavalry, the French Army entered Mulhouse on August 8, an hour or so after the Germans simply withdrew. Willy and his family emerged from their cellar, where they'd been told to take cover, and went with the rest of their neighbors to welcome their liberators on the rue de Bâle. As the soldiers marched by, singing "The Marseillaise," Willy was crestfallen to discover that the French infantryman didn't cut much of a military figure. "I noticed they weren't even carrying their rifles on the same shoulders," he said many years later. "And they had poppies in the muzzles of their guns. They'd picked them from these huge fields near town. Like any good little German, I'd been taught in school to admire efficiency and discipline. It took me a while to realize what was important."

At City Hall crowds gathered in the square to observe the momentous change in their status. Officials lowered the imperial German flag. Then, to the accompaniment of the French national anthem, they raised the tricolor for the first time in forty-three years. A military band played

"Sambre et Meuse." The cavalry in shiny battle armor and horsehair plumes passed in review. But soon after dawn the next day, the sound of artillery shells and distant gunfire announced that the first fierce struggle for Mulhouse had begun.

The German Seventh Army sent reinforcements from Strasbourg to deploy around the city. Willy and his family found themselves again taking cover. "When the battle broke out, the three families in our house went down to the cellar," he recalled. "So there we were—Catholic, Protestant and Jewish—all in the middle of the cellar praying in our different ways. We could hear shooting outside. There was a kid from one of the other families, and the two of us tried to look out the cellar window. We had to climb up on a pile of coal or something. All we could see were feet going back and forth. One time a soldier fell right in front of the window, and we couldn't see anything. So we got hold of a broomstick and shoved it through the grating. We pushed him away, then rolled him over so we could watch the battle."

Shelling stopped on August 10. The French, fearing encirclement, retreated about twenty miles southwest of Mulhouse. The Germans reoccupied the city. But the struggle was far from over. The French Army cashiered the local commander, reinforced his troops and ordered a fresh attack. Within four days renewed shelling began. Before August ended, Mulhouse changed hands several times. "We'd spend the night in the cellar until the battle was over," he recalled. "Then we'd come out in the morning to see whether we were French or German." Each time the same performance took place in front of City Hall. Both sides repeated the ceremony: Down came the enemy's flag, up went its own. Depending on whose victory it was, the band played "The Marseillaise" or "Die Wacht am Rhein," the German hymn to the Western troops. "We used to stand outside in front of our house when the armies went by—French or German, it made no difference—and we'd hand them cups of coffee," he remembered. "My mother would get them something to eat, a tartine or a piece of cake. I'd give the coffee cup to a soldier and trot with him till he had drunk up so I could bring back the cup. All the kids in the neighborhood did this."

By September, the Germans reoccupied Mulhouse and held onto it until the end of the war. They established their trenches just west and south of the city, built an electrified wire fence snaking through the suburbs around the city and choked off all traffic except through military checkpoints. Since the front was only a few miles away, Willy could see the flares at night and the big guns going off. Mulhouse had a blackout that lasted four years.

When he wasn't at school, Willy hung around the main railway station and the Altkirch Bridge that crossed the train tracks near his house. He watched the troop transports arrive with fresh soldiers and depart with the wounded. Sometimes, from his rooftop, he witnessed dogfights as German planes engaged Allied bombers heading over the city toward Germany. In one spectacular aerial combat, he saw a plane shot down so close to his house that he reached the wreck in a nearby field before anybody else. It turned out to be a French fighter. The pilot was dead in the cockpit. Willy cut a piece of canvas from the airplane wing, a rare souvenir possessed by no other boy he knew.

His French lessons came to an end when the Germans made it illegal to speak the language in 1915. But Thursday afternoons were still devoted to violin lessons. "Willy is no Eugene Ysaye," his teacher liked to joke, referring to the famous Belgian virtuoso. "But he has an ear for music. Now if only he would practice with his fingers." Melanie started a vegetable garden after the authorities introduced food rationing, and she continued going with Willy to the movies, a habit they'd developed not long before the war.

Mulhouse had at least three movie houses. The privations of war somehow did not interfere with them. The only difference for Melanie was that now, in Robert's absence, Willy became her movie companion. Her taste ran to Asta Nielsen, the Danish actress who achieved enormous popularity playing fallen women in German-made silents. It is a measure of Melanie's openness that she took Willy to see them. By the standards of the time, if not by ours, they were risqué sex dramas. *Die Arme Jenny*, which they'd seen in 1912, featured Nielsen as a scullery maid who turns to street walking after her caddish lover betrays her. *Engelein*, seen the following year, showed her as a droll, sultry, teenage vamp whose uncle falls in love with her.

Willy's own taste ran to the action serials epitomized by *Fantômas*, his favorite. Made by Louis Feuillade and issued between 1911 and 1913, the popular series traced the exploits of Fantômas, the Emperor of Crime. He wore a mask and black tights and was a master of disguises. He invariably outwitted detectives and reporters, his two chief enemies, leading them on chases through secret doors and hidden chambers and leaving behind so many false leads that the audience, too, was likely to be baffled.

The French literary surrealists Louis Aragon and André Breton and the Spanish filmmaker Luis Buñuel discovered Feuillade in the twenties. He was then forgotten and rediscovered in the thirties by film archivist Henri Langlois, whose Cinémathèque Française resurrected

him in the forties for the edification of the future *nouvelle vague* auteurists. Alain Resnais, among them, praised Feuillade's "prodigious poetic instinct for surrealism," declaring him the artistic equal of D. W.
Griffith. The irony is that Feuillade regarded himself strictly as a commercial craftsman. "He had no artistic pretensions and disapproved of
cinema aesthetes," film historian David Robinson has noted. Moreover,
the same auteurists who admired Feuillade later disparaged Wyler as
the ultimate Hollywood craftsman, painting him unfairly as a corporate
filmmaker because of his commercial success.

In addition to movies, Willy now began attending concerts, stage
plays and operas as never before. Despite the war, productions came to
Mulhouse in a steady stream from larger cities like Frankfurt and
Stuttgart. With the front stabilized, the military command saw fit to encourage whatever German culture could be imported for their own di-
version as well as the public's. Sometimes the army itself offered
amateur productions of classic plays. But most often, Willy went to the
professional productions staged at the Mulhouse Municipal Theater or
the outdoor presentations at the Zoological Gardens and the summer
theater in Badenweiler, near the Black Forest, where the Wyler family
still spent vacations.

"We had some of the best opera companies," he remembered. "Everything was shown. My mother always got me to go to the theater and to
all the operas. I sat there fascinated."

More than a decade later, when Wyler completed his apprenticeship
as a director of silent Westerns, he would gravitate to theatrical material. During the thirties alone, seven of his movies were based on plays.
At the time, Hollywood naturally looked to Broadway for premade material. But his passion for theater went beyond the ordinary. His familiarity with it from adolescence on bred a sense of its strengths and
weaknesses as a medium. He would draw upon it with intuitive skill and
evident confidence, consistently transferring plays to the screen with
greater mastery than any other Hollywood director of the period.

THE WORST PRIVATION OF THE WAR YEARS, PARTICULARLY FOR
Melanie, was Robert's absence. Although Lausanne was little more than
a hundred miles away in neutral Switzerland, it might as well have been
on the other side of the world. The Wylers, despite their Swiss passports, could not cross the border without some risk of being refused
reentry to Alsace. Willy, too, experienced certain privations because of
the war. His older brother had had an extravagant prewar bar mitzvah

to mark the arrival of Jewish manhood at age thirteen. By contrast, Willy's celebration was an inconspicuous affair, coming as it did during the summer of 1915.

The war raged on, decimating troops and civilian populations on both sides even while grinding to a stalemate on the battlefield. But with the landing of American troops in France by June 1917, the military balance began to tip in favor of the Allies. It took another year, however, before certain defeat loomed for the Central Powers. At last on November 11, 1918, according to the terms of an armistice dictated by the French, all the guns on the Western front fell silent.

The liberation of Mulhouse occurred five days after the armistice, and had no military significance. But it was far from an anticlimax when French troops, led by officers on horseback, marched into town on a Saturday afternoon. Crowds lined the streets, waving flags cut from bedsheets and pillowcases because cotton cloth was so scarce. The homemade flags — American, British, Belgian, Italian and, of course, the French tricolor — hung from virtually every window.

The Mulhouse newspaper recorded a wildly happy scene: "The troops passed through rows and rows of cheering people. Everyone was shouting 'Vive la France!' and waving their handkerchiefs. Flowers rained down on the soldiers from windows and balconies. Young boys climbed onto passing gun carriages and straddled the artillery cannons. Seeing officers and soldiers holding hands with children was immensely touching. It never occurred to the Germans to fraternize this way. The French know how to speak to the heart of the population."

Many in the city had suffered reprisals for their French sympathies during the war. "After the defeat of the Germans the whole population went crazy," Wyler recounted. "They were in a furor. I was with a bunch of kids who went after German officers in the street. We harassed them, terrorized them like gangs." The mob's anger spent itself in a matter of days, however, eclipsed by the arrival of American troops, which lent an exotic note to the liberation.

"All the kids went out into the streets looking to bring an American home for dinner," he remembered. "We didn't have much to offer in the way of food. But we made whatever we had. I found this big black fellow. There used to be one black man in Mulhouse, the doorman at one of the movie theaters. We used to take a detour from school just to look at him. Well, I brought this black American soldier home and another Jewish fellow from New York who spoke a little Yiddish. We didn't really speak Yiddish, but it was all very exciting from a kid's point of view."

Willy preferred the Americans of all the soldiers because of their easygoing camaraderie—so much so that at one point he spent three days nosing around with a pair of them "on reconnaissance." His memory of driving through the outskirts of Mulhouse in their truck, employed as a local scout while they explored the battle-scarred vicinity, lingered like a sentimental emblem of some vanished childhood friendship.

3

~~~~~~~~~~~~

TROUBLEMAKER

With the end of the war in 1918, Willy was free to join his older brother at the Institut Bloch in Lausanne, and Melanie was determined to see that he did. Regardless of the expense, she believed Willy needed the discipline of intensive schooling if he were to amount to anything. Robert had not only done well, showing particular promise in mathematics, but he had become completely fluent in French. Further, the headmaster, Benjamin Bloch-Katz, had the reputation of being a stern disciplinarian. That too would be beneficial for Willy, she believed. His extroverted nature, like hers, made him popular. But he had a streak of wildness in him, which drew angry if ineffectual disapproval from Leopold and sometimes drove Melanie to tears. She hoped the change of atmosphere, besides engaging Willy's interest, would subdue his unruliness.

By this time Willy was almost fully grown. Stockily built, he had nearly reached his adult height of five feet seven inches. He had thick curly brown hair, a largish nose, twinkling hazel eyes and an impish, gap-toothed grin. Despite his early maturity, however, there was nothing physically prepossessing about him. You could never have called him handsome. Yet even then he had an earthiness, a temperament that would make him, as Lillian Hellman said years later, "an absolute charmer with the ladies." While not yet the insouciant figure he would become in his Hollywood bachelor days, giving orders on a sound stage with quiet assurance and a cigarette perpetually dangling from his lower lip, he was already flirtatious and self-deprecating. His dry and wicked sense of humor made him most appealing.

Apart from its attraction as a quaint year-round resort with steep mountain streets, the city of Lausanne was known throughout Europe for its excellent boarding schools. They catered to a privileged international clientele ranging from the extremely wealthy to the merely upper middle-class. The Institut Bloch, which had been established in 1902, occupied a stately mansion known as the Villa Grammont on a quiet, rustic lane just off the avenue des Alpes. Its four stories overlooked Lake Geneva in the distance from a graceful neighborhood resplendent with such villas, all of them ensconced behind tall pines, manicured hedges and wrought-iron gates. Classified by the city as "a Jewish institute for boys," Bloch's establishment had room for about two dozen boarders.

The period Wyler spent in Lausanne was among the fondest chapters of his youth, despite the difficulties he would encounter there. Later, he tended to embroider on its excitement, as he did the short time spent soon afterward in Paris. You might almost have thought from Wyler family lore that his Swiss education took years. In fact, Willy's stay in Lausanne lasted fewer than ten months. But the time proved to be a defining experience in terms of his clash with authority, which, to Melanie's chagrin, brought about his dismissal from Bloch's premises. It also tested Willy's independent character and, though indirectly, set him on the unorthodox path that eventually led to Hollywood.

Dora Picard remembers Willy and Melanie arriving by train in Basel on their way to Lausanne during the winter after the war. Records indicate that he registered as a boarder at the Institut Bloch on March 1, 1919. He had already completed two years of a rather undemanding business curriculum at the École de Commerce in Mulhouse. The plan now was for him to live at Bloch's, perfect his French and enter a higher school division: Lausanne's École Supérieure de Commerce.

Willy crammed for two months with Robert's help and on April 28 enrolled at the École Supérieure. Fortunately, he did not have to pass an entrance exam but simply entered a class reserved for German-speaking transfer students. If the eighty-two-year-old school was not the most exacting educational institution in Lausanne, its imposing new edifice was second to none. Designed to inspire awe, the building had opened in

1915 at a cost of nearly a million francs and looked like a huge neoclassi-
cal wedding cake. It was attended by eight hundred students of both
sexes.

As usual Robert's scholastic record was far superior to Willy's. He
had entered Lausanne's elite public high school—the Collège Scientifique—for future engineers and mathematicians. But he continued to
board at Bloch's until May 1919. Thus, less than two months after Willy
arrived in Lausanne, Robert was already on his way elsewhere, returning to Mulhouse in June and entering university at Zurich's Technische
Hochschule in the fall.

Before Robert left Lausanne, he introduced Willy to his circle of high
school friends. Among them were René and Bruno Traveletti, sons of a
well-to-do civil engineer. They would room with Willy three years later
in Hollywood. The Traveletti brothers usually got together with Willy
to play tennis on weekends. Because there weren't any public courts,
they would rent a court at the chic Hôtel Alexandra for a few cents
an hour. "Tennis was actually a glamorous name for what we played,"
Bruno recounted. "None of us were any good."

Robert had become especially close to René during the war. In the
summers and on holidays, when Robert couldn't go home to Mulhouse,
he stayed with the Traveletti brothers at their family's mountain chalet
near the Wiermat. Now Willy was invited there, too. More often, they
socialized at the chaperoned parties thrown by one boarding school or
another. In their immediate circle were Alex Manuel, a handsome
would-be stunt man from a wealthy family who would also room with
Willy in Hollywood, and Blanche Brunswig, a distant cousin Willy already knew from childhood, whose ravishing beauty by various accounts turned the heads of many young men. Indeed, Willy himself
would become infatuated with Blanche a decade later on a return visit
to Europe in 1930 as a rising American director. The two of them would
exchange torrid letters and begin a secret affair.

For entertainment, there were plays at the Théâtre Municipal and
lectures by musicians and writers. Jean Cocteau, André Gide and Igor
Stravinsky were all invited to speak to the arts fraternity at the University of Lausanne by the precocious Maurice Abravanel. "Willy was part
of our little social group," said Abravanel, who would become an inter-
nationally known conductor. "I was a little younger but already well
ahead of him in school. I realized even then that he was an artistic fellow. I introduced chamber music to the fraternity, and we did an Offen-
bach operetta one night. He liked it very much. But the big story that
went around about Willy was that he did not like what his headmaster

said to him, and he threatened to throw the headmaster out the window. That was an accepted story."

In fact, the clashes between student and headmaster became so intolerable that Willy was dismissed from the Institut Bloch toward the middle of July. "I was kicked out and they wrote to my mother to come get me because I had made trouble," Wyler recalled. Before Melanie even received the letter of dismissal, Willy packed up his belongings and hauled them out of the villa onto the street. "He bought a cart for two francs from a little boy and put all his stuff in it," Blanche recalled. "I'll never forget, he pulled it up the hill to our house and said, 'Well, here I am. Where do I live now?' He was a wonderful fellow but always full of mischief. He wanted to strangle the owner of that school."

Blanche's mother took Willy in and found a place for him at a boys' boarding house known as "The Monastery." It stood at the edge of a large sylvan park with a lake. Name notwithstanding, the Monastery was a pleasure dome compared to Bloch's. As Willy soon discovered, an upstairs window peeked over a wall into the courtyard of an exclusive finishing school for girls.

"Very proper," Wyler recalled years later. "The girls were not allowed out of the grounds alone. Chaperoned all the time." The Monastery's adolescent boarders had been sneaking upstairs nightly, trying to catch sight of naked girls in the dormitory across the courtyard—but without success. Willy sized up the situation and decided that stealth was the wrong stratagem. They needed to be more inventive. Since one of the boys was a natural with electrical gadgets, why not have him string together a series of light bulbs? They could lower them from the window into the courtyard and flick them on at a crucial moment. The sudden burst of light would catch the girls' attention and, with any luck, they'd come rushing to their windows just as they were preparing for bed. "The prank worked," Wyler recalled, "except for one thing. All the girls came running in their nightgowns."

While living at the Monastery, Willy began going to the Cinéma-Théâtre Lumen with Alex Manuel from the Collège Scientifique. Both were drawn by the riveting screen stunts of the early silent pictures. Manuel had even begun testing his own daredevil skills. He often walked the iron handrail of the Pont Bessières, the city's newest land bridge, one hundred fifty feet above a steep ravine. "Manuel did all kinds of stuff like that," Bruno Traveletti recalled. "Stunts were his hobby." Willy also frequented the Lumen with his roommates from the Monastery for the latest Charlie Chaplin movies. As the largest and most elegant of Lausanne's five movie theaters, the Lumen got the choice bookings. Deceptively plain from the outside, its interior resembled an ornate opera house with three luxurious tiers totaling a thousand seats.

"There were a few of us who were particularly eager about Chaplin," Wyler recalled. "When a new picture of his came out we'd rush over to see it. We'd go about a half hour before the picture would start. We'd take loge seats — spent our entire weekly allowance on loge seats. And we'd just sit there looking at the blank screen. Pretty soon one of us would start chuckling, another would start grinning, another would start laughing until we were all in stitches. Nothing had happened yet. The picture hadn't even come on."

School held no such allure. By the fall of 1919 Willy was totally bored with his classes. Only five months after he had enrolled at the École Supérieure de Commerce, he knew he would not be able to last long enough to qualify for the minimum two-year certificate, let alone the four-year diploma. In letters to his mother he let her down gently, noting that perhaps he'd be better off continuing his studies elsewhere. "I had this idea I wanted to go to Paris, to the École des Hautes Études Commerciales," Wyler said. "My mother was for it." His father, however, had another idea: Willy, who was now seventeen, would be better off coming home to work for him.

Willy hesitated at the thought. The prospect of one day taking over his father's haberdashery shop was implicit in the proposition. That appealed to him no more than his high school regimen. And so he stayed on in Lausanne through the fall. Finally, on December 12, he left the École Supérieure without completing his studies. After a brief winter holiday spent with the Traveletti brothers at their country chalet, he took the train back to Mulhouse three days before Christmas, 1919, hoping to persuade his father that going to Paris held more promise than going to work in the shop.

4

⋙⋙≡⋙⋙

His Mother's Sorrow

WHEN WILLY CAME HOME, HIS family no longer lived on rue de Zurich. Leopold and Melanie had bought a two-story house with a garden not far from the old apartment. They now lived in a neighborhood dotted with parks on the other side of the Rhône Canal. Robert had gone off to Zurich. As an engineering student, his future seemed mapped out. There was no question about his having to follow Leopold into the family business. Willy, on the other hand, appeared to have no choice for the moment. Before he could persuade his father otherwise, he would have to live down his bad-boy reputation. And so, during the winter of 1920, he did not object to working in the shop, learning how to sell ties and cuff links.

That Willy had a reputation to live down there can be little doubt. His habitual misbehavior had led his mother to fear the worst. The light bulb episode at the Monastery had not escaped her notice, indeed had rattled her faith in Willy. Free spirit though she was, Melanie shared the era's prudishness about adolescent sexual stirrings. Poumy Moreuil recalled from a visit to Mulhouse that winter as a girl of nine that everyone seemed on edge about his escapades. Poumy and her mother were sitting in the downstairs parlor when she got a sense of the cloud he was

under. Blanche's mother, Fleur, was also visiting from Lausanne with
Blanche, who was upstairs with Willy. Suddenly all the lights in the
house went out.

Melanie fairly leaped out of her chair. "Mon Dieu! They're alone up
there!"

"Yes," Fleur replied drily. "But what are you worried about? It's my
daughter he's with."

Nevertheless, the cloud began to lift. After three months at the shop,
which he regarded as penance for his school failure, Willy acquired a
certain finesse with the customers. Leopold himself pointed out that his
son wasn't a bad salesman. What he needed now was to broaden his retail experience with the sort of training only a large department store
could provide. Leopold took him to Paris and introduced him around
the wholesale circuit.

As long as going to work in a department store meant remaining in
Paris on his own, Willy was very happy to give up the idea of school.
And by mid-April his father found him a bottom-rung job in Charenton,
a blue-collar suburb on the southeast side of the city at a retail store that
sold ready-made clothes and goods on the street. Willy put out the man-
nequins and did the sweeping. He lived near the Gare du Nord across
the city, so it took him nearly an hour to get to work. He would leave by
seven in the morning and get home by eight in the evening. "Finally, I
got fed up and told off the boss," he recalled. "I said something really
nasty. He wasn't happy about that, and he kicked me out the door."

Willy kept the news of his firing to himself. He hadn't been on the job
for more than a few weeks. He went looking for another at a chain
called "100,000 Shirts," and was hired to clean and sweep in one of its
branch stores near Les Halles, the working-class market at the center of
Paris. His salary came to two hundred francs a month, or about eight
dollars. Because he had some experience selling ties and cuff links, the
boss soon put him in charge of "the department of collars, ties and cuff
links." In reality it was nothing more than a tiny counter. "I had some
pretty long-winded speeches for selling ties, especially to the married
ladies who came in to buy for their husbands," Wyler remembered. "But
that got to be an awful bore."

He had brought his violin to Paris with the idea of getting advanced
instruction, though he never intended to become a professional musician. "I studied the violin as an amateur," he said, "the way young
people in Europe study a musical instrument as part of their general education." He entertained the notion of enrolling at the renowned Conservatoire National de Musique. In later years he sometimes claimed to

have attended it. Hollywood publicists and newspaper profiles amplified that to "conservatory graduate." His official United States Army service record indicated that he spent a full year at the music conservatory in Paris. But there is no trace of him in the registration records, as either a full- or part-time student. His entire Paris sojourn lasted only about three months. It's possible he took private lessons with a member of the faculty. In the meantime, he discovered the poor man's nightlife.

"I couldn't afford concerts, so I went to a place where they had records," Wyler recalled. "I'd never seen a store like that. You could put in a few cents and hear a Beethoven symphony on the earphones. I'd sit there for hours." Unlike his schoolboy experience in Lausanne, the interlude in Paris appears to have been intensely solitary. He often sat in the cheap cafés of Pigalle near the Gare du Nord, observing the neighborhood demimonde before going home to bed. He went to the theater as often as his pocket money allowed, which wasn't often. One time he managed to get a balcony seat to see Sarah Bernhardt "in one of her last performances," he recalled. "It was *Atalie,* by Racine."

Willy celebrated his eighteenth birthday wandering after work from the Boulevard des Italiens to the Boulevard St. Martin, both well known for their prostitutes. "There were girls all over the place," he recalled. "I had no money. I was scared anyway, an innocent. But I let myself be accosted by one. I walked along as if I was interested. I had her tell me all the things she would do to me. By the time I got to the end of the block I had come in my pants." These excursions became fairly regular. They were a cheap form of excitement. "I'd go up one street, then at the end of the block I'd say I had no money," Wyler remembered. "The girl would get mad. I'd say, 'Thank you very much,' then I'd cross the street and go up the next block, and the next girl would tell me what she'd do."

He eventually lost his virginity before returning to Mulhouse in July of 1920. "I went with one of these girls up to her room. She was kind of pretty. I told her I had never been with a girl before. She wanted to throw me out, but she didn't. I finally got laid for the first time. When I got home, I went to see a doctor. I told him what had happened. I said, 'Maybe I have syphilis.' He laughed like hell."

Melanie knew nothing of her son's boulevard outings. But she did know that Willy's three months away had settled one thing: Willy would never be a shopkeeper. Nor did she want him to be—not in Paris, not in Mulhouse, not anywhere. Willy was home little more than a week when she announced he would be coming to Zurich with her to meet her mother's first cousin, Carl Laemmle. If anyone could provide a fresh start for Willy, she reasoned, it was her cousin, who had become a rich and famous movie tycoon on the other side of the Atlantic.

According to Dora Picard, Melanie had read a newspaper item that Laemmle was in Lucerne, traveling through Switzerland on his annual summer vacation. He customarily came to Europe in June and returned to New York in September. Without telling Leopold, she'd written cousin Carl. His assistant had written back, inviting her to the Dolder Hotel in Zurich, where they would be staying.

Melanie had a double claim on Laemmle. Her mother was not only his first cousin but her father had seen him off to America thirty-six years before at the train station in Laupheim, the small Württemberg village where Laemmle was born. Indeed, when Laemmle's father needed the ninety marks to pay for his son's sea passage from Bremerhaven to New York on the S. S. *Neckar*, Melanie's father, Ferdinand Auerbach, had offered to lend him the money. That, at any rate, is what she told Dora Picard many years later.

NOBODY ON THE STATION PLATFORM IN LAUPHEIM COULD HAVE guessed that Carl Laemmle's steerage ticket, a gift for his seventeenth birthday, would take him from Germany to a place not yet called Hollywood, where he would become captain of an industry not yet invented. The group of friends and relatives seeing him off that day in 1884 had waved good-bye to a homely young man. He was small in physical stature, modestly ambitious and barely educated. Born in 1867, the tenth of thirteen children (five survived childhood), Laemmle started working as an indentured clerk at thirteen for a wholesale stationer in a Bavarian town forty miles from Laupheim. He rose from bookkeeper to office manager and might have become a partner in the business had he stayed. But he gave up that prospect to follow his older brother Joseph to America, where he settled in Oshkosh, Wisconsin, spending twelve years as branch manager for a large Midwest clothier.

Laemmle had married the boss's daughter. "The store is full of relatives [who] won't pay any attention to what I say," he complained. "They go over my head when I try to make them do anything."

At thirty-nine, Laemmle moved to Chicago to be his own boss and hoped to buy a clothing store with his savings. One night he walked by a movie theater on State Street, took in the picture for ten cents—it was a Hale's Tours travelogue showing scenery filmed from a moving train—and three weeks later owned his first nickelodeon. The year was 1906, the total investment twenty-two hundred dollars. Laemmle switched businesses without a qualm, having spent two days counting heads outside the Hale's Tours theater. He rented a building, converted it to an auditorium and painted it white to create an immaculate impression. A couple of months later he opened a second nickelodeon. Between the two of them, he was soon netting two hundred dollars a week. Within a decade, Laemmle would head a chain of movie houses throughout the Midwest, along with the world's largest film exchange and a production studio in southern California that dwarfed all others in size and output. By 1910 he turned to producing his own films and launched Independent Moving Pictures, later to become Universal Pictures. He also introduced the star system by luring Florence Lawrence and Mary Pickford away from the Biograph Company with promises of more money and better billing. Until then the public did not know screen actors by name.

Willy's first impression of Carl Laemmle was disappointing. The movie mogul had a small potbelly and an elfin grin and was barely five feet in height. Wire-rimmed glasses sat on the bridge of his nose. One hand was thrust into the pocket of a wrinkled jacket. The other held a half-smoked cigar that apparently had just gone out. Melanie had talked about "Uncle Carl" with such family pride on the train to Zurich that Willy couldn't help feeling puzzled.

"So you're your mother's sorrow," Laemmle teased.

The bantering tone caught Willy by surprise. Laemmle's pale gray eyes were amused. But they also seemed to be reading his own, as if by some sort of mental computation he could tell what Willy was thinking. Willy said nothing.

Laemmle indulged the young man's silence for a moment, then asked, "Do you want to make something of yourself?"

Willy knew the question was coming. His mother had said, and everybody in the family had claimed, that if Uncle Carl thought you were ambitious, he would offer his help. He had been coming to Europe every summer since 1906, except for the war years, always returning to America as the benefactor of yet another young man. Avuncular to a fault, he had so many relatives on the payroll—at least fourteen by the late 1920s—that his habit of bringing them over from Europe became a joke both in and out of the movie colony. As Ogden Nash, the satirical poet of the *New Yorker*, once put it: "Uncle Carl Laemmle / has a very large faemmle."

Naturally Willy wanted to make something of himself, but at what, he admitted, he couldn't exactly say.

"Well, maybe we'll find out," Laemmle said, and relit his cigar.

You didn't have to be a relative to attract Uncle Carl's help. He'd hired Irving G. Thalberg as his assistant because of some astute remarks the unemployed nineteen-year-old made one night in 1918 at Laemmle's summer home on Long Island. Thalberg soon became the youngest boss in Hollywood, not even old enough to sign the payroll checks when Uncle Carl promoted him to head of production. Before Thalberg it was Harry Cohn, the future head of Columbia Pictures, who was his assistant.

As they also proved, you didn't have to come from the Old Country to catch Laemmle's attention. But it didn't hurt if you did. Though Uncle Carl could be as shrewd, paranoid and penny-pinching as any of Hollywood's rapacious founding moguls, he was a notorious sentimentalist. The legendary story of how the German-Jewish émigré Erich von Stroheim got him to finance his directorial debut in 1919 was a case in point. Unable to talk his way past the underlings on the Universal lot, he went to Laemmle's home without an appointment. The butler was just turning him away when Laemmle overheard von Stroheim's protests and came to the door. Laemmle invited him into the library. Five minutes became five hours. Uncle Carl, who was a gambler as well as a sentimentalist, agreed to put up twenty-five thousand dollars for *Blind Husbands*, which established von Stroheim as a director and, not incidentally, ended up costing ten times the agreed-on amount.

Years later, Wyler could not recall many details of his first meeting with Laemmle, except what happened when they went to an elegant restaurant. The self-made tycoon dined on chicken. To Willy's amazement, he ignored his utensils and picked the chicken bone clean with his fingers. After their plates were cleared, Laemmle turned to him.

"How would you like to come to America?" he asked.

Melanie beamed.

Willy replied that he'd be thrilled to go. He said so as firmly and soberly as he could, trying not to reveal how giddy he really felt. It was, he often said in retrospect, like being offered "a trip to the moon."

"Okay, I'll give you a job," Laemmle said. "After that you're on your own."

Willy's salary at Universal would come to twenty-five dollars a week, with five dollars to be deducted from each paycheck until the company recovered the cost of his one-way sea passage. Harry Zehner, Laemmle's current assistant, would make all the travel arrangements. Willy would sail first-class on the Cunard liner *Aquitania*, joining Laemmle and his two children, Julius and Rosabelle. They would leave for New York from Southampton, England. In the meantime, Laemmle would go on to the Hotel Pupp in Carlsbad, the famous spa near Prague, for several weeks of curative baths, massages and pedicures.

Not long afterward, on August 20, 1920, Leopold wrote the American embassy in Paris, enclosing Willy's Swiss passport and asking for a visa to allow him to enter the United States. Five days later, he, too, got a taste of Laemmle's far-reaching influence.

The embassy's Second Secretary replied that according to State Department rules visa requests must be made in person. But, his letter added, "in view of a request by your cousin, Mr. Carl Laemmle, on the subject of a visa for your son, the Ambassador has advised the passport office to ease as much as possible the necessary formalities." The Second Secretary was kind enough to return Willy's passport with the visa inside.

5

LIKE A TRIP TO THE MOON

THE *AQUITANIA* PUT TO SEA FROM Southampton, England, on September 10, 1920, with Willy comfortably installed in a single-berth stateroom on the boat deck. Throngs of wealthy upper-crust Americans had resumed their annual summer rites at the fashionable resorts of Europe now that the Great War was over, and it must have seemed to Willy that all of them were returning to New York that season aboard the *Aquitania*. Among its nearly three thousand passengers were more than seven hundred sailing in first class, including such notables as Solomon R. Guggenheim, the New York philanthropist; Marshall Field II, heir to the Chicago retail fortune; and Dorothy Gish, the younger sister of Lillian Gish and a movie star herself. Also aboard was a contingent of American athletes, most of them medal-winning boxers returning from the Olympic Games held earlier that summer in Antwerp.

If you wanted to cross the Atlantic in stately British luxury, you couldn't do better than the six-year-old *Aquitania*. It was the pride of the Cunard fleet, newly refitted with engines that burned oil instead of coal. This nine-hundred-foot-long "ocean greyhound," as the press referred to it, could take "the Big Pond" in less than seven days, making an average speed of twenty-two knots. But speed was the merest of its glories. Refurbished staterooms were full-size affairs with bed and settee. Many had private dressing rooms. A fresh Pompeii period design graced the dining salon. The ship's staff catered to personal tastes. If you liked a fine cigar at sea, as Uncle Carl most certainly did, you had more than two dozen brands to choose from.

On Friday afternoon, September 17, the *Aquitania* put into its berth in Manhattan at the foot of West Thirteenth Street just as news of Bloody Thursday, a terrorist maelstrom of death and destruction, gripped the city. The very morning of Willy's arrival the dailies splashed pictures of the macabre scene. The *New York Times* bannered a three-deck headline across eight columns, the sort usually reserved for war declarations and national emergencies: WALL STREET EXPLOSION KILLS 30, INJURES 300; MORGAN OFFICE HIT, BOMB PIECES FOUND; TORONTO FUGITIVE SENT WARNINGS HERE. No less than eight reports on the day's havoc made the front page of the staid newspaper of record, to the exclusion of all other news.

For Willy, who disembarked looking like a picture of youthful innocence and privilege—a violin in one hand and a pair of skis over his shoulder—this stark introduction to New York City outstripped the improbable but common immigrant fantasy of streets paved with gold. Waiting at the dock for his ride to Brooklyn, where a Universal employee was to put him up for the weekend, he sat on his steamer trunk with a cadged newspaper, deciphering in his rudimentary English what had happened.

The blast erupted at the stroke of noon as lunchtime crowds streamed into the streets of the financial district. Witnesses told of seeing a horse-drawn cart standing at the curb in front of J. P. Morgan and Company across from the Stock Exchange. The next thing they knew, a deafening explosion had sent up a white fireball with tongues of green and yellow flame. The heat from the explosion kindled office fires high above the street. People's hair burst into flames. The horse that drew the bomb-laden cart had vaporized, except for its head and hooves. Two hundred detectives were now fanning out across the city to canvas blacksmith shops for matching horseshoes.

Willy raced around the city like an amazed tourist. After being taken by car to Brooklyn, he rushed downtown to the financial district to see the spectacular devastation, along with thousands of gawkers. But his interest was drawn to the nearby Woolworth Building on lower Broadway, where he rode the elevator sixty stories to the top of what was then the world's tallest, most elegant skyscraper. "It was all fantastic," Wyler recalled. "I also climbed to the top of the Statue of Liberty."

The recollection of his initial excitement remained vivid in Wyler's memory to the end of his life. Coming to America "was something fabulous for a young man," he said. "And don't forget, I was not a poor immigrant. I had a job, a certain amount of protection through Laemmle." Indeed, the flood of destitute immigrants during the week of Willy's arrival was so great that landings had to be halted for forty-eight hours to relieve congestion on Ellis Island. The temporary closing of the nation's main entry point left more than six thousand steerage passengers stranded on various liners by week's end.

Willy reported to work at the Mecca Building, a drab twelve-story office tower that belied its name, at 1600 Broadway just north of Times Square. The Universal Film Manufacturing Company occupied the entire third floor. Willy learned for the first time what his duties would be from one of Uncle Carl's minions, who assigned him to the company mail room next to the stenographic department and the telephone exchange. Fronting Broadway and West Forty-eighth Street were Universal's executive offices, impressively furnished in heavy mahogany and plate glass. Fronting Seventh Avenue were the scenario department and the Mecca branch of the Universal Film Exchange. As a shipping clerk Willy would deliver messages, disseminate the mail and carry film cannisters to and from the executive screening room.

Another young man, Paul Kohner, also reported to work that Monday and was given the same menial assignment. Like Willy, he was eighteen years old, spoke German and had met Laemmle less than two months before. Unlike Willy, he had a background in film reportage. His encounter with the diminutive mogul had been a case of self-generated enterprise. Kohner wanted to interview Laemmle at the Hotel Pupp in Carlsbad, for his father's Czech film magazine. When informed that Laemmle was there strictly on vacation and would not consent to an interview, the tall, plucky reporter left his business card with a note on the back: "If I have taken three hours to come here, surely you can spare three minutes to see me." Laemmle invited Kohner up to his suite. Then after lunch, he offered him a job.

As ambitious as he was resourceful, Kohner had arrived in New York the week before Willy, his transatlantic passage also paid with the proviso of future deductions from salary. When he went to the Universal office, however, he discovered Laemmle was not yet back. Nor had word been received of the new hire. Somewhat dismayed, Kohner got an audience with Laemmle's cigar-chewing office lieutenant, Manny Goldstein.

"Are you by any chance a nephew?" Goldstein wanted to know.

"No," Kohner told him, "no relation."

In that case, Goldstein advised, come back in a week. The boss wasn't expected at the office until then.

It didn't take long for the two young men to become friends. "Willy didn't like the room he had," Kohner recalled. "I think it was in Far Rockaway. He had to travel by subway for an hour and he hated that. He asked me, 'Isn't there a room where you're living?' I was staying in a building near Eighty-sixth Street and Park Avenue. It was not yet *the* Park Avenue. It was just the center of Yorkville. We had two very tiny rooms—I could almost say two holes—right next to each other. Both of us had big steamer trunks. We had to push them into the hallway just to move around."

They each paid seven dollars a week for rent, took the subway to the office every morning and walked home to save the fare. For six weeks neither of them saw Laemmle. Then one Saturday, the phone rang in the mail room with an invitation for the two of them to dine with Laemmle at the Progress Club, a sedate West Side speakeasy near Central Park. It served decent food but, more important, it had back-room gambling.

By the summer of 1920, six months after the National Prohibition Amendment went into effect, thousands of speakeasies had opened in Manhattan. Like the rest of the country, the city winked at the new law of the land. "Speaks" operated at all levels of the social strata, from peepholed neighborhood hangouts to posh society nightclubs. As one famous Jazz Age madame scoffed: "They might as well try to dry up the Atlantic with a post office blotter."

Uncle Carl, who didn't drink and wasn't a gourmet, made no pretense about the Progress Club. He was a regular customer for one reason only: gambling. Following dinner, he excused himself, gave each of the boys ten dollars for the dice tables and went off to a card game.

"After half an hour or so," Kohner recalled, "Willy had a fistful of money. I had plenty, too. I said, 'Well, this seems to be the beginning of a big career in America.' A half hour later we didn't have a penny. We couldn't even tip the hat-check girl."

They had not only run through Laemmle's twenty dollars but both of their paychecks as well—and their landlady expected fourteen dollars from them. The next morning Willy eyed Paul's "Uncle Sam" coin bank, which looked like a toy cash register and held nearly seventeen dollars in nickels, dimes and quarters. The time had come to rifle the bank. But the cash drawer was engineered to pop open only in multiples of ten dollars.

"I'll take care of that," Willy said.

He dressed and took the coin bank to the corner grocery with the idea of buying a grapefruit. But the grocer wouldn't cooperate. He refused to deposit the three dollars and change needed to spring open the drawer, which would have enabled Willy to make the purchase and repay the deposit.

"One store after another nobody would do it," Kohner recounted.

Willy finally went into a restaurant and ordered a royal breakfast: bacon and eggs, coffee and muffins. When the waitress brought the check for seventy-five cents, he brandished the coin bank and explained his problem. He also promised to throw in a large tip if she would make the necessary deposit.

"Willy came home with a bagful of coins," Kohner said. "That's how we paid the rent."

6

~~~~~~~~~~~~

NEW YORK

AROUND THIS TIME THEY
became inexhaustible moviegoers. Paul used his father's magazine
connection to get them free passes to the city's prime movie houses. He
presented himself to the house managers, along with a letter of introduction, as the New York correspondent for *Internationale Filmschau*.
During one week in late November, they saw *Dinty* at the Strand; *The
Life of the Party* with Fatty Arbuckle at the Rivoli; *The Great Lover* at the
Capitol; *Idols of Clay* with former Ziegfeld Follies star Mae Murray at
the Criterion and *His Wife's Caller* at the Rialto.

They made no effort to take in plays, though the season on Broadway
was strong and occasionally even spectacular. Had they done so, they
might have seen the world premiere of George Bernard Shaw's dark
comedy, *Heartbreak House*, about the moral bankruptcy of prewar Eu-
rope. It opened at the Garrick Theatre that November just as Eugene
O'Neill's startling expressionist drama, *The Emperor Jones*, went up on
MacDougal Street in Greenwich Village. They also could have seen
Fanny Brice and Eddie Cantor in *The Ziegfeld Follies of 1920* at the New
Amsterdam; or George M. Cohan in *The Meanest Man in the World* at the
Hudson; or Ethel and John Barrymore appearing together in *Claire de*

Lune, which packed the house at the Empire even though the play itself was a grandiloquent dud.

But even if their movie habit had left them the time for it, playgoing was simply too expensive. The cheapest ticket to a Broadway show cost two dollars or more. The language also presented difficulties. Silent movies offered no such problem. They were almost entirely a visual medium. As for the title cards, both Willy and Paul understood them easily. Willy already read English by the time he left Mulhouse. Among his many boyhood lessons, he'd had English grammar and vocabulary drilled into him for three years by an elderly expatriate British teacher. And Paul, a quick study, had been taking evening classes in English twice a week ever since his arrival in New York.

To sharpen his language skills, moreover, Paul gave himself a rigorous homework assignment. He sat down with a German-English dictionary and patiently began to read through the articles in Universal's free trade paper for exhibitors, *Moving Picture Weekly.* The idea soon dawned on him that German-language film magazines and trade papers abroad might be willing to buy the articles in translation. So he undertook the tedious work of translating what were, almost without exception, awkwardly written pieces turned out by the studio's publicity hacks.

Kohner made up duplicate packages of his translations on mimeographed sheets, enclosed publicity stills touting Universal's upcoming movies and mailed them off at his own expense to a flock of publications, including his father's magazine. The translated articles sometimes contained real news about where, in Laemmle's view, the American movie industry was headed. One editorial in January 1921 noted: "The Universal chief predicts there will be less production during the coming months. This state of affairs he welcomes as a much-needed correction. It is his opinion that both the producer and the exhibitor will be brought successfully through the coming year by concentration on big pictures with high exploitation value."

More often there was the unabashed filler masquerading as news: " 'Eddie Polo has taken Havana by storm,' Universal reports. 'He has made personal appearances in many of the leading theaters on the Cuban island and causes a youth riot each time he leaves his hotel. At the Campoamor, one of the best theaters in Havana, the management had to call out the police to handle the crowds.' "

But the preponderance of material that Kohner and, later, Wyler worked from almost invariably fell into a few time-honored categories of unadulterated movie puffery.

There was the purple-prose star profile: "Youth, animation, vivacity and life—they are written in Carmel Myers's eyes. Big, lustrous and gray-green are those eyes—and direct. It is fascinating to watch them not only for their singular beauty but because they are so expressive. They can be merry and sad, scornful and sympathetic; they can flirt and they can 'freeze'—indeed they seem able to express every shade of human feeling."

There was the pseudo-insider's look at the working life of the stars, intended to arouse both envy and sympathy: "They have automobiles and yachts; they have charming homes and gorgeous clothes; they seem to travel to the most delightful places and put up at the most exclusive hotels—their life seems to be one big *snap*—so exclaimed *someone who did not know*, in a conversation turning on movie stars, not so long ago.

"But that *someone* forgot that movie stars are often dragged out of bed before dawn to 'shoot' a scene; that sometimes they work from morning until late at night; that their lives are often endangered by the perilous stunts they are compelled to perform. And not the least trying part of their lives is that they must act the same scene over and over again, with undiminished patience, until it suits the finicky eye of the director."

And, of course, there was the inevitable celebrity item filled with breathless gossip about stars and starlets long since forgotten: "Of late there have been some notable romances among the player-folk at the Universal studios in Universal City. Priscilla Dean and Wheeler Oakman, Josephine Hull and Jack Perrin, Erich von Stroheim and Valerie Germonprez—these are the most prominent of the marriages which have taken place. And now comes the announcement that Alta Allen, leading lady in *A Shocking Night*, has just been married to the famous director, Mr. Hampton Del Ruth."

Laemmle knew nothing of Kohner's enterprise. Willy hardly did either, until tear sheets from an assortment of illustrated magazines and trade papers—German, Austrian and Swiss—began to arrive for Paul in the mail room, along with foreign-currency payments equivalent to a few dollars each. Kohner recalled years later, "I received all sorts of papers back from Europe, and they all printed this material. They were just delighted to have news from America. . . . One day I had a whole stack of these papers assembled, and I thought maybe I should send them over to Mr. Laemmle. So I did."

Kohner heard nothing for several hours. Then he was summoned to Laemmle's office, where the secretary warned him in no uncertain terms, "Oh boy, you are in bad trouble." A little dazed by this unexpected reaction, Kohner entered the inner sanctum and waited silently in front of Laemmle's desk as the tiny movie magnate leafed through the clippings. He could see the boss's face turning red.

"Have you gone mad, Kohner?" Laemmle seethed.

Kohner wondered what he had done wrong. He felt like a schoolboy being called to account for a particularly nasty prank.

"This will cost us a fortune!"

He shouted that Kohner would have to pay the bills when they came in. And just where did he think he could get that kind of money?

Humiliated, Kohner replied that the articles had cost the company nothing. He pulled several uncashed checks from his pocket.

"Here's what they paid me," he said.

"Paid you?"

What should have been Kohner's moment of triumph became instead a quaking apology. He expressed his regret for not turning the checks over to the company sooner.

As he described his efforts of the past several weeks, Laemmle pushed a buzzer to call in Manny Goldstein, which was an ominous sign. The sour-faced office lieutenant had a reputation as the company hatchet man. His presence often meant that someone was about to be fired.

"I want you to see what this young man has done," Laemmle said, pointing to the clippings. "We have not paid one penny for this. What are we going to do?"

Goldstein seemed to take only grudging notice of the clippings, except one. It included a large photo of Laemmle. "Very good, Kohner," he said.

"Good?" asked Laemmle. "I think the boy deserves a break."

The turnabout came as a complete surprise to Kohner, he later recalled. Goldstein wondered if he shouldn't get a raise in salary.

"Of course," Laemmle said. "But I want more than that. I want him to have an office. What's your salary?"

"Eighteen dollars," Kohner told him.

"Make it twenty-five."

Emboldened, Kohner asked if the words "Foreign Publicity Department" could be printed on the door to his office with his own name in smaller letters.

"Sure, yes, you do that."

Laemmle handed back the checks Kohner had given him.

"You keep these. But from now on any money coming in belongs to Universal."

. . .

THUS LAUNCHED, THE ONE-MAN DEPARTMENT SOON DOUBLED IN size. After Kohner rounded up a painter and had his name and the department's stenciled on the glass door of his new office, Wyler showed up from the shipping room.

"Willy wanted to know what I was doing there," Kohner remembered. "Well, I could see his mind beginning to work. And sure enough, after two days Willy came back one morning and said, 'I'd like to talk to you.'"

Wyler was not enamored of lugging heavy film cannisters back and forth between the shipping department and the projection room. He proposed translating into French the same stories Kohner was translating into German.

"Willy spoke German and French equally well," Kohner recalled. "I said, 'I think that's a good idea. Why don't you go ahead, and we'll see if you get the same results.' Sure enough, Willy sat down, worked night after night. He translated the articles and sent them out to various papers in France and Belgium and Switzerland.

"Pretty soon papers came in with big pictures of Laemmle and photos of Universal stars. When we had enough of them, we both went to see Mr. Laemmle. He was delighted. I said, 'Mr. Laemmle, would you mind if Willy works with me in the department, and we both send out articles?'"

Laemmle happily assigned Wyler to Foreign Publicity, though without a raise in salary.

The creation of a permanent publicity mill to grind out copy aimed strictly at European markets—a Universal precedent emulated by rival studios—made Paul Kohner a young man to watch. The "foreign department" marked him as someone with audacious promotional skills and signaled a fertile talent for the business side of movies generally. In a short time he would become one of Laemmle's trusted advisers and his career would take him to the top of Universal's executive ranks.

The new job proved to be little more than a way station for Wyler, however. It was marginally useful in acquainting him with the studio's workings, but, what is of greater importance, it whetted his appetite to go to California. He admitted to Kohner, "I don't think I'm a good publicity man. I don't want to sit and write stories." He said he hadn't really come to America to be cooped up in an office.

. . .

LAEMMLE, ON ONE OF HIS FREQUENT TRIPS TO THE COAST, HAD left his capable, twenty-year-old secretary Irving Thalberg at Universal City and then put him in charge of all production to keep a lid on rising expenditures. But Thalberg was unable to rein in Erich von Stroheim, who had begun filming one of his typically extravagant productions, *Foolish Wives*, in July 1920. Laemmle's editorial prediction that Hollywood would be relying on "big pictures" was more well-founded than he knew. The budget for *Foolish Wives*, which also starred von Stroheim, soared from two hundred-fifty to seven hundred-fifty thousand dollars as the months wore on.

By fall, Universal executives were grappling with negative publicity within the industry about the picture's runaway cost and by winter were determined to put the best face on it. They touted *Foolish Wives* as "the first real million-dollar picture." They exploited von Stroheim's reputation as Hollywood's *enfant terrible*. They played on his vintage billing as "the man you love to hate," for the fetishistic Prussian officers he personified in First World War pictures. Studio ads noted, "He's going to make you hate him! Even if it takes a million dollars of our money to do it!" Indeed, despite Universal's official figure of $1,053,290.80, the picture "actually cost one million six," *Variety* reported.

But it took a Kohner brainstorm to capitalize on the astronomical numbers in the grandest possible style. He suggested that the company put up a colossal electric billboard in Times Square to bombard the public with news of the picture's galloping expense. If you're spending so much, you might as well flaunt it. The billboard would read, "The cost of FOOLISH WIVES up to this week," while showing a seven-digit number for the latest amount in blazing incandescent light bulbs. Also, Laemmle's name would be spelled out in letters five feet high, as tall as the boss himself. All during the summer of 1921 the crowds who passed through Times Square couldn't help but notice Universal's extravagance. The figure in lights announced $1,250,000 before the sign came down. For this idea, Kohner got a bonus of fifty dollars.

Wyler, in the meantime, hadn't gained any special notice, despite finally receiving a five-dollar raise. "Willy was a little restless," Kohner recalled. "He was a daredevil. He loved all sorts of excitement." When the giant billboard for *Foolish Wives* went up—it covered three floors of the Astor Hotel at Broadway and Forty-fifth Street—Wyler climbed to the top of it to take snapshots of Times Square. He particularly liked going to the roof of the Mecca Building to experiment with time-lapse photos of the Great White Way at night. Pleased with the results, he began lugging a tripod and camera around Manhattan. Instead of writing home now, he sent photographs captioned in white ink and marked with Xs to show what he'd been doing or what unlikely ledge he'd clambered to.

Wyler also kept up his violin, often performing on street corners for spare change. "Willy would go wherever there were people who'd listen," Kohner remembered. "They would throw a few coins into his hat." When the two friends were invited to a party, they'd sometimes team up, with Kohner playing the piano. "We'd usually do some Hungarian or Viennese waltzes, or something by Strauss," he said. Their music-making was not memorable. But Kohner could never forget one Wyler performance. Coming home to their rooming house at 149 East Ninety-second Street on a sultry summer night, Kohner noticed a crowd gazing up at their wide-open, third-floor window. They looked entranced. "There was Willy fiddling away," Kohner said. "The only thing was, he was standing there stark naked. He got great applause."

Though Willy's ambitions had yet to jell, he knew he wanted to remain in the United States. Misinformed that volunteering for military service would shorten the residency requirements for citizenship, he joined the New York State National Guard on February 7, 1921. While his soldiering did not take up a lot of time, it did provide a certain amount of excitement. Just how much is illustrated by what he termed "two minor episodes."

In the first, a sergeant caught him brawling with another enlisted man. For punishment, the two of them were ordered to settle their argument in the ring. According to Wyler, they fought a preliminary bout at a Manhattan armory on a regularly scheduled card of National Guard match-ups. "I won the decision," Wyler said of his three-rounder. "But it was a short-lived prizefight career."

In the second episode, he was knocked cold by an officer's horse during artillery maneuvers that summer at Camp Upton in Brookhaven, Long Island. "We would come in from the field dead-tired. We had to take care of our horses before we could go to our tents, clean the hooves, brush the horses, feed them, clean the stables. One day this lieutenant was leading his horse, and I was the first man he spotted. 'Here, take care of him,' he told me. Which meant I had to do the whole thing all over again. I was annoyed. I took his horse into the stables. I grabbed his leg to clean the hoof. But I was careless. This horse didn't know me. He kicked me right in the face. I passed out and woke up in a hospital with a face out to here."

Meanwhile, the lieutenant paid the barely conscious Wyler a visit and was greeted with a stream of invective in French. "I don't remember what happened," Wyler said. "It seems I called him every dirty name in the book. Unfortunately, he understood what I was saying because he'd been in France during the war. So when I got out of the hospital, they gave me guard duty *and* latrine duty."

Toward the end of the year, with Paul branching out beyond the Foreign Publicity Department, Willy decided the time had come to arrange his escape from the drab corridors of the Mecca Building. It seemed to him that "all the fun was in California." He knew it not only from the silent movies he saw and the stories he translated but also from the uproar over the latest industry scandal—the sensational Fatty Arbuckle affair in San Francisco—which made front-page news all through the fall of 1921. Willy had no doubt that a job at Universal City, in any capacity, would be a raffish adventure.

Despite Laemmle's admonition that he could not rely on personal privilege, Willy had two unmistakable advantages over other Universal employees. For one, his mother now kept up a solicitous correspondence with Uncle Carl. She peppered him with reports of his Bavarian relations and inquired with keen interest about her son's welfare. For another, Willy could get an appointment to see Uncle Carl, which wasn't easy under any circumstances, and he could put his plea for a transfer on a family basis. Even Paul, a favored non-relative, didn't have that prerogative. He often wished he did. In fact, when his friendship with Willy gave higher-ups the idea that he, too, might be a relative, Paul took pains not to correct their impression. "At times it probably saved me from being fired," Kohner later recalled.

Of course, Willy's request for a transfer still had to be made with great deference and had to be couched in the sort of high-minded terms Uncle Carl cultivated—even if they just barely applied. And so Willy went through the required ritual. He spoke of wanting to learn all aspects of movie production, which couldn't be done if he remained in New York. He spoke of how he had worked diligently for the past seventeen months to earn that chance. Above all, he spoke of his gratitude to Uncle Carl.

"Do you have any money?" Laemmle wanted to know.

Willy replied that he didn't have much.

"Okay," Laemmle agreed rather unceremoniously. "I'll pay the trip and you pay back five dollars a week."

Within a matter of days—by late January 1922—Willy packed up his steamer trunk, bid Paul a temporary farewell and took his leave of the National Guard. On February 1, almost a year to the day of his three-year enlistment, he was granted an honorable discharge by "special order" because of "removal from the state." He'd never risen in rank. At the time of his discharge he was still a buck private, seventh grade, the lowest of the low. Afterward, in California, Wyler would be dismayed to learn that his military service, such as it was, had no bearing on the residency requirements for citizenship.

Uncle Carl was generous but, as Willy had come to expect, frugal. The loan of a hundred sixty dollars for his one-way transcontinental rail fare did not cover the cost of a ticket on any of the first-class trains.

Instead of taking the New York Central Railroad's Twentieth Century Limited or the Pennsylvania Railroad's Broadway Limited, Willy boarded the less expensive Western Express for the first leg of his trip. He departed from Grand Central Station at six in the evening and arrived at Dearborn Station in Chicago the next night at nine fifteen. That gave him little more than an hour to cab to La Salle Street and catch the Scout on the Atcheson, Topeka and Santa Fe, a less expensive alternative to the Chief, for the second leg of his trip.

After four days and five nights Willy disembarked in Los Angeles, grateful for the warmth of the California sun outside the train station. Even at eight in the morning in the dead of winter it soothed the stiffness in his bones. Uncle Carl's loan not only hadn't paid for a first-class fare, it hadn't covered the price of a sleeping berth on a second-class train. Willy had made the entire journey sitting up.

7

"WORTHLESS WILLY"

THE BOOM OF THE ROARING
Twenties changed America from a comfortable prewar world of tra-
ditional values and Victorian ideals to a clamorous new age of flappers
and jazz babies. Out went the deprivation of the war years. In came the
consumer society. It was suddenly the era of the automobile and the
radio. Cars brought independence, especially for the young. Merchandising filled the air. The public fell in love with home appliances from
electric toasters to refrigerators. Women got the vote. They also went to
work, gave up corsets, showed their legs and bobbed their hair.

In southern California the era dawned with remarkable force. Probably no city anywhere experienced a more radical transformation than
Los Angeles. It grew overnight from a sleepy nineteenth-century village
into a sprawling postwar metropolis that caught the world's attention
with sunshine seekers of every stripe. The influx made Los Angeles the
nation's fastest-growing city. Its 1920 population of five hundred
seventy-six thousand doubled in slightly more than five years. People
poured in from all over the country, lured by a combination of tourist
promotions and cheap land, newly discovered oil fields and the glamour
of motion pictures. Many were eager to get rich or famous, usually both.

Failing that, they were content just to survive in a semitropical desert setting until their luck turned. So many stayed that the Los Angeles phone directory for 1922 gained sixty thousand permanent listings over the previous year.

This naturally created cheap labor. Large industries began moving in. First came the tire factories, then the aircraft and automobile plants. Tourists were attracted through a relentless advertising campaign begun in 1921 by the city's semiofficial All-Year Club. "No sedate public relations office," one historian has written, "it functioned like a ministry of information . . . working overtime to get out the message that Los Angeles was the most favored spot on earth." Promotions in national magazines and major newspapers proclaimed that California could make you "a new man in two weeks!" At the very least, you could "exchange your winter for the smiles of spring."

But through all of these developments, the making of motion pictures held the limelight economically and culturally. Movies were the sine qua non, the original industry to set up shop in Southern California in a big way, and focused attention on the region as no other had. Much more than radio, movies were the great medium of national expression. They not only reflected the twenties ethos, they helped spawn it, in all its wild contradictions. They glorified the changing social mores and magnified fashionable notions of the new sophistication: easy sex, free spending, marital infidelity, ready divorce, fast cars, booze, smoking, drugs.

Paradoxically, movies also bolstered the old values of middle-class respectability. For all their ballyhooed "midnight revels" and "petting parties in the purple dawn," they prized the Victorian clichés of virtue rewarded and virginity protected. They thrived on happy endings or, at the very least, moralized about decadence. This reinforced their popularity with an audience that still harbored ambivalent feelings about society's enormous changes, proof of which was readily apparent in the passage of Prohibition laws and immigration quotas, the revival of the Ku Klux Klan and a general conflict between city and country.

Movies were, in addition, the great social leveler. Where else could Fatty Arbuckle, a former plumber's assistant, become a star making thirty-five hundred dollars a week? In what other industry could the deposed Romanov Czar of Russia be offered the same line of work? The producer Lewis J. Selznick's notorious cable to Nicholas II in 1917 was a surreal portent of the industry's leveling power: "When I was a poor boy in Kiev some of your policemen were not kind to me and my people. I came to America and prospered. Now hear with regret you are out of a job. Feel no ill will what your policemen did. . . . Can give you fine position acting in pictures. Salary no object. Reply my expense."

Such noblesse oblige was a condescending joke, of course. But it nonetheless suggested the global influence of the American movie industry, real and imagined. Three of the world's most famous people—Mary Pickford, Douglas Fairbanks and Charlie Chaplin—were movie stars. They were also the highest-paid employees in any industry. Each netted more than a million dollars a year before the twenties began. They were the new royalty.

Still, when Willy arrived in Los Angeles, the studios were not shooting many movies. Production activity, always cyclical, had ebbed so low in early February 1922 that most of the film colony was temporarily out of work. The fully employed people were the sheriffs. In the land of the dollar-down-dollar-a-month installment plan they were working overtime repossessing automobiles and auctioning off bungalows. Even at Universal, usually one of the busiest studios, just three serials were under way and a minor comedy was finishing up. But for Willy, whose salary was guaranteed, the picture slowdown meant little more than an unhurried introduction to life in Los Angeles.

Willy moved into a downtown rooming house near Vermont Avenue for six or seven dollars a week. His old friend, the would-be stunt man Alex Manuel, was already living there. Manuel had written Willy earlier from Lausanne of his intention to seek work in the movies. When Manuel reached New York, Willy provided him with a letter of introduction and told him to look up Julius Stern in California. Willy didn't actually know Stern, a Universal executive working for Thalberg, the wunderkind production chief. But he knew Stern was part of Uncle Carl's inner circle and a nephew through marriage who might take at least some notice of a family referral.

Manuel had managed to land occasional parts as an extra during the few months he'd been in Los Angeles. Now he was trying to get a stunt job in *The Adventures of Robinson Crusoe*, one of the three Universal serials commencing production. Scheduled for eighteen episodes, the serial required action thrills, of course, and called for a live boa constrictor at one point. Manuel wasn't hired. But Willy remembered watching six men on an outdoor stage holding the snake down as a "scared-to-death" artist applied makeup to its taped jaws.

Nothing could have taken the luster off Willy's first impression of that vast open-air circus, Universal City. Cradled between sloping hills and rugged mountains four miles north of Hollywood over the Cahuenga Pass, it was by far the largest of the movie studios and truly seemed a dazzling factory of dreams. Before Disneyland was ever imagined, the studio had a fantastic mélange of "streets" with life-size mockups of medieval villages and frontier towns, desert sheikdoms and city tenements. The original two hundred fifty acres had been a poultry farm when Laemmle made the purchase in 1912 with a down payment of thirty-five hundred dollars. Now, seven years after its official opening in 1915, Universal City was worth millions. It had an artificial lake, a remote back lot large enough to film several rampaging posses at a time, the world's largest completely electrified indoor stage, roughly the size of a football field, and another indoor stage almost as big.

There were also many outdoor stages and elaborate standing sets: European castles, Western saloons, blacksmith shops, Mexican pueblos, cabins, Moslem minarets, cafés and palaces. The lot had its own zoo, restaurants, shops, police force, hospital and school and the mundane essentials of the movie business—an administration building, bungalows where employees bunked, film-processing labs, cutting rooms, costume shops, a garage for the auto fleet, a barn for the frequently cast farmyard animals. What Laemmle especially liked to brag about was the post office, which gave Universal City the trappings, if not the official status, of a municipal entity.

Just getting to the studio furnished palpable excitement for Willy. "Hollywood was like a village on the outskirts of the big city," he recalled. "Where I worked was way out in the valley beyond Hollywood. You took the streetcar from downtown to the corner of Hollywood Boulevard and Cahuenga. And there you hitched a ride over the pass on a small dirt road. Once you got over the pass, it was wide open country." Sometimes it was even bandit country, with open season on commuters. Holdups on the lonely stretch of Cahuenga Pass occasionally made the newspapers: "Bert Roach, who usually plays 'crook' characters in the films, was stuck up by a real crook on his way home from Universal City." Though robberies weren't frequent, they were sufficiently threatening to unnerve Erich von Stroheim. He armed himself with a pistol for his commute through the pass.

Willy started on the lot as an errand boy. "They'd send me out to buy cigars," he recalled. Although Thalberg worked in the office, he rarely deigned to speak to Willy. "He was very demanding," Wyler remembered fifty years later. "I didn't have much contact with him. He was way up there, and I was way down here. But this one time, on a Friday, he gave me a book, and he said, 'You read German, don't you?' I said, 'Yes.' He said, 'Bring me a synopsis in English on Monday.' Well, I didn't know how to do it. It took me longer than that just to read the book. I had absolutely no experience writing a synopsis. It was some-thing von Stroheim was thinking of making. Came Monday, I didn't have the synopsis. A couple of more days went by before I could really tell him what it was about."

Thalberg's assignment seems to have been a missed opportunity. The book, a novel by Ludwig Ganghofer called *Castle Hubertus*, was an-nounced in April 1922 as von Stroheim's next project. Someone eager to prove himself—a Paul Kohner, for example—would have gone out of his way to capitalize on the assignment. Willy didn't. He lacked more than experience. He lacked focus, which is perhaps not surprising in a nineteen-year-old whose only ambition was to seek excitement. This poor performance helped Thalberg form an opinion of him that was even lower than he deserved. Not long afterward, in connection with stories Thalberg was to hear about Wyler's motorcycle escapades, the boss of Universal city nicknamed him "Worthless Willy" and dismissed him from serious consideration.

ALL THROUGH THE SPRING WYLER FLOUTED THE SPEED LAWS. "WILLY was a cowboy—on a motorcycle instead of a horse," recalls Arthur Hurni, who met Wyler in April 1922 and began rooming with him by the middle of the summer. "He loved his motorcycle with a passion. He was crazy for speed." In fact, Wyler's passion started out as a practical solution to a daily problem. The commute to Universal City from his downtown boarding house, thrilling as it was at first, covered some thirty miles and became a time-consuming trek despite the widely touted virtues of the Los Angeles streetcar system. In May, for example, riders had to be rerouted so regularly because of track-laying efforts to keep up with growth that even the chief of police swore off the city's so-called "electric railway paradise."

"My automobile was out of order, and I took a streetcar," the chief said. "It looked all right and ran all right, but it never got me to where I wanted to go. I take an automobile or I walk."

The Yellow Car trolley, which Wyler rode, followed a circuitous route. It trundled east on Pico, north up Broadway and Lake Shore, and finally headed west along Sunset and Hollywood boulevards before depositing him at Cahuenga in front of the city's newest skyscraper, the five-story Security and Savings Bank, where he thumbed his ride the rest of the way. Getting a motorcycle made sense, especially when his work began shortly after dawn and lasted until dark six days a week.

But if, as Wyler later recalled, speeding around town on a motorcycle was considered raffish, then all the better. He bought a large, loud, throbbing Henderson with a loan from Manuel and a hundred dollars borrowed from Julius Stern, who'd been promoted to a top managerial production job. At the same time Manuel bought his own motorcycle with an allowance from his well-heeled family. The two young men exuded a dangerous charm as they gunned their engines in tandem and swept by motorists on the road. "We'd come up like cops alongside a car," Wyler recalled. Once "somebody made a quick turn and ran Alex into a pole. He had his head split open. We got him to a hospital, but how he lived through that I'll never know."

On Sunday larks the pair thundered north to Santa Barbara or south to Tijuana. They sent postcards home to Europe from the Mexican border town. "My mother wrote back immediately, 'Don't go there any more!'" Wyler remembered. "She was thinking of bandits." Meanwhile, on his way to work, Wyler often got caught speeding, usually at the Cahuenga pass, where he liked to let out the engine. When his citations piled up unpaid, he eventually had to serve a three-day sentence on a prison farm in the San Fernando Valley. Thalberg was amused. He began calling him ".Jailbird" as well as "Worthless Willy."

For all that, Wyler's nightlife was fairly dull. Despite the film colony's notoriety, it did not have many wild or glamorous hot spots. The working folk tended to gravitate to a few eateries such as the Montmartre at Highland Avenue and Hollywood Boulevard, near several of the studios. It was chic yet had a relaxed Parisian atmosphere, as well as a dance floor and an energetic twelve-piece band. The music jumped ("Toot, Toot, Tootsie," "Ain't We Got Fun?"), teased ("Do It Again") and crooned ("Carolina in the Morning," "L'Amour, Toujours L'Amour"). Not surprisingly, the colony's French-speaking contingent made the Montmartre their home away from home. Stars sometimes threw private parties, and you could hang around the fringe without an invitation.

"That's where Willy ran into Robert Florey," Arthur Hurni recalled.

Robert Florey, a Parisian-born filmmaker two years older than Wyler, had come to Los Angeles in September 1921. He is best remembered today for writing or directing dozens of "B" pictures during the thirties, among them Universal's *Frankenstein* and *Murders in the Rue Morgue*. In 1922 he was earning his living interviewing stars for *Ciné-magazine*, a popular French publication, and freelancing as a low-level technical advisor at Fox. By year's end Mary Pickford and Douglas Fairbanks hired him as their foreign publicity director. He also caught on with Charlie Chaplin as a scenario writer and with Rudolph Valentino, who made him his press agent. Despite this heady success, Florey remained friendly with a whole circle of fellow émigrés on the bottom rungs of the industry. He knew Hurni originally from their school days in Geneva. Tall and strapping, Hurni was as suavely handsome as Valentino himself but could barely get walk-on work. Florey tided him over from time to time with small loans. By July, though, it was Wyler's turn.

"I met Willy at Florey's house on Formosa Avenue in Hollywood," Hurni recalled. "Willy got me some jobs." Then Wyler offered to take him in. "I was appointed to find a room for three of us. Me, Willy and René Traveletti, who was coming over from Lausanne."

His search ended at 1719 Mariposa Avenue, conveniently located a block north of Hollywood Boulevard, in a neighborhood of big old frame houses with deep porches and wide front lawns. A family by the name of Walker offered to rent them a room and a bath. "Two of us had beds and the third slept on a couch," Wyler recalled. "I was the only one who had a job." Which is not to say he always covered the bills. On Saturdays he received his weekly paycheck at the studio and regularly got into a crap game. Hurni and Traveletti knew that if Wyler wasn't home by nine he wouldn't be bringing back any groceries.

Wyler recalled, "I'd come home at four or five in the morning — busted. Then I'd borrow five dollars from an assistant director, and somehow we'd manage." He made such a habit of losing his weekly pay, however, that they turned to petty theft. "We stole milk from the neighborhood stoops," recalled Bruno Traveletti, who moved into the Walker house in 1923. "We considered food community property."

Among their more risky capers, they also "turned an old Maxwell into community property." There were more than a hundred sixty thousand automobiles on the streets of Los Angeles, and apparently the owner of this one didn't seem to notice its absence. "That car became our collective means of transportation," Traveletti said.

8

SIN CITY

WHEN WYLER ARRIVED IN LOS Angeles, the movie industry was caught up in a historic crisis. With the lurid Fatty Arbuckle case providing a long fuse, moviedom had lit a time bomb waiting to explode. Arbuckle's three trials for manslaughter, lasting on and off from November 1921 to the following April, would have been sensational in any context. But as a symbol of Hollywood's excesses they brought the public's moral outrage to the flash point and set off a national firestorm that nearly wrecked the industry.

Roscoe "Fatty" Arbuckle had started out in Mack Sennett's Keystone Cops and rose to fame as a moon-faced, roly-poly comic idolized by legions of young moviegoers for his innocent buffoonery. In the summer of 1921 he was shooting three pictures simultaneously on the Famous Players–Lasky lot, when Paramount signed him to a three year, three-million-dollar deal. To celebrate, he motored up to San Francisco in his custom-made Pierce-Arrow and threw a party over the Labor Day weekend at the posh St. Francis hotel.

Arbuckle, who was far from immune to the blandishments of money and star worship, had a tendency to revel in lavish style. The party in his twelfth-floor suite degenerated into a three-day binge fueled on bootleg liquor. Fatty presided drunkenly over a crowd of swells invited up from the film colony who were more than happy to share in the pleasures of a bacchanal. On the third day, screams were heard from Fatty's bedroom. When he emerged, revelers found a disheveled actress and reputed prostitute groaning in pain on his bed. She died several days later, though not before claiming that Arbuckle "did this to me." The press had a field day wondering, among other things, whether she was sexually violated with a champagne bottle.

Arbuckle's first trial ended in a hung jury favoring acquittal, the second in a hung jury favoring conviction. A third jury found him innocent after deliberating for about forty-five minutes. Though the party had occurred beyond Hollywood's precincts, it defined the public's exaggerated notion of routine depravity throughout the industry. *Variety* headlines of September 23, 1921, indicated the depth of the reaction: WORLD-WIDE CONDEMNATION OF PICTURES AS AFTERMATH OF ARBUCKLE AFFAIR. MUST RID FILMS OF DOPESTERS, DEGENERATES AND PARASITES—CLEANLINESS IN PRODUCING AND ACTING RANKS WILL BE REFLECTED ON SCREENS—CHURCHES AGITATING AGAINST PICTURES. Two suicides were fresh in memory: Olive Thomas, the Selznick Pictures star just out of her teens, who took poison and died in Paris following her marriage to Mary Pickford's brother, Jack, a widely rumored narcotics addict; and Zelda Crosby, a screenwriter for Famous Players–Lasky, who took a drug overdose in New York.

Carl Laemmle reacted immediately to the Arbuckle case with a company edict. Universal's lawyers announced they would insert a "morality clause" into all existing and future contracts. The clause required players to conduct themselves "with due regard to public conventions and morals" and not to bring "public hatred, contempt, scorn or ridicule" on themselves or the company. Public interest ran so high that the fan magazine *Photoplay* printed the entire clause verbatim, its dry legal language notwithstanding.

Then came a thunderclap in the heart of the film colony itself. The prominent director William Desmond Taylor, a man-about-town with a murky past and a penchant for the ladies, was shot to death in his bungalow home in Los Angeles. When the police arrived at the scene, they found Mabel Normand, who'd gained fame as Charlie Chaplin's beautiful but funny co-star, rummaging through the bungalow in search of love letters. While Normand was not incriminated in the murder, she was implicated in a drug-and-blackmail tale uncovered by the newspapers in their pursuit of the Taylor case. Apparently, she was spending two thousand dollars a month on cocaine and paying to keep her habit a secret. As one film historian has written, "By 1922 Hollywood had gained the reputation of being not only the most glamorous but also the most corrupt city in the United States."

Laemmle responded to the Taylor case by telling the press: "Hollywood is not a nest of immoral people. Living there does not harm one's morals any more than living in New York or London or Paris. It is a clean, beautiful place, and it does not even need as much defense as I have given it. To say that the Taylor murder hurts the moving-picture business is utterly foolish. If it turns out that a banker committed the murder, it won't hurt the banking business, will it?"

The public didn't have to wait long for the year's crowning Hollywood scandal. It began to unfold when Dorothy Davenport, a Universal actress whose real name was Florence Reid, quietly announced she was committing her husband, Paramount star Wallace Reid, to a sanitarium for nervous exhaustion. In fact, the handsome leading man was being committed for alcohol and morphine detoxification. Without Florence's knowledge, he rented a cabin in Laurel Canyon and turned it into an opium den where friends could come to smoke with him or, if they preferred, shoot morphine and snort cocaine. So said angry Hollywood insiders without actually naming Reid.

Unfortunately, the star did not survive detoxification. Kept at the sanitarium for a long "cold turkey" cure, he wasted away physically, had a nervous breakdown and died in January 1923, at age thirty. These revelations came as such a shock that even the ultrastaid *Los Angeles Times* made them front-page news.

Meanwhile, the moral outrage threatening Hollywood was scarcely limited to concern over the dissolute lives of the film colony's famous and not-so-famous. There was a growing federal investigation into graft, which was said to be rampant within the industry, and an alarming probe of fraudulent stock trading among the top executives. But even more dangerous were the mounting attacks, from church pulpits and civic rostrums, on movies themselves.

"We have been plunged into an abysmal morass of fornication, adultery, pandering and prostitution," the chairman of the Pennsylvania Board of Censors wrote in 1922. "The seduction of mill girls and stenographers by their employers, men living with mistresses and women consorting with men without marriages are flashed into the eyes of old and young, willy nilly, in our 'movie' houses."

Such boiling sentiment was so common that government censorship loomed as an increasingly real possibility. And nothing frightened Hollywood's founding moguls more than censorship. They feared it not because it would have meant a collapse of artistic autonomy, regrettable as that might have been, but because it would have meant losing control at the box office. With ten million people going to the movies daily, by the industry's official estimates, too much money was at stake to allow outsiders to dictate what would be commercially appealing. Moguls like Adolph Zukor, Samuel Goldwyn and Carl Laemmle were not about to give up that right. Faced with strong regulatory moves toward censorship on the federal as well as state levels, particularly in New York and Massachusetts, they proposed to reform the movie industry themselves.

"We don't care about anything except a united front against censorship," Zukor professed.

Taking a cue from professional baseball, they decided to co-opt their critics and hire an unimpeachable movie czar. They wanted him to do for them what former United States District Judge Kenesaw Mountain Landis was doing for the major league team owners in the wake of the 1919 Black Sox betting scandal.

With Zukor as ringleader, the moguls turned to a politically influential cabinet officer in President Warren G. Harding's administration, Postmaster General Will H. Hays. He had recently engineered the president's election campaign as chairman of the Republican National Committee. Hays resigned from the cabinet with Harding's blessings and in March 1922 took over a newly formed organization called the Motion Picture Producers and Distributors Association of America. At first he soft-pedaled his mandate: "I hope to help develop the highest moral and constructive efficiency in films but will be neither a censor nor a reformer. I have no leaning toward eradicating sex from pictures—it would eradicate interest."

Soon, though, the film colony got its first real taste of what was to come from the Hays Office. The new movie czar sent a jolt through the rank-and-file with an ultimatum. "A bulletin was posted in all of the coast studios," *Variety* reported, "to the effect that instant dismissal would be meted out to anyone, whether star, director or executive, who fails to follow the straight and narrow path."

No matter what he said about not being a censor, Hays was out to sanitize pictures.

9

~~~~~~~~~

LIGHTS! CAMERA! ACTION!

AN OLD HOLLYWOOD AXIOM
says that anything worth doing once is worth doing twice, especially
with embellishments. If the producer Lewis J. Selznick could offer Russia's Nicholas II a job in pictures, then Carl Laemmle could do no less
for the Austrian emperor Charles I, who abdicated his throne.

In March 1922, hearing that the former monarch was broke and living in a dilapidated mansion on the Madeira Islands, Laemmle sent him
a cable from New York offering two hundred fifty thousand dollars for
the emperor's appearance on screen with the empress. The royal couple
would be cast in a spectacular movie with a prewar Vienna locale, called
The Merry-Go-Round. It was being prepared for production at Universal
City by one of the emperor's former subjects, Erich von Stroheim.

Laemmle's cable did not produce the desired result. Like Selznick's
offer five years earlier, it may have been nothing more than a grandiose
publicity stunt to begin with. But it did indicate that the mogul had un-
commonly sanguine expectations for a majestic production by his most
flamboyant director. Indeed, as the pace at Universal City quickened toward summer, the studio was looking to several extravaganzas.

One of them, Tod Browning's *Under Two Flags*, had already been shot.

Filled with "corking action," it starred Priscilla Dean, then the reigning queen of the lot, and featured climactic battle scenes between hordes of Algerian Arabs and the French Foreign Legion. At the end of May, with the editing still to be done, a huge explosion from an electrical short-circuit rocked the studio. Several buildings were engulfed in flames, including the cutting room. Hundreds of thousands of feet of film were destroyed, not least the finished footage of *Under Two Flags*. Virtually the entire movie had to be reshot.

Also on the horizon was *The Hunchback of Notre Dame*, Thalberg's pet project. He intended to make it the most spectacular movie ever mounted at Universal, surpassing *Foolish Wives* in histrionics and rivaling it in expense. Thalberg had persuaded Laemmle to let him spend more than one million two hundred fifty thousand dollars on *Hunchback*. But before that happened he would have to deal with von Stroheim's latest.

When the summer began, an uneasy truce prevailed between producer and director. Von Stroheim delivered a screenplay for *The Merry-Go-Round* in June, having chosen not to make *Castle Hubertus* after all. Thalberg, anxious to retain control of the production, refused to let him star in it. He did not want a repeat of *Foolish Wives*. This time if costs soared higher than he deemed reasonable, Thalberg wanted to be free to fire the director without the prospect of losing the leading man.

Filming started at the end of August amid Viennese sets of authentic prewar period splendor. Within six weeks, production costs spiraled to two hundred twenty thousand dollars. Von Stroheim spared no expense. For scenes in which Austrian officers were shown getting drunk, he served champagne to the extras "by the bucketful." He also filmed nude bathing scenes that couldn't be used. And he threw tantrums when the colors of the set design weren't perfectly accurate, which seemed beside the point in a black-and-white movie.

Thalberg decided he'd seen enough. On the evening of October 6, with a fraction of the movie completed, he called von Stroheim into his office and had the company lawyer fire him on the spot. *The Merry-Go-Round* would be finished by another director, Rupert Julian, who'd been kept waiting in the wings for just such a purpose.

Von Stroheim's firing was a signal event in Hollywood, the coup de grace in a power struggle of long standing between directors who represented art and producers who represented the bottom line. It was the first time a director of such stature had ever been fired. News of the humiliating dismissal swept through the film colony from top to bottom. Even Wyler was shocked. He heard what happened while sitting with friends in a restaurant and telephoned the studio to make sure he'd heard correctly.

Not that Wyler had anything at stake in the struggle. His own artistic conflicts with Universal would come sooner than he or Uncle Carl could possibly have expected, but now they were inconceivable. He was, after all, getting his first taste of movie production, no more likely to develop into a director than Joe Martin, Universal's star orangutan.

Wyler ran errands for the chief casting supervisor, who oversaw all performance assignments on the lot. He checked in extras. He worked as a prop boy, served as a script clerk, swept the sets. "It was like being an apprentice," he recalled. "Maybe I was too young. I didn't take it seriously." Which helps explain the vagueness of his recollections about his earliest practical training.

He worked for Irving Cummings, a former matinee idol with long experience as a director, and Jack Conway, another actor-turned-director known for his technical competence. Each made a handful of hour-long routine five-reelers for Universal from the time Wyler got to the studio to the time he became a third assistant director almost a year later on *The Hunchback of Notre Dame.*

Wyler never identified which of Cummings's or Conway's pictures he worked on during this period. As nearly as can be determined they were *The Jilt*, about a blind war veteran whose girlfriend drops him, and *Paid Back*, about a wealthy orphan who is being blackmailed (both directed by Cummings); *The Long Chance*, a Western about a gambler who protects a young girl from being swindled out of her mine claims, and *The Prisoner*, about an American traveler in Europe who discovers his former sweetheart is engaged to a murderer (both directed by Conway).

WYLER WAS ALLOWED TO WIELD A MEGAPHONE FOR THE FIRST time during the filming of *The Hunchback of Notre Dame*, which lasted six months from December 16, 1922, to June 3, 1923. Various authoritative sources credit him as an assistant director on the picture, though he actually was little more than a glorified "gofer" who helped control the milling crowds of extras during the shooting of the epic night scenes.

"How it really was," Wyler once recounted, "was there were two assistant directors, Jack Sullivan and Jimmy Dugan, and they needed a boy. I was the assistant directors' errand boy. . . . I did whatever chore came along. I was the lowest on the ladder."

The picture, a melodramatic simplification of Victor Hugo's 1831 classic novel, *Notre-Dame de Paris*, starred Lon Chaney as Quasimodo, the bellringer of the Cathedral of Notre Dame, who is so deformed and wart-eyed as to seem subhuman.

Though the screenplay stripped down Hugo's panoramic story of Louis XI's Paris, circa 1482, the physical production was literally gigantic. The Gothic sets alone took six months to build and were insured by Lloyd's of London for half a million dollars. A full-scale facade of Notre Dame, cast in concrete, duplicated the cathedral's huge main entrance to the top of its three arched portals. A hanging miniature of the cathedral's upper facade and bell towers was mounted for optical alignment between the camera and the full-scale set. The resulting visual blend looked perfectly matched on the screen.

Tons of cobblestones were brought in and laid by hand for the cathedral square, which covered eleven acres. The streets of old Paris and a castle courtyard covered another eight acres. Besides the cathedral, other buildings included a castle, taverns, houses, shops and a hotel. The Bastille and a drawbridge were built a quarter mile from the courtyard. Concrete arches constructed over the bed of the Los Angeles River served as the sewers of Paris.

Wyler recalled that one of his main errands was to help round up extras. *Hunchback* used as many as twenty-five hundred at a time. The assistant directors would send him downtown to pick people up and haul them back to the set in buses. "The running price of extras in those days was five dollars," he recalled. "For dress extras it was seven-fifty." But Universal paid only three dollars because it provided the transportation and the costumes. Wyler also was assigned to help round up lighting equipment. Film stock was so slow in those days that night scenes required extraordinarily intense illumination. "We had every sun arc in Hollywood on the set every night," Wyler remembered. "We'd get them from the other studios and bring them back in the morning. Some were spots, some were arcs—but they were all coal burners." The director Wallace Worsley and cameraman Robert Newhard used about three hundred individual pieces of lighting equipment each night.

Once the extras assembled on the set for the mob scenes, Willy became, for the first time, "more than an errand boy." As he recalled years later with dry self-deprecation, "I became the assistant directors' *assistant.*"

Worsley made use of an electric public address system, with loudspeakers hidden beyond camera range, to give orders to the crowds. But about ten assistants to the assistant directors actually patroled the set and saw to it that Worsley's orders were carried out. Arthur Hurni, who appeared in the mob scenes along with Alex Manuel and René

Traveletti, remembered Wyler, megaphone in hand, working with fierce energy. "Willy never stopped running back and forth," Hurni recounted. "He'd be yelling commands: 'Everybody! Light your torches! Pull up your tights! Everybody! Do you hear?' Getting us to do anything as simple as that wasn't so easy. He had to bully us into it. The whole place was basically in an uproar."

Patsy Ruth Miller, who co-starred as the kidnapped Esmeralda, would chat in French with Wyler between scenes. She, too, recalled his sense of purpose on the chaotic set: "I was impressed by how quickly he seemed to catch on to everything, the camera work, the setups and the crew preparation."

Coincidentally, it was during the filming of *Hunchback* that Paul Kohner made his first trip to Universal City with Laemmle's lieutenant, Manny Goldstein. Although they arrived in Los Angeles after dark, they drove straight out to the studio. And Kohner, too, saw Wyler amid the pandemonium. But he caught a rather different glimpse of his old friend.

"I made my way for the large gates of Notre Dame and stood around watching all these hundreds of people," he recounted. "There was no way to find Willy. But then I saw a small door in one of the gates. People kept coming and going through that door. Well, I was curious, so I snuck in. And there behind a black curtain were rows and rows of tables. Extras were standing around these tables. They had big bunches of daily checks in their hands. There was a terrific crapshoot going on. And there, at the head of the tables, was Willy—shooting craps."

Ever since going their separate ways, Wyler and Kohner had retained a warm affection for each other. During the visit "Kohner stayed over at the Walker house on Mariposa," according to Hurni, who recalls having to surrender his bed to Wyler's friend from New York. "We had a little party. Willy got out his violin and gave us a good performance. Someone put on the Victrola. Willy grabbed Mrs. Walker's daughter, Gladys, and swung her from one end of the drawing room to the other. Willy danced with gusto. The fox trot was popular at the time."

Afterward they decided to go to the neighborhood poolroom. In their rush to leave, "Willy couldn't find one of his shoes," Hurni recounted. "This amused Kohner no end. René was exasperated. 'The hell with Willy's shoe,' he said. 'We're going to lose our table.' So we told Willy he'd have to catch up with us. About fifteen minutes later, Willy finally appeared. He was wearing one brown shoe and one white shoe. He had this big grin on his face. I don't think he ever found the missing shoe."

Hurni's recollection of the incident, minor though it is, provides an impression of the post-adolescent Wyler as likably outgoing, devil-may-care and rather haphazard. Wyler's fond regard for Kohner seemed baffling to Hurni, considering the differences in their personalities. Indeed, Wyler's playful charm was the very antithesis of Kohner's controlled and careful manner, which epitomized the smart (and smartly tailored) style of a young executive on the rise.

Professionally, too, the contrast between them could not have been greater. While Willy had swept sets and run errands, Paul had spent the year as Uncle Carl's protégé. He'd accompanied the boss to Europe, arranging meetings with foreign dignitaries, organizing his personal publicity and generally operating as Universal's ambassador-at-large. Paul had risen so far above Willy by this time that when Irving Thalberg defected from Universal midway through producing *Hunchback* Paul could actually make a bid for Thalberg's job.

The defection proved to be as big a bombshell as the firing of von Stroheim. On February 15, 1923, Thalberg went to work for Louis B. Mayer, a feisty deal-maker who recognized that he needed a production chief with better taste than his own for his small but thriving studio. If Thalberg's resignation came as a shock—especially in view of his seeming attachment to Laemmle's attractive, headstrong daughter, Rosabelle—it had been brewing for some time and for a combination of reasons best summed up by Thalberg's dictum, "Never remain in a job when you have everything from it you can get."

His most basic reason for quitting was money. He was making four hundred dollars a week at Universal and felt he deserved more, including a share in the company. When Laemmle offered him a mere hike in salary to four hundred fifty dollars, Thalberg quietly began casting around elsewhere. Mayer signed him for six hundred dollars a week and made him a corporate officer. Fifteen months later Thalberg was awarded a share of profits in the newly merged Metro-Goldwyn-Mayer company. By October 1925 his weekly salary vaulted to two thousand dollars. The following October it doubled. Through guaranteed bonuses, moreover, the twenty-eight-year-old executive's minimum annual compensation was set at a phenomenal four hundred thousand dollars.

Kohner's hope of replacing Thalberg ultimately did not pan out. When he suggested himself for the job, the boss demurred.

"You're running too fast, Kohner," Laemmle told him. "You know next to nothing about the production end of the business. Also—very important—if you want to be a producer you must know what to produce. How do you find out? From the exhibitors. That's how I started. Listen to the exhibitors. They know what audiences like."

Kohner couldn't very well disagree. His only production experience amounted to giving director Rupert Julian some technical advice about the look of imperial Vienna after von Stroheim was sacked from *Merry-Go-Round*. And so, Kohner was maneuvered into spending a year on the road, canvassing theater owners from Maine to Montana as Laemmle's personal representative.

The irony, of course, is that Thalberg believed Laemmle had his ear cocked to the wrong exhibitors. Money aside, that was the other reason he quit. He did not believe, as Laemmle did, in catering almost exclusively to second-run markets with an endless stream of cheaply made fare. That policy, essentially unchanged from Laemmle's earliest days as a struggling independent producer, seemed hidebound and restrictive. Movies of quality and scope were aberrations at Universal, notwithstanding the lavish productions of *Foolish Wives*, *Merry-Go-Round* and *Hunchback*. Thalberg wanted to concentrate on producing prestige movies for first-run theaters. By the end of 1922 he'd concluded that Laemmle would not agree to his ideas for change.

Universal's huge output of routine melodramas, Westerns, and shorts—its so-called "balanced program," which Laemmle flogged to mom-and-pop exhibitors in America's hinterland—was, in Thalberg's opinion, anything but balanced. Such pictures never drew first-run bookings in the big cities, where profits were most lucrative. Thalberg was no less a proponent of cost control than Laemmle. But he believed that while classier pictures entailed greater financial risk, they brought better returns. They just had to be chosen wisely, scripted adroitly and produced efficiently—all areas in which he'd proved himself an expert supervisor.

Laemmle fumed over the loss of his boy wonder. Yet he made no effort to retain him, and neither did Rosabelle. Many executives who had chafed under Thalberg were happy to see him go.

WHEN THE FILMING OF *HUNCHBACK* CAME TO AN END, WYLER received a promotion to second assistant director and a raise in salary to forty dollars a week. His friend Alex Manuel, tamed perhaps by his motorcycle accident, figured he was not cut out for a career as a stunt man. He soon left for New York to study medicine at Columbia University's College of Physicians and Surgeons. Arthur Hurni had other plans, too.

He hitchhiked to San Francisco, took up the life of a bohemian painter and in 1928 moved to Tahiti with money Willy lent him for boat fare.

René Traveletti, who wanted to become an architect, stayed on as Willy's roommate. After working in Universal's art department, where he helped make the Notre Dame miniatures, René got a part-time job as an architect's assistant. René's younger brother, Bruno, also stayed on. Before the end of 1923, they would move with the Walker family to a house on Los Feliz Boulevard. "Since we were always behind in the rent, we had to move with them," Bruno recalled. "Nobody else would give us credit."

Encouraged by his promotion, Wyler wrote Laemmle in New York to ask for an advance of a thousand dollars against future salary deductions. He wanted to make a visit to Mulhouse to see his family. It must have been an unexpected blow to receive Laemmle's reply, a lengthy letter dated the day after Wyler's twenty-first birthday:

"My dear Willy . . . I often wondered whether you are lacking in judgment or what is wrong with you. Ever since you have been here, you have been a 'borrower,' and you no more pay off one debt than you want to borrow three or five times as much as you had before. I tell you frankly, Willy, I have very little confidence in you, and I am satisfied that if you continue as you do now, you will never be a success."

Laemmle adopted the hectoring tone of a put-upon headmaster. He threatened to communicate his displeasure to Willy's parents, "because they have already asked me one favor this year, namely, to bring your brother Robert over here."

What irked him most was Willy's "chutzpah" in demanding such a burdensome loan. "It is high time that you became sensible," he noted.

Coming from a millionaire who routinely squandered large sums at poker or on the horses, this righteous indignation over Willy's infractions seems laid on. Laemmle is said to have lost thirty thousand dollars in one weekend at the Agua Caliente racetrack in Mexico. Despite his legendary stinginess, he would pay seven hundred fifty thousand dollars in 1925 for a palatial Beverly Hills mansion with a living room more than thirty yards long and a fireplace ten feet high. It surely gave the lie to Laemmle's taste for the plebeian. Fifteen gardeners and six thousand dollars a month were needed just to keep up the twenty-eight-acre estate under its former owner, the famed producer Thomas Ince.

Yet Laemmle seemed to believe every pious word of his reproachful letter to Willy. "If you hope to have my goodwill and my friendship in the future, you must save your money and quit making debts. And if you ever want to go to Europe, you will have to go with your own money. Get that. Not with borrowed money."

Finally, however, he offered encouragement. Willy had "done splendidly on the *Hunchback*." As soon as he showed he was "capable enough to become a first assistant," Laemmle would instruct Julius Bernheim, the general manager who had succeeded Thalberg, to give him another promotion. Thus, he could "immediately earn more money." For the moment, though, Willy was "being well paid" as a second assistant.

It would take Wyler more than a year to put together a trip to Europe. Long before then, his brother Robert arrived in Los Angeles under Laemmle's sponsorship. Bob, as his friends now called him, joined Willy and the Traveletti brothers at the house on Los Feliz Boulevard in the fall of 1923. "The Walkers were very accommodating," Bruno Traveletti remembers. "Mr. Walker was a retired police chief from a small town in Illinois, and I don't think he had any pension. I guess they needed the extra income." Paired off in two upstairs rooms — Willy with Bob, René with Bruno — the quartet lived there through the spring of 1924, when they moved into a rented bungalow at Universal City.

Robert Wyler's recently acquired engineering degree was of no use to him on the movie lot. He went to work as an office boy doing what Willy had been doing in previous months. But he swiftly made an impression. "He was the one I'd have bet on," Patsy Ruth Miller recalled. "He was taller than Willy and quite good-looking." Everyone who met Robert seems to have been struck by his sensitivity, his jaunty Gallic manners and especially his handsome, delicate features in comparison with his gap-toothed younger brother's. Even three decades later, the writer Jessamyn West was so taken with "Robert's pulchritude" she remarked that he "may well have been the most beautiful young man in France at one time."

Willy did not exactly turn over a new leaf, as Uncle Carl had urged. "We still had the Maxwell, so we'd all go up to Reno to gamble," Bruno recalled. "Willy wanted to try out a betting system for roulette. This was typical of him. The thing is you had to stick to the system, and we didn't. We always came back losers."

Willy also had a more successful idea: to build a one-room beach house in Santa Monica for weekend romps. "We used to take the car and spend the night on the beach," Bruno said. "Willy figured, 'Why not put up a little cottage?' He took the lead. He thought René and Bob had the technical know-how. So we all scraped around for the money. The whole thing cost seven hundred dollars. We bought the land. In those days you got it for nothing. We bought the lumber. We did the work ourselves. It was just a square room with some cots. We had parties once or twice a month. We brought girls. If Willy wanted to, he could always get girls to come along, girls he met at work. But it was all pretty innocent."

"I was just playing the field," Wyler remembered. "I had a little black booklet with girls' names. But if a girl looked like she would want to get married, I ran like hell. I was determined I would never get married, or maybe when I was forty. The first two years [in Los Angeles], I just had dates—occasionally. I had no money. I was very short of girls. We were this group of fellows. You might have a date with a girl for a soda, but there was damn little sex. Getting laid? Sometimes you'd work on a girl for a week, for two weeks, and maybe make it and also maybe not."

At the same time, he didn't forget Laemmle's admonitions. He enhanced his professional skills by attaching himself to several of the studio's bigger, more promising pictures. Following *Hunchback*, he worked as a second assistant for Irving Cummings on *Fool's Highway* (originally titled *My Mamie Rose*) and *The Rose of Paris*, and for King Baggot on *The Gaiety Girl*. The first was released as a Super Jewel, the Universal imprimatur denoting a major film of the highest quality and prestige. The other two were Jewels, indicating top features with somewhat less status. All three starred Mary Philbin, whom von Stroheim had discovered in 1920 at a Chicago beauty contest and had cast as the virginal ingenue in *The Merry-Go-Round*. A radiant-looking brunette with innocent, wide-set eyes, Philbin would become Universal's most important dramatic silent star of the late twenties.

Cummings, who went on to direct musicals and comedies at Twentieth Century–Fox—notably *Curly Top* and other Shirley Temple pictures—is said to have drawn a sensitive performance from Philbin as Mamie Rose, a seamstress in a tailor's shop.

Wyler, who always took a modest view of his beginnings, never indicated what he learned, technically or otherwise, from working on these now-forgotten pictures. But, by his own account, assisting Cummings and Baggot helped him make up his mind on a career. "I decided that directing was what I'd like to do," Wyler recalled. "Maybe it seemed glamorous. It was something I felt I could do. I had a certain eye for the camera. I used to watch where they would put it and how they did things. Occasionally, I would come up with a suggestion. Directing was something that intrigued me. I never felt I could act or write. But I felt I could direct."

. . .

THALBERG'S ASSESSMENT OF THE PRODUCTION DEFICIENCIES AT Universal came back to haunt Laemmle by the beginning of 1924. Profits had fallen, and a new national sales manager hired to reverse the decline came to the same conclusion as Thalberg: "Exhibitors want bigger pictures and will pay to get them because they make more money with them. This is thoroughly borne out by the experience of Jewel pictures. So I am going to propose to Mr. Laemmle that he give us thirty-six Jewels for the next season."

Considering that Universal had made only six such features in 1922 and six in 1923, it was a stunning proposal, made more so by Laemmle's agreement to implement the change despite having to spend "five million dollars more than we have ever put into a production program." The company offered stock to the public to raise the necessary capital. And while output did not quite meet the ambitious new quota, Universal did release sixteen Jewels in 1924, twenty-six in 1925 and twenty-nine in 1926.

But the change was not intended to reverse the studio's overall policy. Formulaic Westerns and serials continued to be main ingredients of Laemmle's marketing campaign. In fact, the Vitagraph "serial king" William Duncan, who had been brought over to Universal in 1922, was given complete control of his own production unit to help bolster the popularity of the genre. A top Western star who had earned ten thousand dollars a week at his peak in 1919, Duncan not only directed most of his own movies but wrote them, shot them on location and did his own stunts.

Wyler went to Idaho with the bluff, well-liked actor-director to make *Wolves of the North,* a 1924 Northwest melodrama about fur pirates. "We shot it in six to eight weeks," Wyler recalled. *Wolves,* one of three major serials Duncan made for Universal, closed out his long and successful career. It had twelve episodes and ran for a total of twenty-four reels, which was the equivalent of a four-hour movie. Serials typically delivered lots of action, but Duncan's were highlighted by unusual (and unusually dangerous) stunts. If they were sketchy on character (also typical of the genre), they went out of their way to make the action seem authentic.

Wyler would soon be applying a similar recipe on the studio back lot to his own two-reel Westerns, almost two dozen of them. As he recalled years later for film historian Kevin Brownlow, "They were all very elementary stories. They'd start with action, finish with action and have some action in the middle. There was very little time for plots or characterization or anything like that. You'd have a little love story, but mostly villains, heroes, a sheriff or some such complication. . . . To characterize someone quickly, I remember in one film I had him come out of the bar, kick the dog. Another man comes out of the bar, pets the dog. Now you know who's the hero and who's the villain."

Before Wyler got to direct, however, he returned to Mulhouse for the first time in four years. He booked passage on the S.S. *De Grasse* and sailed cabin class from New York on October 7, 1924. When the ship docked ten days later under the slate-gray skies of Le Havre, he looked very much the fit young American in his single-breasted suit and tightly knotted tie. He was tanned from the California sun. His shock of dark brown hair was as thick as ever but now had golden highlights. His stocky frame had filled out, yet his round face had lost its pudginess.

Indeed, at twenty-two, Wyler seemed to have taken on a certain degree of maturity. He even carried a glowing letter of introduction from William Koenig, Universal's latest production chief, which was the closest thing to a diploma that Willy ever received. Citing Wyler's work on "some of our largest productions," Koenig noted, "we will be more than pleased to have him return to our Company after his trip abroad." Although the letter probably was intended to ease Willy's reentry into the States — it was no-tarized for use by immigration officials — Koenig went further than he had to in praise of the young man. "I can heartily recommend him for a posi-tion in the Motion Picture line," he concluded, "and am positive that he will more than satisfy any Director in need of a first-class Assistant."

As 1924 drew to a close, Wyler's two-month stay in Mulhouse con-firmed his earlier realization that "my roots were European but America was already my home." He saw his family and childhood friends, went to the Salzburg music festival in Austria and by the middle of December was back at Universal City in time for the departure of René and Bruno Traveletti.

The pair had decided to move back to Lausanne. They drove off, heading east, in a new Model T Ford bought with their share of pro-ceeds from the sale of the Santa Monica shack. But they never got fur-ther than Chicago. "We stopped there to make a little money," Bruno recounted, "and we stayed forty years." René became an architect. Bruno went into the travel business.

The Wyler brothers continued living together in their bungalow on the Universal lot. Bob earned a promotion to the scenario department. Willy was about to turn a corner that would mark a decisive change in his career.

10

~~~~~

GIVE HIM A TWO-REELER

In a stroke of luck, Wyler landed an assignment as first assistant director to William Craft, an old-timer who had directed more important pictures than the two-reel Westerns handed him at Universal. When filming took Craft and his crew out on location to Mulholland Drive or up to the Sanchez Ranch in Newhall, as often as not Craft ducked out for the afternoon and left Willy to shoot scenes on his own.

"He'd say to me, 'I've got a doctor's appointment at four o'clock,' or something like that. 'You know what happens here.' Then he'd go home. I was delighted, of course."

Wyler also served as first assistant to director William Crinley on a pair of two-reelers filmed in Lone Pine, a little California town in the Owens Valley near Mt. Whitney, some two hundred miles north of Los Angeles. It had become one of Hollywood's favorite Western locations. The surrounding terrain was rugged, even exotic. Gnarled stone hills rose from the valley floor like totemic monuments to wind, water and earthquake, the powerful forces of nature that had shaped them over eons. West of town were the foothills of the Sierra Nevada mountains, which soared in the distance like towering steeples. To the east, a desert stretched as far as the horizon.

In June 1925, Crinley and Wyler and a company of roughly twenty players spent several weeks in Lone Pine making two Mustang "stunt thrillers" starring Fred Humes. Although many Universal companies had come there before, this was the first time for both Crinley and Wyler. The two pictures were shot among the rocky hills of Lone Pine Creek Canyon. The same landscape was eventually stamped in memory by the *Hopalong Cassidy* and *Lone Ranger* serials of later decades. For some scenes Crinley and Wyler also trekked into the desert flats across the Owens River. Neither picture is extant, and neither was named by the local newspaper that noted both productions. But in all likelihood they were *Taking Chances* and *The Gold Trap,* each released before the end of the year.

Wyler worked for Arthur Rosson as well. Rosson was a young director trying to get to Paramount with a crime picture he and Ben Hecht had written called *Underworld.* Rosson was making two-reelers at Universal as a way of marking time. When Paramount finally called, Rosson dropped everything and went to the supervisor of Westerns, Isadore Bernstein, to suggest that Wyler be allowed to complete the two-reeler. But Bernstein turned down the idea, pointing out that Wyler was "just an assistant."

Hollywood legend has it that Wyler then demanded a meeting with Laemmle on one of his frequent West Coast visits to the studio. Wyler, who told the tale himself, is supposed to have bluffed his way into his first full-fledged directing assignment. Laemmle supposedly called Wyler into his office to settle the issue. He is said to have asked if Wyler thought he really knew how to make a two-reeler on his own. Laemmle then called Bernstein into his office and told him: "This boy here says he can direct. Let's see if he can." When Bernstein reiterated his objection, Laemmle silenced him with a command: "Let's see if he's telling the truth. Give him a two-reeler."

It is a dramatic story, but apocryphal. Laemmle was not on the coast. He was back in New York. Wyler did not plead his case. And Bernstein was not ordered against his better judgment to give Wyler his first two-reeler. What actually happened, according to Wyler's personal records, is that a few days short of his twenty-third birthday, Wyler wired Laemmle in New York asking for a promotion from first assistant director. Laemmle simply wired back his approval. Bernstein's objection would come six months later, when Laemmle assigned Wyler his first five-reel Western, starring Art Acord. By then Wyler had already made a half-dozen two-reelers.

On July 3, 1925, two days after he turned twenty-three, Wyler wrote Laemmle: "Please let me extend to you my heartfelt thanks for the wonderful opportunity you have just given me. Although I expected to become a director within the next few months . . . your favorable answer to my wire is beyond words. As it happened, it was on my birthday anniversary . . ."

Wyler's letter goes on to thank Laemmle for "the most wonderful gift" and adds: "Now, the rest is up to me, I know, and I feel fully confident that I will make good; in fact I feel surer of myself this time than in anything I have ever attempted. . . . I frankly believe that I have the material within me to develop some day into one of your best commercial directors."

The promotion made Wyler the youngest director on the Universal lot and probably among the youngest at any of the studios. It irked him several years later to see *Variety* calling Mervyn LeRoy Hollywood's youngest, though LeRoy didn't become a director until 1927 at the age of twenty-seven. Normally Wyler did not care about such distinctions. But LeRoy's self-promotion rankled him. "It used to make me angry because he had press agents," Wyler remembered. "And I didn't."

Wyler began shooting his first Mustang two-reeler, *The Crook Buster*, on July 13, 1925. The movie was twenty-four minutes long, the usual length of two-reelers, and featured Jack Mower, a third-rank cowboy actor who never became a star. Wyler would make a total of six two-reelers with Mower over the next six weeks. He began his second Mustang picture, *The Gunless Badman*, on July 21, followed by *The Fighting Romeo* (retitled *Ridin' for Love*), *The Fire Barrier*, *Flashing Spurs* (retitled *Don't Shoot*), and *The Pinnacle Rider.*

Thus, in less than two months, Wyler gained considerable experience as a full-fledged Western director. His six Mustang pictures, lasting a total of three hours, were the rough equivalent of three or four full-length Westerns, which generally ran forty-five minutes to an hour each. He also spent many hours shooting cowboy tests for the studio, although not necessarily for his own two-reelers.

"One time they were looking for a new cowboy star," Wyler remembered. "The test was a very simple matter, because the main thing was how well you rode and how good you looked on a horse. That was the first qualification, not how much or how well you acted. Of course, acting was a consideration, but the riding was the most important thing."

Wyler shot the tests on the Universal back lot. Over and over he had cowboys "ride down a hill as fast as they could, make a flying dismount in front of a bar, go in, come back out, make a pony express." This last trick was a form of stunt riding. It consisted of mounting a horse in motion. "The horse goes by, and you grab the saddle horn," Wyler explained. "Bang, you're back into the saddle and you ride out."

One of the unknown cowboys he tested was Gary Cooper. When they made *The Westerner* together fifteen years later, Wyler had completely forgotten the encounter. Cooper reminded him. "He told me he made the test and flunked it."

Notwithstanding its trend toward feature production, Universal had no less than four separate units turning out two-reel Westerns during the summer of 1925. The studio was, in fact, the only one still eager to keep the market supplied with them. These short films—intended mainly as attractions for Saturday matinees in neighborhood theaters— cost very little to make, perhaps two thousand dollars each. Because they were so cheap, Universal earned profits on them even if they couldn't generate the earnings of first-run features. And Wyler, on a weekly salary of sixty dollars, now became part of the factory process. He joined Crinley, Vin Moore (for whom he'd also worked as an assistant director), Ernst Laemmle, Victor Nordlinger and Ray Taylor, among other low-budget journeymen.

They shot Mustang two-reelers at the rate of one every three days. With script preparation and editing, it took five days on average to complete these films of twenty-four minutes or so in length. Between 1925 and 1927, Universal would release a total of one hundred thirty-five Mustangs. Wyler made twenty-one of these. The recipe for each was basically the same: strong hero, love interest, villain, several chases, fights, a rescue, a happy ending and nonstop action throughout. The casts invariably had players who'd been real-life cowboys, along with a complement of actors. Wyler always related that the making of two-reel Westerns was his film academy: "It was a hell of a good school for learning the fundamentals of making films, which lie in movement. Movies are not stills. They are movement. And those Westerns—all routine, elementary stories—had to *move*." Sometimes he sat up nights "trying to think up new ways of photographing a man getting on or off a horse," he recalled. "That was my preoccupation."

But for all the ingenuity that went into them, the chases were more or less interchangeable from one two-reeler to the next. "We had a circle out in the country on Frenchie's ranch, where we used to shoot," Wyler noted. "We put the camera in the middle of it on a platform. I sat under the platform in a swivel chair, and the chase went around in a circle. Once it's photographed like this you can't tell they're going in a circle. You were able to shoot close shots, long shots, medium shots, all sorts of shots. And you made a whole chase in that one position without having to move the camera. I'd have the prop boy turn me around in the swivel chair as they were riding around, so I could see what was happening in comfort."

Universal generally tried to shoot Westerns during the spring and summer months to avoid the rainy season, a policy it often broke. Even so, this meant the winter months tended to be slower for production; and by the end of that summer, Hollywood was facing another of its periodic downturns. All the studios began to cut their payrolls. Universal alone laid off three hundred employees, claiming it wanted to save money on a precipitous rise in filmmaking costs of some two hundred percent. In late September, with none of his pictures yet released, Wyler suddenly found himself without a job.

A friend of Wyler's and fellow employee, Bruce "Lucky" Humberstone, found himself out of work as well, though not because of the massive layoff. Humberstone was a first assistant director. He had gone to Universal's production chief, William Koenig, and asked to be assigned to *The Phantom of the Opera*. Koenig turned him down, but offered a smaller assignment. Rather than accept, Humberstone walked. He heard that Metro-Goldwyn-Mayer was making a big picture out in Culver City called *Ben-Hur* and suggested to Wyler that both of them apply for jobs. The studio had built a Roman stadium, the Circus Maximus, on a vast tract. It had hired thousands of extras for the chariot race, the picture's monumental action sequence, and MGM needed sixty assistant directors for a few days' work.

Wyler's experience on the MGM epic was one of the more vivid memories of his early career. It did not play as crucial a role as he liked to remember, but it did put him at the heart of the most spectacular production Hollywood had ever attempted until then, far surpassing *The Hunchback of Notre Dame*.

On the day of the chariot race, he and Humberstone reported to the set at six-thirty in the morning. Each of the sixty assistants was posted on the edge of the vast oval track in front of the grandstand, dressed in Roman costumes to blend with the crowds of extras who poured into the seats above them. By nine, Fred Niblo was ready to begin shooting. Niblo, who ranked as Hollywood's top contract director at twenty-five hundred dollars a week, stood on a tower several stories high. Next to him were the chief assistant and the head cameraman, who was supervising forty-two cameras at strategic points throughout the stadium and an airplane circling overhead for aerial shots.

Behind and below Niblo, assembled in a tier of makeshift seats, were many of the film colony's stars, studio executives and city officials. So many directors and production people turned out to watch the filming that work had come to a virtual halt throughout the rest of Hollywood. Douglas Fairbanks, who was making *The Black Pirate,* saw the spectacle with Mary Pickford. They'd planned to stay for an hour but ended up staying six. Harold Lloyd, the comedy star, even climbed to the top of the director's tower and watched the chariot race at Niblo's side.

Estimates varied about the size of the throng in the grandstand that day. They ranged from thirty-five hundred to ten thousand. Whatever the number, the crowd was costumed in full regalia as Romans, Egyptians, Jews and Assyrians. No expense was spared. A Berlin costume company, which dressed the Berlin and Vienna Grand Operas, provided the biblical outfits. The extras had been rehearsed for several days by the assistant directors to cheer wildly, rush pell-mell from their seats, place bets on the charioteers and generally act like frenzied spectators caught up in the drama of triumph and defeat.

The first riders to appear on the track were mounted horsemen of the Roman Imperial Guard, played by cavalry officers of the United States Army. They cleared the race course of the Roman rabble and rode off for a quick costume change to reappear again as buglers on horseback. When they blew their final note and galloped off, huge curtains were flung back at one of the arena entrances and twelve chariot teams dashed out onto the track. Each chariot had four horses. The track was so wide that a phalanx of forty-eight horses could circle in unison before the race got underway. Ten chariot teams had stunt men for drivers. Two were driven by the stars, Ramon Novarro, playing Ben-Hur, and Francis X. Bushman, playing Messala.

Niblo gave orders through an oversized megaphone taller than he was. Wyler recalled, "You were signaled to have your section get up and cheer or sit down." Just before Niblo started shooting, he wanted something from Wyler's section. "Suddenly I heard my name called. So I came running. As I looked up behind him I saw this gallery of all the important people in Hollywood, including the guy who'd just fired me. I don't remember what Mr. Niblo said or why he called me over. But it must have looked like I was his right-hand man."

When work on the chariot race was finished, Wyler got his job back at Universal. He always claimed he was rehired and, for the first time, made a director because he'd been spotted that day on *Ben-Hur.* In fact, the chariot race wasn't filmed until October 3, 1925—long after Wyler had already directed his first six two-reel Westerns. What actually happened was that Laemmle sent word assigning Wyler to direct *Lazy Lightning,* his first five-reeler. And here is where he encountered objections from Universal's supervisor of Westerns. Bernstein felt Wyler wasn't seasoned enough for the assignment and strongly protested in a memo imploring Laemmle not to give it to him:

"Wyler has not had enough experience to tackle a five-reeler at the speed we are going—*ten days to a picture.* The two-reelers he did make averaged *four and one half days* to a picture. Give him a chance at a few more before you insist upon him taking a five-reeler. . . ."

Thus, from the very beginning of his career, Wyler was dogged by the sort of complaint that was to bedevil him time and again in later years. He would gain a reputation for being too slow, too deliberate, too careful, too demanding and, consequently, for tending to run over schedule and over budget. But the litany of complaints, though justifiable at first glance, often had to do with factors beyond Wyler's control even when his artistic taste and attention to detail compelled him to work at a pace some found intolerable. And more often than not, it turns out to be unjustified on closer examination of the actual shooting schedules for his major pictures.

In any case, Bernstein did not get his wish. Laemmle refused to budge. Wyler began filming his first five-reeler, *Lazy Lightning,* on January 12, 1926, less than a month after *The Crook Buster,* his first two-reeler, had been released without the slightest notice.

The melodramatic plot of *Lazy Lightning,* a Blue Streak Western with Art Acord, capitalized on the leading man's riding ability and his image as a "white hat." Acord was a silent Western star with a large following in small towns across the country. Raised in Oklahoma, he was a real cowboy whose roping skills had made him a great rodeo attraction. He had had a successful career performing cowboy stunts with several Wild West shows and, when he got to California, found himself featured in a number of Westerns. He'd been at Universal making two-reelers since 1919. They became so popular that in 1925 he was jumped up to five-reelers. Though he eventually starred in fourteen of them, he was not much of an actor, nor was he able to make the transition to talkies. He achieved popularity because, according to Wyler, "he had a kind of sincerity." His weather-beaten face "wasn't handsome," but he was physically rugged and "he looked good on a horse."

The movie told the story of Dickie Rogers, an invalid child who lives on a ranch with his Uncle Henry, who is in over his head to gamblers.

The uncle will do anything to pay off his debts. That includes trying to get possession of little Dickie's inheritance. As Rance Lighton, Acord plays a lazy wanderer whose name is mistaken for "Lightning." He is arrested for vagrancy and hauled off to the ranch, where he not only befriends Dickie but saves his life and his inheritance and wins the love of Dickie's older sister, Lila.

Fay Wray played Lila. As a teenager she had haunted casting offices and, beginning in 1923, got to play bit parts in such pictures as *Gasoline Love* and *Coast Patrol*. A pretty redhead who later donned a blond wig, she soon would catch the eye of Erich von Stroheim and land a starring role in *The Wedding March*. Wray also would become a world-famous Hollywood icon as the terrified love object of the giant ape in the 1933 sensation *King Kong*. But in *Lazy Lightning* she was still an unknown ingenue.

Wray recalls that Wyler was immediately put to the test by his star. Acord "sometimes had to be awakened by the assistant director on the way to location. It seemed that he wouldn't stir out of bed until pulled from it. We would all wait in the car until he came out, looking grim, saying nothing, smelling of alcohol." Though Acord looked sad, she said, "he wore his cowboy clothes with style. But because of his sadness and silence and the alcohol, it wasn't comfortable to do scenes with him."

What Wray remembers most about making *Lazy Lightning* was Wyler's willingness to take time and trouble over her performance. "I had a scene with the little boy," she said. "He is dying. As someone who cared for him, I was sitting by his bed in the candlelight. All of this had a quality that was richer and more thoughtful than anything you found in those films. I mean, a Western was mostly action. But this had a mood and a moment. Willy wanted to give the scene a rich feeling. I appreciated him for the values he was trying to achieve.

"I remember he wanted tears from me. He was sitting on the other side of the bed by the camera. He talked very quietly to me. It was very intense. I'm not sure my tears were as abundant as Willy wanted. But he took time over the scene. That was not normal. He wanted to dwell on it. That was exceptional. It made me understand why he became one of the greats. There was a tenderness beneath his exterior."

By the time *Lazy Lightning* was released eleven months later in December 1926, Wray had been named one of the year's WAMPAS Baby Stars. The selection of these starlets was part of an annual publicity campaign by the Western Association of Motion Picture Advertisers that continued through the end of the twenties as an accepted industry measure of glamour potential. Wyler's first five-reel effort showed much less promise. *Variety* said "the picture in the main is a 'weak sister,' despite its sentimental tug." Before its release, Universal's in-house critic savaged it. He objected to the very texture that Wray had appreciated:

"This would make a great two-reel western, putting all of the first four reels into one and running the fifth reel as it is. But to have to wade through four meaningless reels full of just exactly the wrong kind of thing to put into a western picture to get to anything which is interesting or spectacular from the audience standpoint is going to be a hard thing to advertise, and a still harder thing to sell.

"This picture should be shown to every director on the coast as an example of the thing not to do in making Blue Streak Westerns. There isn't a single element in it which is in line with the policy of five-reel western pictures, and I certainly hope that nobody will ever try to make another one like this."

Nevertheless, ten days before that memo was written, Wyler was already shooting another Blue Streak with Acord, called *Riding Honor.* Begun in April, the picture was released a year later as *Hard Fists*. Again Acord plays a fancy-riding ranch hand, this time with a shady past. Again Acord saves the life of an elderly woman who has a daughter. Again he falls in love with the daughter.

Despite the opinion of the in-house critic or the obvious second-rate status of *Lazy Lightning*, Universal put together its usual publicity campaign glorifying both the star and director. Just before its release, Acord was trotted around to Hollywood public schools to deliver homilies on laziness. He was credited with saving the life of Bobby Gordon, the child actor playing little Dickie, not just on film but in reality. Describing a scene in which Gordon's wheelchair is headed over a cliff, the studio noted: "For safety purposes a net was placed below the cliff out of the camera's range. As the chair was wheeling down the incline it suddenly struck a small rock that threw it out of its course toward a part of the cliff where there was no net. Acord whirled his lariat and let fly. [The rope] settled about Bobby Gordon's waist and lifted him bodily from the chair just as it plunged over the cliff."

Wyler, meanwhile, was named a "Gold Medal Western Director" and awarded a trophy "given annually to the maker of the best Western production by the Boy's Cinema Club of Hollywood." The club probably was a figment of Universal's publicity department, which also manufactured a German university education and theatrical experience for him. Wyler was said to have "spent time studying the drama and working about the theatres in Berlin." Universal claimed Laemmle "was at-

tracted by the young man's knowledge of the drama and his intense enthusiasm for the stage and screen."

Wyler began shooting his third Blue Streak Western, titled *Smiling
Sam*, by May of 1926. It had Fred Humes as the star opposite a petite,
vivacious blonde, Ena Gregory, who was still in her teens. This picture—renamed *Blazing Days* for its release—represented something of a
step up for Wyler if only because Humes was Universal's favorite lead
among its five-reel cowboys, after Hoot Gibson.

Humes came from Pennsylvania and worked as a cowpuncher on
ranches from Texas to Montana. Eventually drifting to Hollywood, he
began appearing in two-reelers as one of the Universal Ranch Riders.
Supporting roles in a few Hoot Gibson features led to starring roles in
twenty-one features between 1924 and 1927. Unlike Acord, though,
Humes had a handsome, youthful face. But he was less physically imposing, and so wore a ridiculously high ten-gallon hat to make him look
taller. It was a white hat, of course, leaving no doubt as to his heroic
stature.

Gregory was only twelve years old when she came to Hollywood
from Australia with her mother. Eighteen when she made *Blazing Days*,
she remembers Wyler was "all business" on the film. "He didn't josh
around. He was definitely the director in charge of everything. He
wasn't tough, but he was serious. He wanted to get things done. I remember we were on awfully hot locations. They had to put ice on the
camera to keep the film from melting."

Gregory also remembers she didn't know how to ride a horse and lied
about it to Wyler. "I told him I could ride. But all I'd ridden was a pony,
never a horse. They put me on one in front of twenty-five horses and
riders. We had to ride down into a gully. They were all yelling and
screaming. And I remember thinking, 'My God, I'm going to fall off.' I
grabbed the horse's mane and hung on. When I got to the bottom, I
started to cry. That's when I told them I'd never really ridden a horse.
Wyler laughed."

In fact, Wyler couldn't ride a horse either. He soon learned though,
frequently putting on a cowboy hat and joining the posse in his pictures.

When *Blazing Days* was released, it came in for ridicule as a prime example of the dumb Western. *Variety*'s reviewer thought it a howler for
schoolboys: "This is a pic-ture, a wes-tern pic-ture. Not a good pic-ture;
not a bad pic-ture. It is a-bout cow-boys and love. Of course, you are
not old e-nough to really know what love is, but it is a-bout kis-sing.
You will like this pic-ture. It has a stagecoach rob-ber-y—what a big
word. It means naught-y steal-ing."

Wyler was not impressed either. The scripts he had to shoot were so worthless he sometimes threw them away. He once reshot a story that he'd made a few months earlier. "Nobody knew the difference," he recalled. "Part of another script we used for toilet paper, because that's all it was good for." Still, he worked steadily. In the ten months following his twenty-third birthday, Wyler made nine movies. And on June 24, before he turned twenty-four, he started his tenth: *True Blue*, another full-length Blue Streak again starring Fred Humes and this time co-starring Acord's wife, Louise Lorraine.

Later retitled *The Stolen Ranch*, it tells the story of "Breezy" Hart and his war buddy, Frank, who suffers from shell shock. Frank is the heir to a ranch that a tough hombre named Hardy has claimed as his own after Frank's departure for France. Now that Frank is back, Hardy naturally wants to get rid of him. But Breezy is determined to help his friend and see justice done. Frank gets the ranch back, of course, thanks to Breezy. He also falls in love, just as Breezy does, which cures his shell shock.

Three weeks later, Willy began making *Martin of the Mounted*, another routine two-reeler. He would shoot fifteen of these in a row at the rate of roughly one a week through the end of October: *Dangerous Game* (retitled *The Two Fister*), *Haunted Homestead*, *Tenderfoot Courage*, *The Red Rider* (retitled *Galloping Justice*), *Lone Star*, *The Ore Raiders*, *Kelcy Gets His Man*, *Silent Partner*, *Range Courage* (retitled *The Phantom Outlaw*), *Gun Justice*, *The Home Trail*, *Square Shooter*, *The Horse Trader* and *Hollywood or Bust* (retitled *Daze of The West*).

USUALLY, WYLER SHOT HIS WESTERNS ON UNIVERSAL'S BACK lot or in nearby locations. One pair of films, however, took him north to Lone Pine — *Square Shooter* and *The Horse Trader* — which he made simultaneously. Both starred Fred Gilman, a third-rank cowboy star who filmed eleven two-reelers with Wyler and eventually went on to make Universal's *Texas Ranger* series in 1927 and 1928.

"The only way we could get up to Lone Pine was to make two pictures at the same time because everyone had to be fed, the hotel bill paid and so on," Wyler recounted. "Well, we had some bad weather, and I was a day behind schedule and the studio called and said, 'Come home tonight.' I needed another day to finish, because everything was shot around a cabin that was out there on a beautiful location with the mountains in the background. I couldn't possibly leave it. They said, 'Shoot everyone going into the cabin and coming out of the cabin. We'll shoot the rest at the studio.'

"Well, I hadn't worked out the plot. I'd changed the script. In those days we were allowed to change things any way we wanted as long as the action kept going. So I got the villains and the hero to come riding in fast, single, double, from one direction, from the other direction. I got them coming out of the cabin, shot up, crawling, riding fast, with the girl, without the girl, rescued, not rescued. That way I could make up anything I wanted to on the following day when we didn't know what we were going to shoot inside the cabin. We had all the entrances and all the exits in every possible combination."

Many of these silent Westerns were so similar, Wyler could barely recall one from the other. But the last of this batch, *Daze of The West*, was somewhat different. A send-up about a movie company going on location to do a Western, it involved a film within a film.

"The star, who wears a cowboy hat and silver spurs, is supposed to be kind of a pansy," Wyler remembered. "He's effete, can't ride a horse well, can't do any stunts. So the movie company starts looking among the ranch hands for someone to double him. And that's where the real star comes in.

"I had the first guy play a very exaggerated pansy. Then the ranch hand comes on and does the stunts. The leading lady naturally falls in love with *him*. It's very corny. But we had to have [players] acting as the director and the crew. It was a takeoff. Well, I ran into Vin Moore, who was one of the directors on the lot. I'd worked for him as an assistant. He'd been a comedian. So I asked him to play the director. He said he would if I played his assistant.

"We're making the movie. He's got a big megaphone and puttees, like De Mille. He'd walk around and I'd be right behind him with his director's chair. He'd sit down, get up, move, sit down, get up. Everything he did kept breaking me up. I couldn't stop laughing. It was ruining the shots. So I arranged to have him fire me on camera to get myself out of the picture."

Wyler didn't have to look far for this sort of parody. Universal had long catered to tourists and other visitors on the lot. Guided tours of the studio gave them a glimpse of how films were made. To amuse themselves, however, the studio's directors sometimes turned these tours into filmmaking spoofs.

"When visitors would appear on the set, we'd stage a little act," Wyler recounted. "Sometimes these acts were better than anything in the pictures. I would shoot a scene, for instance, and by prearrangement a couple of cowboys would be behind the set arguing over something. I would say, 'Stop the scene. Who's shouting there?' And then I'd say, 'Bring those fellows out here.'

"Out came the two cowboys.

"I'd say, 'Hell, you're making all this noise. How do you expect me to make a picture?'

"And they'd say, 'Who are you?'

"And I'd say, 'I'm the director of this film, and I require silence.'

"They'd say, 'Oh, to hell with you.'

"One thing would lead to another and there'd be a fight. Well, we had breakaway bottles, and we had chairs that were made of very light wood. They couldn't hurt anything. So we would be hitting each other over the head, and finally somebody would pull out a gun.

"Bang. One guy would shoot the other guy.

"We also had ketchup in a rubber tube in one of the guy's shirts. It would burst and what looked like blood would come spurting out. Then the guy would drop dead.

"The visitors would run away screaming. We put on a good show. The cowboys acted better than they did in the pictures."

Wyler's parents, Melanie and Leopold were also entertained. They had come to the States for the first time in October of 1925 to spend the winter. Melanie, in particular, liked visiting the studio. According to Fay Wray, she often showed up on the set of *Lazy Lightning* to watch her son work.

"She always gave me little gifts," Wray recalls, "a little crystal perfume bottle, miniature ivory figurines, things she collected. There were other people at the studio who interested her besides her son. Universal had a kind of family feeling about it, and to a great extent she symbolized that for me. Willy's mother played mother to all of us."

Melanie was so taken with California that she decided to stay longer than the few months initially planned. But she had more in mind than simply enjoying herself. Settling into a house Wyler had rented, Melanie hoped to have an influence on his bachelor life as well as his brother Robert's. She wanted them to begin thinking of marriage.

Neither of her sons had any intention of settling down any time soon. Wyler had found, to his unconcealed pleasure, that being a director brought certain benefits to the bachelor life.

"I dated little actresses from the studio," he said. "Some of the girls were on the two-reel Westerns. The first romance I had was with Evelyn Pierce. She was a beautiful girl. She had won a beauty contest somewhere. She and her sister had a little apartment. We had a helluva time getting to be alone. We'd go up on Mulholland Drive and lie on the grass or we'd go to Griffith Park under a bush. I had a Chevrolet. Try to get laid in a Chevrolet coupé. This kind of thing went on for a few years."

Pierce, who was to play a dance-hall siren in Wyler's five-reel Western, *The Border Cavalier,* never turned her beauty into much of a film career. In the 1931 Marx Brothers movie *Monkey Business* she plays a shipboard manicurist who does Zeppo's nails and has one line: "You want your nails trimmed long?" Zeppo wants more than that, of course, and chases her around the room.

She apparently had plenty of sex appeal in real life, too. Wyler recalled making the round-trip drive from Lone Pine to Los Angeles just to see her one night during the middle of a shoot. "I left the location at six o'clock," he recalled, "drove six hours, spent a couple of hours with her, and drove back another six hours to be back at eight the next morning without any sleep."

Besides Evelyn Pierce, Wyler also had a fling with Lotus Thompson, who would soon star as the heroine in *Desert Dust,* another of his five-reel Westerns. A bright and cheerful party girl, Thompson made no emotional demands on Willy. In fact, her savvy, bantering attitude appealed to his own breezy personal style.

Typical of their easygoing relationship was a letter she wrote him from the Santa Fe Chief while traveling across Kansas on her way to Europe: "However can you bear up under the strain of not gazing on my beautiful visage . . . All those hectic Hollywood orgies just won't be the same. As for the casting couches— Well! They will all probably wear out through lack of use. I can always use your reference, regarding my capabilities re: the sexy afternoons spent on one's back being cast for the next Jewel Production. . . . Sadly enough I still remain virtuous—it is an awful burden to be *pure.* It really isn't fair to the men for me to hold out this way. I am denying them the spice of life, and not doing myself too much good either."

BY THE TIME WYLER MADE *DAZE OF THE WEST* IN OCTOBER 1926, he had shot a total of twenty-five movies over a period of little more than fifteen months. But he was still a complete unknown. Just five of his earliest two-reelers had been released. Now, however, he was about to gain consistent exposure. From December 1926 through October 1927, Universal would release a Wyler-made Western once every few weeks. And over the next eight months, including pre- and post-production, he would shoot four five-reel Westerns.

The longer films earned run-of-the-mill action reviews in the trade journals. But more important, the studio supervisors felt he was making Westerns with "more pep in his stuff then the other directors." One Universal in-house critic wrote that "Wyler has turned in the best Western for next season" with *Spurs and Spark Plugs* (released as *The Border Cavalier*).

Wyler also earned plaudits for his keen visual sense, which capitalized on the natural splendor of the locations. "What a beautiful start this is!" a Universal film editor wrote in a memo about *Frontier Courage*, which Wyler began filming in Palmdale in April 1927 with Ted Wells. "Desert stuff with big beautiful clouds. Photography soft as velvet, and action fast and dramatic. The director has made fine artistic use of the Joshua trees. Composition beautiful enough to be framed on a wall."

Wyler came in for even more praise over his handling of troublesome scenes that could have been censored. And his creative eye for romantic moments was especially appreciated. He shot "a very nice love scene in the kitchen," the editor pointed out. "They do not play it in profile as is the case in the work of some directors on the lot. It would be a good thing if some of those profile shooters would study this love scene, especially those that have been saying that it can't be done. Here it is. These other directors not only should want to see it, they should be made to see it."

Frontier Courage, released the following October as *Straight Shootin',* drew a spectacular in-house report during the final phase of production: "At last a real western picture—one that holds your interest from first to last reel—action, suspense and laughs. Let's hope Willie Wyler keeps on directing such Westerns—it is a pity that the other Ted Wells pictures shown prior to this [not by Wyler] are not of the same calibre."

But Wyler had begun taking his career more seriously and had no intention of continuing as a Western director. He believed that if he did, he risked being typed as a second-rater. With a hard-won reputation for solid work to his credit, Wyler asked for a promotion. Specifically, he wanted to begin directing Jewel features. They had name stars, were more expensive to make and were guaranteed bigger marketing campaigns.

In May 1927, Universal executed Wyler's first director's contract. It offered him a salary of two hundred dollars a week for the first six months and six-month options for the next five years. Each option called for a salary increase of fifty dollars, so that by the end of the last option he would be making six hundred fifty dollars a week.

Although it would be four months before Wyler was to receive his first non-Western assignment, he signed the contract in the same week that Charles Lindbergh made his triumphant transatlantic flight from New York to Paris. Coincidentally, nothing could have been more emblematic of the overnight change in American heroes. Aviators soon took the place of cowboys, and Wyler could not have picked a better time to get out of Westerns.

11

—⟫⟫⟫⟫⟫⟫⟪⟪⟪⟪⟪—

LAST OF THE SILENTS

WYLER DREW *THE GIRL SHOW* AS
his first non-Western assignment, but temporarily abandoned it over
casting problems. Originally written by Charles A. Logue as *The Grap-
pler*, it told the story of a brutish wrestler who traveled from town to
town with a burlesque show and took on all comers in the ring. The
script was eventually combined with an adaptation of a Damon Runyon
story called "The Geezer" and rewritten as *The Frame-Up*. It ultimately
became Wyler's second non-Western feature, retitled *The Shakedown*.

In the meantime, Wyler began prepping *Anybody Here Seen Kelly?*, an
"Irish" program comedy about a former World War I soldier who is
pursued by a French girl he romanced overseas. Wyler was given the
script and told he could do anything within reason as long as he kept
costs to no more than sixty thousand dollars. So he took the cast and
crew to New York City to shoot the key exterior sequences of the girl's
search through the city for her boyfriend.

Bessie Love starred as Mitzi, the young girl. Invited to the States, as
was every girl Pat Kelly romanced, Mitzi goes looking for him at the
Metropolitan Museum, where he once told her he lived, not for a moment believing she would actually look him up. But where she finds him

is in Times Square. He is a cop directing traffic at the intersection of Broadway and Forty-second Street.

Wyler began making the picture in November 1927. He used hidden cameras everywhere—in cars, in taxis, in windows, even in a closed laundry pushcart—to follow Mitzi in her search. The crowded streets of New York were filmed without filming permits, paid extras or rehearsals. At the climactic moment, Mitzi recognizes Kelly (played by Tom Moore) and rushes into the street to kiss him. Kelly, still directing traffic, turns toward her with his arms outstretched and causes a traffic jam. The line of dialogue on the title card is: "I told you, I just have to lift my hand and everything stops." Years later Wyler recalled the traffic jam: "I almost went to jail for that."

When the picture was completed it had a documentary look. The studio execs loved the spontaneous technique. Although the reviews would be only mildly favorable, Wyler's stock had risen considerably. A few months after the picture was completed but well before its release in September of 1928, Universal buzzed with word of his success—all the more so when it became evident that rewrites of *The Frame-Up* were muddling along without much to recommend them. Reviewing the script the following April, the dialogue writer Alfred De Mond, who wrote the title cards for *Anybody Here Seen Kelly?*, noted that Wyler deserved better.

"The story in its present form could do nothing but hurt the career of Willy Wyler, in whom Universal has a big potential asset," De Mond commented. "This story lacks everything that *Anybody Here Seen Kelly?* possessed. In that story a simple plot was introduced early and Willy had two characters and a sweet love story to play with. Consequently, he was able to give the production the sweet, whimsical touches of which he is so capable. In a story like *The Frame-Up*, in its present form, which is overloaded with cheap, scheming intrigue and characters, I don't see how Willy is going to benefit. In place of the lovable, headstrong Irish cop in *Anybody Here Seen Kelly?* we have a blasé, vacillating nincompoop; in place of the demure, ingenuous French girl, we have a colorless character who comes into the picture four or five times and does nothing."

Nearly six months of rewrites were needed before filming started in July of 1928. Wyler balked at the assignment. But the general manager of Universal, Henry Henigson, pressured him to cooperate and offered a future reward. "I promise to do my utmost on the next picture you make. In other words, if you play ball, I will."

The Shakedown, which cost no more than fifty thousand dollars, was released in two versions: a silent and a part-talkie. The picture told the story of a young orphan (Jack Hanlon) and a waitress (Barbara Kent), who reform a crooked boxer (James Murray) involved with a shake-down ring. Universal's production executives knew the story would make a fair picture at best. But once they'd seen the finished product, various department heads gave Wyler raves.

"This is the second good one he's made," one memo said. "Wouldn't hurt a bit to give him good play in our advertising. Say something like this—ANOTHER WILLIE WYLER WINNER." Said a second, "Should be a cinch to sell. Mr. Wyler comes through 100%." A third summed up the feeling of many executives on the lot: "One of the most entertaining pictures we have made this year. Above all, Willy Wyler's direction should be highly recommended. He is developing like a million dollars and his picture shows a sense of realism and pace that endows every little incident in it with charm and entertainment value."

While those memos focus on commercial worth, they recognize Wyler's growth and show a prescient regard for the style that was to characterize his art. In later years, whether praised by James Agee for their "purity, directness and warmth" or derided by Andrew Sarris for their "meticulous craftsmanship," Wyler's pictures brought to the screen a compassionate honesty and a dramatic intensity in their vision of American life. They managed to combine poetic truthfulness with social awareness, yet struck a popular chord in a mass audience that went to the movies for pleasure as well as enlightenment.

Universal's enthusiasm notwithstanding, the reviews for *The Shake-down* were mixed—and not just for the picture. The *New York Times* said, "It is fairly well acted, but far better results could have been obtained from the players had the director, William Wyler, not been so keen to win sympathy." *Variety* called it "a not bad 50 percent talker." Moreover, its dual release as a silent and a part-talkie in March 1929 was a holding action for the studio.

The silent film had died a quick death. Sound was what the public wanted ever since the release of *The Jazz Singer* fifteen months earlier by Warner Bros. To stay competitive, all the studios rushed talking sequences into pictures that had gone into production as silents. And within a year of sound's introduction, every important picture was made as a talkie.

Of the twenty thousand five hundred theaters across the country at the end of 1928, only thirteen hundred had sound installations. A year later, there were more than nine thousand theaters playing talking pictures, and by 1931 thirteen thousand. Filling these houses with moviegoers was not a problem. Paid admissions jumped from sixty million a week in 1927 to a peak of one hundred ten million in 1929.

Critics and moviemakers recognized that sound often robbed films of their artistry by sacrificing visual drama for dialogue. Nevertheless, the public's enthusiasm for this latest cinematic innovation was overwhelming. The novelty of sound even proved strong enough to carry the industry through the early years of the Depression.

The transition from silents to talkies couldn't help but revolutionize the industry. Stars who lacked attractive voices, whether because of an inappropriate accent or tone, were out. On the other hand, stars with effective voices were in. Dialogue writers and playwrights were in. Many producers of silents who thought they knew what people wanted in entertainment found their expertise discounted, if not worthless. Directors lost control to the demands of the microphone. Sound experts suddenly had power.

Universal built four sound stages during the summer of 1928 in hopes of making all future pictures with sound. It would be another year, though, before that would happen. In the meantime, the studio added as many talking scenes as possible to all its silent productions.

Universal was, in fact, the slowest studio to make the changeover to sound. The decision had been a tough and costly one for Carl Laemmle, whose skeptical attitude toward talkies derived from his personal experience. During his earliest days in the motion picture business he had experimented with sound and suffered heavy losses. Ever since, he had vehemently opposed the possibility of making sound films. But when it finally became clear to him that talking pictures were popular and that far better silents were dying at the box office, he relented.

THE SPRING OF 1929 BROUGHT WYLER A ROMANTIC COMEDY— *The Love Trap*—starring Laura La Plante, among the biggest names on the Universal lot. The picture had a larger budget than *The Shakedown*, approximately seventy-five thousand dollars and a longer shooting schedule.

La Plante and her husband William Seiter, himself a director, had to give final approval for Wyler. They arranged a screening of *The Shakedown* to see what his work was like. Hearing of this, he showed up without telling them and joined the projectionist. Anything even slightly humorous in the film drew loud laughs from inside the booth. Wyler hoped La Plante and Seiter would conclude that the scenes must really be a hoot if the projectionist was laughing.

The Love Trap, though not sterling material, was regarded by Wyler and others as a step up from *Anybody Here Seen Kelly?* and *The Shakedown*. La Plante, an attractive blonde, had real skill as a comedienne. The picture was a risqué bedroom comedy about a chorus girl who marries a young taxi driver after she has been fired from her job and evicted from her apartment. He is an upper-cruster down on his luck, and his family doesn't approve of her. His uncle, a judge, tries to buy her off, then finally realizes she's not so bad after all.

The story was typical of the period, and the film received mixed reviews. Wyler was commended, however, for drawing high-calibre performances from the actors—especially from La Plante as the chorus girl. Universal executives continued to be pleased with his work—so much so that Willy's next assignment was a plum and would help put him in the limelight. But it didn't happen automatically.

Just two weeks before shooting began on *Hell's Heroes* in early August 1929, there was still no director assigned to the project. Carl Laemmle Jr.—recently promoted on his twenty-first birthday to general manager of the studio—was considering the screenwriter Tom Reed. But Junior, as everybody referred to him, had doubts. "In my heart I feel this is too good a property to give to a new man for his first picture," he wrote his father, who was traveling in Europe on his annual visit to Laupheim. "This may be one of the surprise packages from Universal for 1929–30."

Wyler, meanwhile, was busy dealing with a flurry of studio tasks. After he finished cutting *The Love Trap*, he shot special scenes of La Plante in Spanish for a film exposition in Barcelona at Carl Laemmle's request. Then Junior asked Wyler to reshoot some scenes for *The Mississippi Gamblers*, a melodrama that had been filmed on the same riverboat as the recently released musical *Showboat*. At the same time, Junior also assigned Wyler to direct *The Cohens and Kellys in Scotland*, the latest installment in the popular and profitable Jewish-Irish serial that had begun in 1926. This assignment Wyler flatly refused, which made Junior angry.

Wyler described the effects of this refusal in a letter to his parents: "Right now the situation is not as bright here as it could be. Though my most recent film was very successful in its preview last week, I've had plenty of trouble lately. You know that Junior is now General Manager, and we are not getting along at all. Over the last two weeks I've turned down two stories I didn't like and didn't think could be made into good films. . . .

"Junior is furious with me. As you know, my contract gives the company the right to lay me off for four weeks every six months, and at the moment I am not working. This past May my contract was renewed again. But I'm almost certain that next October it will not be. On the one hand, I'm happy about that because I believe I can improve my situation elsewhere. . . . If I were to work somewhere else, without a doubt I would be earning double what I make here.

"I probably would be considered one of the large army of ingrates who got their starts with Carl Laemmle and then left him. But I don't want to sacrifice my future for the past. There are too many people in Hollywood who have confidence in me for me to be walking around on tiptoe without any reason, especially after having made three excellent films for Junior. He wants to reign here like a petty tyrant, requiring everyone to do only what he wants, as if they didn't have brains of their own."

Finally, two considerations forced Junior to rethink the *Hell's Heroes* directing assignment: Wyler's proven ability to elevate mediocre material beyond expectations and his doubt about giving an important picture to the untried Tom Reed. Junior decided to assign the routine *Cohens and Kellys* to William Craft and named Wyler as the director of *Hell's Heroes*.

The movie, which was to be Universal's first all-sound outdoor picture, took its story from the short novel *Three Godfathers* by the popular Western writer Peter B. Kyne. The book had been made twice before as successful Universal silents, the first a six-reeler in 1916 and the second a John Ford remake called *Marked Men* in 1920.

The plot of both those film versions followed the original tale in most details, including the survival of one of the three outlaws. Three bank robbers, escaping across the desert, discover a dying woman about to give birth in a covered wagon. Before she dies, they become the infant's godfathers and promise to take it to its father. During their desert crossing, two of the bandits die. The third manages to bring the child safely through the ordeal.

In Wyler's version the child survives, but none of the three bandits do. Wyler also insisted on shooting the picture in the Mojave Desert and the Panamint Valley. He wanted the film to have a gritty realism. Though he recognized that the sweltering August heat would create huge discomfort and technical difficulties, he believed it was worth the trouble because it would lend authenticity to scenes showing three fugitives dying of thirst. Because Reed's screenplay darkened Kyne's famous story, Wyler felt the need of especially harsh conditions. His interpretation would turn out to be the bleakest and least sentimental version (including a second John Ford remake in 1948 with John Wayne).

WYLER BEGAN SHOOTING *HELL'S HEROES* ON AUGUST 9, 1929, confident that the scorching sun would help him elicit convincingly "distressed" performances. Also, the scenic reality of the desert as captured on film would convey the raw adversity these men had to face. But primitive sound techniques caused problems that Wyler had not anticipated.

Since the bandits were being chased by a posse, they had to keep moving and their dialogue had to be captured on the run. To allow moving shots the crew improvised a soundproof booth with a sealed window to house the camera and cameraman. Mounted on rails, the booth was pushed by a dozen men in absolute silence. Microphones were hidden in the sagebrush. With desert temperatures at a hundred ten degrees Fahrenheit, the heat in the booth reached a hundred thirty. Sometimes the cameraman would be discovered passed out on the floor.

A still greater problem Wyler hadn't counted on was the attitude of the lead actor Charles Bickford, a popular New York stage star who had been brought out to Hollywood by Cecil B. De Mille. Because he came from the theater, Bickford believed he knew all there was to know about dialogue. Accordingly, he felt Hollywood directors knew nothing about it. When he didn't agree with Wyler's instructions, he refused to follow them. To make matters worse, he also tried to get the other actors not to take Wyler's suggestions. Ironically, Bickford's attitude led Wyler to invent the most talked-about scene in the movie.

Bickford played the last surviving bandit dying of thirst. Wyler remembered the incident in detail: "He's staggering, so the next scene begins slowly. He begins to shed things. First the rifle, then the backpack, then the gold and finally he thinks of leaving the baby. So we discussed it.

"I said, 'I think you should be walking along and the rifle drags in the sand and you let go of it.'

"He said, 'That's lousy.'

"I said, 'What's your idea?'

"He said, 'I'll show you.'

"He staggers along, finally he looks at the rifle, which is heavy, and he throws it. No matter how far you throw it in the desert, it's gonna look like nothing.

"I said, 'I don't think that's good.'

"He said, 'Well, that's the way I'm going to do it.'

"We argued, but I couldn't get him to do it the way I wanted. So I let him do it. And one day when he wasn't working, I got somebody to wear his boots and I shot it again. Not the boots, just the tracks.

"First the tracks went straight. Then you saw a place where he falls and picks himself up. Then suddenly you saw a crease along the track. You didn't know what it was—you just saw this crease in the sand, and after a while you saw the rifle lying there. I thought, 'Why stop here?' I went on. I made a longer track, and finally there was his backpack. Then more tracks. Then the gold. Gold was spread all over the sand. Then his hat. And finally the baby was lying there. I did this whole thing, this long tracking shot without Bickford even knowing it."

Because of that scene, Darryl Zanuck, the savvy producer who was running Warner Bros. at the time, sent a memo to all his directors ordering them to see "this picture by this new director." It was just the beginning of the recognition that Wyler was to receive for *Hell's Heroes* throughout the industry.

Yet all through the making of the picture Wyler had to fight a running battle with those Universal executives who were unsympathetic to him, especially Junior. Despite a grudging respect for Wyler, Junior basically failed to appreciate his methods, his style, his taste, his expertise, his obsession with realistic details or his sense of humor.

The day before shooting was to begin, Junior notified Wyler that he must work fast because Bickford had to be back at Metro within three weeks. Ten days later a production supervisor assigned to keep Junior informed of what was happening on location complained about Wyler's apparently unorthodox technique: "Not enough reflectors being used. The faces are very shadowy and it doesn't look right. It may be true that that is natural on the desert, but it's [not] as natural anywhere else."

Another memo complained about Wyler's inclination to change lines and risk censorship by the Hays Office: "Some censorable stuff. However, a lot of it can be salvaged by judicious cutting. . . . Not so good was the variation in the script line, 'Reach for Heaven or you'll be going there' to 'Reach for Heaven or you'll be going to Hell.' Wyler should protect himself by shooting both versions." To which Junior appended his own remark: "Wyler, why don't you use good judgment?"

With Universal profits at rock bottom, Junior scrutinized all the studio's expenditures. He reprimanded Wyler about "film wastage" throughout the shooting of *Hell's Heroes*. In addition to weekly reports outlining what he thought was Wyler's use of too much footage, he kept harping on Wyler's unapproved script changes. He objected, in particular, to Wyler's alterations of dialogue. "I must ask," Junior wrote in one memo, "that you have such changes as you may desire to make submitted to this office for my approval before being shot."

The barrage of objections and admonitions reached its peak by mid-September, during the editing process. The supervisor assigned to keep tabs on Wyler let Junior know that he thought the picture had been ruined completely by the director's unyielding realism. His memo of September 16 noted: "In the most gruesome scene we have ever seen on the screen, the director swings wide of the script and ends the picture not only sadly but in a way that will give audiences nightmares for a week."

The memo summarized the movie's climax under Wyler's guiding hand, revealing in fact a mature director not only making the most of the material given him but taking it to its logical conclusion: "The surging, angry crowd has surrounded Bickford. A dance-hall girl snatches away the child from the dazed bandit. The crowd knocks him down, ties him. A rope is thrown around him and a horseman begins to drag him through the street. The Sheriff rushes up, claims Bickford in the name of the law. He picks up the fallen man, promises to hang him. We see the bandit's face—inhumanly gruesome, nightmarish. The Sheriff shakes him. No sign of life. He slaps his face again. With his finger he pries open the bandit's eye, and we see the dead, glazed white. The Sheriff announces him dead. Ugh!"

Referring to the beginning of the movie, the supervisor continued: "Other shots show close-ups of the robbery in the bank: front views of bandits Kolk at the counter, firing their revolvers almost into the camera. Close-up of cashier Frank Edwards as he is shot and falls dead to the floor. Close-up of the safe showing the surviving cashier getting the gold bags for the bandits. . . . In other words, the robbery is shown in detail. It is a moving picture lesson in crime."

Junior, for his part, agreed without even taking a look at the scenes himself. He scribbled his comment to Wyler on the supervisor's memo: "It looks from this report that you have evidently butchered a great picture."

There are no extant prints of the sound version of *Hell's Heroes*. But the silent version shows that instead of being dragged to death by a cold-blooded mob Bickford's character dies because he has drunk poisoned water in an effort to save the baby. He staggers the last few miles into town, where he finds the townspeople in church, hands over the baby, then collapses and dies. Wyler's version of the last bandit's death was not just softened visually. The manner of the bandit's death, without its implied social critique of the townspeople, has been altered so radically as to vitiate Wyler's meaning.

Nevertheless, Wyler apparently was able to impose most of his ideas: *Hell's Heroes* was hailed as an uncompromisingly realistic Western both in story and in look. Unlike his formulaic two-reelers of a few years before, it became an enormous critical and commercial success.

The public was ready for the film's unusually downbeat approach to the story—perhaps in reaction to a movie market saturated with musicals, revues and inept melodramas. When Universal previewed the finished movie on December 1, opinions solicited from the audience were striking. "A great picture beautifully done," one moviegoer wrote on a reaction card. "I'm afraid the only way you'll ever make money with it is to sell water to the audience during the performance at a dollar a glass. The picture is a work of art."

The *New York Times* review didn't mention Wyler by name but said, "despite its title, which means little to the story, *Hell's Heroes* happens to be an interesting and realistic bit of characterization" and went on to praise the acting. *Variety,* incorrectly listing the director as Wilbur Wylans, said it was "gripping and real. Unusually well cast and directed. Any class house can book it and not only make money but satisfy fans with something convincingly out of the ordinary."

Released January 5, 1930, the picture did eighteen thousand dollars at the box office during its first week in New York, a whopping gross for a movie not priced as a special attraction. It also did excellent business elsewhere across the country and in Europe. Later it made several best-of-the-month lists, as well as a few best-picture lists for 1930.

Surprisingly, one person who hated both the film and the directing was the author Peter B. Kyne. Screenwriter Tom Reed, who was an acquaintance of Kyne's, asked the author to write a complimentary letter to Wyler so it could be used for personal publicity. Kyne wrote back, "Frankly, I think your Mr. Wyler murdered our beautiful story. I can shoot holes in every sequence. . . . It is dreadfully directed and dreadfully played by that leading man. . . . I don't care how much money the picture makes, my conscience will not let me cheer for the atrocious murder of one of the few works of art I have ever turned out. . . . I will not write any letter to Mr. Wyler. The young gentleman must fight his weary way through life without a helping hand from me."

JUNIOR FOUND IT CONVENIENT TO OVERLOOK THE FACT THAT many of Wyler's changes had improved *Hell's Heroes*. That Wyler had taken it from the level of a good Western adventure to a higher plateau seemed to irritate Junior, even though it temporarily softened him.

"The success of this film has changed Junior's attitude toward me," Wyler wrote his parents three weeks after the picture's release. "He has condescended to be normal, and we're now close friends. How long that will last I can't say, unfortunately." And for all the success of *Hell's Heroes*, Wyler received no guarantee about the quality of his next assignment. Nor did his ostensible rise in stature help Robert, who desperately wanted to become a director himself.

The two brothers, who were living together, had collaborated on many of Willy's pictures. Willy particularly valued Robert's advice on story construction and, in later years, on all aspects of production. By 1927 Robert had worked his way up from assistant director to production supervisor. In his first official credit on one of Willy's films, he was listed as the producer of *Anybody Here Seen Kelly?* Although Laemmle had named Robert a director and given him a picture to do just before Junior took over the studio, Robert had not begun working on it.

"Junior, despite his father's orders, has not allowed him to make the film in question," Willy wrote their parents in the summer of 1929. "And I don't know if he will ever be authorized to make it, even if Carl Laemmle gave a new order. Robert is right now working as a supervisor on a completely different production. It goes without saying he is very discouraged at the way Junior has, for the last six months, thrown cold water on his first big chance.

"At the moment [Robert] is trying to find a directing job in England. I doubt he'll succeed in finding one from here. But he is determined to take his chances in Europe next autumn, if he doesn't begin directing here when Carl Laemmle gets back. It's possible and even probable that with the experience he has had here and with the beginning of talkies in Europe that he could find a very good job there."

In fact, Robert wouldn't leave Hollywood for almost two years. When he did—as a Universal producer sent to Paris in May 1931 to help develop the overseas market—conditions in Europe turned out to be less promising than he'd hoped. And even though he got to make his own pictures there, with Willy's help he was soon angling to have Junior bring him back to the States under a director's contract.

Gloomy stories did well for Universal in 1930. *All Quiet on the Western Front,* the somber film about the World War I nightmare of trench warfare, was the studio's first Academy Award winner. Junior always felt he would have a hit with it, largely because the prestigious antiwar novel by Erich Maria Remarque, on which it was based, had sold hundreds of thousands of copies in the United States and Europe and had received millions of dollars' worth of national publicity in the Hearst newspapers.

Here again, though, Junior dithered over who would direct it. His decision came down to a choice between Lewis Milestone and Herbert Brenon. He picked Brenon. But as often happened with Junior, money changed his mind. Brenon wanted a hundred thousand dollars. Junior finally let Milestone have the picture not because of greater directorial prestige (Brenon's was greater), but simply because he came cheaper. Milestone was willing to do the picture for seventy-five thousand dollars.

Wyler's next assignment, in keeping with the prevailing mood of gloom, was a remake of *The Storm*, which had been a successful silent. The original, based on a play by Langdon McCormick, had been made in 1922 and was best remembered for its spectacular shots of a raging forest fire. Not surprisingly, special effects also played a major role in Wyler's 1930 version of this routine melodrama about a love triangle starring Lupe Velez, Paul Cavanagh and William Boyd. Wyler managed to include everything from avalanches and snowdrifts to pounding rapids, blinding storms and howling gales.

Initially, he tried to avoid the assignment. But threats by Junior to demote him back to programmers caused him to reconsider. In addition, Wyler recalled, he was offered a bonus to direct *The Storm*, which made it doubly hard to turn down. Though he would come to regard the film as "one of the worst pictures I ever made," Wyler always remembered making it as great fun.

Shot near Truckee, just north of Lake Tahoe, the cast and crew went on location in the dead of winter. Filming began February 17, 1930. Wyler enjoyed the snow. He even brought his skis. The company lived in train cars on the tracks.

"We had berths, a dining car and a flatcar where we put the gear and shot from," he remembered. "We had three or four miles of track that was at our disposal. I could tell the engineer to go this way or that way, to go fast or slow. It was a great toy. After work I'd get on a pair of skis and get behind the train and have it pull me. The whole crew would sit on the flatcar and watch me."

One day, he was being pulled along the track, skiing on the embankment outside the rails. "I couldn't see ahead because there was a curve," Wyler recalled. "All of a sudden I notice there's nothing but trestle below me. We'd come to a bridge. I had to jump in between the tracks. Luckily, there was enough snow on the railway ties, and I got across practically on one ski." The dumbstruck crew broke out in cheers, real-izing he'd just missed falling into the gorge below.

Before filming began, Wyler had sought Claudette Colbert for the starring role. But she was not available. He then wired Charles Bickford in Mazatlan, Mexico, asking his opinion of Sylvia Sidney. Bickford, with whom Wyler had managed to keep a professional rela-tionship, knew Sidney from the New York stage. AM CONSIDERING HER FOR LEAD, Wyler telegraphed. CHARACTER VERY VIVACIOUS PRIMITIVE HUMOROUS AND EMOTIONAL REQUIRING FIRST-RATE ACTRESS.

Ultimately, Wyler ended up using Lupe Velez, a young Mexican dancer who had recently come to Hollywood to work for Hal Roach Studios and was under personal contract to Douglas Fairbanks. In 1927 she'd appeared opposite Fairbanks in *The Gaucho* as a fiery leading lady. Wyler remembered Velez with special affection: "She was quite a girl. She spoke freely. She was supposed to play this sweet innocent French-Canadian girl. Off the set, she was having a big romance with Gary Cooper.

"One day she asks me, 'Did you know Gary was an artist?'

"I said, 'No.'

"She said, 'He can draw good pictures. Look.'

"And she pulls out one of her tits and there was a nose with two eyes and a mouth. He had drawn a face with lipstick around her nipple."

The reviews for *The Storm* were mixed. Natural performances and beautiful photography were the movie's chief assets. For many reviewers, the movie was handicapped by a forgettable story about two war veterans in love with the same damsel in distress, all three of them snowbound. "Presumably a yarn of . . . primitive passions, *The Storm* peters out into pretty mild stuff before the inevitable and expected fade-out," the *Motion Picture News* concluded.

But other reviewers were more enthusiastic. The *Los Angeles Times* called it "one of the real red-blooded melodramas of the year—a straightforward, unpretentiously illuminating segment of three lives in an isolated cabin deep in the Canadian snows. . . . The story has been so improved and strengthened [from the silent original], its psychology so shrewdly built, that the elements are never allowed to obscure the human actors or concern for their fate."

On completing *The Storm*, Wyler requested a vacation. With his brother Bob living and working in Los Angeles and with periodic visits from his parents, he had no reason to long for a visit to Mulhouse. Nev-ertheless, after working steadily for more than five years since his last trip there, he was eager to go back. But Universal wouldn't let him. Determined to get his way, he arranged for a physician's letter declaring that he needed a sabbatical for health reasons.

"Mr. Willy Wyler is suffering from acute nervous exhaustion," it said. "For his recovery it is imperative that he is away from his surroundings for several months. Any further strenuous work at this time might cause a nervous breakdown."

In all likelihood this letter from a Dr. Frederic Waitsfelder was bogus. But it worked. In August, Wyler emptied his bank account of nearly three thousand dollars and left for Europe. He stopped in London and Paris, then spent more than a month exploring his old haunts in and around Mulhouse.

Wyler had written ahead to his cousin Blanche, whose beauty had once smitten the young men of Lausanne, and she had written back encouraging him to visit her. Still living in Lausanne, Blanche was now in her late twenties, a mother of two young children and, not incidentally, feeling somewhat bored in her marriage. She enjoyed the prospect of seeing Wyler again. He had, after all, attained success tinged with glamour. He was charming, funny, adventurous, intense, certainly an appealing figure impeccably dressed in custom-tailored clothes. And he could tell wonderful stories about the exotic world of Hollywood.

Blanche did more than merely encourage a visit. As she confided in a letter: "I like Willy very much. I love to flirt with him, it's true. Above all, I'm taking advantage of a little momentary freedom." She went on to say her feelings were "all very innocent" and that "Willy knows very well that nothing will happen. . . . We're not going to do anything silly. We're taking advantage a little, me especially."

With Blanche's husband away on business, Wyler went to see her in Lausanne during the last week of August. What transpired between them must have been seductive—certainly enough to have aroused his romantic interest.

Several days later, he wrote from Mulhouse: "Dearest Blanche, If we don't see each other this week it certainly won't be my fault. When for the love of God are you going to Strasbourg? If I had known that your husband wasn't going to Lausanne, I could easily have come Monday or Tuesday and stayed a day anyway. But thinking every day that he was on his way down there to come and get you, I sit here in Mulhouse wasting my time with nothing to do but wait for you to arrive in Strasbourg. Even yesterday I would still have gone to Lausanne had I known that you would be alone—but I'm afraid three is a crowd, one that might not get along so well."

Wyler decided to go to Strasbourg, about two hours north of Mulhouse by car. "I may as well wait there for you as here," he wrote. On the way he took a detour to Badenweiler, the famous international spa in the Black Forest, where his family used to spend summer vacations. Blanche reached him at his Badenweiler hotel. "When shall we meet again? I am longing to."

The two of them then spent two days together, at the end of which she wrote him on his return to Mulhouse: "Why did you ask me if I loved you? Do you think I should take so much trouble for someone I did not care for? Just think a little and you'll find out for yourself without my help."

Then disaster struck. Wyler saw Blanche on a Saturday at her home, while her husband was away. The next day he took her to a casino in nearby Niederbronn-les-Bains. Her husband was there, playing baccarat. On Monday morning, according to a letter Blanche wrote, her husband came home and found them alone. He erupted with verbal insults.

Wyler left but soon returned, which was a worse mistake. The classic cousins' romance exploded in recriminations. Later, explaining to Wyler's mother part of what had happened, Blanche wrote: "All would have gone a thousand times better if Willy hadn't come back. But no, at two o'clock, he came back instead of leaving as I begged him to, and started to fight like a beast, in spite of my cries."

Blanche maintained that, although her husband "spoke too quickly," it was Wyler who struck the first blow. After the melee, Blanche shrank from the affair to protect her family and confessed in still another letter: "My husband is anxious that Willy apologize by letter, and I hope you will make him do it for me, for my happiness and for that of my children."

With the affair over, Wyler drove off to Berlin, where *Hell's Heroes* was scheduled to premiere several weeks hence at the Mozartsaal. He checked into the Eden Hotel. Berlin's glitterati welcomed him. The German film impresario Eric Pommer gave him a personal tour of the UFA studios. Universal arranged for his first press conference. Wyler was so impressed with all the attention that he thought of getting a picture deal in Berlin without Universal's permission.

Shortly after his arrival, Wyler wrote on Eden Hotel stationery to Blanche's husband. It was not the sort of humble apology Blanche had demanded, but rather a denial and even a reprimand whose cool, commanding tone clearly was intended to put her husband in his place.

"Monsieur," Wyler began. "I am writing you this letter for only one reason. I want to be of some use to my cousin Blanche. I will not try to explain here what I had come to your house to explain . . . since I am certain you will always succeed in seeing only the worst. . . . Believe me when I say I am very much aware of the wrong I did. . . . However, I hope you are aware of the wrong you did. . . . This is not even to say anything about your attack. With the help of several metal and bronze instruments, you seemed to be having fun on my skull. Fortunately, it was a little bit tougher than you might have hoped."

Wyler enjoyed his transatlantic celebrity. As he later told a *New York Herald-Tribune* reporter, he was fascinated by what he found to be the "wild, mad city" of Berlin. It had "the gaiety of Paris before the war — only more so." He considered staying on. But he was not blind to the fact that its sense of abandon was "an artificial excitement," which made Berlin "at once the most interesting and most pathetic city in Europe."

One reason for its "glittering, harsh gaiety and its wild night life" was the poverty and unemployment throughout the country, but especially in Berlin. "Everything in Germany has a political angle," he told the *Tribune* reporter. "It is torn by groups of radicals and reactionaries, each fighting for a different government. . . . The people in Berlin seem to be hopeless in all this chaos. They have very little money and what they have they spend lavishly at the nightclubs, almost in a gesture of defiance."

Enticed by Berlin nevertheless, he asked Max Magnus, *Variety*'s German correspondent and agent, to explore possibilities of getting him a movie contract. He also cabled his brother in Hollywood to find out . . . IMMEDIATELY WHETHER [Universal] CONTRACT RENEWED IF SO CABLE DETAILED ADVISABILITY ACCEPTING OFFER ONE PICTURE. . . . Three days later Robert Wyler wired back: DUE ABSENCE OPTION EXTENDED TWO MONTHS JUNIOR CLAIMS WILL RENEW OPTION WHEN DUE NOT BEFORE BELIEVE WILL DO SO INSPITE DISLIKING YOU JUNIORS PERMISSION UNOBTAINABLE SAYS WILL STOP YOU EVER WORKING AMERICA AGAIN IF MAKE PICTURE ABROAD.

Coincidentally, in the time it took to hear back from Hollywood Wyler began to reassess the Berlin situation. "Business conditions over here are generally poor and I would not advise you or anyone else to go to Europe except on a pleasure trip," he wrote Robert. "There is much glamour, and for the stranger it is very worthwhile, but there is very little behind it, and everyone in business here, particularly in pictures, is complaining. With only very few exceptions, such as Pommer, pictures are being made fast and cheap and working conditions are much inferior to ours."

Wyler decided to return to Hollywood. By the end of November he was back in New York.

12

<hr>

Dialogue in Small Doses

As the novelty of sound wore off and the Depression deepened, movie attendance dropped off. The New York banks, struggling to maintain their stability, were no longer an easy source of capital for Hollywood. Big budgets necessary to fund talkies led to a steady decline in the number of features produced each year. Hit on all sides, studios battled to remain solvent by cutting costs. Production financing was slashed, salaries were reduced and employees told to "take it or leave it." Of the eight leading studios only MGM and tiny Columbia remained in the black during the early thirties.

Despite such pressures, Wyler was seen as a rising director whose value could not be overlooked. Universal offered him a new contract. In 1931 his salary leaped to seven hundred fifty dollars a week and was supposed to jump to a thousand dollars the following year. Conditions at the studio became so bad by 1932, however, that he had to accept a compromise on his raise. Realizing he was one of the fortunate few with a long-term contract, Wyler agreed to take eight hundred seventy-five dollars a week instead. But he liked to tweak the studio bosses.

"Although there is nothing in my contract about where to, or where not to park my car," he wrote Henry Henigson, "I will gladly make this concession to the Company and park it in the space given me — in return for other such small concessions that may come up from time to time in *my* favor, also not provided for in the contract."

At the same time, Wyler graduated in social status. On Saturday nights he was now part of the weekly poker games that Laemmle hosted for his inner circle. Each player had his tab. Checks for winning and losing amounts were exchanged the following Monday. It wasn't unusual for Wyler to pay or collect several hundred dollars each week.

Robert Wyler found himself in a very different position. In the spring of 1931, after spending eight years in Hollywood, he arranged to go to Universal's Paris office with an assignment to develop French and German films.

The two brothers were extremely close. Eager to help promote each other's career, both of them recognized this as an opportunity for Robert to emerge from Willy's shadow. And within a short time Robert did have some success directing two French films, *Papa Sans Le Savoir* and *Une Étoile Disparait.* If times had been better, he might have made a name for himself. But the poor economy, political tensions and a lack of savvy in manipulating opportunities kept him from achieving real momentum.

By contrast, Willy was astute in his dealings with the industry's power brokers. Quite apart from his artistic talents, he had a strategic comprehension of the industry and a shrewdness easily masked by his personal style. Though he seemed more playful than serious, he knew how to strum the strings of the Hollywood system.

Writing his older brother on June 14, 1932, Willy gave him the sort of tactical career advice that revealed his thinking: "There are a great many directors here who would jump at the chance of having an assured income of $8,000 next year. . . . I can't blame you for trying to get more money, but remember, the important thing for you at present is to keep working. This is far more important for the next year or two anyway than the amount of money you may earn. Regardless of how well you're doing, I would not lose contact with Universal. I've often told you to drop a line to Junior now and then, possibly suggesting a play or a good piece of property. I know he would appreciate that thoughtfulness, particularly since you have no ulterior motives. Of course, don't do it unless you really have something fine to suggest."

Four months later, when Robert was negotiating with Universal to come back to Hollywood, Willy gave him more advice: "I think you will be far better off to make a deal with C. L. Senior than making it out here with Henigson or Junior, and my advice is by all means to conclude the deal with C. L. I happen to know—as a matter of fact, Junior told me himself—that he told his father to make you an offer of $300 a week and pay $350 if he had to, but no more. You can see for yourself that the Old Man ignored that procedure, and offered you $350 straightforwardly. Although Junior wants you he wouldn't want you, I know, if you began to make things tough.

"Remember," Willy continued, "you are not a businessman, and if they want to put one over on you they can do it anyway. . . . Don't forget, I still think the best method is to leave this entirely in the old man's hands. Tell him that you will sign anything he wants you to. But you cannot tell him that you will sign his contract and also argue about it before signing it. Either sign it blind and talk about it later, or discuss the details and try to arrive at a happy conclusion. Regardless of which way you do it though, you must make him understand that you trust him entirely."

LOOKING FOR A QUALITY STORY TO DIRECT HIMSELF, WILLY tried to convince Junior to purchase a successful French comedy, *The Weak Sex*, which he had seen in Paris the previous summer. When that didn't get Junior's approval, he tried to spark some interest by suggesting *The Road Back*, a sequel to *All Quiet on the Western Front*. This time Junior deferred a decision. Finally, a studio property that Robert recommended became Willy's next project: *A House Divided*.

Vaguely inspired by Eugene O'Neill's *Desire Under the Elms*, it told the story of a middle-aged fisherman, who, shortly after his wife's death, marries a young, attractive mail-order bride. The marriage creates a disastrous rivalry between the fisherman and his grown son. The picture, originally titled *Heart and Hand*, begins as it will end—with death and the sea as overpowering images. The opening burial scene establishes a grim tone, which Willy maintained throughout. He refused to allow the troubled atmosphere to be romanticized and kept dialogue to an absolute minimum, imbuing the picture with a stark and brooding aura that made it both dramatically and psychologically convincing.

Filming took thirty-four days from August 4 to September 12, 1931, running ten days over schedule and fifty-three thousand dollars over budget for a total cost of two hundred eighty-four thousand dollars. "It was a difficult picture as far as shooting was concerned," Wyler wrote his brother that October. Indeed, the daily reports indicate Wyler was improvising on the set. He shot seven scenes from the script on the first day and added two new scenes; on the second day he shot six scenes and added two; on the third day he shot eight scenes and added four. By the fourth day, when he shot eight new scenes and only four from the script, the picture was already two days behind schedule. On the eleventh day, he rehearsed the company and shot nothing, which put him three days behind.

Moreover, the actor playing the fisherman's son, Kent Douglass, sprained his ankle, causing further delays. "We couldn't shoot him, so we just plodded along, waiting for the leg to heal," Wyler noted.

In all, he added roughly a hundred scenes to a script that had three hundred thirty-two to begin with. Even before photography commenced, the script had problems. Jack Clymer the screenwriter, had been asked to transform an already existing silent into a talkie. His story changes required a nearly total rewrite. Clymer did it in two and a half weeks, "working nights, Sundays and holidays," Wyler said. And he stood over Clymer, pushing him like "the proverbial slave driver." So the backing and filling on the set should not have come as a surprise.

But none of this softened Junior's attitude. He blamed Wyler for the entire overrun. Early in the shoot, Junior cautioned him: "Understand you are falling behind. I am really surprised after our conversation in the office." Midway through filming, Junior admonished him further: "You do not have to shoot every scene from three different angles. Confine yourself to the shots necessary to cover the action." Nearing the end of production, Junior was thoroughly disgusted and fired off a memo: "For your information, permission for retakes must be given by me and I don't want this ever to happen again."

Everyone else on the lot was pleased with the results, as were the critics. Walter Huston's fine performance as the stern father of the love triangle came in for especially positive notices.

But a month after its domestic release in December 1931, box office prospects were nil, and the movie was considered a dud. The film lost money in several key cities. First-run houses in New York wouldn't book it. In Los Angeles it played the Orpheum Theatre, along with eight vaudeville acts. Exhibitors found the picture too morbid. Although a great many people did like the film, many more felt it was too grim a story for release during the Christmas holidays. A dramatic situation with no comic relief was not what the movie audience wanted.

Box office results in Europe, however, proved different. The picture turned out to be a commercial success overseas. Wyler was convinced that spare use of dialogue had helped put it over. "Strange as it may seem, Europeans like their dialogue in small doses," he told a reporter. He recalled attending a "German talker at the Mozartsaal, one of the finest movie houses in Germany," during his trip the previous year. "At the end of the third reel there were 'catcalls.' At the end of the fourth, people started walking out. At the end of the fifth, the picture was withdrawn. Trite dialogue was the reason."

On the other hand, one of the most popular talkies he'd seen in Germany was a French movie with "very little dialogue," he pointed out. "For that reason American talkers made for European consumption must get the European angle—and the European positively demands action first, good drama and as little dialogue as it takes to put that story and action over." Interestingly, this became a Wyler credo. If it was partly a residue of his silent days, it nonetheless served as a useful way to measure screenplays.

The making of *A House Divided* also brought together Wyler and Walter's son, John Huston. John had been doing some writing for Sam Goldwyn when he read his father's copy of the Clymer script and had some thoughts that Walter repeated to Wyler. Impressed with the ideas, Wyler arranged to have John hired to rewrite some of the dialogue.

The two of them became pals immediately and would maintain a lifelong friendship. "Willy was certainly my best friend in the industry," John remembered. "In fact, Willy was my very beginning. We seemed instantly to have many things in common, and not only was it a relationship that was bonded by motion pictures, but many other things. Willy liked the things that I liked. We'd go down to Mexico. We'd go up in the mountains. And we'd gamble. He was a wonderful companion."

Those early trips to Mexico were mostly to Ensenada. "There was a beautiful hotel there," Huston said, recalling the Riviera del Pacifico. "Jack Dempsey was the front man, and it was a gambling establishment. Very well done. It was the best hotel, I think, south of San Francisco. My check was rather meager. I think I was making about a hundred fifty, two hundred dollars a week. Willy was making rather more. But we used to go down every week or two and lose everything we had. We would hang around the door waiting for a familiar face to come in, so we could borrow money and go back and try to recoup our fortune—which never worked out. Sometimes we did this week after week. Willy was a very daring gambler."

The bohemian Huston particularly admired Wyler's charisma. The young director was equally capable of playing Beethoven on his violin, speeding around town on his motorcycle, or schussing down steep virgin snow trails. Though he projected confidence, he also had an unassuming manner.

"Willy was not a hell-raiser," Huston explained. "He never created scenes. I never saw Willy drunk, for instance. He was a great man for walking a narrow ledge at a dizzying height. He'd do anything that had a touch of physical challenge to it. He loved thrills. He was an extremely modest man, highly egocentric, but not egotistical in any way."

Wyler also had Old World taste, which Huston, a tall, raw-boned Missouri native, admired and cultivated from recent European jaunts. Still, refinement did not prevent Wyler from being "hell on wheels." Huston recalled that "Willy used to put Universal into a state of abject terror if any sound stage over there had two doors open. Why, he would buzz through them at seventy miles an hour on his motorcycle. People would have to jump to make room for his passage."

For all their revelry, Wyler rarely got into fights. Two of his later films—*Friendly Persuasion* and *The Big Country*—would have pacifist themes. Nevertheless, he once asked Huston, who'd been an amateur boxer, how to protect himself in a street fight.

"I told him to watch his opponent's eyes," Huston remembered. "Just before he is going to hit you, he'll get a look in his eyes. When you see that, you beat him to the punch with a straight jab and nine times out of ten the fight will be over.

"Well, not more than a week went by when Willy began seeing that look. He was taking a girl to dinner one night and she had a little white dog which the parking attendant objected to. Willy saw the look and hit the guy in the nose. There were several other occasions from then on. One time somebody made a racial remark. Willy called him on it. He saw that look and decked him. But that was Willy. He acted. He knew exactly what to do, and he did it. Thereafter, I always thought twice about giving Willy the benefit of my advice."

During the next year and a half the pair collaborated on several projects, none of which materialized. First, they turned out a script based on a long-owned Universal property called *Steel*. Junior claimed he wanted to produce the film with Wyler as director, but changed his mind on seeing the script. "Junior seriously said it was too good—and, therefore, not box office—to make into a picture," Wyler wrote his brother. "This is certainly a shameful confession.

"So now I am assigned to do Pirandello's play, which was bought for John Stahl—*As Before Better Than Before*, which we have retitled *The Marriage Interlude*. The starring part, you will be surprised to hear, will be played by Tala Birell, whom you will probably remember from the

German version of *Command to Love*. Junior thinks he has another Garbo. I doubt it."

Ironically, the work on *Steel* saved Wyler from a layoff notice he'd received for refusing to direct the Western star Tom Mix in *Destry Rides Again*. After a three-year absence from the screen, Mix had agreed to do his first movie for Universal. Wyler at first gave his pledge to direct the Mix film, having been assured that the assignment was a professional concession to the company and not some form of punishment. The studio's idea was to do a whole series starring Mix. The salesmen at Universal felt that if Wyler directed the first installment, it would go a long way toward helping them sell exhibitors on the rest of the series.

But Mix threw a monkey wrench into the plan when he laid down an ultimatum: He would not appear in any picture that required him to drink, smoke or pull a gun.

Wyler received word of this in an edict from New York sent by Carl Laemmle's son-in-law Stanley Bergerman, who had married Rosabelle and was now serving in an official capacity as Laemmle's executive assistant. Boiling down "our New York Cabinet meeting," Bergerman let Wyler know he was passing on Laemmle's strict instructions: "Far more riding, thrills and stunts should be incorporated" in the picture "and less gunplay," especially since "the big Mix audience [is] children." Moreover, Wyler should see to it that the screenwriter cut innocuous bits of business from the script. Moments like "Mix rolls cigarettes" were deemed offensive and had to be excised.

Wyler, who did not want to go back to Westerns, wanted even less to deal with Mix. He regarded Mix as a self-important star whose celebrity had gone to his head—and he said as much. The press was soon reporting that Wyler had "refused to make a Pollyanna Western."

His next attempt to work up a project with John Huston was *Laughing Boy*, a more ambitious film than *Steel*. It would preoccupy them for much of 1932. In addition to preparing the script, based on Oliver La Farge's 1929 Pulitzer Prize-winning novel of the same name, they spent months scouting locations in Arizona, New Mexico and Oklahoma. Because they were determined to make an authentic movie of a tragic Navajo love story, they wanted to cast Native Americans in the lead roles and hoped to show actual customs. Wyler and Huston traveled to Indian reservations throughout the Southwest to see various tribal ceremonies and find a pair of actors. In doing this, they were taking a cue from La Farge himself.

An anthropologist as well as a writer, La Farge had used material from his ethnological and archaeological expeditions to authenticate his

fiction. Consequently, *Laughing Boy* was unusual for its time. Not a prettified story, it dealt with real issues of prostitution, racism and poverty,
as well as cultural dispossession and spiritual alienation. In its tale of the
love affair between Laughing Boy and Slim Girl, the novel spelled out
implicit conflicts that lay hidden in the folds of American history.
Laughing Boy is seen as a Navajo uncorrupted by the dominant white
culture. Slim Girl, however, has been victimized by it. Taken from her
home and educated in government schools, she has been forced to assimilate yet ultimately faces rejection by both cultures.

Although the plot involved serious subjects—and censorable scenes
showing Slim Girl, for example, as a prostitute with a white clientele—
Junior felt the movie could be made into an entertaining spectacle.

"We anticipate an Epic," he wrote in a memo to Henigson, who was
shepherding the project through its early stages. "While the script is
good, it is not big enough . . . even though probably it is more artistic
the way it is written now. But to Hell with artistry—we want action and
box office."

Wyler believed from the beginning that he could make a beautiful
picture and a great love story. But he always doubted its commercial
possibilities. Still, he was not averse to having the studio spend thirty-
five thousand dollars on his and Huston's research around the country—money that would not have been available except for Junior's
enthusiasm.

Separately and together, Wyler and Huston made three trips to Arizona and camped out for two weeks at a time with the Navajos. The two
of them flew to Oklahoma City and Lawrence, Kansas, to visit reservations there. They traveled through Texas, Nevada and Utah as well.
They witnessed sacred snake dances and sand paintings, initiation rites
and prayer meetings. They even conferred with medicine men. Over a
two-month period the pair toured reservations of the Hopi, Piute,
Apache, Comanche, Crow and Blackfoot.

Meanwhile, the search for a nonwhite actor to play Laughing Boy
brought an avalanche of international publicity and an outpouring of
unknown hopefuls. Hundreds turned up for screen tests from as far
away as Ecuador. Universal, happy to milk the publicity for all it was
worth, tested more than fifty of them.

The casting of Slim Girl also started out as part of the campaign for
authenticity. But it was Hollywood-style authenticity. In April of 1932
Huston sent Wyler a wire from Flagstaff, Arizona: "Found made-to-
order Slim Girl. Speaks perfect English and is very beautiful. Have

taken photographs of her. As soon as developed will send them on. Going into reservation tonight. Wish you were along to see this girl."

Despite their search, Universal decided to cast Zita Johann, a Hungarian-born stage actress who became Huston's lover. As for Laughing Boy, La Farge recommended Franchot Tone, a new Hollywood arrival who was hardly an authentic Navajo. The studio also considered using two other Caucasian actors, Lew Ayres, who had starred in *All Quiet on the Western Front,* and Gary Cooper. But the role ultimately went begging when Junior abruptly decided to shelve the project because of the combination of casting difficulties, Hays Office warnings and mounting costs. (The property eventually was sold to MGM and made into a vehicle for Ramon Novarro and Lupe Velez. It flopped.)

While Huston was working on the screenplay for *Laughing Boy,* Wyler had his hands full directing another film, *Tom Brown of Culver.* Shot partly on location at the well-known Culver Military Academy in northern Indiana, it was a juvenile programmer, and Wyler regarded it without much enthusiasm. "The picture is a different type from anything I've done so far, and I believe (and so does Junior) that it will make a lot of money," he wrote his brother. "It's not artistic in any way but purely commercial in subject and treatment, maybe a little too much so."

The plot centered on the life of the Culver cadets, with the primary focus on one rebellious boy, Tom Brown, and his relationships on and off campus. Universal's intention was "to make a wholesome, virile picture to counteract the sensational gin-and-jazz pictures that were so sadly misrepresenting American youth." That, at least, is how one studio executive explained it in his initial request to use the academy campus. Carl Laemmle had so much enthusiasm for the picture that he visited the military school during filming.

The generic Tom Brown character had been filmed before, for example in MGM's 1926 silent *Brown of Harvard.* But the type was first described in *Tom Brown's School Days,* a British story published in 1857. It told of Squire Brown being sent off to Rugby School, where he is to become a "brave, helpful, truth-telling Englishman, and a gentleman, and a Christian." The boy's rite of passage requires initiation on the playing fields and in the dormitories. The school bully must be faced. A stiff upper lip must be kept. To cry or cringe was tantamount to moral defeat.

To obtain an inside view of life among the cadets and to acquaint himself with the atmosphere, Wyler spent two weeks living in their barracks. His script girl, Freda Rosenblatt, who accompanied him to Culver, recalled that the academy was filled with "rich spoiled kids" and that discipline was spotty. "Smoking was forbidden," she said. "Naturally you found mounds of cigarettes all around the place."

Wyler had heard that the upperclassmen often terrorized the freshmen. "I wanted to see how they did it," he recalled. "So one day I got a couple of the older boys to hide me in a closet." He watched as naked plebes came running into the dormitory, where the upperclassmen grilled them and "slapped them around for no reason." Wyler made use of the experience. "I copied this kind of scene in the picture," he said. But the superintendent of the academy, General L. R. Gignilliat, had final approval of the film before it could be released. He objected to the "plebe scenes" after screening the film and requested changes, claiming "the element of harshness has been unduly emphasized." Otherwise, he was more than pleased with the results.

It fell to Henry Henigson to harass Wyler whenever the filming of *Tom Brown of Culver* ran behind schedule. And by April 9, Henigson was fuming. In his view, Wyler had failed to comply with a directive limiting the number of times a scene could be shot either from different angles or with different lenses. In fact, bad weather was largely responsible for Wyler's production delays, not excessive camera setups. Also, despite the academy's cooperation, it strictly limited the amount of time and the number of cadets that Wyler could use on any given day. The commandant notified Henigson that "Mr. Wyler was rather impatient" about that. When the weather kept him from filming, Wyler and the crew would pile into a car and drive to the auto races in Indianapolis. "Even with that," Rosenblatt said, "the project came in close to schedule."

Praise for the picture was overwhelming across the country. On its release in July 1932 the public and the critics felt it was the sort of family viewing that gave a true impression of American youth. The *New York Times* liked the "fact that the boys act like boys instead of road company Hamlets." The *Chicago Daily News* wrote: "West Point, Annapolis, Yale, Harvard and Notre Dame have all been sung in pictures before, but no picture perhaps has been screened with greater fidelity to fact and with greater credibility." The *Detroit Free Press* hailed it as "the most poignantly beautiful story of boyhood ever seen pictured on the screen."

Pleased at its success but unimpressed by all the raves, Wyler was still trying to make *Laughing Boy,* and spent much of that summer on Navajo reservations. When the project fell through, he tried once again to make a socially relevant picture with Huston — this time about a very different class of boys from those at Culver.

In the fall of 1932 stories were circulating in the press about the multitudes of children on the road, perhaps as many as half a million between the ages of ten and seventeen, who had to endure the Depression under the harshest possible conditions. They ran away from home, often because their families couldn't support them. Many rode the rails in flatcars and boxcars, shunted from one state to the next. Nobody wanted them. Various towns and cities wouldn't let them off the trains. Fatal incidents created a scandal. In Texas, for example, a dozen children died in a boxcar of starvation and thirst.

To research their project, called *The Forgotten Boys,* Wyler and Huston took to the road themselves. "We went on the boxcars, like hobos," Huston remembered. "We went up to Fresno, Bakersfield. There was a whole other world, a stratum of society moving at that level in every town, every city. Each had its skid row, and those skid rows were overpopulated. I remember one place in Fresno we spent fifteen cents to sleep on ropes, like a boxing ring. You sat on a bench and leaned forward and slept on the rope.

"I remember our being in a flophouse in Los Angeles for I think twenty-five cents a night. You got just a bed and you could shower in the morning. We were in the shower and there was a big redheaded, toothless bum in there with us. He opened the towel, and the towel had the name of the flophouse on it: Deluxe. He asked us, 'What does Deluxe mean?' That broke Willy up."

Wyler had a reader from the studio comb the files of the *Los Angeles Examiner* for stories about youths caught committing crimes. He also arranged to attend night sessions of juvenile court with Huston.

"I wrote a script," Huston said, "and then Willy and I went to La Quinta to do the final version. While at La Quinta, two world-shaking events occurred, the earthquake [in Japan] and the first Inauguration of Franklin Delano Roosevelt. We came back to the studio. The picture was going into production. But before it did, these kids were off the road and working in the reforestation camps [for the Civilian Conservation Corps]. With FDR's first hundred days, the whole social scene had changed. Overnight, it seemed, there was a new spirit in the air. There was no need for the picture, and it was called off."

13

<hr/>

WILD TIMES

In June 1932 Willy took his own apartment for the first time since his parents had come to live with him in Los Angeles. "I can't be living at home all my life and remain a true bachelor," he wrote Robert, who was still in Paris. "I know you will understand the circumstances. I have for two years endured the restrictions of a respectable family life. I feel some wild times coming over me, which I must give proper quarters. Anyway I have gotten the parents a dog to take my place, and he seems to be less trouble and more fun around the house."

Unlike Huston, Wyler was not a reckless womanizer. But he had plenty of sexual charm. And according to Freda Rosenblatt, by then his all-around Girl Friday, "he knew how to turn it on, really turn it on. He was very likable." His flirtations could become elaborate. "Willy was always sending roses and perfumes to some actress or other," Rosenblatt recounted. "A date with Willy might include a candlelight dinner or an intimate soiree. He was always taking someone to Agua Caliente for the weekend." But when he went in for one-night stands, he didn't advertise them. "Willy was very courtly," she said, "very European, always a gentleman."

That fall Wyler met a blond, blue-eyed actress with a porcelain beauty. A former Miss California, she came from San Francisco and had just turned twenty-one. Her name was Sheila Bromley. "She looked like a Dresden doll, very delicate," the director Vincent Sherman remembers. Bromley, who later appeared in films as Sheila Manors and Sheila Fulton, soon became Wyler's steady girlfriend. He got her a bit part in his next film, *Her First Mate*, which would begin filming in April 1933. "Willy was quite serious about her," Rosenblatt said. "They didn't always get along. Sheila had a temper. But she *was* beautiful."

As serious as he felt about Bromley, Wyler was not tempted to join what he termed "the marriage club." He had as much family as he needed. Mama, Papa and Gaston were ensconced in Crescent Heights. He still ate with them three times a week, often bringing friends along. Mama was becoming famous in the film colony for her Viennese dishes. Even when Paul Kohner got married in October — to Lupita Tover, a Mexican actress working for Universal — Wyler didn't feel the temptation. He wired best wishes to his old friend, who was now in Berlin heading European production for Universal: HEREWITH UNREQUESTED BUT HEARTY APPROVAL. CONGRATULATIONS IN SPITE OF HELL OR HITLER. ALSO WISHING YOU OCCASIONAL BLESSED EVENTS. THE MIXTURE SHOULD PROVE A NOVELTY.

Mama wished it had been Willy at the altar. He was already thirty. But she knew better than to insist.

TOWARDS THE END OF 1932, ROBERT MANAGED TO WORK OUT A one-year deal with Universal and returned to Hollywood expecting to direct and hoping to get a long-term contract. The family was thrilled to have him back, but the joy would be short-lived. As Willy later related, Junior and his assistants "were out to get him and they *got* him."

Soon after Robert's arrival, the studio closed for several months. A number of directors already under contract continued on the payroll under the shutdown, including Willy. But Junior let Robert know that keeping him on the payroll with nothing to do, especially after bringing him all the way back from Europe, was an embarrassment. After six months of indecision, Robert arranged a deal with Metro enabling Universal to swap a story, *She*, for one of Metro's, *Candle-Light*, which he would direct. The picture was cast. The sets were built. Then Universal discovered it didn't own *She*, whereupon the swap fell through and Junior called off the production.

Having worked so long on arranging the deal only to see it fall apart,

Robert went to Junior and asked him to buy *Candle-Light* outright. Junior refused. Robert then went to Carl Laemmle and told him the whole story, explaining how much money had already been spent preparing the production. Laemmle promptly bought the rights—not, however, without giving Junior hell about mismanaging the project.

The day before shooting began, though, Junior told Robert that he didn't believe in his ability and thought he would have to take him off the picture after a week. As soon as Laemmle left for Europe, Junior kept his word. He pulled Robert off *Candle-Light* on the pretense that the rushes did not look good. James Whale, one of the directors on salary but not then occupied with a picture, was assigned to take over. Whale protested, notifying Junior that all of the rushes were not only "very good but had a charm and delicate humor."

Meanwhile, Junior indicated that Robert would get another directing assignment only after Willy signed a new contract. "Naturally knowing my interest in Bob, they used him as pressure on me," Willy wrote Kohner. When Willy refused to sign, "they went as far as dismissing Bob entirely and threatened to tear up his contract in an effort to bring me to terms."

Willy refused to bow to the pressure. With the termination of his own contract in January 1933, he left Universal. He could see that other studios were turning out the overwhelming majority of prestige pictures. If he were to have a shot at them, he would have to go elsewhere. It had been a dozen years since he stepped off the *Aquitania* in New York. He had learned a craft, gained respect and reputation, considerable money and even some fame. Though the country was still in the throes of the Depression, his skill had shielded him from it.

Willy believed he owed an enormous debt to Carl Laemmle, so it was difficult to leave Universal. But Uncle Carl no longer ran the company on a daily basis. Junior did, almost exclusively. Uncle Carl's goodwill still commanded loyalty, however. With great difficulty, Willy wrote a letter a week before his departure.

"It is not without a good deal of regret that I will be leaving . . . I have made every effort to reach an agreement. I have given the Company extension after extension, concessions both financial and otherwise and have accepted each and every bona fide offer made me—except the very last one—only to find that upon acceptance the offer no longer held good, or had been considerably modified.

"Even though I will no longer be connected with Universal I do not regard my indebtedness to you as being at an end. I will never be able to fully repay you for your many kindnesses. . . ."

After posting the letter, Wyler walked through the gates of Universal on January 7, thinking it would be for the last time. He had no specific prospects, but he did have expectations. He wired Paul Kohner in Germany asking about the possibilities of doing a film in Europe. Kohner wired back that Germany was out. Maybe there would be a chance in England or France. Willy then got Robert to wire Gaumont in London for any nibbles. He talked with Frank Orsatti, a bootlegger-turned-Hollywood-agent, to see if he could line up a directing assignment at one of the major studios. Willy even tried peddling the script of *Laughing Boy* to Paramount when he heard Universal was willing to sell it. There were no takers.

Stumped by his inability to find work, Wyler then did a complete about-face and went back to Universal. On February 23, he signed a one-picture deal for a flat fee of eight thousand dollars to do *Her First Mate*, the third in a series of four comedies starring the husband-wife team of Zasu Pitts and Slim Summerville. Filming would start April 3, and he would have eight weeks to shoot it.

Wyler told his newly acquired agent, Myron Selznick, that he had buried his qualms and signed because he still hoped to do *The Forgotten Boys*. What he didn't tell his agent was that his return to Universal was largely motivated by the hope of getting work for Robert. Junior's blackmail had, in fact, proved effective. And now, with Willy under contract again, Junior promised to bring Robert back into the fold with a new directing assignment.

Wyler began *Her First Mate* as scheduled, spending a week on location in San Francisco Bay. The entire picture, based on a Broadway play called *Salt Water*, took place aboard a ferryboat. "There was no real friction on that set," Rosenblatt remembered. "It was light and fluffy." Wyler added enough fresh gags and comic touches to make the film a popular one with audiences and critics.

"It was almost slapstick," he said. "[But] it was sort of advanced in content for its time, because the girl thinks she's pregnant and she's not, and he lies about his job. She thinks he's the captain of the ferryboat. All he does is sell peanuts on it."

After completing *Her First Mate*, Wyler signed another contract with Universal for a year at a weekly salary of one thousand one hundred twenty-five dollars. And he promptly received a prestige assignment: Elmer Rice's *Counsellor-at-Law*, the Broadway hit.

Meanwhile, Junior failed to keep his word regarding Robert. As *Variety* would report, "Robert Wyler, director, has left Universal voluntarily after ten months of cashing salary checks without an assignment. He had about two months longer to go on his contract but preferred to tear it up." Willy, despite his anger, could do nothing.

COUNSELLOR-AT-LAW NOT ONLY RAN ON BROADWAY, IT HAD PRO-ductions in Chicago, Los Angeles and San Francisco. Now Junior was going to put the play on the screen. The price tag for the rights to this 1931 smash hit came to one hundred fifty thousand dollars, steep for the Depression and for Junior. Despite his reluctance to spend large sums on production, he tried to guarantee a certain number of quality pictures each year. To help ensure the Hollywood success of *Counsellor-at-Law,* moreover, Elmer Rice was hired to do the screen adaptation.

The playwright went back a long way in the American theater. In 1914, at the age of twenty-two, he took Broadway by surprise with his first effort, a courtroom melodrama called *On Trial.* It relied heavily on Rice's experience two years earlier as a precocious attorney just out of his teens. It also earned him roughly a hundred thousand dollars in royalties.

Rice could write with sophisticated craft. *On Trial* introduced the "flashback" technique on the stage, for example. But he did not have another hit until 1923, when his expressionistic fantasy, *The Adding Machine,* became a succès d'estime with its intellectual critique of American capitalism. Centered on an office drudge trapped by technological regimentation, it foreshadowed the leftist stance his plays largely took throughout the thirties and beyond. *Counsellor-at-Law* came during the flush of his greatest success. Two years before, he had won the Pulitzer Prize for *Street Scene,* an unflinching slice of New York life. This latest play represented a return to the legal world.

Hoping to get a jump on the script, Universal sent Wyler in early August to Mexico City, where Rice was vacationing with his family. Wyler flew on the first Mexican airline to the border town of Juarez, across the Rio Grande river from El Paso. "It was a hell of a big flight in those days," he recalled. "The railroad would have taken three days. When I got on, I was the only passenger. We flew and flew, and suddenly we came down and landed in a place called León. The pilot said we couldn't go any further because of the weather in Mexico City. Well, there I was stuck in a crummy hotel full of cockroaches in this town where no one spoke English. Finally after three days, I went back to the airport. The pilot said we still couldn't leave because the weather wasn't any better."

Wandering the airport, Wyler spotted a Mexican worker whose eyes were heavily bandaged. "He was going to Mexico City to have an operation on his eyes. So I told the pilot this poor fellow is liable to go blind if he doesn't get to the hospital, and it will be your fault." The ploy worked. The pilot decided to risk the bad weather.

When Wyler met Rice, he was pleased to learn from the playwright that "vacation and work don't mix." Rice said he would be in Hollywood in a few weeks. They could begin collaborating on the screenplay then, but not before. Wyler stopped in at Universal's Mexico City office to give the news to the home office, spent a couple of days sightseeing and decided to take the train back to Los Angeles. In all, the round trip took him ten days and cost the company less than five hundred dollars. He was back by August 17. Screen tests for a large cast of players began within two weeks, and principal photography started on September 8, 1933.

Rice must have shortened his Mexican vacation or had a screenplay already written, because by August 22 he arranged to have a draft of it shipped to Universal from his New York office. Wyler agreed with the cuts Rice made from the stage production. But when it came to actual shooting, he found that excised material often was needed for the "build" of the scenes. So he began putting material back in to make the scenes effective. In fact, during the entire shoot, Wyler worked from the screenplay and the play script at the same time. The procedure, unorthodox and undesirable as it was, allowed Wyler to test his choices on the spot. Interestingly, Wyler would repeat the procedure some years later on the set of *The Little Foxes* during the shooting of Lillian Hellman's drama.

The studio had intended to engage Paul Muni to recreate his Broadway success in the role of George Simon, a shrewd, highly successful Jewish lawyer who has worked his way up from the poverty of New York's Lower East Side. Muni refused to reprise the role, however, claiming he was afraid of being typecast as a Jewish actor. So Universal turned to its list of alternatives. The names ranged from Edward G. Robinson to Joseph Schildkraut and William Powell. But at the top of the list was John Barrymore. Though Barrymore seemed an improbable actor to play a driven Jewish lawyer from the ghetto, the studio could not resist the extraordinary marquee value of his name. Even his staggering fee and reputation for heavy drinking did not deter Junior from hiring him.

The plot of *Counsellor-at-Law* involves several days at a critical juncture in George Simon's life. Earlier in his career, he'd gone along with a guilty client's perjured testimony because he believed the man could be rehabilitated. Now a rival is threatening to expose the incident, which could result in George's disbarment. He gets no sympathy from his gentile wife, a beautiful socialite who is horrified that her name might be associated with scandal. Desperate to save his marriage and his career, George fights back and seems to succeed. But then he discovers his wife is about to leave for Europe with another man. The revelation devastates him. As he is about to jump from the window of his office — it occupies a high floor of the Empire State Building — his devoted secretary, who is secretly in love with him, stops him from jumping. But melodrama and romance are not the point. Slice-of-life realism is. The phone rings. Simon picks it up. A client is calling. Shaken though he is, Simon regains his self-possession. Work goes on. Life goes on.

When *Counsellor-at-Law* went into production, most of the supporting roles were filled with Hollywood actors. Among them were Bebe Daniels as the loyal secretary, Doris Kenyon as the selfish wife, Melvyn Douglas as the wife's lover. Both Rice and Wyler had suggested taking actors from the Broadway production. Screen tests were made in New York of several of them. Other tests were made of actors from the Chicago and San Francisco productions. But, finally, only four were cast from New York and only one, Vincent Sherman, from Chicago. Sherman, later to become a director at Warner Bros., was brought to Hollywood to reprise his cameo role as a young communist firebrand.

Having seen the play in New York, Wyler knew *Counsellor-at-Law* was a huge artistic opportunity. Also, to direct a star of Barrymore's caliber was heady stuff. Wyler seemed visibly nervous at their first meeting in Henigson's office. Recognizing this, Barrymore immediately tried to put the young director at ease. He took him into a corner and put his arm around him.

"You and I are going to get along fine, you know," the star said. "Don't worry about all the stories you've heard about the Barrymores. That all comes from my sister and she's full of shit!"

The shooting schedule was set for a mere twenty days. Junior had agreed to pay Barrymore twenty-five thousand dollars a week and had signed him for two weeks. All scenes involving Barrymore were to be shot as swiftly as possible. Wyler was under orders not to stop for close-ups of anybody in Barrymore's scenes. They were to be picked up later.

"It was a terrible way to make a picture," Wyler commented.

But even working at a breakneck pace, it took three and a half weeks to complete Barrymore's scenes, largely because the star had so much trouble remembering his lines. On the second day of shooting, the pattern of delays began. A half day was lost "on account of Mr. Barrymore not knowing his lines," a production report notes. On the fifth day another half day was lost for the same reason, and again on the eighth day. These delays did not include later retakes or time lost for the same reason with other members of the cast.

"My roommate Johnny Qualen came home from the set one night at ten o'clock," Sherman recounted. "We were supposed to have dinner at seven.

"I said to him, 'What the hell happened?'

" 'Barrymore couldn't remember his lines,' he said. 'We did fifty-six takes. Then Wyler called it off.' "

Qualen and Sherman joked that the young director would soon be known around town as "Fifty-take Wyler," a prediction not far off the mark.

Sherman got a firsthand taste of the grueling experience as well. He had a climactic scene with Barrymore that crystalized one of the movie's key themes. Playing a young rabble-rouser who is beaten and arrested for making anarchist speeches, Sherman refuses George Simon's legal help and accuses him of denying his Jewish roots and betraying his class origins.

"I thought we'd be through in a couple of hours," Sherman said. "It took four days to do that scene. Barrymore kept forgetting his lines. We had to do twenty-seven takes."

The star's memory lapses got so bad that Wyler finally came up with a mutually acceptable solution: cue cards. Ordinarily, Barrymore's lines would be written on a signboard placed where the star could glance at it without giving any indication to the camera. "But sometimes we had to write on the walls for him or on a piece of the ceiling," Wyler said.

The star became rather adept at this system.

"There was constant motion in some of the scenes," Sherman remembered. "Barrymore could walk and read the cue card, while it was held up by Willy's script girl. She'd be riding backwards on a dolly. It was quite an operation."

More impressive, though, was Barrymore's ability to negotiate his lines at all, especially since they had to be rattled off with speed.

"He was playing the part of a fast-talking, very glib lawyer," Wyler said. "A lot of the talk was legal phraseology, which had to be studied, and it was fashionable in those days to talk very fast on the screen."

Barrymore's drinking created other delays. "At times it was impossible for him to be in front of the camera," Rosenblatt recalled. "He always had a companion with him to make sure he showed up. And someone had to be assigned to him to make sure he was dressed for scene continuity."

Sherman recalled that Barrymore's face looked so puffy from time to time that the makeup department "had to tape his jowls up with fish skins" before he could go in front of the camera.

In the midst of all these problems, Junior kept after Wyler to shoot quickly. "Every day pink slips would come from Laemmle's office," Rosenblatt recalled. "They'd have a notation that if Willy didn't finish within a certain time, he was going to be taken off the picture. That didn't help his mood any. So sometimes when these slips came in, I'd hide them until he finished shooting the scenes."

Wyler responded to Junior's pressure by being tough on the cast. Most of the actors "were scared to death of him," Rosenblatt said. He particularly took his frustrations out on the supporting players. "Willy wore down everybody on the set," she added. "The actors were ready to kill him."

In addition to pressure from Junior, the front office wanted Wyler "to open up the movie," that is, to use as many exterior locales as possible. But he felt the focus of the story was the public and private life of George Simon at work and therefore insisted that all the action had to take place in his law office. To do otherwise, he also felt, would slow the frenetic pace of the original production.

"I retained the construction of the play and gave an illusion of movement," Wyler said. "We never left the lawyer's offices. But no critic ever wrote that it was just a photographed stage play. I avoided that feeling by using several offices, instead of two as in the play, and by having the actors walk or move around at certain moments.

"This, too, can be overdone. Many great scenes have been ruined because the director thought it was time the characters got up and said, 'Shall we dance?' You have to apply great judgment as to when and where and how you open things up and, equally important, when you don't. The studio was constantly after me to leave the offices, but I wouldn't do it.

"There was a scene in *Counsellor* that had great suspense because George Simon sent somebody out on an errand to get some piece of information, and the fellow comes back and he's telling Simon, and Simon is dying to know, 'Did he get this information?' The fellow goes into a lot of superfluous detail, how he got there, when he took a taxi and so on. And Simon is going crazy trying to get the answer. Every time he wants to get to the point, this guy goes into a long story. It was a funny scene. Well, Universal said, 'You've got to show the fellow getting into a taxi and going to a house and eavesdropping and finding something important.' I said, 'No,' because the interest in the scene lies in the man who's listening, not in the man who's talking. In a case like that you don't open up. You sit still.

"A film can be accused of being a photographed stage play. But I've seen where directors have opened up and squandered all the emotions. So they show a panorama. So they show a city. A street. A house and a taxi out front. What's so emotional about that?"

Exactly three months after shooting began and two weeks before Christmas, *Counsellor-at-Law* opened at Radio City Music Hall in New York City to both critical and commercial acclaim. Rice, an anti-Hollywood curmudgeon, was pleased with Wyler's results. He wired effusive praise to Junior. The *Hollywood Reporter* said the movie proved "the value of having a playwright adapt his own brainchild to the screen." But the review also emphasized the contribution of the director. "William Wyler gives the film a far better tempo than the play possessed—and that is saying a great deal," the reviewer noted. "He milks each situation and speedily lets it go without stressing . . . many scenes which could easily have ensnared a less capable director."

Apart from the speed at which he worked—all those takes notwithstanding—Wyler managed another feat: He drew from Barrymore what is now regarded as possibly the actor's best film performance. "This is one of the few screen roles that reveal his measure as an actor," Pauline Kael wrote in a retrospective critique. "His 'presence' is apparent in every scene; so are his restraint, his humor, and his zest."

For Wyler, *Counsellor-at-Law* stood out as his most significant work of the early thirties and represented the high point of his career at Universal in terms of artistic achievement. Only *Hell's Heroes* and *A House Divided* can lay claim to such serious stature.

WITH THE PICTURE COMPLETED AND ROBERT'S ASSOCIATION with Universal recently terminated, the two brothers flew off to New York and checked into the Essex House on Central Park South. Every night except for the premiere of *Counsellor* at Radio City, they took in the Broadway hits—fourteen plays in all. Robert returned to Europe thinking he would find more opportunities for work there, and Willy flew back to Hollywood. Of the plays he saw, he recommended three to Junior as having commercial possibilities.

First on Wyler's list was *The Dark Tower*, which he described as an intelligent comedy melodrama with an extremely interesting twist. What appealed to him was its human perversity. He noted, "A perfectly honorable person commits justifiable but nonetheless cold-blooded murder and gets away with it, due to the fact that he is a clever actor." Wyler, who was a great believer in plot, thought the structure of the play "could be implanted in the picture to an even greater extent" than it was in the Broadway production. Equally revealing of Wyler's taste perhaps, he wrote that the play treated the story "more in the light of comedy, and so the curse is taken off the melodramatic incidents."

Significantly, he also thought the play's love story could be amplified and that the role of the actor "was ideally suited" for Barrymore. Wyler was not making idle recommendations. He was keeping his own interests in mind. Universal executives in New York had suggested that, given the popularity of *Counsellor-at-Law*, there should be a follow-up Barrymore picture. The natural implication was that Wyler should direct it.

The other two plays he wrote Junior about were *The Pursuit of Happiness* and *Jezebel*. Wyler felt *Pursuit* could be a charming and delightful picture along the lines of *Little Women*, which had been a big success for RKO earlier that year. Regarding *Jezebel*, despite its weak stage reviews, Wyler thought it was "an excellent foundation for a picture—in fact, more so than for a play." It would make a better movie because it could be opened up. Contrary to his practice in *Counsellor*, he wrote that sequences only talked about on stage could be shown in the movie. He also thought the dramatic love story of *Jezebel*, which was set in the antebellum South, would lend itself to a beautiful-looking production complete with lush countryside and sumptuous costumes.

Thus, in December 1933, long before Margaret Mitchell's novel *Gone With the Wind* was even set in galleys, Wyler strongly recommended *Jezebel* as a vehicle for Universal's new star, Margaret Sullavan. Little did he guess that he would marry Sullavan eleven months later and would direct *Jezebel* for Warner Bros. four years hence, with Bette Davis, who would claim he was the love of her life.

He also gave Junior a list of the other plays he saw, including Eugene O'Neill's *Ah Wilderness!* and the stage adaptation of Erskine Caldwell's *Tobacco Road*, with a reminder that he'd be happy to answer any questions about them. But Junior showed no interest in Wyler's suggestions. Instead, Junior assigned him to *Glamour*, which was loosely based on a short story by Edna Ferber.

THE BEST THING ABOUT *GLAMOUR* WAS ITS ATTRACTIVE LEADING lady, Constance Cummings, Junior's fiancée (within weeks of filming she would marry someone else). Forced into doing the picture, Wyler felt it was "a real disappointment" and couldn't muster the enthusiasm to save it. He always remembered it as "kind of a screwy picture."

Cummings plays an ambitious chorus girl who callously dumps her husband (Paul Lukas) for her younger dance partner (Philip Reed), after she makes it professionally as a dancer. She, in turn, is jilted by husband number two, which sets up a return to husband number one.

First impressions of the picture were so favorable within the industry that Radio City Music Hall booked it for an opening in April 1934. Universal was overjoyed, because it had been unable to get a booking there since *Counsellor-at-Law*. But audiences didn't like it, and all Wyler ever said in its defense was that "it was made in four weeks at a total cost of only a hundred sixty thousand dollars."

Again trying to interest Junior in a story that he would like to make, Wyler suggested an idea about the life of Tchaikovsky given him by Max Magnus, the *Variety* reporter-cum-agent he'd met in Berlin. In a memo to Junior, Wyler wrote: "I think it is high time that a musical picture with a serious story were made and I think it will be very profitable to whoever may be the first to make one." Wyler continued, "I have always wanted to make a picture about a classical composer with his music but was always fearful that it might be a little too highbrow to be box-office, but the music of Tchaikovsky offers the happy combination of truly great and at the same time popular music."

Wyler told Junior that he heard Zanuck at Twentieth Century–Fox was preparing a story on Franz Liszt to star George Arliss. Wyler also mentioned that Paul Lukas, whom he'd just finished working with in *Glamour*, would be "swell as Tchaikovsky." Several weeks later Wyler planted an item in Louella Parsons's syndicated gossip column about the Tchaikovsky story. That finally ignited Junior's interest. The day after the item appeared he sent Wyler a memo: "Get me a price on the Tchaikovsky story and discuss it with me today." For all that, the project failed to materialize.

At the same time, Universal had two properties in mind for Wyler to direct. The first was *Fanny*, a story that Robert had brought to the studio's attention the previous year when he was still working there under his short-lived contract. Now, having recently acquired the rights to make an English version of *Fanny*, Universal needed approval from the Hays Office.

The story, the second in a trilogy by Marcel Pagnol, had already been successful in France. It told of a woman who marries one man while pregnant with another man's child. Surprisingly, Junior had great enthusiasm for the story and made the picture his pet project. He and

Henigson fought to gain the censor's approval. He decided the script would be rewritten. To do this he hired Preston Sturges and paired him with Wyler.

They made a remarkably compatible team. Both men had Continental backgrounds. Sturges, though an American, had spent most of his youth in Europe. Both spoke French. They took to each other instantly and would maintain their friendship until Sturges's death in 1959. But they were very different types as personalities. Wyler was a great listener, all his drive notwithstanding. Sturges was a great talker. Wyler thought of him as "a genius and also a tremendous egomaniac." Sturges was the life of the party, the great host, the marvelous friend. But he needed to take control of everything and everyone around him.

Within five weeks, Sturges turned out a script that, according to Wyler, "retained most of the humor and the characteristics" of the people in Pagnol's story. Wyler believed the script completely captured the spirit of the original, changing only what might "bring it within censorship requirements and within the understanding of the average American." It did not even transfer the locale of the story from the Marseilles waterfront. Yet Pagnol suddenly began making last-minute requests in cables from Paris, raising questions about ownership of the rights as well as the screenplay itself. Willy informed Robert, "He wants to make sure his play won't be massacred on the American screen. I can't say that I blame him."

Though Hollywood newcomer Jane Wyatt was being brought from Broadway to play the title role of Fanny, Universal's New York office did not want to venture further in an expensive project that probably would be held up by disputes with the Hays Office. The company needed a quick infusion of profitable movies to shore up its financial weakness. Also, Wyler was having problems finding the right actor to play César, the male lead. Walter Huston, his first choice, was tied up in a play in New York. Charles Laughton and Wallace Beery, his second and third choices, were unavailable as well. After testing George Bancroft and a number of others, Wyler found that "none of them have the necessary humor to play the part as it ought to be played."

Wyler didn't really mind that the picture might not get underway. In fact, that secretly suited him because he had an ulterior motive in helping to develop the project in the first place: Willy wanted the picture for his brother to direct. He thought it would be ideal for getting Robert on his feet.

If approval from the Hays Office was not forthcoming, Willy reasoned, Robert would be able to buy the script cheaply and perhaps get it produced at another studio more willing to buck the censor. In a letter to Robert in April, he outlined the problems Universal was having with *Fanny* and indicated that Robert could benefit from them:

"This material is much too good to let it slip through our fingers because considerable attention has been called to it and someone will come along and snap it out of the hands of Universal or Pagnol or whoever owns it; they will make it and if properly made will be a great picture. . . . I believe that with *Fanny* you can put yourself on top with one single picture. . . . All this information I give you in the strictest confidence. I feel like somewhat of a traitor towards Universal in the matter but I have such confidence in *Fanny* that if at all possible I would like to see you do it."

As it happened, Henry Henigson felt so positive about *Fanny* that when he left Universal in April 1935, he took the script with him and tried to arrange a deal with Ernst Lubitsch to do it at Paramount. But the deal never came off. Twelve years later, when Wyler was looking for projects to do at Liberty Films, he tried to buy *Fanny* from Pagnol. Again it was not to be made. (In 1961 Joshua Logan finally produced and directed it with Leslie Caron, Maurice Chevalier and Charles Boyer.)

The project Wyler really hoped to direct instead of *Fanny* was *Sutter's Gold*, which Universal also had in mind for him. Based on the story "l'Or" by the French writer Blaise Cendrars, it was to be a biopic about Johan Sutter, the American pioneer who established a colony in California and later discovered gold at his mill in 1848. The studio had been accumulating facts on Sutter's life for several years in hopes of making a movie with mass appeal.

The Russian master filmmaker Sergei Eisenstein had tried unsuccessfully to interest Paramount in *Sutter's Gold* on his trip to Hollywood back in 1930. Wyler obtained the forty-three-page, English-language scenario that Eisenstein had prepared from the Cendrars story in 1932. Wyler also read several plays based on the life of Sutter, including Bruno Frank's *The General and the Gold* and Caesar von Arx's *John Augustus Sutter*. So he was reasonably well informed on the subject.

Cendrars, a major poet as well as novelist, got in touch with Wyler in March to offer his services as a screenwriter and hoped perhaps to install himself in Hollywood. "I am ready to be present on the set to give you advice and collaborate [in] the development of the scenario," he wrote. "Should this film be successful, I have several other first-class American scenarios."

But Universal was not interested in bringing Cendrars over. Henigson insisted on replying in Wyler's name that the studio had already engaged William Anthony McGuire, "who is a very well-known American dramatist" to write the screenplay. McGuire had been successful in the twenties with librettos and musical sketches for Florenz Ziegfeld and potboiler plays like *Six Cylinder Love*.

Cendrars persisted, however, even offering to read the script and suggest possible improvements "absolutely gratis." It would be "just a few extra ideas from the author to a friend." Wyler couldn't resist such an offer. He wrote back that as soon as the script was completed he would send it on. But by July he was pulled off *Sutter's Gold* and Howard Hawks was assigned to it. Eventually James Cruze directed, turning out a mediocre picture. When it was released in 1936, *Sutter's Gold* produced no gold for Universal. Along with *Show Boat*, it proved to be one of the studio's two biggest flops of the year. A poor script was its undoing.

14

"THAT BATTY BROAD"

WYLER'S NEXT PICTURE WOULD mark a turning point in his life. He had no inkling of that, nor was he even interested in making the picture. "My soul may belong to me, but my body belongs to Universal," he complained to his brother, now living in London. Wyler had hoped to go to Europe that July. "Have been unable to get the studio's permission to take my layoff at this time," he wrote. "I'm supposed to make Molnar's *The Good Fairy* immediately — that is, beginning in about three weeks."

Hearing Robert's stories about nights on the town with John Huston, who had also moved to London, Wyler added: "Tell that long-legged, lobster-nosed, shark-livered, mutton-fisted, pernivorous Presbyterian land-lubber that I'm getting out a vigilante committee who will cut him in two for a carrot and pitch him to the flatfish if he ever tries to shorten sail in these parts again, unless he comes in poop-first or makes an honest effort at squaring himself with a complete account of his activities."

Wyler wanted to take his brother and the Hustons — John was married by then to his first wife, Dorothy — on a trip to Switzerland and the south of France but instead began to work with Margaret Sullavan, for whom *The Good Fairy* was intended as a star vehicle. At twenty-three, she was a quick-tempered, somewhat seasoned stage actress and a darling of the critics. She had already starred in two hits for Universal (*Only Yesterday* and *Little Man, What Now?*), having signed a three-year contract in 1933 to do two pictures a year at twelve hundred dollars a week.

Sullavan had a flair for both drama and sophisticated comedy. Her magnetic, winsome manner quickly made her popular with the public in this country and abroad. "She was an absolutely adorable, charming creature," according to the screenwriter Philip Dunne, who dated her. Sullavan was also complicated. She had a pixie slyness and a headstrong tomboy style. These qualities were combined with a reputation for sexual promiscuity. Married at twenty to Henry Fonda, another newcomer to Hollywood, she divorced him at twenty-two and had numerous liaisons, including an obsessive relationship with the powerful Broadway producer Jed Harris. Later, she would marry her agent, Leland Hayward, who became a top producer both on Broadway and in Hollywood.

Rights to *The Good Fairy*, one of the Hungarian dramatist Ferenc Molnár's lesser plays, had been acquired by Universal after a respectable run on Broadway with Helen Hayes in the starring role. Preston Sturges got the assignment to adapt the comedy to the screen. He was fascinated by the ingenuous sweetness Sullavan projected on film, in contrast to the reality of her saucy, high-strung temperament. Sturges altered the play dramatically to suit the star's image. He wrote a new beginning and changed the general tone of the story from cynicism to optimism. Also, to get the story past the Hays Code, he sanitized many of the play's observations on marital infidelity.

Though hardly a line of Molnár's dialogue went unchanged, Sturges did manage to retain the play's basic charm. The picture is a light-hearted tale of good deeds gone awry. Sullavan plays a naive young woman who grew up in an orphanage. Her helplessness totally disrupts the lives of three very different men: a hotel waiter (Reginald Owen), a rich businessman (Frank Morgan) and an unsuccessful lawyer (Herbert Marshall). Sturges also wrote in a movie-within-a-movie scene, a device that became one of his trademarks.

Wyler was extremely pleased. But the writing process was slow, and the adaptation needed many revisions. A completed script that met with the studio's approval was still not ready when shooting began. Consequently, Sturges stayed on the set throughout the shooting schedule to complete the screenplay and rewrite scenes as needed.

Sullavan, despite the success of her first two pictures, had a disdainful attitude toward Hollywood. Further, her quick temper meant troubles for Wyler during production. His script girl, Freda Rosenblatt, remembered that while Sullavan seemed "very cute and had a winsome sort of appeal, she didn't care what happened to anybody."

"She did spiteful things to get her way," Rosenblatt said. "If she was tired and wanted to go home and Willy had one more scene to do, she would smear the makeup on her face. That would mean everything had to stop so she could be made up again. Which might take hours. So they couldn't shoot." Another time, she added, "Maggie got so bored between scenes she went behind one of the sets and purposely lay down on the dusty floor. The beautiful white dress she was wearing was a wreck. That stopped everything."

Sullavan's willfulness also extended to artistic disagreements with her director. Wyler remembered, "We fought over the interpretation of her part. We fought over everything. We didn't get along at all. She had a mind of her own, and so did I. I knew more about pictures than she did. She was a good actress in a way, but she was not terribly ambitious."

The fights between director and star took their toll on both sides. But while Wyler could nurse his anger in private, Sullavan's moods showed up on the screen. Watching dailies with the cameraman Norbert Brodine, Wyler noticed something wrong in her expression.

"The girl looks terrible," he said. "You didn't photograph her well. What's the matter? The other day she looked good, now she looks terrible."

Brodine replied, "You had a fight."

Wyler didn't see what that had to do with anything.

"Each time you have a fight with her, she's unhappy and doesn't look good," Brodine explained. "When she's happy, she looks beautiful. You have a fight with her. She looks terrible."

Wyler decided for the sake of the picture, he would make peace. So he asked Sullavan to dinner. They went out a second time, and a third. A romance blossomed virtually overnight. To his surprise Wyler found he was absolutely crazy about her.

The dread thought of marriage popped into his head one evening while they were watching dailies of the picture's wedding scene. Unable to decide which takes were best, they reviewed the scene together in the projection room long after the rest of the staff had left. By coincidence, they'd met for the first time eighteen months earlier in that same projection room. Wyler had been running off a print of Julien Duvivier's *Poil de Carotte*, brought over from France, when Sullavan burst in, thinking that dailies from *Only Yesterday* were being shown.

Now, as he sat next to her in the dark, he smoked a cigarette and watched Sullavan in the picture's closing scene. She looked radiant in a wedding gown.

"Do you think," he whispered, "there is any law against a star marrying her director?"

Sullavan leaned in and squeezed his arm.

"I'll tell you tomorrow," she whispered back.

Wyler didn't sleep that night. Needing to talk to someone about his feelings, he confided in Sturges.

"What do you think of my marrying Maggie?"

"Well, she's not marrying you for your money," Sturges said, pointing out that Sullavan had the greater earning power.

"Should I go ahead with this?" Wyler persisted.

Sturges was typically cavalier.

"Sure. Why not?"

The night after he proposed, Wyler nervously paced the set as he waited for Sullavan to arrive. She came in, smiling demurely.

"There is no law against an actress marrying her director," she said. "I looked it up."

There was, however, the question of Wyler's marrying outside the Jewish faith. Though he was scarcely a practicing Jew, his parents were. When he brought Sullavan home to dinner, his father, who did not understand English very well, took Willy aside.

"What did you say her name was? Solomon?"

His mother, who was anxious for Willy to marry, had already tried to arrange meetings for him with eligible Jewish women. Wyler's response to her matchmaking had been blunt.

"If I find the right woman," he once told her, "I'll marry her whether she's a Jew or a Christian."

To avoid the three-day waiting period required in California, Wyler and Sullavan decided to fly to Yuma, Arizona, just across the state border, on a chartered DC-3. Though their wedding plan was secret, industry gossip about their romance had gotten out, and Sullavan's former lover, Jed Harris, suddenly appeared at the studio.

"He turned up on the set," Rosenblatt recounted. "I don't know what he knew. But he was there. He took Maggie aside and pleaded with her to marry him right there. Maybe that had something to do with Willy's urgency."

Wyler reflected years later: "There he was, out of the blue. He stood there like Svengali. In those days flying out from New York was something. He made her very nervous, but I think she was fascinated by him. He had a kind of hold on her. I think she desperately wanted to get away from him. For what reason I don't know. I think trying to get away from Jed Harris contributed to the fact that she married me."

On the morning they chose to elope, Harris tried to stop them. Sullavan asked Wyler to let her speak with Harris alone. Wyler waited for half an hour in a hotel lobby.

"Is she going to come now or isn't she," he recalled thinking. "It seemed like forever."

Then Sullavan appeared, her face totally composed.

"Okay, let's go," she said, as if nothing unusual had happened.

They were married on a Sunday, November 25, 1934, by Yuma's "marrying justice" Earl A. Freeman. It was a perfectly horrible ceremony, Wyler recalled. The justice was dressed in his bathrobe and slippers. The radio was blaring. The justice's wife, who "witnessed" the ceremony, was in the bathroom and couldn't come out. So they slipped the marriage certificate under the bathroom door for her to sign. Afterwards, the newlyweds celebrated with a snack at a local coffee shop, where the waitress recognized Sullavan and made a fuss over her.

By Monday morning they were back at the studio. The surprise marriage had made a big splash in the press.

The Good Fairy finished filming on December 15. It had been a long shoot: sixty-four days. When the picture finally went into post-production, Wyler asked to be released from his contract. Although he had no definite prospects, he once again felt he had to get away from Universal. He also reasoned that now that he was married to a movie star he "had to do better." And to his surprise, the studio agreed to let him go.

In late January 1935 star and director attended the opening of *The Good Fairy* at Radio City Music Hall in New York. It was the first time in the history of the Music Hall, the nation's most prestigious venue, that a picture had been booked there without having to be previewed for the theater's executives. They took it on faith.

The Good Fairy turned out to be a smash hit. The notices were mixed, though mostly favorable. The movie was faulted for being too talky. The critics all agreed that Frank Morgan and Reginald Owen gave hilarious performances. The *New York Times* reviewer wrote, however, that "Miss Sullavan is not the expert comedienne that her role demands." Even so, he added, "she is frequently able to persuade us that she is at home in a part for which she is temperamentally unfitted."

Seen today, both *The Good Fairy* and Sullavan definitely seem over-

rated. The movie strains for humor. The dated story doesn't hold up.
And the vaunted charm of its star has gone flat. Marshall's portrait of a
befuddled, poverty-stricken, idealistic lawyer has warmth. But the only
performance that still translates is Owens's in the small comic role of the
waiter who keeps coming to Sullavan's rescue.

WITH NO SCHEDULED WORK COMMITMENTS, WYLER AND SULLA-
van took a European honeymoon in February. Shortly before sailing
from New York on the *Ile de France,* she wired his parents in Los Angeles: I SHALL TRY TO BE VERY DIGNIFIED AND NOT DISGRACE YOU IN MULHOUSE.
Before leaving, Sullavan also decided to see her former husband, Henry
Fonda, who was starring on Broadway in *The Farmer Takes a Wife.* She
told Wyler she had tickets to a show but didn't tell him which one or
that Fonda was in it until they arrived at the theater. After the curtain
Sullavan insisted on going backstage.

"I don't think I took it gracefully," Wyler remembered years later. "I
felt sort of funny. Fonda turned out to be charming, delightful, attractive. I had never asked her why they broke up. It bothered me. Why
had she divorced him? He was a really handsome fellow, better looking
than I was."

Arriving in London, they stayed at the Dorchester and spent several
days visiting Robert and his French girlfriend, Sandra Ravel, as well as
John and Dorothy Huston. British movie fans mobbed Sullavan at the
hotel. Wyler was amused by the autograph hounds. "One girl felt sorry
for me," he recalled. "She came over and stuck out her scrapbook and
pencil. 'Here,' she said. 'You too.' I said, 'Thank you very much' and
signed: 'Mr. Sullavan.'"

Crossing the English Channel, the couple made Paris their first stop
on the continent. They joined Wyler's old friend Paul Kohner and his
wife, Lupita, who recalls that Wyler seemed especially happy and
prankish.

"One evening in front of the opera house in the Place de l'Opéra,
Willy took out his harmonica and started playing," she said. "This was
right in the middle of Paris. You couldn't have picked a busier place. He
stood on a corner under a lamp post. There was nothing self-conscious
about it. Paul went over and joined him. He held out his hat for change.
People stopped to listen. They put coins in the hat. These two grown
men were like kids. They said it felt like 'the old days' in New York."

On another occasion, the two couples were leafing through the pages
of an interview that Sullavan had given to a French magazine. "At that

time Maggie Sullavan was a big name even in France," Lupita recalled. "A *vedette*, as they say. The press came to the hotel and interviewed her. Do you know how they referred to Willy? It's hard to believe it now. They said, he was 'the little Jew, her husband.' We actually laughed about that."

In Mulhouse, Sullavan was introduced to all the Wyler relatives and his childhood friends. He showed her his old haunts—the house he'd lived in, the school he'd attended, the river where he'd almost drowned and, of course, the zoo. No return to Mulhouse was ever complete for Wyler without a visit to the zoo. Then they went on to Switzerland, where he bought new skis and headed for the slopes at Grindelwald and Davos. In Vienna, they visited the set of *Episode*, which was being directed by Walter Reisch.

From there it was on to Munich, where Wyler had plans to see Walter Laemmle and Walter's father, Siegfried, a brother of Carl Laemmle. Willy and Walter, who were distant cousins, had met at Universal in the twenties when both were lowly assistant directors. Walter had found the movie business not to his liking. He'd returned to Munich, where his family ran a prosperous business as antique dealers. Now, however, the family was increasingly worried by the Nazification of Germany. Wyler's visit, in fact, was partly intended to gauge the situation. He was acting as an emissary of sorts for the rest of the Laemmle family in America.

Wyler and Sullavan stayed at the luxurious Regina Palace Hotel, the city's most elegant hotel. "It was too conspicuous for me to be seen there," Walter remembered. "A Jew stayed out of places like that even by then. But Willy called us to come see him. I didn't want to go there. My parents were afraid to go. But finally I went.

"We ate dinner downstairs in the bar. There was a dance floor. The two of them were dancing.

"Willy said, 'Why don't you dance with Margaret?'

"I said, 'Willy, I'm Jewish.'

"He said, 'Oh, what the hell, you can dance. You speak English.'

"So I danced with Margaret for maybe two minutes. I said to her, 'I feel uncomfortable.' She said she understood so we sat down. Everything was already under the Nazis, and I didn't want to have any difficulties."

Walter told Wyler that he and his parents had been given six months to close their antiques shop. One day they had received a letter from the official German antique association saying that only members of the association were authorized to deal in antiques. As Jews, the letter explained, they could not be members. Therefore they had had to vacate their shop. They were now operating illegally, as many Jews were doing. They had rented two rooms in an apartment house to store their goods.

Despite the ominous portents, Walter and his parents were not ready to leave Munich. They clung to the hope that things would not get worse. Indeed, even though anti-Jewish legislation had begun to take hold in all aspects of life, Jewish property was not yet being confiscated. Nor were Jews as yet required to identify themselves in public by wearing the infamous yellow stars.

Wyler was struck by Walter's fears, nonetheless. He had noticed storm troopers on the streets while driving around the city. He had seen a pair of them standing at attention in front of a Nazi flag in the Odeonplatz, their unnerving presence commemorating the spot where the Führer was once arrested for the Munich *Putsch* in 1923. To his astonishment pedestrians gave the Hitler salute as they passed by the flag.

Almost four years later, on the night after Kristalnacht in November 1938, Walter was caught in a round-up of thousands of Jews and hauled off by truck to the Dachau concentration camp outside Munich. His parents had left Germany just weeks earlier. Planning to follow them, he had even obtained his American visa.

One morning, after nearly a month in Dachau, he heard his name called for a special lineup. "I was marched off to the railroad station with many other prisoners," he recounted. "We boarded a train that took us back to Munich. Dachau was so overcrowded because of the roundups they decided not to keep us. They just let us out into the street. It was still early then, before the ovens. I was let go on a Monday. The next Saturday I left for America."

WYLER AND SULLAVAN WENT ON FROM MUNICH TO THE SOUTH of France. In late April they sailed home from Cannes, aboard the liner *Rex*. He had spent nearly ten thousand dollars on their honeymoon. "I came back broke," he recalled years later. "She didn't come back broke." He had no one to blame but himself, though, having refused to let Sullavan spend any of her own money.

Their arrival in New York was heralded by celebrity interviews. Everything seemed fine on the surface. They posed for pictures over breakfast, sipping coffee on board the *Rex* and looking for all the world like globe-trotting socialites.

What did not appear in the interviews or the press photos, of course, was the slightest hint that their marriage already seemed headed for trouble.

"The battles started out from the very beginning," Freda Rosenblatt said. "They didn't get along. Maggie didn't really know what she wanted. Deep down she was not a happy person. She had a very sharp tongue, and she could be very mean-spirited. Willy was not mean to her at all. He was a gentleman. But he could be obstinate."

Titanic battles would erupt at home. Philip Dunne visited the couple at their home on St. Pierre Road in Bel Air and found "pieces of busted furniture lying around from one of their fights," he said. Neighbors overheard them shouting insults at each other. She called him "Kraut" and "Hogface." He took her measure with such colorful epithets as "Pussy-Shit."

"You could hear them yelling from their house all the way up the canyon," the actor Charles Starrett told one of Sullavan's biographers. When Starrett's wife wondered whether Wyler was beating Sullavan, the actor thought the opposite.

"And sure enough," he recounted, "Willy appeared in their garden one day with a badly bruised face. Later we saw her getting into her roadster, cool as a cucumber, and there wasn't a mark on her."

Knowing Wyler was jealous of her former lovers—particularly Jed Harris—Sullavan would bait him about Harris's reputed sexual endowment. "She enjoyed making Willy squirm," said one Hollywood press agent. Even at dinner parties, Sullavan would tell anybody who listened that her husband couldn't bring her to sexual climax. She complained that he was no better in bed than Fonda, by her account "a fast starter and a lousy finisher."

Willy, in private, would accuse her of being frigid, despite her provocative talk. "She castrates a guy," he later claimed with wounded male pride. "She makes him feel like two cents—and two inches." At the same time, the sexually predatory Sullavan was jealous. She believed, wrongly, that Wyler was having an affair with Merle Oberon, whom he was soon to direct in *These Three.*

Lillian Hellman, who would become one of Wyler's closest confidantes, remembered the marriage as a disaster: "She made him completely miserable—miserable and jealous. She was very nasty to him. . . . He was jealous of Maggie. As a matter of fact, she saw to it that he would be jealous of her. Because there were a great many other gentlemen along the way to tease him with. I don't know what she did about them, nor do I care, but he was in great pain about them. . . . I used to say, 'Willy, be very careful of Maggie.' He would say, 'She doesn't care about me, she doesn't care what I do.'"

Gossip about the Wyler-Sullavan battles spread through the film colony. Beverly Hills hostesses stopped inviting them to dinner for fear that their stormy, sometimes obscene confrontations would erupt over cocktails. Wyler hardly cared about being dropped from the social circuit. What bothered and confounded him was that Sullavan had managed to twist him in knots. Looking back, he told friends that his marriage to "that batty broad" was "the roughest and meanest [time] of my life."

Sullavan's star status coupled with Willy's old-fashioned expectations about marriage didn't help their relationship. "You have to know how to handle this kind of thing — I didn't," he admitted. "It was one of the reasons why we had to break up finally. . . . We had about a year and a half together. Lots of fights, lots of good times, adventurous fun. It was fighting and making love and fighting."

The three-month European honeymoon had magnified the reality of being married to a star. The scene with the autograph hounds outside the Dorchester in London was not an isolated incident. Sullavan received all the attention, he virtually none. Wyler knew that when they returned to Hollywood, he had to have a new project waiting for him.

BEFORE GOING ABROAD, HE HAD LEFT INSTRUCTIONS WITH Myron Selznick, his agent, to scout for possible deals and to cable details of any serious prospects. It was only a matter of weeks before Wyler received the script for *Alice Adams* with a possible offer to direct Katharine Hepburn, who was set to star. But, when the final decision was made, RKO decided to go with George Stevens, a staff director. As Wyler and Sullavan traveled, he also received tantalizing cables about interest from Paramount, Zanuck at Twentieth Century–Fox, United Artists and even a potential deal in Paris for a film with Hellman. These nibbles all seemed promising, yet no actual offers materialized.

Sullavan, on the other hand, had no problem landing her next assignment. On April 1, while they were in Vienna, a cable arrived from Leland Hayward, advising her: ARRANGEMENTS PRACTICALLY CONCLUDED FOR YOU TO DO *SO RED THE ROSE*. FIFTY THOUSAND DOLLARS FOR EIGHT WEEKS. STARTING DATE NO LATER THAN MAY SIXTH. Universal agreed to lend Sullavan to Paramount for the picture, a sentimental post-Civil War love story based on a popular novel by Stark Young. It was to co-star Randolph Scott as her romantic interest, with King Vidor to direct. It was that assignment, in fact, which brought the honeymoon to a close.

Luckily for Wyler, within days of their return to Los Angeles, he clinched an assignment. Jesse L. Lasky, a former production executive at Paramount who had been one of Hollywood's founding moguls and was now an independent producer at Fox, offered him a light comedy with a Cinderella plot, *The Gay Deception*. Wyler wired Robert the good news in May 1935: SIGNED ONE PICTURE FOX. It was his first free-lance job, the first picture not for Universal.

Pleased with the idea of making another comedy and anxious to collect a paycheck, Wyler happily agreed to Lasky's terms of twenty-five hundred dollars a week. Roughly six months earlier he was collecting less than half that from Universal. The only catch was that the salary would be payable for just ten weeks, the amount of time Lasky expected the picture to take.

To celebrate the signing of his new contract, Wyler bought Sullavan a two-carat diamond ring for eleven hundred dollars. But the impulse to give her expensive gifts soon faded. Wyler remembered his first payday at Fox like this: "With great pride, I came home and showed her my check for twenty-five hundred dollars and she showed me hers for eighty-five hundred bucks. That's tough. I couldn't buy her gifts that she couldn't buy herself."

At the same time, Sullavan knew precisely what sort of extravagant gift would surprise him most. For his thirty-third birthday she picked out a shiny new Harley Davidson motorcycle and had it delivered to the Fox lot. "It would make you turn green with envy," he wrote a friend.

Wyler had never given up his love of motorcycles or his brand of motorcycle antics. And Sullavan, as adventurous as he was, loved to ride with him. Lupita Kohner remembered, "They used to come up on Sunday afternoons to where we were living in Toluca Lake. She'd be in jeans on the back of the motorcycle holding onto Willy. He zoomed around like a wild man. Willy would drive right through our front door into the living room and out the back door onto the patio."

Lupita continued, "They used to fight like the dickens. In our house. In their house. Then she'd run off. Then they'd make up. Willy would say to Paul, 'I want you to come to dinner, Maggie's coming back.' At dinner, on Maggie's plate, there would be a bottle of perfume, and by my plate a bottle for me."

Freda Rosenblatt, who left Universal to continue working for Wyler as his script girl and personal secretary, recalled that Sullavan sometimes disappeared for days at a time. "He would go searching for her," she said. "One time he ran after her all the way to New York. He didn't want the press to know, so he went under an assumed name. I bought him a ticket but neglected to give him money. He got on the train and went hungry for three days."

Meanwhile, Sullavan bet Lupita Kohner that she would get pregnant.

"One day Maggie said to us, 'I want to make a bet: The couple that gets pregnant first wins a thousand dollars,' " Lupita said.

"I thought that was much too much money. But Paul was a gambler. He said, 'I'll take you up on that.' Several months later I did get pregnant. By that time Willy and Maggie were separated.

"I never took this thing about the bet seriously. We never mentioned it. But several years later, at Christmas, an envelope came in the mail with a check for a thousand dollars and a note to my little girl, Susan. It explained that Maggie had made a bet with me, and now she was paying up."

In fact, Sullavan won the bet but the Kohners didn't know it. Sullavan was the first to conceive. Many years afterwards, Wyler revealed to his eldest daughter, from a later marriage, that Sullavan had had an abortion without telling him. It was the abortion that ultimately caused their breakup.

"He told me she got pregnant with their child," Catherine Wyler said. "She didn't feel like having it. I imagine career reasons. She told him after she aborted the child, not before. He said that's what ended their marriage, getting rid of it without telling him. She knew he would have wanted it."

By the beginning of 1936, Wyler and Sullavan had separated. In early March she went to Juarez, Mexico, to get a divorce. The reason cited on the divorce papers was "incompatibility of character."

Wyler would hear the news while staying at the Waldorf Towers in New York, where he was working with the playwright Sidney Howard on changes in Howard's screen adaptation of *Dodsworth*.

Freda Rosenblatt remembered, "The doorbell rang and the bellhop handed me a telegram for Willy, which I opened. It was from Margaret Sullavan in Mexico saying she had just divorced him. I didn't know what to do, whether to hand it to him or to tell him. I finally handed it to him. It was a terrible moment. His face fell. He didn't say much. After a while we just talked about what it was we were talking about before the telegram came. That was that. A terrible moment."

The tempestuous Wyler-Sullavan marriage had lasted not quite sixteen months.

. . .

OF ALL THE MOVIES WYLER MADE DURING THE THIRTIES, HIS picture for Lasky is perhaps least appreciated today. In part that is because *The Gay Deception* is a rarely seen light comedy that has not been preserved in the major film archives. But contemporaneous accounts gave the picture high marks. The two stars — Francis Lederer and Francis Dee — came in for most of the critical acclaim.

Dee played Mirabel, a small-town stenographer who tries to crash high society by checking into the Waldorf with her five-thousand-dollar winnings from a sweepstake prize. The hotel staff mistakes her for the heiress to a melon fortune and gives her the Waldorf's most elegant suite. Sandro, the bellhop who carries her bags, played by Lederer, happens to be a European prince working incognito to learn the hotel business. He has a lot to learn. As the bell captain informs him along with his cohorts: "You must receive a tip — no matter how small — with a look of shy surprise, followed by a timid smile. You're not bellhops, you're the Waldorf's angels of assistance."

Sandro's zealous, outspoken manner doesn't quite fit his position. He is fired as a bellhop, then reinstated as a waiter, fired again, reinstated as an elevator boy and fired again. Meanwhile, he keeps running into Mirabel. A romance develops. She confesses her real identity. He doesn't confess his. But he comes to her rescue when she can't find a socially impressive escort to take her to the charity ball. He promises to accompany her in the guise of a prince and then steals the proper evening clothes to wear for their date.

At the ball they create just the right impression, turning heads and setting the socialites agog. Mirabel is thrilled. But when Sandro starts bidding for items at the charity auction, she worries that he's going overboard. Indeed Sandro is soon discovered by the guests whose clothing he has stolen. They denounce him as a fraud. The police trundle him off to jail. There, at last, his true identity is revealed. Prince and stenographer are reunited, and they live happily ever after.

"It was a cute picture," Wyler said, recalling that midway through filming he had to alter his shots to accommodate Dee, who confessed to being pregnant after he noticed she seemed to be putting on weight. This explains the unusual number of closeups, which surprised some critics. They were not used to seeing so many in a Wyler picture. They ran counter to his fluid style. "I *had* to shoot her mostly from the chest up," he remembered.

The Gay Deception received an Academy Award nomination — the first of Wyler's pictures to get one—for best original story, co-written by Stephen Avery and Don Hartman. Hartman would become a close friend of Wyler's as well as a professional associate. During the early fifties, they would work together at Paramount, with Wyler directing and Hartman in charge of production.

But a far more significant relationship was to result from the picture, changing Wyler's career and setting a creative standard of exellence for taste and maturity in Hollywood's Golden Age. *The Gay Deception* would bring together Wyler and Samuel Goldwyn.

Goldwyn's recent pictures had not been doing well, critically or commercially. He was looking for a star actress to help turn things around. One of Goldwyn's contract actors, Joel McCrea, who was married to Dee, wanted the producer to see his wife's work. McCrea brought a print of *The Gay Deception* to Goldwyn. They screened it together, and both of them loved what they saw.

But each of them saw something different. When the film ended, Goldwyn was not interested in Dee. He was interested in the man in charge of her performance.

"Who directed this?" he asked.

"A funny little guy named Wyler," McCrea told him.

15

~~~~~~~~~~

THE WYLER TOUCH

Samuel Goldwyn ranked as Hollywood's most notable independent producer. Born Schmuel Gelbfisz (Goldfish) in the Warsaw ghetto in 1879, he made his way to the United States by way of England and Canada at sixteen years of age. Alone and penniless, he found work as an apprentice glove-maker in Gloversville, New York. By the time he was twenty-one, he had become one of the best glove salesmen in the business. But in 1912 the tariffs on foreign glove manufacturers were lowered, and the American glove industry took a nose dive. He knew it was time to get out.

Gelbfisz (Goldfish) joined forces with his then brother-in-law Jesse L. Lasky, a vaudeville promoter and musician, and with the aspiring director Cecil B. De Mille, to form a motion picture firm called the Jesse L. Lasky Feature Play Company. Their first film, *The Squaw Man*, was a huge success. Made in 1914, it led to the production of twenty-one films within a year. By 1916 the company merged with Adolph Zukor's Famous Players. But only months later his partners would buy him out for the huge sum of nine hundred thousand dollars, not least because they couldn't abide his bullying, overbearing personality.

Gelbfisz (Goldfish) used that money to form a partnership with the producer Edgar Selwyn. The new company was called Goldwyn, a name Gelbfisz (Goldfish) grew so fond of that he took it legally as his own. They hired famous actors and top writers, also to become Goldwyn's lifelong professional credo. But while the Goldwyn Company had some successes, profits were scarce. In 1922 he was again pushed out, and the company merged soon after with Metro Pictures and Louis B. Mayer Productions to form Metro-Goldwyn-Mayer. Although the Goldwyn name made it seem that he was part of the merger, in fact he was not. From then on he chose to go the route of an independent producer. He would make all decisions himself and would spare no expense, putting together the best talent money could buy. That trademark style effectively set him apart from other independent producers.

Goldwyn would be a new and welcome experience for Wyler, who was still making the transition from Universal. The relationship represented a chance to make important pictures. "Goldwyn," he said, "was not afraid to spend money. His pictures had publicity, big stars, good casts, good writers." Summing up their meeting and subsequent relationship, Wyler took a generous view shaped by his years with Junior, who was a marked contrast to Goldwyn: "I was surprised to find a man who didn't just want to do things as cheaply and as quickly as possible. He wanted the same thing I wanted—to make a fine picture. We didn't always agree on what would make a good picture. If he wanted something, money was no big object with him; it was quality. There were facets of Goldwyn which were humorous, sometimes irritating, sometimes ugly. He could be very unreasonable at times. There were good fights, but we were always trying for the same thing—to do it better."

Goldwyn, for his part, needed a skillful director with a subtle touch, someone creative enough to execute the psychological intricacies of *The Children's Hour*, Lillian Hellman's controversial, seemingly unfilmable Broadway drama. After watching *The Gay Deception*, its lightweight material notwithstanding, Goldwyn felt sure that he'd found his man and offered Wyler a five-year contract.

Wyler at first couldn't fathom how *The Children's Hour* would pass the scrutiny of the Hays Office. The play had a lesbian theme and was the sensation of the theater season—it opened in November 1934 to rave reviews and packed houses—in part because of "that taboo subject." But Hellman always recalled being able to sell Goldwyn the screen rights by persuading his story editor, Merritt Hurlburd, of the play's deeper implication.

"It's not about lesbians," she told him. "It's about the power of a lie. I happened to pick what I thought was a very strong lie."

Years later, she remembered, "That fascinated him, and he flew back to tell that piece of news to Goldwyn."

Hellman was willing to back up her claim by writing an adaptation that would pass the scrutiny of the censors by avoiding the issue of homosexuality. Goldwyn paid fifty thousand dollars for the play with the understanding that the Hays Office would not permit him to use *The Children's Hour* as the movie title, or even to publicize the fact he had purchased the screen rights.

Wyler, intrigued by Hellman's argument, agreed to direct. But still wary of a long-term commitment tying him too closely to one producer, he insisted on a three-year contract instead of the five-year contract Goldwyn wanted.

Wyler signed with him on September 19, 1935. The contract called for a first-year salary of eighty-eight thousand dollars on forty paid weeks a year, and it allowed Wyler to accept outside projects. Even by Hollywood standards the pay was high, vaulting him into the top ranks. He would get two thousand five hundred dollars a week to direct *These Three* for the first fourteen weeks; two thousand eighty-three dollars a week for the next fourteen, and two thousand dollars a week for the balance of the year. In its third year, as the nation would begin to climb out of the Depression, his contract called for a base salary of one hundred thousand dollars. It also included a typical "suspension and extension" clause, which meant that Wyler had no right to refuse an assignment. If he did, he could be suspended and the length of the suspension tacked on to the end of the contract. During his professional association with Goldwyn, Wyler was often suspended. As he explained, "I always chose the best material he had. I refused to do the things I didn't like. . . . When I refused, I would be on suspension and extended. [Once] I had a three-year contract that ran five years."

Hellman produced a brilliant adaptation of her first play, notwithstanding the almost total reversal of its tragic ending. The original told the story of how a spoiled, malicious student, Mary Tilford, ruins the reputations and lives of two teachers, Karen Wright and Martha Dobie. Mary, who is a habitual liar, seeks revenge for a minor punishment by telling her wealthy grandmother that the two teachers are secret lesbians. This sets off a rumor that eventually results in Martha's suicide and ruins Karen's plan to marry Joe, a local doctor who lives nearby.

In Hellman's screen version, the vindictive Mary whispers to her grandmother that Martha is having an affair with Joe, Karen's fiancé. Thus, the accusation of an unmentionable homosexual relationship is replaced with a more acceptable love triangle. At the same time, however, the new twist adds a complicating element of subtle competition between the two women. It creates an undercurrent of distrust—chiefly Karen's unconscious loss of faith in both Martha and Joe—that is ultimately resolved by the exposure of the truth.

By the time Wyler was hired for *The Children's Hour,* Goldwyn had already set the three major roles with contract players. For Karen he chose Merle Oberon, a young brunette who would make her most notable mark in *Wuthering Heights;* for Martha he picked the newly signed Miriam Hopkins, an established stage actress who had worked for Ernst Lubitsch; Joe would be played by Joel McCrea, a tall, handsome leading man whose career would peak in the forties with roles for Alfred Hitchcock and Preston Sturges.

Hellman, who signed with Goldwyn earlier in 1935, had a three-year contract guaranteeing ten weeks' salary a year at two thousand five hundred dollars a week. She already had worked on one script for Goldwyn: *Dark Angel,* a sentimental love story that starred Merle Oberon and Fredric March. Much more was at stake with *These Three* since the original material was hers. Not surprisingly, she wanted to work with a director she respected, especially because her experience with Sidney Franklin, the director of *Dark Angel,* had been very discouraging.

"It was I who suggested Wyler [to Goldwyn]," Hellman maintained. "I'd seen *Counsellor-at-Law,* and I didn't want to work with any of the standard directors. I'd met Wyler and liked him. We had fun. And I must say for Goldwyn, he was quite open to bright, new young men. There, he deserves some credit."

Hellman recalled that she had "walked out" of *Dark Angel* because she "got sick of Franklin." Wyler, on the other hand, "was a joy. Willy left you alone. He said things like, 'Don't bother about the shots. Just do the dialogue. Don't tell me where to put the camera.' And I thought, 'This is heaven.'"

These Three would be the first of several collaborations between Wyler and Hellman and the beginning of a lifelong friendship. On the surface their affection for each other seemed unlikely. Hellman, living by then with Dashiell Hammett, was a difficult, tough-minded literary author born in New Orleans, bred there and in New York, and not particularly impressed by Hollywood. But Wyler's lack of self-importance appealed to her.

"We had to become friends," she told Goldwyn biographer Scott Berg, "because we were the only two people in the Goldwyn asylum who weren't completely loony."

Cinematographer Gregg Toland was the other key artistic force in the making of *These Three*. A quiet and sensitive craftsman from the Midwest, he'd started in the business as a teenager, worked for a decade as an assistant cameraman and had been Goldwyn's head cameraman since 1929. Toland felt resentful of Wyler at first.

"After we'd worked together a few days," Wyler recalled, "I heard that he wanted to quit, and I couldn't understand why. I was in the habit of saying, 'Put the camera here with a forty-millimeter lens, move it this way, pan over here, do this.' Well, he was not used to that. Making Westerns at Universal, I directed the camera work. I considered it part of my job. You don't do that with a man like Gregg Toland."

When Toland explained his feelings, Wyler accommodated him. "I saw he was absolutely right," he recalled. "You didn't tell him what lens to use, but what you wanted. And he would help you by suggesting the best way to photograph it. We discussed every move. He was an artist."

The pair soon developed one of the most fruitful director-cinematographer relationships in filmmaking history. Both of them believed in the perfection of a fluid photographic style that underscored the paramount importance of the story. It prized realism and clarity, but not at the expense of poetic effects or psychological complexity. Over the next decade, Wyler and Toland would make six films together, including *These Three*, and some of them—*Wuthering Heights*, *The Little Foxes* and *The Best Years of Our Lives*—would become landmarks of Hollywood achievement.

Toland had the creative freedom to experiment with lighting and optics. Modern camera techniques benefitted from his mechanical experiments: coated lenses, high-speed stock, Waterhouse stops, a sound-deadening camera "blimp." But it was his innovative "deep focus" shots, although not yet evident in *These Three*, that enabled Wyler to layer scenes with sharply etched images at varying distances from the camera. Visual cues could be used to draw the eye and let the audience notice subtle details without having to point them out. This enhanced the smooth flow of the story, allowing Wyler to establish foreground and background with fewer shots and less editing.

"When photographing a thing, he wanted to catch the mood," Wyler explained. "He and I would discuss a picture from beginning to end. The style of photography would vary, just like the style of direction. In *Dead End*, we had a different style of photography than in *Wuthering*

Heights or in *These Three.* In *These Three,* we were dealing with little girl things. What was good was rather simple, attractive photography. In *Dead End,* we had flat lights, hard lights. We used open sun-arcs from behind the camera, flat sunlight, sharp. We didn't try to make anybody look pretty. We would discuss the style of photography that would fit the picture, then the style of sequence. I would rehearse and show him a scene. Then we would decide together how to photograph it."

Once the filming of *These Three* began, Wyler discovered that he and the temperamental Goldwyn had clashing opinions. Although the producer didn't mind that Wyler took the time to get things right, script girl Freda Rosenblatt said, "they differed about *what* was right. Goldwyn liked to throw his weight around. They would have discussions, and Goldwyn would tell Willy he didn't like something. Or he did like something but he wanted Willy to change it. Yet Willy tended to get his way."

Filming moved along steadily, though not without insecurity and jealousy among the cast. "McCrea probably thought Willy was a bastard," Rosenblatt said. "They got along, but McCrea always resented the number of takes he had to do." The actor knew that Wyler would have preferred Leslie Howard in his role. Goldwyn gave McCrea this piece of intelligence one evening over dinner, although Wyler had asked the producer to keep it to himself. At the same time, Merle Oberon resented the careful attention Wyler was paying to Bonita Granville's performance as the evil-minded little girl, Mary. Oberon told McCrea that Granville was walking off with the picture and asked him to complain to Goldwyn. Which McCrea did. But nothing ever came of it.

Not especially thrilled with the ensemble he was handed, Wyler had chosen the twelve-year-old Granville himself. Her performance earned an Academy Award nomination for best supporting actress. It was the movie's sole nomination.

Forty years later, Granville recalled her first meeting with Wyler and how he treated her: "Dozens of girls had already tested on film for the coveted role. As I entered Mr. Wyler's office I really had little hope. He was a quiet-spoken man with penetrating eyes. Lillian Hellman was also present.

"After explaining the character of Mary Tilford in depth, he asked if I would do a 'cold' reading. I was petrified, but knowing there were at least six other girls waiting in the outer office to get the big chance, I took the scene, looked at it for a few minutes and did my best.

"I could tell nothing about the reaction of either Mr. Wyler or Miss

Hellman from their faces. At that point, Mr. Wyler said, 'Let's take a little walk.' "

Shortly, she found herself in the largest most impressive office she had ever seen—the inner sanctum of Samuel Goldwyn. She reread the scene for Goldwyn. The only comment came from Wyler. He betrayed no excitement but conveyed something reassuring in his matter-of-fact tone.

"Will you go sit down on the couch on the other side of the room?" he asked. "We want to talk about you."

A few minutes later, Wyler called her back. Goldwyn asked if she would like to play "this very important role." Wyler handed her the script. She felt as though she had just been initiated into a rare club.

During filming, Wyler "had infinite patience and never once raised his voice," Granville said. "Without putting it into specific terms, I realize now that each day he was teaching me something important—the technique of how to move, when to build to a climax, how important it is to listen in a scene—but most of all, he taught me that integrity was absolutely vital in acting. He taught me that you can't fake. A scene, a line, a look, even a single moment must be from the heart."

When Granville did not win the Oscar, she was devastated. Wyler braced her with words of wisdom from Rudyard Kipling. He told her if she really wanted to be a fine actress she would have to treat triumph and disaster as "two imposters."

WYLER ALSO ASKED DANIEL MANDELL TO BE PART OF HIS artistic team for *These Three*. A veteran film editor at Universal, he had cut *Counsellor-at-Law* and *The Good Fairy*, and Wyler liked him personally. Mandell would stay on with Goldwyn for the next twenty-five years, editing nearly all his pictures. During the late fifties, when Goldwyn's output declined, Mandell would become Billy Wilder's favorite film editor.

Working for Wyler under Goldwyn "was a bit of a difficult situation," Mandell remembered. "[They] very often didn't see eye to eye about things, and you might say I was in the middle. . . . If they disagreed about anything, I'd just sit there and let them fight."

Although the arguments tended to revolve around artistic issues, they often reflected Goldwyn's pettiness toward his director. He would pick an argument with Mandell to provoke Wyler. Small disputes occurred regularly. But the first big explosion between producer and director came three days after shooting was completed on *These Three*. Wyler and Mandell wanted to preview the picture. Goldwyn objected.

"I don't want a preview," he told them. "I want to see it first. I don't like surprises."

So the picture was run in Goldwyn's projection room. The producer didn't say anything until the lights came up. Then, in a hushed voice, Goldwyn said, "I'm terribly disappointed."

Everyone waited for him to say why. Goldwyn looked at Mandell, his tone suddenly sharp and accusing.

"How can anybody louse up a picture the way you did? I saw this picture four days ago and it was perfect. You loused up the whole thing."

"I didn't do anything to louse it up," Mandell replied.

When the producer and editor got into an argument, Wyler jumped in.

"I will not tolerate you abusing this man," he told Goldwyn. "He's done a very good job."

As Mandell recalled, "That's all Goldwyn wanted. He forgot about me and he pounced on Wyler. The argument went on until three o'clock in the morning. Wyler wanted to quit. It was really something."

Mandell realized afterward that Goldwyn's objections had less to do with what he'd seen than with the fact that he hadn't been consulted by Wyler, who'd instructed the editor to make cuts in certain scenes just before the private screening.

"The main thing was the picture opened with a graduation exercise, and it was a long drawn-out thing," Mandell recounted. "So Wyler got to me and said, 'Let's get this over with as quickly as possible and just keep the essential bits.' "

In fact, Wyler's instructions were detailed. His memos to Mandell on how to cut various scenes were full of well-reasoned explanations.

Goldwyn's disagreements with Wyler didn't always flare up into an explosion. One time, Goldwyn objected to the way Wyler had shot a scene in which Martha confesses that she has been in love with Joe from the day she and Karen met him.

"I had just shot it the day before," Wyler said, recalling that the producer brought his nine-year-old son Sammy to the projection room with him. "At the end of the scene Goldwyn got up and said, 'I don't understand this scene. What's it all about?' "

Wyler thought the scene was so simple even a nine-year-old would get it. He turned to Sammy and asked: "Did you understand it?"

The boy explained exactly what the scene meant.

"Since when are we making movies for children?" Goldwyn fumed.

THESE THREE OPENED AT THE RIVOLI THEATER ON MARCH 18, 1936, to virtually unanimous raves. Even before its premiere the trade papers served notice that audiences would be seeing something unusual. The *Hollywood Reporter* called the picture "sensitive, tasteful and moving" and "a smashing directorial triumph" for Wyler. *Daily Variety* put out word that the "play has lost none of its power and penetration and emotional percussion in the translation" to the screen.

Graham Greene, then a movie critic for the *Spectator* in England, published the sort of glowing review that becomes part of film history:

"I have seldom been so moved by any fictional film as by *These Three.* After ten minutes or so of the usual screen sentiment, quaintness and exaggeration, one began to watch with incredulous pleasure nothing less than life. . . . Never before has childhood been represented so convincingly on the screen, with an authenticity guaranteed by one's own memories."

All the newspaper reviews chimed in with superlatives. Goldwyn, according to his biographer Scott Berg, had never seen such unanimous acclaim for any of his pictures. It was a clear demonstration that despite all his money and taste Hollywood's notoriously self-aggrandizing producer needed Wyler as his creative mainspring. The storied "Goldwyn touch" should have been called, more accurately, "the Wyler touch." Indeed, as the film historian David Shipman points out, the eight pictures Wyler made for Goldwyn during their long and turbulent association "are virtually the only Goldwyn products worth serious consideration." Mandell admitted he "never knew what 'the Goldwyn touch' was." He believed it was "something a Goldwyn publicist made up." Wyler thought it was a transparent myth. It was Goldwyn's attempt "to make a name for himself as an artist. But as far as being creative? He was zero."

Of all the bonds that Wyler forged on *These Three,* his relationship with Hellman turned out to be the deepest and most personal. Their attraction to each other was magnetic from the start. They met when she was thirty and he thirty-three. She had already been married and divorced. Neither counted on their looks, but both possessed an appealing force of personality.

"We had a hold on each other," Hellman said. "I've often thought about it, and I don't know that there is any explaining it. When we first met we fell in love in the most simple and easy fashion, without any kind of romantic attachment or even any notion of one. We loved each other. And I think that was true all of our lives."

Hellman admired Wyler as an artist, of course. "I honestly believe that Willy was the greatest of all American directors," she said. But she was also drawn to his talent for trouble. "He was as mischievous as anybody I knew," she said. "Full of fun. It was what made him such fun. He was willing to do anything, *anything*." That included driving his motorcycle off the diving board into the swimming pool at the Beverly Hills Tennis Club.

"He used to take me to work on that motorcycle almost every morning," Hellman said. "He would call for me at my house, and we'd go zooming around Hollywood, in and out of traffic. I had the most wonderful time, and I looked forward to him taking me home on it almost every night."

Wyler was, in her opinion, "a very adventurous man. He wasn't a cherub at all." One time, they went water skiing together. "I remember him coming up out of the water behind a very fast boat," Hellman said. "Willy circled into land, jumped off in a very dangerous fashion, walked up the pier and said to Orson Welles, 'Well, Orson, you talk about it and I do it.' "

Some of that mischief spilled over onto the set. "Part of those retakes he did was just to annoy the actors," Hellman believed. "That wasn't his primary reason. His primary reason was to keep on going until he got what he wanted. But it was behind those retakes a little: *Come on, we'll press you a little harder than you meant to go. Let's see what happens.*"

TWO WEEKS AFTER *THESE THREE* OPENED — WITH WYLER ENJOYing the pleasures of a bona fide hit for his first serious film since leaving Universal — Carl Laemmle officially lost control of the studio he'd built from scratch. Universal had been the subject of takeover rumors for years, dating back to the mid-twenties. Laemmle always rejected the offers, even a 1925 buyout proposal of fifteen million dollars. But now, with Universal verging on bankruptcy, Laemmle was forced out because he could not repay a loan of less than a million dollars. The lenders, a syndicate of New York and London bankers, exercised their option to purchase the studio for slightly more than five million dollars, loan included.

Though Laemmle's demise at Universal was a long time coming, all of Hollywood was thunderstruck. But nobody was more surprised at the outcome than Laemmle. He'd given the option as a condition of obtaining the loan, fully believing that even if he defaulted, the lenders could not raise the money to pick up their option.

"Don't worry," he'd told Kohner, who was incredulous that Laemmle would risk everything for so little. "They will never come up with the balance — five million in cash. Never."

Kohner had every reason to worry. Unlike Junior, who was protected by a long-term contract allowing him to stay on as a producer, he had no guarantee of future employment. As one of Universal's top production executives, Kohner was drawing his five-hundred-dollar salary week to week. He needed some sort of protection. But when he asked for it, Laemmle told him his hands were tied. Regrettably, the terms of the option did not allow him to offer new employment contracts.

Feeling angry and betrayed, Kohner sought a production deal elsewhere and landed at MGM. The job didn't last long, however. After another detour to Columbia, he set up his own talent agency in 1938, eventually representing a gold-plated clientele such as Greta Garbo, Rita Hayworth, Lana Turner, Henry Fonda, John Huston, Peter O'Toole and Mick Jagger. Wyler helped his old friend establish the agency with a one-third investment as a silent partner.

16

JUST DO IT AGAIN

GOLDWYN COULD HAVE BOUGHT the rights to *Dodsworth* for a fraction of the amount he paid. The playwright Sidney Howard first called the Sinclair Lewis novel to his attention in 1932. Howard thought it would make a great movie, but Goldwyn rejected the idea. He felt *Dodsworth* was a non-starter. The fact that it had been a best-seller in 1929 and that Lewis had won the Nobel Prize for literature the following year—the first American author to do so—left him unimpressed.

As far as Goldwyn was concerned, *Dodsworth* had no box-office prospects because it was a long-winded romance about mid-life crisis. "You can't sell a middle-age love story," he once told Garson Kanin. "Who the hell cares about a middle-age love story? Nobody. Not even middle-age people are interested in a middle-age love story."

Howard, who'd just adapted Lewis's *Arrowsmith* to the screen, decided to acquire the dramatic rights himself. And in November 1934 his stage adaptation of *Dodsworth* opened on Broadway, a smash hit starring Walter Huston and Fay Bainter. Goldwyn suddenly had a change of mind. He snapped up the screen rights for a whopping hundred sixty thousand dollars and hired Howard to write the screenplay.

"I don't understand you," Howard told him. "Two years ago you could have had it for twenty thousand."

The producer's reply was classic: "I don't care. This way I buy a successful play. Before it was just a novel."

Goldwyn's first choice to direct *Dodsworth* was Gregory La Cava, who is best known for the stylish charm of the screwball comedies *She Married Her Boss* and *My Man Godfrey* and the comedy drama *Stage Door.* But now, impressed by the praise for *These Three*, Goldwyn wanted Wyler for the job.

Wyler threw himself into the making of *Dodsworth* with unmitigated enthusiasm. The play had not only run on Broadway for six months but had toured the country on and off for another year. Wyler had seen it in New York and in Cincinnati, where the tour ended in March 1936. Ever since their collaboration on *A House Divided*, he had wanted to work with Walter Huston again. Apart from their personal attachment, Huston's ideas about acting meshed with his own. Unlike many Broadway stars, Huston had absorbed the techniques required by the screen. "I was certainly a better actor after my five years in Hollywood," he said. "I had learned to be natural—never to exaggerate. I found I could act on the stage in just the same way as I acted in a studio: using my ordinary voice, eliminating gestures, keeping everything extremely simple."

Goldwyn's first reaction to the novel was not uncommon. Literary critics have acknowledged its ambition but tend to rank it among the Nobel laureate's lesser works. The narrative rambles, the tone seems contradictory and the plot sprawls, often reading like a travelogue. Lewis was more admired and better known for *Elmer Gantry*, a withering attack on religious evangelism. He had gained fame for satirical portraits of middle-class America—first with *Main Street*, his 1920 novel about small-town life in the Midwest, and then with *Babbit*, his 1922 novel about a self-satisfied businessman destroyed by conformity. His scathing depiction of the medical profession in *Arrowsmith* won him the 1925 Pulitzer Prize, which he refused.

But *Dodsworth* did address serious themes: aging, marriage, divorce, cultural snobbery and the clash between American and European manners. It also painted a warm, authentic portrait of middle-aged Sam Dodsworth, a self-made automobile magnate from fictional Zenith, Indiana, whose pretentious wife Fran fears growing old and desperately wants to take up a new life abroad as her only chance to stay young.

Sidney Howard's play, while remaining true to the large spirit of the novel, brought the story down to manageable size by focusing on the crumbling marriage. Sam, who sells his auto plant for millions to take an

early retirement, is seen as a figure of strength and innocence, a noncon-
formist utterly without pretensions despite being hugely successful in
business. Fran, on the other hand, is willful, selfish and calculating.
Bored by the Midwestern matrons of bourgeois Zenith, she thinks of
herself as a cultured sophisticate who can fit in with European high society.

On their trip to the continent for an extended vacation, Fran's delu-
sions of grandeur lead to the collapse of the marriage. She has contempt
for all things American, especially Sam's guileless manners, which embarrass her beyond reason. Not knowing what she is really after, Fran
jumps from one foolish affair to another, playing out her obsessive urge
to remain young. First there is a brief shipboard romance with an English playboy. In Paris she becomes involved with a charming and
debonair banker. In Vienna she is wooed by an Austrian nobleman half
her age. These liaisons make her feel like a woman of the world, even
though she is clearly out of her depth.

Sam struggles to save their marriage, patiently enduring Fran's in-
fidelities. At the same time, he accidentally meets a shipboard acquaintance, the graceful and understanding expatriate divorcée Edith
Cortwright, who lives outside Naples. Seeing how depressed he is,
Edith offers to put him up in her modest villa. Their friendship blos-
soms. His enthusiasm for life returns, and he falls in love with her, real-
izing at last that his marriage to Fran is over.

When Wyler joined Sidney Howard in New York at the Waldorf-
Astoria Hotel in March to help rework the *Dodsworth* script, Huston's
casting in the title roll was assured. He had a virtual guarantee in his
play contract that the role would be his to reprise. If not, he was entitled
to ten percent of the fee for the screen rights. Meanwhile, instead of Fay
Bainter, who originated the role of Fran, Goldwyn chose Ruth Chatterton, a movie star with two Oscar nominations and a long Broadway career behind her.

Edith was yet to be cast. Huston's wife, Nan Sunderland, who'd
played the role on Broadway and on the tour, hoped to get it. Goldwyn
wanted Rosalind Russell, who still hadn't made a name for herself in the
movies, or possibly Dolores Costello, a beautiful star of the twenties recently divorced from John Barrymore and eager to return to the screen.
"We are going to make a definite effort to get Rosalind Russell," Merritt
Hurlburd wrote Wyler, "but the chances are slim enough that we should
not give up the search for someone else."

Wyler thought Costello was "a good idea" but that Russell wasn't.

"I'm not at all sorry that the chances of getting [her] are very slim," he wrote back. "I think her personality is not striking enough." In the end Goldwyn picked Mary Astor, a popular and intelligent actress whose many off-screen liaisons with everyone from John Barrymore to the playwright George S. Kaufman drew more notice than her supporting roles on screen.

Wyler surprised Howard with his feeling for character and dialogue, and the two of them worked easily together. "He had written a good script. I wanted to loosen it up a little more," Wyler said. In Howard's notes for a motion picture treatment, the playwright pointed out the "danger that on the screen *Dodsworth* may seem a hard story." Wyler agreed, particularly when it came to Fran's characterization.

He believed she came off as "a bitch at the outset." And he reminded Howard of his own notes about the character: "She'd like to sell the house and be done with Zenith forever. She wants Sam to retire and learn to enjoy his leisure. Sam is pretty well bowled off his feet, but Fran won't be stopped. 'I'm begging for life, Sam. No, I'm not. I'm demanding it!' But the all-important point for Fran—and this never satisfied me in the play—has been to establish a case for her as a woman who has done her job, even though her husband, along sound American lines, has too often thought more of his business than his wife. This is important because Fran will never convince an audience if she is presented merely as a demon of vanity and social ambition."

In fact, the play went a good deal further than the novel in developing Fran's fear of growing old. Howard believed it "a good justification for practically anything any woman may elect to do." Unfortunately, the idea of a woman trying to hold on to her youth touched a nerve in Ruth Chatterton. It was "exactly what Ruth herself was trying to do," Mary Astor recalled.

The result was a battle royal with Wyler over Chatterton's interpretation of the role from the moment shooting began in June. "It was like pulling teeth with her," Wyler said. "She played Fran like a heavy, and we had momentous fights every day. She was very haughty. She had been a big star."

Chatterton hated and feared Wyler. "She hadn't worked for awhile—this picture was very important for her," Freda Rosenblatt recalled. "She was uptight about the whole thing." Even before her first day on the set, her agent sent Wyler a wire: "I beg you to have a talk with Miss Chatterton before you start shooting. Please put her mind at ease. Needless my telling you how miserable she's been surely through no fault of yours as she has terrific respect for you. Therefore think if you could have understanding she will give you a great performance and no trouble."

But no matter what Wyler said or did, it made no difference. He wanted more dimension from her portrayal, and she couldn't, or wouldn't, give it to him. "She disagreed with his direction of every scene," Astor said, "and he was stubborn and smiling, and it drove her to furious outbursts."

Chatterton was used to being pampered. She took daily facial massages to preserve her looks, but her petite beauty no longer photographed well. "Her figure was gone," Rosenblatt said. "She swaggered like a truck driver when she walked. Willy didn't like it. He thought it was all wrong."

Asked to do one more take, Chatterton would pout.

"Mr. Wyler," she said, "we've done it so many times already. I really don't know what you want."

"Miss Chatterton," he replied. "I'm not making these takes for my personal health."

At times the actress gave as good as she got. "When Ruth and Willy weren't yelling at each other, they were exchanging polite poison darts," Astor recalled, citing an acerbic incident that summed up the animosity between them.

"It was in the summer, and very hot. Willy had on his usual white linen slacks and white shirt and was sitting immediately under the camera. It was lined up on a big close-up of Ruth, and just before Willy gave the order to roll, she said:

" 'Willy, darling, that *white* suit of yours! It's very distracting with you sitting so close. It's all I can *see!*'

" 'Would you like me to leave the studio, Miss Chatterton?'

" 'I would indeed, but unfortunately I'm afraid it can't be arranged.' "

Another actor on the set who disliked Wyler was David Niven. He described himself as "bloody miserable" while doing the small role of Major Lockert, a British playboy. Wyler was "a Jekyll and Hyde character" and "a sonofabitch to work with," Niven said. Wyler could be "kind, fun and cozy" off the set, but "he became a fiend the moment his bottom touched down in his director's chair."

Wyler didn't have much respect for Niven's talent. But he believed they had gotten along "all right" on the set. "He was not really an actor at first," Wyler said. "He was sort of a playboy around town. He and Merle [Oberon] had a romance. But he fit the part in *Dodsworth*. He played himself." It was on *Wuthering Heights*, two years later, that Wyler felt he had notable difficulty with Niven in the role of Cathy's husband Edgar Linton. "When he had to cry in her death scene," Wyler said, "the tears came out of his nose instead of his eyes."

Astor, on the other hand, had no trouble with Wyler: "We got in step very quickly. He was meticulous and picky, and he had a sharp tongue, sometimes sarcastic and impatient. . . . But he knew somehow that sharp criticism bottled me up completely. Nothing would come out. He could use spurs, but not a whip."

Astor worked well with Wyler partly because most of her scenes were shot with Huston, who invariably brought out the director's admiration. "He was not an actor you had to hold down," Wyler said. "If anything, he was underacting. He was first-class." The Broadway version of *Dodsworth* had been a smash hit largely on the strength of Huston's performance. It was the greatest personal triumph of his stage career. Huston's familiarity with the role minimized the need for the director's shaping hand. "He had played the part on the stage and was letter-perfect in the film," Wyler said. "No acting ruses, no acting devices, just the convincing power that comes from complete understanding of a role."

ASTOR'S TROUBLES ON *DODSWORTH* AROSE OFF THE GOLDWYN lot. From her earliest days in Hollywood, she had lived a sexually liberated life. She'd had her first affair, at the age of seventeen, with John Barrymore, who was then forty-one. She married Kenneth Hawks, the brother of director Howard Hawks, but carried on an extramarital affair that resulted in an abortion. When Hawks died in a plane crash, she married a Hollywood gynecologist, Franklyn Thorpe. While married to Thorpe she fell in love with the playwright George S. Kaufman, divorced her husband and was now involved in a custody battle.

To keep Kaufman's name out of court during the divorce proceedings, Astor had agreed to give Thorpe custody of their daughter for six months of the year. But she had since gone back to court to have the custody revoked, and the case came up for trial in the middle of filming. At first, the judge agreed to hold night sessions so that Astor could continue working during the day. Things might have been resolved quietly if Astor's private diary, which was in Thorpe's possession, hadn't been leaked to reporters.

When her attorney persuaded the judge to keep the diary from being introduced in court, Thorpe revealed titillating excerpts in the press to discredit her. Astor supposedly kept a sexual "box score" on her lovers. The *Daily News* in New York, which set the tone for the nation's tabloid coverage, began one story: "Almost three pages of closely scribbled notes in her diary were devoted to one night when Kaufman revealed himself to her as a superman . . ." Published passages from her diary suggested graphic details: "He fits me perfectly . . . twenty—count them, diary, twenty . . . I don't see how he does it . . . he is perfect."

Astor wrote in her biography, "I had achieved the reputation of being the greatest nympho-courtesan since Pompadour."

Photographers camped out at the gates of the United Artists studio on Formosa Avenue, where the picture was being made, and at her home. In early August, bowing to the practical necessities of a major Hollywood production, the judge suspended the trial for a week so that Astor could complete her work. To avoid reporters, she never left the lot, living under "studio arrest" in a comfortable dressing room suite with a kitchen. All through filming the set was closed except to approved personnel.

Wyler was unfazed by the scandal.

"Before the story came out, she told me, 'This is going to make a big stink.' I said, 'What the hell, nobody's going to pay much attention.' So much for my prophecy. Reporters came out by the planeload. Some people pressured Goldwyn to take her out of the picture, some of the puritans. I don't know who they were. Fortunately, he ignored them."

In fact, Goldwyn summoned Astor to his office to meet with him, Harry Cohn, Jack Warner, Irving G. Thalberg, A. H. Giannini, Louis B. Mayer and Jesse Lasky, all flanked by their lawyers.

"They had heard of, or had seen, certain pages in the diary that contained sexual acts with almost every well-known actor in the business," Astor recounted. "All I could say was that it just wasn't true, and if there were such pages they had to be a forgery. I was not believed, naturally."

Acting as a surrogate for Kaufman, the playwright's friend and collaborator Moss Hart was allowed a confidential look at the diary pages in question. He told friends that the most notorious entry—"twenty, count them, diary, twenty"—referred not to Kaufman's sexual performance but to his prolific output of plays.

The judge found in Astor's favor, but only marginally. He awarded her custody of the child for nine months a year instead of six. Goldwyn, when asked if he would invoke the morality clause in Astor's contract, replied: "A woman fighting for her child?" Of course not.

· · ·

MANY OF THE *DODSWORTH* LOCATIONS WERE SITUATED ALL OVER Europe. It did not make economic sense in 1936, and it certainly was not Goldwyn's custom, to send a film company abroad. Instead, a camera crew went to London, Paris, Vienna, Montreux and Naples to shoot background scenes. Wyler knew some of the locales from personal experience and gave detailed instructions of what he wanted.

"In Paris," he wrote, "get the buses with the low steps. Get a bus starting off with a man running after it. The people on the platform eagerly wanting that man to make the bus. It looks as though the bus is running away from him, but he finally makes it, with several people giving him a hand as he gets on. The front of the bus, first class practically empty. Second class with a few people in that compartment, but the bus platform jammed with people.

"If possible try to get some French drivers into an argument. (Stage this.) They argue and gesture and look as though they are going to have an awful fight. Then each walks away in a different direction.

"[In] Switzerland: There is a little island near Vevey with a house on it. It is private property. Get an establishing shot of the house that Fran rents, with the mountains in the background. In this shot, as per diagram, get a piece of the lovely house in the foreground. . . . Pick a clear day. Go to Basel, take a train to Montreux, get a shot from the electric train, shooting across the lake."

To eliminate the sense of a travelogue, most of the atmospheric shots of places that figured in the novel did not get into the picture: Westminster Abbey, Victoria Station, a cozy English cottage, a big old castle. "Get a huge castle," Wyler noted, "terrifically large, so that Dodsworth is scared to death at the sight of it." The few that made it in—a glimpse of Paris, views of Lake Geneva and the bay of Naples—play key roles in the story. And through the use of rear projection, Wyler blended these actual locations with scenes he staged in the studio. So, for example, Dodsworth has coffee in the Café de la Paix, a realistic set made up of a few tables, while the authentic flavor of the Place de l'Opéra surrounds him.

But the scenic design of *Dodsworth* consists mainly of interior settings, some echoing Jo Mielziner's set for the play. The picture's opening tableau in Dodsworth's office, with Sam's back to the camera as he looks out through a vast window over the roof of his auto plant, is basically taken from the opening of the Broadway production. Wyler played with other locales to suit his imagination. In the Vienna nightclub where Fran has gone dancing with her Austrian suitor Kurt, Wyler gets into the act as an inside joke. The camera pans across the small orchestra, revealing the director playing the violin front row center. "Don't cut shot of orchestra, whatever you do," he told Mandell, who was editing the film.

The cinematographer for *Dodsworth* was Rudolph Maté, not Gregg Toland, who was working for Howard Hawks on *Come and Get It*. Maté had recently arrived from Europe with extensive experience as a cameraman for Alexander Korda, Fritz Lang and René Clair. He was a fine craftsman, in Wyler's opinion, but no Toland. Still, if proof were needed that Wyler did not depend on Toland's eye for mastery of the screen — pictorially or dramatically — *Dodsworth* provides it. Even more than *These Three*, it shows the spare elegance of his fluid style, balanced compositions and steady takes.

Wyler always credited Toland with being a technical genius. But his own concern with the spatial arrangement of characters in a scene to tell a story or create an effect — whether psychological or symbolic — predated his work with Toland. In *Dodsworth*, moreover, there is plenty of evidence to indicate that Wyler conceived of "deep focus" shots, even without the technological means to perfect them.

A case in point is his treatment of the accidental meeting of Sam and Edith in the American Express office in Naples. The two characters, each unaware of the other, shift back and forth between foreground and background. Wyler's pictorial division of the scene develops a sense of expectation in the viewer. Visually, if not dramatically, the configuration foreshadows the sort of pattern Wyler would use again, most notably in *The Little Foxes* and *The Best Years of Our Lives*, which were benchmarks of the Toland-perfected "deep focus" technique.

Wyler also was painstaking in his attention to other kinds of compositional detail. Astor remembered "one entire afternoon spent shooting a scene of a crumpled letter being blown gently along the length of a terrace. He wanted it to go slowly for a way, then stop, and then flutter along a little farther."

The scene takes place in Montreux, on the terrace of the villa that Fran has rented for the summer. It is evening. She is sitting with Arnold Iselin, her soon-to-be lover. Dressed in white, an image of virginal purity, she looks for a moment at the letter that has just arrived from Sam, who is back in Zenith, and decides not to open it.

"Would you do something for me?" Arnold asks.

"Within reason. Why not?" Fran replies.

"Read your husband's letter."

"That's an odd request."

"I have my reasons," he says.

Fran takes the letter and goes off. The sound of a violin comes up. It is playing the plaintive melody of Debussy's "The Girl With the Flaxen Hair." When Fran returns, she is petulant.

FRAN: Why did you make me read this letter? I was having such fun today. This letter spoiled everything. Switzerland, the lake, the house. All of it's just so much Zenith now.

ARNOLD: Presently he'll be taking you back to Zenith.

FRAN: What are you doing? Trying to torture me?

ARNOLD: I'm making love to you.

Fran protests.

ARNOLD: Afraid, Fran? Surely not afraid. If your husband had saved for you some of the love he had lavished on carburetors — My dear innocent Fran.

FRAN: I'm not innocent, and Sam does love me. And no matter what he lacks I've always been able to trust him.

ARNOLD: I live in the present. Why don't you? This letter is the past.

FRAN: It's the future, too. At least it is for me.

ARNOLD: Let's get to them both, past and future.

FRAN: How?

ARNOLD: Will this be of any use to you?

He flicks his lighter and ignites the tip of the letter. It flares quietly in his hand. The breeze takes it and wafts it gracefully, turns it into a flame in the air and sails it across the terrace. The camera follows. As the letter flutters to the ground and burns, the last poignant notes of Debussy's melody are heard. The shot quickly fades to black.

Far from being an instance of time-wasting perfectionism, the shot sums up what *Dodsworth* is all about in a single emblematic image: failed marriage, illusory dreams, capricious fate. It may have taken an entire afternoon to shoot, but that is a small price to pay for one of the most stunning moments of visual poetry in all of Wyler's movies.

DODSWORTH PREVIEWED AT THE WARNER BROS. HOLLYWOOD Theater in Los Angeles to an elite crowd of invited guests and opened a week later on September 23 at New York's Rivoli Theater. Sinclair Lewis wired Goldwyn: I DO NOT SEE HOW A BETTER MOTION PICTURE COULD HAVE BEEN MADE FROM BOTH THE PLAY AND THE NOVEL. Sidney Howard cabled Wyler: I CAN ONLY THANK YOU FOR SUCH A DISTINGUISHED AND LIVELY JOB OF DIRECTING. The critics applauded wildly, some declaring it better than the play. Walter Huston won the New York Film Critics Award for his performance and was nominated for an Oscar. Wyler received his first Oscar nomination. The picture itself got seven nominations.

Despite the praise and expectations, however, *Dodsworth* picked up only one Oscar (for art decoration) and did only moderate business at the box office. Goldwyn maintained that he took a financial bath on it. "I lost my goddamn shirt," he claimed. "I'm not saying it wasn't a fine picture. It was a *great* picture, but nobody wanted to see it. In *droves*." He also maintained that it was "one of the biggest hits I ever had. It made a *fortune!*"

17

≈≈≈≈≈≈

GOLDWYNITIS

Not long before filming ended on *Dodsworth,* Wyler was summoned for the first time to Goldwyn's home. He arrived at Laurel Lane in a pleasant frame of mind, having heard his boss was happy with the nearly completed footage. But Wyler was not greeted by a happy man.

Goldwyn, recovering from a gall bladder operation and the extraction of his appendix, had been unable to keep his usual close watch on the day-to-day progress of his productions. Though he liked what he'd recently been shown of *Dodsworth,* he positively loathed the footage of *Come and Get It,* which Howard Hawks was filming.

Hawks had rewritten some of the script, based on the Edna Ferber novel about a Wisconsin lumber dynasty, and improvised scenes apparently without regard for the original story line. An infuriated Goldwyn had called Hawks on the carpet and when Hawks threatened to quit, fired him. Now Goldwyn needed someone to finish *Come and Get It.* With *Dodsworth* just about wrapped, his new favorite, Wyler, quickly came to mind.

Goldwyn suggested the idea gently. Wyler begged off gently.

"I can't just walk into another man's picture," he said.

Goldwyn insisted. He said Hawks was off the picture. And, in fact, Hawks was already preparing to make the screwball comedy *Bringing Up Baby* for RKO with Katharine Hepburn and Cary Grant.

Wyler declined, more firmly.

This sent Goldwyn into a temper tantrum.

"We had a scene I'll never forget. Sam was in bed, but he raised such hell that Frances, his wife, ran in with a flyswatter and started beating him over the legs while he was screaming at me. He said he was going to ruin me, fix it so I'd never be able to get another job in Hollywood as long as I lived."

Wyler left the house in disgust and went to his lawyer, Mark Cohen, who informed him that he didn't have a leg to stand on if he refused the assignment. He could turn it down and take a suspension. But, according to his contract, he could not work anywhere else in the meantime.

"I ended up doing it because in those days guys like Goldwyn and Louis B. Mayer *could* ruin you. I was talked into doing it, and I've been sorry about that ever since. The picture wasn't very good. Goldwyn wanted certain things shot over. I was the new golden boy, and he thought I was going to turn this picture around."

On September 14, with Wyler on the set doing retakes, news came of Irving Thalberg's sudden death from pneumonia at the age of thirty-seven. Wyler halted work to say a few words about Thalberg. That evening he went to dinner with Walter and Nan Huston, whom he'd invited to town from their mountain retreat in Running Springs, to celebrate the next day's preview of *Dodsworth*. But the death of Thalberg cast a pall over Hollywood.

Wyler never believed he improved *Come and Get It*. He thought the first half hour of the film, shot by Hawks, and the footage of logging operations, shot by second-unit director Richard Rosson, were "the best parts" of the picture.

Estimates vary as to how much Wyler actually shot or reshot. At the time, trade reports claimed it was eighty percent, an unlikely amount. Wyler said he did perhaps fifty percent, and even that seemed high. Though Daniel Mandell didn't edit the picture, he contended that "by actual measurement" Wyler directed more than half.

When *Come and Get It* was finished, Wyler and Goldwyn had another quarrel—this time over the directing credit. The producer wanted to drop Hawks's name and give Wyler sole credit. Wyler was shocked. "I said, 'Absolutely no!'" For that matter, he preferred not to have his own name used at all. Goldwyn retreated. Both names would appear, he said.

Wyler insisted that Hawks come first in the billing, which he did, a small victory of sorts. The Directors Guild, just being established that year, had yet to be recognized by the studios. Goldwyn could have done whatever he wanted. In any case, Wyler never considered *Come and Get It* one of his pictures and disowned it every chance he got.

Ironically, the slap-dash concoction turned out to be a bigger commercial success than *Dodsworth*, despite its higher cost. And it drew considerable praise from the critics. When it opened in November 1936, Frank Nugent of the *New York Times* went so far as to rate it "as fine in its way" as both *These Three* and *Dodsworth*.

Today, if the picture is remembered at all, it is for neither Hawks's nor Wyler's direction, but for Walter Brennan's first Academy Award in a supporting role and for the best screen performance of Frances Farmer's brief career.

WYLER'S NEXT ASSIGNMENT FOR GOLDWYN WAS TO BE *DEAD END*. He and Goldwyn had seen the play together on Broadway back in March, when Wyler was working at the Waldorf on the *Dodsworth* script with Sidney Howard. The drama, a social document by Sidney Kingsley about life in the slums, had opened the previous October as something of a spectacle.

The production boasted a grim urban setting, the likes of which was rarely seen in the theater. On the tiny Belasco stage, set designer Norman Bel Geddes created an entire neighborhood of crowded, unrelenting starkness. A narrow tenement street dead-ended at the East River and ran smack up against a swanky new high-rise. The pier had pylons and rotting timbers constructed over the edge of the stage into the orchestra pit. You could see the thick ribbing of a coal bin. A steam shovel blocked the street. Filthy mattresses hung on ghetto fire escapes. Clotheslines sagged with torn garments. Dirty milk bottles stood in doorways. Newspapers lay in the gutter. The dank atmosphere sulked with gaslight in evening and burned under a harsh, white sky in day.

The realistic details didn't stop there. Bel Geddes marshaled the sounds of the city and the waterfront to lure the audience further into the panorama. The asphalt sidewalk rang with the click of heels. (There were seventy-one people in the cast.) The dock whispered underfoot with the crunch of cinders. A phonograph rasped tinnily in the distance. Bel Geddes also prerecorded a sound track for the play, as if it were a movie. The audience heard the hum of the streets in the background, the East River tide lapping against the pier, foghorns in the harbor, a speed boat sputtering by, the splash of water when characters leaped off the pier into the orchestra pit.

There was no water in the pit. "That would have been disastrous," Kingsley said. "The theater was drafty. The kids simply leaped into a net. Once they jumped, the assistant stage manager threw a geyser of water up in the air, representing the splash. He then rubbed them down with oil, and they came out glistening as if they were wet, but actually the oil protected them from the chill."

The main strands of the plot brought together a gang of teenage hoodlums, a big-time killer wanted by the police and an unemployed architect. The kids in the gang threaten the passersby, beat up a privileged kid from the fashionable high rise and spend most of their time taunting each other. "Baby Face" Martin, who has committed eight murders, returns to the old neighborhood on a sentimental whim to see his mother. But she wants no part of him. Gimpty, the architect who is also back in the old neighborhood, recognizes Martin and eventually turns him in for the reward.

Kingsley rooted his drama not so much in a great story of winners against losers, rich against poor and good against evil—though it examines all of that—but in the warped mood of the crime-ridden slums and the foul-mouthed heart of its vernacular language. Much of *Dead End* had epithets which the playwright regarded as "a shocking jargon that would put a truck driver to shame." Critics of the time remarked on the freshness of the slang, though today it's wholly outdated.

Kingsley's preoccupation with social inequality and the influence of environment was not uncommon for many playwrights of the thirties. Gimpty might as well be speaking for all of them when he says: "The place you live in is awfully important. When I was in school, they used to teach us that evolution made men out of animals. What they forgot to tell us is that it can also make animals out of men."

Every night as the curtain came down, the Belasco Theater rang with cheers. *Dead End* ran for sixty-five weeks. Hollywood wags claimed that David O. Selznick was willing to pay a hundred fifty thousand dollars for the screen rights. The night they saw it together, Goldwyn asked Wyler his opinion of the play.

"Great! Great!" Wyler enthused.

Filing out of the theater, Goldwyn put another question to him: How would he like to direct it? The answer was obvious. He would be thrilled. The next day Goldwyn bid a hundred sixty-five thousand dollars for the rights and put up a twenty-five thousand dollar deposit.

"That was the good thing about Goldwyn," Wyler recalled. "If there was some great material and he wanted it, he would buy it just like that. He just paid it and said, 'Okay, we've got it.' "

Nevertheless, Goldwyn's bullying tactics were equally notable. In November 1936, having gone on vacation with the *Dead End* screen adaptation being written and a shooting schedule still months away, Wyler suddenly found himself being pressured to direct a screwball comedy called *Woman Chases Man.*

It had taken two years to write and roughly a dozen writers, among them Dorothy Parker and Alan Campbell. But Wyler thought their collective brainstorm "just plain stupid." He'd told Goldwyn, "It's absolutely hopeless. I can't do anything with it." Wyler felt certain the film would bomb.

(He was right. When *Woman Chases Man* was released in June 1937 with journeyman John Blystone directing, the critics panned it and moviegoers avoided it. Goldwyn, too, would later acknowledge it as one of his worst films.)

Wyler had already spent a month in New York and was about to leave for Paris when Goldwyn reached him by phone. First the producer tried to cajole him to return to Los Angeles, despite Wyler's obvious distaste for *Woman Chases Man.* Then Goldwyn's tactics changed. He berated Wyler in a repeat performance of his temper tantrum at Laurel Lane, only worse.

Goldwyn used "the worst language I had ever heard," Wyler recalled. "He said he was through with me and that I'd be finished in Hollywood."

This time, however, Wyler stood his ground. He hung up the phone and decided to call Goldwyn's bluff. Later that day, he wired the following cable:

DEAR MR GOLDWYN AM STILL TRYING TO FIND SOMETHING PLEASANT ABOUT OUR CONVERSATION OF THIS MORNING STOP I HAD HOPED THAT AFTER MY FIRST YEAR WITH YOU WE COULD BOTH ENJOY A MUTUALLY HAPPY AND SUCCESSFUL ASSOCIATION BUT JUDGING FROM YOUR MANY COMPLAINTS TO ME ABOUT ME ITS EVIDENT THAT THIS IS NOT THE CASE STOP WELL FRANKLY I AM NOT VERY HAPPY EITHER STOP SO WITH BOTH OF US UNHAPPY WITH EACH OTHER WHY NOT TERMINATE OUR AGREEMENT TO OUR MUTUAL BENEFIT STOP I SHALL ALWAYS BE GRATEFUL FOR THE OPPORTUNITIES YOU HAVE GIVEN ME BUT CANNOT FEEL THAT I HAVE FAILED YOU COMPLETELY STOP I WILL OF COURSE REFUND YOU ALL SALARIES RECEIVED DURING MY VACATION STOP SINCERELY WILLIAM WYLER.

Then he sailed off to London, where he received a wire from Freda

Rosenblatt: PUBLICITY OUT POTTER TO DIRECT DEAD END. Goldwyn had ordered his publicity department to announce that H. C. Potter would be
replacing Wyler.

Within a couple of weeks, though, Goldwyn backed off and called
the whole affair a misunderstanding. Wyler was reassigned to *Dead End*
and placed on suspension until the script was ready. Goldwyn also took
up Wyler's refund offer. When Wyler returned to Hollywood in late
February 1937, Goldwyn docked his pay a thousand dollars a week for
five weeks.

THAT WINTER WYLER WAS A BUSY TRAVELER. HE SPLIT HIS TIME
on the ski slopes of Switzerland and California. Returning from Paris,
he spent the Christmas holidays with Walter and Nan Huston at their
retreat in the San Bernardino mountains and skied daily with John
Huston.

They preferred virgin ski trails in high country where no one ever
went. "Willy would go first," Huston remembered. "Then I'd start down
the slope after him. On these occasions, we always came in bloody."
One time, Huston caught sight of Wyler disappearing over a cliff. "He
was going too fast. I thought, 'Willy's had it.' I got down to him as
quickly as I could. He fell, I guess, thirty-five or forty feet. He was
buried in a drift. Willy came back shaken, but he loved it."

In February, Wyler found a new thrill. He entered the novice-class
races in the Bobsled World Championship held at St. Moritz, Switzerland. The one-mile course, an icy speedway called the Cresta Run,
wound along the top of a steep ridge. As reported in the British newspaper *Daily Manchester*, Wyler captured second place for the Fairhurst
Cup, a race against the clock that combined the aggregate time for three
separate runs, and third place for the Martineau Prizes, a handicap race
also over three separate runs.

By the beginning of March, Wyler was back again in Hollywood to
prepare *Dead End* for production. Rehearsals were scheduled to begin in
April. In the meantime, Wyler's fondness for speed landed him in trouble with the police. Back in the twenties, when he was caught speeding
through the Cahuenga Pass once too often, he ended up "planting tomatoes for three days" on an honor farm in the San Fernando Valley. This
time he ended up in the Los Angeles city jail.

"The cop who pinched me says, 'Just go to court, don't bring a
lawyer. The judge will see you in his private chambers. He'll probably

bawl you out, give you a lecture and then maybe a fine and that's it.' So I didn't bring a lawyer.

"I get there at quarter to ten. Nothing happens. The courtroom fills up. At ten, the judge walks in and sits down. The bailiff calls my name. He reads the charges.

"The judge asks me, 'Guilty or not guilty?'

"The moment I say, 'Guilty,' he raises his head. He has this big smile.

" 'So you're Wyler,' he says.

" 'Yes, your honor.'

" 'You have a brother,' he says. 'He gets pinched, too. I know your brother, too. I'm going to teach you a lesson. I'm going to put you in jail.' This guy is still smiling.

"I said, 'Your honor, I'm working on a picture. Dozens of people will starve if I go to jail.'

"He said, 'You work weekends also?'

" 'Yes, weekends too.'

"He said, 'Well, you've got to take a weekend off because I'm putting you in jail. You pick your weekend, but you're going.'

"I waited a couple of weekends, and I thought I'd better get this thing over with. So I pick a night, pack a bag. I had a good last dinner and I went downtown to the jail at six o'clock. But the fella there can't find my name.

" 'Look,' I told him, 'I'm not looking to break in here. You've got to have my name.'

"He said, 'The bailiff gave you a slip. You've gotta have a slip.'

" 'How did all these fellas get in here?'

" 'They all had their slips.'

"Finally, I said, 'Make a note I was here.' And I went to a party and came home about midnight, and Sam [Wyler's butler] tells me, 'The police are looking for you.'

"It seems they'd made a mistake. They had my name. They were just looking on the wrong list. So Sam drives me down, and they put me on the elevator and take me up.

"There must have been fifty cots. I never heard so much snoring. They took my clothes and gave me prison clothes. I went to sleep and got up the next morning at five o'clock. I was in there till Monday. Everybody in there was innocent, except this one fellow. He said he was in for embezzlement and he was on his way to San Quentin. His only complaint was he didn't steal as much money as they said he did.

"I got out with two bums. They were obviously in for vagrancy. They thought I was, too. So we come out together, and there's Sam waiting for me in the Cadillac. Their eyes opened wide. They couldn't believe it. So much for my prison record."

LILLIAN HELLMAN GOT THE JOB OF ADAPTING *DEAD END* FOR THE screen because Sidney Howard, Goldwyn's first choice, was already under contract with David Selznick to write the screenplay for *Gone With the Wind*. She came up with a thoughtful script that captured the spirit of the original but softened it to comply with Hollywood values. The tone of the play's realism—the saltier bits of slang so admired by the Broadway critics, for instance—had to be less strident to pass the Production Code. Some of Kingsley's pointed themes about the slums as a breeding ground for crime and disease had to be muted, if not muffled. A scene she wrote showing cockroaches had to be cut to satisfy the censor. Production Code chief Joseph Breen informed Goldwyn, "We would like to recommend, in passing, that you be less emphatic throughout, in photographing of this script, in showing the contrast between conditions of the poor in tenements and those of the rich in apartment houses." As Hellman recalled, Goldwyn "wanted me 'to clean up the play.' What he meant was 'to cut off its balls.'"

The characters, too, had to be changed. The architect Gimpty is no longer crippled, embittered and self-pitying. And he doesn't turn in his former boyhood friend "Baby Face" Martin for anything as tainted as reward money. Gimpty is transformed into the handsome, rugged idealist Dave, who wants to tear down the slums and build housing for the poor. Now he kills "Baby Face" in a rooftop shoot-out to rid the neighborhood of evil. He doesn't even know there's a reward. The small role of the passive working-girl Drina has been enlarged and activated, not just as Dave's love interest but as a saintly union marcher who wants to make a better world.

Wyler believed *Dead End* would be most effective if shot in New York in an actual riverfront slum. But Goldwyn routinely frowned on location shooting. It would have meant less control over his directors. Richard Day, who had just won an Oscar for the set design of *Dodsworth*, built a huge, multitiered ghetto street more or less duplicating the stage production but on a much grander scale. One end of the sound stage was excavated and filled with water as a stand-in for the East River. Day's set was the talk of the industry, rumored to have cost nearly a hundred thousand dollars. Wyler found it artificial.

"We built the whole damned street and it all looked phony," he said.

"It was very fashionable in those days to build in the studio, even when the real thing was standing somewhere. That was one battle I lost."

Director and producer also had many arguments over the look of the set during the course of filming. Wyler wanted to heighten the realism by dressing the set with props appropriate to a slum. "Goldwyn didn't like dirt," Wyler said. "You'd never see him in shirt-sleeves or with his tie undone. He was absolutely immaculate. He never carried money or anything in his pockets for fear it would cause a wrinkle in his pants."

The day before shooting was to begin, Goldwyn arrived on the set and looked around, horrified.

"This set is filthy!" he shouted. "Clean it up! Clean it up! I won't have it!"

Wyler didn't reply.

"Clean it up! Just clean it up!" Goldwyn ordered.

As Hellman recalled, "Willy had quite rightly littered the street with garbage and garbage cans. Goldwyn wandered down the set and thought it was disgusting. Willy didn't clean it up."

Toward evening, Goldwyn returned to the set. When he saw nothing had been changed, he was furious.

"He fired Willy," Hellman said. "I said, 'Goodbye, I'm going home, too.' And he said, 'You'll be here tomorrow morning?' And I said, 'No, I won't be here tomorrow morning. I work with Wyler. I won't work with anybody else.' "

"The next day Goldwyn called me up and said, 'We've got Lewis Milestone.' I said, 'Well, you keep Lewis Milestone. You don't get me.' Two days later we got Wyler back."

ONE PERSON ON THE SET WHO WISHED WYLER HAD NEVER COME back was top-billed Sylvia Sidney, a beautiful but waiflike actress with expressive eyes and a delicate face. Goldwyn had signed her to play Drina for seventy-five thousand dollars.

"Wyler was not very pleasant to me," Sidney recalled. "He was a sadistic son of a bitch. Really, really nasty."

The Bronx-born actress had been a leading lady on Broadway and was under personal contract to Paramount Pictures producer Walter Wanger. Having played the pregnant factory girl Roberta Alden in Josef Von Sternberg's *An American Tragedy* and the anguished tenement heroine Rose Maurrant in King Vidor's *Street Scene,* two major pictures of 1931, she was invariably cast in similar roles as the oppressed working girl.

One day after rehearsing with Wyler at the studio, she went to Elizabeth Arden's for a massage, where she fell and split her forehead on the edge of a glass table. When she came to, she was lying on the floor and a panicked masseuse was yelling for a doctor.

The injury, which required hospital treatment and stitches above the bridge of her nose, held up the picture for two months.

"Willy didn't believe I was under a doctor's care," Sidney said. "He did not believe I was suffering from a concussion. Once we started shooting he told me he could have gotten any actress for a hundred dollars a week to do a better job than I was doing."

Sidney was having trouble remembering her lines. She blamed it on the injury. Wyler didn't believe her. The more takes he made her do, the more tearful she became. Not surprisingly perhaps, Drina's pathos called for tears. But Wyler's way of getting them undermined her confidence as an actress and made her despise him.

"I found him very distasteful," Sidney insisted.

Fifty years after making *Dead End*, she still believed Wyler had nearly ruined her talent. This, despite the fact that the critics hailed her performance as one of her best and praised it for its sensitivity, power and restraint.

"He had a habit of treating you badly," Sidney said, "and then trying to make love to you. At least that was my experience with him. He was not nice to me on the set. But he tried very hard to get into bed with me.

"He followed me all the way home. I had a wonderful little hideaway in Palos Verdes, and he showed up there one night. It was after we had a fight, and I left the set. I just tore down to the beach. I guess he thought I was alone.

"Fortunately, Luther Adler was there with me. Nobody knew I was having an affair with Luther," she said, referring to the New York stage actor she soon married. "If it hadn't been for him, I might have ended up in the crazy house. Wyler almost put me there."

Wyler got along better with Humphrey Bogart, who was on loan from Warner Bros. Bogart had been cast by Goldwyn as "Baby Face" Martin when George Raft turned down the role because he thought it too vicious. Bogart didn't seem to mind playing such an unsympathetic killer. He had just scored his first real Hollywood success as the ruthless hood Duke Mantee in *The Petrified Forest*, a role he originated on Broadway. Treated as a Warner Bros. backup to Raft, James Cagney and Edward G. Robinson, he portrayed stereotypical gangsters in twenty-eight pictures between 1936 and 1940.

Bogart never appreciated having to do as many takes as Wyler demanded. The Hollywood reporter for the *Detroit News* noted that Wyler "took six days to kill Bogart and the actor was frantic about it." But the only real difficulty Wyler and Bogart had on *Dead End* involved a scene with Marjorie Main, who played "Baby Face" Martin's mother.

Freda Rosenblatt remembered the day they shot it. "Bogie was not the great Humphrey Bogart that he became later," she said, "but he was a good actor. The mother had to slap her son on the face. Bogart comes in and the mother says, 'Why did you come back? You dirty rotten bum.' And she slaps him.

"Well, this went on for many takes because Marjorie Main came from the stage and she didn't know how to hold back. She was still playing to the gallery. The slaps went on and on, and pretty soon Bogart said to Wyler, 'If she slaps me one more time, I'm going to wipe up the floor with her.' His cheek was swollen. You could see it. Bogie was very upset."

WYLER GOT ALONG BEST WITH THE REAL STARS OF THE PICTURE, the six boys who'd played the slum kids in the original Broadway production. He felt strongly about casting them. But Goldwyn was up and down about it. Kingsley, acting as a consultant on the screen adaptation, endorsed the idea. He told Goldwyn the boys were so good it would be "a big mistake not to use them." The playwright's recommendation sounded too hard to ignore. Goldwyn brought them out to Hollywood.

The tough-talking gang of wiseacres—soon known all over town as "the Dead End kids"—became a sensation in their film debut. Except for Leo Gorcey, all were actors still in their teens: Billy Halop, Huntz Hall, Bobby Jordan, Gabriel Dell and Bernard Punsly. And Wyler felt a special kinship with them, serving as mentor and ringleader, disciplinarian and cutup.

"He rode us around the lot on his motorcycle," Hall remembered. "He'd put the six of us on it pyramid-style. Goldwyn went crazy.

"There was a line of parked cars on the lot. He'd tell us we could drive any of them because they were the studio's cars. So we'd go out and take a car and drive around. One day some guy says, 'Will you get out of my car?' It was Gary Cooper."

Cooper was lucky his car came back in one piece. The boys bought a vintage 1924 Ford. On the first day they had it Gorcey wrapped it around a telephone pole.

On the set Wyler was not so easygoing with them. "He was the man who taught us," Hall said. "He wanted you to be good, so he was tough with your performance. He made you get it. One time Bobby Jordan did thirty takes just putting on a coat. He could be very strict. He told us not to get tan. Well, on Sunday I went to the beach and I'm the type who gets red. I didn't know about the California sun. He put my back to the camera for three days. He said, 'Huntz, when you're told something to do, you do it.' After three days, he turned me around and shot all my close-ups."

The East River had an important role in the film as the gang's playground. Hall remembered that Goldwyn, perhaps to save money, tried his best to avoid changing the water in the tank. "It started to stink worse than the East River," Hall said. "We asked the crew to change it, but they wouldn't. So one day we all peed in the water and told them we weren't jumping into somebody else's piss. That was the only way we could beat them."

The water tank also became the chief instrument of initiation into the Dead End Club. If the gang wanted you in the club, you were thrown into the tank. The first to be initiated, Hall said, was Bogart. Later they got Wyler and Joel McCrea, who was starring as the architect Dave.

One day Leslie Howard came by to watch the filming. Dressed in tails, he was on a break from *Stand-In*, which he was filming on another set. Wyler dared the boys to "give it to him," Hall remembered. Bogart egged them on. When Howard emerged from the tank, the boys fled. But the British star surprised them. He loved the dunking.

"Where are you running to?" he shouted. "Come on back here." Howard wanted to shake their hands.

In spite of their clowning, the boys worked hard and gave Wyler tips to make *Dead End* more authentic, which earned his appreciation. "What amazed me most of all was their ability to ad-lib and to invent little bits of business that enhanced the value of the picture considerably," Wyler wrote in the *New York Mirror* two days after the August 24 opening. Heralded by great reviews for their performance — "The show undoubtedly belongs to the six incomparable urchins imported from the stage production," said the *New York Times* — Hall, Gorcey and some of the others went on to make a long-running series of low-budget pictures called *East Side Kids* and, after that, *The Bowery Boys*.

The reviews for *Dead End* itself were, if anything, grander still. *Film Daily* called it "a gripping, realistic picture that has been brilliantly acted and directed." It turned out to be one of the year's most prestigious successes. Four Academy Award nominations followed, including the one for best picture. Wyler's direction, which had also come in for extraordinary praise, was overlooked. And rightly so.

Today, the picture doesn't hold up. It looks set-bound, for one thing. Despite some interesting camera work, especially a long opening shot that swoops over the ghetto rooftops, the staging has a locked-in look. Once the camera lands on the street, a static feeling sets in. As for themes and characters, far from retaining any of their punch, they now seem passé. In any case, *Dead End* came away from the Oscars empty-handed.

18

<center>~~~~~</center>

"I'll Know It When I See It"

I<small>N LATE SUMMER</small> H<small>AL</small> W<small>ALLIS</small>, the production chief at Warner Bros., made an unsolicited bid for Wyler's services. He wanted Goldwyn's star director to put *Jezebel* on the screen. The Owen Davis play about the antebellum South had bombed on Broadway in early 1934, closing after only thirty-two performances. Yet Bette Davis, the studio's top dramatic actress, had spent more than a year trying to persuade her boss Jack Warner that it would be a good vehicle for her.

On stage the role of the beautiful, selfish, high-handed socialite Julie Marsden was played by Miriam Hopkins, who'd stepped into the part when Tallulah Bankhead took ill during rehearsals. Coincidentally, Wyler saw the show on a trip to New York when he was still working for Universal and had recommended it to Carl Laemmle Jr. as a possible film project.

"Despite this morning's review in *The [Hollywood] Reporter,*" he noted in a December 1933 memo, "I believe *Jezebel* contains an excellent foundation for a picture. It's a very dramatic love story. . . . The weaknesses of the play can be overcome in a picture through the addition of many incidents and sequences only suggested and talked about. A good deal of action can be added. The atmosphere and costumes lend themselves to beauty in production."

Wyler suggested it would be an excellent vehicle for Margaret Sullavan, Universal's rising star at the time, and even mentioned that *Jezebel* might be turned into a musical. Junior had ignored the suggestion.

Now, almost four years later, Warner Bros. was offering Wyler seventy-five thousand dollars to make it over a period of twelve weeks. He was promised a name cast, a quality production and generous personal publicity. Unlike Goldwyn, Warner Bros. would go out of its way to promote the director.

Not long before, Bette Davis and Jack Warner had been embroiled in a court battle over her contract. Every time she had refused what she considered an unsuitable role, Warner had forced her to take a suspension. So, objecting to her many contract extensions, she went to England to make pictures and tried unsuccessfully to break her ties with the studio. Warner not only won the suit, but out of spite dropped his option on a soon-to-be-published novel, *Gone With the Wind*, which he had thought might be a good vehicle for Davis.

David O. Selznick grabbed the opportunity that Warner had left him. He purchased the screen rights to the Margaret Mitchell epic for fifty thousand dollars—a record for an unpublished work. Selznick then launched a nationwide search to "discover" an actress worthy of its heroine, Scarlett O'Hara. The publicity surrounding *Gone With the Wind* drummed up a national frenzy. It became a massive best-seller and more than fifty-six million Americans, fully a third of the population, wanted to see it as a movie, according to a Gallup poll.

Warner, having second thoughts about his fight with Davis, decided to capitalize on the Scarlett O'Hara mania by coming out with his own picture about another tempestuous southern belle. He purchased *Jezebel* with the idea of releasing it before Selznick's magnum opus. But he needed Davis's cooperation. To soften her up, he paid the legal expenses for her losing court battle. Then he let her know the role of Julie Marsden was hers.

Jezebel would be Davis's first A-level picture, with a top director *and* a production budget of almost eight hundred thousand dollars. But she was upset to learn it was Wyler who would direct her—and not just because of his reputation for endless retakes, though she couldn't believe the Warner front office was prepared to spend a chunk of the film's budget on retakes. Davis remembered her one and only encounter with Wyler at Universal six years earlier when she tested for the role of the mail-order bride in *A House Divided*.

The wardrobe department had put her in a dress with a low neckline that showed too much cleavage for the role. As Davis recalled the incident, Wyler had humiliated her on sight by remarking loud enough for others to hear: "What do you think about these dames who show their tits and think they can get a job?" She felt mortified and, needless to say, didn't get the part. Now she decided to exact revenge for the personal insult.

Davis recounted in her autobiography: "Licking my chops that I was in a position to refuse to work with Mr. Wyler. I asked for an appointment to talk to him. . . . Mr. Wyler, not remembering me or the incident, was, to put it mildly, taken aback. . . . He actually turned green."

Wyler apologized, telling her he "had come a long way since those days." Davis graciously accepted the apology. "I could not help but believe he was sincere."

When filming began on October 21, he welcomed her to the set in courtly style but then proceeded to work in his usual way, which could not have been less reassuring. "The first day on *Jezebel* he made me do forty-eight takes," Davis recalled. "I never in my life had done more than two takes, ever."

The scene required Davis to dismount from a horse and rush into a formal gathering. Wyler had invented an inspired bit of business to complement Julie Marsden's cavalier character. He wanted Julie, who is arriving late for her own engagement party, to hike up the long train of her riding dress with a riding crop and, in a rather unladylike gesture, hook it over her shoulder as she strides into the house.

Wyler had told her to practice with the riding crop before shooting began. The gesture had become second nature to her, and she felt she'd got it right on the first take. But Wyler apparently didn't think so. He asked for another take, then another. After a dozen more, Davis was exasperated and confused.

"What do you want me to do differently?" she asked him.

"I'll know it when I see it," Wyler said.

Thirty-three takes later, without so much as a thank you, he commented, "Okay, that's fine," and called an end to the day's filming.

Furious, Davis demanded to see the takes. Wyler obliged by screening them for her that night. They were a revelation. What she thought she had done exactly the same proved to be different each time. The early takes looked practiced. The later takes not only looked more natural but showed that when she had felt irritable and fatigued she seemed vigorous and excitable. And that was precisely what the scene required.

At first, she couldn't get used to Wyler's undemonstrative style. Whether he liked a take or not, his reaction seemed the same.

"After about a week," she recalled, "I went up to him and said, 'I may be very peculiar, Mr. Wyler, but I just have to know if what I'm doing pleases you in any way. I just have to know, after every scene if possible.

"So the entire next day, he went, 'Marvelous! Marvelous!' And I couldn't stand it. I said, 'Please, go back to your old ways.' "

As filming continued, Wyler convinced Davis that every moment need not be played with equal fervor. During rehearsals he had realized that was her greatest weakness.

"She comes in during the morning eager to do it right, maybe to overdo it," he noted in a memo to Wallis and associate producer Henry Blanke. "I tell her to take it easy. I tell her a scene is important, but not every scene . . . so she learns not to act everything at the same pressure, as though her life depended on it."

Davis learned how to modulate her performance and tone down her mannerisms. She was not angry when Wyler snapped, "Do you want me to put a chain around your neck? Stop moving your head!" Nor was she offended when he demanded, "Don't wiggle your ass so much." Though he was, in her words, "quite rough" with her, she didn't mind because her own professionalism demanded excellence at any cost. Wyler had met his match as a perfectionist.

"No detail, however minor, ever escaped him," Davis said years later. "He would probe like a fiend, then turn sarcastic; or he'd be aloof and drive you crazy. He had a disarming, gap-toothed grin that could melt a dragon. But sometimes he had an evil eye. I had an evil eye, too! After a while we knew each other so well that he'd look at me, and I'd know what he wanted in the scene. He'd remain silent, take after take after take, then when I was exhausted, he'd give a suggestion that turned the whole scene around and made it live. When I wasn't hating him, I was loving him."

It eventually became clear to everyone around them that Davis had more than a professional reason for accepting such rough treatment. The star had fallen for the director.

"Her love affair with Wyler was the talk of the studio," Hal Wallis recalled.

Davis admired Wyler's masculinity. He challenged her. "I *adored* Willy," she said. "He was the only male strong enough to control me." It made no difference that Wyler wasn't handsome. "Willy was *enormously* attractive," she said. "The sexual sparks were there from the beginning."

Wyler was everything her husband Harmon Nelson, a childhood

sweetheart, was not: successful, secure, disciplined, amusing, forceful, direct. Davis's relationship with her husband was already on the rocks when *Jezebel* started filming. But Davis had not yet separated from him or even contemplated divorce. It was she more than Wyler who needed to keep their adulterous affair discreet. Above all, she was afraid of its getting into the gossip columns. "Our romance was doubly difficult because we could not be seen in public," she recounted. So they spent evenings at Wyler's home, where Sam prepared dinner for them.

Yet all did not go smoothly on the shoot. Though Wyler had a leading lady who adored him, there were other problems. He was not thrilled with Henry Fonda's performance as Pres, Julie's fiancé. Fonda was basically miscast in the role, and he, too, suffered the indignities of Wyler's demands. After a couple of weeks of production, the many Fonda retakes caught the attention of the studio front office. Wallis wondered whether Wyler had a secret grudge against the actor over Maggie Sullavan.

"Do you think Wyler is mad at Fonda or something because of their past?" he memoed associate producer Henry Blanke. "It seems that he is not content to okay anything with Fonda until it has been done ten or eleven takes. After all, they have been divorced from the same girl, and bygones should be bygones. I wonder if he wouldn't be satisfied to okay a fourth take or a fifth take occasionally."

Wallis joked that since "Wyler likes to see these big numbers on the slate . . . maybe we could arrange to have them start with the number six on each take, then it wouldn't take so long to get up to nine or ten."

Later, Wallis was less amused.

"In spite of hell and high water and everything else, Wyler is still up to his old tricks. In last night's dailies he had two takes printed of the scene where Donald Crisp leaves the house and Davis comes down the stairs and finds out that Pres is coming. The first one was excellent, yet he took it sixteen times. . . .

"What the hell is the matter with him anyhow—is he absolutely daffy? Is he on the level when he says he is going to speed up and try to get through? If he is, this is a poor indication of it. Will you please tell him I said so."

Wyler also had a problem with the screenplay. The last half seemed implausible to him. In addition, he felt Julie's character needed to be strengthened. A week into production he approached Wallis with a request to put John Huston on the script. Wallis complied.

"[Wyler] maintains that Huston knows exactly his feelings and thoughts about the script. . . . He explains that he himself cannot devote the time to consult with the writers. . . . In view of this, and in order to keep Wyler happy on the picture, I have agreed. . . . I told Wyler I did not want him to come in and start writing a new story."

Set in 1852 against the backdrop of Southern plantation life and a yellow fever epidemic that eventually decimates New Orleans, *Jezebel* revolves around a spoiled vixen, Julie Marsden, who destroys her chance at happiness. Her fiancé, the straightlaced banker Preston Dillard, breaks their engagement after Julie defies convention to spite him. Pres transfers to the bank's New York branch. Julie, meanwhile, regrets her foolish action and secludes herself from the social whirl.

When Pres returns a year later, Julie humbles herself and asks his forgiveness in the belief he will propose. What she does not know is that Pres has come back from the North with a wife. Julie schemes to win him back and, when she can't, to emasculate him. Her vengeful plan inadvertently results in the death of her longtime admirer Buck Cantrell, the pride of Southern manhood. When Pres comes down with yellow fever, however, Julie finds redemption in self-sacrifice. She volunteers to nurse him on a quarantined island, where the contagious population is being shipped to die, even though it means probable death for her as well.

The picture's idealization of the South cannot help but seem a Hollywood cliché. Also, there are blatant examples of racist stereotyping characteristic of movies in the thirties. *Jezebel* features a large contingent of happy plantation "pickaninnies." But if the picture can hardly be said to escape the era's paternalistic racism toward blacks, Wyler went out of his way to humanize them. In addition, he bolsters the political themes of North vs. South and abolition vs. slavery with a debate of ideas during a powerfully staged dinner sequence. The scene illuminates the psychology of individual characters and spells out why Southern society as a whole was doomed to crumble with or without the Civil War.

The huge production went slowly. It wasn't long before Wyler fell almost a month behind schedule. Davis, exhausted by his exacting demands, struggled to keep from becoming depressed. At times, she became hysterical. She caught a cold, which kept her at home for two days. Her face broke out in pimples. That meant no close-ups for a while. The slow progress made Fonda jittery. He had a clause in his contract allowing him to leave the production by December 17 so he could be in New York for the birth of his first child. The deadline was fast approaching.

As filming began to go over budget, Wallis also lost whatever sense of humor he may still have had. He threatened to dismiss Wyler and bring in William Dieterle. "They tried to fire him about four times and replace him," Davis recalled. "And there was no way to replace the work of this man. It was just impossible." As drained as she was, Davis wouldn't stand for it. She told Wallis that "after all she had been through" she would not "tolerate anybody else taking the picture on." She knew she was on the verge of a career-making performance. She pleaded with Jack Warner: "If you don't fire Mr. Wyler, I will work every night until nine or ten o'clock and be ready to shoot the next morning at nine — whatever it takes to finish."

Davis's stand saved Wyler's job. But he didn't work any faster. Twelve days before shooting was completed, Wallis sent Blanke an especially nasty memo: "The only thing that bothers me on *Jezebel* is that the little nigger boy will be a full-grown man by the time Wyler finishes the picture."

Were it not for Wyler's creative imagination, however, *Jezebel* would not have the sweep, size or grandeur that makes it so impressive even today. A case in point is the movie's pivotal Olympus ball sequence, which launches Julie on her headlong rush to destruction. It not only highlights Davis's formidable performance but underscores the movie's themes about Southern chivalry and male honor, social convention and the price of defiance.

The elaborate scene came to a few lines of description in the script and was allotted a mere half day in the production schedule. Wyler virtually turned it into a movie-within-a-movie. "Willy took five days!" Davis said. Crackling with tension, the scene had its own beginning, middle and end. Ernest Haller's mobile camera swooped behind pillars and traveled from ceiling to floor, showing off Robert Haas's gorgeous art direction as well as Orry-Kelly's lavish costume design (especially Julie's scandalous "red" dress). And all of this was set to the tempo of Max Steiner's lush yet portentous waltz music. Not surprisingly, Selznick would hire Haller and Steiner for *Gone With the Wind*.

Wyler and Fonda knew of the rumors about their supposed personal animosity toward each other. One story even claimed Davis was having an affair with both of them, explaining the alleged tension between them. Wyler didn't give it a second thought. He and Fonda actually liked each other. Together they decided to deflate the rumors by playing an elaborate practical joke on their agent Leland Hayward, who had married Margaret Sullavan after her divorces from both Fonda and Wyler.

"I forgot whose idea it was," Wyler recounted years later, "but one of us said, 'Let's call Leland and make some trouble for *him*.' So Fonda called him and said, 'Come on out here. I've gotta see you.' And I called him, too, and said, 'You've got to come out. I've got trouble here.'

"So Leland came out, and he went to Fonda and said, 'What's up?' And Fonda said, 'Get me out of this picture. That sonofabitch Wyler, I don't want to work for him another day.'

"Then Leland comes over to talk to me, and before he could say anything, I said, 'Get me another leading man. I want him out of this picture.' And Leland said, 'But you're almost finished!' I said, 'I don't give a damn. I'd rather reshoot the whole thing. Get him out.' "

It took a while, but Hayward finally coaxed the two men to calm down. They reluctantly allowed him to bring them together. As soon as they did, a photographer took their picture. Fonda and Wyler grinned. "Welcome to the Maggie Sullavan Club," Wyler told him. Hayward was amused.

Delays notwithstanding, Fonda made his deadline. He got to New York in time for the arrival of his daughter Jane, who was born December 21. To announce her birth Fonda sent Wyler a telegram: I ADMIRE YOUR PICTURES AND I WOULD LIKE TO WORK FOR YOU I AM EIGHTEEN MINUTES OLD BLONDE HAIR BLUE EYES WEIGHT EIGHT POUNDS AND I HAVE BEEN CALLED BEAUTIFUL MY FATHER WAS AN ACTOR SIGNED JAYNE SEYMOUR FONDA.

Wyler replied the same day by cable: MY DEAR MANY THANKS FOR YOUR KIND WIRE HEARTY CONGRATULATIONS ON YOUR ARRIVAL AND HEARTFELT CONDOLENCE ON YOUR CHOICE OF FATHER HOWEVER WE FEEL IT OUR DUTY TO CORRECT ANY ILLUSION YOU MAY HAVE BEEN UNDER IN THE PAST AS WE FEEL YOU ARE OLD ENOUGH NOW TO BE TOLD THE HAPPY NEWS YOUR FATHER NEVER WAS AN ACTOR STOP WE ARE SMOKING TO YOUR HEALTH WYLER WANTS TO MAKE A TEST OF YOU SOON AS POSSIBLE UNDER CERTAIN PROVISIONS YOUR CONTRACT AND HEREWITH REQUESTS YOU CALL HIM UNCLE BECAUSE HE FEELS THERE IS AN UNDEFINABLE BUT NONETHELESS DEFINITE RELATIONSHIP SOMEWHERE SOMEHOW LOVE AND GOOD WISHES TO YOU AND YOUR MOTHER AND YOU KNOW WHAT TO YOUR FATHER SIGNED THE JEZZIES.

With Fonda gone, Davis did her close-ups out of sequence. Since she didn't have her co-star to play off for reactions, she made use of Wyler instead. "All those close-ups of me showing my love for Hank were shot after he had finished his scenes for the picture and left the lot," Davis explained years later. "It was Willy—off camera—I was looking at!"

But their romantic relationship was short-lived. By the time the shoot was over, the affair was almost over. For Wyler, Davis's temperamental nature, free spirit and focus on her career did not augur well for a lasting match. It reminded him too much of his stormy experience with Sullavan. For all his admiration of Davis's talent and dedication, he was not in love with her.

Davis, for her part, didn't want to be dominated. Though Wyler intrigued her, the idea of giving up her independence and submitting to his forceful personality was too frightening for her. Nevertheless, she *was* in love. Years later, she admitted, "Looking back, I should have married Willy after my divorce . . . and taken the chance that it would work out. It just well might have, but, of course, that's hindsight. After four husbands, I know that he was the love of my life. But I was scared silly. As good as we were together, I was afraid that I couldn't handle the bit at home. I was in no way the hostess that he wanted a wife to be."

Wyler ended the affair, Lupita Kohner remembered. "He lost interest," she said. "Many times we would be having dinner with Willy. Just the three of us, Paul, Willy and myself. The telephone would ring. Sam would come in and say to him, 'Miss Davis is calling.' Willy's answer was, 'Later.' He would ignore the call."

The end of the affair did not end their professional relationship, however — not when it had proved so effective. Davis was always grateful to Wyler for improving her technique in *Jezebel* and deepening her art. "He made my performance," she said. "It was all Wyler. I had known all the horrors of no direction and bad direction. I now knew what a great director was and what he could mean to an actress." But he also did more. "Willy really is responsible for the fact that I became a box-office star," she said.

Jezebel opened in New York at Radio City Music Hall on March 10, 1938, to long lines of moviegoers and mainly favorable reviews. Davis herself received dazzling raves. If some critics underrated the picture, it was because of the ending. They remained unconvinced of Julie's climactic soul-cleansing. They would have preferred that the ruthless anti-heroine remain unregenerate to the bitter end, a point not lost on Wyler himself. He knew, given Wallis's script constraints, that John Huston's rewrites would not be able to resolve that problem. Even so, *Jezebel* did smashing business. Although it had run over budget and cost slightly more than a million dollars, it took in a million and a half dollars, for a tidy profit. It also won two Academy Awards on five nominations — Davis's for best actress and Fay Bainter's (she played Julie's aunt) for best supporting actress.

19

~~~~~~

A Little Hook That Gets You

Wyler's last four assignments had solidified his reputation. But he was in for trouble. Goldwyn had two losers waiting for him: *The Cowboy and the Lady* and *The Adventures of Marco Polo*.

The first, to star Gary Cooper and Merle Oberon, was a light comedy that Wyler disliked as much as *Woman Chases Man*. Not wanting to take a suspension, he pursued a new strategy to get out of the assignment: Accept it and work at a snail's pace that was slow even for him. When Goldwyn saw the amount of footage from Wyler's first three days on the job, he replaced him with H. C. Potter.

The second assignment was no better. *Marco Polo* looked like another low-grade vehicle for Cooper. This time director and producer got into a shouting match.

"I'm here to make good pictures," Wyler insisted. "If I don't see it, I won't touch it. I may not make a good picture, but I still gotta believe in it!"

Goldwyn suspended him.

Both pictures reached the screen, the worst Cooper ever made, and both turned out to be disastrous flops.

Wyler did have a script he wanted to direct: *Wuthering Heights*, based on Emily Brontë's 1847 novel, a Gothic tale about the doomed passion between Catherine Earnshaw and Heathcliff.

Various stories have circulated as to how Wyler became interested in it. His own, repeated in one version or other to many interviewers, essentially contends that actress Sylvia Sidney tipped him off to Ben Hecht and Charles MacArthur's screen adaptation.

"During *Dead End* Sylvia Sidney told me there was a very good script of *Wuthering Heights*," Wyler maintained. "It was for her and Charles Boyer. They were both under contract to Walter Wanger, who owned the property. But she said she wasn't going to do it because it wasn't right for her or for Boyer either. She asked if I wanted to read it. I read it and loved it. It was a marvelous script. I took it to Goldwyn. He read it and didn't want to do it. He didn't like stories with people dying at the end. He considered it a tragedy. I told him it was a great love story."

While making *Jezebel*, he and Bette Davis realized they wanted to do another picture together. "She asked me if I knew of anything," Wyler said. "Although I didn't think she was right for it, I gave her the script. She loved it. She took it to Jack Warner and asked him to buy it. But my loyalty to Goldwyn got the best of me because, after all, I was under contract to him.

"I went back to Goldwyn and told him what had happened with Bette Davis. I told him she wanted to do it and Warner was going to buy it. Well, he said, 'Can Merle do it?' I said, 'Of course.' He was looking for a picture for Merle Oberon, so he stepped in and bought it."

When Sylvia Sidney was asked in 1990 about this story her reply was: "Total lie. Total lie. First of all, my relationship with Wyler was so weird I wouldn't have opened my mouth to him about anything. Second of all, I was dying to do it. What happened was the script was bought by Wanger for me and Charles Boyer, but I had a terrible fight with Wanger because I refused to do *Algiers*. So he turned around and sold the script to Goldwyn."

Whether Sidney gave the script to Wyler, who took it to Goldwyn, or Wanger sold it to Goldwyn to spite Sidney, remains a question. Whether Wyler let his loyalty to Goldwyn take over or, as legend has it, connived with Bette Davis to interest Warner as a ruse to draw Goldwyn in, also can't be settled. But nobody disputes the fact that Wyler persuaded Goldwyn to buy the rights or that Goldwyn did so with great reluctance.

. . .

ON JUNE 30, 1938, WYLER SAILED FOR EUROPE ON THE *NOR-*
mandie. He had a twofold objective: to select a British cast for *Wuthering*
Heights and to acquaint himself with Yorkshire's windswept moors,
where Brontë's novel is set.

Although Wyler and Goldwyn had yet to settle their differences over
what changes needed to be made in the script, they both agreed the picture required a British cast. For the role of Heathcliff, Hecht suggested
the seasoned stage actor Laurence Olivier. Wyler thought him a great
choice. In 1934 he had caught Olivier's Broadway debut in Mordaunt
Shairp's *The Green Bay Tree,* a dark and puzzling drama about a homosexual relationship that left audiences astonished. Olivier was still relatively unknown in America, but Wyler thought that all to the good.
When he arrived in London to offer the young actor the "plum" role,
however, Olivier was nowhere to be found. He had gone on a leisurely
vacation to the south of France with his lover, Vivien Leigh, in her old
Ford V8.

So Wyler took to scouting secondary players for the film. With the
help of Hugh Percival, the casting director at Alexander Korda's London Film Productions, he got a thorough look at the current crop of
English actors and actresses. He made his selections only to discover
later that Goldwyn would not consider the added expense of importing
actors for minor roles. Wyler was forced to replace them with English
and Scottish actors available in Hollywood: Leo G. Carroll, Donald
Crisp, Miles Mander and Cecil Kellaway. But he did manage to bring
over Flora Robson for the role of the narrator Ellen Dean, who recounts the entire history of the Cathy-Heathcliff love affair.

Wyler's search also turned up Robert Newton, a young actor with a
thundering voice and a wild look in his eyes. He arranged a screen test
for Newton to see if he was suitable for Heathcliff as an alternative to
Olivier. It seemed possible, after all, that Olivier might not be available
or even interested in the role. His first experience in Hollywood in the
early thirties had ended disastrously when Greta Garbo refused to accept him as her leading man in *Queen Christina.* Unhappy with his treatment, Olivier had gone back to England with small faith in movies and
no desire at all to return to Hollywood.

Wyler reached Olivier by cable through his agent: ARE YOU INTER-
ESTED GOLDWYN IDEA FOR VIVIEN YOURSELF AND OBERON IN WUTHERING
HEIGHTS? ANSWER AS SOON AS POSSIBLE. Olivier was in no hurry, either to

reply to the cable or to rush home from the French countryside. It took him several weeks to wire back a rather noncommittal response: HAVE BEEN MOTORING ON CONTINENT THANKS YOUR INTEREST AND KINDNESS. . . . HOPE TO SEE YOU BEFORE YOUR RETURN.

Newton had appeared in just a handful of films. He was soon to begin what would be Alfred Hitchcock's last British picture, *Jamaica Inn.* Wyler wired Goldwyn: HAVE FOUND HEATHCLIFF AMAZING YOUNG ENGLISH ACTOR. Newton was rugged and had the gypsy look he wanted. But Goldwyn found Newton physically unattractive. He wired back: NEWTON OUT OF QUESTION. Given Olivier's ambiguity, Wyler pressed the idea of Newton and made further screen tests. But Goldwyn was adamant. (He later agreed to give Newton the role of Cathy's brother Hindley, a mean, bullying and dissolute coward. Newton declined the offer.)

Hearing that Olivier would not be back in London before early August, Wyler headed to the south of France himself. He spent a week at Juan-les-Pins on the Riviera, not far from the Italian border. In April, he had donated two hundred dollars to the anti-Franco Loyalists for an ambulance fund through the Motion Picture Artists' Committee, headed by such luminaries as Nathanael West and Dorothy Parker. But the horror of the Spanish Civil War seemed a distant reality.

Wyler and Olivier finally met at the actor's London home in Christ Church Street. The actor was not keen on accepting the role if it meant a separation from Vivien Leigh, whom he'd met the year before while making the British film *Fire Over England.* Their adulterous affair—both were married, he to the actress Jill Esmond and she to Leigh Holman— had stirred a huge sensation in the British press. Olivier was worried that if he left Leigh for any length of time she might be persuaded to go back to her husband and daughter. He also had disdain not just for Hollywood but for the notion that movies could compete with the high art of the theater. For Olivier, the stage was a calling. Movies were, at best, a career. Still, the actor thought Wyler had charm and intelligence. It was also clear he loved making movies and just as clear that he understood Brontë's work of literary genius.

"I presented what I considered a 'plum' part for any actor, particularly for one who was relatively unknown in America at the time," Wyler recalled. "But Mr. Olivier was less than enthusiastic, though he agreed that it was a good script and that Heathcliff was a good role."

The more he saw of Olivier, the more convinced he became that Olivier "was right for Heathcliff." Contrary to subsequent reports, he never thought the actor was "too handsome" for the role. "Only when he hesitated about accepting the part and refused to commit himself did I consider casting someone else," Wyler maintained.

At first, nothing Wyler said could get a commitment from Olivier. It was only after the actor took him to see the premiere of *St. Martin's Lane,* which starred Charles Laughton and Leigh, that Wyler realized what Olivier was really angling for: He wanted a solid offer for Leigh to play Cathy, not just some vague "Goldwyn idea" that she would be in the picture, too. Wyler knew there was no way that could be arranged. But Wyler thought he had the perfect compromise. He offered her Isabella, the second female lead, not yet cast.

"She immediately rejected the offer," Wyler remembered. "I told her Merle Oberon had the part [of Cathy], that Merle was the reason Goldwyn was making the picture. She said she still didn't want [Isabella]. Now I was back to square one.

"Thinking Larry wouldn't come unless they came together I made another attempt to convince her. I said, 'Look, Vivien, you're unknown in America. You may become a big star, but for a first part you'll never get better than Isabella. Never.' I guess she showed me. Six months later, she had the role of Scarlett O'Hara in *Gone With the Wind.*"

Olivier finally changed his mind for a combination of reasons. In his memoir *On Acting,* he recounts, "I went to see [Wyler's] current success, *Jezebel,* and realized that he had a telling way with a camera and with dialogue. Vivien saw that I liked Wyler, liked the part of Heathcliff, and persuaded me." And Ralph Richardson, his colleague and closest friend, also gave his stamp of approval: "Bit of fame! Good!"

Happy to have the answer he'd come for, Wyler sailed home from London on September 1. The day before he left, he received a letter from Leigh that she might well accept the role of Isabella after all: "Would it be possible, Willie, to let you know definitely in two weeks or so. This is not because I am still fencing about the part but purely because it is only fair to my theatre management to wait and see. . . . Subject to the usual conditions, which can be negotiated in the meantime, I shall be very happy to play Isabella for you."

Olivier caught the *Normandie* bound for New York on November 5, Vivien's twenty-fifth birthday. She stayed behind to await rehearsals for *A Midsummer Night's Dream.* But three weeks later she could no longer bear their separation. On an impulse she booked passage on the *Queen Mary* and sailed for New York herself, then took a plane to Los Angeles.

No deal was ever made for her to play Isabella. Goldwyn decided her price was too steep. But a month later, on Christmas Day, she snared the role of Scarlett O'Hara. Olivier had introduced her to the agent

Myron Selznick. He in turn had brought her to the set of *Gone With the Wind* in Culver City, where his brother David was supervising the spectacular burning of Atlanta.

The director George Cukor, later replaced by Victor Fleming, tested her the following week. Candidates for the role had been narrowed down to Paulette Goddard, Jean Arthur and Joan Bennett. But it would be no contest. Selznick knew the outcome in advance. "Shhhhh," he memoed his wife. "She's the Scarlett dark horse."

ON HIS RETURN TO THE GOLDWYN STUDIO AT 1041 FORMOSA Avenue, Wyler found a special directing request awaiting him. The boss needed him to shoot the concert sequence of a planned Jascha Heifetz movie eventually to be titled *They Shall Have Music*. The celebrated violinist earlier had agreed to appear in a Goldwyn picture, but the screenplay wasn't even close to finished. Unfortunately, time was running out for Goldwyn. He had paid Heifetz seventy-five thousand dollars for any four weeks of the virtuoso's time that summer. It was already September, and the contract was about to expire. To get his money's worth, Goldwyn arranged for a sound stage concert that could be inserted into a finished script at a later date.

Wyler's violin training and love of music made him the obvious choice. He had no objection. He'd gotten a kick out of using small orchestras on camera in both *Dodsworth* and *Jezebel,* when they weren't absolutely necessary, and would again in *Wuthering Heights.* So, for more than a week, Heifetz and a seventy-seven piece orchestra took direction from Wyler as they played selections by Saint-Saens, Tchaikovsky and Mendelssohn.

"I loved doing this," Wyler wrote his brother, not just "because Goldwyn was in a spot." Perched on a boom, he swung "from the orchestra pit to the chandelier" and synchronized the camera movements to the music, creating what the *New York Times* reviewer called "an effect of transcendent beauty." Wyler was so pleased to be working with Heifetz, Freda Rosenblatt remembered, that when technicians or anyone else made the slightest noise he went out of his way to rebuke them.

With Heifetz playing and Wyler directing, Goldwyn's sound stage was the "in" place to be. Paul Kohner paid a visit one day, escorting a prospective client for his agency. Her name was Margaret Tallichet— Talli, as friends called her—and she was an up-and-coming actress from Dallas. She had striking looks, a broad Texas accent and, at twenty-four, little acting experience. Kohner introduced her to Wyler.

"Willy was standing next to Heifetz and showing *him* how to hold the bow," Kohner recalled. "Talli was fascinated."

Though Margaret Tallichet did not know it, the meeting wasn't entirely accidental. Lupita Kohner explained the impetus behind Paul's introduction: "Willy wanted to have a family. He used to come and visit us all the time. After we had our daughter Susan, he went absolutely crazy. You would think nobody had a baby but us. Willy would say, 'I envy you having a child and family. Find me a nice girl.' He'd always ask us to find him a *nice girl.* So one day Paul said, 'Willy, I've got just the girl for you. I'll bring her by.'"

The way Talli remembered it, "We chatted and he asked me if I liked tennis. When I said yes, he said he had box seats at the Pacific Southwest Tennis Tournament and asked if I wanted to go. I said yes. So we went to the tennis tournament. We went for several days in a row. Then we started going out to dinner. I stopped seeing everybody else.

"About ten days later we were having dinner with John Huston, who was Willy's closest friend at the time. John was with his second wife, a lovely Englishwoman named Leslie Black. They had a house up on Outpost Drive. We came out on a moonlit night, and Willy proposed.

"I said yes. Willy had charmed me. I remember he played the harmonica. He loved to play the harmonica. At the tennis tournament he played this little tune from *Hansel and Gretel,* the opera. I was so enchanted that he knew this. It was just very special. Sounds silly? With love it's always something intangible. Just a little hook that gets you."

Wyler remembered, "It happened very quickly. In about four weeks. You find out a lot about a person in four weeks. I don't know what she saw in me, but I saw a bright, attractive, educated college graduate. She wasn't like the Hollywood girls. She was no pushover."

To keep their wedding plans out of the papers, Willy and Talli went to San Bernardino for a marriage license. Sam drove them because Willy had had his driver's license suspended again. A week later, on October 23, they were married at Walter Huston's home in Running Springs. It was a surprise to most of the wedding guests themselves. They thought they'd been invited for an uneventful weekend getaway. On hand were John and Leslie Huston, Paul and Lupita Kohner, Willy's parents Melanie and Leopold, his brother Robert, his attorney Mark Cohen and Talli's girlfriend, Jane Rose. (Walter Huston was back East, doing the Broadway musical *Knickerbocker Holiday.*)

"I didn't know about the wedding plans, and I don't think anybody else did, except for John and Leslie," Lupita recalled. "We got to this beautiful house on a Saturday, and all of a sudden the doorbell rings. It was Myron Selznick, who had a big place nearby. And he says, 'There are rumors around. Is there going to be a wedding here?' We were mystified.

"So everybody is laughing, and John says, 'Yes, we're about to make an honest woman of Lupita.' I was very pregnant with my second child. And everybody was laughing. Leslie was pregnant, too.

"Well, Myron left. Then John says, 'Lupie, we'd better let you know because we don't want you to have the baby drop just yet. There *is* going to be a wedding. Willy and Talli are getting married.'"

The next afternoon, a justice of the peace conducted the ceremony in the living room. Lupita supplied the flowers, which she gathered from the garden. The cake, arranged by Leslie, had violets on top. The bride and groom left for a two-day honeymoon at the Racquet Club in Palm Springs because Willy was due to begin making *Wuthering Heights*.

Though Wyler's parents didn't know in advance of the wedding plans, they were fairly suspicious. Willy had brought Talli home for dinner and, Melanie later told Talli, "Willy never brought ladies to the house." The Tallichets in Dallas hadn't even received that sort of clue. Talli decided to break the news to her parents after the wedding. She knew they would be horrified by her haste and might try to talk her out of it.

"I've always regretted the fact that I hurt my parents in that way," Talli recalled. "I knew it was absolutely crazy to marry so soon after meeting. I knew it was a long shot. But I had the strongest instinct that this man was genuine and special and unusual. I knew it was just the right thing to do."

John Huston never had any doubts either. "It was a perfect marriage," he said. "Talli was the ideal person for Willy and he for her. She had unlimited patience, the ability to love and a fund of deep affection."

Lillian Hellman concurred: "Willy was an absolute charmer with the ladies. He had a lot of girls before both of his marriages, and he was a charmer until the end of his life. However, his relationship with Talli was the real thing. Willy was devoted to her. Their marriage turned out to be one of the wisest marriages *I've* ever seen."

MARGARET TALLICHET HAD COME TO LOS ANGELES IN MARCH 1936 with the vague hope of getting into pictures. A Dallas native, she was a graduate of Southern Methodist University who worked during her senior year as a reporter for the society pages of the *Dallas Times-Herald* for fifteen dollars a week. When she graduated, she switched to the *Dallas Morning News*, which offered more money.

"I was sent out to interview some talent scout from Paramount," Talli recalled. "When I was getting ready to leave he said to me, 'If you ever think of being an actress, come out to Hollywood and look me up.' Well, I had done a couple of plays in college, and I guess I was just looking for some excitement. I didn't want to settle down in Dallas."

The excuse that pried her away and made her family give their blessing was that her great-aunt was going out to Los Angeles with her grandson, who would be attending UCLA for a semester. And Talli was invited to go with them. On their arrival, they stayed in Santa Monica and Talli looked up the talent scout.

"Of course all he said was, 'Oh, hello. How nice you're here.' Period. That was it," she recalled. "But I wanted to stay, and I had this bug for excitement. So I got myself a job at the Paramount studio in the publicity department, based on my newspaper experience."

She took acting lessons at night and diction lessons to get rid of her Texas drawl. When her great-aunt went home, Talli moved to a room at the Studio Club in Hollywood. Meanwhile, her job at Paramount turned out to be "the lowest of the low," she said. "I typed publicity copy and ran the mimeograph machine. The trouble was I couldn't type well." Her boss didn't have the heart to fire her, so he promoted her. She was made secretary to the executive who handled out-of-town journalists, no typing necessary.

One day the film critic of the *Louisville Courier-Journal,* Boyd Martin, showed up to interview Carole Lombard. Talli escorted him to the star's dressing room. Lombard, divorced from William Powell and living with Clark Cable, had emerged as one of Hollywood's most sophisticated comedy stars. She had wit, sass, elegance and beauty. And she had an unselfish personality.

"Towards the end of the interview I think Mr. Martin ran out of things to ask," Talli recounted. "Probably to make conversation he pointed to me and said, 'Don't you think this is a pretty girl?'

"Miss Lombard said, 'Yes, I do.'

"Then he asked, 'Don't you think she ought to be in pictures?'

"She said, 'Yes, why not?'

"Then he said, 'Well, how about doing something to help her?'"

Talli was floored.

Lombard spoke to Paramount chief Adolph Zukor and tried to get her a contract. When that didn't work, Lombard got her an agent, Zeppo Marx, and took her to Paramount's stills department for portrait shots. "She loaned me her clothes to pose in," Talli said. "She told me about the perils of Hollywood. She invited me to her home. I was picked up by her chauffeur and taken to her house in Bel Air to have dinner with her and Clark Gable." Lombard's extraordinary generosity "totally changed my life," she said. "It made me believe in luck. You can't beat good luck."

Making the rounds of the studios with Zeppo Marx, Talli got a screen test for David Selznick at United Artists, where he produced his pictures. He gave her a job as an extra in *A Star Is Born* and signed her to a seven-year contract, then put her in *Prisoner of Zenda* as a walk-on. Her beauty was dazzling on the screen, but she clearly needed training. In January 1937 Selznick sent her to New York for acting lessons.

Six months later Talli was doing summer stock at regional playhouses. She first appeared in Mount Kisco, New York, and then in Westport, Connecticut, where she played the ingenue for two weeks opposite Henry Fonda in *The Virginian*. After more seasoning in New Orleans and Louisville, where she had roles in small productions arranged by Selznick, she was brought back to Hollywood just in time for the casting hype of Scarlett O'Hara.

"I made a couple of tests in Scarlett's scenes, and I got an enormous amount of publicity," Talli said. "It was all undeserved and unearned. Russell Birdwell had signed with Selznick as his chief publicist, and he wanted to prove to David how much publicity he could generate for a total hundred percent nobody.

"I was all over the papers as this 'new discovery' who's up for Scarlett in *Gone With the Wind*. I have a scrapbook just jammed with the stuff Russell did. I was Miss Perfect Teeth at some dental program. I was Miss This and Miss That. One of the crazier things was Miss Cellophane. Cellophane had just come in. Birdwell got the idea of doing shots of me on the beach in Santa Monica in a cellophane bathing suit. I was wearing a flesh-colored body stocking, of course. What it looked like was a transparent nothing with blue and white stripes across the top and bottom. Needless to say, it drew a crowd."

On loan-out from Selznick, Talli soon had several roles in B movies. At Republic Studios she played the romantic interest in *A Desperate Adventure,* a melodrama intended to revive the career of Ramon Novarro. At Columbia, she played a haughty society deb in *Girls' School,* a vehicle designed to launch Anne Shirley after her splash as Barbara Stanwyck's daughter in *Stella Dallas.*

In the meantime, Birdwell arranged a "romance" for Talli with another of Selznick's unknown contract players. "It was really ridiculous," she said. "We had to go out once a week for the publicity. All this stuff is coming out about us in the gossip columns, none of it is true. I felt rather embarrassed by the fraudulence of it all."

Talli did go on real dates, including several with Howard Hughes, the millionaire playboy, aviator and movie producer who had recently flown around the world in record time. But her social life was rather innocent. She was part of a group of young Hollywood hopefuls like herself, among them Lana Turner and future producer "Cubby" Broccoli, who often went roller-skating together at a rink on Sunset near Western.

Some of Bette Davis's biographers allege that Wyler married Talli to get back at Davis for spurning him. They contend he sent Davis a letter containing an ultimatum that unless she agreed to marry him he would marry Talli. Charles Higham, for example, writes in *Bette:*

> No sooner had she begun the picture [*Dark Victory*] in October than she experienced another trauma. She had been quarreling with Wyler, who wanted to marry her desperately, but who was also seeing a beautiful young girl named Margaret Tallichet. One evening, when Bette returned home after a day of shooting, she found a letter from Wyler, which had been hand-delivered, on her entrance-hall table. She was too angry with him after their latest collision to open it.
>
> A week later she finally decided to read the letter. She put it down and burst into tears. It said that unless she agreed to marry him then and there, he would wed Margaret the following Wednesday. The day she read the letter was a Wednesday. And the moment after she finished it, a radio announcer stated that William Wyler and Margaret Tallichet had been married that same morning.

The tale is untrue on the face of it. Willy and Talli were married on a Sunday, not a Wednesday. What's more, it would have been impossible for Davis to marry Wyler "then and there," since she was still married to Ham Nelson. The letter, if it exists, has never surfaced. It was never found among Davis's personal papers, all of which are stored in a massive and carefully catalogued collection at Boston University.

"Bette had great fun repeating that story. It amused her very much," said Howard Gotlieb, the director of Special Collections at the university's Mugar Memorial Library.

In any case, it seems highly unlikely that Wyler ever wrote such a letter or even thought of it. Friends who knew Wyler well say it would have been totally out of character for him. Talli herself never gave the story a second thought. "Anything is always possible," she said lightly, "but I think if Willy had wanted to marry Bette Davis, he would have.

Willy generally did what he wanted to do and I'm sure if that's what he wanted, he would have done it."

FOLLOWING THEIR TWO-DAY HONEYMOON, WYLER INTENSIFIED his preparations for *Wuthering Heights*. Hecht and MacArthur had performed major surgery on Emily Brontë's novel, lopping off its entire second half and narrowing a multigenerational epic to the climactic tale of Heathcliff and Cathy. Wyler admired the script's efficiency. Nevertheless, he wanted John Huston to tinker with it and asked Goldwyn to hire him. Hecht and MacArthur had written "a beautiful screenplay, but it was almost in treatment form," Huston recalled.

Wyler got his wish. Then producer, director and writer met for story conferences.

"There would be great arguments between Willy and Sam," Huston recounted. "Sam's voice would go up in pitch. Willy, not to be intimidated, would go an octave higher. Pretty soon it would be a screaming match."

To cure this, Huston made a suggestion. Each one of them would put up fifty dollars, and whoever raised his voice first would forfeit his money to the others.

"Fine," Wyler said.

He reached into his pocket and desposited his money on the table.

"I'm good for it," Goldwyn said.

The story conference proceeded in virtual whispers. When it was over, Goldwyn stood up triumphantly.

"I win!" he declared, and raked in the money.

"Wait a minute," said Wyler. "What do you mean, you win?"

"I didn't yell, not once," Goldwyn replied.

Wyler often cited the incident as typical of Goldwyn's maddening egotism. "We had a helluva time explaining to him that that was not the bet."

The filming of *Wuthering Heights* began in early December 1938 and was, by most accounts, a less than serene experience. In Chatsworth, north of Los Angeles among the hills of the San Fernando Valley, some five hundred acres were stripped of their natural vegetation. Fifteen thousand pieces of tumbleweed were brought in to replace it and topped with purple sawdust to create the illusion of heather. A thousand genuine heather plants were planted for close-ups. Unused to California sunshine, the heather grew so tall that within a week it no longer resembled anything seen on a Yorkshire moor.

Feelings between Merle Oberon and Laurence Olivier were far from congenial. They had gotten along the year before when making *The Divorce of Lady X* in Britain. But Olivier did not think much of her acting abilities then and it irked him now that Oberon, rather than Leigh, was playing Cathy. Olivier also felt that Oberon took a dislike to him partly because she lacked confidence and envied his wealth of stage experience. More to the point, he explained years later, "she may have thought that I looked upon her as a little pickup by [Alexander] Korda, which she was."

Oberon grumbled about their love scenes. At one point she stopped a scene in the middle of a take.

"You know, you spat at me," she said. "You had a drop of spittle come flying across in your goddamned passion. You spat, and it hit me."

"Oh Merle, I beg your pardon," Olivier said testily. "But these things do happen between actors."

On the retake Oberon lost her temper.

"That was worse than anything I've ever seen in my life," she snapped. "I don't think I've ever seen such a badly played shot if I may say so—and you spat again!"

"Why you amateur little bitch," Olivier fumed. "What's a little spit for Chrissake between actors? You bloody little idiot, how dare you speak to me . . ."

Before he could finish, Oberon fled in tears.

Wyler lost his patience. "Go on after her and make it up," he said.

"No, sir," Olivier told him. "I [won't] be insulted by snippets like that."

Wyler insisted that he apologize, though he didn't think much of Oberon's acting either.

"You called her an *amateur*. . . . I think you'd better stop all that, or I'll begin to get angry. And if I get angry, it'll hurt."

Olivier sulked, still refusing to go after her. Gregg Toland, who was photographing the scene, came up to him and patted him on the back.

"Come on, come on," he said. "It's all right. I understand what you're going through."

Olivier felt that Toland was his one friend on the set. The actor certainly didn't think he'd made a friend of the director.

"I was abominably pompous with Wyler, who detested me quite rightly," Olivier remembered. "I was so goddamned conceited. I thought I was the cat's whiskers. I thought I knew all about acting. I thought I knew all about films. I thought I knew all about the stage. I thought I knew all about everything to do with the art or the craft.

Well, I didn't. But that didn't stop me thinking so, and it took Wyler to bully that out of me."

At first, Olivier considered Wyler vicious and cruel. He couldn't understand the director's method of doing take after take without communicating what it was he wanted. When Olivier asked him to explain, Wyler typically cut him off with a curt reply. "It's just lousy," he'd say. "Do it again."

Olivier finally couldn't bear doing another retake. He went up to Wyler and confronted him.

"For God's sake, I did it standing up. I did it sitting down. I did it fast. I did it slow. I did it with a smile. I did it with a smirk. I did it scratching my ear. I did it with my back to the camera. How do you want me to do it?"

Wyler stared at him, bemused.

"I want it better."

Wyler was, in Olivier's words, "a marvelous sneerer" whose demand for the truth could humiliate. If his critiques usually were short and to the point, they were not less devastating for their brevity. Once he gave the star a dressing-down in front of the entire cast and crew.

"I was overacting appallingly and doing some extravagant gestures," Olivier said. "Wyler stopped me and said, 'For Chrissake, what do you think you're doing? Do you think you're at the Opera House in Manchester? Come down to earth. I want it so I know you mean it. I don't want a "great performance." Tell me, Larry, what dimension do you reckon you've got to now?'"

In front of everybody Olivier heard himself say, "I suppose this anemic little medium can't take great acting." As soon as he said it, he regretted it. Laughter rolled from the gantries. The other actors, indeed the entire crew, were vastly amused.

"I thought Willy would *never* stop laughing," Olivier remembered. "He bawled me out and made me feel a jackass. He was right. I was a fool, a stupid, conceited, pompous little bastard."

NERVOUS ABOUT THE COMMERCIAL POSSIBILITIES OF A BROODING and rather gloomy love story, Goldwyn kept a close watch on production with frequent visits to the set. He examined the dailies with an eye toward the amount of footage Wyler was using. He worried over the performances. He could see that Oberon was in over her head and Olivier was mugging. And he disliked Olivier's makeup. It made him look as though he'd been rolling around in the mud. With all these thoughts on his mind, Goldwyn went to the set one morning ready to burst.

Olivier had been limping around on crutches with a bad case of athlete's foot contracted from shoes provided by the wardrobe department. When Goldwyn came on the set to confer with Wyler, the star thought he could appeal to the producer's sympathy for a day off.

"I couldn't put any shoes on at all," Olivier recounted. "I had to wrap my feet round with bandages and simply hobble about. I thought if I went up to him, Goldwyn would hold out his arm and say, 'Willy, you must send this poor unfortunate fellow home. He looks dreadfully tired. We've got to rest him now.'

"Sure enough, as I approached him, he held his arm out and I put my shoulder underneath his hand where it rested. And he said, 'Will you look at his ugly face? He's dirty! His performance is rotten! It's stagy! It's just nothing! Not real for a minute. I won't have it, and if he doesn't improve I'm gonna close up the picture.'"

Olivier was shocked, Goldwyn seemed to be working himself into a tirade.

"Look at him!" he said. "He's filthy!"

Wyler didn't bat an eye.

"He's playing a stable boy," Wyler said. "What did you expect? A choirboy?"

Goldwyn had no answer for that.

"He's a stable boy who lives in a barn," Wyler went on. "He takes care of the horses. He shovels manure. He can't be clean. Wait till he goes to America and comes back rich. He'll look very clean. Don't worry, he'll look elegant!"

Olivier's relationship with Wyler turned a corner after that incident. The director invited the actor home to dinner, where they talked seriously about film. Wyler tried to convince Olivier of its unlimited artistic potential.

"You despise this medium, don't you," he said. "You think the theater is better. Can't you understand that your attitude is just pure snobbery and nothing else?"

"I wouldn't say that."

"Please don't say it, because you'd be making a fool of yourself. There's nothing you can't do on film. You tell me you can't do *Hamlet* on it. You *can* do *Hamlet* on it. You could do *Oedipus Rex* on it. You can do any goddamed thing in the world on it. All you've got to do is find out *how*."

Wyler's respect for the medium changed Olivier's outlook. He came to regard the director so highly that when he decided to put *Henry V* on the screen six years later, he asked Wyler to direct it. Though Wyler begged off, claiming Olivier knew enough about pictures by then to do it himself, they eventually worked together again on the screen version of Theodore Dreiser's *Sister Carrie.* Moreover, Olivier always felt grateful to Wyler for opening his eyes.

"If any film actor is having trouble with his career, can't master the medium and, anyway, wonders whether it's worth it," he said, "let him pray to meet a man like Wyler."

David Niven would not have agreed. Though he was broke and had to let Errol Flynn pay the rent on their shared apartment, Niven declined the role of Cathy's husband Edgar. He preferred to take a suspension on his contract rather than work for Wyler again.

To cajole him into changing his mind, Wyler invited him to lunch at Chasen's and asked what the problem was. Niven made the excuse that Edgar was "an awful part."

"You're one of the few people in the business who can make it better than it is," Wyler told him.

Then Niven revealed the truth. He "just couldn't go through" another humiliation on the set, as he had on *Dodsworth.*

Wyler laughed.

"I've changed," he said. "Come and play the part . . . and I'll make you great in it."

Niven gave in, only to discover that the director hadn't changed and that the role was even worse than he feared. Greatness was not in the cards.

Wyler rarely brought his work home with him. But *Wuthering Heights* was an exception. Talli remembered "Willy thrashing around in his sleep" over it. When she would ask him the next morning if he'd had bad dreams, he would tell her: "I was arguing with Goldwyn."

Relations between producer and director were heated over their differences about the ending of the picture. Cathy and Heathcliff don't merely fail to connect. During Cathy's death scene, both of them know they've botched their lives. Years later, Heathcliff disappears in a storm, seeking her ghost. Goldwyn wanted Wyler to create the illusion of a happy ending by resurrecting them, if only momentarily, and having them walk off into the proverbial sunset.

"He didn't want to look at a corpse at the fadeout," Wyler said. "So he asked me to make a shot of them walking hand in hand through the clouds to show that they were together in heaven. I told him there was no way I would shoot it."

Undeterred, Goldwyn ordered H. C. Potter to do it. Potter used a pair of doubles for Olivier and Oberon. They are seen from the back climbing upward together along their favorite path, toy figures superimposed in the sky.

WUTHERING HEIGHTS OPENED ON APRIL 13, 1939, AT THE RIVOLI in New York and the Pantages Theater in Hollywood. The reviews gushed: "brilliant and bold" (Archer Winsten in the *New York Post*), "marked by a rare integrity" (Howard Barnes in the *New York Herald-Tribune*), "a thing of beauty that will remain forever" (Kate Cameron in the *Daily News*).

On their thirteenth ballot the New York Film Critics voted *Wuthering Heights* the year's best picture over *Gone With the Wind* and *Mr. Smith Goes to Washington*. No Goldwyn production had ever taken such a prestigious honor. The award made up somewhat for the picture's showing in the Oscar race. Nominated for eight Oscars, it won only for Gregg Toland's black-and-white cinematography. (*Gone With the Wind* took the Oscar for best picture that year.)

Wuthering Heights turned Olivier into a matinee idol. Moreover, news reports noted that in the months following the movie's release as many as one out of three newborn girls were named Cathy. Goldwyn took such enormous pride in the picture that he proclaimed it his own greatest achievement. "I made it," he insisted, "Wyler only directed it." When he threw an intimate dinner party at home for the Hollywood premiere, he invited Eleanor Roosevelt, Irving Berlin, Norma Shearer and Merle Oberon, among a few others, but not his star director.

Wyler was miffed but also amused. He knew why he hadn't received an invitation. "It griped Goldwyn that the story got around about how much trouble I had selling him the idea," he recalled.

Goldwyn felt the need to assert his social and professional rank because his claim to artistic superiority was patently untenable. He didn't invite his star director to the premiere of *Wuthering Heights* in New York or to the opening-night party there, either.

"I came to New York anyway," Wyler recalled. He didn't go to the party, but he did attend the premiere at the Rivoli Theater on Broadway. "When Goldwyn saw me, he asked: 'What are you doing here?'"

20

GOOD-BYE, SAM

WILLY AND TALLI SETTLED INTO married life. They leased a cozy two-bedroom house with a small pool in Beverly Hills from Loretta Young's mother. Willy liked to joke that its look, that of a New England farmhouse, hardly matched its address, 1712 Tropical Avenue. Willy also liked to joke about Talli's cooking. She didn't know how to cook. She recalled that on their second night home she served salad greens for dinner. Willy smiled politely but couldn't help asking, "What the hell is this?" Talli soon hired a full-time chef to prepare the German dishes Willy loved.

For their first Christmas together, they invited Talli's parents from Dallas. The Tallichets were eager to meet Willy, and not a little nervous about it. The man who had swept their daughter off her feet might be a successful Hollywood director, but he was also divorced, twelve years older than Talli, and Jewish.

Willy had made it a point to discuss his heritage with Talli "because of all the terrible things happening in Europe," she recalled. His religion hadn't mattered to her. She was not religious, nor was he. (Her own Protestant heritage reached back to French Huguenots.) Her parents, however, "might have had some reaction in their hearts," Talli said. "But it wasn't really a problem. My father's brother had married a Jewish girl in the South." Not surprisingly, Willy charmed them as easily as he had charmed their daughter. When he heard that Talli's mother played the piano, "he got out his violin," Talli recounted. "The two of them had a great time playing music together."

In early March, after *Wuthering Heights* was completed, the Wylers went to Sun Valley, Idaho, for a skiing holiday. Talli had never been on skis. Almost five months pregnant, she decided not to attempt the downhill slopes. Ironically, she fell while walking their three dogs a month later at home, nearly causing a miscarriage. Her doctor ordered her to bed for several weeks. "My mother was appalled at the idea that the baby might come before nine months," Talli said. On July 25 — precisely nine months and two days after her wedding — she gave birth to a daughter, Catherine, named for Brontë's heroine.

Meanwhile, Willy bought out Talli's contract with Selznick. "He didn't like the idea of his wife being at the beck and call of any producer, especially David," she said. But Willy was too smart to tell his wife she couldn't have a career. Over the next three years, Talli appeared in two movies: *It Started With Eve*, a romantic comedy in which she lost a boyfriend to Deanna Durbin, and *A Stranger on the Third Floor*, a crime thriller in which she played Peter Lorre's near-victim.

"I enjoyed making the pictures up to a point," Talli said. "But Willy's pictures were a lot more interesting than the stuff I was doing. I began to think, 'What's so great about being in movies?' I was sitting all day on a dark sound stage. All you did was wait and wait. So a movie career sort of fell away. Soon I had another child coming, and then World War II came and Willy went off into the service. The whole thing petered away absolutely painlessly."

Cathy's birth, and plans for more children, prompted a search for larger living quarters. By their first anniversary the Wylers purchased their first home at 125 Copa de Oro in Bel Air, behind the University of California campus above Sunset Boulevard. The living room was large enough for a grand piano at one end and a regulation-size pool table at the other. "Unfortunately," Talli remembered, "the pool table was right under the master bedroom. When John Huston came over, which was very often, he and Willy would play pool until all hours of the night. I could never get to sleep because of the racket they made."

MONEY WAS NO PROBLEM. IN JUNE 1939, WYLER HAD SIGNED A new two-year contract with Goldwyn at a salary of a hundred fifty thousand dollars a year. The contract called for "not more than two pictures" to be made annually and added compensation of ten percent on net profits. Also, if Wyler went on loan-out to another studio, he would get a flat fee of at least seventy-five thousand dollars per picture.

Wyler's lucrative contract had its roots in the prestige of his pictures even more than it did in their profitability. Though he was loath to admit it, Goldwyn was so dependent on Wyler for his artistic reputation by now that without him he could not have maintained his status as Hollywood's most tasteful, if distastefully self-promoting, producer.

"Willy was one of the few people Sam had much respect for," Huston said. "Willy stood up to Sam, who was dictatorial in his approach to everything. Sam was an overlord, but Willy wasn't affected by that. When there was a difference of opinion, Willy invariably came out well. I think that Sam tested ideas. In trying to dominate someone, he was testing to see the value of the ideas. Of course, when he came up against Willy, he came up against real value."

"There must have been a dozen times when Wyler packed his things and said, 'Good-bye Sam,' and Goldwyn ran after him and brought him back," said the director Billy Wilder, a longtime Wyler friend. "Willy respected authority. But he fought Sam on what he thought was important."

Artistic values apart, Goldwyn needed Wyler to show that his studio was a viable entity. The producer had become embroiled in an unsuccessful boardroom battle for control of United Artists. When he could not take it over, he went to court to get out of his distribution deal with the company. As the battle dragged on, Goldwyn's output slowed almost to a standstill. In 1939 he released two pictures, including Wyler's *Wuthering Heights*. In 1940 he would release two, including Wyler's *The Westerner*; and in 1941 just one, Wyler's *The Little Foxes*. When the fight with United Artists was finally resolved and Goldwyn was let out of his distribution deal, he had either dropped or lost most of his contract players and had Wyler under contract as his only notable director.

LELAND HAYWARD HUSTLED TO GET WYLER A FREE-LANCE project all through the spring of 1939. There was interest from Metro, RKO, Universal and especially Selznick. Deep into production of *Gone With the Wind*, Selznick was already making plans for his next picture. His foreign film scout, Kay Brown, had interested him in Gustaf Molander's *Intermezzo*, largely for the sake of its promising Swedish actress, Ingrid Bergman. Selznick liked the story, though, and purchased the rights. Then he decided to have Bergman re-create her role in an American version.

Wyler couldn't have been more pleased when Selznick asked him to direct it. Ever since his unsuccessful attempt to persuade Junior that a biopic about Tchaikovsky was bankable, he had wanted to do a serious treatment of music. The cornball story surrounding Heiftez in *They Shall Have Music* did not interest him. The material of *Intermezzo* did. It was not a composer biopic, true. But its love affair between a brilliant young pianist and a renowned violinist provided an opening for thoughtful consideration of a musical subject.

Wyler began by making tests of the music. Toscha Seidel of the Los Angeles Philharmonic was hired to play the violinist's score. The two became so friendly that Wyler even began taking private lessons from Seidel. He remembered, "I'd be playing and Seidel would stop me and ask, 'Do you hear how you're playing? Let me show you.' He'd take the violin and scratch and scratch. It was terribly exaggerated. He'd say, 'That's how you're playing.' I'd hang my head in shame."

Bergman sailed from Sweden and arrived in May to begin shooting. She looked eighteen but actually was twenty-five, married and the mother of a seven-month-old daughter. On Bergman's first morning at work she was sitting in her trailer waiting for her opening shot when she heard "a big argument going on outside" between Wyler and Selznick. "They hadn't even called me for the first scene yet," she remembered. The next thing she knew Wyler slammed past her door "like a tornado." Bergman peeked out of her trailer and said to Selznick, "What happened?" His reply was unruffled, even cheerful. "Oh," he said, "you've just lost your director."

Selznick was notorious for his high-handed treatment of everyone who worked for him. "He liked to fire directors," Wyler said. "He said I walked out, and I say he fired me. The truth is somewhere in between. Our contracts weren't signed. We got into an argument. Anyway, I left. I don't remember the reason. He made things difficult for me and I said, 'To hell with this.' I worked about six weeks on the picture — story conferences, tests, that sort of thing — and I never got a penny. That I do remember."

Selznick replaced Wyler with Gregory Ratoff, an actor who had turned his hand to directing some years before without much distinction. When Wyler saw the completed picture, he was so stunned that he dashed off a letter to Selznick: "I know this will sound like 'sour grapes' to you. But in looking at *Intermezzo* last night, I was shocked beyond description. I was prepared for a certain amount of disappointment, but how it was possible to completely miss *every* point in *every* scene is beyond my comprehension. . . . The original Swedish picture was a masterpiece compared to yours because at least it told the story.

"You may have received satisfaction out of some good reviews that I've read in the local trade papers. But . . . those reviews [are] nothing short of perjury. One of the purposes of this letter is to correct any impression they may have made on your mind."

His feelings vented, Wyler thought better of sending the letter. Nothing would be changed by it.

THE SUMMER OF 1939 SIGNALED NEW BEGINNINGS WITH THE birth of his daughter, but it also brought tidings of closure. His father, Leopold, suffered a stroke and died just days after Wyler's thirty-seventh birthday in July. Carl Laemmle also died in late September. Hollywood mourned the passing of one of its founders, and Wyler eulogized him as "a kindly, excessively tolerant man" with "an amazing gift for gambling on personalities."

But that summer's momentous event turned out to be the German invasion of Poland. Willy and Talli heard the news in San Diego, where they had gone with the Kohners for the Labor Day weekend. Word came while they were in Tijuana just across the Mexican border. At a bullfight they ran into Franz Planer, a Czech cameraman who had fled Germany and come to Hollywood two years before. He was now living in Mexico as a refugee waiting to reenter the United States. News of the invasion dominated their conversation, Talli recalled, and soured their holiday.

WITH HITLER MAKING WAR IN EUROPE, WYLER'S NEXT PICTURE, *The Westerner,* seemed rather inconsequential. He had begun preparing it in July, when Goldwyn assigned it as a rush job. The popularity of John Ford's *Stagecoach* earlier that year had brought renewed interest in Westerns. Hopping on the bandwagon, Goldwyn figured he had the perfect match in Wyler and Gary Cooper. His director had the expertise—he could do a Western in his sleep if he had to—and Cooper had the star power.

Wyler, with his new contract just signed, had gone along because he thought it might be fun. It seemed a chance to do something different with a Western. But Cooper balked. He thought his role, the cowboy drifter Cole Hardin, was undernourished. "I couldn't figure for the life of me why they needed me for this picture," he said. "I had a very minor part."

Cooper had already been stung twice by Goldwyn, who had saddled him with *The Adventures of Marco Polo* and *The Cowboy and the Lady,* and he was not about to step into a secondary role that gave him star billing in name only.

"Goldwyn bought a ten-page original based on the life of Judge Roy Bean," screenwriter Niven Busch said. "There was really only a slim tracing of story and no character for Cooper at all." Jo Swerling had finished half the screenplay, which nobody liked, when Busch was brought in to rewrite it. He created a new story out of the mix of biography and 1880s Americana about the crusty hanging judge who was infatuated by a woman he'd never met, the beautiful English actress Lily Langtry. Busch invented Cole Hardin, a saddle bum who is accused of horse stealing when he passes through Judge Roy Bean's Texas territory. Sentenced to hang, Hardin talks his way out of the noose by pretending to be an acquaintance of Langtry.

Busch's rewrite still couldn't get around Cooper's objection: Bean, and not Hardin, was the central role. Cooper believed Goldwyn simply wanted to exploit his name. Wyler conceded that the role, as written, was not great. But he tried to persuade the star to take it because he thought Cooper's laconic style would play off nicely against the frenetic Walter Brennan, who was cast as Judge Roy Bean. Cooper remained unconvinced. He was under contract, though, and Goldwyn threatened to sue him for every penny of the four hundred thousand dollars spent so far on the picture. Under protest, Cooper agreed to do the role.

Wyler shot the picture in four weeks on location near Tucson, Arizona. Goldwyn wanted *The Westerner* to be made quickly but still budgeted more than a million dollars to produce it. No expense was spared to capture the atmosphere of the Texas frontier. For the climactic shootout between Bean and Hardin, a replica was built of the Fort Davis Grand Opera House, where Lily Langtry once put in an appearance. For the range war between the cattlemen and the farmers, local cowboys rounded up a herd of seven thousand cattle, the largest ever put on screen up to that time. Cost notwithstanding. Wyler went out of his way to keep the picture from looking glamorous. Much of it takes place in Judge Bean's plain saloon, a boozy outpost set in a bare, dusty little town.

What interested Wyler most was the love-hate relationship between Hardin and Bean, which Busch had invented to propel the plot. "There was subtle comedy in there," Wyler said. "It gave me the opportunity to do some improvising in the scenes between Cooper and Brennan." Brennan was full of ideas for bits of business, something Wyler always appreciated. And working with Cooper was a breeze: "If you tell Gary that here, after this line, is a chance for a funny look, he'll get the idea. . . . He'll do something with that look no one else could do."

Talli, too, marveled at Cooper's screen magnetism, especially after watching him work on the set. "This was one of the more interesting experiences I ever had," she said. "Cooper would do a scene, and it looked like nothing. He just seemed to stand there like a block of wood. The next night, I'd go to view the rushes. It was incredible. Everything showed in his face. It was all there. He had something special with the camera, really extraordinary."

Wyler had wanted to cast Talli in the picture as the female lead. It was a small role, a farmer's daughter who falls in love with Hardin. Goldwyn wouldn't hear of it. He wanted to use an unknown actress, Doris Davenport, whom he believed showed great promise.

"She's marvelous in your test," Goldwyn contended.

Wyler demurred. He thought Davenport sweet but untalented. Ironically, he'd gone out of his way to make her look good in the test for Goldwyn, because she told him that some years before he had slighted her in a screen test at Universal.

Freda Rosenblatt was relieved that Talli didn't get the role. "Their marriage could have gone down the drain," she said. Talli agreed. Her screen test for the picture had given her a taste of her husband's professional demands. "I had a prop in one hand, a hand mirror," she said. "Willy was telling me what to do and how to do it. I don't remember why, but I got so angry at him I wanted to throw the mirror at his head. I remember being perfectly furious. It was odd because I'd never felt that way as his wife."

What's more, *The Westerner* was not an easy shoot. "We'd get up at six in the morning and drive eight miles out of town to the set," Rosenblatt said. "There would be snow and ice on the ground. By ten the sun would come out and we'd bake. We'd shoot till sundown. Then we'd go back to the Santa Rita Hotel in Tucson and have dinner. At night we'd watch rushes from the day before. Lots of times Willy would want a rewrite for the next day. The crew, including Willy, didn't get much sleep. In the morning we'd start all over again."

Filming went smoothly nonetheless. "Willy made it look easy," said Jules Buck, a photographer who visited the set for *Life* magazine. "I watched the way he talked to everyone. He had this graceful body language. He had a shorthand everyone understood. He'd snap his fingers, not in any supercilious way, and people would say, 'Sure, Willy.' He had this quiet authority. I watched him talk with Cooper. He'd go up to Cooper and say something you couldn't hear. It was just a murmur. Then he'd come back and sit down on this little dolly ranger he had. I remember thinking, 'Boy, he makes it look easy, and it's not.'"

Though shooting ended in November, Wyler did not complete post-production on the *The Westerner* until late January. The picture was scheduled for release in February, but Goldwyn withheld it until the following September, partly because of his dispute with United Artists and partly because he had Alfred Newman rewrite much of Dimitri Tiomkin's score.

Willy and Talli flew to Fort Worth, Texas, for a spectacular premiere tied to a charity show hosted by Bob Hope. Cooper joined them along with a contingent of Hollywood celebrities. The hoopla included a rodeo-style parade through the downtown streets and some three hundred thousand onlookers.

Critics agreed that Wyler had made something unusual, a horse opera that subverted the genre's conventions. It had shoot-outs, cowboy chases, an epic range war and a spectacular fire. But it was also an intimate character study filled with comic overtones about the peculiar friendship between a hanging judge and the mild-mannered drifter who outfoxes him.

Wyler himself described *The Westerner* as a comedy disguised as melodrama. He didn't mind creating a certain amount of ambiguity. "There isn't a thing at stake," he said, "not even the heroine's life or the father's mortgage." Reviews were positive but mixed, and everybody lauded the performances of both Cooper and Brennan. When the 1940 Academy Awards rolled around, Brennan won his third Oscar for best supporting actor. The irony, of course, is that his was the starring role—and everybody knew it.

AT THE START OF THE NEW DECADE, WITH THE WORLD PONDER-ing Hitler's next move during the oddly quiet months of the "phony war," Willy and Talli made plans for a belated honeymoon. They knew Goldwyn's court battle with United Artists meant Willy would be going on loan-out for his next picture. Now was the best time to leave, before he had to make a commitment. As one of Hollywood's most sought-after directors, he was assured of offers.

The first came from Warner Bros. to direct a remake of *The Constant Nymph,* a stately romance. Using his planned honeymoon as an excuse,

Willy declined. RKO followed with a proposal to do *Kitty Foyle,* a dramatic love story that would bring Ginger Rogers an Academy Award. Wyler passed again. He had his eye on another Warner picture in the works for Bette Davis, a remake of Somerset Maugham's short story and play, *The Letter.* The first movie version, an early 1929 talkie, was best remembered for the magnificent performance of its leading lady, Jeanne Eagels. Davis couldn't wait to work with Wyler again. "After *Jezebel,* I would have jumped into the Hudson River if he had told me to," she said. "That's how much belief I had in his judgment as a director."

A treatment of *The Letter* had been written by Robert Stevenson. Howard Koch was still to write the screenplay when Willy and Talli left for the ski slopes of Lake Placid, New York. Six-month-old Cathy was packed off with a nanny to her grandparents in Dallas. All seemed promising. Lake Placid, however, proved well-named. "Willy didn't like the skiing there," Talli said. "The slopes were too flat."

They drove north to Montreal, heading for Quebec's rugged Laurentian Mountains. At their hotel they had an ugly incident.

"We'd heard the best skiing in the Laurentians was at Mont Tremblant," Talli recounted. "Willy talked with the hotel clerk in Montreal about getting a reservation on the mountain. Well, the clerk began to hesitate. He hemmed and hawed and looked very embarrassed."

"What's the problem?" Willy asked.

The clerk finally said, "Are you Jewish?"

Willy told him he was and wondered what that had to do with anything.

"I'm terribly sorry," the clerk said. "I can't make a reservation for you there. Jews are not allowed."

Jews could ski on the mountain and eat at any of the Mont Tremblant lodges, but an overnight stay was prohibited.

"We were stunned," Talli remembered. "We had never run into anything like that. Certainly nothing as overt as that. It was so bald it was shocking."

The next day they drove on anyway and found accommodations fifteen miles from Mont Tremblant at the Gray Rocks Lodge, now a famous resort with its own ski runs but in those days a charming little winter outpost. Slightly inconvenienced, they went skiing on the mountain for a week and then caught a train back to New York, where they booked a cruise to the Caribbean.

Their ship, the *New Amsterdam,* had a huge Dutch flag painted on its deck as a wartime precaution. If by some remote chance they encountered a German U-boat the flag was intended to signal the ship's neutrality. (Hitler's invasion of Holland wouldn't come until May, still two months off.) The send-off at the dock had a party atmosphere. "We embarked from one of those lovely old piers," Talli recalled. "Everybody was throwing confetti."

After two weeks, having stopped at the ports of St. Thomas, Curaçao and Havana, they decided to leave the cruise ship. "Nice as it was," said Talli, "we got sick of all that togetherness." They disembarked in Miami and went sportfishing with the screenwriter Dan Taradash (later to win an Academy Award for *From Here to Eternity*). Talli hooked the only catch, a skinny sailfish. Willy had it stuffed and shipped home for mounting on the wall of their den.

21

—— ⊰⋙⋙⋘⋘⊱ ——

HE PLEASED HIMSELF

Back home by early April 1940, Wyler signed a Warner Bros. contract to direct *The Letter.* Shooting would commence at the end of May. He would be paid six thousand two hundred fifty dollars a week, and he felt secure in the knowledge that Bette Davis would be able to carry its intriguing story.

Maugham had written a psychological study of Leslie Crosbie, the wife of an English plantation manager, who murders her secret lover out of anger and jealousy and then coolly uses her social position to hide the truth by claiming self-defense. Set in the tropics on a Malay rubber plantation, the tale addressed themes that had long fascinated Wyler, but in a more exotic way than usual.

Wyler would have a field day exploring murder and sexual infidelity, erotic tension and psychological suspense, class snobbery and racial hypocrisy. Leslie is blackmailed during the inquest by her dead lover's Eurasian wife. She has an incriminating letter that Leslie wrote on the day of the murder. To keep it from coming to light and exposing her lies, Leslie buys back the letter for ten thousand dollars—her husband's life savings—and also submits to a mortifying demand to deliver the money personally, a "loss of face" that compounds her humiliation.

The picture gets off to a breathtaking start with a long opening sequence. It is a calm tropical night. Light from a full moon floods the plantation. The camera moves steadily, panning through the trees and over the sleeping natives in their hammocks, then through their crowded bunks. The air is thick with humidity. The silence builds. The shadowed darkness menaces. A sudden shot rings out, frightening a bird from its perch. A man stumbles down the front stairs of the main house. A woman follows. She fires a pistol into his limp body until she has no bullets left.

Without a spoken word or a single cut, the opening scene establishes the mood, the scenario and the main character. Wyler created the entire sequence out of his imagination from little more than a single sentence in the screenplay. The day before filming was to begin he laid out the camera moves with cinematographer Tony Gaudio.

"The script said something like, 'You hear a gunshot and you see a woman coming out shooting at a man,'" Wyler said. "I thought the shot should shock you. To get the full impact of it I thought everything should be very quiet. At the same time I wanted to show where we were — and in a single camera move.

"This two-minute sequence was all we did on the first day. And since all of this was not in the script, we ended the day with only a quarter of a page filmed. Normally, you're suppose to do three or four pages a day. Jesus, the whole studio was in an uproar. But when they saw the shot they didn't mind."

Screenwriter Howard Koch, who wrote the taut, smart screen adaptation, marveled at Wyler's instinct for staging. A precocious mix of *film noir* effects and straightforward melodrama, it drew Koch's admiration not just because of nuances that illuminated character and established subtext but because of symbolic details that enlarged the drama.

"Willy was not completely satisfied with all his planning," Koch recounted. "He came to me and said, 'I don't know what it is. There's something missing. An image. Something to unify the story that isn't there now.'

"I thought about it for a while. He was searching for a fundamental image — something that by its recurrence would reveal the woman's suppressed guilt behind the facade of her protested innocence. Finally I came up with an idea and went to Willy. 'Why don't we use the moon?' He thought that was interesting. We had decided to have a full moon the night she did the shooting. Now we would really make use of it. From then on, starting with that night, she would draw away from the moonlight to avoid the memory of what she'd done."

Wyler took the moonlight even further. During production he "doubled the dramatic import of my image," Koch said. Using louvered blinds on the windows, Wyler cast the moonlight on Leslie as though "printing prison stripes on her dress." Thus, he manufactured a visual emblem of guilt and sin for Leslie, not unlike the "A" worn by Hester Prynne, the adulteress in Nathaniel Hawthorne's novel, *The Scarlet Letter.*

"Willy never claimed to be an 'auteur,' " Koch said, "but his interpretation of a writer's work was creative, enhancing the values of the screenplay."

Warners had "an unwritten law" that screenwriters did not go on the set once they turned in their final scripts, Koch noted, but Wyler "broke the rule for me." In fact, it was common practice for Wyler to keep a screenwriter at his side to help improvise during filming, regardless of where he worked.

"I criticize and I leave alone the things that are good," Wyler explained. "All on the basis of my own likes and dislikes. On the set I follow the story line of the finished script, but sometimes a scene's significance isn't apparent until you see the actors playing it. Reading it is one thing, seeing it played is another. Also, actors sometimes make good suggestions, which require script changes *on the set.*"

Such collaboration could just as easily lead to clashes. Bette Davis, who was thrilled to be back working with Wyler, nevertheless walked off a set for the first time in her career over his interpretation of a scene. She and Wyler fought bitterly about the delivery of a key line in one of the picture's climactic moments.

Leslie tries, when her husband learns of her adultery, to make up for the wrong she has done him. But when he asks if she still loves him, Leslie cannot bring herself to lie. "I still love the man I killed," she admits. Wyler felt her declaration was such a brutal admission that Leslie must look her husband directly in the eye.

"If she says it turning away from him, she just lessens the impact, and she's ashamed to admit it," Wyler contended. "But if she says it to him in a desperate moment of honesty and self-flagellation, then, it seemed to me, it hits him twice as hard *and* it's a terrible confession to make. You can't say that looking away."

He did not want to deflate the significance of the scene and turn it into a cliché. "If you try to soften the blow," he said, "you shouldn't say it at all."

Davis protested.

"It was such a cruel thing to say to the husband, I felt I could not say it to his face," she explained. "I couldn't conceive of any woman looking into her husband's eyes and admitting such a thing."

But after walking off the set in a huff, the star relented.

"I came back eventually—end result, I did it his way," she recounted in her autobiography. "It played validly, heaven knows, but to this day I think my way was the right way. I lost, but I lost to an artist. . . . So many directors were such weak sisters that I would have to take over. Uncreative, unsure of themselves, frightened to fight back, they offered me none of the security that this tyrant did."

THE ROMANCE BETWEEN WYLER AND DAVIS HAD LONG SINCE ended. He, now happily married, was not tempted to rekindle the sexual liaison with his star. For her part, she had had several affairs after Wyler broke theirs off, some rather indiscreet. She'd slept with Howard Hughes, the actor George Brent and the director Anatole Litvak. She'd already met Arthur Farnsworth, the hotel manager whom she would marry six months later, on New Year's Day 1941. Also, just before starting *The Letter*, she'd spent a month in Hawaii, where she'd had a brief fling with the Warner Bros. publicity chief Bob Taplinger. And while making *The Letter* she took up with Bruce Lester, a young actor who had a minor role in the picture.

So it is perhaps no surprise that Davis was pregnant during filming. As she confided years later to a friend, "Tony Gaudio, the cameraman, kept looking at me sideways. Obviously, I couldn't have the baby and I was upset as hell. I had already had two abortions. I was only thirty-two and thought to myself that if I married again and wanted to have a baby, my insides might be such a mess that I couldn't. I cried and cried, but I knew what I had to do. . . . I went to the doctor on a Saturday and showed up for scenes on Monday morning wearing a form-fitting eyelet evening dress for a scene and that damn Tony said, 'Jesus, Bette, it looks like you've lost five pounds over the weekend!' "

What is surprising, however, is the implication that the baby might have been Wyler's. One Davis biographer says she offered "an oblique clue" to the father's identity when she opined that she "should have married Willy." But the likelihood that Wyler fathered the child seems as improbable as the supposed letter he was said to have once sent her proposing marriage.

THE ROLE OF LESLIE'S UNSUSPECTING HUSBAND FELL TO HER- bert Marshall. Ironically, he had played the thankless role of the slain lover in the 1929 version of *The Letter*. But the starring male role was that of the honest lawyer, the husband's old friend, who reluctantly takes Leslie's case. Wyler always found it amusing that he had to fight with Warner Bros. to cast one of its own actors in the role.

"I have a fellow here under contract," Jack Warner had said before filming began. "I signed him last year, very good actor named Stephenson, James Stephenson. Have you got a part?"

"I've got a very good part," Wyler told him. "But I never heard of this actor."

"Take my word," Warner said. "He's a very good actor, but I can't get anybody to give him a good part."

Wyler replied that he'd be glad to consider him but wanted to make a screen test first. The test turned out so well that he told Stephenson, "You're in," and notified the front office.

No sooner had he done that than his phone rang.

"I didn't realize this was an important part," Warner said. "Shouldn't you get somebody better? Somebody with a name?"

"Jack, remember what you told me about this fellow? How good he was? It's all true. He *is* good. He's actually first-rate."

"Look," Warner said, "I appreciate what you're doing, but . . ."

"I'm not doing this for you," Wyler asserted. "I insist I get this man."

Stephenson played the role, and his performance drew exceptional praise. Wyler was so taken with him, "he expected really great things in his future," Talli said. Unfortunately, within a year Stephenson would die of a heart attack.

THE SHOOT, WHICH HAD BEGUN MAY 27, 1940, WENT RELATIVELY quickly. "I am delighted you are off to a flying start," Warner memoed him. A month later, the picture was two days ahead of schedule and was projected to finish four days early. Nevertheless, Wyler's repeated takes annoyed the increasingly restive studio boss. On June 26 Warner saw a cameraman's report listing nine scenes shot that day. Not bad. But sixty-two takes? Six scenes were shot in six takes or fewer, one required fourteen takes, another twelve and another eight.

Warner fired off an angry memo: "I will not stand for this practice and you must discontinue it immediately. You are a very good director and no one can tell me you can't make a scene in at least two to four takes tops and print the one you really know is right. . . . This is a serious matter, as far as this company is concerned, and I am not going to let any one man put us out of business."

Wyler drafted a reply:

"Please be assured that I have no intention of putting your company out of business. If I found it necessary to make fourteen takes of one scene there must have been a very good reason. Since it is difficult to judge from a pink sheet just exactly what happened on the set, I would consider it a favor if you did not. . . . I have made a particular effort towards speed and economy (even at occasional sacrifices of quality) and shall continue to do so. . . . I had hoped that you would be aware of this, and I must admit that I was somewhat surprised by the tone of your note."

Warner, who ran the studio with an iron hand, was famous for his penny-pinching. But he ultimately chose not to pressure Wyler too much, recognizing him as "an important director." For his part, Wyler "didn't play politics at the studio," Koch said. "He didn't try to please the front office. He pleased himself."

One thing Wyler could not avoid, though, was having to satisfy the Production Code by creating what he termed a "stupid" ending for *The Letter*. Unlike the ending of *Wuthering Heights*, which had been tacked on by Goldwyn, this one he "had to tag on as a concession" to the censorship of the day.

Koch initially wrote a screenplay that adhered to Maugham's short story, in which Leslie's guilt is established and she faces prison. Maugham's play, however, ended with Leslie suffering a different sort of punishment. She is condemned to live out a dreary existence with her husband after confessing to him that she loved the man she killed.

But the picture needed something "less prosaic," Koch realized. He wrote a new ending intended as Leslie's "act of expiation." Leslie would walk out "alone into the moonlit garden, knowing that the wife of the man she'd murdered was waiting for her, knife in hand."

Wyler agreed that Leslie's death could be a logical conclusion to the tragedy. His staging of it, filled with *film noir* overtones, again enhanced the dramatic effect while enlarging the symbolic content.

"The way Wyler directed it," Koch noted, "the actual stabbing was left to the audience's imagination. As she walked out into the garden toward the avenging knife, a slight wind brushed her white scarf. The ghostly figure seemed to dissolve into the moonlight as though her dead lover had reclaimed her."

But in those days, Wyler said, "you couldn't leave anyone unpunished. Even the Eurasian widow somehow had to be punished. We had to put in two cops to apprehend her. That was silly, but we had to do it. I wish when they show *The Letter* on television they would cut off the ending where she is arrested."

. . .

ON NOVEMBER 22, *THE LETTER* OPENED AT THE STRAND IN NEW York and went on to do solid business everywhere. Bosley Crowther of the *New York Times* wrote an extraordinary rave both for the picture and for Wyler's direction, which he thought deserved "the ultimate credit for as taut and insinuating a melodrama as has come along." But he, too, objected to the final scene. He did not like having "Miss Davis pay for her criminal deed with her own violent death." Despite its logic, he felt her death was an obvious concession to the Production Code's demand for "compensating moral values."

The Letter earned seven Academy Award nominations, including best picture, best director, best actress and best supporting actor. But it didn't win a single Oscar. This was the fifth Wyler picture in a row to receive a best-picture nomination. (The others were *Dodsworth, Dead End, Jezebel* and *Wuthering Heights.*) It was also Wyler's third nomination for best director in five years. According to Talli, he never seemed to mind not winning, although that year's loss proved slightly embarrassing.

"Whenever Willy was nominated, we'd go to the ceremony," she said. "Frank Capra was presenting the best director award that night. Capra wanted to highlight the director's award, make it more important. So he called the nominees to the podium." George Cukor, Alfred Hitchcock, Sam Wood and Willy followed orders and came forward. But when Capra opened the envelope he was horrified to discover the winning director was John Ford, who wasn't even at the ceremony. He won for *The Grapes of Wrath.* The four losing directors were at a bit of a loss. They were empty-handed *and* they had no one to congratulate. "They all had to slink back to their tables," Talli recalled.

Oscars or no, *The Letter* holds up today as few movies of that era have. Indeed, many film scholars rank it as a high point for Wyler. Davis's performance also turns out to be among the greatest of her career, more powerful and subtle than her superb Oscar-winning portrayal of Julie Marsden in *Jezebel.* Pauline Kael, in a retrospective review, hailed her portrait of Leslie Crosbie as incomparable. "Davis," she wrote, "gives what is very likely the best study of female sexual hypocrisy in film history."

TOWARD THE END OF SUMMER 1940, THE GOLDWYN STUDIO WAS still virtually shut down. Lillian Hellman's adaptation of her play, *The Little Foxes,* was the only work in progress, and it was all on paper. Goldwyn had purchased the rights shortly after it became a hit on Broadway in 1939, although his story editor Edwin Knopf had misgivings that the subject was "too caustic for films."

Wyler anticipated that when Goldwyn resumed production, *The Little Foxes* would be his next project. Months earlier, he had read Hellman's first draft of the screenplay and couldn't wait to get started. He thought it "a literary masterpiece." Hellman had done a great job in opening up the play, keeping the best scenes intact, creating others and coming up with entirely new places and characters.

In the meantime, Goldwyn put him on loan-out to Warner Bros. again. On September 6 Wyler was notified that a tentative agreement had been reached for him to direct *Sergeant York,* a patriotic tribute to a hillbilly World War I pacifist-turned-soldier. He was to be reteamed with Gary Cooper, also on loan-out in what was basically to be a "star swap" for Bette Davis.

Jesse Lasky owned the film property, having paid the former war hero fifty thousand dollars for the rights to his life story. Lasky believed Cooper was the ideal actor for the role, perhaps the only one. Warner Bros. agreed to do the picture but told Lasky he'd better forget Cooper. The star had just finished making Frank Capra's *Meet John Doe* for Warner, and Goldwyn was unlikely to let him go back there so soon.

Over on Formosa Avenue, though, Wyler told Goldwyn the only actress who could possibly play Regina Giddens, the central character in *The Little Foxes,* was Bette Davis. Which meant they had a problem. Jack Warner *never* loaned her out. She was his biggest star, and he didn't want anyone even flirting with the idea that she was available to other studios.

So when Lasky asked to borrow Cooper, he was surprised and not a little pleased to hear that Goldwyn, his old enemy and former brother-in-law, was amenable to the idea. Perhaps he shouldn't have been surprised. The star's contract was costing Goldwyn a pretty penny. Though it amounted to less than half of what Cooper earned—the United States Treasury reported in 1939 that the actor's annual income of four hundred eighty-two thousand dollars made him the nation's top wage earner—another loan-out would help defray at least some of Goldwyn's cost. Besides, Goldwyn needed Bette Davis.

It didn't take a genius to see the advantages of a swap. The two studio heads, Goldwyn and Jack Warner, arranged it by phone. Ironically, a week after getting the *Sergeant York* assignment, Wyler was notified that his services in the deal were no longer required and he would be loaned out instead to Twentieth Century–Fox for *How Green Was My Valley.*

. . .

Twentieth's legendary production chief, Darryl F. Zanuck, had been a longtime admirer of Wyler's pictures, going back to *Hell's Heroes*. Now he wanted to make a prestigious follow-up to John Ford's *The Grapes of Wrath*, which had been a huge hit for Twentieth. With Ford busy on another picture, Wyler was his director of choice to put Richard Llewellyn's best-selling novel on the screen.

Zanuck had bought the rights to *How Green Was My Valley* for an unprecedented three hundred thousand dollars. He had the novel turned into a screenplay by Ernest Pascal, then asked Philip Dunne to rewrite it. But Dunne told him the screenplay was so bad it made him wonder "what had persuaded him to buy the book in the first place." Zanuck replied by sending it to him.

On reading the novel, Dunne quickly changed his mind. Llewellyn had written a sprawling, earthy, inspiring tale of a family of Welsh coal miners. Their green little valley was being destroyed by industrial pollution and they were caught up in a divisive, intergenerational conflict over the right to strike. But Pascal's script had reduced all of that to a turgid union tract, missing the passionate core of the characters themselves.

Dunne wrote a new screenplay from scratch. He and Zanuck agreed it could go long, but when he turned in a rough draft for a four-hour movie, Zanuck told him it was "twice too long." By the time Wyler came to the project, Dunne was struggling with the cuts and needed a sounding board. Wyler suggested they go to a mountain resort at Arrowhead Springs. They could "have a good time," he said, "take the mineral baths and—incidentally—work on the script."

Zanuck agreed to pick up the tab for a two-week trip on condition they phone him with daily progress reports. After a week the duo succeeded in cutting ten pages. But for every page they cut out, they added two. When they got back to town, the script was even longer than before. "We'd meet at Willy's house on Copa de Oro," Dunne remembered. "The picture was very episodic. That was the nature of it. There were all kinds of stories and subplots. The book had no structure, so one of the difficult things was to find out how to arrange the scenes. We spent most of our time transposing them. That's most of what we did."

Between production chores—casting had begun and a Welsh village was being built in the Malibu hills—Wyler eventually spent ten weeks working with Dunne on the script. "Willy couldn't write a line, but he knew what *you* could do and he *made* you do it," Dunne recounted. "I'd shout, 'What's wrong with this goddamned scene?' And he'd keep say-ing, 'You can do it better.' I'd go home grousing and mumbling and I al-ways did do it better. I worked harder on scenes for Willy than I ever worked in my life."

Their single greatest difficulty was trying to tell the entire life story of the central character Huw, who looks back on his Welsh mining family and his childhood. The solution to cutting the script surfaced only after Wyler cast twelve-year-old Roddy McDowall as the young Huw.

McDowall, who had appeared in some British pictures, came to New York with his mother and sister to escape the war. They arrived on the last convoy from England in 1940, though not as refugees. Wyler found him on a hunch. "I wanted an English boy," he said. "So I asked Twenti-eth's New York office to check the ships for a boy who could act."

Meanwhile, Mrs. McDowall contacted an agent who took her son to MGM to test for *The Yearling*. He was wrong for the part but was sent over to Twentieth to test for *How Green Was My Valley*, along with four other boys. When the tests were sent to California, Twentieth's casting director wildly opposed showing McDowall's test to Wyler.

"You don't want to see this kid."

"Why not?" Wyler asked.

"Because he's bowlegged and walleyed. He has a gap in his teeth, and he's ugly."

"Let's see it anyway."

It became instantly obvious to Wyler that he had found someone to portray the young Huw who was captivating enough to carry a whole picture. Therefore, Huw need not grow up, and the picture only had to deal with the first half of the novel. He sent for McDowall, and within two weeks of landing in America, the awkward-looking boy with the big brown eyes had a role. This suited Dunne and pleased Zanuck. The producer was losing patience with the snail's pace of the project and was threatening to get involved in writing the script himself.

Zanuck had started out as a screenwriter and had earned a reputa-tion for speed as well as story construction. He couldn't understand what was holding them up, since they'd already found the key to solving their problem.

"I have stood on the sidelines offering what advice and counsel you would take," Zanuck notified them in early December a month after Wyler saw the test. "The very fact that you have both worked very hard and so far have failed . . . leads me to believe that you are never going to achieve [your goal] unless you get some help. When I spent two hours trying to convince you that your own idea of carrying young Huw through the story as a boy is correct, and you agree with me and then you come back two days later and tell me that the conception is all wrong . . . you can hardly blame me for suggesting that you need assistance—and you need it badly."

Wyler's contract with Twentieth called for a fourteen-week loan-out. Time was running short. Even if filming were to begin immediately there was little chance he could bring it in without an extension from Goldwyn. Quietly, Zanuck and Wyler talked about postponing production until the following summer. Just before Christmas, however, Wyler ran into the agent Frank Orsatti, who told him he'd heard the picture had been called off.

"As I had treated our conversation on the subject with strict secrecy," Wyler memoed Zanuck, "I was naturally very surprised that [Orsatti] should know, and he in turn was surprised that I did *not* know. . . . Today there are already all sorts of rumors and I fear there may be an item in tomorrow's trade papers with perhaps the wrong interpretation of the facts—which might do everyone harm—including the picture."

But before the year was out, it was clear that Wyler's chances of making *How Green Was My Valley* were slimmer than ever. Relations with Zanuck remained cordial nonetheless. When Zanuck went off to Sun Valley for a Christmas ski holiday, Wyler cabled him: WOULD YOU PLEASE WIRE ME ABOUT SNOW CONDITIONS STOP IF AS GOOD AS HOTEL CLAIMS WILL WORK OFF THE REST OF MY SALARY WITH SKIING LESSONS.

Wyler also had his chauffeur deliver a Christmas gift to the young actor. "The doorbell of our little duplex rang and I was handed a magnificent package," McDowall recalls a half-century later. "Willy was no longer involved with the film, but he was wishing me luck. I was deeply moved. I still have the gift. It was an elegant leather jacket."

Dunne always regretted that Wyler never got to direct his screenplay. He blamed Twentieth's board of directors for pulling the plug, not Zanuck. "The New York office hated the script," Dunne said, "hated the absence of real starring roles, hated Willy's reputation as an extravagant director, predicted disaster for the entire project, and refused to put up the money for it."

Months later Zanuck called the writer to his office. There sat Jack Ford, Dunne recalled, "chewing on his handkerchief and greeting me with insulting remarks about the script. Ford had agreed to bring in the picture for a million dollars, and on that basis New York had told Zanuck he could go ahead."

Wyler, too, regretted not making *How Green Was My Valley*. He always took pride in discovering Roddy McDowall. When the picture came out, moreover, Zanuck got his wish for a serious follow-up to *The Grapes of Wrath*. The picture scored not just at the box office but took five Academy Awards, including those for best picture and best director.

Dunne was nominated for the screenplay but didn't win the Oscar. He was in good company. Neither did fellow nominees Lillian Hellman for *The Little Foxes*, John Huston for *The Maltese Falcon*, nor Billy Wilder and Charles Brackett for *Hold Back the Dawn*.

22

DEEP FOCUS

LILLIAN HELLMAN'S SCREENPLAY for *The Little Foxes* still needed fine-tuning by late January 1941. The playwright, worn out from work on the third rewrite of her latest play, *Watch on the Rhine*, could not go to Hollywood to deal with the script changes for the picture. She notified Goldwyn that she had to remain in New York because the Broadway opening of her play was only two months away and casting was to begin immediately.

"The script doesn't need actual rewriting," Hellman explained in a letter. "It needs cutting in places and perhaps expanding in others, in general someone able to put some of the scenes so that they come through the camera's eyes rather than through the theater's eyes. And that is all I honestly believe it needs."

Hellman suggested that Goldwyn hire someone else and recommended several people she trusted not to tamper with the basics of her script: her former husband and friend Arthur Kober, her friend Dorothy Parker and Parker's husband Alan Campbell. Goldwyn hired all three.

Filming began April 28. Ironically, midway through production, Wyler wrote to Hellman, "I am carrying on under difficult conditions and doing the best I can. . . . There are many things in the picture that are not well done, and only a few that are, and believe me, I miss your final work on the script, even more now than I did during preparation. I'm directing with the new script in one hand, your old script in the other and a copy of the play in the third. I have also grown an extra head for headaches."

Set in a small Southern town at the turn of the century, *The Little Foxes* is a stinging drama about the Hubbards, a rapacious family not unlike the Snopes clan of Faulknerian legend. Lacking a conscience, they use any means to make a dollar. In need of seventy-five thousand dollars to build a cotton mill, which is sure to make a fortune by exploiting cheap labor, Ben and Oscar Hubbard scheme with their duplicitous sister Regina to get her husband Horace, who disapproves of them, to invest in the venture.

For all his enthusiasm, Goldwyn worried that the picture might be subversive, a leftist attack on capitalism. The second day into production, according to a story Parker told Hellman, he appeared on the set and announced that he'd heard *The Little Foxes* was "a Communist play."

"Oh, Mr. Goldwyn, I don't think that could be true," Parker said. "The play takes place in 1900 and the Communist Manifesto was written in 1848. That makes no sense at all."

"Wonderful," Goldwyn replied. "I'll tell everybody that."

Wyler's biggest headache turned out to be his leading lady. Bette Davis vehemently disagreed with him about how to play Regina. Davis wanted to play her as a sinister, callous, greedy bitch — not unreasonable, given Regina's behavior. When her brothers resort to stealing negotiable bonds from Horace's bank vault for their investment, after he has turned them down, she blackmails them for a larger share of the cotton mill. She also lets her husband die — he has a weak heart — by refusing to get him his heart stimulant during an attack of angina.

But Wyler's vision of Regina was more complex. He believed she had many shadings, that she was charming and funny as well as evil, that she was also very sexy. "I wanted Bette to play it much lighter," Wyler said, unwilling to settle for a one-note performance. Davis, however, thought the outlines of the character had been set in stone. The role was so clearly defined by Hellman, she believed, that Regina could be embraced only as written and only as Tallulah Bankhead had portrayed her on the stage.

Bankhead had played Regina with heartless brass in the Broadway production. Wyler had urged Davis to see that performance to give her an idea of what he did *not* want. But just the opposite happened. Davis came away so convinced of the truth of Bankhead's interpretation that she chose to play the role in the movie "with scarcely an accent's difference." Doubly ironic, the critic James Agee presumed Wyler had shaped Davis's performance to that mold. "This was not Miss Davis's idea," Agee wrote. "She quarreled with [Wyler] for her own version. He—or the play—won. Result: the film's foremost dramatic actress not only acts like Tallulah but looks like her."

In fact, director and star fought over Davis's choice of makeup as well. The actress believed she looked too young, at thirty-three, to play a woman of forty-one who has a seventeen-year-old daughter. She whited her face with calcimine to give her the appearance of a powdered Southern matron. The effect made her so pale that cinematographer Gregg Toland had to do extensive tests to balance her lighting with that of the other actors.

When he saw her makeup, Wyler demanded, "What's *that* for?"

"It's to make me look older," she said.

"It makes you look like a clown. Take it off!"

Her refusal brought out Wyler's nasty side.

"He hated the way I looked, spoke, moved, delivered my lines, my false eyelashes—everything else about my performance," Davis said. "Nothing escaped his scathing tongue."

Two weeks after shooting began, she walked off the set and went home to Laguna Beach, where she had rented a house.

"I was a nervous wreck," she said. "My favorite and most admired director was fighting me every inch of the way. I just didn't want to continue."

Flatly refusing Goldwyn's entreaties to return to the set, she stayed away for nearly three weeks. Rumors swept Hollywood that she was pregnant and had collapsed from the heat, that she was not only feuding with Wyler and Goldwyn but that she was being replaced by either Miriam Hopkins or Katharine Hepburn.

Wyler shot around his star. Fortunately, *The Little Foxes* was more of an ensemble piece than a star vehicle and he could rearrange the schedule. He filmed without a break during her absence. At the same time, he asked Hellman to write Davis a letter to help exorcise Bankhead's ghost from her performance. She wrote on May 20:

> I am bewildered that you are having so much trouble with Regina. . . . I never meant Regina to be a violent woman or a fiery woman: it is obvious that a woman of the violence that Tallulah showed would never have stayed with Horace or with the

town . . . I was very pleased when you agreed to do the picture, and only because I thought that it was the kind of casting that was right for the play. You will be better as Regina than Bankhead ever could have been: better by looks, by instinct, by understanding. Tallulah's performance should not worry you: It should make you far more sure of what your own could be. I have great faith in Willy as a director and great faith in his ability to project character. . . . There are many . . . who can testify to my very great objections to the way Tallulah was playing the part. It was vulgar and it was cheap, and it was a complete misinterpretation.

After missing sixteen consecutive days, Davis came back on June 2 because, as reports had it, she "wasn't a quitter." That she was being paid three hundred eighty-five thousand dollars for her services also may have had something to do with it.

But when she returned, she continued to play the role as a monstrous bitch, precisely as before. "I wasn't pleasing him," she said of Wyler, "but he'd grit his teeth and let me play it my way."

The tension between them took its toll on him. One evening over dinner, after Davis had resumed work, Talli innocently asked how things were going. "I don't want to talk about it here," he snapped. "It's bad enough having to be there." Each day was a form of combat. Teresa Wright, who played Regina's daughter Alexandra, remembered: "Bette had it in her contract that she could leave at six. We were working towards that time doing a scene over and over again. She said to Willy, 'It's getting time for me to leave.' We continued, and when it got past that time, she said, 'Willy, I'm really sorry. I've been up since dawn and I'm too tired to do the scene.' It became a clash of wills. She was going to go and he was going to get the scene. Finally, he said, 'Okay. If you want to leave, I'll print it the way it is. But it's not good.' Well, she couldn't leave."

Wright was making her movie debut in *The Little Foxes*. Hellman had suggested her to Goldwyn. The young Broadway actress had made her professional stage debut in the fall of 1938, right out of high school, understudying Martha Scott's Emily in *Our Town*. A year later, she played the ingenue in *Life with Father* and was still playing it when Goldwyn went east to see her performance.

Wright's arrival in Hollywood caused a stir not because of her star power but because of an unprecedented clause Goldwyn agreed to write into her contract. It said she "shall not be required to pose for photographs in a bathing suit unless she is in the water. Neither may she be photographed running on the beach with her hair flying in the wind. Nor may she pose in any of the following situations: In shorts, playing with a cocker spaniel; digging in a garden; whipping up a meal; attired in firecrackers and holding skyrockets for the Fourth of July; looking insinuatingly at a turkey for Thanksgiving; wearing a bunny cap with long ears for Easter; twinkling on prop snow in a skiing outfit while a fan blows her scarf."

Herbert Marshall, who had played Davis's husband in *The Letter*, did so once again as Horace Giddens. Charles Dingle and Carl Benton played Regina's brothers Ben and Oscar Hubbard, reprising their roles from the Broadway production. Dan Duryea, also reprising his role, played Oscar's sniveling son Leo. Wyler admired them all as performers. But his favorite was Patricia Collinge, though only after a struggle.

She thought her stage performance didn't need to be changed for the movie. Wyler disagreed. They argued so heatedly she complained to Goldwyn about her rough treatment, and he asked Wyler to ease up. It was then Wyler took her by the hand and led her into a projection room, where he made her look at the dailies.

Collinge saw the problem immediately. Everything came out bigger on the screen. Her slightest gesture seemed magnified. She was overacting terribly. At the end of the session, she begged Wyler's forgiveness.

"Willy, whatever you ask me to do, I will," she said humbly.

The result is evident. Collinge nearly walks off with the picture in the role of Birdie, Oscar's wife, a woman reduced to alcoholic despair by a husband who married her long ago for her wealth and, now that he has spent it all, treats her with contempt. The pathos of Birdie's character shines like no other.

"Willy thought Patricia Colinge was absolutely marvelous," Talli recalled. "She gave him a soulful performance, and he loved her for it. It was such a relief for him."

HELLMAN'S SCREENPLAY OPENED UP THE STORY. SCENES WERE moved outside the Giddens home. She also created a love interest for Alexandra: David Hewitt, a young man who works for the town newspaper. The romance between these two is predictable, but it provided some breathing room in the drama's poisonous atmosphere—and Wyler used it as an opportunity for comic touches.

At one point, for example, Alexandra departs by train for Baltimore and David insists on accompanying her to the station. Dishevelled from working all night without sleep, he rushes into the street in his night shirt and overcoat. Alexandra, shocked by the impropriety of his outfit, protests that he can't accompany her to the station. Wright said the scene mystified her at the time. "You know he couldn't possibly have gone out like that in the South. We had done all this period stuff for authenticity. I thought, 'Gosh, why are we doing this?'" But Wyler was after the humor of the situation. He has David look himself over, hurry back into the house and rush right out again—wearing a black bowler.

"That," said Wright, "was Willy's touch."

Collaborating with Toland also enabled Wyler to exploit the camera in ways that opened up the production with striking results. The most famous instance is the "shaving scene," in which Oscar discovers that his son Leo has sneaked a peek into Horace's safe deposit box.

The play has them discussing this over coffee in Regina's dining room. The screenplay put it in Oscar's bedroom, where he is shaving and Leo passes by in the hall. Wyler shifted the scene to the bathroom, where Oscar and Leo are now shaving back to back but talking directly to each other through their respective mirrors. Their doubled reflections are not just clever camera work. Leo's face, seen in a small round mirror over Oscar's shoulder, seems to be looking through a key hole. It underscores the idea of prying eyes.

The master Russian filmmaker Sergei Eisenstein prized *The Little Foxes* so highly he showed it over and over at private parties, according to Hellman. Eisenstein told her several years before he died in 1948 that the shaving scene was an inspired moment of genius. For its staging alone Wyler deserved "motion picture fame for the rest of his life," he said.

Another sequence frequently cited for its inventive brilliance is the "staircase scene," which demonstrates Regina's terrifying ruthlessness. It begins with Regina telling Horace, who is sitting in his wheelchair, that she never loved him but married him only for material gain. What she cannot see, but we can, is the pained expression on Horace's face, as her remarks precipitate a heart attack. He tries to take his medication, but the bottle drops and breaks.

By now Regina has come over to the sofa in front of him. When he pleads for her help, she recognizes an opportunity and sits stock still not lifting a finger or blinking an eye. Horace staggers out of his wheelchair toward the staircase behind her. He struggles up toward the bedroom where he has more medication. But the camera doesn't follow him. It remains fixed on Regina's stony face, which is rigid with anticipation in the foreground. She listens keenly for his collapse in the background.

Instead of using deep focus in this scene, which could have kept both planes of action sharply etched, Wyler chose to blur the focus on Horace in the background, where the external drama is. The camera keeps Regina in sharp focus, where the internal drama is, both to draw attention to her cruelty and to underscore her steel will. It is only at the very last moment, when Horace collapses on the stairs, that the camera brings him suddenly into focus, directing our eye to the consequences of her ruthless immobility and releasing the psychological tension.

"What is interesting here is the wife," Wyler explained. "The scene is her face, what is going on inside her. You could have him out of the frame completely, just hear him stagger upstairs. . . . Gregg said, 'I can have him sharp, or both of them sharp.' I said no, because I wanted audiences to feel they were seeing something they were not supposed to. Seeing the husband in the background made you squint, but what you *were* seeing was her face."

The picture drew extraordinary admiration from André Bazin, the foremost French critic and film theorist of the time who later founded the influential magazine *Cahiers du Cinéma*. "There is a hundred times more cinema, and better cinema at that, in one fixed shot in *The Little Foxes*," he wrote, "than in all the exterior traveling shots, in all the natural settings, in all the geographical exoticism [through] which the screen till now has ingeniously tried to make us forget the stage."

Though not a writer himself, Wyler had advice for screenwriters that frequently went against the conventional wisdom. He may have helped "open up" Hellman's play, but he also questioned the presumed virtue of automatically dramatizing implied narrative material buried in a stage work.

"A mistake often made in adapting a play to the screen," he said "is actually showing a piece of action that in the play was only talked about. The adaptor believes he is taking full advantage of his medium, when in many cases the incident was only talked about not because of the limitations of the stage but because it may have been far more dramatic to hear it discussed by interested parties than to actually see it happen."

Hellman herself lavished praise on Wyler for clarifying her work and improving on it. "I think most of *The Little Foxes*, a good fifty percent, is better in the picture than it ever was in the play," she said.

When filming ended on July 3, 1941, the production was nine days behind schedule. Wyler felt happy just to get it over with. Collinge and Wright had been out sick time and again, a fire from a short circuit had destroyed part of the set during the filming, and the summer's heat had been unbearable. And, of course, Davis had made it a grueling experience.

"I'm not knocking Bette—she is a great actress," he told the New York *World-Telegram.* "But I am relieved the picture is done. Maybe she is just as relieved."

Davis *was* relieved, but also heartbroken. She regretted her fights with Wyler. *The Little Foxes* was their third and last picture together. Davis opined years later that he "never asked me to be in one of his films" again. "I have few ambitions left," she told a friend. "One is to do one more film with Willy before I end my career."

In fact, Wyler had not written off working with her again. After five years elapsed, he suggested they meet for lunch to talk over the possibility. Davis replied in a letter on her thirty-eighth birthday: "The war should be over between us. It is so long ago, and so much has happened to both of us in the meantime. It seems sort of unimportant, the only important thing being, we should be friends. We should work together again. . . . It will always be for me the only right direction—yours. . . .

"Without seeming a coward or pompous let me say, no lunch or meetings. Sherry [her third husband, William Grant Sherry] would not like it. And in a town where our row has been common talk, as well as the other feelings we had for each other, such a proposed lunch or meeting would start it all up again and could only hurt Sherry very much. . . . You have had so much to do with what I am at thirty-eight. . . . So here's to all of it, and to a picture together again. Please God, soon. . . ."

Six months later, in January 1947, they were still corresponding about the prospect of finding a mutual project. Wyler suggested a comedy. Davis preferred doing a drama and asked him to think about directing her in *Hedda Gabler.* But by then he was under contract to Liberty Films and still owed Goldwyn a picture. "Under my present setup it's utterly impossible," he wrote her, "but if an opportunity should arrive for *you* to make a picture away from Warners I wish you would let me know. . . . I think we have both done a lot of healthy growing up since working together, and so have pictures in general. There's so much wonderful work left undone I long to do some of it with you."

ON AUGUST 21, 1941, *THE LITTLE FOXES* OPENED TO HUGE LINES at Radio City Music Hall. It was a smash hit around the country, as well as in Europe. Critics liked the story's bite. Howard Barnes claimed in the New York *Herald-Tribune* that the play's adaptation to the screen "charts a whole new course of motion-picture making." Many reviewers raved about Bette Davis's acidic portrait of Regina. But in a retrospective critique Pauline Kael was closer to the truth when she wrote that her "tight, dry performance was probably a mistake."

The Little Foxes swept nine Academy Award nominations, more than any Goldwyn picture up to that time but two less than that year's Sergeant York and one less than How Green Was My Valley. Wyler would be shut out again, along with his picture. The Little Foxes didn't win a single Oscar. Yet seen today, more than half a century later, it has far more impact than either How Green Was My Valley (five Oscars) or Sergeant York (two Oscars). Neither of those can hold a candle to it on any artistic level, whatever the flaws in Davis's performance.

Wyler clowns with Audrey Hepburn during the filming of *Roman Holiday* in Rome, summer of 1952. She won the Oscar for Best Actress.
(COURTESY THE WYLER FAMILY)

From left, Wyler plays the first assistant director; Elaine Forest and Fred Gilman star; and Vin Moore plays the director in *Daze of The West*, Wyler's last two-reel silent, made in 1926.
(UNIVERSAL PICTURES. COURTESY THE WYLER FAMILY.)

Wyler gives Olivia de Havilland some hints on needlepoint in *The Heiress,* 1949.
She won the Oscar for Best Actress.

Walter Huston, starring as Samuel Dodsworth, falls in love with Mary Astor's Edith Cortwright in *Dodsworth*, 1936. The role was also Huston's greatest triumph on Broadway.

Dana Andrews and Teresa Wright in *The Best Years of Our Lives*, 1946. Wyler considered her the most accomplished young actress he worked with.

Bette Davis and Henry Fonda in the pivotal Olympus Ball sequence in *Jezebel*, 1938. Wyler was allotted a half day to shoot what was written as a sketchy scene. He spent five days on it, reinventing everything but the dialogue. Davis won the Oscar for Best Actress.

Wyler directing Laurence Olivier and Merle Oberon in *Wuthering Heights,* 1939. The two stars despised each other.
(SAMUEL GOLDWYN PRODUCTION. COURTESY THE WYLER FAMILY.)

Bette Davis as the adulteress who kills her lover in *The Letter,* 1940. Moonlight seen through louvered blinds suggests prison stripes, an emblem of her guilt.
(WARNER BROS. COURTESY THE WYLER FAMILY.)

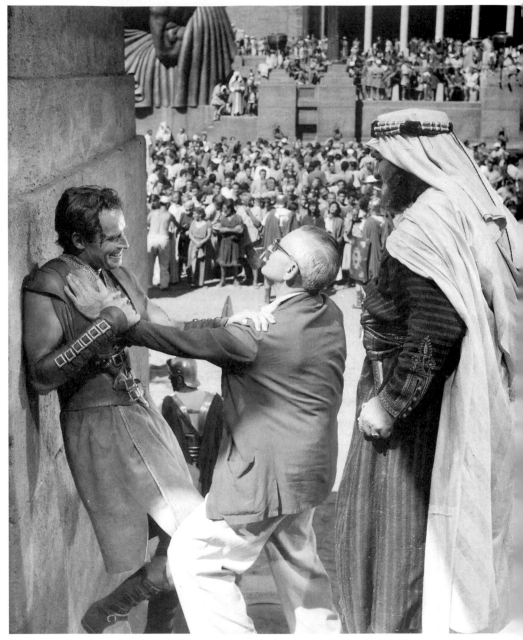

Wyler directs Charlton Heston as Hugh Griffith looks on during the filming of *Ben-Hur*
in Rome in the summer of 1958. Heston, Griffith, and Wyler all won Oscars.
The picture won eleven Oscars, still a Hollywood record.

From left, Stephen Boyd (Messala) and Charlton Heston (Ben-Hur)
drove their own chariots in the spectacular race at the Circus Maximus.

(METRO-GOLDWYN-MAYER. COURTESY THE WYLER FAMILY.)

Gregory Peck *(left)* as a reporter and Eddie Albert as his freelance photographer in *Roman Holiday,* 1953. Peck was the star. Audrey Hepburn stole the picture.
(PARAMOUNT PICTURES. COURTESY THE WYLER FAMILY.)

Wyler with Bette Davis *(right)* and Teresa Wright on the set of *The Little Foxes* during the summer of 1941. Lillian Hellman wrote the play and the movie. She said the movie turned out better than the play because of Wyler's direction.
(SAMUEL GOLDWYN PRODUCTION. COURTESY THE WYLER FAMILY.)

Wyler with his pal Paul Kohner *(left)*, circa 1926. Kohner became a top Universal executive and later the dean of Hollywood agents.

From left, Wyler with Lillian Hellman, Talli Wyler and an unidentified friend during the 1960s. Wyler and Hellman had what they called a lifelong platonic love affair.

Wyler with *(from left)* Samantha Eggar, Terence Stamp and Federico Fellini on the set of *The Collector*, 1964. Stamp says Wyler and Fellini, who later cast him in the title role of *Toby Dammit*, were his two best directors. (UNITED PRESS. COURTESY THE WYLER FAMILY.)

Wyler discusses a camera setup with cinematographer Gregg Toland on *The Little Foxes*, 1941. (COURTESY THE WYLER FAMILY.)

Wyler on his seventy-fifth birthday with Barbra Streisand.
She considered him a father figure. (COURTESY THE WYLER FAMILY.)

Instant pals Wyler and John Huston
(*right*) pose as Mutt-and-Jeff
lifeguards in Long Beach, California,
circa 1931.

(COURTESY THE WYLER FAMILY.)

Hollywood's odd couple, Wyler and producer Samuel Goldwyn, on the set of *Dead End* in the spring of 1937. They made eight pictures together.

(COURTESY THE WYLER FAMILY.)

Wyler got a kick out of showing virtuoso Jascha Heifetz *(beneath camera)* how to play his violin in the summer of 1938.

(COURTESY THE WYLER FAMILY.)

Wyler *(center)*, with the B-17 crew of the *Memphis Belle,* gazes at the perky pinup on the bomber's nose in the spring of 1943. He memorialized the crew in a live-action aerial combat documentary, *The Memphis Belle,* 1944.

Wyler checks footage during post-production on *The Big Country* in 1958 with his longtime editor, Robert Swink, who reshot the final scene at Wyler's request.

Billy Wilder presented
Wyler with an Oscar for
The Best Years of Our Lives at
the Academy Award
ceremonies in March 1947.
Wilder called *Best Years* the
best-directed picture he'd
ever seen.
(COURTESY THE
WYLER FAMILY.)

Wyler and his two
youngest children,
Melanie, five, and
David, three, in 1955.
(COURTESY
THE WYLER FAMILY.)

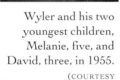

Wyler with Margaret Sullavan,
his first wife, in the Piazza San
Marco, Venice, on their
European honeymoon, 1935.
(COURTESY THE WYLER FAMILY.)

Willy, three (*right*), and brother
Robert, five, in Mulhouse, 1905.
(COURTESY THE WYLER FAMILY.)

Wyler's daughter,
Catherine, was born in
1939, the first of five
children, and was named
after the heroine of
Wuthering Heights, which
had recently opened.
(COURTESY THE WYLER FAMILY.)

Wyler married Margaret
Tallichet a few weeks after
they met in 1938. They drove
to Walter Huston's home in the
San Bernardino Mountains for
a secret ceremony, with John
Huston and a few other friends
present. This is their wedding
picture. The marriage, one of
Hollywood's happiest, lasted
until Wyler's death in 1981.
(COURTESY THE WYLER FAMILY.)

After the death of their
son Billy, the Wylers
put on a brave front in
Sun Valley, Idaho,
Christmas 1949.
From left, Willy,
daughter Judy, seven,
Robert Parrish, Talli,
Kathleen Parrish and
Catherine, ten.
(COURTESY THE
WYLER FAMILY.)

Talli was five months pregnant when
she got on skis for the first time,
mainly to have this picture taken
with Willy in Sun Valley, Idaho,
March 1939.
(COURTESY THE WYLER FAMILY.)

Wyler in his upstairs
study on Summit Drive,
June 1979, with his many
awards, including three
Oscars, the Irving G.
Thalberg Award, the
D.W. Griffith Award, the
Palme d'Or, his war
medals, a dozen Oscar
nominations for directing
and three for producing.
(COURTESY STEVE BANKS
© 1995.)

23

VELVET GLOVE

W HEN FILMING OF *MRS. MINIVER*
began November 11, 1941, a small box for the director arrived on the
MGM set. Inside was a pair of black velvet gloves, a gift from his leading lady. The card read: "For the iron hand of William Wyler."

Greer Garson had a sense of humor.

"I shopped and shopped for those gloves," she said, "and when I
found them I sent them to him in a lovely box with lots of ribbons. He
wore them with great panache on the first day of shooting. But they
were soon put aside, both figuratively and actually."

Teresa Wright, borrowed from Goldwyn for a supporting role in the
picture, told the columnist Sheilah Graham: "If you handle Mr. Wyler
right you can put across your ideas. I wish you could have seen how
Greer Garson got her way with him. She'd be very sweet and charming
and say, 'Don't you think, Willy, we ought to do it this way!' That's the
way to handle him."

Louis B. Mayer wasn't quite as deft. The MGM chief called Wyler
on the carpet a couple of weeks into production. Why, he wanted to
know, was Wyler departing from the script and injecting so much anti-
German sentiment? He had just heard about a sequence in which a

young, wounded Luftwaffe pilot—shot down over a London suburb and found by Mrs. Miniver in her backyard garden—was being remade into a self-righteous, fiendish killer. To have him spout Hitler's master race slogans was unacceptable, Mayer told him.

"Mr. Mayer," Wyler said, "you know what's going on, don't you?"

"Look," said Mayer, cutting him off, "maybe you don't understand. We're not at war with anybody. We don't hate anybody. This picture shows [the British] having a hard time, and it's very sympathetic towards them—but it's not directed against the Germans."

"Mr. Mayer, if I had several Germans in the picture, I wouldn't mind having one who was a decent young fellow. But I've only got one German. And if I make this picture, this one German is going to be a typical little Nazi son-of-a-bitch. He's not going to be a friendly little pilot but one of Goering's monsters."

"Look, this is a big corporation," Mayer retorted. "I'm responsible to my stockholders. We have theaters all over the world, a couple in Berlin. This is not a hate picture. We don't hate anybody. We're not at war."

"You love the Germans?" Wyler asked.

Mayer gave him a hard stare. "Well, we'll look at the scene when it's finished. Just remember what I told you."

In fact, the loss of overseas markets, particularly in Germany, was not Mayer's primary concern. That might have been true five years earlier when official German policy against importing American films began to take hold. By 1936 the German Ministry of Propaganda had excluded most run-of-the-mill Hollywood features from the Third Reich. Moreover, in the summer of 1940, three days before all American films were banned outright, MGM closed its Berlin office and effectively ceased its German operations.

What really worried Mayer was a threat that originated much closer to home, in Washington, D.C. For nearly three weeks in September 1941 a Senate subcommittee had held hearings to investigate the purported link between anti-Nazi propaganda in Hollywood films and monopolistic practices by the major studios. Spurred by a pair of rabidly isolationist senators, Gerald P. Nye of North Dakota and Bennett Champ Clark of Missouri, the hearings had attacked the studio heads as a Jewish conspiracy trying to draw the United States into a European war allegedly to protect their British interests. Nye, who was a darling of the Fascist-friendly America First Committee, set the bigoted tone of the hearings. But he had plenty of support from his Senate colleagues, who vented their own prejudices in a display of anti-Semitism and Anglophobia so outrageous that it prompted a general outcry in the press.

World events resolved Wyler's argument with Mayer just days after they clashed.

December 7, 1941, was a beautiful Sunday morning. John Huston had come over to Wyler's house to play tennis. That afternoon they were to meet with director Anatole Litvak to discuss a planned trip to China.

Huston's first film as a director, *The Maltese Falcon*, had been released in October and was a big hit. He was midway through making *In This Our Life*. Litvak's *Blues in the Night* was to be released later that week.

"Willy and I wanted to get out of Hollywood for awhile," Huston said. "We wanted to see a bit of the outer world. I'd never been to the Far East, nor had Willy or Tola. I suggested it would be great to go on a proper trip to China. Willy thought it was a wonderful idea and that we should do it."

Halfway through their tennis game, the telephone rang. Talli Wyler picked up the phone. It was Paul Kohner, with news that would alter their lives and the lives of millions. The Japanese had bombed Pearl Harbor. Talli rushed out to the tennis court, stopping the game instantly with the news.

"We all three jumped into the car," she recalled. "We drove to the beach to Tola's house in Malibu. Suddenly there was enormous talk about how they could get into the service."

The talk was not idle chatter. On December 18, Wyler wrote Lillian Hellman: "I've enlisted in the Army Signal Corps, and I am anxiously awaiting confirmation." Wyler was thirty-nine. Talli was four months pregnant with their second child. Both conditions would have exempted him from the draft.

The morning after the attack on Pearl Harbor, Mayer called Wyler into his office. "I've been thinking about that scene," he said. "You may be right. You do it the way you want, that's fine with me."

MGM PRODUCER SIDNEY FRANKLIN HAD COURTED WYLER FOR the picture even before *The Little Foxes* finished post-production. Franklin, with a reputation for elegance and taste, had had a major career as a director dating back to the early twenties. A favorite of Irving Thalberg, he became a producer after Thalberg's death.

Franklin insisted on personally reading the script aloud to Wyler. It was based on Jan Struther's stories, published in the London *Times*, of a middle-class suburban London family seen before and after the dark days of the blitz and the retreat from Dunkirk. Wyler's personal ties, both his European and his Jewish heritage, tugged strongly for the Allied cause. He wanted America to enter the war against Hitler. He knew from the beginning that he wanted to make *Mrs. Miniver* into a strong piece of pro-British propaganda.

"I was a warmonger," Wyler said flatly. "I was concerned about Americans being isolationists. *Mrs. Miniver* obviously was a propaganda film."

Before Franklin was halfway through reading the script, Wyler told him he would make the movie. "I jumped at the chance," he recalled.

Greer Garson, on contract with MGM, got the title role after Norma Shearer turned it down. Garson did not want it at first. After all, Mrs. Miniver was supposed to be in her forties and the mother of three children, including a son in college at Oxford. Garson, who had just turned thirty-three, felt rather sensitive about playing older.

"I couldn't possibly have a nineteen-year-old son," she told Wyler when he offered her the role. "How do I make up to look like that?"

"Don't do anything different," Wyler said, recalling his experience with Davis's makeup in his last picture.

He couldn't have said anything worse to an obviously beautiful actress whose vanity was showing. But Garson liked Wyler instinctively, despite his embarrassing remark, and he played on her patriotic obligation to take the role. The Irish-born Garson was a British subject, after all.

"Most of my family and friends were in the services," she recalled, "and those who were not were suffering from the blitz back in London. I had wanted to break my contract and go back for volunteer work."

The pro-British sentiment of *Mrs. Miniver* depended for its appeal on an idealized portrait of domestic bliss and suburban life with which Americans could identify. As the picture opens, Mrs. Miniver has just indulged her weakness for an expensive hat and wonders if she is doing the right thing. She feels mildly guilty about the price. This is a woman who likes to shop, although with an endearing twinge of conscience. Mr. Miniver is a prosperous architect, played by Walter Pidgeon. He has just made his own purchase, somewhat more extravagant than his wife's: a new sports car. Except for their slight British accents and manners, the Minivers could pass for transatlantic Scarsdale suburbanites. They are a model family, exemplars of upper-middle-class aspirations.

The screenplay also developed a bit of light satire on British class conflict. The Miniver son, Vin, comes down from Oxford with newly learned ideas, not to be taken seriously, about the social injustice of the class system. The local aristocrat, Lady Beldon, holds an annual flower competition and always wins for her rose. But she is challenged this time by the local stationmaster, a commoner whose more beautiful rose has been named, not incidentally, for Mrs. Miniver.

With the advent of war, domestic bliss is shattered and the Minivers prove their mettle. Vin joins the Royal Air Force and marries Lady Beldon's granddaughter Carol. Mr. Miniver in his motor launch joins a motley flotilla of civilian boats and crosses the Channel to help evacuate the retreating British Army from the beaches of Dunkirk. Mrs. Miniver not only rounds up the downed Luftwaffe pilot in her garden but braves the blitz in a cramped bomb shelter with her husband, two children and their cat. For bedtime stories, the family reads from *Alice in Wonderland*. Indeed, the picture strikes one sentimental note after another. But it also has a fair amount of incidental humor spontaneously created on the set, a clever plot twist that illustrates the paradoxical tragedies of war and an elegiac final scene imbued with eloquence about the bravery of the English and the value of freedom.

EACH OF THOSE ELEMENTS CONTRIBUTED TO THE SUCCESS OF *Mrs. Miniver,* which became not just the top-grossing film of 1942 but the biggest box-office hit in a decade, second only to *Gone With the Wind*. Two weeks before the picture opened at New York's Radio City Music Hall in May 1942, Wyler received a cable from David Selznick: DEAR MAD WILLIE I SAW MRS. MINIVER LAST NIGHT IT IS ABSOLUTELY WONDERFUL YOU REPEATEDLY AMAZE ME WITH THE DEMONSTRATIONS OF YOUR TALENT AND I ASK YOU TO BELIEVE THAT IT IS WITH GENUINE PLEASURE THAT I SALUTE THIS LATEST AND GREATEST EXAMPLE OF YOUR WORK.

Mayer boasted that Winston Churchill had written him a letter calling the picture an indispensable part of the war effort. It was, in Churchill's words, "propaganda worth a hundred battleships." Franklin Delano Roosevelt, also impressed after a private White House screening, asked MGM to distribute *Mrs. Miniver* across the country immediately instead of relying on its usual marketing plan for a limited first-run release.

Perhaps more astonishing, Roosevelt was so taken with the vicar's sermon, delivered from the pulpit of a bombed-out church in the picture's final scene, that he asked to have the text broadcast over the Voice of America in Europe, translated into several languages and air-dropped in millions of printed leaflets over German-occupied territory.

Wyler believed in the vicar's words with his whole being. In a hasty rewrite of the script he and Henry Wilcoxon, the actor who played the vicar, had put the text together the night before shooting the final scene. "Willy felt it needed a quintessential statement and a climactic speech from the vicar," Greer Garson recounted years later. "He and one or two others batted it out." Wyler recalled that he "hardened the speech," making it a more principled declaration and giving it both a more contemplative and more ringing tone. The vicar tells his congregation to turn its grief for victims of the blitz into inspiration for the coming test of national wills:

> We, in this quiet corner of England, have suffered the loss of friends very dear to us—some close to this church. . . . The homes of many of us have been destroyed and the lives of young and old have been taken. There is scarcely a household that hasn't been struck to the heart.
> And why? Surely you must have asked yourselves this question. Why, in all conscience, should these be the ones to suffer? Children, old people, a young girl at the height of her loveliness. Why these? Are these our soldiers? Are these our fighters? Why should they be sacrificed?
> I shall tell you why.
> Because this is not only a war of soldiers in uniform, it is a war of the people—of all the people—and it must be fought, not only on the battlefield, but in the cities and in the villages, in the factories and on the farms, in the home and in the heart of every man, woman and child who loves freedom!
> Well, we have buried our dead but we shall not forget them. Instead, they will inspire us with an unbreakable determination to free ourselves and those who come after us from the tyranny and terror that threatens to strike us down! Fight it, then! Fight it with all that is in us! And may God defend the right.

Listening to Wilcoxon deliver the sermon on the first take, Greer Garson was so moved that tears formed in her eyes. Wyler noticed them, of course.

"Willy came over to me and said, 'The tears in the eyes. That was very good. But you let them spill over just a second too soon. Now, if you can get the tears again, I want you to hold them there. And *then* I want you to let that tear run down your cheek.'"

Garson recalled that she nearly "burst into hysterical laughter" at the impossibility of Wyler's demand. But discipline prevailed.

"I got myself back into Mrs. Miniver's skin and into the moment," she said, "and I could feel the tears stinging my eyes. The camera moved in and, wonder of wonders, the tear obligingly and obediently rode out and down my cheek."

Wyler was delighted. He sent a bottle of champagne to Garson's dressing room.

MORE THAN ONE CRITIC MADE THE POINT THAT WYLER HAD done the impossible: He had shot a war movie without a single battle scene. *Mrs. Miniver* was hailed as "a study in reaction, not action." Its personalization of the issue made it powerful.

The notion of a "people's war" had not originated with the vicar's speech, of course. The phrase itself was borrowed. As Edward R. Murrow had remarked in one of his famous radio broadcasts from London during the blitz, "The politicians who called this a 'people's war' were right, probably more right than they knew at the time." Naturally, *Mrs. Miniver* drew furious opposition from the America Firsters.

In a radio interview for the British Broadcasting Company after the picture's release in England, Wyler commented on his motive for mixing propaganda and entertainment: "The finest sermon ever preached on the screen—or off it—never converted an empty row of seats." He told the syndicated Hollywood columinst Hedda Hopper: "People say we should be making escapist pictures today. I say, 'Why?' This is a hell of a time to escape from reality. We're in an all-out war—a people's war— it's the time to face it. Let's make propaganda pictures, but make them good. Pictures go in trends. *Mrs. Miniver* has had the success I wanted for it, but, more important, it will make producers realize that a propaganda picture doesn't have to be filled with blood and brutality."

Wyler always took a modest pride in the worldwide popularity of *Mrs. Miniver.* Besides grossing more than six million dollars domestically, it broke foreign box-office records everywhere from Cairo to Trinidad to Buenos Aires. He was far more pleased, however, that the picture had rallied opinion to a cause he fervently believed in. But once he went into the Army Air Force and saw the war firsthand, he felt somewhat embarrassed that *Mrs. Miniver* had offered the public a sugarcoated myth. With its prettified hardships and saccharine nobility, the picture "only scratched the surface of war," he said. "I don't mean that it was wrong. It was incomplete."

24

HE DIDN'T WANT TO MISS THE WAR

L IKE THE REST OF THE COUNTRY
in the aftermath of Pearl Harbor, Hollywood went to war with a burst
of patriotism and pride. The film industry had already helped popular-
ize the Lend-Lease Act, which enabled Roosevelt to supply Great
Britain with planes, tanks and other basic weapons to defend itself
against Germany. Stars toured the country to raise millions of dollars in
war bond drives. A lock of Veronica Lake's hair, for example, brought
two hundred thousand dollars at auction. Theaters held "bond pre-
mieres." By the end of 1942 some twenty-five thousand civilians from
the movie industry joined the service. They included Jimmy Stewart
and Clark Gable, Frank Capra, John Ford and Darryl Zanuck. As
early as January 1942, Hollywood took its first stunning casualty when
Carole Lombard was killed in a plane crash on her way home from an
Indianapolis bond rally.

Wyler's fervor to enlist was apparent to his pregnant wife. "He just
didn't want to miss the war," Talli said. "He couldn't stand the thought
of sitting on the sidelines." It had taken him until early February to finish shooting *Mrs. Miniver*. During all that time he had heard nothing
about his application to join the Army Signal Corps. The day after he

finished the picture, he wired Lieutenant Colonel Richard T. Schlosberg, head of the Army's Photographic Division, who had initially recruited him: WILL ARRIVE IN WASHINGTON REGARDING MY STATUS AND WHAT ACTION HAS BEEN TAKEN. He would be flying in from California with Zanuck, the head of Twentieth Century–Fox. On leave from the studio, Zanuck had a lieutenant colonel's commission and was assigned to supervise the production of training films.

But no amount of pressure seemed to work. When Wyler got to Washington, he was simply put on hold. What he didn't know was that Schlosberg disliked Zanuck and, for that matter, all the star directors he'd been ordered to recruit. Capra, who'd received a major's commission at the end of January, reported to Schlosberg for duty a few days before Wyler's arrival. "One Darryl Zanuck around here is enough," Schlosberg told Capra. "You Hollywood guys just won't fit in with the Army way of producing films." And, to his dismay, Capra found himself detached from the Photographic Division and assigned to Special Services, a newly created branch where he would supervise films designed to boost military morale. In Capra's view, Schlosberg "had the charm of a bag of cement . . . and wasn't about to help any outsiders muscle in on him."

Impatient with the runaround, Wyler took a different tack. That winter he and Lillian Hellman had discussed making a documentary about the Soviet Union, which was battling for survival against the Nazi invasion. The idea had been instigated by President Roosevelt through his intimate friend and adviser Harry Hopkins. Goldwyn volunteered to produce the documentary for commercial release. Now Wyler met with Hellman, who came down to Washington from New York, and the two of them arranged to see Soviet ambassador Maxim Litvinov. A friend of Hellman's, Litvinov heard them out but regarded their proposal—to fly to the Soviet Union and make a picture in the midst of the fighting—as impossible. Nevertheless, he told them he would take up the project with the foreign minister, Vyacheslav Molotov.

The next afternoon, Litvinov telephoned Hellman. Molotov had arrived in Washington, and to Litvinov's surprise the foreign minister thought the movie "a fine idea." The Russian government would supply a bomber, camera crew, and whatever else they needed.

Thrilled by the news—"This was unheard of, Americans allowed in up to the front for a documentary," Hellman remembered—she phoned Goldwyn, who had come east. Wyler met with Hopkins. The writer and director flew to New York to confer with Goldwyn at the Waldorf. The meeting began well. "We got, or thought we got, Goldwyn to say he'd put up the money," Hellman recalled. She, Wyler and cinematographer Gregg Toland would fly to the Soviet Union to scout locations and develop material. The script for what they expected to be a full-length picture had yet to be written.

Goldwyn agreed with their ideas, not least because he expected his financial risk to be minimal. He knew "a large part of the cost . . . would be supplied by the Russsians," Hellman said. Then Wyler mentioned salary. He wanted Goldwyn to send his to Talli in weekly installments while he was gone. Goldwyn's mood darkened. Hellman tried to make a joke. She said she'd take hers in two installments, half when photography began and half on her return home—"even if I come back in a coffin."

Goldwyn wasn't amused. He turned his resentful glare not on Hellman but on Wyler. "You're taking salary for this? For a patriotic mission?"

Hellman was startled. "What? What are you saying?"

"You and Willy are taking salary for this?"

"Excuse me?" she said. "I'm a little puzzled. Aren't you releasing the picture for money?"

"What does that got to do with it?" Goldwyn replied. "You say you love Russia. You say you are radicals. So you say."

"I don't know what you mean," Wyler retorted. "Who is radical and who says they love Russia? What's that got to do with anything?"

"You say you love America; you are patriots, you tell everybody. Now it turns out you want *money* from me, from *me*. [I'm] sacrificing a fortune for my government because *I* love my country."

"Are you really suggesting that we take no salary?" Wyler asked. He was incredulous. "You take the profits, and that makes you a patriot and us hypocrites?"

Goldwyn stood up.

Wyler told him, "You're not putting up a nickel. . . . The Russians, as a matter of fact, are giving you most of a free ride."

"You know what's the matter with you, Sam?" said Hellman. "You think you're a country. You've got rivers and mountains. We're not doing it for the country, we're doing it for Sam Goldwyn. I guess we get paid or we don't go."

"Well, then, don't go," Goldwyn replied.

Wyler laughed. Hellman called the debate ridiculous. The conference came to an end. The next morning her phone rang. It was Goldwyn. "I thought it over," he said, "and I guess you're right."

Hellman believed he "never intended not to pay us, he only hoped we'd reduce our usual fee." But frayed relations stalled the project, and no decisions were made.

By mid-April, when Wyler heard from a Schlosberg aide that there was "no vacancy in the Signal Corps to which you could be assigned," he took up an offer from Capra.

Capra's transfer out of the Signal Corps to the Information Division of Special Services actually hadn't been arranged by Schlosberg, as he initially thought, but by higher-ups. General George Marshall, the army chief of staff, wanted Capra to produce military films to train recruits and educate the civilian population. It was Brigadier General Frederick H. Osborn, a friend of Roosevelt working directly under Marshall, who had sent Schlosberg to Hollywood to recruit top directors. And it was Osborn who had arranged Capra's transfer to Special Services.

Capra had invited Wyler to make a picture in the "Why We Fight" series he was planning. Wyler had chosen *The Negro Soldier* and asked Hellman to write the script. In early April Capra wired him: WHEN CAN YOU LEAVE FOR PICTURE PROJECT WE DISCUSSED? HELLMAN AGREEABLE. Wyler finished dubbing and scoring *Mrs. Miniver* for its final preview and returned to Washington at the end of April ready to work. Capra told him he would be attached to Special Services as a civilian "expert consultant." His salary would be ten dollars a day. Meanwhile, Hellman wired Wyler that she had asked Goldwyn to finance *The Negro Soldier.* GOLDWYN WILLING. DELIGHTED BECAUSE I THINK WE CAN DO A REALLY IMPORTANT SHORT PICTURE. She also asked Paul Robeson, then at the peak of his fame, to be in it. But by mid-May her plans fell through, and Wyler prepared to leave for Kansas City and the South with two other writers: Carlton Moss and Marc Connelly. Eager as he was to get started, however, Wyler now had to wait for his official travel orders. That, Capra told him, could take weeks. So he headed home to be with Talli for the birth of their second daughter, Judy, on May 21. Four days later his orders came: first stop Kansas City, followed by Fort Riley, New Orleans, Alexandria, Camp Claiborne, Montgomery and Tuskegee, Fort Benning and Fort Bragg.

Despite losing Hellman from the project, Wyler liked the idea of working with Connelly and Moss. Connelly, best known for his 1930 Pulitzer Prize-winning play *The Green Pastures,* was a veteran writer who had collaborated with George S. Kaufman on a string of Broadway hits during the twenties. Moss, a black writer-actor, had worked with Orson Welles and John Houseman for the Federal Theater in Harlem.

But from the moment Wyler reached New Orleans, he was put off by the South. "In those days everything was strictly segregated," Wyler said. "Mr. Moss couldn't ride in the same compartment as us on the train. He couldn't go into the same hotel with us." Working their way north through Georgia, they visited a black Army Air Force squadron. "We talked to the colonel in charge," Wyler said. "He was the only white. I asked, 'Do you have any problems around here?' He said, 'Well, a little bit.' He said the local population was unhappy about seeing black boys fly airplanes. They felt it was 'very uppity.' He told me some fanatic would get on the phone one day and call the local KKK, and they'd all come charging in." Wyler got the sinking feeling that the Army would not like seeing any of that put on the record, certainly not in a film to boost morale. Also, at Tuskegee Institute, the famous black university, its most eminent scientist, George Washington Carver, declined to meet with him. "He received Mr. Connelly, not me," Wyler recalled. Back in Washington a week later, he decided to bail out. "The timing just wasn't right," Talli said. "His heart was really for getting into the service."

By June, Wyler found his opportunity in a chance meeting with Sy Bartlett, a former Columbia screenwriter. It was Bartlett who had accompanied Schlosberg on his Hollywood recruiting mission back in December. Now no longer in Schlosberg's Signal Corps unit, Bartlett was a staff aide to Major General Carl A. Spaatz, one of the Army Air Force's top commanders. "Everybody was going overseas," Wyler said. "And that of course is what I wanted." Bartlett asked him to a cocktail party being held the next day at Spaatz's home to celebrate the general's departure for the European Theater. Spaatz had been ordered to organize the Eighth Air Force for combat. It was to be based in Great Britain. Four months earlier—in February 1942—it had six officers and no planes. By December 1943, Spaatz would have under his command a hundred eighty-five thousand men and four thousand planes. "Sy introduced me to the general as a Hollywood director," Wyler said.

Mrs. Miniver had just been released at New York's Radio City Music Hall, where crowds were lining up to see it, and he was being hailed as Hollywood's man of the moment. Only days before, the New York critics were unanimous in their praise. "Perhaps it's too soon to call this one of the greatest motion pictures ever made," Bosley Crowther raved in the *Times*. "But certainly it is the finest film yet made about the present war." The *Herald-Tribune*'s Howard Barnes told readers: "There has been nothing to touch the understated eloquence of this magnificent dramatization of the Battle of Britain." Archer Winsten in the *Post* called it the year's best picture. Wyler didn't waste his introduction or his extravagant notices.

"General," he said, "I don't know where you're going and I don't know what for, but whatever you're going to do I think it should be recorded on film."

Spaatz turned to his chief of staff, Brigadier General Claude E. Duncan, who was standing at his elbow.

"Take care of him."

Duncan told Wyler to come to his office at Bolling Field. When he got there, the paperwork for his induction had been completed except for two things.

"Rank?" asked Duncan

Wyler didn't know what to say. Duncan tried to be helpful.

"Would you like to be a major?"

Wyler thought he was joking. "Yes, sure."

"Okay, Major," Duncan said.

Wyler was ushered down the hall for a physical. At five feet seven and a hundred sixty-five pounds, he was over the recommended weight. He also had too many false teeth. The conditions were waived.

"An hour later, I was a major," Wyler recounted. "No training, nothing. I was simply sent someplace to buy a uniform. The next thing, I put on this uniform. It didn't fit at all. I walked down the street. I've got a cigarette and a briefcase. And here comes a general. I don't know what to do. Swallow the cigarette? Throw away the briefcase? I threw away the cigarette. How do you salute? I did something. The general laughed like hell."

25

⎯⎯〜〜〜⎯⎯

IT COULD BRING YOU BACK ALIVE

WYLER FLEW BACK TO LOS AN-
geles with orders to recruit a crew and round up camera equipment. He
didn't have a clue about military operations, proper channels or what it
took to motivate the army's bureaucratic chain-of-command. All he had
was zeal and Hollywood contacts. First he planned to attach Irwin
Shaw to the unit as his writer. But Shaw, a screenwriter who had made
his mark in New York as a wunderkind playwright with a one-act, antiwar drama *Bury the Dead*, was ruled ineligible for an officer's commission
because of his A-1 draft status. Wyler pressed to get him anyway.

Shaw turned him down. AFTER SOBER REFLECTION, he cabled Wyler,
IVE DECIDED THAT GOING WITH YOU AS A PRIVATE WOULD MEAN A LONG
SUCCESSION OF FRUSTRATIONS MILITARY ARTISTIC ECONOMIC AND SOCIAL.
AND THE WAR EFFORT WOULD SUFFER IN CONSEQUENCE. SO IM GOING INTO
THE REGULAR ARMY THIS MORNING AT 645. I FEEL IVE WAITED TOO LONG AS
IT IS.

Ironically, the Army drafted Shaw and shipped him to the Signal
Corps picture unit at the converted Paramount studios in Queens, New
York.

With Shaw eliminated, Wyler chose Jerome Chodorov, a reporter-turned-screenwriter-playwright who already was a lieutenant in the Army's Directorate of Photography. For one of his two cameramen, Wyler enlisted William Clothier, an experienced aerial photographer who had worked on *Wings* back in the twenties. Clothier received a captain's commission and would make his reputation as a cinematographer more than a decade after the war working for John Ford, Raoul Walsh and Sam Peckinpah. The second cameraman, Captain William Skall, was a longtime journeyman recommended by the Army. An RKO sound man, Harold Tannenbaum, also joined the film unit at Wyler's request. Tannenbaum had served in the Navy during the First World War. He was the oldest man in the unit—five years older than Wyler—and he would die ten months later on a bombing mission.

Wyler returned to Washington, knowing he would soon be getting orders to go overseas. But his frustration mounted over lack of cooperation from the movie industry. "I have seldom been so busy or worked so hard and accomplished so little," he wrote Talli in mid-July. "We tried to enlist the help of MGM—it's shameful how we got *no* cooperation—nothing but evasion when it came to giving up some equipment they really could spare. They all talk big, but when it comes to doing something the tone changes. . . . Sometimes I feel I should just get on a ship and go—I'm offered a seat two or three times a week, and it's awfully hard to refuse it. But there's no sense in my going without proper equipment. . . ."

Wyler looked into an experimental combat camera being built by an independent engineer living in Hollywood. "Better than any hand camera so far made," he noted in a memo. The Army didn't take his recommendation. Wyler left for England equipped with nothing more than an ordinary, hand-held, sixteen-millimeter camera. On August 6, he boarded a PBY in New York and arrived two nights later at Eighth Army Air Force headquarters near London. Clothier, Skall and Tannenbaum were still in the States, trying to acquire cameras for later shipment by sea. Despite his frustration, Wyler hadn't lost his sense of humor. The night he arrived he mailed a postcard to Talli:

> *And here is the young man from Limerick —*
> *Who thought he had been thru thin & thick —*
> *Until he went to war*
> *For good reasons or*
> *Such reasons he thought might give him a kick.*

When Wyler reached England, the first American B-17 bomber squadrons had just begun flying combat missions across the Channel. The Eighth Air Force's first base, at Polebrook, began operating in July with thirty-five planes. Other air bases were soon established in the countryside. At first there were so few Yanks in London, Wyler recalled years later, that "kids would stop on the street and say, 'Look! An American!' We were a sensation." By October that had changed. As fresh arrivals poured in, an already acute housing shortage worsened. "The trouble with London at the moment is too damn many Americans," Wyler wrote Talli. "The British call it 'the invasion.' Sometimes you have to apologize for being here."

He considered getting a flat but, finding that difficult, settled on a hotel room at Claridge's. Alexander Korda was living there, as were other top British film executives. Korda, the most important of them, went out of his way to make Wyler feel welcome. "A few people I know have put themselves out to be nice to me," he wrote. The director Carol Reed, who'd been a friend of his brother Robert, took Wyler around London and gave him a glimpse of life behind the polite English facade. "Food at homes is not so hot. Dinner invitations are few and far between. Also, whiskey is at a premium. So being invited just for a drink is already quite a gesture."

Apart from its social convenience, Claridge's had another advantage. It was centrally located, only a short walk from General Spaatz's headquarters and Wyler's office at 33 Davies Street. Although the Blitz was now a memory, London still lived with wailing air-raid sirens and blackouts at night. "The blackout is something I thought I could never get used to," he explained to Talli. "It's blacker than black. But after a few moonlit nights, you discover a hidden beauty in a large city that I had not seen. You hear people, autos—you know just where the curb is, and the door—and you develop a sense that you didn't seem to possess before."

Though Wyler had to spend much time early on at Bomber Command headquarters in the city, he soon began touring the newly built air bases to observe bombing missions being prepared and launched and made three visits to bases in Ireland. All this travel qualified him for a car and driver, plus a truck and command car for his crew. "People here say the sign of a big shot is when he has an army car assigned to him," he joked. But Talli knew that he felt like a small cog in an enormous machine.

Wyler's orders were to produce films about the Eighth Air Force "for public morale and education" and "training and orientation" and to record "events of historic value." He drew up a list of five projects by early September. Two contained key elements of what later became *The Memphis Belle*, the most widely seen and acclaimed Air Force documentary of the war. He called one project *Nine Lives*, the story of a bombing mission and the crew of a single bomber. "This will, in some way, resemble the British film *Target for Tonight*," he noted, "but will differ by its emphasis on *American* crews, *daylight* bombings and American characteristics and methods." The other he called *Phyllis Was a Fortress*, to be based on the experiences of a B-17 crew in a bomber named *Phyllis* during a single combat mission over occupied France.

The three other projects held less interest for Wyler, but he dutifully proposed them as part of his unit's mandate: *Ferry Command*, a short documentary to be kept classified until the war's end about transatlantic bomber deliveries; *The First Americans*, a ceremonial short about members of the Eagle Squadron who were the first American pilots in the war; and *R.A.F.–A.A.F.*, an ambitious documentary that would show how well the British and American air forces were cooperating. The last he took rather seriously, notwithstanding its public relations agenda, trying at various times to enlist Thornton Wilder, Ring Lardner, Jr. and the British playwright Terrence Rattigan as scriptwriters.

During the summer months, air raids across the English Channel on enemy targets usually consisted of thirty to forty B-17 bombers at a time, rarely more than sixty or seventy. But by the fall, those numbers began to climb, The Boeing-made bombers rolled off assembly lines in Seattle at an increasingly rapid pace. Men and matériel embarked for Europe in transport ships that stretched like a pipeline across the Atlantic. And by late 1943, the Eighth Air Force could mass hundreds of B-17s, sometimes more than five hundred on a given day, in awesome raids with multiple targets. On one raid in 1944, with twelve hundred and ninety-one planes, lead bombers were crossing into Germany three hundred miles away as tail bombers were still forming up over England.

Of all the heavy bombers that saw action during the Second World War, none earned as much admiration, gratitude and affection from their crews as the B-17. It was durable, maneuverable, easy to fly. It was fast for its size and well-armed. It could bring you back alive even with its tail shot off, or with gaping holes blown in a wing, or with three of its four engines out and a fuselage ripped by hundreds of bullets. It could cruise six miles above the ground, beyond sight of the naked eye. It could dive at speeds of more than four hundred miles per hour and was known to do complete loops without tearing off its wings.

Dubbed the "Flying Fortress" by a reporter back in 1937, when an early model was being tested, the B-17 carried a ten-man crew: pilot, co-pilot, navigator, radio operator, bombardier, engineer doubling as top-turret gunner, tail gunner, two waist gunners and a ball-turret gunner. It was a loud plane, primitive in its amenities. The noise of four Wright Cyclone engines, each throbbing with twelve hundred horsepower, made conversation impossible except on the radio intercom. The Plexiglas nose gave the pilots and bombardier a wraparound view of the huge sky above and the ground laid out below. The fuselage had a thin catwalk running lengthwise above the bomb bay, which looked from the inside like an empty metal drum. The plane was not pressurized. When it flew above ten thousand feet, the crew needed walk-around oxygen bottles. At higher altitudes they worked in subzero temperatures that fell to sixty below. On bombing raids lasting anywhere from three to nine hours frostbite was not uncommon.

The Germans at first were not impressed by the Flying Fortresses, at least not when the British were flying them before the American entry into the war. No single bomber could defend itself against a concerted fighter attack. Though it bristled with fifty-caliber machine guns—ten in all, making it the most heavily armed bomber until then—the B-17 needed to follow certain tactical rules for protection against fighters. The main rule was to fly in tight formations, with enough B-17s grouped together to create a wall of overlapping machine-gun fire in all directions. The British sent their B-17s on daylight bombing raids in twos and threes, not enough to keep from being picked off by swarming Messerschmitts and Focke-Wulfs. It wasn't long before the Germans took to calling the new American bombers "Flying Coffins."

Pending the arrival of his equipment, Wyler borrowed cameras wherever he could. "Things are progressing slowly," Wyler wrote Talli. "The great difference between the army and the studios is that here they always try to slow me down. I am continually after somebody so that I can move faster." Often, he stood on a runway with "no film, nothing," watching bombers take off. "My equipment had a very low priority," he remembered later. "It was coming across on a surface vessel. Suddenly John Ford showed up, eyepatch, cigar, and all. He was in the *Navy* and his equipment was *flown* over by the Army Air Force. I don't know how he did it." To Talli, who relished her husband's lengthy, handwritten letters, his impatience was palpable. "Willy didn't know the Army ways," she said. "He couldn't requisition even a typewriter, much less cameras. When Ford came over with *two* camera crews, it just drove Willy crazy. He finally went to the generals and said, 'Look! What is going on here?'"

On November 4, Wyler learned that his unit's equipment, bound from Wrigley Field, Ohio, had been "lost in transit." The shipment included a pair of thirty-five millimeter, motor-drive Eyemo cameras with turrets, lenses and tripods, four hand-held Eyemos, and a silent thirty-five millimeter Akeley, plus a portable sound system and all the accessories. Wyler never was able to replace the loss with equivalent professional equipment. He made do largely with forty hand-held cameras subsequently obtained in London, all sixteen millimeter. Finished film would have to be blown up to thirty-five millimeters.

In early November he requested that he and his officers be put on flying status. They had been allowed on training flights for target practice, but not bombing raids. The real experience of the air war had yet to be captured on film. To get flying status Wyler and his officers had to qualify as aerial gunners by attending gunnery school at Bovington. Approval didn't come through until February 1943, which meant instructing B-17 crews to take their own pictures with stationary cameras mounted in the planes. If the crews remembered to turn on the cameras, and if the cameras didn't jam or otherwise malfunction in the subzero temperatures, maybe the footage would be useful. More likely not. This was no way to make movies.

At the same time, he appealed to the top commander of the Eighth Air Force, Major General Ira B. Eaker, for the sort of endorsement that would guarantee his unit a higher priority.

In early December, Eaker issued new orders for Wyler. They broadened the scope of his mission, pointing out his need to go on actual bombing raids. "These films are to portray the U.S. Army Air Force carrying the air war to the enemy," Eaker wrote. "These films are conceived as documentary motion picture stories exploiting the human element, as contrasted to factual and newsreel material." Wyler was to be provided with all "the necessary directives . . . funds . . . and authority" to make his films. The orders could not have been better tailored to Wyler's purpose had he written them himself. But Eaker didn't stop there. He also assigned a Yale-educated career officer and pilot, Beirne Lay, to smooth the way for Wyler by taking over the unit's logistical operations.

Lay, a lieutenant colonel, had written the script for the prewar movie *I Wanted Wings* and after the war would cowrite *Twelve O'Clock High*. He met Wyler for the first time over dinner at Claridge's. "I was supposed to be his commanding officer, temporarily," Lay recounted, "because all his military experience consisted of was a change of wardrobe into a major's uniform." One problem Lay solved immediately was to clarify that Wyler, and nobody else, would decide what films were made. The Hollywood producer Hal Roach, also recruited and assigned to make films for the Eighth Air Force, was transferred to eliminate any confusion. "The job calls for a creator," Lay told Roach. "Wyler has that reputation, and you're more of a businessman."

Lay also arranged Jerome Chodorov's transfer back to the States. Wyler and Chodorov did not see eye to eye about the films they were to shoot. "From the beginning, Willy wanted to make a picture that was authentic," Lay said. "He wanted every piece of combat footage to be shot in combat. Chodorov, who was supposed to be his writer, had a falling out with him. They had an argument right in front of me the first night at dinner."

Wyler and his crew attended gunnery school, where they took a four-day course in "aircraft recognition." The most difficult part of the training, he recalled, was "identifying aircraft in a fraction of a second." With a sky full of fighters—British Spitfires, German Focke-Wulfs and American Mustangs—instant identification was essential. Film projectors flashed their silhouettes across the ceiling of a dome-roofed building. Trainees simulated machine-gun fire to shoot them down and were rated on their hits.

If that skill was difficult to learn, getting the hang of the machine guns on the live firing range was out-and-out dangerous. Wyler nearly had his head blown off. On February 4, 1943, the *New York Times* reported that he "narrowly escaped serious injury when a 50-mm aerial cannon with which he was training exploded near his face." Other newspapers picked up the story. Wyler made light of the accident in an attempt to reassure Talli. "I hope that silly item in the papers didn't scare you. I was bombarded with cables, and although I was sorry anyone was frightened, I was also glad to see I wasn't forgotten. The whole thing was really started by Goebbels to undermine the morale of our home front."

Wyler wasted no time going on his first combat mission with the Ninety-first Bomb Group, stationed at Bassingbourn. The Ninety-first consisted of four squadrons of three dozen bombers—three flights to a squadron, three planes to a flight—which had come over to England in September 1942 and had been flying missions since November. Wyler left London just past midnight on February 26 and got to Bassingbourn at four in the morning for a briefing. The group's primary target would be the harbor facilities at Bremen, with a secondary target the naval base at Wilhelmshaven. Wyler would fly in a B-17, nicknamed the *Jer-*

ley Bounce, piloted by Captain Robert K. Morgan, a tall, slim, curly-haired twenty-four-year-old from North Carolina.

Wyler scribbled a last-minute note: "Darling Talli — Just before leaving for Bremen — All my thoughts are with you & the children — just in case — But I'll be back — Love darling, Willy."

Ordinarily, Morgan and his equally young crew flew another B-17, the *Memphis Belle*. But it was grounded for repairs from damage on Morgan's last mission, a raid ten days earlier on the well-defended submarine pens at St.-Nazaire. The *Belle* had taken two bad hits. One damaged the right wing and the other knocked out the number-two engine. The bomber had managed to limp home on three engines, its crew unscathed. Six B-17s from other groups were lost.

The Ninety-first Bomb Group had so many B-17s laid up for repair that it could muster only twenty planes for the Bremen raid. The mission was Morgan's twelfth, the crew's thirteenth — not a lucky number. "This was one of those missions when nothing happened as it should," according to waist gunner Clarence Winchell's diary. Some squadrons assigned to the mission from other bases near Bassingbourn arrived late at the rendezvous point and had trouble forming up. Over the North Sea, the lead navigator miscalculated the wind velocity, which put the formation on a heading south of the intended course. The planes encountered heavy antiaircraft fire. Then, as the formation approached Bremen, clouds obscured the harbor. "We turned off and headed for Wilhelmshaven, constantly accompanied by and attacked by German fighters," Winchell wrote.

To the bombardier Vincent Evans, Wyler looked like "this over-age major" who didn't seem fearful of anything. He marveled that Wyler kept "walking the open catwalk of the bomb bay five miles above Germany, breathing out of a walk-around oxygen bottle." The major, dressed in a bulky flight suit for protection against the forty-five-below temperature, kept pointing his hand-held camera at the flak bursts, then at the German fighters, which were trying to break up the formations.

"We could hear him cuss over the intercom," Evans recalled. "By the time he'd swing his camera over to a flak burst, it was lost. Then he'd see another burst, try to get it, miss, see another, try that, miss, try, miss. Then we'd hear him over the intercom, asking if [Morgan] couldn't possibly get the plane closer to the flak."

Evans couldn't believe it.

Approaching its secondary target, the *Jersey Bounce* was forced up to twenty-eight thousand feet. Morgan informed Wyler he would have to stop moving around the plane and choose a stationary position either at the waist or the nose. Wyler now moved to the nose, explaining in his debriefing report that he wanted "to photograph frontal attacks." But all three of his cameras kept freezing up. Even when they didn't, he still lacked "sufficient time to prepare." Also, "flak was considerable . . . mostly aft of our element." Visibility over Wilhelmshaven turned out to be poor as well. A partial overcast of clouds and a heavy smoke screen obscured the naval base. The *Jersey Bounce* dropped its payload, then veered for home. Waist gunner Winchell could see that "many of the bombs fell in the water, doing little if any damage."

When the bomber groups returned to their bases around two in the afternoon, roughly six hours after takeoff, the casualties were tallied. Seven planes didn't come back at all, the worst losses for a single day until then. Forty-one men—the equivalent of four full combat crews—were wounded in the Ninety-first alone. Among those, nineteen suffered from frostbite.

"I have come back from an assignment to hell," Walter Cronkite, then a special correspondent for the British United Press who also went on the raid, reported. "A hell of burning tracers and bursting flak; of crippled Fortresses and burning German fighters; of men going down in parachutes and other men not so lucky."

Wyler had exposed only two hundred fifty feet of film, "the quality of which is doubtful," he wrote in his debriefing report. But his baptism by fire left him feeling confident and strangely exhilarated. It also alerted him to technical problems. He explained in a letter to a friend back in Hollywood, "Aerial warfare takes place in altitudes where the oil in your camera freezes, where you have to wear oxygen masks or die, where you can't move around too much and keep conscious, where the world below you looks like the map of another planet, where human resistance and wit are taxed to the maximum, where things happen faster than any man can think. These and many other conditions are far removed from the comforts of Stage 18 in Burbank or Culver City. This is life at its fullest. With these experiences, I could make a dozen *Mrs. Minivers*—only much better."

In fact, the more Wyler experienced, the less he believed in *Mrs. Miniver.* This was embarrassing, since it had just been nominated for the Academy Award. With the list of nominees made public in early February, a London screening was arranged "for all the big brass," Lay recalled. Wyler declined to go until pressured into it. "Willy told me he couldn't watch it. He said, 'Here I made this picture and I didn't know what I was doing. Not for an audience like this.' He almost chickened out. Well, halfway through the picture it was a handkerchief job. You could hear people sobbing and sniffing all over the room. It obviously gripped them. I sat next to Willy, and when the lights came on I turned to him. There were tears on his cheeks, too. He said, 'Christ, what a tearjerker!'"

Hollywood looked smaller and more unimportant to him than ever. He made fun of show-biz gossip in his letters to Talli: "Heard about Garson Kanin marrying Ruth Gordon; isn't it grim. And Greer Garson and Richard Ney; revolting." In *Mrs. Miniver* the baby-faced Ney had played Garson's nineteen-year-old son. In real life he was ten years her junior. "I feel very responsible," Wyler wrote. "I think back to when I picked him out of a bunch of silly kids [for *Mrs. Miniver*] because he seemed the silliest.

"If some of my letters sound a little sad," he added, "it's only because at the time I write you I naturally feel that way." But he liked the camaraderie of his new military life. "We're sort of a little gang here, everything from colonels to lieutenants, and after five o'clock we take down our ranks and get together over a bottle of bad scotch. Usually in my room, now called the Wyler Mortuary."

At the same time he didn't completely give up his former life. "I've seen Larry and Vivien several times," he wrote, alluding to Laurence Olivier and Vivien Leigh. "They always ask about you and are both very well. Larry is in the Fleet Air Arm but is presently out to make a picture." The British Ministry of Information used Olivier from time to time in films with patriotic themes. The actor invited Wyler to see Leigh in a London revival of Shaw's *The Doctor's Dilemma*, which had been a hit on Broadway two years earlier with Katharine Cornell. "Vivien is very good in it," Willy informed Talli. "She fits the part better than Cornell, though she plays it less profoundly, which I think is more the way it was intended. . . . Anyway, Larry and Vivien are still very much the newlyweds—and it's very refreshing to see."

Olivier now asked Wyler to direct him in a film version of Shakespeare's *Henry V.* The project had begun as a fifteen-minute radio program for the BBC called "Into Battle," for which Olivier had done King Henry's famous St. Crispin's Day speech. It had since grown into a fullscale attempt at a Hollywood-style epic designed to inspire a battle-weary nation with Henry's martial spirit.

"I'm not your man," Wyler said. "I'm not a Shakespearean."

"Don't worry," Olivier replied. "I know Shakespeare. You know how to make pictures."

"Larry, I'm in the army."

"I can get you out. I'll go and see Churchill."

"Well, that's very nice. But I'm more interested in what I'm doing."

Wyler told him he ought to direct it himself, which Olivier did several months later.

On March 4, a week after his first bombing raid, Wyler won his first Oscar. The Academy Award had eluded him for years. From 1936 to 1941, he had made seven pictures. Six of them had been nominated for best picture, one in each consecutive year—*Dodsworth, Dead End, Jezebel, Wuthering Heights, The Letter, The Little Foxes*—and he had been nominated five times for best director. As a joke he started bringing a suitcase to the ceremonies, on the chance he might be carrying an Oscar home. This time it fell into his lap for a picture he valued largely because of its effectiveness as propaganda rather than art. At the awards banquet in Los Angeles, there was a patriotic motif. Jeannette MacDonald sang the national anthem. Tyrone Power and Alan Ladd, both privates in uniform, marched out with the flag. Bob Hope, the emcee, joked about the lack of leading men in Hollywood. When it came time to present the Oscar for best director, Frank Capra in his Army uniform made his way to the dais through the jam-packed tables at the Ambassador Hotel's Cocoanut Grove. He opened the envelope and announced the winner— "William Wyler for *Mrs. Miniver*"—to prolonged applause.

Standing behind a cluster of radio microphones and gripping the Oscar with both hands, Talli looked out at the audience and beamed. There was a catch in her voice as she delivered a speech that took less than thirty seconds: "Thanks so much everybody. It makes me very happy to accept the award for Willy. I wish he could be here. He's wanted an Oscar for a long time. I know it would thrill him a lot, almost as much as that fight over Wilhelmshaven."

The ceremony was crawling toward a conclusion when Greer Garson came to the dais to accept the best actress Oscar, the evening's final award. "I am practically unprepared," she said, and then launched into a prepared speech about the arbitrary nature of awards. The hour was late—well past one o'clock in the morning—and her remarks long-winded. The Hollywood press would deride her mercilessly for sounding pretentious. When Talli described the evening to Wyler, he wrote back: "I could have guessed the kind of pompous speech Greer would make; she would have been out of character otherwise, but it's too bad she was so ill-advised. I wonder if she ever remembers the times she didn't think it was a good part for her, and didn't want to do the picture. . . . While I couldn't be more pleased at having won the award, you're right: It doesn't seem to have the same importance it used to have."

Back in London, British and American officers feted Wyler with a stag dinner. He appreciated the gesture. But he wore his fame lightly at the Bassingbourn air base, where he now spent most of his time. "He never once mentioned Hollywood," recalls Robert Hanson, who was a radio operator on the *Belle*. "He was just a genuine guy, real down-to-earth, easy to talk to."

Charles Leighton, the crew's navigator, appreciated Wyler's reputation. "I knew he was this great Hollywood director," he said. "But I liked the way he worked. He seemed to make decisions, get things done his way. He wasn't bossy or offensive. What amazed me was why a guy like him would do something he didn't have to. I remember thinking, 'What a way to make a living. Coming along with us just for pictures? Taking that kind of risk?' The guy had guts."

In a bomber operation that sustained terrible combat damage—"We lost over eight-two percent of our group," Morgan says—Wyler's personal courage should not have stood out. Yet even the *Belle*'s pilot, who went on to fly B-29s in the Pacific and led the first bombing raid on Tokyo, remembers: "The man had a lot of nerve. The nerviest thing he ever did is something I would never have let my own men do. He rode in the ball turret under the belly of the plane on takeoff and landing. It was completely unsafe, totally against regulations. All you had to do was have a tire blow out and the guy in there is in bad shape, probably dead. We lost planes on takeoff that tore their bottoms off. But he wanted pictures of the wheels and the runway. You see the shots in the film."

The turret was a semispherical Plexiglas bubble that hung beneath the fuselage behind the bomb-bay doors. It allowed the ball-turret gunner, positioned on a swivel seat, to turn and fire in all directions below the belly of the plane. Wyler's best cameraman, William Clothier, also took pictures from the ball turret. But he did it by hooking up a remote-control camera. "You wouldn't have caught me getting in there, not on a landing or takeoff," Clothier said. "If the landing gear failed you'd have been flattened."

Wyler's second bombing raid didn't come until six weeks after his first, largely because Lay had gone to the States on temporary assignment, and the film unit's administration was left to Wyler. But on April 16, with Lay still not back, he joined Morgan and his crew, this time in the *Memphis Belle*, on a two-pronged raid of the U-boat bases at Lorient and Brest. The targets lay in occupied France along the Atlantic coast some three hundred miles away. Brest was on the northern tip of the Brittany peninsula and Lorient on the Bay of Biscay.

The Ninety-first Bomber Group mustered twenty-one planes. Ordered to climb as fast as possible so as to reach their targets before enemy fighters knew they were coming, the planes labored under the weight of their bomb loads. The formation soon became dangerously strung out. Some planes had engine problems and were forced to turn back almost immediately. The accelerated climb had burned up so much fuel that others were forced to turn back short of their targets even after making it to western France. The *Belle* was one of these. It turned back before reaching Lorient. Still others got to their targets but had to make emergency landings on their return routes.

The film unit's sound man, Harold Tannenbaum, also went on this raid, assigned to take pictures from a B-24 Liberator bomber. Lieutenant Tannenbaum never came back. His plane was shot down returning from Brest over the Atlantic. The B-24s, though larger and heavier than the B-17s, were not as well armed. Indeed, whenever Liberators went on a raid, they tended to draw fighter attacks away from the Fortresses because of their greater vulnerability. "We were always glad to see a B-24 outfit in our bombing missions," Morgan recalled. "We knew the German fighters would concentrate on them and leave us alone."

Tannenbaum's death stunned Wyler. "While I knew sooner or later I'd have to lose somebody," he wrote Talli, "it was a shock when it happened. So far I've seen a good many go over and not come back. But it makes a difference when it's one of your own men, and you got him into the army and sent him on the particular job. . . . It doesn't help anyone, but somehow I'm glad that I went on the same mission."

To Tannenbaum's widow, he wrote a long heartfelt letter: "I wish I were able to find words of comfort for you, but I know I should fail. . . ."

Wyler's third bombing mission, again with the *Memphis Belle*, was another strike on Lorient. This time, May 17, the four-hour daylight raid scored direct hits on the U-boat pens, and the attack was rated a huge success. Swarms of German fighters, some forty to fifty Focke-Wulf 190s, came up to meet the formation. But they were beaten off. Winchell shot down a fighter as it bore in on him. "Wyler kept shouldering me to get a picture," he recounts. "Fighters were buzzing around. It's not so bad when you've got a gun in your hands and you can shoot back. You feel better. But just hanging out the window with a camera in your hand? It was hard to believe." Wyler, in his field report, described his experience as "uneventful."

Not long after Beirne Lay got back to London in mid-May, the commander of the Eighth Air Force started to worry about Wyler's safety. "General Eaker became concerned that Willy—because he was a Jew and because he'd made *Mrs. Miniver*—would not have an easy time if he were shot down on a mission," Lay recalled. "*Mrs. Miniver* was having great success, and the Nazis didn't appreciate the picture. So he gave me a direct order that Willy was not to fly any more missions. I passed this on to Willy: No more combat missions. The next morning he didn't show up in the office, so at ten o'clock I called Bassingbourn, and they said, 'If you want to reach Major Wyler he's probably over Hamburg.'"

In fact, he was over the shipyards of Kiel, Germany, on his fourth mission in a B-17 dubbed *Our Gang*. Wyler recorded what happened in a pocket diary he sometimes kept: "Kiel—learned a lot about it in school—and Kaiser Wilhelm Canal—never thought I'd see it this way—counted one hundred sixty B-17s in perfect formation— Got good pictures— Then passed out (bad show) good thing I came to— Don't know how either happened— Was so dopey I thought I was dead— Thought of Talli and Cathy— What a fool I was to go— Who asked me?" The tube to Wyler's walk-around oxygen bottle had broken loose, which is why he lost consciousness. "When I came to I found myself in the bottom of the ship between the pilot and the nose— Moved to the pilots' compartment— It's only two crawls and two steps but on oxygen carrying camera, bottle, chute, it's a five-mile run."

Lay confronted him on his return: "Willy, this is in direct violation of orders. You can be court-martialed for that."

Wyler insisted, "If anybody wants to court-martial me for doing what I think is my job, I'm willing to leave it to the judgment of the readers when they read the headlines. I think I know who'll win that one."

Lay decided not to tell Eaker. Several days later, an exhausted Wyler decided to catch some sleep and not join the predawn briefing for another raid on Wilhelmshaven. "Lucky stiff," he recorded in his diary. "They came back all shot to hell— Three planes missing from the 324th alone. . . ." One of them was *Our Gang*.

26

〰〰〰

A Battlefront Like No Other

W YLER AND HIS CAMERAMEN HAD
shot enough footage for the feature documentary that now took total
precedence over his other ideas projects. Eighth Air Force bomber
crews who completed twenty-five missions were to be shipped home on
combat leave. The *Belle* was closing in on that number, as were several
other B-17s—the *Hell's Angels, Delta Rebel, Jersey Bounce* and *Connecticut
Yankee.* He decided to structure the story around "the twenty-fifth mission."

Initially, Wyler obtained considerable footage of the *Invasion II.* One
day it did not return from a raid. "Suddenly it was gone," Clothier remembered. "So we got in a Jeep and started driving around the base
looking planes over." Wyler noticed one with a leggy redhead painted
on its fuselage. "There was that perky Petty bathing suit girl staring us
in the face and that romantic name, *Memphis Belle,*" Clothier said. "Willy
pointed his finger at the name and said, 'That's it.'"

Virtually all the crews invented names and logos for their planes.
Morgan had a girlfriend back in Memphis, and Air Force legend was
that he named his B-17 for her. In fact, it was named for the saucy heroine of a movie he and his co-pilot had seen in Bangor, Maine, before

they took off for England. In the movie, *A Lady for a Night,* Joan Blondell played the sexy queen of a Mississippi River gambling boat that comes to Memphis. She and the boat are called "Memphis Belle." Morgan also had the leggy pinup in a red swimsuit painted on the fuselage. It was an imitation of the vampish George Petty drawings he often saw in *Esquire* magazine.

When Wyler heard that King George and Queen Elizabeth were scheduled to tour Bassingbourn as a morale booster, he arranged with the base commander for a special inspection of the *Belle.* "They lined us up," Winchell recalls, "and out comes this entourage of Rolls-Royce limos. It was a surprise to all of us." Wyler knew he was playing up the *Belle*'s significance and that other crews were equally deserving. But casting the king and queen with Morgan's crew for a brief moment seemed too good an opportunity to pass up. Besides, the *Belle* was scarcely undeserving. It had a reputation for durability, having returned from bombing raids nine times with at least one engine out. It also was held in high esteem for shooting down eight fighters and five "probables" and for damaging twelve others.

Wyler would fly one more raid on May 29, four days after the king's visit—though not with the *Belle.* As his fifth mission, it would qualify him for the Air Medal. "The fifth was the toughest," he told an interviewer years later. "I almost didn't come back. It was a stupid thing to go on." He already had enough footage for his film, but he wanted the medal. The raid, capping the heaviest month of bombing yet, had three targets: St.-Nazaire, Rennes and La Pallice, all in western France. It was the largest raid till then. The U-boat pens at St.-Nazaire, where Wyler went, were so well defended by antiaircraft emplacements that bomber crews had long since dubbed them "Flak City." Thirteen Flying Fortresses were lost that day.

General Eaker now wanted the film footage turned into a finished product. Wyler explained that the footage needed to be blown up from sixteen to thirty-five millimeters, and that had to be done in the States. On June 4, three days before receiving his Air Medal, he wired Talli: SUGGEST BRUSHING UP CATHY ON USE OF WORD DADDY AND PREPARE JUDY FOR AN EARLY INTRODUCTION. He would be coming home for ninety days to put together a two-reel feature documentary.

Morgan and his crew were shipped home as well. In mid-June they flew to Washington in the *Belle* and received a tumultuous greeting. Welcomed back as heroes, they began barnstorming the country from Memphis, Nashville, Hartford and Boston, west to Pittsburgh, Akron, Cleveland, Detroit, and eventually to California.

Wyler returned home by way of Iceland, Greenland and Nova Sco-
tia, cadging space on military cargo planes. It took him five days to get
to Washington. When he arrived on June 25, Talli was already waiting
for him in New York. Their year-long separation had drawn them closer
together. Both of them had poured out their feelings to each other in
long, handwritten letters, deepening their relationship with declarations
they otherwise might not have made but for the need to bridge the physical distance between them. Sometimes passionate, always affectionate
and with a graceful lightness of humor, Wyler reaffirmed his commitment to Talli, their marriage and their future.

"Each day, no matter how dull or exciting," he had written, "amounts
to practically the same thing, come evening. By that time the most
prominent thing in my mind is the fact that I miss my family, that I hope
they miss me. And I'm glad I have such a nice family to miss. And I
think about all the wonderful things we'll do when this mess is over.
And what a fine life together we'll have. And how glad we'll all be that
we did the things we felt. And how much closer we will be than those
that have been together. How we will then have another child just for
the hell of it, and to show that we're still young *and* useful. I love you."

He had also written: "I see the house and the pool and Cathy running
around screaming and you looking very domestic and lovely. I'm sorry I
don't see Judy, poor Judy. But I do see Boy [their St. Bernard], and the
bicycles and the walks through Bel Air and the lazy life and the good
life, and I see you in your bed or walking about in your transparent
nightgown. And I'm sorry we didn't stay together more often than we
did. But that was my fault. Anyway you can't store up things like that,
or eat in advance and digest the food when you want it most. I see you
especially well when I'm alone. And I'm often alone. I say good-night to
you as I go to bed and I see you when I get up and have a thing called
breakfast. But *our* breakfasts were the best. You must think of them too.
That's what I call *breakfast*—with wife, child, dog, pool, sunshine and
eggs. But we shall have it again. We won't be quite so young maybe. But
we'll be just as happy because we *were* happy and we knew it. It didn't
pass us by. I was very happy. My life was full and rich, and you made it
so.

"I also *hear* you. . . . I finally got a radio and often hear one of the
many symphonies we used to wear out together. Then I'm sitting in our
library and watching you read and hearing you laugh. So, you see, I do
see you and hear you. But I want so much to touch you, all of you, with
all of me. My darling wife . . .

"By the way, what do you think of my love letters—I hope they don't sound too silly — as I was never able to say this sort of thing. But it's easier to write, and anyway I'm sure you always felt it just the same."

Talli recalled their reunion at the Hampshire House on New York's Central Park South, "You're strangers but you're not supposed to be — yet you are for a moment. You've been very intimate, you've been away from each other for so long, and suddenly you're intimate again. It's lovely but it's awkward."

Wyler would use their meeting as the model for the famous reunion scene in *The Best Years of Our Lives*, when homecoming Army veteran Fredric March surprises his wife.

"I got the room number," Wyler remembered, "I couldn't find it at first. Finally, I saw Talli at the end of a long hallway. It was just a little unusual. We had to run to each other. When I did the same thing for the movie, it was no great invention."

As soon as Wyler returned to California, he set up shop at the Hal Roach Studios in Culver City, then being used by the Army Air Force's First Motion Picture Unit. He would be able to cut, print and record at Fort Roach, as the studio was called. But editing couldn't begin until he received his thirty-five millimeter work print from the Technicolor Company. That wouldn't happen until the end of August, because of a huge backlog of training films with higher priority. By the end of July, Wyler realized that making a twenty-four-minute two-reeler would short-change his feature documentary, now tentatively titled *Twenty-Five Missions* — especially since the *Belle* was creating a sensation. Besides raising money for war bonds at factory rallies, Morgan was putting on a demonstration of acrobatic flying that dazzled the crowds in city after city. He not only buzzed airfields but downtown rooftops, sometimes slipping his big bomber sideways between tall buildings. As the tour came west it made headlines in Oklahoma City, Wichita, San Antonio, Las Vegas.

Wyler cabled Beirne Lay at Eighth Air Force headquarters: POSSIBIL-ITIES OF THIS PROJECT FAR GREATER THAN PREVIOUSLY ANTICIPATED DUE TO COMPLETE AUTHENTICITY AND FACT THAT MORGAN AND CREW HAVE BECOME NATIONAL HEROES STOP EXPECT FINISHED FILM WILL RUN FOUR TO FIVE REELS. He requested that the *Memphis Belle* be sent to Fort Roach to help him complete the film. He needed the crew for dialogue voice-overs. To make the picture a two-reeler, he argued to Pentagon higher-ups, would be to make "an ineffective presentation . . . sure not to be accepted for public release." He wrote to Major Tex McCrary, the well-known radio personality then working for General Eaker: "A picture cut down to merely the operational material" would make it "nothing but a pretentious and glorified newsreel with very little idea behind it and no feeling at all."

By the time Morgan and the crew reached Los Angeles, they had barnstormed nonstop for two months. Now Wyler threw them a party at his home on Copa de Oro. "He had all kinds of movie stars there for us," recalled Casimir Nastal, the nineteen-year-old waist gunner who was the baby of the crew. Hanson, the radio operator, remembers Wyler asked each man what star he would like to meet. "I said, 'Anyone?' He said he'd guarantee that anybody we picked would be there. I'll never forget, Veronica Lake was there. She had her hair done up instead of down over her eye. And she says, 'Boys, I'm Veronica Lake.' And Quinlan, our little tail gunner, just looked at her and said, 'Ma'am, that's nice. Why don't you sit back down and I'll buy you a drink.'" Morgan asked for a date with Hedy Lamarr. "I didn't get it," he recounts. "Evidently, she was unavailable." He was happy to settle for Olivia de Havilland. Danny Kaye and Dinah Shore, about to make a war comedy for Goldwyn called *Up In Arms*, provided the entertainment.

In the studio at Fort Roach, Wyler put the crew to work evoking the atmosphere of aerial combat with intercom dialogue that typically occurred aboard a Flying Fortress. He had brought back nineteen thousand feet of original color footage—all of it silent—and he needed to re-create the crew's conversation in the heat of battle. None of the Fort Roach technicians working on the picture had ever been in battle. Until the crew showed up for voice-overs, they didn't have a clue as to what aerial combat sounded like during a bomber raid.

Morgan and the crew intoned matter-of-fact phrases, their voices intense but steady, as the screen showed approaching fighters.

"There's four of 'em."

"One o'clock."

"High."

"They're comin' round."

"Watch 'em."

"Two fighters six o'clock."

"Comin' in."

"Divin' at us, Chief."

The waist gunners fire. Voices are heard again in a monotone.

"Comin' round at ten."

"Watch 'em, Chuck."

"Keep your eyes open."

"They're breakin' at eleven."

"Breakin' at eleven."

"I got 'em."

By the time Wyler obtained thirty-five millimeter work prints of all his color footage, he had just two weeks left to edit the film before he had to return to Eighth Air Force headquarters. "I couldn't get it finished in three months," Wyler remembered. "It needed sound effects, narration, composing. It was a *job*." He cabled London for sixty days more. Eaker's replied: YOU COME BACK OR I GET A REPLACEMENT. "He didn't know what I was doing," Wyler recalled, "so I went all the way to England to explain. It took seventeen hours in a bucket seat on a C-54 transport from Los Angeles to New York, then way up through Greenland and Iceland again."

Eaker bought Wyler's idea, when it was presented in person, and gave him a promotion to lieutenant colonel, then shipped him back to Fort Roach. Now that he had a freer hand, Wyler junked the three-reeler assembled in his absence and hired Lester Koenig to rewrite the script.

Koenig was a technical sergeant attached to the Fort Roach Motion Picture Unit. But he was not your average sergeant. He came to Hollywood in 1937 after attending Dartmouth with Budd Schulberg, the son of Paramount studio head B. P. Schulberg. B. P. had taken a shine to Koenig's college film reviews. When Koenig dropped out of Yale Law School, B. P. invited him to Paramount to try his hand at screenwriting. Koenig wasn't your average Ivy Leaguer, either. His Jewish family came from Manhattan's Lower East Side. His grandfather and father both rose to eminence as New York State magistrates. His mother's parents were the well-known screenwriters Victor Heerman and Sarah Y. Mason. They'd won an Oscar in 1933 for the script of *Little Women*, which starred Katharine Hepburn. Heerman also was highly visible in Hollywood as a director.

Nothing much ever came of Koenig's job at Paramount. But now he came into his own. He wrote a spare prose narration that verged on poetry and proved to be what is the most eloquent script of all the World War II documentaries made by the military. Wyler himself believed that "in large measure it was Koenig's superlative commentary and the ideas expressed in it" that made the film such a notable success.

Working seven days a week at top speed, Wyler assembled seven reels of material and began cutting it down. "It looks like it will be four reels long," he wrote McCrary at Eaker's headquarters in late November. "After much sweating it is beginning to look pretty good, if I say so myself." By the end of December, the picture was basically completed, except for sound effects, music and finishing touches. In the meantime,

Wyler lobbied for commercial distribution through his Hollywood contacts. He arranged personal screenings for Goldwyn, Mayer, Hal Wallis, Selznick and Twentieth Century–Fox production chief William Goetz, and even showed it to Nelson Rockefeller, the State Department's Coordinator for Inter-American Affairs. "I don't consider my job finished," he noted, "until I get the picture into thousands of theaters all over the country."

With the arrival of the new year and the fate of *Twenty-Five Missions* still to be determined, Wyler found himself in demand for another picture project. The playwright Moss Hart wanted him to direct a screen version of *Winged Victory,* his smash hit about the Air Force then running on Broadway. Wyler wrote a friend, "The success of the play means that Moss Hart can have practically anything he wants . . . and he can have me drafted for the job." Indeed, by mid-January Wyler was ordered to New York to see the show.

Rights to *Winged Victory* had been purchased for a million dollars cash by Twentieth Century–Fox. The studio, being run by Goetz in Darryl Zanuck's absence, was set to co-produce it as a fund raiser for the Army Emergency Relief Fund. Wyler went East with mixed feelings and stalled. He didn't get around to seeing the show until late February. Instead he took advantage of the trip to arrange screenings of *Twenty-Five Missions* for General Arnold, head of the Army Air Force, his staff generals and top War Department personnel at the Pentagon.

"It had a terrific reception," Wyler recalled. So terrific, in fact, that another screening was arranged for President Franklin Delano Roosevelt.

Wyler should have been nervous that evening in early 1944. But he felt almost jaunty as he stood in the basement of the wartime White House, a lieutenant colonel among generals. When an aide wheeled the president into the screening room, everyone snapped to attention. Roosevelt wasted no time in small talk.

"Which one of you did this?" he asked.

"I did, sir."

Roosevelt glanced at Wyler and saw an officer of medium height and sturdy build—leaner by twenty pounds than the day he enlisted. The colonel also had a rugged-looking face, not handsome but self-assured.

"Okay," said Roosevelt, "you come here."

The aide indicated a chair next to the president. The lights dimmed and the forty-one minute film began. It opened with shots of the quiet English countryside.

"*This,*" a voice-over intoned, "is a battle front."

Images of green splendor gave way to shots of an airstrip tucked into the landscape.

"A battle front like no other in the long history of mankind's wars."

A B-17 bomber stood in silhouette against the bright blue sky of day. All over England the countryside hid a patchwork of similar airstrips, where the nation's defenders were launched in the shadow of rural churchyards and villages.

"*This*," said the voice-over, "is an air front."

As the hypnotic rhythm of Koenig's words and Wyler's images took hold, Roosevelt watched with a rapt gaze. Several minutes into the film, he took out a thin, elegant cigarette case and leaned over the arm of his wheelchair.

"Cigarette?"

Wyler took one. He noticed that the president, who was nothing if not patrician, smoked Camels. Roosevelt snapped shut the case and drew a long black cigarette holder from his jacket pocket, without taking his eyes from the screen.

"Which kind of bomb is that?" he asked. "A thousand pounder?"

"No, sir. A five-hundred pounder."

Wyler had been instructed not to put his hands in his pockets when in Roosevelt's presence. But it became apparent the president was waiting for a light and nobody was offering one. In the dark, Wyler dug into his pocket for a match and lit both their cigarettes.

The film showed live-action footage of a bombing raid. But it didn't just capture what the crews saw as they flew wing to wing in tight formation: the white vapor trails that gave away their position to antiaircraft batteries on the ground; the harmless-looking puffs of black smoke from exploding flak; the swarms of enemy fighters coming up to meet them over the North Sea. It captured the experience of their daily lives, if briefly, reaching its climax with the stirring last mission of a particular Flying Fortress that stood for all of them.

When the lights came up, Wyler could see that Roosevelt's eyes were brimming behind his rimless glasses. The president hadn't said another word through the entire screening. He hadn't smoked another cigarette. He'd sat absolutely stock still, transfixed. Now he turned to Wyler.

"This has to be shown right away, everywhere."

The room buzzed, and so did Washington. *Twenty-Five Missions* became must viewing. Over the next few days, Wyler ran it a dozen times at the Pentagon for everyone from Secretary of War Henry L. Stimson to the Army Chief of Staff General George C. Marshall to the head of military espionage Colonel "Wild Bill" Donovan. The National Press

Club held a preview screening and piped in General James H. Doolittle's remarks from London on a radio hookup.

At forty-one, though nearly twice the age of the bomber crews, Wyler felt like he was in the prime of life. Certain now of backing at the highest level, he turned down *Winged Victory* as his next project. On February 20, he wired Hart in Beverly Hills: DEAR MOSS, TERRIBLY SORRY ABOUT THE DELAY BUT COULDN'T BE HELPED. FINALLY SAW WINGED VICTORY LAST NIGHT. IT IS A MAGNIFICENT SHOW . . . [BUT] I WANT TO MAKE MORE DOCUMENTARY FILMS. I STRONGLY FEEL THIS IS WHERE I CAN DO THE MOST GOOD. AFTER THE WAR, LET'S DO ONE TOGETHER IF YOU ARE NOT TOO DISGUSTED WITH ME.

To cover himself at Twentieth, he wired his old friend: DEAR DARRYL, I KNOW YOU WILL MAKE A GREAT PICTURE OF 'WINGED VICTORY' AND I JUST WANT TO WISH YOU GOOD LUCK ON IT. SOMEDAY LET'S DO A REAL BANG-UP JOB TOGETHER AND NOT JUST STOP TO SCARE EACH OTHER. IF THE FIRST TWO TIMES DIDN'T TAKE, MAYBE THE THIRD TIME WILL.

Wyler hoped to return to Europe as soon as possible "to get into the Spring fighting." His boss, General Eaker, had moved to the Mediterranean and wanted him to make another live-action documentary, this time about P-47 fighter pilots flying air support for ground troops on the Italian front. All Wyler had to do was complete arrangements for the distribution of *Twenty-Five Missions* — now retitled *The Memphis Belle* — and he would be free to go. Ironically, he almost got himself court-martialed some two weeks after the screening for Roosevelt, nearly muffing his chance to rejoin Eaker.

On March 10, 1944, Wyler was staying at the Statler Hotel several blocks from the White House, expecting new orders to come though any day. Washington was jammed. The morning began with a cold drizzle that turned by afternoon to gusts of bone-chilling rain. Cabs were hard to catch. He happened to be waiting in line for one in the Statler's crowded motorway when a bellman directing traffic got into a heated argument with a guest. As the guest hopped into a cab, the bellman slammed the door shut behind him and turned to Wyler.

"One of these goddamned Jews," he muttered.

"You're saying it to the wrong guy," Wyler replied.

"Whaddya mean? I wasn't saying it to you. I meant him!"

Visibly angry, the bellman wouldn't back off. He was a head taller than Wyler, considerably heavier and clearly intimidating. "That doesn't make a goddamned difference," Wyler said — and pasted him in the jaw with his fist. It was a short, swift blow that seemed to explode from nowhere. The bellman collapsed in a heap.

Wyler's indignation subsided as soon as he saw the man go down. Another army officer, who was standing nearby, stepped out of the crowd of onlookers, glared at Wyler and helped the bellman up from the sidewalk into the hotel lobby. Then he reported what he'd seen to the military authorities.

Wyler recalled, "The next day I go to New York and I get a telegram: RETURN TO WASHINGTON. ORDERS CANCELED."

Back at Bolling Field, a preliminary investigation found his behavior in violation of the military code. A stern-looking captain took him into a hearing room for questioning.

"Anything you say can be held against you."

"Okay."

"Do you know the articles of war?"

"No."

A stenographer sat opposite the captain, recording their conversation.

"You've never heard of them?"

"No."

"How did you become an officer?"

Wyler told him he'd volunteered; that he received a major's commission and a promotion sixteen months later; that his decorations included the Air Medal and that he had just been recommended for the Distinguished Service Medal.

"Did you ever hear the expression 'conduct unbecoming an officer and a gentleman'?" the captain asked.

"Yes, I've heard of that expression."

"What does it mean to you?"

"Well, it means what it says. But I'd like to remind you I was a gentleman long before I became an officer."

"Oh, put that down," the captain told the stenographer.

For Wyler's information, he added, "The articles of war prohibit an officer from striking anyone except in self-defense. Was this self-defense?"

"No, I can't say that it was. But it was something more important to me, a matter of honor."

The captain asked if he had anything else to say.

"What happened," he replied, "is the kind of thing happening in Germany. Without that I wouldn't be in uniform."

His statement didn't help.

"He was arrested," says James Parton, the Eighth Air Force historian. "For an officer in uniform to strike a civilian is a very serious offense. He was threatened with court-martial. General Arnold had to go to bat and pull strings to get him out of it. A letter of reprimand was the outcome."

Wyler received notification that he could either accept the letter of reprimand in his permanent record or plead his case at trial. He preferred going to trial but soon discovered it might not occur for months, which meant he would miss the Allied advance toward Rome and the liberation of Europe. On the advice of colleagues, he accepted the reprimand and hoped Eaker would press to renew his orders.

While waiting, Wyler continued to campaign for *The Memphis Belle*'s commercial release. Before winter was out Paramount Pictures had five hundred prints made and agreed to distribute them to its more than ten thousand theaters. And on April 14, 1944, the day before the picture opened, the *New York Times* review by an admiring Bosley Crowther appeared on page one, marking the first time in the newspaper's history that an American film had ever been reviewed on the front page. The next day the *Times* followed up with an editorial. So did the New York *Herald-Tribune*.

Crowther, in still another piece two days later, described *The Memphis Belle* as a "brilliant report" from the front. It was "as vivid and actual and informative as any film that we have yet seen," he wrote. But what thrilled him most was its emotional impact. The film "pervades the spectator with an illusion of personal experience." Wyler's exacting demand for the authentic had paid off in urgency and immediacy.

It didn't take long for his renewed orders to come through. By mid-May, with brief stops in Casablanca and Algiers, he flew to Caserta, Italy, the Allied headquarters for the Mediterranean theater. When he got there, he learned his reputation had preceded him, not so much for being a big Hollywood director, which was to be expected, but for the fracas at the Statler.

"They'd heard about what happened and rather respected me for it," Wyler remembered with pleasure many years later. "They understood my attitude for hitting that guy."

Minor in itself, the fight signified something larger. It was an emblem of both his principles and his personality and would be invoked after the war in his much-loved masterwork *The Best Years of Our Lives*. He would even re-create the incident in the famous soda fountain scene with Dana Andrews and Harold Russell, catching the ethos of a generation.

27

ITALIAN ASSIGNMENT

JOHN STURGES MET WYLER FOR
the first time at Fort Roach. Sturges, the future director of *Bad Day at
Black Rock, The Great Escape* and *The Magnificent Seven,* had been a cutter
for David Selznick and was then editing routine Air Force training
films. "Wyler was recording the narration for *Memphis Belle,*" he recalled, "and he had this guy read one line about twenty-five times. He
could sense that I thought that was the most ridiculous thing I'd ever
seen, and he came over and said hello. 'You're wondering why I'm doing
this. Well,' he said, 'let me tell you—when this line is right, I'll know it.
And when you hear it in the picture, it'll give you a lump in your throat.'
And my God, it did."

What appealed to the thirty-three-year-old lieutenant about Wyler's
next project was not his persistence so much as the chance for an overseas adventure. Sturges readily agreed to join the tight little team about
to leave for the Mediterranean. Wyler asked him to be co-director.
Koenig would be scriptwriter. They would take no cameramen with
them but would rely on combat photographers already in the field.
Their assignment was to film "tactical air operations in support of
ground forces," chronicling the story of the snub-nosed P-47 Thunder-

bolt fighter-bombers of the Twelfth Air Force—specifically the Fifty-seventh Fighter Group at Alto air base on Corsica.

The Fifty-seventh was one of the Air Force's oldest and most experienced fighter groups. It had gone overseas in July 1942, to join Montgomery's British Eighth Army, which had been pushed back to Egypt by Rommel's Afrika Korps. Handicapped by lack of supplies and makeshift air bases against an extremely effective Luftwaffe, the Fifty-seventh's three squadrons nevertheless distinguished themselves in the desert campaign. After Montgomery finally defeated Rommel at El Alamein, they fought their way west to Tunisia. There, at Cape Bon, they intercepted a fleet of German fighters and shot down twenty-seven planes in a single battle. Then they took part in the invasion of Sicily and the Italian mainland, moving on the heels of the infantry and occupying air bases as soon as they were captured from the Germans.

During the five-month stalemate at Cassino, the key to the German-held Gustav Line across the narrowest and most mountainous part of Italy, the Fifty-seventh received P-47 Thunderbolts and went to Corsica to act as a separate task force. Affectionately dubbed "the seven-ton milk bottle," the P-47 was a rugged, single-pilot fighter capable of matching the Focke-Wulf 190 in air combat at any altitude. But it also served as a dive bomber, carrying a five-hundred-pound bomb under each wing, as well as rockets and eight machine guns for strafing.

The Allied Command had decided to isolate and weaken the German Army by cutting off all shipping to the front. This strategy, called Operation Strangle, meant using air power to attack enemy supply routes and communications deep behind the German lines instead of using it to hit front-line positions. Wyler would be filming the Fifty-seventh's role in Operation Strangle.

Because he couldn't get cameramen aboard the P-47s, Wyler would have to use cameras mounted in the nose, in the cockpit, on the wings, even on the tail—all timed to the firing mechanism of the aircraft's guns—if, that is, the pilot agreed to it. Many of them wouldn't.

"With so many units involved," Wyler informed higher-ups, "it becomes very hard to reduce the complications to the level of a short film that must have a structural unity and be entertaining as well as instructive. Since we can't go along with the fighter-bombers, there are many things we can't put a camera on, many things that can't be photographed." Given those limitations, he decided to see as much of the war as possible from the ground. And because he now had high-priority orders urging "the closest cooperation" from local commanders, he could roam virtually at will. Thus, within days of landing at Caserta on June 2, Wyler commandeered a jeep and followed the infantry into Rome for the city's liberation. Working as his own cameraman, he caught the jubilant mood of "GIs rubbernecking" and "soldiers whipping around" the Colosseum in their jeeps, "in a modern version of the chariot races." He filmed children begging for candy. "All through Italy our advances into various cities and towns have been marked by the children's cries of *'Caramelli!'* Rome ran true to form."

Next on Wyler's itinerary was Mussolini's balcony, "another place the GIs wanted to see." The big square below the balcony, where Il Duce gave his speeches to the Fascisti, now shook with the rumble of tank treads. "The cries of welcome to the liberators didn't sound much like the cries of *'Duce! Duce!'* " Wyler remarked in a memo. He filmed a Roman civilian scraping a Nazi sign off a wall and noted drily: "The old order changeth on Via Poli." Finally he went to the Vatican for the Pope's first press conference with Allied newsmen and photographers. "The scene was unusual," he wrote, "with flashbulbs popping and correspondents edging in for better shots while His Holiness tried to speak of peace." As Pope Pius XII talked with a hundred or so members of the press corps, the Swiss Guard could barely maintain order. When a news photo of the audience appeared in the *New York Times*, Wyler could be seen in the crowd next to the Pope, staring at him with an owlish intensity. "You have a most holy and uplifted expression," Talli teased in a letter. "An expression never seen on your face before — positively saintly." The papal audience did not appear in *Thunderbolt*, but it generated an idea for the final scene of *Roman Holiday*, which Wyler would direct eight years later.

Wyler spent the next months careering around Italy, staying no longer than a few days in any one place. He flew between Eaker's headquarters in Caserta, near Naples, and Alto air base on Corsica. He traveled north from Rome following a zigzag path toward the front in central Italy. He filmed bomb damage where Thunderbolts had destroyed bridges and railroads in the battle against Field Marshal Kesselring's forces.

"We were together for hours on end riding around or sitting in tents," Sturges recalled. "He drove like a bat out of hell. He was a wild man in a jeep. One time in Rome he gave a ride to some nuns. They were terrified and hopped out the first chance they got. This embarrassed him. He was actually blushing. I don't think he realized how terrified they were."

With Koenig coordinating production plans at Alto, Wyler and Sturges got a taste of the ground war as seen through the eyes of a British tank corps near Florence. "They were Monty's people, and they were firing artillery back and forth with the Germans. We fit right in. We would scrounge eggs, do our laundry and go up to the front. One time we made it to the command post. It was sitting on a hill. You could look out the window, and there was the war right in front of you. We asked how come they knew just where the German post was and the Germans knew just where theirs was but didn't blow each other off the face of the earth? They explained there had to be a compromise of convenience. It let them live to fight another day, each side in their own mudhole."

This unwritten arrangement didn't mean you were safe, though. On the way up to the command post, Wyler and Sturges were spotted by a German tank with an eighty-eight-millimeter cannon. "That gun could cut a telephone pole a mile away," Sturges said, "and it made a helluva noise. All these sounds were rushing over our heads, but one of them was different. The guy with us said, 'Drop.' Willy and I fell into a shallow ditch. I remember a whistling sound and a big explosion. All the bushes and grass around the top of the ditch were cut. It looked like a scythe did it. The guy said, 'We've been spotted. They'll give us three shots. That's all. If we have any luck, he won't hit us.' All three shots missed. But when we moved up to the command post, you could tell everybody was nervous. An attack had started. They wanted us the hell out of there."

Wyler's status in the Air Force rose immeasurably with the acclaim of *The Memphis Belle* back home, in part because the movie had brought the top generals unusual public appreciation. Pentagon memos exulted over the praise and publicity he had garnered for the Air Force. Wyler's treatment was no longer that of a mere lieutenant colonel. When it came to social contact, the generals welcomed him as an equal. In early July, Eaker, who now commanded all the Allied air forces in the Mediterranean, ordered him to Naples for a meeting with Spaatz, who was still in command of the Eighth Air Force in England.

"Willy thought they were planning the invasion of France," Talli recounted. "So he sent back a note: 'I think I should bring Koenig and Sturges with me.' Word got back to him: 'Come alone and bring a camera.' He's on the dock in Naples at eight o'clock. They get in a boat and go to Capri, where they spend the next forty-eight hours in a poker game at a beautiful villa. It was bizarre."

Eaker's poker games were legendary. In Caserta, whenever high-ranking officers came through, "we'd always get them into a game," Parton, Eaker's aide, recounted. "The idea was never to let a stranger leave without being poorer in pocket." One time the Army's top intelligence officer "Wild Bill" Donovan showed up. He was fleeced. "I picked up two thousand bucks from him," Parton recalled. Wyler preferred gin rummy. He would hang around the poker table at Eaker's Nissen hut looking to snare someone into his own game. "Willy was a shark," said Parton. "He removed nine hundred dollars from me one evening."

In August, with the Allied invasion of southern France, Wyler supervised film coverage of the beach landings. "It was a walk-through because the Germans were just sitting there waiting to be captured," Sturges recalled. "The Free French and the Resistance had everything under control. We landed at St. Tropez, of all places. It was a joke."

For the next month, they worked their way north past Lyons. By mid-September they reached Besançon, fewer than a hundred miles from Wyler's hometown. "Willy was dying to be in on the capture of Mulhouse," Parton, who joined them, recalls. "But the front stalled, and we didn't get anywhere near it." They did, however, come under attack. "We went with a company of infantry who were going off to pursue Germans. We trudged across fields with a platoon of thirteen infantrymen and got into a firefight. We took refuge in a tiny hamlet when this Volkswagen flying a Red Cross flag came ripping around a corner. A Red Cross man got out with a wounded German colonel. He was bleeding copiously. We put him on the ground and started giving him an intravenous feeding from a bottle of white plasma. The German colonel was puzzled. He didn't seem to know what was in the bottle. He muttered something. '*Vas ist das?*' Willy was the only one of us who could speak German. He said to him: 'That's blood, you bastard! Negro blood! How do you like that, you stinkin' Nazi?' Meanwhile, we're being fired on from a mile away. So we went up the line and found a farm, where Willy and I spent a night in a hayloft out of harm's way."

WYLER FELT BY THE END OF SEPTEMBER THAT HE HAD ENOUGH material to take to London and begin processing. He and Sturges flew to England, where they spent nearly a month cutting and editing. Wyler didn't mind the break from combat life. He informed Tex McCrary, "As I seem to have come down with the almost-flu, I have decided to stay at Claridge's Hospital. After many months of sleeping in open tents and on airfields and in stables and what-nots, the luxury of Claridge's has been really too much for me. I am afraid I will live."

Around Christmas Wyler spent ten days in Paris, where he ran into fellow director George Stevens, who headed a film unit documenting invasion tactics for the Sixth Army. "I wanted to go to Luxembourg, Belgium and the Bastogne," Wyler recalled. "I needed a driver with me. And I said, 'Do you have somebody you can assign?' He said, 'Yes, I've got a fellow—Leicester Hemingway. The kid brother.'" The reference, of course, was to Ernest Hemingway.

Wyler couldn't take immediate advantage of the offer. He first had to gain clearance in London, so it was back to England. There he wangled permission to travel as "a self-contained unit" among forward elements of American forces in the Ardennes, where the Battle of the Bulge was being mopped up. Again using *Thunderbolt* as an all-purpose passport, he persuaded the staff of the Ninth Air Force, headquartered in Luxembourg, that he needed more pictures "illustrating tactical air power in cooperation with ground forces." He also persuaded the top brass of the First French Army, which had taken Mulhouse, to let him into its sector.

Leicester Hemingway, tall and rangy, was a private in the Army Signal Corps. In his late twenties, Leicester was seventeen years younger than his brother. He also drove like a maniac, which Wyler liked. On the other hand, "he was never happy unless we were getting shot at," Wyler recalled. When they reached Bastogne, where the American army had covered itself in glory during the Battle of the Bulge, the pine trees were blanketed with snow in the dying gray light of day. They stopped to sleep in a bombed-out farmhouse. A soldier wakened them in the middle of the night with news that eight German tanks were headed their way. Startled, Wyler asked: "What do we do?" Hemingway's reply was typical: "Nothing. We wait." To Wyler's relief, the tanks never came.

In Mulhouse, which had been heavily bombarded by Allied planes, they drove through whole neighborhoods of blasted houses and deserted, rubble-strewn streets. When Wyler couldn't find any of his childhood friends, he went to see the mayor. "I asked him where everybody was. He said to me, 'Take my advice, don't look for anybody. If you see somebody you know, be glad to see him. But don't go looking for people, because you won't find them.'"

Wyler directed Hemingway to rue du Sauvage and found his father's old haberdashery shop. Miraculously, it stood undamaged. The caretaker he remembered from childhood, Madame Henriette Helm, greeted him at the door as though he had never left. She "thought it was the most natural thing in the world that I should come back as an American officer," Wyler recalled. "She managed to preserve the shop because my father was Swiss. The Germans harassed her, but she carefully obeyed every law. For instance, on Hitler's birthday every store window had to have a picture of Hitler. She always bought the smallest one. If my father knew, he would have turned over in his grave."

Back in London, Koenig and Sturges completed the first cut of *Thunderbolt* by mid-February. As they prepared to leave for Culver City, Wyler flew back to Italy. He wanted to get "atmosphere shots" of Rome from the air and other fill-in material to lend the picture some finishing touches. Ironically, that footage would be his costliest of the war. Filming from a B-25 camera ship one day in late March, he made several passes over Rome and the coast. He also shot bomb damage inland and aerial shots of Corsica. Then it was back to Rome to drop off an Italian intelligence officer who had come along. Finally, the long day at an end, they flew north to Grosseto, forty-five minutes away, where the Twelfth Air Force had moved its headquarters.

Wyler recalled, "I usually flew with the pilot up front. A B-25 is a very noisy plane. This time I got in the waist, where the windows were open, because the cameraman complained about his camera setup. This was a routine flight, no flak, no guns. My hearing just went. I thought it was nothing. A lot of times you step out of an airplane, and you can't hear for a while. But this time I couldn't walk straight when I got off. They thought I was drunk. I went to see the flight surgeon. He said, 'This is serious.'"

Wyler had gone deaf in both ears.

Two weeks later he still couldn't hear and was ordered back to the States immediately. On April 10, he boarded a troopship in Naples bound for Boston. The trip took ten days. Some hearing had returned to his left ear, but so little that he became increasingly depressed. As soon as he got to Boston, he phoned Talli. "Instead of a happy voice, I heard an absolutely dead voice," she recalled, "toneless, without any timbre, without emotions. I couldn't imagine what had gone wrong. It was not the cheerful phone call I had expected. He sounded totally unlike himself, terribly disturbed. He talked as if his life was over, not only his career. I was shocked." Air Force doctors sent Wyler to New York for observation and treatment in a hospital at Mitchell Field on Long Island. Lillian Hellman saw him there. "I'd never seen anybody in such a real state of horror in my life," she remembered. "He [thought] he never would direct again."

The doctors believed that Wyler had sustained irreparable nerve damage in his right ear. They decided they could help conserve the minimal hearing he still had in the left by removing his adenoids. Talli wanted to rush East, but he asked her not to come. After shuttling between military hospitals in New York and Washington for three weeks, he finally took a train to Los Angeles. When Talli saw him for the first time in a year, she felt she was facing a stranger. "He was terribly thin," she recalled. "He wasn't eating. His face was so drawn, I almost didn't recognize him. You had to talk directly into his left ear. And you had to speak with great clarity or he couldn't understand you. He felt very isolated."

Desperate for any kind of medical treatment, Wyler sought out hearing specialists to give him a definitive diagnosis. "He went to everybody there was," Talli said. Finally, the Air Force sent him to a military hospital in Santa Barbara, where he submitted to psychiatric therapy with sodium pentathol treatments. Injections of the so-called "truth serum" were supposed to reveal whether his deafness had a psychosomatic component. The therapy consisted of intense scrutiny and deception. Psychiatrists told Wyler he was able to hear so well under the influence of the drug that he had understood what was being said in the next room. They even told that to Talli. "When I picked him up to bring him home from the hospital, he was in a padded cell," she recalled. "He could barely stand up. It was all I could do to get him out to the car." The drug treatment accomplished nothing. As compensation for his hearing disability, Wyler would get sixty dollars a month from the government for the rest of his life.

The war in Europe had already come to an end. Mussolini was executed by partisans on April 28. Hitler committed suicide two days later. The last German holdouts surrendered unconditionally on May 7. And in late July—as Talli and Willy went off to Lake Arrowhead for two weeks of rest—Truman, Stalin, Churchill and his successor as prime minister, Clement Attlee, were meeting in Potsdam to shape the postwar world. They also issued an ultimatum to Japan: Surrender or face total destruction. On August 6, four days after the Potsdam Conference ended, the first atomic bomb devastated Hiroshima. Three days later another destroyed Nagasaki. The Japanese surrendered on August 14.

The end of the war short-circuited the impetus to get a commercial release for *Thunderbolt*. Even within the Air Force enthusiasm waned. "We went through the mechanical process of finishing it," Sturges said. "We got it timed, cut and scored and sent out to Technicolor for processing by the middle of August." When it came back about six weeks later, he and Koenig personally delivered a five-reel print to the Pentagon in Washington.

"We ran it for General Arnold, the top general of the Air Force, and about fifty officers," Sturges said. "The lights went up, and Arnold stood up and says, 'Is Willy here?' And Willy stood up. Arnold said, 'Willy, what's this picture for?' Willy was literally speechless. Maybe it was because of his hearing, but he didn't say a word. He could have given fifty reasons why we made the picture. He knew them all. Hell, I could have given them. I even considered popping up and saying something. But I was only a captain. There were enough generals there for ten armies. Willy finally mumbled something. He was fumbling around. Arnold needed positive answers. He just walked out, and that was the end of that."

Wyler arranged a screening for the Hollywood trade press in October and tried to enlist the help of the War Department. But by then commercial distributors were strongly resisting government war documentaries. It wasn't until two years later, in July 1947, that Monogram Pictures released *Thunderbolt* to admiring but ultimately inconsequential reviews. With the public having long since put the war behind it, the picture was of little interest. Even a short introduction by Jimmy Stewart, tacked on to *Thunderbolt* to give it timeliness, acknowledged that viewers were about to see a combat chronicle of "ancient history."

28

NOT HOLLYWOOD-AS-USUAL

WYLER CAME BACK FROM THE war a changed man. Like millions of returning veterans, he had been radically altered not just physically but emotionally. The experience of combat had thrown their lives into high relief, forcing many to question their values and transform their outlook. "No one could live through that experience and come out the same," he said. Wyler did not kid himself about his own wartime activities. He never confused the twenty-four months he spent overseas, often at a safe remove from the fighting, with the daily grind of battle. But he had seen enough firsthand to understand its transformative power. He felt he could take nothing for granted, especially not Hollywood as usual.

"The war had been an escape into reality," he said. "In the war it didn't matter how much money you earned. The only thing that mattered were human relationships—not money, not position, not even family. Only relationships with people who might be dead tomorrow were important."

By the time he was officially discharged from the Army in October 1945, Wyler had plans for a different future. He still owed Goldwyn a picture under his old contract. But in July he also had accepted an invitation from Frank Capra and Samuel Briskin to join their newly formed Liberty Films, an independent production company that would allow him to be his own boss.

Capra had various reasons for starting the venture, primarily a stated belief in overhauling the studio system. But the fact was, despite his prewar success, the major studios had lost interest in him and wouldn't give him the sort of long-term deal he wanted. "Like it or not, going independent . . . was his only postwar option," according to Capra's biographer Joseph McBride. Indeed, Wyler would be key to Liberty's financing. It was only after he signed on as a partner that RKO agreed to distribute future Liberty pictures. Though Wyler worried about his deafness and whether it would affect his ability to direct, nobody else seemed to be giving it a second thought.

Goldwyn initially wanted him to make a picture about the life of Dwight D. Eisenhower. As early as June the producer had wired the War Department asking for permission to bring Wyler to Washington with Robert Sherwood, who was writing a treatment, to meet the five-star general. But Wyler did not show great enthusiasm. "It would have been a regular dramatic film with someone playing Eisenhower," he explained. Acknowledging Wyler's lukewarm response, Goldwyn "changed his plans and went alone" to meet the general.

Of course, Goldwyn was nothing if not a mass of contradictions. The other picture he had in mind happened to be *The Bishop's Wife*, a sentimental Christmas fantasy with Cary Grant. This possibility, in line with Goldwyn's proclaimed policy of making frivolous pictures to help the public forget the war, held absolutely no interest for Wyler.

What did appeal to him, however, was a story Goldwyn had commissioned in 1944 and dropped after the author turned in a manuscript in blank verse. Goldwyn had asked McKinlay Kantor, a screenwriter and historical novelist, to create the story. Prompting the assignment was a *Time* magazine feature about Marines on furlough who were finding it hard to adjust to the home front. Kantor, who had flown missions with the Eighth Air Force as an overseas correspondent, delivered a manuscript about three servicemen back from the war, *Glory for Me*, in January 1945. It had cost Goldwyn twelve thousand five hundred dollars, but he showed it to Wyler almost as an afterthought. In fact, when his ace director told him he liked it, Goldwyn tried to talk him out of it. "He thought it was nothing—ten thousand wasted," Wyler recalled. Unswayed, he told his old boss: "This is what I want to make."

The Kantor story, which would become *The Best Years of Our Lives*, attracted him because it depicted "the ordinary GI—not a general," and he brought the material to Sherwood's attention. Three-time winner of the Pulitzer Prize for drama (*Idiot's Delight, Abe Lincoln in Illinois, There Shall Be No Night*), Sherwood also was a veteran screenwriter (*The Divorce of Lady X, Rebecca*) and a former Roosevelt speechwriter who'd headed the Office of War Information. He, too, preferred Kantor's material. Goldwyn heard them out and finally agreed. In November 1945, Sherwood switched from writing about Eisenhower to writing the *Glory* script.

When millions of veterans turned in their army uniforms, the problem of becoming civilians again surfaced as a paramount social issue for the nation. Soldiers often came back to families that had learned to get along without them. Many veterans felt alienated. They needed jobs, housing, education. They had left school to join the service and had no real training for anything but war. "I've come home twice myself from the war and I know just how these fellows feel," Wyler said at the time. "No man can walk right into the house after two or three years and pick up his life as before."

Wyler scarcely qualified as a hardship case, hearing loss notwithstanding. Under his old contract with Goldwyn, he'd earned a hundred and fifty thousand dollars a year in 1939—the equivalent of two million dollars today. For this new picture, he would be making the same salary as before (less a thousand a week deducted against a twenty-five thousand dollar advance). And for the first time he would be getting a twenty percent royalty on the picture's profit, twice the royalty he'd previously earned.

Also, whatever his personal sense of dislocation, Wyler came home to a loving wife and family. By the time of his discharge, Talli was already several months pregnant with their third child. Needing a larger home than their three-bedroom place on Copa de Oro, they bought Fred Astaire's comfortable, rambling Beverly Hills manse on Summit Drive in January 1946, for ninety-five thousand dollars. It had twelve rooms and came with a pool and tennis courts. Charles and Oona Chaplin lived next door. Astaire built another home up the street beyond Mary Pickford's estate, the legendary Pickfair. Glenn Ford, who soared to stardom that year opposite Rita Hayworth and Bette Davis, lived just down the street with Eleanor Powell. The Wylers couldn't have been better situated.

Yet as Wyler repeated time and again in press interviews and written remarks, "no subject was as important" to him as veterans and their problems. When he went on the set in the morning, "it was no problem to imagine what they would do in a situation, because I already knew it in my heart." Making their postwar return the subject of a picture, moreover, "imposed a responsibility . . . to be true to these events and refrain from distorting them for our own ends."

In *Glory for Me*, Kantor told the story of three returning veterans of different social standing to the same home town in the Midwest. Wyler clearly identified with all three, each for different reasons. One, Fred Derry, was a B-17 bombardier. Another, Homer, was a seaman hobbled by war injuries. The third, Al Stephenson, a former infantry sergeant verging on middle age, seems to have been something like an alter ego.

Summarizing the character in Kantor's novel, Wyler could have been writing about himself: "His first night home, memories of combat came back to contrast with the soft and easy life he will lead. . . . He has a sense of guilt in accepting the luxuries of a home and family, when he thinks of his friends who are not coming back. Stephenson had been a banker before the war and has no problem in making a living. His problem becomes that of working in a bank and reconciling the sharp business practice he sees with the social conscience he developed during the war."

Sherwood would alter some details of the original story but would keep many essentials. As in the original, Derry was a drugstore soda jerk before the war and lived on the wrong side of the tracks. "He had married a girl while training in Texas and had only a few days of marriage before being shipped overseas," Wyler noted. "His first night home, he finds her making love to another man."

In Sherwood's screenplay, however, Derry can't find her on his first night home and so does not discover her infidelity. Their bad marriage is drawn out and a love story develops between Derry and Al Stephenson's grown daughter. Derry's wife "would be kept throughout the story," Wyler explained,"not merely as the third side of the conventional [love] triangle but as a symbol of a way of life" that Derry would leave behind.

Kantor's Homer also underwent change. In *Glory for Me* he returned from the war a spastic because of his combat injuries. "Unable to coordinate his movement, awkward, even grotesque," Wyler noted, "he finds homecoming sheer misery because his people don't understand him. His situation is aggravated by his love for the girl next door, his high school sweetheart, Wilma, and his fear that she will go through with marriage only through pity for him." Sherwood retained all the details of that characterization. But the physical disability had to be altered. "I realized," Wyler said, "that no actor, no matter how great, could play a spastic with conviction."

Stumped by the problem, he and Sherwood briefly considered cutting the character even though they preferred not to. The solution presented itself to Wyler one day at a war bond rally to raise funds for disabled veterans. Documentaries were being shown to educate the public about the effectiveness of rehabilitation. One of them, *Diary of a Sergeant,* chronicled the story of Harold Russell, a former meat cutter who lost both of his hands in a training accident and had mastered the use of prosthetic hooks.

What most impressed Wyler about Russell was the way he faced his disability, especially compared with the amputees he had seen on a tour of several military hospitals. At the Sawtell Veterans Hospital in West Los Angeles, Wyler and Sherwood had looked in on three armless veterans who were particularly bitter and resentful. It turned out to be a shocking experience.

"So you're gonna make a picture about fellows like us," one said. "You're gonna make a lot of money. You're gonna exploit these things."

Wyler told them he regretted their feelings. He wanted the picture "to show that disabled veterans were thoroughly capable of doing ordinary things with artificial hands."

Then he mentioned Harold Russell.

"Yeah, Russell," said one of the vets, "we know him. He's a lucky guy."

"How come?"

"He's got his elbows. When you've got your elbows, they can put claws on."

Wyler understood their resentment. As he later told an interviewer, "We're the ones who are maladjusted since we annoy and embarrass them with our patronizing attention."

Hedda Hopper leaked word in her syndicated gossip column that Wyler was considering a real amputee for his next picture and named Russell as the prospect before anyone contacted him. When a Goldwyn executive subsequently phoned the thirty-two-year-old veteran to invite him to Hollywood for an interview, Russell thought it was a prank. He couldn't have been a less likely candidate for pictures. After getting out of Walter Reed Hospital, he had toured some bond rallies with *Diary of a Sergeant* and returned home to Cambridge, Massachusetts, to a job at a local YMCA.

"I flew out in an old DC-3 and met with Wyler," Russell recounted. "He took me to lunch at the Brown Derby. Now this is a funny story, but it really put me at ease — and it's the truth.

"When we left the restaurant, he stopped to pay the bill. Somebody who knew him came up and said, 'Gee, that guy does a pretty good job with the hooks.' Wyler said, 'Yeah, he does a fantastic job. He did the shrimp cocktails. He ate the salad. He cut the steak. But the one thing he can't do is pick up the check.'"

Meanwhile, Goldwyn gathered a cast. His first choice for the role of Milly, sergeant Al Stephenson's wife, was Olivia de Havilland. Even if she hadn't turned it down, she would have been far too young. Wyler's first choice was Myrna Loy, adored as "the perfect wife" by millions for her portrayal of Nora Charles, the sophisticated mate to William Powell in *The Thin Man* series of the thirties and forties. To get Loy for Milly, which was not a large role, Goldwyn gave her top billing. Fredric March, a personal favorite of Wyler's, took the role of Al Stephenson when he lost the lead in *Life With Father* to Powell. The other principal roles went to contract players: Dana Andrews played Fred Derry; Virginia Mayo was his unfaithful wife, Marie; Teresa Wright portrayed Stephenson's grown daughter, Peggy, who falls in love with Derry; and newcomer Cathy O'Donnell, later to marry Robert Wyler, was introduced in her first screen role as Homer's high school sweetheart, Wilma.

Wyler made clear from the beginning that the pictures would be "honest" and have nothing to do with the grand Hollywood manner. Costumes, even for the women, were to be bought off the rack in department stores. The cast would be asked to wear them for weeks before production started, so they would not look new. Makeup would be used sparingly, if at all. Wyler instructed the art director to create smaller-than-life sets, the opposite of customary practice.

In February, before filming began, Wyler wrote Fredric March that since he would be playing a sergeant just back from two years of combat duty, "it's very important that your figure suggest a K-ration diet rather than the 21 Club. . . . You should make every effort to be as trim and wiry as possible. . . . I know it's not easy for fellows our age. I've gained twenty pounds since coming back. . . . But the entire approach to this picture will be along realistic lines. . . . I would hate to have something like the proverbial little 'pouch' spoil the illusion."

Perhaps more than anything else, realism colored the script. In a lengthy article written in 1947 soon after the picture's release, Wyler elaborated on what that meant:

"We had to be honest in ending the three stories, for we felt the picture would be seen by millions of veterans. We could not indicate any solution to a problem which would work only for a character in a movie. Bob Sherwood felt, for example, that it wasn't a fair solution to let Al Stephenson quit his job at the bank and go into something else where he could avoid problems"—as Kantor's *Glory for Me* had it—"because millions of other veterans would have no such easy alternatives to a job they did not like."

Homer's tale required special care.

"We wanted to have a scene," Wyler explained, "in which Homer tells Wilma the reason he has been avoiding her is not that he doesn't love her, but that he doesn't feel it fair to her to marry her."

" 'You don't know, Wilma,' he says. 'You don't know what it would be like to live with me, to have to face this every day—and every night.'

"Wilma replies, 'I can only find out by trying, and if it turns out that I haven't courage enough, we'll soon know it.'

"This was intended to lead to a scene in Homer's bedroom in which, in order to prove his point, he demonstrates his difficulty in undressing, removes his hooks, and explains how helpless he is once they are off. . . ."

Wyler had to decide whether he could put that sort of scene on the screen without violating the Production Code.

"There were delicate problems in bringing a boy and a girl to a bedroom at night, with the boy getting into his pajama top, revealing his leather harness, which enables him to work his hooks, and finally, taking the harness off," Wyler recounted. "We solved the problems without the slightest suggestion of indelicacy, and without presenting Homer's hooks in a shocking or horrifying manner. As a matter of fact, we felt we could do quite the opposite and make it a moving and tender love scene."

The third story of Captain Fred Derry, the former B-17 bombardier, also required a change from Kantor's original. But the climactic transformation of the character lay less in Sherwood's script than in Wyler's directorial imagination.

"We wanted to have [him] relive one of his war experiences," Wyler noted, "and as a consequence have him realize that in order to win his personal battles as a civilian, it was necessary to apply the same courage and strength of character that he and twelve million others applied to win the war.

"This was the climax of Fred's story; unlike most movie stories, it had to be resolved in terms of a basic change in attitude, which is always difficult to handle in such an objective medium. 'You'll have to do something cinematic here,' Bob told me. 'I know just what we want to say, but it isn't to be said in words—it must be said with the camera, and that's your business.' He was right. In such instances, the author has a right to expect the director to do some 'directing.' "

Sherwood's script set up the situation: Derry leaves town defeated, unable to get a job, no longer with his wife or Peggy, whom he loves. He goes to the airport to hitch a ride on an army plane. While waiting, he wanders over to a vast military scrap heap, where there are endless rows of dismantled bombers.

"In long moving shots," Wyler wrote, "we follow Fred as he moves through the gigantic graveyard. At once the parallel was apparent: for four years Fred was trained, disciplined, and formed into a precise human instrument for destruction. Now his work is done, and he too has been thrown to the junk pile."

Filming the scene on location in Ontario, California, Wyler had Derry climb into one of the abandoned Flying Fortresses and crawl into the bombardier's seat in the nose of the plane.

"We did nothing in the interior of the B-17," Wyler pointed out, "except show Fred Derry seated and staring out through the dusty Plexiglas. Then we went to a long exterior shot of the plane, in which we could see the engine nacelles [housings], stripped of engines and propellers. We panned from nacelle to nacelle, as though there really were engines in them, and the engines were starting up for takeoff. Then we made another long shot, on a dolly, and also head on. We started moving our dolly in toward the nose of the B-17, through which we could see Fred seated at the bombardier's post. This shot created the illusion of the plane coming toward the camera, as if for a takeoff. To these shots we planned to add sound effects of engines starting and then let the musical score suggest flight. We then cut inside to a shot of Fred's back, and as we moved in, we saw his hand reach for the bomb release. We continued moving until we reached an effective close-up of Fred, framed against the Plexiglas nose of the bomber."

To give the feeling that Fred was reliving his combat experience, Sherwood created a preceding scene in which his father picks up Fred's discarded citation for the Distinguished Flying Cross and reads from it.

"The citation gave us not only a capsule form of exposition," Wyler explained, "but allowed us to make a sharp and ironic comment on Fred's reward for his war record, [his] discouragement and hopelessness and defeat as a civilian. The reading of the citation tells the audience the story of Fred's determination and courage, and the audience remembers it subsequently while Fred sits in the nose of the wrecked B-17. As a result of reliving his experience, Fred decides to take a job as a laborer, which isn't well paid but which may lead to a future in the building business. And so his story is resolved, not by letting him have a good job"—as in the Kantor original—"but by a change in his attitude to a realistic appraisal of himself. . . ."

Wyler worked closely with Sherwood in preparing the script. But while they got along well the script did not come easily. In early February, Wyler wrote Lillian Hellman, "We are having plenty of trouble with the Goldwyn picture, and it doesn't look like we'll get started shooting until sometime in March, if that." Meanwhile, he was keeping an eye out for projects to collaborate on with her. "I am so determined to make every effort to find something for us to do together," he wrote, "that I will keep searching for a story that you would be willing to do, and I hope you keep doing the same thing on your end. The only notion that I have about it is that I would like to do a truly great picture. The closest I have come to that in the past has been with your scripts. . . ."

By late March, with Sherwood's script completed and Talli about to give birth, Wyler couldn't wait to get started on the picture, now retitled *The Best Years of Our Lives.* He sounded chipper about the prospect of becoming a father for the third time. "Any day now," he told Hellman, "I expect to take a fast trip to the hospital with Talli, and if it's another girl you are invited to the drowning!" At the same time, as *Best Years* got closer to a shooting date, the strain in his relations with Goldwyn became more evident. "I am about to get started on the picture and have occasional attacks of 'Goldwynitis,'" he confided. "I thought the war had toughened my skin, but it has made me less immune than ever."

Goldwynitis could manifest itself in any number of forms and cause minor irritations or serious explosions. Wyler blew up, for example, when he learned the producer had ordered Harold Russell to take acting lessons.

"Mr. Goldwyn arranged for me to work with a coach," Russell says. "I went two days and the third day I was on the set for a wardrobe call when I ran into Mr. Wyler. He said, 'I haven't seen you. Where've you been?' And I said, 'I've been taking acting lessons.' Well, he hit the ceiling. He said, 'What do you mean, acting lessons?' I told him. And he said, 'You're not taking any more acting lessons. I didn't hire an actor. I hired a guy to play a role.' And that was the end of the lessons. Wyler didn't usually display his anger. But this time he was steamed."

The screenplay faced its last hurdle on March 30 when Joseph I. Breen, the head of the Production Code Administration, outlined various code violations in a meeting with Wyler and Sherwood at Wyler's home. Breen objected to "the breakup of the marriage between Fred and Marie." He also cited Wilma kissing Homer "passionately." All kisses between any of the characters "should not be prolonged, or lust-ful, and there should be no open-mouthed kissing." Some of the dia-logue was unacceptable: "Come here, Peggy, and give me a great big kiss," "a *hot* blonde baby," "bum," "Jew-lovers." A belch would have to be eliminated. And it was suggested that twin beds be shown in the Stephenson master bedroom.

In all, Breen's advisory amounted to eight typed pages of recommen-dations. Though Wyler and Sherwood agreed to some minor changes — "bum" and "Jew-lovers" were killed — they did not alter the structure or the substance of the script. Goldwyn gave them his full support, and the Breen office ultimately backed down.

On April 2, Talli gave birth to a son, William, Jr., nicknamed "Billy." Wyler's joy seemed boundless. "The family was complete," Talli remem-bered. "It was possibly one of the happiest days of our life." Two weeks later, on April 15, Wyler began filming *Best Years* and quickly found an-other reason for joy. He discovered that by sitting beneath the camera and attaching a headset and amplifier to the sound equipment, he could hear the actors with no trouble at all. In fact, the hookup even had cer-tain advantages. He heard precisely what the microphone heard on the set, with no distractions.

"Pretty clever, no?" Wyler boasted to Russell. "I put on this little in-novation, like you with your hooks, and I can work."

To Teresa Wright, who had appeared in two previous Wyler pictures, *The Little Foxes* and *Mrs. Miniver,* he seemed positively jaunty, eager to work, happier than she had ever seen him. As far as she could tell, there were no tensions on the set.

"He adored Freddie," Wright says. "They got along so beautifully. And he was very fond of Myrna. She was bright and intelligent and she had a lovely sense of humor. And he was thrilled to be getting back with Gregg Toland. It couldn't have been a better picture for him to come back to from the war. It seemed like an absolutely natural continuation for him. His knowledge of the war reinforced everything. I'm certain the script wouldn't have been as good without him."

Some things hadn't changed, of course. Despite running scenes in re-hearsal, Wyler still insisted on taking them over and over on camera. In-deed, for the first time it occurred to Wright that his quest for perfection may have been motivated to some degree by a sadistic impulse. That, at least, is how it seemed to her while watching Wyler direct a scene with Dana Andrews.

"Dana, who had a drinking problem, didn't report one day," she recounted. "They had to go find him, and we had to wait. They discovered him at some motel and brought him to the set and fed him a lot of coffee. He could work, but he was having a hard time.

"We were doing a scene that we started the night before. It was when the three guys come home—they've been out drinking—and they take Fred Derry home by car. Unfortunately, Dana hit his head getting out of the backseat. It was an accident. But Willy said, 'Hey, that's good. I like that. Do it again.' And that went on and on for about twenty-five takes. Dana was not going to complain. He just kept hitting his head harder and harder. I just cringed.

"What is so strange is that it was such a contradiction of the Willy I knew. He was not the milk of human kindness, but he was always so much fun to be around. And he *loved* Dana. He had the best rapport with him and Freddie and Myrna that I had ever seen."

Russell's hooks caused some minor discord. March cautioned him that his hooks were stealing scenes. In one bar sequence, Russell had to pour a bottle of beer. After one of the takes, March rolled his eyes. "When I say my lines, keep those goddamned hooks down!" he commanded. "Don't lift that bottle because I want people listening to what I'm saying, not watching you drink beer!"

The only real tension on the set, Wright says, occurred whenever Goldwyn came around and began giving Wyler advice. That would bring everything to a halt. "Willy just stalled and stalled," she remembered. "The lighting man stalled. The sound man stalled. Goldwyn got the message that nothing was going to be shot while he was there. So he would leave."

Usually Goldwyn went quietly, but sometimes his meddling ended in a nasty argument. "It's gotten to be an apocryphal story by now," Wright said, "but I'm sure I saw it happen. Goldwyn started yelling and screaming at Willy. 'You're so many pages behind schedule!' And Willy said very quietly: 'Okay, Sam. How many pages? Tear them up. We're back on schedule.'"

Russell confirms that the two butted heads often enough for everybody to notice. "Wyler came late to the set one morning. Apparently he'd just had a meeting with Goldwyn, and he was steamed. 'This goddamned picture!' he said. 'Goldwyn wants it *Produced by Sam Goldwyn. Directed by Sam Goldwyn. Acted by Sam Goldwyn. Written by Sam Goldwyn. Seen by Sam Goldwyn.*' The fact is, it was Wyler's picture, no question about it. It was Wyler's heart and soul. It was Wyler's wisdom that went into everything."

Certainly that personalization is nowhere more evident than in a key

scene in which Fred Derry comes to Homer's defense and socks a civilian who claims the Nazis and the Japanese were on the right side during the war. ("We fought the wrong people," he says.) Derry's blow
knocks the man down, smashing a drugstore display case. Derry gets
fired. The situation almost replicates Wyler's own fracas at the Statler.
Even Derry's lines to his boss — "I know, 'The customer is always right.'
But this customer is wrong"—have a familiar ring from the comments
Wyler made during the military investigation that nearly ended in his
court-martial.

Once filming began, Gregg Toland became Wyler's closest collaborator in translating the script to the screen. Even before production got
under way they had had many talks about the style of photography
Toland would use in this, their sixth and last, picture. "We decided to
try for as much simple realism as possible," Wyler noted. "We had a
clear-cut understanding that we would avoid glamour close-ups, and
soft, diffused backgrounds. . . . [And] since Gregg intended to carry his
focus to the extreme background of each set, detail in set designing,
construction and dressing became very important."

But more important, "carrying focus" in black-and-white cinematography provided crisp images with "good contrast and texture . . . establishing a mood of realism." Also—and this was paramount—it not only
allowed Wyler greater freedom in staging his scenes but imposed a
more rigorous, fluid and involving aesthetic. "I can have action and reaction in the same shot without having to cut back and forth from individual cuts of the characters," he explained. "This makes for smooth
continuity, an almost effortless flow of the scene, for much more interesting composition in each shot, and lets the spectator look from one to
the other character at his own will, do his own cutting." As useful as the
technique was, however, Wyler's concern really lay elsewhere. "I have
never been as interested in the externals of presenting a scene," he
pointed out, "as I have been in the inner workings of the people the
scene is about."

These comments would be echoed and elaborated upon in 1948 by
André Bazin, the leading intellectual among French film scholars. His
seminal essay about Wyler's body of work has remained the essential
analysis. Subsequent critics and scholars have either agreed or disagreed with it but have not been able to ignore it. In sum, Bazin regarded *Best Years* as the epitome of Wyler's "invisible style"—that is,
when the director chose to use it. He was an eclectic filmmaker, who lets
the content of each picture determine its own style. By "invisible," Bazin
meant his signature was honest, democratic and stripped down, in con-

trast, say, to that of Orson Welles, which he regarded as mannered, even sadistic.

Wyler's point, Bazin wrote, "is not to provoke the spectator, not to put him on the rack and torture him. All [he] wants is that the spectator can (1) see everything; and (2) choose as he pleases. It's an act of loyalty toward the spectator, an attempt at dramatic honesty." Bazin compares the neutrality and transparency of Wyler's staging—*"un style sans style"*—with André Gide's literary technique, which maximized clarity, immediacy and directness. He even counted the number of shots in *Best Years* to prove his point, noting that it used roughly one hundred-ninety per hour compared with three to four hundred an hour for the average picture. This meant longer, therefore less deceptive, shots that allow the audience to choose what it sees. Unlike Welles's use of "deep focus" to create effects (such as foreshortening perspective or heightening suspense), Wyler makes functional use of the technique.

"It is through professionalism, not as esthete but as craftsman, that he has become the consummate artist," Bazin wrote, noting this was already evident in *Dodsworth*. "When we talk about his direction, we must keep in mind . . . that his first and only worry is to make audiences *understand*. . . ."

When the filming of *Best Years* ended on August 9, four months after it began, the exposed footage came to about four hundred thousand feet. Wyler had met every morning with his longtime editor, Danny Mandell, to pick out the printed takes from the previous day that he wanted to use. He would tell Mandell how he intended to cut the scene and every few weeks would spend an evening running the assembled footage to see what they had. "By working this way," Wyler recalled, "I was able to avoid making mistakes on the set because I had a feeling of the picture as a whole." Moreover, the day after shooting was completed, Mandell had a first rough cut ready to show. It ran just a few minutes under three hours at sixteen thousand feet.

The picture was previewed for the first time in Long Beach on October 17 to test audience reaction to such a long film. Wyler expected he would have to make cuts. They already had done "quite a bit of reshuffling, intercutting the sequences to keep all segments of the story alive," Mandell recounted. This altered the continuity of some scenes from the original script, he noted, but the picture was still "very close to three hours." To their delight, the audience loved what it saw. Goldwyn, bursting with pride, wouldn't hear of further cuts or changes even though he knew a long picture would be more difficult to distribute. He initially planned to release *Best Years* in early 1947 at the Pantages Theater in Hollywood, but Wyler convinced him to move the opening up. He argued that the response to the previews had been so positive that the picture ought to be released in time to qualify for that year's Academy Awards.

Goldwyn went to New York with a print and managed to book *Best Years* on short notice at the prestigious Astor Theater in Times Square, where it opened on November 21.

To qualify for the Academy Awards, *Best Years* also had to play in the Los Angeles region before the year was out. And so the picture opened Christmas Day at the Beverly Theater in Beverly Hills. "After a euphoric opening, there was a party at the Brown Derby," Talli Wyler recalled. "We had a driving rainstorm, but that didn't seem to hinder anybody. The movie went over beautifully." Goldwyn threw nearly half a million dollars into an advertising campaign. Newspapers and magazines promoted benefit screenings. The cast went on radio programs to spread the word. The New York Film Critics named it the Best Movie of the Year on December 30. And in early January it garnered eight Oscar nominations, including the best picture and best director categories.

If anybody needed proof that Wyler still had "the golden touch," not to mention the artistic force that gave meaning to "the Goldwyn touch," this was it. *Best Years* drew acclaim across the social and political spectrum. The conservative *Los Angeles Times* editorialized that it represented "the better American spirit," while the liberal New York daily *PM* said "it must merit the gratitude of the whole country." The lowbrow *Daily News* declared it "the best picture from Hollywood since the end of the war," while the highbrow *New York Times* hailed it "not only as superlative entertainment but as food for quiet and humanizing thought." And Wyler came in for personal accolades across the critical spectrum. Dorothy Kilgallen declared that he "means more to filmgoers than they know. He is full of unexpected magic." James Agee wrote: "William Wyler has always seemed to me an exceedingly sincere and good director; he now seems one of the few great ones."

When the Academy Awards were held on March 13, 1947, Goldwyn tearfully accepted the first and only Oscar for best picture that he would ever receive. The ceremonies went public, also for the first time, at the mammoth Shrine Auditorium in Los Angeles. And for another first, Wyler got to collect his Oscar personally. Handing him the statuette, the previous year's winner Billy Wilder declared *Best Years* "the best-directed film I've ever seen in my life."

The picture swept five of its six other nominations: Fredric March for actor, Harold Russell for supporting actor (he also received a special Oscar "for bringing hope and courage to his fellow veterans"), Robert Sherwood for screenplay, Daniel Mandell for film editing and Hugo Friedhofer for musical score. Only Gordon Sawyer, nominated for sound recording, did not win. But the great irony, of course, was that Gregg Toland had not even been nominated for his black-and-white photography.

Despite its size and length, *Best Years* cost only two millon one hundred thousand dollars. Goldwyn spent as much on run-of-the-mill extravaganzas. *Up in Arms*, a forgettable 1944 war musical that introduced Danny Kaye to the screen, cost two million dollars. Of no interest today except for Kaye's debut, *Up in Arms* became one of Goldwyn's biggest money-makers. "Best Years," by comparison, not only became a long-lasting classic but an even bigger money-maker. It grossed almost ten and a half million dollars by the end of 1947, putting it ahead of *Mrs. Miniver* as the highest-grossing picture after *Gone With the Wind*. In London, it ran for more than a year and did better in England than *Gone With the Wind*. And it had a huge success worldwide, running for more than half a year in Sydney, nearly that long in Rio de Janeiro, Stockholm and Buenos Aires, and picking up best picture awards from Tokyo to Paris.

Best Years also drove a final stake into the heart of Wyler's professional relationship with Goldwyn. Besides not getting the promised screen credit of "A William Wyler Production," he discovered that Goldwyn had "cooked the books" and failed to pay him all royalties owed him. Wyler did not want to sue. As he had once told Teresa Wright during the filming of *Best Years* when she was having problems with the producer: "What you have to understand about Sam is that he can scream at you, and he can scream at the makeup man, and he can scream at me, and we'll all go home upset. But when Goldwyn goes home, he forgets about it and has a great time. I'll meet him that night to play poker and he'll be a marvelous host. All the anger is gone. His screaming is just a rite of passage. He gets to yell at everybody and then it's done."

But their latest disagreement festered. Wyler could get no satisfaction without a suit. He finally took Goldwyn to court in 1958, alleging that the net profits of *Best Years* had been understated by two million dollars between 1947 and 1951. Thus, he claimed, Goldwyn owed him an additional four hundred and three thousand dollars.

Goldwyn rebutted the claim in a statement to the press: "Willy Wyler, a very fine director and a good friend of mine," has received "something over one million four hundred thousand dollars for direct-ing" the picture "but this suit seems to indicate that he thinks he is enti-tled to more. This is a free country, and if Willy feels he has been mistreated by being paid such a paltry sum, he is certainly entitled to the great American privilege of going to court."

Wyler's reluctance to sue stemmed from the wish to avoid nasty pub-licity, but also from a certain fondness for Goldwyn. He did not want to personally embarrass his old boss. "I don't much like the use of words like 'fraudulent,'" he instructed his lawyer. "I assume they are necessary in an action of this kind, but, whenever possible in the future, please avoid saying anything that sounds insulting to Goldwyn. We are simply asking an impartial jury to make a decision on a difference of opinion, and that is what the courts are for. . . . P.S. But since we *are* suing, let's *win!*"

By the time Wyler filed the suit, *Best Years* had earned another five million dollars, for a total of fifteen million after distribution fees were deducted. Goldwyn fought the suit for four years. In 1962 they finally settled out of court, when Wyler agreed to a payment of eighty thou-sand dollars.

29

〰〰〰〰〰〰

ARE YOU NOW, OR HAVE
YOU EVER BEEN?

AT THE HEIGHT OF HIS SUCCESS, Wyler's bid for independence ran into an unexpected detour. He and Capra had a congenial relationship based more on mutual professional respect than deep personal friendship. Their business association, Liberty Films, rested on similar agendas to the extent that they both wanted total artistic control over their pictures without interference from the likes of a Goldwyn or a Harry Cohn. But even as Wyler's first postwar picture swept the Academy Awards in March 1947, their fondest wish was beginning to unravel. Ironically, the huge response to *Best Years* contributed to Liberty's demise before the company could get off the ground.

Capra had started the venture in early 1945 with Samuel Briskin, a top executive he knew from his years at Columbia Pictures. After Wyler became a partner later that year, they turned for a fourth to George Stevens. Briskin would manage the mechanics of production, distribution and finance, leaving the three directors free to concentrate on filmmaking. Their aim, spelled out in a Liberty policy statement, was "complete freedom in planning" and "absolute authority," over the creative process. Each of the partners put up a hundred fifty thousand dollars—Wyler borrowed on his life insurance to raise his share—and each drew weekly salaries of three thousand dollars against their investment. Although they were equal partners, they owned slightly different amounts of stock. Capra had thirty-two percent, Wyler and Stevens twenty-five percent and Briskin eighteen percent. Liberty then signed a deal with RKO, calling for each director to make three pictures. RKO agreed to provide facilities and arrange bank loans. The nine productions were expected to cost a total of about fifteen million dollars.

Regarded by the industry as a bellwether for the future, Liberty's high-minded policy statement could not have been more idealistic in tone. "The time element in production will be relegated to a place of secondary importance," the shareholders maintained. "Cost of production likewise will have a yardstick of its own, unique in filmmaking." It is hard to believe experienced Hollywood hands, even principled studio renegades with reputations for painstaking craft, could have expected to operate on that basis without unusually deep pockets—which they did not have.

Liberty ran into trouble with Capra's first picture, *It's a Wonderful Life*. He began filming at the same time Wyler started on *Best Years*. They kidded each other in an exchange of telegrams. Wyler cabled: LAST ONE IN IS A ROTTEN EGG. WILLY. Capra replied: MY FIRST DAY WAS EASY BUT DO YOU KNOW THEY'RE USING SOUND TODAY. FRANK. *It's a Wonderful Life* not only ran over budget by a not-so-wonderful million dollars—production costs came to more than three million—it floundered at the box office. To qualify for the Oscars, RKO released the most expensive picture of Capra's career around Christmas in New York and Los Angeles, where it went head to head with *Best Years*. It failed to earn back expenditures—nearly four million dollars including distribution fees—and was shut out at the Academy Awards despite five nominations. The financial problem arising from Capra's popular and critical rejection was compounded by a shrinking market. All-time high attendance of eighty million movie patrons a week in 1946 dropped rapidly the following year to just sixty-two million. While *Best Years* cleaned up at the box office and vaulted Wyler into the country's top ten wage earners, Capra's picture dried up Liberty's cash flow. "I can't begin to describe my sense of loneliness in making that first film, a loneliness that was laced by the fear of failure," Capra wrote in his autobiography. With movie attendance declining and his picture a flop, Liberty lost its nerve. Capra thought it best to sell the company as quickly as possible and salvage what they could of its assets. He broached the idea to his partners. Briskin agreed. Wyler hesitated. He was willing to stick with Liberty.

But he also knew it was Capra's call. Stevens objected, until he discovered that another independent company he'd considered joining also was on the block. In fact, all the independents created in Liberty's wake were folding their tents.

Paramount and MGM made offers for Liberty's assets, valued at about four million dollars. Among other things, the company owned film rights to literary properties like Jessamyn West's *The Friendly Persuasion* and Alfred Noyes's *No Other Man*. The greatest assets, though, were the future services of its three directors. Paramount, feeling the need of "prestige" pictures, offered a block of stock worth slightly more than three million dollars to be divided four ways by Liberty's partners. For his percentage in the company, Wyler received Paramount stock worth three-quarters of a million dollars. He also agreed to make five pictures for Paramount at a flat fee of up to a hundred fifty thousand dollars a picture. Capra agreed to make three pictures, Stevens four, for the same fees. Briskin became a Paramount executive who would supervise their projects.

"They assured us we would have the same independence as before, which didn't turn out to be true," Wyler explained years later. "We still had to have their approval of subject and budget."

Advised by his agent "to be smart and knock off the five in two years," Wyler would try to do that in his fashion. First he worked with his former Air Force buddies, Sy Bartlett and Beirne Lay, who were writing *Twelve O'Clock High*. Paramount turned him down. The picture, about the psychological pressure on American fliers during the war, went to Darryl Zanuck at Twentieth Century–Fox. Then, while making his first picture for Paramount, *The Heiress*, in 1948, Wyler helped screenwriter Michael Wilson prepare an adaptation of Thomas Wolfe's *Look Homeward, Angel*. But he could not get approval to make that either, even though Paramount had purchased rights to the novel for him. Miffed, Wyler drafted a memo calling the decision "entirely unreasonable."

He reminded the studio, "This is the second time I wanted very much to make a picture and spent a great deal of time and energy on it, only to have the project turned down."

Over the next year, Paramount rejected one proposal after another: *No Way Out*, formerly Capra's project at Liberty about a young black doctor; a biopic about Roosevelt with a script by Sherwood; Wilson's *Olympus*, a picture about a nuclear physicist; and Marcel Pagnol's *Fanny*, a property Wyler once wanted to make at Universal. It would take

Wyler seven years to fulfill his obligation to Paramount under his five-picture deal. Capra and Stevens never fulfilled theirs.

With the sale of Liberty being concluded, Wyler decided it was time to take Talli on her first "grand tour" of Europe. Because much of the continent was still in ruins, it would not be the usual grand tour. But it was, as Talli later recalled, "unforgettable." Her parents came up from Dallas and stayed with the three children. In June the couple left for a three-month vacation. Doctors did not want Wyler to fly, for fear he would lose more of his hearing, so they took the train to New York, where they departed for Southampton, England, on the *Queen Elizabeth*. Accompanying them aboard ship was a spanking new Buick convertible, which they bought in New York.

They saw Olivier and Leigh and spent a weekend at their country home near London. They met Carol Reed and his future bride "Pempie" (actress Penelope Ward), the Ralph Richardsons and Alex Korda. "I was so excited to be there I practically developed a fever," Talli remembered. "We stayed at Claridge's. Willy was thrilled to be back and eager to show me the scenes of his war escapades. The city still hadn't recovered from the war. Waiters wore threadbare uniforms and served the smallest portions from magnificent silver trays. No meal was more than three courses, and a slice of bread was considered a course. Paris was no better for food." They drove to Mulhouse, where Willy introduced Talli to childhood friends and toured his old haunts. He also pulled some military strings and obtained credentials as a war correspondent, allowing them to enter American-occupied Germany.

"There wasn't a car on the road in Europe," Wyler remembered. "The Buick was the first car with automatic transmission, power windows and automatic convertible top. When a cabdriver in Paris came over to give me hell about something, I pushed the button and the window went up. He nearly fainted. In little towns, I'd wait till there was a good crowd, then I'd push the button and the top would go back. It was pandemonium, people came running. A kid once asked me if the car was amphibious."

Talli recalled, "The summer was incredibly hot. You can imagine how delicious it was driving through the deserted countryside. Whenever we got to a river, we would pull the car off the road, strip off our clothes and leap in."

They drove as far east as Berlin and back to Switzerland, where they stopped in Bern and Geneva, finally heading through the south of France to the Riviera. There, they joined Lillian Hellman in Antibes at the Hôtel du Cap. Coming home on the *Queen Mary,* they ran into Merle Oberon, Cary Grant and his wife-to-be, the actress Betsy Drake.

THE SPECTER OF HOLLYWOOD'S "RED SCARE" GREETED THE WY-lers on their return. In late September 1947, more than forty people working in the movie industry received subpoenas to appear before the House Committee on Un-American Activities, headed by J. Parnell Thomas. He was about to convene a congressional hearing in Washington, D.C., on "alleged subversive influence in motion pictures." Within days Wyler met with two old friends, John Huston and the screenwriter Philip Dunne, as well as Alexander Knox, a prominent Canadian character actor. The four decided to rally opposition to the hearing. They called their campaign "Hollywood Fights Back," soon after known as the Committee for the First Amendment.

"Our first meeting was at Lucey's," Dunne recounted. "It was a restaurant across from the RKO and Paramount studios. I called the meeting. I talked it over with Willy first. It was Willy who called John in on it. [Huston was an officer in the Screen Directors Guild.] Alex just wanted to be part of it. After that meeting we all went home and began making phone calls. The thing snowballed. The next meeting, the big meeting, was at Ira Gershwin's house. He had a large house and the place was packed. We changed the name of our group to the Committee for the First Amendment because we believed the 'unfriendly' witnesses who'd been subpoenaed would adopt a clear-cut constitutional defense."

J. Parnell Thomas, the HUAC chairman, was a tiny, pink-faced Republican congressman from New Jersey who craved headlines and believed the easiest way to get them would be to attack the film industry. He had been out to Los Angeles five months earlier in May and had taken secret testimony at the Biltmore Hotel from fourteen so-called "friendly" witnesses. Thomas and HUAC's chief investigator Robert E. Stripling briefed the press daily on what had been said behind closed doors.

Lela Rogers, Ginger's mother, reportedly testified that she believed writers Dalton Trumbo and Clifford Odets were Communists. Her daughter, she said, had declined to utter a line ("Share and share alike, that's democracy") in one of Trumbo's screenplays. The actor Adolph Menjou had called Hollywood "one of the main centers of Communist activity in America." The infiltration of Hollywood by subversive elements, according to Thomas, had resulted in "flagrant Communist propaganda films," among them *Song of Russia, Tender Comrade* and *The Best Years of Our Lives.* This cried out for exposure. Among others who gave secret testimony were actors Robert Taylor and Gary Cooper and, reluctantly, Warner Bros. production chief Jack L. Warner.

With HUAC's Washington hearings scheduled to begin October 20, 1947, the Committee for the First Amendment convened at Gershwin's house in a defiant mood. A huge crowd of top stars gathered that night, including Edward G. Robinson, Danny Kaye, Judy Garland, Gene Kelly, Humphrey Bogart, Lauren Bacall, Burt Lancaster, Evelyn Keyes, Sterling Hayden, Jane Wyatt, Marsha Hunt, John Garfield, Henry Fonda, Ava Gardner, Myrna Loy, Gregory Peck, Paulette Goddard, Katharine Hepburn. They prepared a declaration, went public with it several days later in full-page newspaper ads across the country and presented it to Congress in the form of a petition.

"We the undersigned, as American citizens who believe in constitutional democratic government, are disgusted and outraged by the continuing attempt of [HUAC] to smear the Motion Picture Industry," it said. "We hold that these hearings are morally wrong because: Any investigation into the political beliefs of the individuals is contrary to the basic principles of our democracy; any attempt to curb freedom of expression and to set arbitrary standards of Americanism is in itself disloyal to both the spirit and the letter of the Constitution."

During the meeting prearranged phone calls came from Washington with an update on the latest HUAC developments. After further discussion, the Committee for the First Amendment decided to send a delegation to the hearings as a further show of support. They chartered a TWA Constellation from Howard Hughes for thirteen thousand dollars. The tycoon "had no interest" in the protest, Huston told the press. "It was strictly a business deal." The plane was called, by an unfortunate coincidence, *Star of the Red Sea.*

According to Dunne, the CFA founders retained control of the ad hoc group with the help of an informal steering committee: director Anatole Litvak, screenwriter Julius Epstein, actor Sheppard Strudwick, producers Joseph Sistrom (a conservative Republican) and David Hopkins (the son of FDR confidant Harry Hopkins). Volunteers recruited for the flight to Washington included many of the stars who had gathered at Gershwin's. Wyler wanted to go but was advised by his doctors not to fly. "Originally Huston was going to go alone, without the two of us," Dunne recounted. "But he called me in the middle of the night and said, 'You're not going to leave me with this bunch of mani-acs.' So the two of us went, and Willy stayed behind. We wanted some-one to run things, anyway, while we were gone."

The night before the October 26 flight, Wyler called a meeting at Chasen's restaurant and reminded the delegation that they were likely to come under political attack. According to Dunne, Wyler cautioned, "If anyone aboard the plane is in the slightest degree vulnerable, our en-tire group and its cause could be discredited. If there is anything in any of your pasts that could hurt you or us, don't go. You don't have to tell us about it. Just don't show up at the airport tomorrow morning."

(Lauren Bacall remembers his warning rather differently: "Wyler told us we must not look like slobs. We were representing a lot of people in the industry, we must make a good impression—the women were to wear skirts, not slacks; the men, shirts and ties.")

Wyler himself has recounted that he told the delegation to maintain a distance from the unfriendly witnesses. "I told them that the newspa-pers would say they were there to defend the Communists, but that they were going to Washington to attack the House Un-American Activities Committee and not to defend any Communists."

The distinction later became a matter of controversy. Detractors of the CFA would claim that its stance ultimately betrayed the unfriendly witnesses by seeming to equivocate. Why wouldn't the CFA stand up for Communists, if it believed that citizens in a democracy had a right to their political beliefs? Defenders of the CFA would claim that the un-friendly witnesses themselves had muddied the constitutional waters by engaging in a vociferous debate with HUAC. Instead of declining to an-swer questions on the grounds of their First Amendment rights, many chose to answer some questions but not others. According to Dunne, that was a misguided attempt to defend themselves with self-righteous pronouncements.

"We had two specific goals," Wyler recalled in his autobiography. "First, we timed our flight to Washington to support the scheduled testi-mony of Eric Johnston, the [president and] spokesman for the [Motion Picture] Production Association, who had publicly declared that the motion picture companies would never impose a blacklist nor submit to censorship. Second, we intended to confront Richard Nixon, the only congressman on the House Committee from our home state, and re-quest that he either call off the hearings or insist on a reformation of its procedures."

Wyler's concern about sending a CFA delegation to Washington that might include Communists stemmed not just from fear of attacks by the press. (In fact, as the hearings progressed, it was HUAC that came under editorial attack by the responsible press while the CFA drew favorable coverage.) Wyler, Dunne and Huston worried even more that once the CFA delegation entered the caucus room of the House Office Building, where the hearings were being held, Thomas very well might subpoena the delegates and put them under oath. According to Dunne, this possibility unsettled them. "It caused heated discussion as our chartered Constellation droned toward Washington," he said. "We had to have a principled defense to the question: 'Are you now or have you ever been a member of the Communist Party?'"

The delegation aboard the plane "finally agreed on a unified course of action," Dunne noted. "If any or all of us were called to the stand and asked the question, we would reply, 'I must respectfully decline to answer that question, on the grounds that the information is privileged under the First Amendment to the Constitution.' We would then call a press conference, ask a Supreme Court justice to put us under oath . . . and answer all questions the newspapermen cared to ask us, including the Sixty-Four-Dollar one. We felt that this second step, though it might to some extent detract from the purity of our stand, was necessary to protect the major stars on the flight."

Moreover, by proving it had nothing to hide, the CFA delegation felt it might sway public opinion not so much about its principles but about HUAC's lack of them. "I didn't like that compromise," Dunne recounted, still eager to set the record straight forty-two years later. "But there was no other way. We would make that statement before the congressional committee and there would be nothing it could do except to dismiss us and cite us for contempt. Then Supreme Court Justice Felix Frankfurter, who was a friend of my father's, would swear us in on the radio and we would express our political affiliations. We would 'come out.' But it would not be under the direct duress of the committee."

Thomas chose to play a different game. He switched witnesses. Instead of calling Johnston, as scheduled, he called John Howard Lawson, a co-founder and former president of the Screen Writers Guild, who, Dunne said, "could be counted on to foul things up." Johnston had a likable personality. He'd made persuasive speeches against HUAC (though in secret he was advising producers not to keep "proven Communists" on their payrolls). Lawson, on the other hand, was "the grand old man of Hollywood Communism." He had a notoriously self-dramatizing personality. As the first of the unfriendly witnesses, his contentious testimony set the tone for what would follow.

Lawson tried to assert his rights. "I am not on trial here, Mr. Chairman," he said. "This committee is on trial before the American people. Let us get that straight." He had a prepared statement to read, but Thomas wouldn't allow it. Lawson denounced the committee for "the old technique . . . used in Hitler's Germany . . . to create a scare here!" Thomas threatened him with contempt. Lawson shouted that his rights were being trampled. Correct though he was, the witness succeeded in making a high-handed spectacle of himself. (In the prepared remarks that he never got to deliver, Lawson accused the committee of relying on "stool pigeons, neurotics, publicity-seeking clowns, Gestapo agents, paid informers and a few ignorant and frightened Hollywood artists.") When Thomas dismissed him, Lawson refused to leave until forced out of his chair. That he was grandstanding immediately became clear to the press. After being hustled from the caucus room, his bitter demeanor turned to smiles for the photographers. Following Lawson's testimony, an FBI agent testified that he had copies of registration cards for the Communist Party from 1944, Lawson's among them.

The rest of the Hollywood Ten — so named because ten of the original nineteen unfriendly witnesses were called to testify — included six other screenwriters of varied talent and reputation: Dalton Trumbo, Albert Maltz, Ring Lardner, Jr., Lester Cole, Samuel Ornitz, Alvah Bessie, as well as director Edward Dmytryk, producer-director Herbert Biberman and producer-writer Adrian Scott. (An eleventh unfriendly witness, the German playwright Bertolt Brecht, left the country after he testified.)

As the Hollywood Ten's testimony played out, and the CFA's advice was all but ignored, the notion of a principled defense seemed to dissolve in pandemonium. "I think their tactics were abysmal and self-defeating," Dunne recalled. "They wound up yelling and shouting and saying, 'I'm trying to answer your question.' Even my friend Ring Lardner, who was one of the two people among the Ten for whom I had any respect, made that mistake. I think if they had followed our strategy, which we had suggested to them, it would have been very hard to throw them in prison. . . . The First Amendment may have been on the minds of the Hollywood Ten when they evaded direct answers to the questions, but in only a few cases did it fall from their lips. At best it appeared as an afterthought, which could be paraphrased: 'I am trying to answer your questions, which, by the way, I don't think you have any right to ask me.' This is hardly the way to pose a clear-cut constitutional issue."

Meanwhile, the CFA's attempt to confront Richard Nixon, the young Republican congressman from California, also fizzled. He had flown back to California just as the CFA delegation arrived in Washington. "We phoned Willy and asked him to get hold of Nixon," Dunne remembered. "Willy tried to find him, to present our petition personally. But Nixon disappeared. He wasn't home. He wasn't in his office. Nobody knew where he was."

During the first week of hearings HUAC had put on a host of friendly witnesses whose testimony it knew in advance, having interviewed them previously in Los Angeles. Besides Menjou, Cooper, and Warner, it brought on Ayn Rand, Ronald Reagan, Walt Disney and Louis B. Mayer, among others. To counter HUAC's celebrity parade, the CFA put on its own show with two national radio broadcasts directed by Norman Corwin, on October 26 and November 2. The shows enlisted everyone from Joseph Cotten to Frank Sinatra and consisted of fervent partisan testimonials.

Because Wyler had come under attack, Gene Kelly asked the radio audience: "Did you happen to see *The Best Years of Our Lives?* Did you like it? Were you subverted by it? Did it make you un-American? Did you come out of the movie with the desire to overthrow the government?"

Wyler, for his part, told the radio audience: "I wouldn't be allowed to make *The Best Years of Our Lives* in Hollywood today. That is directly the result of the activities of the Un-American Activities Committee. They are making decent people afraid to express their opinions. They are creating fear in Hollywood. Fear will result in self-censorship. Self-censorship will paralyze the screen. In the last analysis, you will suffer. . . . You will be given a diet of pictures which conform to arbitrary standards of Americanism."

Thomas called an abrupt halt to the hearings on October 30, two weeks after they began, citing each and every one of the Hollywood Ten for contempt. Meanwhile, the CFA opposition had struck a chord not only in the press but with public opinion and was beginning to neutralize the impact of the hearings. Thomas denied being "swayed, intimidated or influenced by either Hollywood glamour, pressure groups, threats, ridicule or high-pressure tactics on the part of high-paid puppets and apologists for the motion picture industry." But, as his chief investigator said, the hearings had begun to sound like "a broken record." And in any case, their damage was done.

A month later, on November 24, the House of Representatives voted by nearly unanimous margins to uphold the contempt citations against each of the Hollywood Ten. That same day, the top echelon of the motion picture industry and their minions gathered in New York at the

Waldorf—Astoria to give birth to the blacklist. It took a few days, but the Waldorf Statement—announced by Eric Johnston in a stunning about-face of his public stance—represented total capitulation to HUAC. Johnston announced that each of the Hollywood Ten would be fired immediately and would not be rehired until he was either acquitted or purged of the contempt charges and declared "under oath that he is not a Communist." This edict came with a mind-boggling disclaimer that "we do not desire to prejudge their legal rights."

More broadly, the producers proclaimed they would not knowingly employ a Communist and would root out "alleged subversive and disloyal elements in Hollywood" by combining efforts with the various talent guilds. They acknowledged that some innocent people might get hurt and conceded "the risk of creating an atmosphere of fear." But they would do their utmost to "guard against this danger." Above all, they wanted the world to know that "in pursuing this policy, we are not going to be swayed by hysteria or intimidation from any source." The Orwellian implications were manifold.

"In the aftermath of all that," Dunne recalled, "when we had been pretty well defeated by the producers' cowardice, Willy didn't want to disband the Committee [for the First Amendment]. There was a bit of a pogrom mentality. He wanted to fight that, unlike some naturalized Americans who felt vulnerable to HUAC and had a reverence for authority. Willy was not afraid."

Indeed, Wyler wrote Hellman that J. Parnell Thomas and his ilk "have been an education for many of us" and that the CFA had to continue mobilizing. "My guess, if we learned nothing else," he observed, "is that these gentlemen won't stop attacking or vilifying us because we soft-pedalled. . . . We need to maintain an office and a paid secretary. . . . We want to be able to take out further advertisements, as they may become necessary. . . . We want to send out information to the thousand or more people who consider themselves members of our group. Thomas and the rest of his boys are only quiet for the moment. We want to be able to come out fighting whenever they come back."

Basically, however, there was nothing the CFA could do once the blacklist took hold. In an effort to head it off just days before the Waldorf statement, Wyler and Dunne met with various studio chiefs and the Hollywood Ten and found themselves rebuffed on both sides. Further, their attempt at mediation was "seen as spineless by many on the left," and especially by the Hollywood Ten. Worse, the Red Scare had yet to peak. It would reach a climax in the early fifties with a second round of HUAC hearings and Senator Joseph McCarthy's separate Senate investigation of purported Communist spies in the government.

In 1950, when Edward Dmytryk of the Hollywood Ten was about to go off to prison for six months, he came to Wyler's home unexpectedly. "Willy excused himself and took Dmytryk upstairs to his study," Bob Parrish, who was having dinner with the Wylers that evening, recalls: "They were gone about two hours. I wasn't going home until I heard what that was all about. When Willy came back, we found out."

Wyler said Dmytryk wanted his advice and told him he was not a Communist and never had been. "Why the hell didn't you say that before?" Wyler asked. Dmytryk said he felt pressured by the rest of the Hollywood Ten. But under the circumstances, what should he do? Wyler said to get in touch with him after he began serving his sentence. He would arrange a press conference for Dmytryk, who would say exactly what he had just told him. That might get him parole.

Dmytryk never called. But he signed a statement in prison claiming he was not a Communist. It also said that he felt he was right not to cooperate with HUAC. When that didn't get him off the blacklist, he went before HUAC again and this time admitted he had been a Communist, after all. He also named names. It wasn't long before he was directing *The Caine Mutiny.*

Parrish recalls that Wyler purposely made light of the situation. "Bob," he said. "Never trust anybody, especially a member of the Directors Guild."

The blacklist would continue for another decade.

30

EATING ACTORS ALIVE

ANGERED BY THE PARANOID AT-
mosphere taking hold of Hollywood and frustrated by Paramount's lack
of enthusiasm for his proposals, Wyler was only too happy to answer
the phone one day and hear Olivia de Havilland's voice on the other end
of the line asking him to direct her next picture. She had just come from
New York, she told him, where she'd seen a play called *The Heiress*. It
had a great role for her, she said, and she was certain she could help him
sell Paramount on the idea.

Wyler and de Havilland knew each other socially from just before the
war, when she'd had a passionate affair with John Huston. One of the
film colony's gutsier personalities, de Havilland often chose her own
picture material. She had freed herself from Warner Bros. in 1944 with
a landmark suit that limited studio contracts to a maximum of seven
years, then resumed her career at Paramount in 1946 with an Oscar-
winning performance in a soapy melodrama, *To Each His Own*. Another
Wyler friend, Anatole Litvak, had just finished directing her in *The
Snake Pit* for Twentieth Century–Fox, and industry insiders were
buzzing over her masterly portrait of a woman suffering a mental breakdown.

De Havilland urged Wyler to go to New York and see *The Heiress* for himself. It was a Broadway hit, adapted by Ruth and Augustus Goetz from the Henry James novella *Washington Square*. Wyler saw the play in January 1948, four months after it opened, and couldn't believe the screen rights hadn't been snapped up. Set in nineteenth-century Manhattan, the play centered on Catherine Sloper, the homely daughter of a well-to-do physician who dominates her. Though it captured the stiff manners of an old-fashioned era, it was less a period piece than a psychological power struggle.

The play dramatized Catherine's courtship by a handsome young man whom her father suspects of being a gold digger. Catherine is refined but so painfully shy, plain, and lacking in social graces that her father cannot believe anybody would be attracted to her unless he were interested in her money. He himself resents her, despite an outward show of fatherly concern, because she cannot measure up to his idealized memory of her mother, a ravishing beauty who died giving birth to her. When the charming Morris Townsend turns up out of the blue and sweeps Catherine off her feet, she learns for the first time that her father doesn't truly love her and—shocking to her, though less shocking to us—neither does Townsend.

In New York, Wyler immediately contacted the playwrights through their agent. "We came down from the country and met him at the Pierre Hotel," Ruth Goetz remembered. "He wanted to know all about James's original story, what we had changed and what we had supplied. I'm always amused when people say we simply took everything from the original. It's not true. The James story doesn't have the jilt in it. We also found the key to the story: the cruel fact that Catherine is a child her father didn't love. It was brutal stuff, and nobody had put that in the theater before."

Wyler told them, "It's against the law for me to hire you to write the screenplay until I own the property. But I'm going to own it, so we might as well talk now." They discussed the play for three hours," Goetz recounted, "and by the time we left him that day, we knew he wanted us. I thought he was first-rate."

A few days later Paramount made an offer for the rights. But the playwrights thought it wasn't good enough. They wanted a piece of the gross. Paramount countered that it never made that kind of deal and wasn't going to start with them.

"Then Willy phoned and said, 'Please don't let this fall through,'" Goetz recalled. "Well, both Gus and I trusted him. We asked, 'How do you know we'll be the writers on the picture?' And he said, 'I'm not going to have it deformed by somebody who doesn't know what to do with it.' The next phone call we got, Paramount said we would do the adaptation, too."

The studio upped its bid to two hundred and fifty thousand dollars, which was still a flat fee for the rights, but sweetened the pie by offering the Goetzes an open-ended salary of ten thousand dollars per week to write the screenplay. That, and Wyler's promise of a quality production, brought them to Hollywood.

Although the picture was to be shot entirely on the studio lot, Paramount did not stint on the budget. Studio chief Barney Balaban had decreed that no picture should cost more than a million and a half dollars, but Wyler was allowed a considerably higher sum. Before shooting began, *The Heiress* had an estimated budget of two and a half million dollars. Four hundred thousand alone went to salaries for the cast.

Wyler filled out the roles surrounding de Havilland's with a stunning ensemble. First he persuaded Sir Ralph Richardson to come to Hollywood and reprise the role of Catherine's father, Dr. Sloper, which the great British actor was playing on the London stage opposite Peggy Ashcroft's Catherine. It was a real coup to get him. Richardson had turned down recent Hollywood offers because of his busy theatrical life, especially his devotion to the Old Vic. But he and Wyler had hit it off the previous summer at the Oliviers' country home. Contrary to his austere public image, Richardson had a wicked sense of humor. He also loved the pleasure of good company. To Wyler's delight, he drove big fast cars and owned a motorcycle, which the actor used regularly to zip around London.

For Townsend, played in the Broadway production strictly as a bounder, Wyler thought early on of hiring Errol Flynn to capitalize on his real-life Casanova reputation. Though Flynn's career had peaked, his name also had marquee value. In addition, de Havilland had played Flynn's passive foil in nine swashbucklers for Warner Bros. a decade earlier. Bending that chemistry to a serious purpose just might work, Wyler thought. He sent Flynn the script, but the actor was reluctant and turned him down. "Morris," he replied, "is not for me."

Wyler, for his part, came to the same conclusion. He had decided to soften Townsend's image as a fortune hunter and blur his motives, making them more ambiguous in the movie than they had been in the play or the novel. Needing a subtler actor, he agreed to cast Montgomery Clift, then a promising young stage star who had just made a splashy screen debut in *The Search* and was about to make an even bigger splash in *Red River*, which he had already filmed. Clift had a three-picture deal with

Paramount at a hundred fifty thousand dollars each, beginning with *The Heiress*. But Clift, like Flynn, was dubious about taking the role. He had heard the usual stories that Wyler ate actors alive. He would not accept the part, he insisted, until he first had a private talk with the cannibal himself.

Far from making any forceful demands, however, Clift tried to ingratiate himself with a long speech in a quavering voice. "Mr. Wyler, any actor would be crazy not to work for you. We know you're demanding, absolutely meticulous."

Wyler said nothing.

"You've made some great pictures—more, I guess, than any other one director in town. All right. You're going to be rough on me. . . . I'm willing to take it for the sake of a good picture.

"But when you find things wrong with my work," Clift went on, "would you please take me off quietly in a corner and tell me, and please not shout at me?"

"I don't bawl out actors," Wyler replied. "I might correct something."

Ironically, it was Clift who drove Wyler to distraction and not the other way around. The young star showed up on the set with a personal acting coach and wouldn't talk to anyone but her. The two of them would hide away in his dressing room to run lines. "This annoyed Willy and set his teeth on edge," Talli recalled. Clift also came to work dressed like a beachcomber in a torn jacket, T-shirt and jeans. It seems he was determined to protect the bohemian image that he'd recently created for himself. It became evident to everybody on the set that regardless of his relationship with Wyler, the notion of playing a Victorian character didn't appeal to him in the slightest.

"Monty was brand-new to me," Goetz recalled. "He slouched around in shoes with no backs. He scuffed his feet as he walked, just like a little boy. Monty was a problem, because he came on like a star. I went to Willy and told him, 'He's not serious. He looks like a bum.' Willy said, 'What do you want that he isn't doing?' I said, 'I want him to at least try to have the air of a man of the nineteenth century. His walk is all wrong. It just won't do.' Willy was very thoughtful. 'Okay,' he said, 'tell you what. We'll give him dancing lessons.' So Willy got him a dancing teacher and had him take lessons every afternoon for about three weeks."

Meanwhile, Clift's insecurities turned into disdainful complaints. He wouldn't speak to de Havilland and sniped about her to friends. "She memorizes her lines at night and comes to work waiting for the director to tell her what to do," he observed. "You can't get by with that in the theater, and you don't have to in the movies. Her performance is being totally shaped by Wyler." At the same time, he played his scenes with her as though she didn't exist. De Havilland recalled, "I had a sense that Monty was thinking almost entirely of himself and leaving me out. It was difficult for me to adapt to playing that way. But my having to adapt to him, and not his adapting to me, was really part of my character, so in the end it worked. But there was something . . . well, something in Monty that just stood apart from the proceedings."

Clift also seemed to think there was a conspiracy between director and cast to hurt his performance. He accused Wyler of favoring de Havilland. He claimed that Miriam Hopkins, who portrayed Catherine's Aunt Lavinia, was stealing scenes and that Wyler was doing nothing to stop her. He felt overshadowed by Richardson, whose ability to respond to Wyler's direction intimidated him. "Can't that man make a mistake?" he whined. "I cannot, will not do a scene the same way each time."

In fact, one of Richardson's strengths as an actor was his genius for variation. What impressed Wyler most about him was that he did not have to stick with the same idea. The pattern was set "in the first scene we made," Wyler recalled, "a simple shot of Ralph coming in a door." Dr. Sloper enters his house, hangs up his top hat and cane and wakes Catherine, who has fallen asleep waiting for him to come home, by jangling his keys gently in her ear.

"How would you like me to do this?" Richardson asked.

"There aren't many ways," Wyler said.

"There are several. Can I show you?"

Richardson quickly ran through half a dozen alternatives.

"It was like a symphony," Wyler said. "Each time it was absolute perfection in movement, so effortless. And each time it was a little bit different. I realized this was the kind of actor who doesn't need a director." Richardson had given him "a display laying out his merchandise. He entered the set as if he had lived there twenty years. I suspect that all the time he knew which way he wanted to do it."

There was some truth, however, to Clift's opinion of de Havilland. Her performance *was* being shaped by Wyler, and with a relentless precision that helped her win a second Academy Award for best actress. "She got a lot of attention from Willy because he knew she didn't really have the ass to swing it," Goetz said. "She was no heavyweight. Tola [Anatole Litvak] had gotten a good performance out of her in *The Snake Pit*. That was really her only serious picture. Willy believed he could get a good performance, too, if he kept at her."

Wyler pushed de Havilland hard. The most striking example came in the "staircase scene" near the end of the picture. Catherine has waited hours for Townsend to show up on the night they were to elope. Finally, realizing the awful truth—that he has jilted her—she ends her midnight vigil and climbs the stairs to her room with her suitcase. It was a climactic moment, and Wyler did not like the feeling the actress conveyed. He made her retake the scene so many times, she felt worn out from trudging up and down the steps. In anger she tossed the suitcase to the floor then picked it up and threw it at him. Wyler grinned. Now he knew why the scene had not been working: The suitcase was empty. He ordered it filled with books and made de Havilland climb the stairs yet again. Now she could barely lift the suitcase. Catherine's exhaustion became palpable. Her humiliation and despair seemed to tug at her. She looked like she was dragging herself up from the bottom of the sea. This was the effect Wyler was after.

Indeed, the desolate walk up that staircase was not in the play at all. Nor was a speech Catherine had that was written for the picture. In it, she tells her aunt: "I used to think my misfortune was that Mother died. But I don't think so any more. . . . If she had lived, she too could not have loved me." De Havilland and the playwrights considered it Catherine's most important speech. On the set, Wyler decided to drop it.

"Willy called me to tell me, and I almost fainted," Goetz recounted. "I screamed with horror. It was like a murder to me. In that speech she knows she is being jilted. It is the speech of her breakdown, crucial to the scene.

"I said, 'Willy, you can't do it.'

"He said, 'Ruthie, it will not hold. I cannot make it hold for the whole climbing of the stairs. And Olivia cannot do it. She hasn't got it.'

"We were on the phone for almost an hour. When I got off, I was miserable. Not fifteen minutes later the phone rang again. This time it was Olivia on the phone saying, 'Willy cut the speech.' She was terribly unhappy about it."

As much as Goetz disagreed with Wyler, when she saw the finished picture, she realized he'd been right. Catherine's trauma was conveyed physically. Words at that moment were not necessary. "Willy had a magic timer in his body," Goetz said. "He had a tuning fork in his ears. He was deaf, but he had tuning forks all over him."

Indeed, Wyler felt that music itself would be a key to enhancing the picture's interior landscape. The underscoring of crucial moments in *The Heiress,* to say nothing of the overarching mood, influenced scenic content and shaped audience reaction to characters. The musical treatment had to be sensitive, but it also required an imaginative sweep. He did not want it to be predictable. "The emotion and conflict between two people in a drawing room can be as exciting as a gun battle, and possibly more exciting," he wrote. The score would have to reflect the "deliberately slow unfolding of character in dramatic conflict rather than a rapid-fire unfolding of plot in pictorial action. Unlike so many films which leave their characters pretty much as they discover them, *The Heiress*'s Catherine Sloper undergoes a series of experiences which changes the very texture and inner structure of her personality."

In mid-May, a month before he was to begin filming, Wyler sent the screenplay to Aaron Copland and asked how he would approach the material. The composer had just spent eight weeks in Hollywood scoring *The Red Pony* for Lewis Milestone. Copland liked the prospect of working with Wyler. He had seen *The Heiress* on Broadway, and he had read the original novel. "In my opinion," Copland replied, "the picture does not call for a great deal of music, but what it includes ought to really count." He would try to recreate "the special atmosphere" of the James original, he said, by producing "music of a certain discretion and refinement." What he did not want to do was to write a conventional score. He did not want to "bathe the work in the usual romantic atmosphere."

Paramount still retained veto power over Wyler's decisions. Because Copland also had scored *North Star,* one of HUAC's prime targets, Paramount production chief Y. Frank Freeman preferred not to hire him. But Wyler prevailed, and in mid-July Copland was signed. Along with his contract, the composer received the sheet music of "Plaisirs d'Amour," an eighteenth-century song by Giovanni Martini, which Morris Townsend sings for Catherine. Wyler suggested that Copland incorporate it into his music: "I feel that it is a charming song and comes off very well in the scene as shot. I believe you can use this song to advantage in the score, not literally, but possibly as thematic material for the scoring of the love scenes, the scene of the jilt, and the final sequence between Catherine and Morris."

Copland wasn't needed until mid-November. When the composer reported to Paramount, he was whisked into a screening room for a look at the first cut. It was, in his words, "really very good!" He set to work at a leisurely pace, sketching out ideas and pulling together period music from the 1850s to weave into the score. But *The Heiress* proved more challenging than he had anticipated. "There were no outdoor scenes, which would have given me the opportunity to compose music with a wide instrumental range," he recalled. "Also, I'd never before written a really grown-up love scene."

By mid-December Copland completed only eight minutes of music, and a recording date loomed the day after Christmas. Writing up to the last minute, he went into the recording studio not knowing for sure what he had. "Wyler seemed very pleased," Copland remembered, "but he wanted to try the film at one of those little neighborhood theaters where people don't know they are going to see a new picture."

At the preview, it came as a shock to hear the audience erupt with laughter when Catherine discovers that Townsend has jilted her. Copland had written poignant material for that climactic scene, but it had backfired. Wyler went up to the composer at the end of the preview.

"Copland," he said, "you've *got* to do something about that scene, because if the audience laughs at her then, they'll never take her seriously, and we won't have a picture. We might as well go home and forget the whole thing."

The composer protested, "But how can *I* stop an audience from laughing?"

"I don't care how you do it," Wyler replied, "but do *something*."

Copland rewrote roughly three minutes of music, substituting a dissonant passage for the original. An orchestra was assembled to record it at great expense. The movie was previewed again. This time, the audience didn't make so much as a peep.

The buzz at Paramount was that Wyler and company had done a fabulous job with *The Heiress* but that the picture was too serious to be a hit. The studio was in no rush to release it, waiting until the following autumn to give it a proper send-off.

When the picture opened on October 6, 1949, at New York's Radio City Music Hall, Wyler went east as part of a promotion campaign that included everything from a director's lecture at Yale to product "tie-ins" with chocolate bonbons and "the Heiress look" in fashion design. For the West Coast premiere, *le tout Hollywood* showed up at Grauman's Chinese Theater. Afterward, the Wylers threw a glittering party at Summit Drive. Montgomery Clift came with Elizabeth Taylor. They had just begun making *A Place in the Sun* together. At Grauman's Chinese, Clift had hunkered down in his seat and groused about *The Heiress* all through the premiere. Now, he breezed through the door glowing amiably in his rented tuxedo and with Taylor on his arm. He boasted how he and Charlie Chaplin often played tennis together on Wyler's court.

"We didn't really know Elizabeth Taylor," Talli said. "She was terribly young. It was one of the few times she ever came to our house. I just remember that she and Monty looked absolutely gorgeous together. He was almost as beautiful as she was."

The Heiress opened well in New York. Most of the critics gave it their stamp of approval. They admired its taste and style, its mature subject, its high-calibre acting. They called it superb entertainment for grown-ups. It was, without question, a prestige picture and would garner eight Oscar nominations. But when *The Heiress* rolled out across the country, it lost steam at the box office and took six months to earn back its costs. Though it turned a profit and earned even more overseas, Wyler was crestfallen.

"I expected it to make a lot of money," he told *Variety*, whose critic predicted it would strike most moviegoers as soporific. "It cost too much. It should have been done cheaper. But then it wouldn't have been the same picture. As it was, I didn't go over the estimated budget by more than sixty to seventy thousand dollars."

Later, he claimed the picture had been "sloughed off by the Paramount sales organization" because of Cecil B. De Mille's *Samson and Delilah*. "The company threw its energies behind it and not *The Heiress*," Wyler told David Selznick. "Apparently they are not geared up to give two big pictures special attention at the same time."

Wyler's commercial track record had been so good—his unbroken string of hits dated back more than a decade—that the industry regarded him with only slight exaggeration as a director who couldn't make a flop. But a sense of disappointment hung over the picture even at the Academy Awards. Of its eight Oscar nominations—including best picture and director—it won only four. Apart from de Havilland's, three Oscars came in technical categories. Copland picked up the prize for his scoring. The costume designers and art directors also won. Still, they were not enough to turn *The Heiress* into an easy sell.

Since then, the picture's reputation has blossomed. With time it has taken its rightful place among Wyler's best. In 1993, for example, Tom Cruise and director Mike Nichols screened the original with the thought of doing a remake together. After seeing it, they concluded that "Wyler's version was perfect" and dropped their idea, telling the press they didn't believe anything they could make would hold up against it.

31

He Didn't Want a Yes-Man

WORKING AS HIS OWN PRODUCER now, Wyler put his trust in two long-time associates whose artistic judgment he valued more than ever. One was his brother Robert, who had spent the war in Hollywood serving as a private in the California State Guard. The other was Lester Koenig, who had written the script for *The Memphis Belle* and afterwards went overseas with Wyler for *Thunderbolt*. In a sense, the pair served as Wyler's sounding board. While he invariably made the final decisions, overruling their opinions as often as not, he nonetheless delegated considerable responsibility to them in literary matters and technical aspects of production.

Robert had rejoined Wyler after the war as an unofficial member of the team that made *The Best Years of Our Lives*. He never got any screen credit on that picture, though Wyler regularly debated scripting problems with him and relied on him as something of a script doctor. Koenig came out of the Army Air Force with Wyler and went on Goldwyn's payroll as the director's assistant. He proved so useful in the making of *Best Years* that Wyler thought he deserved a screen credit as associate producer. The tall, thin former Ivy Leaguer had done everything from keeping the production schedule on track to rewriting dialogue and inventing stage business on the set. But he got along badly with Goldwyn, sometimes not speaking to him for weeks. The studio boss took his revenge by not giving him the screen credit Wyler demanded. Goldwyn listed Koenig as "production assistant" instead.

Wyler gave *The Heiress* team its due, however, crediting both his brother and Koenig as associate producers. Their artistic alliance replaced to some extent Wyler's old relationship with Gregg Toland, who stayed with Goldwyn after *Best Years*. Any possibility of working with the cinematographer again ended with Toland's premature death in September 1948 at the age of forty-four. (That year also brought the death of Wyler's younger brother Gaston, and Robert's marriage to the young actress Cathy O'Donnell, whom he had met on *Best Years*.)

But the professional achievement Wyler enjoyed with his small circle of associates suddenly seemed unimportant. Soon after *The Heiress* opened, Wyler's life was rocked by a stunning personal tragedy that left him feeling, as he later recalled, "at the low point of my life."

It couldn't have been more unexpected. The Wyler family—Talli, Willy and their three kids—rented a house in Malibu for the summer of 1949. "Willy loved the beach," Talli recalled, "and we'd had a gorgeous two-and-a-half months there. Ralph Richardson and his wife Meriel also took a house in the colony. We saw quite a lot of them. Our life seemed complete. Our two girls were growing up. Our little boy was about to enter nursery school. We couldn't have been happier." That summer, too, Kathleen Parrish organized the Chaplin-Wyler "Cocka-mamie" Tennis Tournament on Summit Drive. Players who regularly took lessons from Bill Tilden on the Chaplin court and from Tilden's protégé, Noel Brown, on the Wyler court competed for two weekends. Among others, the tournament included Talli, Charlie Chaplin and his wife Oona, Gene Kelly's wife Betsy, Richard Conte, Peter Viertel, Chaplin's son Sidney, who brought his girlfriend Evelyn Keyes to umpire, and Parrish, who played against the men.

When Oona played Talli in the women's singles final, Charlie and Willy each wanted his wife to win and couldn't help showing it. But Charlie put on the better performance. "Every time Oona lost a point," Kathleen recounts, "he would rush into the dressing room, fall on the floor in a faint and mime despair." Just the same, Talli won and took home the "Cockamamie" coffee mug.

With the summer fresh in memory, the family decided to take a Thanksgiving holiday together in Palm Springs. "We all hopped in the car," Talli said. "The weather was wonderful, so balmy and warm you could feel the air." Two days after they got to the desert resort, a three-hour drive from Los Angeles, little Billy became violently ill.

"It seemed like an allergy attack," Talli said. "He began vomiting. He had diarrhea. And it kept getting worse. We didn't know what it was. The food? We'd had a big Thanksgiving dinner, but nobody else was sick. We called our pediatrician in Los Angeles and asked him what to do. He had a broken leg in a cast, so he couldn't drive down, and he didn't seem to know any doctors in Palm Springs. Willy wanted to charter a plane and fly him down. Finally he said he couldn't come and we should get Billy to the hospital.

"By this time Billy was breathing all right," Talli went on, "but he was becoming comatose. At the hospital they said he was dehydrated and they would begin feeding him fluids intravenously. Then they wondered if he had polio. In those days everyone was frightened of polio. So they did a spinal tap. When the doctors told us 'no polio,' we were so relieved. They told us to go get a bite of dinner. At the restaurant there was an orchestra. I remember we got up and danced in each other's arms feeling such relief that Billy didn't have polio. But when we got back to the hospital, something was terribly wrong. His body wasn't absorbing the fluids. He was gone in a few hours. Dead. He wasn't even four years old, a darling child. I can't tell you what a shock it was. That little boy was the apple of Willy's eye. To lose him was just ghastly."

The doctors said the immediate cause of death was dehydration. But the underlying cause was never determined, despite an autopsy.

Wyler felt enormous guilt, as well as grief. He blamed himself for his son's death. "I made the decision to keep him there," he recounted years later. "They asked me, 'Should we take him to Los Angeles or the hospital?' The hospital in Palm Springs wasn't what it is today. But I thought they must know how to take care of children in a hospital. It would take hours to get back. By that time he could get worse. . . . And that night he died."

Numb with sorrow, Willy and Talli tried to comfort their two daughters. Ten-year-old Cathy couldn't sleep. Judy, seven, had screaming nightmares for weeks. "I remember the houseman coming to clear up and taking away little Billy's tricycle," Talli said, breaking down in tears as she recalled the moment forty years later. "It was devastating. All our friends kept trying to be helpful, but I wasn't really there. It was like we didn't know what happened. We kept wondering, 'What did I do wrong?'"

When Christmas came, the distraught family sought refuge in Sun Valley, Idaho, and were joined by Robert and Kathleen Parrish. "We went away to try to cheer ourselves up," Talli remembered. "We needed to carry on. We wanted something to do to take our minds off Billy's death." They put on "a brave front," Robert recalled. As their numbness wore off, anger replaced it. "I was furious," Talli said. "I felt so helpless. So I decided, 'I'm going to have another child.' Willy absolutely agreed. We had a mutual need." A year to the day of their son's death, Talli gave birth to their fourth child, Melanie, named for Willy's mother.

WYLER TRIED TO IMMERSE HIMSELF IN WORK AND BEGAN PREP-arations for his next picture. It would be another literary adaptation, this time based on Theodore Dreiser's turn-of-the-century novel, *Sister Carrie*. He had thought about a movie version long before, hoping Lillian Hellman would write the screenplay. He asked her to consider it as early as June 1947. She'd wired back: POSITIVE WOULD LIKE TO DO SISTER CARRIE. But her availability waned as other projects intervened. Six months later, Robert suggested using *Casablanca* co-writers Julius and Philip Epstein, "in case you can't get Hellman." Still casting around in March 1949, Wyler wondered whether Arthur Miller would be interested and asked Hellman to help get him. MILLER BUSY ON SOMETHING OF HIS OWN, she cabled. IF NORMAN MAILER WERE FREE WHAT WOULD YOU THINK OF HIM. Mailer, then in his mid-twenties, had just burst on the literary scene with his first novel, *The Naked and the Dead*, and she was working on the screen adaptation. Wyler replied: FEEL THAT MAILER MUST BE TOO YOUNG AND INEXPERIENCED TO TREAT SUBJECT LIKE SIS-TER CARRIE. ALSO FEEL I SHOULD HAVE A DRAMATIST FOR THE JOB.

Dreiser's novel—his first, published in 1900—so scandalized the literary world of his time that it was nearly suppressed. The publisher brought it out with great reluctance only because Dreiser demanded strict adherence to the terms of his contract. *Sister Carrie* spurred outrage because its central characters transgressed conventional morality. Worse, Dreiser did not judge his characters so much as illuminate their flaws. They existed in an amoral universe, lashed by sexual impulses and mistaken calculations.

Carrie, a seemingly innocent but thoroughly materialistic farm girl from the Midwest, arrives in Chicago and climbs the ladder of success by surrendering her virtue. Rather than work in a factory, she allows herself to become a kept woman—first by Drouet, a dapper traveling salesman, and then by Hurstwood, the more substantial, middle-aged manager of a fine downtown restaurant-saloon who steals her away from Drouet. That Hurstwood is married to a shrew and sees Carrie as his last chance for happiness prompts him to run away with her, even though it means leaving everything behind: home, family, business and respectability. But once out of his element in New York and out of the money he has stolen from the restaurant safe, Hurstwood cannot hold onto the much younger Carrie. She eventually rises to stardom on the Broadway stage, working her way up from community theatricals, while he sinks to the Bowery and ultimately kills himself.

Wyler turned to Ruth and August Goetz for the adaptation well before *The Heiress* opened. By June 1949, he had their treatment in hand. As usual he kept tabs on the development of the script. Though he liked the treatment, he had doubts about their story construction and offered detailed suggestions to shape it. They needed to tell the tale "more economically," he wrote them, and with greater appreciation for dramatic momentum. When it came to script development, Wyler never pulled his punches.

He focused on "the weakness of the dramatic structure," explaining what made it weak: "There is a narrative quality in the steady downhill progression of Hurstwood. Also, there's a repetitive quality about these scenes not in specific content, but in the general point made by each one: Hurstwood moving one step down, then another step, then another." He further explained his conception of the characters, their motivations, and how to think of their relationship: "First, Hurstwood's downfall stems from his own weakness of character, which led him to run off with Carrie as he did. Without that flaw in his makeup, the blows struck at him by fate need not reduce him to the gas jet. But with that flaw, and with two key moments, which can be dramatized, his total defeat as a human being is more understandable.

"One key moment is the loss of his capital. For a man like Hurstwood, there is no future in a salaried job. When he loses it, he loses more than money. He is a gambler without a stake, who can no longer play in the game.

"His next crucial step down is the result of losing Carrie. That comes in two stages, first the loss of the sex relationship. This really should be dramatized, since sex was all they had to begin with, and when it is gone, their separation is merely a matter of time. The second stage in losing Carrie comes when she leaves him. It doesn't seem likely that Hurstwood, who depends so much on Carrie's presence, even without sex, would ever walk out on her.

"From Carrie's point of view, there is a real problem to dramatize.

What does a woman do in such a case? There are so many conflicting feelings. Carrie is decent and feels a certain loyalty to Hurstwood. She feels that in a way she is responsible for his having given up everything. It is a dreadful thing to do, to leave a man in such circumstances. But then, consider her life. What is to become of her? Is she to be saddled with the responsibility for caring for this wreck of a man, and in so doing to be cheated out of a life of her own?

"Just as we show Hurstwood's retrogression, we want to show some development in Carrie, her growth from the naive country girl on the train to a mature woman with emotional greatness, the fulfillment of the promise that attracted Drouet and Hurstwood, and which will make her a fine actress later. If her decision to leave Hurstwood is dramatized, then the audience will wonder about, and be fearful of, what will happen to Hurstwood when Carrie does leave him. This builds suspense for the last chapter of our story—the gas jet."

Wyler suggested other imaginative ways to expose character, probe motivation and dramatize the story but emphasized that he was not wedded to any of them. He found it useful to offer ideas "even if we decide against using any of them," he said, because merely thinking about them would help clarify themes and issues. Indeed, his interest in the mature presentation of character, motive and drama sets his pictures apart. Whatever else they may be, they are rarely silly. His pictures are inevitably filled with subtle textures, often with humor, and are always intended for grown-ups.

By December 1949, Wyler had the screenplay. Two days before leaving for Sun Valley, he cabled his brother in London asking him to hand-deliver a copy to Laurence Olivier, whom he wanted for Hurstwood. The great British actor was a warm friend by now but still not easy to corral, even though he claimed to like the script. Recently knighted and already considered the greatest actor on the English-speaking stage, Olivier also had come into his own in films. His screen version of *Hamlet*—he directed and starred—won the Oscar for the best picture in 1948 and earned him the Oscar for best actor, as well as a nomination for his directing. Moreover, he had taken over London's St. James Theatre, where he was installed as actor, manager, director and producer, and he was just then preparing to launch Christopher Fry's comedy, *Venus Observed*, in which he was also the star. The opening was set for mid-January. A week after the premiere, Olivier cabled: WITH VERY MUCH REGRET INDEED I HAVE TO TELL YOU THAT MY SHOW IS A HIT AND IT WILL NOT BE POSSIBLE FOR ME TO CONSIDER THE FILM AM SINCERELY SAD TO MISS THIS OPPORTUNITY OF WORKING WITH YOU.

But Wyler refused to take "no" for an answer. He wanted Olivier for the picture so badly that he offered to change his own plans to accommodate him: WILL GLADLY POSTPONE PRODUCTION AWAITING YOUR AVAILABILITY, he wired back. BELIEVE THIS IDEAL AMERICAN FILM VEHICLE FOR YOU ALSO DON'T KNOW WHEN I'LL HAVE AS PROVOCATIVE A SUBJECT AND AS ATTRACTIVE A ROLE TO OFFER YOU. He challenged Olivier's sincerity by sweetening his offer with the prospect of doing something else entirely if necessary. "My schedule of pictures is flexible," he wrote, "and I am always in search of new material. I propose that we look for suitable material and submit it to each other. . . . Also, depending on the subject matter, the picture could be produced in England. Of course, if such a plan could include Vivien, it would be twice as good, and I would like it twice as much."

Olivier responded that he was "most touched" and asked for time to consider *Sister Carrie* after all. By the beginning of summer Olivier decided he would be able to come to Hollywood in August, when *Venus Observed* was expected to close. Not only did Olivier need the money, but Vivien Leigh, who was starring as Blanche in the London production of Tennessee Williams's *A Streetcar Named Desire*, had been signed by Warner Bros. to reprise the role. The play's film version would be directed by Elia Kazan, who had staged the original Broadway production and who brought virtually the entire Broadway cast to Hollywood.

In the meantime, Wyler decided the best choice for Carrie was Elizabeth Taylor. She had just finished shooting George Stevens's *A Place in the Sun*, another Dreiser adaptation (*An American Tragedy*), opposite Montgomery Clift. Taylor was eighteen, just the right age for Carrie, and she projected both the fresh innocence and striking beauty that would easily explain Carrie's mesmerizing appeal. Newly married to Conrad Hilton, Jr., the playboy heir to a hotel fortune, Taylor was in London on her honeymoon. Wyler asked Olivier to see her and help persuade her to take the role. But just as Olivier fixed a date for a chat, Wyler learned that MGM, which held Taylor's contract, had rejected his request for a loan-out. As a result, top Paramount executives insisted on Ava Gardner for their second choice. Wyler rushed off a cable to Olivier to save him from a humiliating predicament and from rumors that Gardner had been signed: ANY REPORT YOU HEARD WAS PREMATURE DEAL NOT YET CONCLUDED WITH HER STUDIO . . . FEEL THAT IF YOU SHOULD STILL HAVE TO SEE HILTON THERE SHOULD BE NO REASON FOR EMBARRASSMENT SINCE WE ALL WANT HER AS MUCH AS EVER.

Wyler also regretted that David Selznick had called Olivier to push for his wife, Jennifer Jones, who had been under active consideration for months. Selznick, hoping to influence Wyler, mounted an indefatigable campaign on her behalf. Always open to advice, Wyler had sent him the *Carrie* screenplay in late 1949 and had been bombarded ever since by Selznick's typically lengthy memos about everything from script revisions to casting suggestions. He, too, wanted Olivier for Hurstwood because the pairing would reflect well on Jones. Under Selznick's careful grooming, she had won an Oscar for her starring performance in *The Song of Bernadette* back in 1943. But her follow-up roles in *Since You Went Away, Love Letters, Madame Bovary* and *Duel in the Sun*—high-budget but mediocre pictures handpicked for her by Selznick—had not fulfilled his ambitions. Playing opposite Olivier, he felt, was guaranteed to increase her prestige. Working under Wyler's tutelage, he also felt, could only make her a better actress.

When Olivier hesitated early on, however, Wyler briefly entertained the notion of casting Spencer Tracy, Fredric March, William Powell, Ronald Colman, Charles Boyer, Humphrey Bogart and even John Wayne—all suggested by Selznick as last resorts. Wyler thought March the best substitute for Olivier. He admired March, long one of his favorite actors, and the Goetzes wanted him instead of Olivier, whom they thought wrong for the part. They mistakenly believed Olivier was too British and could not pass for an American from the Midwest. But the more they pushed for March, the more Wyler resisted.

"The character of Hurstwood was very sophisticated and suave," Wyler explained. "I couldn't find any American actor like that. Any of the American stars, like March or Bogie or Tracy, were not that type of man at all." Powell, who might have filled the bill, was too old. So was Colman, an Englishman. And Boyer had an ineradicable French accent. Also, as discussions about Jones progressed, Selznick virtually demanded casting approval for Hurstwood. He couched his demand with convoluted politeness, while bringing hard-nosed pressure to bear just the same.

"I'm genuinely eager for Jennifer to do the picture," he told Wyler, "but obviously who the man is must play a part in the final decision."

When Selznick learned in June of Wyler's efforts to sign Elizabeth Taylor and of Paramount's negotiations for Ava Gardner, he went ballistic. Feeling betrayed, he fired off a vituperative cable that detailed a bitter litany of grievances for three full pages. His chief accusation was that Wyler had engaged in "double-dealing":

I MUST NOW ASK YOU TO CONSIDER THAT JENNIFER IS NOT AVAILABLE. . . . I DO NOT WISH FURTHER TO DEMEAN [her] OR HER GREAT STANDING AS A STAR BY WHAT I AM FORCED TO REGARD AS THE TYPE OF DOUBLE DEALING WHICH

HAS MADE ME SO FED UP WITH HOLLYWOOD. . . . YOU ASKED THAT I DO NOTH-
ING ELSE WITH JENNIFER WITHOUT NOTIFYING YOU I AGREED AND YOU STATED
IN RETURN THAT YOU WOULD NOT NEGOTIATE FOR ANYONE ELSE WITHOUT
FIRST NOTIFYING ME. . . . YOU REPAID THIS COURTESY BY COMPLETELY VIOLAT-
ING YOUR PROMISE. . . . EITHER YOU OR YOUR ASSOCIATES HAD THE CONSUM-
MATE BAD TASTE AND INGRATITUDE TO USE MY WILLINGNESS TO LET JENNIFER
PLAY THE ROLE AND JENNIFER'S WILLINGNESS TO PLAY THE ROLE WITH OLIVIER
TO ATTEMPT TO GET ANOTHER STAR. . . . YOU OR YOUR PEOPLE EVEN WERE DIS-
HONEST ENOUGH TO STATE THAT JENNIFER WAS DYING TO PLAY THE ROLE BUT
THAT YOU DID NOT WANT HER. . . .

When Wyler learned that Selznick sought to embarrass him by sending a copy of his fulminating telegram to a top MGM executive, he dismissed it lightly as "this desperate and world-shaking event. I think the
only one who has benefitted by it is Western Union."

But he also sent a letter of apology to Selznick: "For the present I
have decided not to reply in kind and just answer the one and only point
on which I cannot deny you a measure of justification—namely, the
matter of our mutual promise. . . . The fact is, no deal has been closed
for anyone. However, I believe I was wrong to wait [to notify you] in
order not to destroy the chances of getting Jennifer should another very
doubtful negotiation fail (as it has) or should the company be willing to
allocate additional money for the casting of *Carrie* . . . Prominent among
the reasons why another actress was being sought was the financial one.
Also, I felt that . . . no harm could come from waiting. However, I repeat that I think you should have received notice from me at the time
when another actress was first considered. For this failure, my sincere
apologies. . . ."

Two weeks later, at the end of June, Selznick did a complete about-
face. Jennifer Jones was signed for *Carrie*. He wasn't entirely mollified,
though, disputing Wyler's contention that financial considerations were
at issue. Selznick claimed the price for Jones had never come up because negotiations had never started. But, in fact, Wyler was accurate
when he described Paramount's concerns about keeping within the two-
million-dollar budget for *Carrie*. Things were not going well in the
picture business, and the studio was caught up in what he called Hollywood's "general economic hysteria." What's more, Selznick had made
plain in his discussions with Wyler that in hopes of getting *Carrie* for
Jones he had just turned down an offer of two hundred fifty thousand
dollars for her to star in a Warner Bros. picture. The going rate for
Olivier's services came to less than that, roughly two hundred thousand
dollars. Paramount did not want to meet the sort of price Selznick was

talking about, and in the end it didn't. Though it isn't clear exactly how much she earned for *Carrie,* her total income that year amounted to a hundred fifty-four thousand dollars—a substantial sum to be sure, but not close to the amount Selznick claimed to have turned down.

Well before production got beyond the planning stage, Wyler sought an editor to cut the picture. His favorite editor, Danny Mandell, whom he had brought to Goldwyn from Universal, did not come with him to Paramount. George Stevens recommended Robert Swink, who had edited his *I Remember Mama* at RKO. Swink got a call one afternoon asking whether he could come over to Paramount for an interview with Wyler.

"I was in seventh heaven," Swink recalled. "I regarded him very highly. I said I'd be right over. RKO and Paramount were next door to each other. All I had to do was take a walk."

When they met, Wyler introduced him to Koenig, who sat in on the interview. They made some small talk at first. "I think Willy was just feeling me out." Finally, they got down to business.

"I saw your latest picture," Wyler said. "I thought it was quite a bit too long."

Swink was being challenged directly. After all, a film editor's job is to cut pictures down to their proper length.

"A lot of people wanted to see more," he countered, although he knew there was no question it was long.

Wyler apparently enjoyed Swink's reply. He smiled and began chatting about other things. Then he became serious again.

"Have you seen my last picture?" Wyler asked, referring to *The Heiress.*

"Yes, I've seen it."

That was all Swink said, so Wyler prodded him.

"Well, what do you think of it?"

"I thought it was a bit too long."   ·

Swink didn't know what effect his terse candor would have. But he was not about to stroke Wyler's ego. To his surprise, the director's face broke into an impish grin.

"Can you get your affairs in order?" Wyler asked. "I'd like you to come over here and work for me."

Swink's gamble paid off brilliantly. "The kind of guy Wyler was, he didn't want a yes-man," he says. This was confirmed for him when production on *Carrie* began. Wyler's methods were totally unlike any he had seen—not just on the set, where he was known for his painstaking craftsmanship, but behind the scenes when it came to working with his technical associates. Wyler gave them rare freedom. This became evident to Swink the first time they ran dailies. Each night after shooting, Wyler would invite a nucleus of key associates into the projection room to watch the previous day's footage.

"It usually included the cameraman, the sound man, the prop man and some others," Swink recalls. "No more than eight to ten people from the set. I sat on Willy's left, right beside him, because he only had one good ear."

Wyler would not comment very much about the dailies, Swink said, unless he saw one take that he liked a lot better than another.

"I noticed everybody would get up and make all kinds of comments, whether this was good or that was bad," he remembers. "This surprised me. I wasn't used to that open approach. I would say nothing. About two weeks into the shoot, Wyler said to me, 'Please come in and see me in the office at the end of the day.' I thought, 'What have I done?' "

When Swink reported to him, the boss had a puzzled expression.

"Bob, why don't you pipe up in that projection room?"

"You've got all those people talking at you and telling you what they think," Swink said. "I didn't want to add to the confusion."

"I'll tell you what, I want to know what you think. So from now on, we'll have a little meeting in my office after the rushes. Just the two of us."

Happy that he had somehow struck up a good relationship with Wyler, he marveled that his new boss's taskmaster reputation was contradicted by the independence he allowed his subordinates. "I was *very* pleased," Swink recalled. Their relationship went so well that from then on they met like that for the next twenty years. Swink became an essential part of Wyler's artistic team—first as editor, then as supervising editor and eventually as second-unit director.

Also contrary to industry hearsay that Wyler wasted footage, Swink was struck by the fact that the director shot a great deal "but didn't print that much. He only printed a few takes. Occasionally he would print more. He knew what he saw, and he knew what he wanted."

OLIVIER CAME OVER FROM LONDON IN EARLY AUGUST, stopping in New York to meet with the Goetzes and tour the Bowery. Wyler wrote him, "I think it a very useful thing to see firsthand what the flophouses are like and how the derelicts live. Actually, not too much has changed since the period of our story, and your observations will be most helpful to you when we come to the latter part of the picture. Ruth and Augustus are prepared to take you downtown and show you the very same places they went to with me earlier this year." He also wanted Olivier to read the latest draft of the screenplay. "If you have any criticisms," Wyler noted, "please don't hesitate to go over them with the Goetzes. They have learned to love criticism after working with me."

Worried about getting the right Midwestern flavor for Hurstwood, Olivier asked Wyler to line up an expert who could "check my accent and intonations so I can feel in tune and happy about this before shooting starts." His own British speech patterns were, of course, "quite wrong for Hurstwood, who was probably bred in Chicago if not points further still from England." Wyler anticipated the need for a language coach. He already had one ready and waiting. Olivier also made use of Spencer Tracy, who had been his houseguest in London the previous year while shooting the British film *Edward, My Son*. Olivier had given the Milwaukee-born star helpful pointers about British speech patterns. Now, eager to repay Olivier's hospitality, Tracy reciprocated as his personal language coach.

To complete the transformation, Wyler had tailored suits made to order for Olivier before his arrival in Hollywood on August 13. He even hired the shoemaker who'd made Olivier's shoes for *Wuthering Heights*. And he asked Olivier to keep the elegant mustache he'd grown for *Venus Observed*, so he could shoot screen tests of it in different shapes for the proper Hurstwood look.

With principal photography to begin August 21, Wyler extracted a promise from Selznick not to venture onto the set. Production would be tense enough without his predictable meddling. Wyler had long since given up reading the deluge of memos that Selznick churned out with obsessive zeal. Four of them alone amounted to eighty-one pages of typed, single-spaced comments. "Almost nightly a messenger would come to our door with pages of notes," Talli recalled. "Willy would read the first few, but then he would throw up his hands. I don't think he bothered with the rest. They exhausted him. David couldn't help it. He must have been in agony that he wasn't in control." Speed was essential to keep within budget and to meet Olivier's tight schedule. He had to be back in London by November, which meant there was time for a ten-week shoot. "As soon as we started, Willy told us we had to hurry," Swink recalled. "We had to get the picture into some sort of shape for a preview almost immediately, which was an unheard-of schedule. If Willy wanted to shoot additional film, it would be very troublesome with Olivier gone. He'd have to pull the whole crew together and shoot

it in London. And that would have cost a lot more than Paramount
wanted to spend."

Other problems added to the tension. For one thing, the Goetzes
were still making changes in the screenplay, partly because of rumblings
from the Production Code administrators in the Breen Office. Breen
didn't like certain story elements and considered the whole tale unsa-
vory. Wyler was informed by Paramount that some aspects of the script
were censorable. Hurstwood's suicide was especially off-putting. Wyler
fumed. He felt the suicide was key to the story. Without it, the picture
would lose dramatic impact. It showed the depth of Hurstwood's despair and made his decline all the more tragic. He decided to shoot the
scene, come what may.

Tension mounted almost immediately for another reason: Wyler was
displeased with Ruth Warrick's performance as Mrs. Hurstwood. A
Hollywood leading lady, Warrick had made a dozen movies in the forties, beginning with *Citizen Kane* as Kane's first wife, opposite Orson
Welles. Wyler cast her over a handful of actresses, including Geraldine
Fitzgerald, Martha Scott and Miriam Hopkins. "Willy replaced Warrick with Hopkins after the first couple of days of shooting," said
Swink. "When he made decisions, they were good and sharp and
quick." Hopkins, who had just worked for Wyler in *The Heiress* as the
flighty, romantic Aunt Lavinia, could play the cold bitch with equal
aplomb. He also knew her socially because she'd married his friend, director Anatole Litvak—her third husband of four—soon after starring
with Merle Oberon in *These Three*. Though he couldn't stand her inces-
sant gabbiness off the set, he admired Hopkins as an actress and would
use her again in *The Children's Hour*, a decade later.

As shooting progressed, Wyler suddenly had to confront a bigger
problem: Jennifer Jones told him she was pregnant. "This was serious
stuff," recalled Eddie Albert, who was cast as Drouet and gave a brilliant performance. "There was not a helluva lot of laughing going on. I
know Willy felt quite irritated because she hadn't mentioned this at the
beginning of the shoot, and she was beginning to show as we got further
along. But Willy didn't display his irritation. He never complained
about her."

Not in public, anyway. He always maintained as late as the seventies
that he was happy with her performance. But privately, he had regrets.
"He told me Jennifer was not quite right for the part," Talli recalled. "I
myself didn't think it was the proper casting. When she told him she
was pregnant, he was horrified because she would insist on being laced

into those tight corsets. He would say, 'Jennifer, please don't do it. I will cut the shot at shoulder level.' But she would have herself strapped into her period costumes anyway, and Willy would cringe. She did lose the pregnancy."

When *Carrie* was released, some critics remarked on the unusual number of close-ups, not knowing the reason, and found the picture's style surprisingly conventional. They were used to a more fluid technique from Wyler. Too many close-ups interrupted the flow and created a static impression. In fact, whenever Jones appears in a scene, it tends to become one-dimensional. At the same time, scenes between Olivier and Albert rank among the best in the Wyler canon for their vivid acting, liquid subtleties and dramatic texture.

Meanwhile, Wyler had to contend with Selznick's blizzard of complaints. Though he was barred from the set, his memos continued to arrive. Selznick took note of his wife's long hours, unmet Paramount promises that she would not have to work on a particular day each month—probably a polite reference to taking the day off at the onset of menses, though it didn't apply now that she was pregnant—and the purported fact that she had taken a pay cut to do the picture. Selznick couldn't keep his numbers straight, which makes them doubtful. When he peevishly reminded Wyler that "we tore up a contract with Warners on a picture for two hundred thousand dollars," he apparently forgot his earlier claim of two hundred fifty thousand. Interestingly, Jones's income the year before came to a hundred thirty thousand dollars—which meant that her salary for *Carrie* actually represented a raise.

In one typical memo, Selznick's complaints went on for four pages and dripped with sarcasm. Selznick began with a warning: "Jennifer tells me that you have asked her to come in 'unofficially.' I suppose the interpretation of this is that Paramount does not want to pay for it. This is satisfactory with me, since Paramount is apparently so very much poorer than we are, *provided* (a) Larry isn't being paid either; (b) You are going to make retakes of Jennifer's close-ups; (c) You are going to make these early in the day . . . and not when she is exhausted after working not only on the most trying scenes imaginable, but hours beyond what is provided for in the contract."

Meanwhile, Olivier became increasingly crabby because of a bum leg. He declined to help publicize the picture, except for a single press conference with a gaggle of Hollywood reporters. And in the midst of filming he demanded a closed set. "I really don't know what was wrong with his leg," Albert says, "but he was in considerable pain. He kept dragging his leg. Larry could be warm and entertaining, but there were temperamental outbursts. And that caused some tension. I remember one time we had some visitors on the set. They were off in the background. Maybe there was a slight murmur. All of a sudden Larry looked up, and you heard that great voice of his: 'Anyone who is not in this picture, would you piss off?'"

Olivier's towering force could intimidate his fellow actors. "It was a real plum for me to play Drouet, and with Olivier no less," Albert says. "Before that I was mostly a singer and light comedian. This was my first dramatic role. In one scene we had, we're standing in the barroom of Hurstwood's restaurant. Hurstwood is angry at me. Olivier whipped himself up to a frenzy and started playing the role. I looked at him, and the guy is looking back at me like he's going to kill me. I was in awe. Of course, he kept complimenting me, helping me along.

"His concentration was incredible. He could narrow that focus in ways you wouldn't believe. After the picture was finished, I had a party at my house and at two or three in the morning we ran out of wine, which meant we drank a great deal of it. I made wine. I had kegs of it. So I went down to the wine cellar to get some more. Larry went with me, and we were both so tipsy we had trouble getting down the stairs. Anyway, there's a lock bolted to the door, and I can't find the key. So I get a screwdriver. I'm going to take the hinge off. The trouble is, I can't see in the dark. I couldn't get the blade into the screw. After watching my maneuvers for a while, Larry said, 'Old boy, let me have a dash at it.' I gladly gave him the screwdriver. He looks at it, looks at the bolt. It was scary. His eyes changed. Everything changed. He became a bloody giant in total control. In no time he had the hinge off. It told you that anybody who got in his way, watch out. If he puts the heat on you, you're in trouble. Try to make it to the border."

On top of all that, Olivier became disenchanted with the gloomy nature of the picture. It seemed to him too dark and depressing. Halfway through production, he began asking Wyler, "Why are we making this?" Olivier had lost faith in the story, despite his superb performance. Wyler himself found Hurstwood's decline more fascinating than anything else. "The thing that intrigued me, the reason I made the picture against so much advice," Wyler said, "was because I think a man's mistakes are more interesting than his virtues. Dreiser's people make mistakes."

Shooting ended November 2, several days over schedule. Faced with Olivier's imminent departure, Swink quickly assembled a rough cut and showed Wyler what he had. Wyler made his retakes by mid-November, bringing the picture in about sixty thousand dollars over the projected budget. This was relatively negligible, just three percent of production costs. It was the political climate that turned out to be the picture's worst liability.

The House Committee on Un-American Activities had not ended its witch hunt for "Commies" in Hollywood. A new round of HUAC hearings was just around the corner, even though chairman J. Parnell Thomas had been convicted and jailed for payroll padding. Widespread word of the upcoming hearings, which began in April 1951, sent Hollywood into a panic. It was the height of the Cold War; American GIs were fighting in Korea; Senator Joseph McCarthy, the demagogue who held hearings against purported spies in government, waved phony lists of names and made headlines daily with unsubstantiated accusations. Alger Hiss, his most famous victim, was charged with perjuring himself before McCarthy's Senate committee and convicted. HUAC's inquisition this time around would reach epic proportions. One screenwriter, Martin Berkeley, named a hundred people as Communists, including Lillian Hellman, Dashiell Hammett and Dorothy Parker.

With all of that looming on the horizon, Paramount executives had nightmares over *Carrie*. Wyler gave them what was basically his final cut in March 1951. They delayed releasing it until July 1952, some sixteen months later, sneaking it out with almost no promotion. They also contributed to the picture's ultimate failure by reediting it themselves.

"I was in Rome preparing *Roman Holiday* when I got a cable from the studio as long as my arm," Wyler said. "It said the picture would be shelved unless I agreed to cuts. They were not allowed to make the cuts without my approval, according to my contract. But faced with the prospect of having the picture shelved permanently, I decided to let them do it.

"The picture frightened them because of the shameful McCarthy era. *Carrie* showed American life in an unflattering light. A sophisticated, cultured man, as we portrayed him, sinks to the depth of degradation. He becomes a derelict, ends up sleeping in flophouses and begging on the street. The super-patriots said, 'This is un-American,' even though it takes place on the Bowery every day and even though Dreiser's story took place forty years earlier. Their answer to that was, 'The picture is not good for America.' So we had a flop instead of a success, which I suppose was better for America.

"We shot a very effective suicide scene, marvelously played by Larry, which was deleted from the picture. It's true that *Carrie* was not a happy story. It *was* a depressing story, and it might not have been a success anyway. But the way it was finally put out, people stayed away by the millions."

It didn't help that domestic movie attendance had hit rock bottom in 1952, down by half from its historic peak of eighty million in 1946. Nevertheless, Wyler accepted final blame for the picture's failure. "It was the wrong time. I think the Goetzes did a good job of adaptation. I guess it was the choice of the original material that wasn't popular, and that was entirely my doing."

The critics panned it. Even Bosley Crowther, who gave it a somewhat favorable review in the *New York Times*, called it a "mawkish reworking" of Dreiser. The screenplay was "a violently sentimental version" of the original, sort of Dreiser Lite. (In fact, Selznick earnestly wanted Paramount to name the picture *The Loved and the Unloved*.) But unlike most of the critics who panned Olivier, Crowther declared his performance "a haunting reflection" of Dreiser's Hurstwood. "When the word first came through that Mr. Olivier had been cast . . . there were those who regarded the selection as a perilously chancy choice. . . . The eminent British actor was thought too elegant and alien for the role of Mr. Dreiser's middle-aged hero who went to ruin out of love for a pretty girl. As it turns out, however, Mr. Olivier gives the film its closest contact with the book, while Miss Jones's soft, seraphic portrait of Carrie takes it furthest away."

Ruth Goetz took a diametrically opposite view of the performances. "Jennifer was much closer to it than Larry was. She had a kind of stupidity, which is part of the character of Carrie."

But Crowther's opinion has become the prevailing one. His view was echoed more than thirty years later by film scholar David Shipman: "Wyler, whatever his motives, has merely made a version of *All for Love, or the World Well Lost*—yet this, because of Olivier, is a moving document." Shipman regards Dreiser's novel as seriously limited material for the screen because it is so downbeat. But "to say that its limitations are not overcome and that this is, nevertheless, one of Wyler's best pictures is to demonstrate his position among film-makers. . . . He cared greatly for both his stories and the intelligence of his audience."

32

~~~∿∿∿~~~

DUPE, IDIOT OR COMMUNIST

IT HAD BEEN MORE THAN THREE
years from the time Wyler saw *The Heiress* on Broadway and first contemplated making a film of it to the time he handed Paramount what he
thought would be the final version of *Carrie.* Eager to quicken his pace,
he "really decided to step on it" with his next picture: *Detective Story,*
based on the Sidney Kingsley play. As early as December 1948, when
Sidney Kingsley asked him to invest fifteen hundred dollars in the
Broadway production, he hoped to make a screen version for Paramount. "It gives me some pleasant ideas about retiring from work,"
Wyler kidded his old friend. "I hope this will be another *Dead End* for
both you and me." And in May 1950, three months before he began
shooting *Carrie,* Wyler announced *Detective Story* as his next project.

First, he asked Kingsley to write the screen adaptation. But the playwright declined. As with *Dead End,* Kingsley did not want to go over old
ground. Besides, he was busy at work on his next play, a stage adaptation of Arthur Koestler's *Darkness at Noon.* Wyler then asked Dashiell
Hammett, thinking "it was something along his line." Three of Hammett's five famous private-eye novels had been adapted for the screen
by others, two more than once: *The Maltese Falcon* three times and *The*

Glass Key twice. *The Thin Man* adaptation proved so popular—it was a combination murder-mystery–screwball-comedy starring William Powell and Myrna Loy as the worldly sophisticates Nick and Nora Charles—that it generated four more *Thin Man* pictures and a flood of imitations.

The height of Hammett's literary career, however, was long since behind him. In 1931 at the top of his game, Paramount signed him to create original stories for gangster melodramas. With a few exceptions, such as Rouben Mamoulian's *City Streets,* most were run-of-the-mill. But Hammett's familiarity with police procedure, his obdurate vision of the criminal world, and especially his feel for hard-boiled anti-heroes, seemed a perfect fit for *Detective Story.* Besides, Wyler wanted to give Hammett work. The writer was broke. He was not in the best of health. And he was a HUAC target.

Hammett took the job—he was now living in California with Hellman—but couldn't write anything. "For some reason he just gave it up," Wyler recalled. With Hammett out, Wyler turned to his brother Robert and Philip Yordan, a novelist who had done screenplays for *Dillinger, Suspense* and many B-movies.

Detective Story immediately ran into censorship problems. The Breen Office gave its "categoric disapproval" to the script. The main problem arose from the original plot of Kingsley's play, which dealt with the crimes of an abortionist. In the original, set in a New York police station during a single day, a self-righteous detective named McLeod, with no pity for anyone who breaks the law, learns to his horror that his own wife once had occasion to use the very abortionist he has arrested.

Just as he was to begin shooting *Carrie,* Wyler lashed out at the strictures being applied to *Detective Story* in the most public forum he could find. "Certain subjects can't even be discussed," he told the *New York Times.* "It's as if they didn't exist. The play forcefully condemns abortion, and it is proper to insist on condemnation of crime in films. But apparently we are not even permitted to condemn. This is ludicrous. The code is old-fashioned. It is fifteen years old, but the company heads won't hear of amendments. Why not discuss reality? I have two daughters who are more important to me than my pictures. There are many things that I wouldn't want them to see. It is my responsibility to keep them from seeing such things. But that doesn't mean it is my responsibility to make pictures for children."

His indignant comments did not score Wyler any points. The Breen Office refused to budge. He would have to come up with a new twist on Kingsley's plot. Wyler and the screenwriters solved the problem by making the abortionist a doctor who delivers out-of-wedlock babies and gets rich by selling them in an illegal adoption racket. That *was* mentionable under the code. In a further plot twist, the detective learns that his wife had a baby before they met. Worse, it was born dead because the delivery was botched, which presumably explains why she hasn't been able to conceive during their eight years of marriage. The twist allowed Wyler to focus with greater poignance on the detective's unbending nature. Having placed his wife on a pedestal, McLeod is unable to accept her transgression. He feels betrayed because she is no longer "pure." Her out-of-wedlock baby was fathered by a rich gangster, no less, which doubly infuriates him. He calls his wife a tramp, though he loves her deeply, and, to his great remorse, drives her away.

Wyler cast *Detective Story* with four actors from the Broadway company: Lee Grant (the dippy shoplifter), Horace McMahon (the precinct chief Lieutenant Monahan), and Joseph Wiseman and Michael Strong (the pair of cat burglars). For Detective Jim McLeod and his wife Mary, he passed over the Broadway leads (Ralph Bellamy and Meg Mundy) and chose two Hollywood actors: Kirk Douglas and Eleanor Parker. Douglas had become a star in 1949 as a vicious, swaggering prizefighter in *Champion*. Parker had been a versatile and beautiful leading lady since the early forties, receiving a 1950 best actress Oscar nomination for playing a hardened criminal in *Caged*. Wyler also cast screen veterans William Bendix as McLeod's partner and Cathy O'Donnell as a naive young woman in love with an embezzler.

Detective Story would be the quickest picture Wyler ever made. It took him just three months from start to finish. Once photography began in February 1951, the shoot itself sped by in five weeks. "The nature of the material makes it possible to shoot fast," he wrote Olivier in March. "I also have the cameraman and crew I wanted. They light while I rehearse, so there is no waiting for the camera; besides, they know how to carry focus, and I can stage long scenes with foreground and background action in single setups. The people at the studio are terribly confused because I am ahead of schedule. They don't know what to make of it. We had a thirty-six-day schedule planned, and it now looks as though we'll finish in twenty-four."

Cinematographer Lee Garmes, who started as a prop boy in silents, was renowned in the industry for his inventiveness as well as his atmospheric lighting. He had a hand in creating the first crab dolly, which liberated the camera from tracks. The dolly could glide in all directions, creating the freewheeling effect of a handheld camera—only steadier.

"We just sailed through," Wyler said, "not a lot of takes, not a lot of close-ups." Garmes's technique also lent a snappy pace to production. Recalling Leo Tover's camerawork on *The Heiress*, Wyler felt an enormous sense of relief. When Tover tried to carry focus, "it took half a day to light a scene, four hours to light a shot." Garmes could do the same thing in half an hour, as Gregg Toland had done.

Further, the New York actors were already familiar with their roles. This, too, enabled Wyler to work speedily. Though it was Grant's first picture and only the second for Wiseman, they adapted smoothly to film acting. McMahon, besides playing the precinct chief in the original, had plenty of camera experience as a Hollywood character actor. He'd made more than a dozen films since the late thirties.

To familiarize Kirk Douglas with his role before filming, Wyler asked him to play McLeod on the stage and sent him to Phoenix, Arizona, where a troupe was doing a revival of the play. "They were delighted to have him," Wyler said. "He got a hundred dollars, maybe." Douglas spent a week on stage. The director came to see several performances, then asked the star to spend some time at a real police station in New York. "After doing the play, I still needed more preparation," Douglas recalled.

He gathered background for several weeks at a precinct in midtown Manhattan. The detectives even dressed him in a uniform and had him sit in on interrogations. One time they let him fingerprint a burglary suspect who gave him a puzzled look and asked: "Ain't you Kirk Douglas?" Playing his role to the hilt, Douglas replied: "If I was him, would I be doing this?" When he got back to Hollywood, Wyler asked him to come along for a night in a patrol car with the Los Angeles police. Douglas pooh-poohed the idea of getting any real background in one night. Before their ride was over, however, the two of them went along for the roundup of a key figure in a forgery racket, watched police pick up a young burglary suspect and sped to the scene of a drugstore holdup that turned out to be a double homicide.

Wyler liked Douglas well enough to invite him home to Summit Drive for dinner, a gesture he rarely made to his actors. "Kirk swept me up in his arms and carried me up the stairs from the living room," Talli remembered. "I was enormously pregnant, probably the heaviest load he ever carried. He may have been sorry halfway up, but he was very gallant." For his part, Douglas considered himself lucky to be working with a director whose talent he put high on his list of Hollywood's best. Of all his directors in a long and stellar career, Douglas ranked Wyler

among the top five—with Howard Hawks, Billy Wilder, Joe Mankiewicz and Elia Kazan. But Wyler always seemed "a bit of an enigma"
to him, "different, much different" from the other four.

"I never knew whether he liked the work I was doing or not," Douglas recalled. "It wasn't until years later when I bumped into Willy that
he said to me, 'Oh, by the way, I saw *Detective Story* on television last
night. You were good, very good.' This is the only compliment he paid
me, and this happened years after we had finished the picture. I don't
think I know much more about Willy now than I did the first day I
worked with him, except that he has a tremendous sense of humor
which is always lurking behind those darting eyes."

On the set of *Detective Story*, Wyler didn't say much. Which couldn't
have come as a surprise: He was famous for that. "He would watch a
scene very carefully," Douglas remembered, "squint his eyes and say,
'Do it again.'" Sometimes Wyler leaned so far forward into the scene, he
would end up nearly face-to-face with his actors. Garmes would tell
him, "Willy, watch your shadow!" And Wyler would have to push his
seat back, so as not to ruin the shot. What confounded Douglas, however, was the lightning speed of production. "Willy was legendary for
doing more takes of a scene than any other director, but I saw none of
that," he said. "We were days ahead of schedule on the first week. The
film was shot in record time. The last day of shooting Willy was actually
rushing, so he could go skiing."

Wyler wrapped up photography not in twenty-four days but in
thirty, six less than scheduled. That saved Paramount roughly a hundred thousand dollars on an already lean budget of a million six. Much
as he had done years before with *Counsellor-at-Law*, he opened up *Detective Story* by showing a slice of life in a busy interior milieu. This time it
was the inside of a seedy police station, where the human traffic comes
and goes around the clock. Society's oddball waifs and common strays,
its low-life criminals and their accidental victims, its liars, squares and
riffraff, all mingle with the fallible detectives and cops who personify society's last hope of keeping chaos at bay.

Except for a few brief exterior shots—a glance outside the station
house and a paddy wagon ride accomplished through effective back projection of city streets—the action took place on a single sound stage. It
housed the station house squad room, lieutenant's office, interrogation
room, upstairs file room and roof. The multilevel set was an illusion.
Wyler had all the rooms built side by side to facilitate Garmes's traveling
camera. "We moved easily and did everything in continuity," Wyler said.

In both style and content, the picture anticipated the myriad of police serials that took hold of television from the early fifties on. Programs as different as *Naked City* and *NYPD Blue* owe something to *Detective Story*. Though tame by today's standards—the camera technique seems conventional now, the melodrama creaky, the documentary ambience too stilted—it galvanized critical attention and became a big hit at the box office. Curiously, after Wyler saw Swink's first cut of the picture, he was disappointed.

"I didn't do my job right," he told Swink.

But Swink had an opposite opinion. "Let's just take the picture out right away and preview it," he said.

"How the hell can we do that?" Wyler wanted to know. "It's got no music, no sound effects. It'll take weeks to put that in."

"It doesn't need music. Just a little piece on the front and back end. We can take it out just like that."

"Well, I'm going to bed. I'll meet you at the preview."

Swink recalls, "I put the music on front and back and left the rest of it the way it was. We took it to a theater in Riverside, and the audience loved it."

So did Douglas. He and Wyler had had a few minor disagreements on the set, one involving the star's objection to being shot with blanks at close range. "The great Willy Wyler had to reblock the scene," Douglas later noted in his autobiography. But the night after seeing the preview, the star dropped Wyler a handwritten letter: "I wanted you to know how proud I feel to be in such a movie. . . . I feel you got out of me one of the best performances I am able to give. . . . The test of the picture for me was that, even while seeing it for the first time, I stopped being critical and got swept away with the story. . . . Thanks, Willy, and please get another role you want me to do—soon."

Wyler kept him in mind, but they never did make another picture together. Nor did Douglas receive an Oscar nomination, though many critics lauded his performance. The *New Yorker*, calling *Detective Story* a "slam-bang melodrama," pointed out that Douglas "was never before so convincing" and added that "the same can be said" of Parker. (She and Grant were nominated for Oscars, along with Wyler and the screenwriters.)

Kingsley, echoing Hellman, believed the picture was superior to the Broadway original: "On the whole, I'd say the impact of the film is greater than that of the play. . . . It's simply because Wyler and Paramount have been able to get wonderful characterizations out of the cast." The playwright singled out Parker especially, claiming she was better than the actress who'd created the role.

If *Detective Story* ultimately did not take home any statuettes, its box-office success nonetheless put Wyler in a better position to negotiate the terms of his next picture, *Roman Holiday*, which he wanted to make on location. More important, it helped earn him the studio's protection from HUAC.

Many of Wyler's close friends and associates were coming under renewed attack by the committee. Some of them, like Hellman and Hammett, would be served with subpoenas and forced to testify. His own political record dating back to the thirties made him vulnerable. Long before he co-founded the Committee for the First Amendment, he had signed petitions and given money to liberal causes. "He was definitely a 'premature anti-Fascist,' as they called him back in the thirties," Talli said. "That was enough to muddy you even though he was not a Communist and had no connection with the Party."

On top of that, despite being denounced in magazines and flyers put out by some of California's worst Red-baiters, Wyler still refused to hide his sympathies. In a meeting of the Directors' Guild, when Hollywood elder statesman Cecil B. De Mille urged that the directors keep tabs on the political views of the actors they hired, both Wyler and Joe Mankiewicz challenged him. De Mille, a ringleader of the Guild's reactionaries, shot back that some directors were traitors—at which point Wyler lost his temper. He jumped out of his chair and looked straight at De Mille. "If anybody doubts my loyalty to my country, I'll punch him in the nose," he retorted, "and I don't care how old he is."

Philip Dunne, who received a HUAC subpoena this time around, believed Paramount "kept Willy safe because it needed him too much to do otherwise. He was a bankable director, a major figure. He made them money." Indeed, the studio chief who ran the Paramount lot, Y. Frank Freeman, told Wyler himself that HUAC investigators "wanted his scalp." But Freeman, an arch-conservative from Georgia with a deep Southern accent and an anti-Communist reputation, vouched for his director: "He's no Commie, he's just a damn fool." On more than one occasion, the studio chief related to Wyler a less folksy version of what he'd said, calling him "an idiot" and "a dupe." Years later, Wyler would entertain his family with an affectionate imitation of Freeman's remarks. "Frank thought he was paying me a great compliment," he remembered. "But I often thought at the time whether, between being a dupe and a Communist, I didn't prefer to be a Communist."

Meanwhile, Wyler stood by his friends. Hellman recalled, "In my own case, he read in the paper one day that Hammett had been arrested and a large bail was going to be required. When I got home that evening, there was a long-distance call from Willy. I remember it came about six o'clock, because I was going to fix myself some dinner. Willy was very fond of Hammett. He said, 'Lillie, how much is the bail going to be?' And I said, 'I don't know, but they think it's probably going to be a hundred thousand dollars.' He said, 'Can you raise that?' I said, 'No, but I can raise some of it.' He said, 'I can raise the rest for you, just say so.' Well, I didn't have to because they refused all bail. It was unspeakable, the first time bail had been refused in such a case. But it was wonderful to hear Willy make that offer. I began to bawl like a baby on the phone."

Hammett went to prison in July 1951 and served a six-month sentence for refusing to tell a grand jury what he knew about a bail fund for four Communists convicted as subversives. They had jumped bail, and prosecutors wanted the identities of contributors to the fund. Hammett did not know them—there were hundreds—despite being a trustee to the Civil Rights Congress, which set up the fund. But on principle, he declined to say so even to defend himself. To give any testimony at all, he believed, was to collaborate with prosecutors who were using the legal system to persecute people for their political opinions.

When Hammett went to prison, his lawyer advised Hellman to leave the country. She was a HUAC target herself, in addition to which she was depressed, blacklisted in Hollywood and unable to get work. That August, after spending several weeks prying a passport out of the State Department, she sailed for Europe with Wyler. Knowing she was broke, he paid her fare and hotel bill. They stayed at Claridge's in London. She hoped to direct a production of one of her plays, and he hoped to meet a young, little-known actress named Audrey Hepburn whom he was considering for *Roman Holiday*.

Before going on to Rome to look into locations and the possibilities of filming there, Wyler promised to do something else for Hellman. "I like Dash and I love you," he told her. "I am opening a bank account in your name and depositing thirty-five thousand dollars. Every six months I will check the balance and make sure it is brought back up." Although Wyler said in later years that he couldn't recall doing so, Hellman vowed he had. "Willy never remembered anything generous he did," she explained. "It wasn't fake. It just went out of his head."

That September Hellman was denounced by Martin Berkeley. At a HUAC hearing the little-known screenwriter claimed she came to his home in 1937 to help form a Communist Party cell in Hollywood. Hammett got out of prison in December. The following February, 1952, Hellman received a subpoena from HUAC. Finally, in May—three weeks after Wyler left for Europe again, to begin filming *Roman Holiday*—she went before the committee and invoked the Fifth Amendment against self-incrimination.

But Hellman's interrogation, grueling as it was, produced a stunning coup. Her attorney, Joseph Rauh, maneuvered the committee into putting on the record a letter she'd written her inquisitors two days earlier, explaining her reasons for taking the Fifth. He then had copies handed out to reporters in the caucus room. It was a brilliantly crafted declaration, proud but humble, full of old-fashioned patriotic sentiment yet ringing with memorable phrases about her personal code of ethics: ". . . to hurt innocent people whom I knew many years ago in order to save myself is, to me, inhuman and indecent and dishonorable. I cannot and will not cut my conscience to fit this year's fashions. . . ."

The letter caused a stir in the press gallery. Hellman was soon excused by the committee, its chairman remarking: "Why cite her for contempt? After all, she's a woman. . . ." The next day she was in the headlines. Some of the most influential columnists painted her as a heroine. But the worst of the McCarthy era was still to come, and the Hollywood studios kept her on the blacklist for years.

33

〰〰〰

ROMAN HOLIDAY

A S THE POLITICAL CLIMATE DARK-
ened in the spring of 1952, Wyler felt relieved to be departing for Europe. Intolerance and paranoia had seeped like toxins into every corner
of American society. Though he'd been spared the worst, Wyler sailed
from New York on the *Queen Mary* that April feeling something like a
fugitive. "It was very unpleasant, even though he knew he was lucky to
be leaving," said Talli, who followed in June with their three daughters.
"Willy and I both felt like somebody was after us."

Even their next-door neighbor Charlie Chaplin had been subpoenaed
by HUAC to testify about purported Communist activities. "Charlie
was hounded out of the country," Talli remembered. "It was awfully
sad." Long a target of ultraconservative groups who reviled his morals
as well as his politics—all four of Chaplin's wives were teenagers when
he married them; two were sixteen and two scarcely older—the world's
most celebrated Hollywood personality defied HUAC by refusing to
testify. I AM NOT A COMMUNIST, he wired the committee. I AM WHAT YOU
CALL A PEACE-MONGER. That Chaplin never applied for American citizenship, despite living in the United States for four decades, gave his
detractors even more leverage to doubt his loyalty. In 1952, while on a

trip to London with his fourth wife Oona, the sixty-three-year-old Chaplin was barred by the attorney general from reentering the country.

But Wyler did not bolt the country just for political reasons. *Roman Holiday* gave him the chance to make his first comedy since the mid-thirties, something he'd wanted to do all along. Also, leaving the country provided a tax shelter. The federal government had created an income tax loophole commonly known as "the eighteen-month law." It exempted Americans who remained outside the country for eighteen months from having to pay tax on their foreign earnings. "That's why we stayed away as long as we did," Talli recalled. "It was quite the thing to do." The Wylers would enjoy the expatriate life and not return to the States until the end of 1953, a year or so after the filming of *Roman Holiday* was completed.

Living in Rome and having unusual freedom to shoot the picture on location turned out to be the most euphoric experience of Wyler's career. Paramount at first resisted the idea. "No, no," Freeman told him. "We've got the studio." When Wyler dug in his heels, Freeman offered a compromise: Wyler could get backdrop shots of the city with a second unit. "The rest we'll do here," he said. "We'll build you the sets." But Wyler flatly rejected that proposal. He already had in mind scenes at the Trevi Fountain, the Colosseum, the Spanish Steps. He wanted to use a sidewalk cafe across from the Forum. Paramount could never build sets like those. Besides, he wanted to avoid stagy back projections. "I'll shoot the whole picture in Rome," he told Freeman, "or else I won't make it."

Paramount finally gave in, provided that Wyler could finance the production with blocked funds the studio had in Italy. This meant getting script approval from the Italian government, which wanted assurances that the picture would not ridicule public officials and would not satirize the culture. It also meant having to work within a budget of roughly a million dollars. That restriction was an especially tall order. Several years earlier, Frank Capra had dropped *Roman Holiday* — it was to be his second picture for Paramount, starring Cary Grant and Elizabeth Taylor — because he would have had to do it for a million five, tops.

"They passed it around to see who wanted it," Wyler recalled. "I'm not sure they offered it to George Stevens. But they offered it to me — I was looking for a story — and I liked it."

To keep costs down, he agreed to shoot in black-and-white. But he wanted to make the picture in color from the very beginning, contrary to his own often-quoted recollection that he thought of color only after getting to Rome, when it was "too late" to switch camera equipment and film stock. In fact, in a letter he wrote Laurence Olivier as early as November 1951, six months before sailing for Italy, Wyler described the project this way: "Our new romantic comedy, *Roman Holiday*, is being readied for Spring production. Ben Hecht just did the screenplay, which is quite charming. We hope to go to Rome to do it properly in color."

Wyler's detractors later claimed that, despite its undeniable success, *Roman Holiday* showed he was timidly old-fashioned—either unprepared to work in color or afraid to do so just when Hollywood was making the transition. As the actress Sylvia Sidney remarked in 1990, echoing other critics of Wyler's postwar career: "Black-and-white film was very cheap, so he could shoot and shoot and shoot. As soon as color came in and it became very expensive, he did not make very good pictures."

But Wyler had always welcomed technical innovation, going all the way back to the first talkies. He felt no different about color. He simply took the heat for the studio's financial decision. Once he made his fifth and final picture for Paramount in 1955—also on the cheap in black-and-white—seven of his last eight pictures were shot in color. These included *Friendly Persuasion* (winner of the Palme d'Or, top prize at the Cannes Film Festival) and *Ben-Hur* (still the record holder for most Academy Awards, eleven). While it can be argued that these were popular hits rather than artistic triumphs for the ages, they and others—*The Collector*, for example, or *Funny Girl*—hardly offer proof of failure.

Roman Holiday is best remembered as Audrey Hepburn's Oscar-winning film debut. She'd had bit parts in a few British pictures and minor roles on stage, mostly as a dancer in West End musicals. When Wyler met her for the first time, in the summer of 1951, she was twenty-two and a total unknown. Colette, the famous French novelist, had spotted her a couple of weeks before in Monaco, where Hepburn was on location at Monte Carlo's Hôtel de Paris shooting another small role for a French-made picture. As Colette has recounted, she was being escorted in her wheelchair through the hotel lobby when she caught sight of Hepburn playing a brief honeymooner's scene. "I could not take my eyes away," Collette remembered. Her short novel *Gigi* was being adapted for Broadway by Anita Loos, and they had yet to cast the title role. "There," Colette said to herself, "is Gigi."

Meanwhile, as the novelist exchanged cables and letters with Loos about her find, Hepburn returned to London and received a message from her agent. "He told me a movie was going to be made called *Roman*

Holiday," she recalled. "They wanted an unknown, and they were going to test a great many girls. To get the test I had to meet a man named William Wyler. I had no idea who he was. So one day I got an appointment to go to Claridge's. I went up to his room wearing my one and only proper dress. I was quite apprehensive. I didn't know what was expected of me. He was very pleasant. He looked me over, and I think I spent five minutes with him."

Even before seeing her test, Wyler recommended that Hepburn be put under contract. "She impressed me as being very alert, very smart, very talented, very ambitious," he said of their interview. But he still had to see whether her personality translated to the screen before he made up his mind about casting her. "I couldn't stay myself to make the test," Wyler said, "so I arranged for one." He also left precise instructions on how to make it. As he explained later, "a test is a precarious thing. A good actress might make a very bad test, depending on conditions. You might not get her true personality, because of nervousness or whatever. So I asked the director to do an old trick." Whoever was assigned should "conspire with the cameraman and the sound man to continue to run camera and sound after the scene ended, in the hope that the girl would not be aware of this." This might allow him to see her "completely relaxed."

Shot by British director Thorold Dickinson, the test became a Hollywood legend. As Audrey Hepburn remembered, "I'd never really acted, never opened my mouth before. There was a young man who read some lines with me. I was so green I didn't really know what to do, and I think Thorold got a little desperate. But he didn't give up, which was what saved the situation. He said, 'Well, we've done this scene now. Why don't you change back into your clothes and then come and have a chat with me. There are a few things I'd like to know about you.' So I got into my sweater and slacks, and I came back and sat down and talked to him. He asked me a lot of questions about myself, about my work, even about my past during the war in Holland. I suddenly realized, little that I knew, a camera was rolling all that time. My face lit up and then I became very rigid. But that's what made the test. He had me on film being as natural as possible, not trying to act."

Hepburn believed, and legend has it, that she clinched the role as soon as Wyler saw the results. But, in fact, this was not the case. He was "very intrigued by her," according to Talli, but he still had another unknown under serious consideration.

"The Hepburn test was very good, as you may have already heard," Wyler wrote a Paramount executive in London in October 1951.

"Everyone at the studio was very enthused about the girl, and I am delighted we have signed her. Please tell Dickinson he did an excellent job. I would like very much to see Suzanne Cloutier tested exactly the same way, however, which would give us an excellent opportunity to compare the two girls. Of course I would like her to have the same freedom and to get the same amount of direction as was given Hepburn, bearing in mind that she's an entirely different type. Thus I don't want her imitating Hepburn. So don't let her see the Hepburn test. She's bound to play things a little differently. The only thing we missed in the Hepburn test was a serious moment. I can understand, with the leading man you had, it would have been difficult. However, if, in the Cloutier test, a serious and romantic moment could be included, it would be very helpful."

Wyler gave Hepburn a hint, after finally casting her, that he'd had certain doubts. But he dissembled. "I remember him saying to me he wasn't all that keen," she recalled. "He said, 'I thought you were a bit fat.' Which was absolutely true. I ate everything in sight, having been undernourished during the war. You know, whole boxes of chocolates. I was ten pounds more than I ever weighed in my life. It's funny to think I might not have gotten the part because I was too fat, because from then on everybody thought I was too thin." Separately, Hepburn also heard that Wyler "stuck his neck out" for her because she was "not only an unknown, but a thoroughly inexperienced unknown."

Wyler couldn't have done this had he not already signed Gregory Peck as the leading man. Paramount wanted a top star in the picture. There are several conflicting accounts as to how Peck was landed. Peck's agent claimed that Paramount "sneaked" the script to him and that Peck loved what he read. Peck himself remembers it was Wyler who called him: "He said he wanted to talk to me about *Roman Holiday.*" Wyler maintained that he engaged Peck, and that Peck initially turned down the picture.

"He said, 'Well, the girl is the best part,' " Wyler recounted. "Which of course was true. So I went to see him. I said, 'You surprise me. If you said the picture wasn't good, okay. But because somebody else's part is a little better than yours, that's no reason. I didn't think you were that kind of an actor.' Then he took it. He said I was right."

According to Peck's version, he needed no coaxing.

"I have no recollection of hesitating at all," he says. "As far as I'm concerned that's apocryphal. The idea of going to Rome and making a romantic comedy after some of the heavier stuff I'd been doing appealed to me immensely. Even more than that, I liked the idea of working with

Willy. With a fellow like that? His track record was well known in our town. His sensitivity and artistry were recognized. You don't hesitate—at least I didn't."

WYLER THOUGHT OF *ROMAN HOLIDAY* AS A FAIRY TALE. IT WAS something of a Cinderella story in reverse, as he'd once termed his 1935 comedy *The Gay Deception.* The plot revolved around an innocent young princess of an unnamed country, Anne, who has arrived in Rome as part of a goodwill tour. Bored by the pomp and ceremony of diplomatic protocol—and frustrated that her whole life has been controlled by official schedules—she impulsively escapes from her embassy for a few hours of freedom among the common people. Drowsy from a sedative administered by the royal physician, Anne falls asleep on a bench overlooking the Forum, where she is found by Joe Bradley, an American newspaper reporter on his way home from a late-night poker game.

Reluctantly, Bradley puts her up in his tiny apartment, not knowing who she is. The next morning when the princess fails to appear for a press conference, he puts two and two together but doesn't tell her what he suspects or who he is. He wants to cash in on an exclusive story of the princess wandering incognito around the city. So he gives her a most unroyal tour, arranging for one of his poker buddies, a free-lance tabloid photographer, to tag along and secretly take pictures. The reporter (Peck) and the princess (Hepburn) fall for each other without revealing their true identities. But in the end, as though at the stroke of midnight, they must separate. She feels duty-bound to fulfill her royal obligations, while he proves himself a gentleman and never writes his exclusive.

The screenplay for *Roman Holiday* had a convoluted history. Ben Hecht's script was not the first and would not be the last. As much as Wyler had liked it, he sailed for Europe knowing he didn't have a shootable blueprint. He took his brother Robert and Lester Koenig with him on the *Queen Mary.* Together they worked on rewrites. "We wanted to get away from all distractions," Koenig recalled in later years. "We had a mess. We worked on the script all the way across the Atlantic. But when we got off the boat, we still hadn't accomplished what we wanted."

According to Ian McLellan Hunter, who won an Academy Award for writing "the motion picture story" of *Roman Holiday,* it was really his friend Dalton Trumbo, one of the blacklisted Hollywood Ten, who wrote the original. "He asked me to front for him," Hunter said. "And my agent sold it to Capra." The deception bothered Hunter. "If some-thing's phony it drives me crazy," he explained. "But I was stuck. I mean, what the hell do you do? Your friend is blacklisted and he needs money. . . ." As an established screenwriter, Hunter commanded a siz-able fee. "My price was about fifty grand." Paramount paid it, and he turned the amount over to Trumbo. Hunter then went on salary at the studio and wrote the first *Roman Holiday* screenplay for Capra. "I was given an Academy Award for a story which was clearly not mine," he said. "Had it been for the screenplay, I could have convinced myself that I had done most of it."

Hunter had no involvement with the picture after Wyler took over the project, but never believed that politics had anything to do with that. "Wyler was a superior sort of fellow compared to Capra in this re-gard," he said. "Capra had two or three properties, all by lefties, and that scared the ass off him." Hunter maintained that Capra shrank from doing *Roman Holiday* because of politics as much as Paramount's budget limitations. "He was scared that people would say he had nothing but Communist stuff."

Hunter eventually shared credit for the screenplay with John Dighton, a British writer Wyler hired and brought on location. Dighton had written a lachrymose romance called *Saraband for Dead Lovers* in 1948. It, too, dealt with the conflict between love and royal duty. "We had Dighton in Rome with us all the time," said Bob Swink, who edited the picture. "He was writing new scenes, new lines, whatever it took. The picture was kind of put together as it went along."

As always, Wyler prized story structure and preparation. But he still liked improvising within fixed scenes to give them spontaneity. In *Roman Holiday* he did more of that than usual, partly because the city's streets provided him with what he called *l'embarras du choix* ("an embar-rassment of riches"). "Filming in Rome in those days was marvelous," he said. "There were practically no automobiles, only Vespas [scooters]. For every scene I could have had six locations, and each one was better than the other." He also made use of the newly renovated Cinecittà stu-dios, Europe's largest production facility. Six miles from the center of Rome, it was the hub of Italian filmmaking and already had a reputation as "Hollywood on the Tiber" because so many American companies were setting up shop there. Up to that time, however, no American pic-ture had been made in Italy from pre-production to final prints. *Roman Holiday* would be the first.

Practically everybody brought their families along. Gregory Peck took an out-of-town villa with his wife and their three boys. Eddie Albert, cast as the photographer, rented a house with his wife and infant son. Robert Wyler and Cathy O'Donnell took a downtown apartment. Lester Koenig had his wife and son come over by plane and moved into the Roman suburbs. Swink brought his wife and three kids. They took an apartment near Cinecittà.

Talli, who was almost five months pregnant, arrived in Naples with thirteen-year-old Cathy, ten-year-old Judy, eighteen-month-old Melanie and their French Creole nanny. At Willy's request, Talli also brought along his big blue Cadillac. He met them on the dock and took them back by train to Rome. They and the Pecks all moved into the Residenz Palace hotel while their homes were being readied. Willy had rented a top-floor apartment overlooking the Piazza Elvezia, near the Via Veneto, across town from Cinecittà. The Venezuelan ambassador to the Vatican occupied the floor below.

"We'd only been in the city for two days when a traumatic thing happened," Talli said. "Judy disappeared. I enrolled her and Cathy at the American School, so they could meet friends. For some reason the children kept teasing Judy. She got so upset she went out into the street. The school called me, 'She's gone. Vanished.' I was absolutely frantic. She knew the name of the hotel, but she didn't speak any Italian. What finally happened was a man saw her walking alone and picked her up. He gave her a ride on the front of his bicycle. When he began to get too friendly she started to cry. He must've gotten scared. He let her off the bicycle and she found her way to our doorstep. The whole episode just made my blood run cold."

It was a steaming hot summer. Between the heat and the language difference—most of the seventy-odd people in the film crew were Italians who didn't speak English—it was reasonable to expect confusion at best. But as Eddie Albert recalled, "working for Willy in Rome was nothing but joy. It was a pity to take the fee." Wyler steered the production with an infectious mood of great confidence and good humor. "He was more in charge than I'd ever seen," Albert said. "He put an invisible wall between him and Paramount and Hollywood. So when they would call with idiot suggestions, he would say, 'Oh my God, we just shot that yesterday. What a shame!' "

Hepburn, too, noticed how easy he was on her. Lacking experience, she felt rather intimidated at first and worried about making mistakes—until they began working. "What I remember most about Willy," she said, "is not at all what most people think of as 'the great director.' He was so dear to me. He never made me feel he had to teach me anything. He just said go ahead and do it. Therefore I felt very relaxed. There was no technique that was visible. It was, 'This is what we're going to do.' We'd rehearse, then he'd say, 'Camera.' And we did it. I was never aware of being put through my paces or that what I did wasn't good enough. He'd say, 'Well, let's just do it again.' He was famous for very many takes, of course. But that was good for me."

Peck regarded Wyler from the quite different perspective of a major star with long experience working for major directors. They ranged from Henry King (*Twelve O'Clock High*) and King Vidor (*Duel in the Sun*) to Alfred Hitchcock (*Spellbound*) and Elia Kazan (*Gentleman's Agreement*). But even in that context, Wyler astonished him.

"In spite of his careful preparation, he was a director who relied a great deal on instinct," Peck says. "He was not one to talk a thing to death. In that sense, he was a pragmatist. What worked worked, and he knew how to recognize it. This may come as a surprise, but not all directors know how to do that. They pick the wrong take, or they're not open to what can happen on the spur of the moment. Willy had a special sensitivity to that. He sensed the interplay between actors. There's a whole parade of moments, with nuances and subtexts. He understood them. This was 'the Wyler touch.' It's why so many actors won Oscars with Willy, because he recognized the moments that brought them alive on the screen."

Unlike some actors, Peck derived pleasure from Wyler's habitual retakes. He felt "privileged" to work with a director who would stay with a scene as long as it took to show everyone at their best. "What I think is *not* true," Peck said, "is that his actors felt browbeaten or put upon. I guess it's fair to say he was not concerned with the interior process of acting, as Kazan was. All he wanted was a good result. He didn't care how you got it. But he had such delicacy and humor, it's also fair to say you could easily fall under his spell. He was an extraordinary person — very subtle, immensely talented, incredibly charming. This made him great fun to be with."

Wyler's ability to improvise infused *Roman Holiday* with a playful allure. In his hands, the airily thin story also acquired an earthy flavor. He mixed the romance with realism, poignance with belly laughs. "It was Willy's picture all the way," Peck said. "Willy invented so many bits from day to day that work seemed more like a game."

A case in point is the now classic scene at the "Mouth of Truth," an ancient stone monument of a pantheistic, round-faced god at the entrance of an old church. Legend had it that a liar would lose his hand if he dared to put it in the god's mouth. A truthful person, however, had nothing to fear. Wyler took his daughters sightseeing one day and came across the monument. To amuse them he stuck his hand in the mouth and pretended his whole arm was being tugged in to the elbow. When he pulled it out, he hid his hand up his sleeve. "It scared them to death," Wyler recounted. "So I thought there must be a place for this in the picture, especially since it's a story of two people who lie to each other."

Peck recalls the origin of the "Mouth of Truth" improvisation somewhat differently. He says he suggested the idea to Wyler as an old Red Skelton bit: "Willy said to go ahead and try it, but don't tell Audrey." Keeping her in the dark is what made the scene work, of course. Her startled look of surprise leaps off the screen. She screams, then dissolves into laughter. It is one of the most candid and indelible moments of *Roman Holiday*.

Wyler would turn on a dime for a good idea. Swink said, "He didn't hesitate a moment. If he liked it, he'd grab it. If he thought it was a lousy idea, he'd say, 'Bob, it stinks.' There was no middle ground. He was honest."

Nor was he above using caddish tricks. Wyler got nasty, for example, to elicit genuine misery from Hepburn when she couldn't produce it on her own. "There was one scene that required tears because I had to leave Greg and go back to my palace," she said. "We were sitting in this tiny little car, and I had to get out, say good-bye to him and rush away very sad, preferably in floods of tears. I was trying desperately and nothing was happening. I just didn't know how to come by these tears. The night was getting longer and longer. Willy was waiting, and out of the blue he came over to the car and gave me hell. He said, 'We can't stay here all night. Can't you cry, for God's sake?' Willy had never spoken to me like that. Never. I broke into such sobs. He shot the scene, and that was it. Afterward he said to me, 'I'm sorry. But I had to get you to do it somehow.' "

Despite Hepburn's lack of experience, everyone on the shoot knew she was a gem. Her image on the screen was so vibrant in the daily rushes—Swink ran them every morning for Wyler—that her performance became the gossip of the set. "We all knew this was going to be an important star," Peck said. "We even began to talk off-camera about the chance that she might win an Academy Award." Hepburn had no idea that Wyler's painstaking effort to get a moment just right was not common Hollywood practice. Certainly, few other directors would have spent days zeroing in on minor details.

"There was a scene of me sitting with Gregory on the Spanish Steps eating an ice cream," she recalled. "It was a complicated scene to get because of the background. So we spent hours at it. It took us two days to get that one shot. Then the film was ruined in the lab, and we had to do it all over again. I think I ate ice cream for five days. I thought everybody shot that way."

Wyler, knowing she was game for anything, got her to jump into the Tiber River more than once for a shot. "And very cold it was — I can tell you," she said. "I was fed on brandy when I came out, and got very tiddly that night."

Giddy feelings extended all around. One night about two in the morning, Wyler invited Swink and his assistant cutter to take a walk with him after a long day's work. "He said, 'Let's go get a plate of spaghetti or something,' " Swink recalled. "So we went over to a café that had a little orchestra. There was nobody there to speak of. Willy was feeling good. We'd had a little wine. He said, 'You guys want to hear me play?' Well, sure we did. So he asked one of the musicians if he could borrow his violin. I don't remember what he played, but he must have played for twenty minutes. It was a happy shoot."

The high point came during post-production in late September: Talli gave birth to her fifth child. It was not without a scare, though. She had taken Cathy and Judy to Switzerland to find them a French-speaking boarding school. "Leaping on and off all these Swiss trains, I took a bad fall," she recounted. "When I got back to Rome I started having trouble, as if I were going into labor. The doctor put me to bed immediately, and for three days I tried to hang on. But I couldn't.

"The moment of truth came about seven o'clock in the evening. I'm alone in the apartment with a couple of servants. Willy is all the way on the other side of the city at Cinecittà. I call him and say, 'Hi.' Before I can say anything else, he launches into how they're missing three days of film, the lab has lost the negative, what a terrible day it's been."

When Talli finally got a word in edgewise, Willy realized he'd never be able to drive home, pick her up and drive back to the hospital, near Cinecittà. He called the wife of his Italian production chief. "She came over," said Talli, "and we commandeered the chauffeured car of the ambassador to the Vatican. Willy met us at the hospital." An hour later, on September 25, she gave birth to a son. "Six weeks premature," Talli said, "but he weighed more than five pounds, so we had no problems." They named him David William. He was their last child.

In no hurry to get back to the States, Wyler strung out post-production through the winter of 1953. He took his family skiing in the Swiss Alps. They went to Klosters. "We had a lot of pals there," Talli recalled. "John

Huston and his latest wife, Ricky Soma; Irwin Shaw and his wife Marianne; the Viertels. Robert Parrish and his wife Kathleen, who'd organized the Chaplin-Wyler tennis tournament, also showed up."

Late that winter the noted French composer Georges Auric came to Cinecittà to conduct the score he'd written for *Roman Holiday*. In the twenties, Auric was one of the Parisian group of avant-gardists known as *"les six,"* with Francis Poulenc and Darius Milhaud. Auric had written the film scores for all of Jean Cocteau's pictures, many for René Clair and Max Ophuls. His subsequent output in Hollywood was prolific.

"He made his music the way he wanted, whether it ran longer than our scenes or not," said Bob Belcher, Swink's assistant. "Willy would say to me, 'How come you didn't give him the right timing?' And I'd say, 'I did.' So Willy would go over to him, and they'd start yammering in French."

As spring approached, Wyler needed Peck to overdub some dialogue and called him back to Rome from London where he was making a British picture called *The Million Pound Note*. Actor and director had become fast friends, a relationship that would turn into a business partnership as well. What's more, Talli liked Peck's new girlfriend, Veronique Passani, a young French journalist. Peck had split up with his wife in the midst of filming *Roman Holiday*. When shooting ended, he sent her home to Los Angeles. "It was leading up to that for a long time," he recalled. "I was gloomy about separating from the boys, but there was no other way." To cheer himself up, he took a trip to Paris and began dating Passani, who had once interviewed him for a magazine.

The paparazzi dogged their every move. "Veronique and I were a hot item for the tabloids," he said. "Willy and Talli were on our side. They loved her." To get away from the press, Wyler suggested the four of them slip away to Lake Como, near the Swiss border. After several days, believing they'd made a safe escape, they took a motor boat to Coccina, a tiny island with Roman ruins, in the middle of the lake.

"It was unbelievably picturesque, and it had a little restaurant," Peck recounted. "We were all having a grand time at lunch. Suddenly Talli froze. Something caught her eye. We all turned around and a hand with a camera went *Click!* from behind a tree. Willy and I jumped to our feet. We were the only customers in the restaurant. We thought we were the only people on the island. Willy and I started chasing this guy up the slope. I didn't want to be photographed with Veronique for obvious reasons. It was an absolute comedy. Willy took a flying tackle and grabbed him by the foot. But the guy's shoe came off in his hand, and the guy disappeared into the undergrowth.

"At this point, the chef was shouting, 'The pasta is ready!' Talli and Veronique wanted us to come and eat. Willy and I looked at each other. We thought this guy was trapped on the island. We hadn't heard a motor boat. Willy said, 'Well, he can't swim ashore. Let's have some spaghetti, and we'll chase him later.' We had our spaghetti, went looking again, no luck. So we finished our lunch. The third time we went after him we were too late. We saw him in a rowboat a couple of hundred yards offshore heading for the mainland. He got away. There was a kind of a blurry picture of us in a tabloid in Milan."

(Fewer than twenty-four hours after Peck's divorce came through in 1955, he married Veronique. Forty years later, they were still happily married.)

A week or so later, Wyler made a brief trip to Hollywood with Swink for a sneak preview of *Roman Holiday*. Up to his old tricks, Wyler had a surprise for Paramount's top executives. During the editing process, many of the Italian-made work prints kept snapping. It was a major headache.

"But," Swink recounted, "this gave Willy a great idea. Keep in mind that the first scene in the picture looks exactly like a newsreel. Willy says, 'Gee whiz. How about after the main title we get the audience to think the print has broken down and the projectionist has switched over to a newsreel while the film is being fixed? That might be really interesting.' So we made it seem that way. We put a big optical scratch after Wyler's name in the main title, then a few white frames and suddenly the whole screen went white, then black. Then the opening newsreel footage came on introducing Audrey Hepburn. The public didn't know her face. For all anybody knew, she really *was* a princess visiting the capitals of Europe.

"Willy says, 'Let's not tell Paramount about this. They'll see it for the first time at the preview.' So when we sneaked the picture, I went up and warned the projectionist. I told him what would happen. 'Don't worry,' I said, 'it isn't you.' Well, the preview starts. This stuff comes on, and it's bedlam. The executives are jumping out of their seats and running around. Willy and I are just sitting there. They're yelling at me to do something. The audience starts clapping. They're thinking the same thing. It worked like a charm, and Willy loved it. But it didn't end up in the picture. It was too distracting. We cut it. After the main title, we went straight to the newsreel."

By June, the Wylers decamped from Rome for the south of France. The Eternal City had been so good for them, Talli said, "I wept when we left." They picked up Cathy and Judy from their Swiss boarding schools. To their father's delight, the girls were fairly proficient in French. The family took a house for the summer in St. Jean-de-Luz, a tiny village in the Basque countryside just outside Biarritz. The Shaws had a place there. The Hustons also turned up, as did a whole colony of Hollywood expatriates.

Wyler missed all the hoopla when *Roman Holiday* premiered August 27, 1953, at Radio City Music Hall. The picture was a big hit with critics and audiences alike, even more so when it opened in Europe. Word of mouth turned it into a long-running hit. Two years later it was still playing at some theaters. William Holden, the Academy Award–winning star who'd made *Sunset Boulevard, Born Yesterday* and *Stalag 17*, returned to the States from an industry tour of Europe in 1954 and told the press that *Roman Holiday* was one of "the two most important films in building American prestige abroad." The other, in his opinion, was *The Best Years of Our Lives*. Holden noted, "All we need is more directors, like Wyler, who realize you don't have to sacrifice honesty to make great films."

Even Dalton Trumbo and Ian McLellan Hunter, who had every reason to believe *Roman Holiday* would not live up to their expectations, were impressed with the result. "When someone directs your picture, it is not yours anymore," Hunter explained. "One is not used to being elated at a production. But I saw that the girl was marvelous. I had never seen her before. Peck I'd always liked. That was one time I came out of the theater and said to myself, 'Well, you got a good deal *that* time.' My reaction was shared by Trumbo. We agreed that Wyler had done a helluva job with this thing."

By early 1955 the picture's gross approached ten million dollars worldwide. When it got to Japan, *Roman Holiday* and its newly discovered star created a sensation. Audrey Hepburn's winsome smile, elegance and grace had made her an international favorite. In the land of the rising sun, women revered her. They made a national fad of her. They cut their hair to look like her. Fan clubs popped up everywhere. Magazines treated her like a screen goddess.

WHEN SUMMER ENDED, THE WYLERS SENT THEIR TWO OLDER girls back to school and went traveling with the rest of the family. Willy, already searching for new material, wrote Paramount: "I have gone through stacks of plays, novels, short stories, manuscripts — in German, French, English and even Italian." He found nothing suitable, however. He went to Manchester, England, to see Vivien Leigh and Laurence Olivier in a pre-London tryout of Terence Rattigan's *The Sleeping Prince.* "I'm afraid it is not for Audrey Hepburn," he noted. "It is, but definitely, for Marilyn Monroe."

In London he saw all the latest plays and gave the studio a rundown on their screen prospects. Among them were Graham Greene's religious drama *The Living Room* ("unsuitable"), *Carrington, V.C.* ("rather dull"), T. S. Eliot's *The Confidential Clerk* ("confidentially, not good") and *For Better, For Worse* ("Take the last"). In Paris he had only slightly better luck. "Most of the French plays are either censorable or not good," he wrote: *l'Heure Eblouissante* ("wonderful, unfortunately too naughty"), Jean Anouilh's *l'Alouette* ("about Joan of Arc and it's too late for that, or too early"). He read the script of Marcel Pagnol's *Judas,* which was in rehearsal. That intrigued him ("a brand-new conception of the biblical character, beautifully written by the master of French writers. I will tell you about it, as I need my hands for it.").

Wyler returned to Hollywood in November 1953. By then *Roman Holiday* was being touted as a strong contender in the Oscar race. When nominations were announced, it got ten, including best picture, director, actress, supporting actor. When the Academy Award ceremonies rolled around in March, Wyler was bested by *From Here to Eternity* and its director, his friend Fred Zinnemann.

As the years went by, *Roman Holiday* gained a huge following and remarkable prestige. In 1960 it wowed paying crowds who jammed the Lenin Sports Palace in Moscow, where it highlighted an American cultural exchange program with the Soviet Union. "Thirty thousand Muscovites fervently applauded three sneak previews," the *New York Times* reported, with the comment that the picture was "sheer enjoyment."

During the Cuban missile crisis of 1962, John F. Kennedy requested a private viewing of *Roman Holiday* at the White House, while awaiting an answer to his blockade ultimatum. He saw the picture on the evening of October 27. The next day the Soviets agreed to dismantle their Cuban-based missiles. Wyler got a kick out of that when told of the coincidence. But he got a bigger kick when he heard that tour guides in Rome were telling tourists at the Forum: "Here is where Caesar is buried. On those steps is where Marc Antony spoke. And over here is where Audrey Hepburn and Gregory Peck played a scene in *Roman Holiday.*"

"All in one breath," Wyler marveled. "Can you imagine?"

. . .

THE RED-BAITING FANATICS OF THE MCCARTHY ERA WOULD
begin to lose ground by the fall of 1954, when the United States Senate
finally censured the demagogic senator from Wisconsin. His unsubstantiated charges of rampant Communist spies and fifth-column traitors
had ruined thousands of lives. But the decline in McCarthyite influence
would come too slowly and too late to save the breakup of Wyler's professional association with Lester Koenig. Ironically, it was *Roman Holiday* that marked the end of their working relationship and, for many
years, their intimacy. They had spent part of the war together and collaborated on all seven Wyler pictures since 1943. It was a bitter blow.

Koenig made the blacklist before going to Rome. Among other
things, he was friendly with the expatriate German composer Hanns
Eisler before the war. Eisler and his wife had put him up in their guest
house in 1939 and became so fond of him that they began taking him to
the regular soirees at Salka Viertel's salon in Santa Monica. There, he
was exposed to Thomas Mann, Arnold Schoenberg, Bertolt Brecht and
all the expatriate German artists who had taken refuge from Hitler. This
came back to haunt him when, in 1947, Eisler was forced to leave the
country or face deportation as a Communist. (Eisler would write the
music for East Germany's national anthem, no less.)

HUAC wanted Koenig's testimony. He had taken the Fifth in hearings in Los Angeles after being named by Martin Berkeley. Wyler inter-
ceded for him with Paramount, persuading the studio he couldn't make
Roman Holiday without him, and reminded the studio that Koenig was
under contract. This resulted in an arrangement whereby Koenig would
be allowed to go to Rome with the unwritten understanding that he
would testify on his return. When Koenig got back he did not testify.
Paramount dropped his name from *Roman Holiday*—over Wyler's objection—and dropped his contract when it came up for renewal. Koenig
went to Malibu and cut himself off from his friends. He got rid of his
telephone, wouldn't speak to professional acquaintances, refused to listen to the radio. "If people saw him on the street," his brother Julian recalls, "they knew to avoid him."

Even after Koenig was fired, Wyler tried to get him reinstated. "My
father was offered some sort of deal from Paramount through Wyler's
intervention," says John Koenig, a record executive and lawyer. "My
father wouldn't take it because he had friends who never had that opportunity. He believed you can't turn around on yourself. That meant,
'If I believe this whole corrupt witch-hunt was illegal and yet take this

deal just to get personal advantage, I'm not being true to my beliefs. I'm betraying everyone who is suffering from this.' "

Though Lester Koenig eventually remade his career, in the record industry—he founded the independent jazz label Contemporary Records—Koenig was dogged by "the pain, almost the agony, of feeling betrayed," according to his son. "I don't think he felt betrayed by Wyler. If anything, Wyler probably was upset with my father for not taking the deal. Those goddamned principles of my father's often got in the way of real life. I won't say he and Wyler *reconciled*, because there hadn't been *that* sort of break, but toward the end of my father's life they were seeing a lot of each other."

On Koenig's death in 1977, Wyler gave a eulogy: "We were among the first American troops at the liberation of Rome. His contributions to *The Memphis Belle* and *Thunderbolt* earned him a Bronze Star. After the war Lester's contributions to my pictures were incalculable and far more than a simple screen credit would indicate. For all of this he was remembered by being blacklisted. Actually he was much more of a patriot than all those self-appointed so-called patriots who made up the lists."

34

~~~〰〰~~~

THE MAN YOU HATE TO LOVE

IT WAS THE SPRING OF 1954.
They were discussing a crime thriller by a little-known writer, Joseph
Hayes, who'd hit the jackpot.

"You really want to play this part?" Wyler asked.

"Sure," Bogart told him.

"It's not really your type."

"Why not?"

"Well," said Wyler, "he's a family man. He has children—"

"Hell," Bogart snapped. "I don't want to play that role. I'm talking
about the gangster."

Hayes's novel, *The Desperate Hours,* was such a hot property that bids
for the screen rights poured in even before publication. It told the story
of three escaped convicts who terrorize a suburban family and hold it
hostage.

On further reflection, Wyler decided it wasn't such a bad idea to
have a cunning, middle-aged ringleader of the trio, *if* he could get
Spencer Tracy to play the father of the family. Pairing the two stars opposite each other seemed like dream casting. So he sent Tracy the script.

"Tracy liked it and said okay," Wyler recounted. "Only we could never make the deal because we could never solve the billing. Neither one of them would accept second billing. It was really stupid. Each one said, 'My name goes first.' As if the public cared."

Humphrey Bogart, through his Santana Productions, had made what he felt would be the high bid for screen rights. He saw the convict role as a throwback of sorts to the character who'd made him famous: Duke Mantee, the sneering, trigger-happy thug he played two decades earlier in *The Petrified Forest.* But Wyler, who'd read Hayes's unpublished manuscript, authorized Paramount to make the purchase by topping any bid.

Hayes signed with Paramount for fifty thousand dollars against a percentage of the gross because, among other reasons, the studio agreed to let him write his own screen adaptation and because of Wyler's reputation. "I cannot imagine anything better happening to an author or a book," Hayes wired.

Meanwhile, the novel soon hit the newsstands as a *Collier's* magazine serialization, then made the book clubs (it was a Literary Guild selection) and topped the best-seller lists before being translated into a dozen or so foreign languages. The press claimed the thirty-seven-year-old writer stood to make a million dollars from all his deals, including a contract for a Broadway stage version. And in an unusual twist the play wouldn't be written until after the movie was made, and the movie wouldn't be released until after the play closed. Wyler never ranked *The Desperate Hours* with his best films. He certainly found its melodramatic possibilities intriguing—suspense, psychological blackmail, class conflict, repressed violence—but he not only didn't get Tracy, he didn't come close to getting the cast he'd originally envisioned. He wanted Marlon Brando or James Dean for the convict, Gary Cooper or Henry Fonda for the father. Hayes, too, was preoccupied with the casting. He endorsed Bogart, noting that he'd "go for him fast" if somebody strong played against him. "Without any desire to add to the Bogart pressure," he explained, "I do think he could give a good performance and his name would be terrific." Hayes also liked the dramatic values to be gained from pitting two men of similar age against each other: It would underscore the essential difference between them, both as real people and as representatives of opposing social forces.

Ultimately, Wyler turned to Fredric March at the suggestion of Don Hartman, who'd recently become Paramount's head of production. In August, two months before shooting was scheduled to begin, Hartman attended a Santa Barbara sneak preview of the studio's Korean War film, *The Bridges at Toko-Ri.* It starred William Holden and Grace Kelly. March played an admiral with a strong paternal streak. "The audience loved him," Hartman told Wyler. "He would be ideal for your picture, I am convinced, if the Cooper or Fonda setup is impossible."

Hayes developed his plot for *The Desperate Hours* from newspaper crime stories—he regularly clipped them for ideas—and a fantasy prompted by the distant prison lights he saw every night from his hilltop home in Connecticut. What if a few desperate inmates broke out? What if they managed to elude the police and came in his direction? The notion was not implausible. Hayes had a sheaf of clippings about innocent people taken hostage by felons trying to evade capture. Now the lights of the Danbury federal prison, tucked in a valley far across the lake, seemed "bright as a carnival, sinister as a gun."

Still, Hayes felt it necessary to set his story in a locale more familiar to a majority of Americans than the rolling hills of suburban Connecticut. A "typical midwestern setting" suited the story best, he told Wyler, "the sort of grown-up or overgrown small town atmosphere of a place like Indianapolis." Wyler zeroed in on particulars. He wanted a house that was "pleasant and very, very comfortable" because Griffin (Bogart) "knows that at this level of society he is safer in making his threats." That would underscore the psychology and status of the Hilliard paterfamilias (March), both as protector of his loved ones and chief target of Griffin's scorn.

Hilliard's home need not be lavish or ornate, "but it and all its furnishings should have the stamp of success on them," Wyler noted. "In an earlier time, Hilliard would have been seen as something of a Main Street Babbitt. He worked as a department store executive with a salary of perhaps fifteen thousand dollars a year. He and his neighbors were not rich. They had middle-class aspirations. They set great store by niceties and outward appearances."

The Desperate Hours also would be the epitome of a squeaky-clean studio shoot, as far from *Roman Holiday* in production ambience as in subject matter. Except for the exteriors, to be shot at night mostly on Universal's back lot, the entire picture would be made on Paramount sound stages. Wyler would have a seven-room home built to order down to the last detail. Lee Garmes would be his cinematographer again. Only this time he would be shooting black-and-white in Vista-Vision, one of the wide-screen formats that Hollywood turned to in the fifties to make movies visually more appealing than television.

Wyler's chief concern, though, had to do with dramatic tension. "In the usual suspense movie, the audience is excited by a single element," he noted. "The audience wishes to see—longs to see—the hero or heroine accomplish certain ends. The villains are very clearly defined.

They're bad, and the audience wishes to see them get their comeuppance. Everything is based on a single threat to sympathetic people." In *The Desperate Hours*, however, he wanted to create not just that element "in an intensified form," but another, ambivalent feeling. "Any ambivalence creates tension, almost unbearable tension," he explained. It was "this added dimension of suspense" that would set the story and his handling of it apart.

At the beginning of the picture "the audience wants to see the police reach the criminals," Wyler elaborated. "Then it wants this even more strongly when the criminals enter the house. It watches the police work, get closer, become stymied. But slowly it dawns on the audience that things might be much worse for the Hilliards if the police *do* come. Still, is there any way out if the police do *not* come? By forcing the audience to face this question, we force them into Dan Hilliard's mind. They take on Dan's anxiety. They worry. . . . This complexity and contradiction, this *uncertainty* on the part of the audience, is the source of the kind of suspense that was created, with intent, by the author. If the audience can be made to want two contradictory things, alternately and sometimes simultaneously, the resulting tension is deepened and intensified."

The shoot would run for eight weeks from mid-October to mid-December 1954. When photography began Paramount celebrated by inviting top stars to the set for a glimpse of "the great Wyler" at work. He did not disappoint. On the opening day, he fully lived up to his reputation. Martha Scott, a New York actress cast as the Hilliard materfamilias, recalls: "We had a lot of people come by to wish us well. So what happens? Willy made us shoot the first scene fifty times for this audience. It was just Freddie coming out of the house, kissing me goodbye and going off to work."

About the thirtieth take Scott went over to Willy. "Is it me?" she asked.

"No," he whispered. "I want to tire Freddie out because he's *acting*. I don't want him to *act*. I want to upset him, so when he comes out of that door he has a harried look on his face. He's late and he's got to get to work."

Scott recalls, "Willy shot that scene for a day and a half, and it was only two pages."

A young Rod Steiger saw enough that day to put him off Wyler for good. Touted as a Hollywood "comer," Steiger had just made a huge splash with Marlon Brando in *On the Waterfront*. After it opened that July, Wyler took Steiger to lunch at Chasen's to talk about a project he had in mind.

"He wanted to do *Look Homeward, Angel*," Steiger recounts. "I told him that was my favorite book. I loved Thomas Wolfe. So he says he's got to make another picture first. Why don't I come over when he starts shooting? I did, and right there I figured I could never work for a guy like that. Three takes, maybe five. That's my limit. After that I'm done."

March went back a long way with Wyler, but on *The Desperate Hours*, he received no quarter. These really were desperate hours for him, not just for the character he was playing.

"He was afraid of Willy," Swink says, "in the sense that Willy wouldn't be pleased with his work. Every once in a while Willy would call me up and tell me to take Freddie March out with another camera and get a close-up or a shot he'd missed. I remember March saying to me, 'I'm so glad when you come to do these things.' I said, 'Why?' He said, 'Because Willy scares me.' Willy scared a lot of people."

In later years, March paid tribute this way: "If Erich von Stroheim was the man you loved to hate, Wyler must be the man you hate to love but must." Having worked for many masters—among them Lubitsch, Ford, Hawks, Cukor and DeMille—March spoke from considerable experience. "It's easier to know that Wyler is Hollywood's finest director for actors than it is to explain it. He doesn't articulate his criticism. But you sense his dissatisfaction. He seems to know when there's more to be gotten than you're giving. And he's relentless until he has it. The released print is the deferred proof."

Bogart, too, got a taste of Wyler's whip hand. Ordinarily Wyler cooperated with him. They had an agreement: Bogart, who was on the set like clockwork at nine sharp, would be free to go at five so he could have his first drink and get home by six. On rare occasions, however, Wyler decided otherwise. "One time, and this was extraordinary, Willy kept Bogie after five because he wasn't getting what he wanted," Scott recounts. "Willy wanted him to be more of a threat, not just the usual heavy. He told everybody, 'We're going to do it again.' It was a short scene. When six o'clock came Bogie started to boil. That's when Willy printed the shot. Bogie's boiling in reality put the threat into his face and the menace into his eyes. He was one helluva'n actor, but Willy was one helluva director."

Scott herself always received kid-glove treatment. She'd made a triumphant Broadway debut in 1938 as the original Emily in Thornton Wilder's *Our Town*, and also reprised the role in the movie. Wyler respected her achievement.

"Willy was especially good to me," she says. "In fact, he confided in me once in a while. He said, 'I would appreciate it if, when I wink at you, you would come and sit by me. You're a stage actress, you know about dialogue. If you hear something that doesn't sound right, you've got to tell me because I don't hear so well.'

"He would talk to me under his breath. 'How is that? Is that okay?' I would say, 'Yes,' or if I didn't think so, 'No.' That never upset him. He was always grateful. Once in a while I'd point out a changed line that was better the way it was written. He'd look at the script and say, 'Yeah, I see what you mean.' One time I said to him, 'You must think I'm a pain in the ass.'

" 'Well,' he said, 'you're a nice pain in the ass.' "

Wyler hired a new assistant for *The Desperate Hours*, who also served as one of his ears. He was a Stanford grad by the name of Stuart Millar, whose father, Mack, had been Wyler's publicist for years.

"Willy's hearing must have been deteriorating," Millar says, "because he was very, very concerned about it. He arranged his whole office so his desk was positioned in such a way that his left ear was available to visitors. But even his left ear had been damaged. He was always cupping it."

Wyler brought Millar in on script conferences and made him his factotum, as if he were grooming him for the business. Millar ran errands, answered his mail and became part of Wyler's extended family. "I think he enjoyed watching me grow up," Millar says, "and now he was letting me in on things. He trusted me. On the set he said, 'Stand behind me and listen. Don't be afraid to tap me on the shoulder after a take and tell me whether I missed something.' I was like a shadow. It felt a little funny. At six foot six, I'm not exactly unnoticeable. Everybody on the sound stage, especially the actors, must have looked at me and wondered, 'Who *is* this guy, and what's he doing?' "

Millar played a more significant role on Wyler's next picture—auditioning actors and dealing with writers—then went out on his own. He eventually became a producer in the sixties (*Birdman of Alcatraz* and *Little Big Man*) and a director in the seventies (*Rooster Cogburn*).

Three weeks after Wyler completed shooting the picture, Hayes's stage version began its pre-Broadway tryout in January 1955 at the Shubert Theater in New Haven, Connecticut. It was an immediate sensation, with Karl Malden in March's role and Paul Newman in Bogart's. "Show gets off like a firecracker," said *Daily Variety*. And *Weekly Variety* predicted: "Hollywood producers may as well lay in a generous supply of dry ice. The already finished film version will probably be in refrigeration a long time if release is contingent upon completion of legit edition."

A week later in Philadelphia, *The Desperate Hours* sent reviewers into a unanimous state of cardiac arrest. The *Evening Bulletin* called it "thrilling, but no play for a weak heart." The *Philadelphia News* called it "blood-chilling . . . a terrifying show that beats its watchers to a pulp." When it opened on Broadway in February, it packed the Ethel Barrymore Theatre and was "standing room only" for months. In spring, it swept the Tony Awards for the top drama categories: best play, production, author and director.

The quiet heroism of an ordinary, law-abiding citizen who manages to out-duel a trio of brutal home-invading thugs obviously struck a nerve. Between the best-selling novel and the Broadway smash, everyone expected *The Desperate Hours* to be an even bigger hit on film. Wyler, Hayes and Paramount figured on a 1956 release, anticipating that the play would run at least through the end of the year. But in midsummer an intense heat wave descended on New York, and Broadway wilted. With nobody buying tickets, Karl Malden, the star of the show, gave two weeks' notice. Hayes shuttered the show on August 13. "Malden's withdrawal was too much," he wrote Wyler. "Pardon my understandable bitterness." Wyler sympathized: "I can understand how you must feel, seeing something so good fade away before anyone ever expected it would."

Paramount pushed up the New York opening of the picture to October 5 and put together a publicity blitz. The cast — Bogart, March, Scott and Robert Middleton, who played Bogart's beefy sidekick Kobish — all went on tour to promote the picture while Wyler put the finishing touches to it with some last-minute trims. Bogart strode into a press conference in Boston, acting the gangster to the hilt. Wearing a brown suit and pale pink shirt with a small gray bow tie, he brushed past a reporter who tried to ask him a question and barked that the press wherever he went was too dumb to ask intelligent questions.

Reporters surrounded him. His wife Lauren Bacall, dressed stunningly in black with a black furpiece, crossed the room and sat down with friends.

"This is a very boring interview," he began. "This woman says Freddie March got a better role than me in the picture. Sure he did, and he's an excellent actor. How's she gonna get a story out of that?"

Bogart fielded the next question: "What's that? Why didn't I get March's role? Now listen here, sister, do you think I could play a father of two kids who was frightened of anybody? Ha! There's a story!"

This sort of thing went on for two hours. Bogart fired back questions on everything from theology and chess to education, sex and the family lives of the reporters. When he got to New York for interviews, he hardly talked about the picture. The *New York Post* columnist Earl Wilson wrote him up and mentioned *The Desperate Hours* as an afterthought.

Wyler and Paramount and everyone connected with the picture, including the exhibitors, were in for a big shock. Despite generally positive reviews, moviegoers didn't turn out in droves. And while the picture made its money back, predictions of a smash proved dismally wrong. Bogart went over; *The Desperate Hours* didn't.

Many postmortems concluded that Paramount's delayed release hurt the picture badly: By the time *The Desperate Hours* came out, a handful of B-movie melodramas with a similar criminals-invade-home-and-hold family-hostage formula had already saturated the market. "Six this season alone," one observer pointed out. Others noted that Hollywood's habit of grabbing off best-selling novels almost before the ink dried backfired in this case because too many people had read the book and knew the thriller's outcome.

Wyler, who always had a healthy respect for box-office success, blamed himself for the flop. He believed that by failing to show "more violence" he strained the credibility of the plot. March is allowed to leave his home and go to work, while his family is held hostage, in order to give the impression of normalcy. But he doesn't take that opportunity to go to the police. Some critics questioned whether any reasonable man wouldn't have done so, even knowing the risk to his family. Wyler concluded that in this sort of melodrama his restraint in not presenting an onscreen beating or two weakened the pressure of psychological blackmail.

It did not occur to him that he was perhaps too successful at creating ambivalent feelings in the audience. Also VistaVision notwithstanding, *The Desperate Hours* didn't offer much of an alternative to the fare on television. However well made, the picture ultimately lacked scope. The nature of the material itself had limitations, not its rendering on film. One Philadelphia drama critic predicted, when he saw Hayes's play, that it would be "long remembered, in the vein of *Death of a Salesman.*" Clearly, he was wrong.

35

〰〰〰

Pacifist's Dilemma

WITH HIS FIVE-PICTURE DEAL AT an end, Wyler was ready to move on from Paramount. The studio didn't want to lose him and offered Wyler profit participation in his future pictures. But Harold Mirisch, an Allied Artists executive whom he'd met in Biarritz, was waiting in the wings with a better deal: profit participation *and* creative freedom.

When Liberty Films was folded into Paramount, Wyler's promised artistic control didn't materialize as he had expected. Though the studio had managed to shield him from the witch-hunters, allowing his career to flourish in the worst of times, he still chafed at the prospect of production executives' turning down his projects. Even before he began shooting *The Desperate Hours*, Wyler decided to sign with Allied. He also knew the picture he would make for them.

In January, while cutting *The Desperate Hours*, Wyler broke the news to his young assistant. He gave Millar a script called *The Friendly Persuasion*, which had been written for Capra by Michael Wilson back in 1946 and was based on a collection of short stories about an Indiana Quaker family during and after the Civil War. The picture had never been made. Still less promising, it had a history of false starts.

"Willy stopped me cold one day," Millar recounts. "He said, 'Here's something wonderful and we're going to do it.' That one hour in his office became the table of contents for the next year of my life. He told me what he thought was wonderful about the script, what he thought was wrong with it, and what he needed to do about it. Then he told me the circumstances under which he was going to make it and what the implications of that were for him and for me. He said, 'We're going to this new place. It's no studio at all, and we're going to have to do this whole movie ourselves.' "

Allied Artists was an offshoot of the low-budget moviemaker Monogram Pictures, which had released *Thunderbolt* after the war when nobody else would. The company wanted to do quality features and needed entree to the big leagues. Mirisch courted Wyler and Billy Wilder, signed them by the end of the year, and in early 1955 landed John Huston. Allied had a small, old, run-down lot at the corner of Sunset and Vermont in a neighborhood of clapboard bungalows. "There were no offices, no departments, no anything," Millar says. "It was a shell. Just ten people huddled together." It had two sound stages, no production staff, a few accountants and lawyers. Wyler's plan to move to the wrong side of the Hollywood tracks seemed to Millar a risky idea at best.

The next morning, however, Wyler's assistant came to work "high as a kite." He'd read the script in one sitting, scrutinized the original collection of stories and praised Wilson's work as "the most incredible job of construction."

"It's brilliant," he said. "It adheres very closely to these stories and weaves them into a seamless whole."

Wyler insisted, nonetheless, that the script would need "a major rewrite." He thought Wilson stressed extraneous characters, and he particularly didn't like the second half. Millar recalls, "Willy felt the script evaded the issue of what a Quaker farmer who doesn't believe in fighting does when he's confronted with violence. He said he did not want to make a movie that ducked that issue."

Wyler asked him to put together a list of writers who might be suitable for a rewrite.

"What about Wilson?" Millar said. "He's the obvious candidate."

Wyler shook his head. "I can't hire him. He's blacklisted. I've got to find somebody else."

Wilson had been banned from employment in Hollywood since 1951 for taking the Fifth under questioning by HUAC interrogators.

Millar came up with another suggestion. "What about the lady who wrote the book?" A former writing student of Wallace Stegner's at Stanford, Millar considered himself a literary connoisseur. He'd been bowled over by the quality of the original stories.

"She must be some little old lady in Indiana," Wyler retorted. "She can't possibly be useful to us."

Besides, the book ducked the issue, too. Jess Birdwell, the Quaker pacifist whom Wyler regarded as the proper hero of the picture, never had to decide whether to fight or let his house be burned down; he never had to fight or watch his wife be raped by marauders.

"Not good enough," Wyler said. "He's off the hook."

But Millar still felt it would be worth contacting the author.

"Nobody knows these characters better," he argued. "And nobody knows better how they would respond to the questions you're posing. If you ask any other screenwriter to do this, they'd have to make up what they *think* these Quakers would do.

"It's not a question of construction," Millar went on. "It's a question of getting into their souls. How can you expect any Hollywood screenwriter to really know what they would do? Would you mind if I at least found out where she lives, and how old she is?"

Wyler gave in.

Millar discovered Jessamyn West not in Indiana but in Northern California. When he phoned her, she hardly took any notice. "Somebody called from Hollywood," West recorded in her diary. "I didn't get his name."

West told him she wasn't interested in discussing any movie. She was busy working on a new novel, and she'd heard plenty of Hollywood talk before.

Millar called again shortly after, from San Francisco. Couldn't he just stop in the following day? Before she could hang up, he explained he'd read her book—a fact that surprised her—and she asked him who he was.

"I am," he told her, "Mr. Wyler's assistant."

She had no idea what that meant, except that "he said it with a pride that sixty miles of telephone wire did not disguise."

In the silence that followed, Millar thought they'd been disconnected.

"Who," she asked, "is Mr. Wyler?"

Now it was Millar's turn to be silent.

"I take it for granted that he is someone connected with the movies," she said.

Millar proceeded to rattle off titles: *Wuthering Heights, The Little Foxes,*

The Best Years of Our Lives, Roman Holiday. He told her Wyler made them all.

West said she'd seen them all. "I thought they were good pictures," she said.

"They were *very* good pictures," he said.

Millar's persistence finally wore her down. West told him she'd be happy to see him. When he drove up to Napa the next day, they surprised each other. The sight of Millar's six-foot-six frame unfolding from the front seat of his beat-up Chevrolet was awesome.

"If the assistant looks like this," she said to herself, "God knows what the assisted will look like: Toscanini, maybe."

To Millar, West looked plain but not little or elderly. She was tall and vibrant and in her fifties. She had an unmistakable earthiness and an outdoor tan. She lived in a ranch house made of redwood. It was surrounded by huge oak trees and had a garden filled with gorgeous flowers: Chinese lilies, daffodils, camellias, red-hot pokers.

Despite her initial coolness, West warmed to Millar's intelligence. They discussed her characters, their motives and so on. But when he asked if West cared whether a good movie were made from her book, she said it was no concern of hers. Besides, she hated the thought of going over old writing. She'd finished the stories in *The Friendly Persuasion* ten years ago.

Millar wondered if she wouldn't at least come to Los Angeles to meet his boss. She countered that she had no screenwriting experience. She would not know what to do and, more than likely, would ruin Wyler's efforts.

"Willy is not a man to let his movies get ruined easily," he assured her.

Finally, she gave up and agreed to see who this Wyler was.

Two weeks later, Millar picked West up at Union Station and delivered her to a posh hotel in Los Angeles. Wyler sent his regrets that he could not see her immediately: His elderly mother had died the day before. Melanie Wyler's death was not unexpected. She had been ill in recent years.

Director and author would look each other over on a bright mid-February morning a couple of days after that. West arrived at Wyler's home in anything but Hollywood style. Millar drove her in his Chevy past the Beverly Hills Hotel and onto a winding road that climbed uphill. West had the feeling she was being taken to an audience with the Pope, "not from anything Wyler had done to foster it," she recalled, but from the briefing his acolyte had been giving her for the past couple of weeks. On the last leg on Summit Drive, as if she weren't sufficiently distracted, Millar warned her that Wyler hated yes-men.

"Stand up to him," he urged. "Don't agree with a thing he says unless you believe it."

On her way past the Wyler living room she glanced in and thought it wonderfully ordinary—except for its considerable size and the original Maurice Utrillo and Diego Rivera paintings on the walls.

Wyler greeted her in his large, second-floor study. He offered her a cigarette—ignoring whether it might offend her Quaker beliefs—and, when she declined, lit one for himself. He asked about the Society of Friends, said he was glad to hear she didn't think of her writing as a religious mission.

"Who have you thought of as the central figure in these stories of yours?"

"Jess, of course," she said, referring to Jess Birdwell, the father of the family. "Jess is the hero from beginning to end."

That was different from the script, he said. Wilson established Jess's wife, Eliza, as the dominant figure.

"Stu tells me you think, if a movie were made, it would have to center on the Civil War story."

The Wilson script matched her view in that regard, but the last half shifted away from Jess so completely that he became an onlooker.

"If *you* were to center [the movie] on the Civil War episode," Wyler said, "how would you get around this?"

"I'd invent something."

Wyler laughed.

"What would you think of Gary Cooper as Jess?"

West didn't have to think.

"Will Cooper play the part?" she asked.

"Not in this script," Wyler said. "Coop says if he starts a movie he likes to be in at the finish. If all he's going to do is watch the last three reels, he'll watch it from a seat in the theater."

West assured Wyler that Jess Birdwell was not only "the whole book" but that "he must be in every scene."

That gave Wyler pause.

"I don't think even Coop wants that much footage," he said.

In their first meeting, West and Wyler not only charmed each other, they entered a working collaboration that would result in one of the more rewarding pictures of the fifties. In that meeting, too, West claims, she invented a key new character for *Friendly Persuasion* and experienced something rare in her life as a writer.

"I can't remember what exactly led to it," she recorded later. "We had been talking about the possible reception of a Quaker picture. Mr. Wyler wondered if I knew (and I did) that there are groups which believe it is un-American to show or even speak of a people whose beliefs run counter to those generally held. Mr. Wyler didn't want me to have any illusions about himself—he was no Quaker. . . . Evil, in his experience, had to be resisted with violence."

Jess needed a friend, she told Wyler. "No Quaker, someone who is a fighter, someone who opposes Jess and loves him, someone as strong in his own way as Jess is in his."

When the meeting ended, Wyler was pleased. He told her to write her ideas down. She went back to her hotel and typed up twenty pages. Millar called to tell her Wyler was sending them on to Cooper and wanted her to come to dinner.

Gary Cooper had to be persuaded to take the role of Jess Birdwell on several counts. Wyler had broached the idea with him some years before, but the star wasn't interested. "I ain't ever played a pappy yet and I ain't aiming to start now," he said at the time. Wyler believed Cooper had gotten over that. He didn't think the star minded playing a pappy now so much as playing a pacifist. It was not the image Cooper's audience had of him.

At Wyler's dinner party for a half a dozen couples—the Coopers, the Dunnes and several others—West found herself all but swooning when the director introduced her to her favorite movie actor. After dinner, when the guests retired to the living room, she, Wyler and Cooper stayed behind for a professional tête-à-tête.

"There comes a time," Cooper said, "when the people who see me in a picture expect me to do something."

"You mean pull a trigger?" West asked.

"Deliver a blow. Fist or bullet. Or sword. They expect it. They feel let down without it."

His most recent outing was a Mexican shoot-'em-up.

"I saw you in *Vera Cruz*," she said. "That was a stupid picture."

"I stank."

"It's a pity for you not to play a complete human being," she said.

"I'd like to play a part like that. But I don't know that I'm very well suited to playing a Quaker."

In a subsequent meeting, Cooper wanted to know what his character would *do* in the way of action. He would do *something*, West told him.

"What?"

"Refrain," she said. "You will furnish your public with the refreshing picture of a strong man refraining."

Precisely how Jess Birdwell would refrain finally wasn't decided until Wyler made up his own mind nearly a year later, when the picture was being edited. According to Swink and Millar, Wyler filmed the action two ways—with Jess picking up a gun and not picking up a gun. "Everybody had an opinion," Swink said, "even John Huston. He thought Jess shouldn't pick up the gun." In the cutting room, Wyler decided to stretch the temptation of violence to the limit and with it the dramatic pressure: Jess does pick up the gun, but finally chooses not to pull the trigger.

COOPER SIGNED FOR *FRIENDLY PERSUASION* IN SPRING 1955, after Willy and Talli returned from a six-week trip to Asia that coincided with the Tokyo premiere of *Roman Holiday*. Meanwhile, West was persuaded to rewrite Wilson's script. She went home to Napa and returned with "excellent raw material," but not what Wyler considered a shootable screenplay. He hired yet another writer, Harry Kleiner, to meld the best of the Wilson-West material together but was so disappointed with Kleiner's version that he tossed it aside and rehired West—this time teaming her with his brother Robert. Indeed, it was Robert who persuaded Willy to get her back. He contended that with her talent and material and his own technical know-how, the two of them could produce a workable script.

Later, West would claim that Willy's ability to draw the best out of them equalled his more famous talent for eliciting great performances. Willy's collaboration was "covert action not open to public inspection," she explained. "I was no longer content with editors who never asked me any questions. . . . I enjoyed discovering an action, a timing, a phrasing which carried my story and revealed its characters better than the original. This scrutiny [Willy] Wyler asked of me."

Filling the role of Eliza Birdwell—Jess's beautiful, bossy and pious wife—also was problematic. Wyler's first choice, Katharine Hepburn, was not available. He tried Vivien Leigh in London. URGE YOU TO ACCEPT, he wired. UNUSUAL AND MUCH SOUGHT AFTER PART ONE OF BEST IN YEARS. ALSO SUITED TO YOU. FILM WE HAVE BEEN TALKING ABOUT FOR SO LONG. Leigh replied from Stratford-on-Avon, where she was doing Shakespeare: DREADFULLY SORRY. QUITE IMPOSSIBLE BE FREED UNTIL END NOVEMBER. MORE DISAPPOINTED THAN I CAN SAY. Wyler turned to Ingrid

Bergman in Italy. She wired back: HOW I WOULD LOVE TO WORK WITH YOU AND GARY, BUT NOT THERE. Hollywood still hadn't forgiven Bergman for deserting her husband and daughter to run off with Roberto Rossellini. Bergman sent Wyler a counteroffer asking him to come to Europe to direct her in a Somerset Maugham adaptation.

"Every woman between the ages of thirty and fifty-five was considered for Eliza," Millar recalls. Jane Wyman, Maureen O'Hara, Teresa Wright, Martha Scott, Eleanor Parker, and Mary Martin led the list. At one point Wyler took West aside and deadpanned: "What do you think of Jane Russell? She's a very pious girl, I understand. Goes to church, teaches Sunday school, sings hymns." In the end, Dorothy McGuire got the role. When Wyler saw she was having trouble getting into character, he suggested a preparatory exercise.

"He had me spending I don't know how many hours a day on the set before production, kneading bread," McGuire recounts. "He never explained why he did something, he just asked you to do it. It was funny. What director would ask you to knead bread? I guess it put me into a different period of time, with a different way of thinking."

Apparently kneading bread didn't quite do the trick. Wyler asked McGuire to move out of her house and not see her husband or her family for a while. He also turned to Jessamyn West for help. West was to take the actress to a prayer meeting in Pasadena and hang around with her, in the hope she might absorb some Quaker culture.

Having just seen *East of Eden*, Wyler approached its young star, James Dean, for the role of Jess's eighteen-year-old son Josh, who needs to test his manhood.

Millar recalls, "Jimmy and Willy spent about half an hour together. I don't think Willy ever offered Jimmy the part because Dean's agent made it clear they would not accept a supporting role. So nothing came of it. I do know that Willy was enormously impressed by Jimmy Dean."

Wyler then looked to New York for a fresh face. He sent Millar ahead to line up interviews for Josh's role, and Millar found Tony Perkins, son of the late Broadway star Osgood Perkins.

Perkins recalled, "I was just a brash kid who really didn't know much about anything. The names William Wyler and Billy Wilder were interchangeable to me. I was just careful to keep my mouth shut, so I wouldn't make any mistakes."

But when Perkins did speak up, in what he described as "a rather austere meeting at the St. Regis Hotel," he was very careful to make himself clear. Millar had coached him about Wyler's hearing problem.

"Stu told me, 'If you want this role, keep your voice up and don't mumble.' It was the age of mumbling actors. He didn't want me to screw up my chances in the great man's presence."

Perkins wasn't altogether unknown. He'd had a small role in a Jean Simmons picture, *The Actress,* and was appearing on Broadway as the sensitive young man in Robert Anderson's *Tea and Sympathy.* Though Perkins hadn't originated the role, "everybody was raving about this remarkable kid who replaced John Kerr," Millar recalls. "Willy went to see the show. Then Tony gave a stunning reading for him. The moment Tony walked out of the room I knew Willy had given him the job."

Wyler conducted rehearsals for *Friendly Persuasion* as though it were a theatrical production. This surprised Perkins. "In those days pictures weren't rehearsed that often," the actor said. "We sat around a table and read the thing several times.

"The first line I came up with, he shot down. He said, 'No, that's not the way it should be.' Then he told us, 'Don't blow this by introducing the serious aspect of these characters too quickly. Get into the fun of it. Get into the family life, the casualness of it.' It threw me. I can even remember the seating arrangement because I felt such chagrin at being ticked up by Wyler not on the first day of shooting or the first week but on the very first line of the first rehearsal."

Perkins also was surprised to discover that Wyler kept the rehearsal process going after filming began. In the early morning hours, when people were gathering around the coffee wagon, Wyler would hold private auditions of what the actors had prepared for the day's shoot.

"Willy was always interested in what the actors brought in," Perkins recounted. "Even if it was a short scene, you'd do four versions for him. He'd run through them quickly and he'd pick and choose elements from each. He'd say, 'Begin with the second one and end with the third one,' or vice versa. So I'd have it pretty much squared away, knowing what he wanted beforehand. What struck me was that he had the patience to listen to a young actor with the pretentiousness and gall to offer him four versions. He actually seemed to enjoy it."

Keeping an eye on how Wyler worked with Cooper, Perkins noticed "they would discuss things in a very, very technical way. Wyler would literally say, 'When you come to this word, stop and swallow, then continue.' Cooper would listen to this, and when he actually did it, it was magic. This was the kind of thing I saw them do often. It was Cooper's artistry that he could translate a technical direction into something very soulful. And I saw him do this time and again."

Friendly Persuasion was Wyler's first picture in color, not counting *The*

Memphis Belle a dozen years earlier. He began shooting August 15, 1955, when Cooper became available. But principal photography didn't start until September, a month before *The Desperate Hours* opened. Wyler wanted to shoot in southern Indiana on a farm, for the authentic look of the mid-nineteenth century. The decision not to go on location that far away, Millar says, "was motivated very strongly by economy." Wyler used the Rowland V. Lee ranch instead, an hour and a quarter's drive from Hollywood in the San Fernando Valley.

Owned by a former actor, the ranch served many outdoor period pictures because directors didn't have to shoot around power lines or telephone poles. It had dirt roads and offered a gently rural landscape unmarred by modern eyesores. But it also had pale brown hills of barley chaff and olive and eucalyptus trees, not the sort of vegetation indigenous to the rich bottomland of the Birdwell farm. So Wyler went to great lengths to dress the exteriors. He had cornfields planted and sycamore trees brought in, and green grass by the acre. He ordered stone walls for the farmhouse—a wood facade, of course, made to look like stone. But he was startled when the art director took it upon himself to erect a stone silo.

"Pull it down," Wyler ordered when he saw it.

"Willy," the art director said, "I understood you to say you wanted Jess Birdwell's barn and house to tell the audience that he was a well-to-do, successful farmer."

"A successful *Indiana* farmer, not somebody farming on the Rhine. That looks like the tower where the rats ate the bishop."

Wyler glanced at a decorative object with fins leaning against the barn. "What's that fish doing over there?"

The art director's face brightened. "It's a weather vane," he said. "Jess is a poetic, imaginative kind of man. I thought he'd be likely to have something kind of offbeat, not the usual horse or rooster on his barn."

"He's not that offbeat. Get a rooster. The audience has got to do something else in the first two reels beside try to figure out this offbeat barn."

The shoot lasted into early December, with Wyler giving over some of the filming to a second unit led by Swink, his key technician and occasional stand-in. Swink shot much of the county fair scene on a Republic sound stage, when Wyler was put out of commission by an unexplained allergy. Swink even subbed for him on a live NBC telecast that Wyler ducked out of at the last minute.

"Willy just wasn't a publicity-hungry guy," he says.

The national telecast, designed to promote the picture, offered a tour of the Birdwell farm for an audience of thirty million viewers. It was to end up on the farmhouse porch, where Wyler would be shown directing Cooper.

Swink recounts, "Willy calls me up at nine o'clock on a Sunday morning two hours before the broadcast. He says, 'Bob, will you go on for me? I've got laryngitis.' So I rush over and Stu Millar gives me a twenty-five-page script he wrote and tells me I've got to memorize it. Stu arranged this whole deal. I looked at the script and said, 'Forget it. I can't memorize that stuff.' " Swink and Cooper winged it.

Wyler chose Robert Middleton for Sam Jordan, Jess's newly created best friend, a cheerful Methodist who likes music, races his horse and follows his instincts with as much fervor as Jess, but without the restraints of Quaker culture. Sam was a complete role reversal for Middleton, who had played the dumb brute Kobish in *The Desperate Hours*. Wyler also cast child actor Richard Eyer, a natural who'd played the son in *Desperate Hours*, as the rambunctious Little Jess. Eyer's running battle with Samantha, the goose, is a priceless touchstone to the picture's buoyancy. Wyler hired his friend Clarence Marks, an old gagman from silents, to help come up with folksy bits of humor.

As for Cooper, Wyler had nothing but high praise. "Coop is a damned good actor," he told Hedda Hopper. "A very smart fella who likes to play dumb."

Throughout the shoot, Wyler asked for constant script revisions. Jessamyn West and Robert Wyler were on the set daily, rewriting scenes even as Wyler was filming them. And he shot a lot of footage. Swink says he cut an hour's worth of material from *Friendly Persuasion* and it still ran to epic length. All that notwithstanding, the shoot went "like a nice boat ride," assistant editor Robert Belcher recalls. "We didn't hit any rapids." They would come later.

On February 8, 1956, Wyler suggested the following writing credits:

Screen Play by Jessamyn West and Robert Wyler
From the Book by Jessamyn West

Michael Wilson immediately protested, and the dispute was submitted to the Writers Guild for arbitration. A month later the Guild made its decision and wrote Allied Artists on March 9 that the credits should read:

Screen Play by Michael Wilson
From the Book by Jessamyn West

In the same letter, however, the Guild informed Allied Artists that, according to its bylaws, if the screenwriter had ever lied about being a member of the Communist Party or taken the Fifth against self-incrimination—which Wilson had done—Allied Artists didn't have to give him the screenplay credit. Allied informed the Guild it would not give credit for the screenplay to anyone.

Wyler was outraged over what he called "this disgraceful bullshit." He got out his contract with Allied and called in his lawyer, believing he had artistic control over the picture. Allied maintained the issue had to do with commercial control. It claimed that if Wilson's name appeared, the American Legion would picket the movie showings and Allied stood to lose financially. Wyler countered that Allied should appeal the Guild's decision and offered a compromise: Give the screenplay credit to all three writers.

This did not happen. In July, Wilson's lawyers filed a civil suit for two hundred and fifty thousand dollars in damages against Allied and Wyler.

Meanwhile, Wyler felt frustrated that West and his brother were deprived of credit and, later, of an Oscar nomination. The screenplay would be nominated, but with no names attached. Before the nominations were announced, the Academy had created a blacklist of its own. Anybody who took the Fifth in Congressional testimony was ruled ineligible for an Oscar.

Wyler's detractors considered him morally and politically culpable for not giving Wilson partial credit in the first place. They claimed he had appeased the blacklisters. As ingenuous as it may seem, though, he believed the picture had changed so radically from the original script that Wilson did not qualify for a credit on artistic grounds.

"I can state flatly," he contended in a sworn affidavit for the lawsuit, "that this picture was made mainly from [West-Wyler] material written either during the final period prior to the shooting or during the period of actual photography."

Millar swore in his deposition that with minor exceptions West-Wyler wrote the entire second half of the picture and that even scenes derived from Wilson's script in the first half were completely rewritten. He had "not the slightest doubt" that West-Wyler were responsible for "structure, continuity and dialogue."

Wyler also maintained—and Millar's deposition supported him in extensive detail—that *Friendly Persuasion* differed significantly as shot from the script examined by the Guild. The changes on the set never made it into the final shooting script "as is not uncommon with my pictures,"

Wyler noted. He and Millar both wondered why the Guild, in assigning Wilson sole screenplay credit, did not actually view the picture.

Ultimately, Wilson's suit was settled out of court with Allied.

Friendly Persuasion had several previews. The first, in Long Beach, was the most significant. Swink recalls, "We must have had nine or ten breaks in the film." The lights in the theater would come on each time and someone in the projection booth would splice the film together. Each time the interruption took five minutes. Ordinarily, an audience might begin whistling and jeering, if it didn't walk out. This one sat through all the breaks without a murmur, and Millar remembers, "it was a really tough sailor-port crowd." He, Swink and Wyler thought they had a big hit. The audience had stayed three and a half hours, to see a two hour and twenty minute picture.

But when it came to the picture's release, Allied Artists was slow to promote it. Besides the bad blood between Wyler and the company over the screenplay credit, *Friendly Persuasion* had cost three million dollars—double its million-and-a-half budget—and Allied was running out of money. A poor showing at the box office by the company's second release, Billy Wilder's *Love in the Afternoon,* even forced the cancellation of John Huston's contract.

Wyler wanted *Friendly Persuasion* to open at Radio City Music Hall, but Allied did nothing to make that happen. "They didn't know how to handle the movie," Millar says. "They were scared of it. They couldn't stand the title. They wanted to call it *Mr. Birdwell Goes to Battle.* They did a real heavy sell on Willy to call it that. Sort of like *Mr. Smith Goes to Washington.*"

Wyler and Swink took a work print to New York themselves and screened it for the top brass at Radio City. *Friendly Persuasion* opened there November 1, 1956. The reviews were generally positive, though many critics found it saccharine. The picture did respectable business but was far from a mega-hit. It was only when *Friendly Persuasion* opened wide around the country that it became popular through word of mouth. The picture's sweetest additive—the theme song "Thee I Love," sung by Pat Boone—climbed the pop charts and increased the picture's popularity. In spring, Wyler took the picture to the 1957 International Cannes Film Festival, where it won the Palme d'Or, the festival's top prize. By 1960, *Friendly Persuasion* would earn eight million dollars worldwide, a slow return for Allied, but profitable.

Since then, *Friendly Persuasion* has had an unusual afterlife, with irony compounding irony.

At the request of the Soviet Union, and with the approval of the U.S.

State Department, Wyler took *Friendly Persuasion* to Moscow in 1960, where he showed it as a symbolic antidote to the Cold War.

Thirty-two years later, with the beginning of *glasnost,* President Ronald Reagan—whose conservative politics Wyler loathed—took a videocassette of *Friendly Persuasion* to Moscow. During a state dinner, he presented it as a personal gift to Soviet premier Mikhail Gorbachev, devoting a large portion of his toast to the meaning of the film and why he had chosen it.

"The film has sweep and majesty and pathos," the president said. "It shows not just the tragedy of war, but the problems of pacifism, the nobility of patriotism, as well as the love of peace."

When the *New York Times* printed the text of Reagan's remarks, it occasioned a ripple of remembrance from Michael Wilson's supporters. Letters to the *Times* pointed out the irony that a movie written by a so-called "Commie" was now embraced by a saber-rattling right-wing president who had made a career of demonizing people like Wilson. From their point of view, Reagan's gesture boggled the mind.

Magazine articles soon followed, denouncing Reagan for hypocrisy. They quite properly picked out the central theme of *Friendly Persuasion,* just as the president's speechwriters had: the moral quandary of a pacifist family confronting violence. But they either didn't realize or didn't care that it was Wyler—not Wilson—who was entirely responsible for injecting that theme into the picture.

"They needlessly lambasted Willy," says Millar, who wrote the *Times* in response to the controversy. "They resurrected the whole business of Michael Wilson's not getting a writing credit to tar Willy, as though he had curried favor with the blacklisters. It's very unfortunate, and it contradicts Wyler's real record."

36

BIG MUDDY

WITH THE ADVENT OF TELEVISION in the late forties, Hollywood faced a huge challenge. By the mid-fifties, the tube was no longer a challenge but a crisis. Wherever TV stations sprang up, people stayed home for their entertainment; movie attendance fell off; theaters closed. Television made dollars and cents. What's more, it offered variety—free—at the turn of a dial.

You could watch Elvis Presley on *The Ed Sullivan Show*, drama on *Playhouse 90*, the Old West on *Gunsmoke*, comedy on *The Life of Riley* and big-money quiz shows like *The $64,000 Question*.

From Wyler's point of view, though, it wasn't novelty, choice or economics that separated the two media. Nor was it mere technology. It was the viewers themselves. "The big difference between TV and movies," he said, "lies in the audience's frame of mind." He had confidence in moviegoers. He could capture their attention. Tube watchers, by and large, were subject to too many distractions.

Still, Wyler decided to take a stab at television on NBC's *Producer's Showcase*. Given his unfamiliarity with the medium, he chose a familiar subject: *The Letter*, which he'd done with Bette Davis. He put his TV version together on a three-week schedule, staging everything the first week and spending the next two weeks on technique. On October 15, 1956, two weeks before the New York premiere of *Friendly Persuasion,* Wyler's eighty-five minute production aired live across the country.

The process felt to him as if he were "making only one take of a motion picture." The result, according to *Time* magazine, was "a slick, highly polished teledrama about a bored housewife who riddles her lover with bullets and gets away with it." The drama starred Irish actress Siobhan McKenna as Leslie, British actor John Mills (making his American debut) as Leslie's cuckolded husband and, as the lawyer who reluctantly helps Leslie beat the murder rap, Michael Rennie, a British actor who'd become popular in American B-movies.

The Letter was considered "adult" material for television because Wyler retained the original plot: The heroine literally gets away with murder. But the network censors insisted on certain cosmetic changes. For instance, "Hell!" became "My God!" and "a woman he had relations with" became "a woman with whom he had a relation." Wyler considered the changes ridiculous. When they wanted to alter "He tried to rape me, so I shot him," he balked.

"What are you going to say? 'He tried to make love to me, so I killed him?' " The line stayed.

Despite its reception as a crack piece of staging, Wyler thought his television outing was "a one-shot experiment." He didn't trust the broadcast moguls. "I don't want to be in the lap of the gods," he said. "I want them to be in my lap." Besides, TV was ephemeral. "One night and it's gone. Movies are always there."

Wyler had long since earned the right to independence. But even as his career and reputation thrived, all his attempts to gain total control of his pictures—in deals with Liberty, Paramount and, now, Allied Artists—had fallen short. So Wyler decided to join forces in a venture with Gregory Peck, who had become a close friend. That December Peck announced they would make a comedy, *Thieves' Market,* about an art heist of El Greco and Titian masterworks from the Prado in Madrid.

"This thing didn't happen out of the blue," Peck says. "Willy and I had grown very close. We spent holidays together at Sun Valley with our families. We were always dining out together. It would be the Wylers at the Pecks or the Pecks at the Wylers. Veronique and Talli really liked each other. We were a foursome. We'd been together in Rome, and we'd been very happy. The idea of doing that again in Madrid seemed quite appealing."

Peck commissioned a screenplay, based on the novel *Thieves Like Us,* from the writing duo Fay and Michael Kanin and sent them to Spain for research. But the script didn't work, and the project was abandoned. Then James Webb, a screenwriter who'd co-written many Westerns, brought Peck a story by Donald Hamilton, "Ambush at Blanco Canyon," which was serialized in the *Saturday Evening Post* and later expanded into a novel, *The Big Country.*

"I took the story to Willy," Peck says, "and asked him what he thought of making a big-scale Western. I told him I thought there were half a dozen very good parts, so we could do some great casting. I also thought the theme would appeal to him. It was kind of an anti-macho Western."

The setup seemed perfect. Peck had a development deal with United Artists, which would finance and distribute the picture, but he and Wyler would be the bosses. The pair divided their producing responsibilities and formed separate companies. Wyler's was World Wide Productions; Peck's was Anthony Productions, named for his infant son. Wyler would be in charge of all things artistic. Peck would have casting and script approval, and he would handle the ranching aspects of the picture: hire the wranglers, rent the livestock, choose the horses, in effect serve as foreman.

"I knew about those things," Peck says. "I had a cattle business. I leased grazing land in Santa Barbara, San Luis Obispo, Merced, Modesto. I had dreams of owning a ranch. I would take part in roundups, the roping and the branding. It was part of my life at the time."

Both hoped to produce a crowd-pleaser. "We wanted to make money out of this," he adds. "We were going after a commercial hit, not the Academy Awards." They knew they had a decent Western yarn with plenty of interesting characters, but they also knew the script didn't measure up. Hamilton, who was hired to adapt his "Blanco Canyon" tale, warned them he was a screenwriting novice. Which turned out to be all too true. It would take another six writers—Webb, Leon Uris, Jessamyn West, Robert Wyler, Robert Wilder and Sy Bartlett—before they came up with a shootable screenplay. And even then Wyler did not have an ending scripted when he began filming. This was rather different from *Friendly Persuasion,* despite its many rewrites. Of all Wyler's pictures, *The Big Country* script would prove the most difficult to get in shape.

But casting went smoothly enough. They signed Burl Ives, Jean Simmons, Carroll Baker, Chuck Connors and, at Peck's suggestion, Charles Bickford. Remembering his experience with Bickford on *Hell's Heroes,* Wyler resisted the idea.

"I had a falling out with that guy years ago," he said. "He was stubborn as a mule."

Peck replied, "Well that's the character. He's self-important, arrogant, opinionated *and* stubborn."

Reluctantly, Willy came around: "I guess we should bury the hatchet. I'll meet with him."

When Bickford came to his office, he seemed genial and pleasant. And when Wyler asked, "How are you in the saddle these days?" the old-time actor skirted the issue: "Oh, you remember how I ride."

Wyler didn't remember. Bickford could hardly get on or off a horse.

A month before the shoot began, Wyler sought Charlton Heston to play the heavy, opposite Peck. A busy leading man with top billing— he'd already played Moses in *The Ten Commandments*—Heston read the script and told his agent, "I'll pass. There are three men's parts better than mine, and the two women's roles are at least as good. I'm pretty far down the line here."

Heston explains: "There's no way to put this without sounding vain. But when you're a leading man, the first thing you ask is, 'Is the picture about me?' It wasn't, of course. The picture was about Gregory Peck, reasonably enough. Then you say, 'Well, is it a great part?' It wasn't a great part, it was a good part. My agent said, 'Chuck, I think you're making a mistake.' Then he called back and said, 'Willy wants to talk with you. I think you should take a meeting.'

"I was delighted to meet him, of course. I never had. He asked me to think the part over, and I went back to my agent"—Henry Citron at MCA, who also represented Wyler—"and told him, 'I still think it's the fifth part.' He said, 'Chuck, you're crazy. Willy Wyler is almost certainly the greatest director in Hollywood. Certainly the best director of performance. It can't *but* be good to be in a picture directed by him.' I thought about it some more and said, 'Okay, I guess you're right. I'll do it.'"

United Artists agreed to the budget—two million eight hundred thousand dollars—and filming began in July. The shoot would last four months on two main California locations. At one, near Stockton, Wyler shot the range scenes and built a spare Old West town for exteriors. At the other location, Red Rock Canyon in the Mojave Desert, he shot more remote scenes. "Willy didn't want to see any signs of civilization," Swink says. With Franz Planer behind the camera—he had filmed most of *Roman Holiday*—the wide-screen color cinematography emphasized the scope and grandeur of the settings. A second-unit director made spectacular aerial shots of the canyon and staged the picture's climactic shoot-out. Interiors were shot on the Goldwyn lot back in Hollywood.

Thematically, *The Big Country* was about "courage and cowardice," Wyler said. "It was about a man's refusal to act according to accepted standards of behavior. Customs of the Old West were sort of debunked."

The picture tells a tale of bitter enemies—the high-falutin' Terrills and the low-life Hannasseys—who are feuding over water for their cattle. The obstinate patriarchs of these clans, Major Terrill (Bickford) and Rufus Hannassey (Ives), have hated each other for as long as they can remember. Terrill and his daughter Patricia (Baker), along with his surrogate son and ranch foreman Steve Leech (Heston), look down their noses at Hannassey, his drunken son Buck (Connors) and their gang. Except for old man Hannassey himself, they are indeed a repulsive bunch. As for the Terrills, especially the Major, they are just better dressed. They're also greedier and more cold-blooded.

Both cattle barons want to take over the Big Muddy, a well-watered but unused spread owned by schoolmarm Julie Maragon (Simmons), who inherited it from her grandfather and hasn't the money to work it. Enter Jim McKay (Peck), Patricia's fiancé from Baltimore, who walks straight into the line of fire on all levels. The Hannassey boys give him a rough hazing because he looks like an Eastern tenderfoot and does nothing to persuade them otherwise. Steve, who covets Patricia, hates McKay and considers his gentleman manners effete. McKay is, in fact, a gentleman—but a tough one with plenty of experience as a veteran sea captain and plenty of money as the scion of a family of shipowners. He doesn't believe in violence and feels no need to prove his courage. Patricia comes to doubt his manhood; McKay falls for her friend Julie; Julie falls for him; and Major Terrill and Rufus Hannassey inevitably have a shoot-out in Blanco Canyon.

Because of the remote locations and constant script revisions, tensions mounted on the set. The atmosphere of the shoot began to reflect the mood of the picture. Tempers flared between Bickford and Wyler. Simmons felt so miserable that she refused to discuss the experience for years. Baker was nervous and frustrated, sometimes offended. Peck stalked off the set toward the end of the shoot and didn't come back for several days. He and Wyler severed relations and wouldn't talk to each other again for three years. Only Heston, Ives and Connors weathered the storm without damage.

"Charlie Bickford was a fairly cantankerous old son of a bitch," Heston recalls. "Very cranky. Sometimes it was a line he didn't want to say that set him off, but he was always grumbling." Peck adds, "Willy liked all those retakes. He was trying to get something new each time, but Bickford was a woodcut. He liked to deliver a fixed performance no matter how many takes. Willy would tell me privately, 'I want Charlie to loosen up.' Charlie didn't loosen up, he blew up. 'What the goddamn hell do you want me to do, Willy?' 'I want you to do it better, Charlie.' Bickford went sky high, yelling and cursing. He had some very fanciful combinations of obscene words. Then he went stomping off to his Winnebago.

"Willy was very calm. He said, 'We'll take a break and let him cool off.' After ten minutes, Bickford hadn't come back. Willy sent the assistant, and the assistant said, 'He's swigging away at a bottle of Jack Daniels. He's mad as hell. He said he's done it nineteen times, and he doesn't know what else to do with it, and he thinks you don't know what you're doing either. He is *hot*.' Willy was still very calm. 'Go back and tell him we haven't got the scene yet.' Well, there was more shouting. The Winnebago was rocking. Bickford was having a tantrum. About a half hour later, Willy said, 'This is getting serious. Go tell him we will call the Screen Actors Guild. He's not fulfilling the terms of his contract. And don't forget to tell him we'll call his agent.' That brought Bickford back on the set, mad as a boiled owl. We commenced to do it again. I think we ended up at twenty-seven takes."

Simmons declined to be interviewed about Wyler and *The Big Country*. But her manager, Jeffrey Barr, said she told him Wyler was "very, very cruel and hurt her deeply." "She still bears the scars thirty years later," Barr added. "I've worked for Jean fifteen years and never heard her say that about any other director."

In the late eighties, however, Simmons did tell a reporter about the shoot. She said the atmosphere on the set felt "very dodgy—the sort of prevailing tension that invites paranoia, causes you to wonder, 'What have I done?'... I guess Willy was in a position to know what it took to achieve great performances, but he also seemed bent on making things difficult . . . and there was all that constant rewriting. We'd have our lines learned, then receive a rewrite, stay up all night learning the new version, then receive yet another rewrite the following morning. It made the acting damned near impossible."

Neither Peck nor Ives remember Wyler treating Simmons with anything but kid gloves.

"I thought Willy liked her," Peck says. "I don't recall any friction. That must have happened off the set. Willy seemed to me very responsive to her work and very tender with her. I don't recall at any time that he was harsh with her. It could have been something he said to her privately. I really don't know."

Ives did recall an incident, however, that might have led to Simmons's hurt feelings. "We were shooting in the middle of the day up in the desert, and it was hot as hell," he said. "Jeannie Simmons was the main person in this particular scene, and since it was hot and everybody was tired, it was an unpleasant time. Willy was quiet, as if he was feeling every inch of that film with his fingers and thumb. There wasn't very much vitality in the scene, so he watched it close up. He was right up next to the camera and so was she. It was an intimate, very strong moment. She tried it several times, and he didn't like it. Again and again and again.

"Then, all of a sudden, Willy jumped up and went over to an electrician or somebody in the crew and really gave him hell. He hollered and screamed and cussed, really ripped this guy apart. Well, that put electricity in the air. We went back to Jeannie Simmons. I could see that it embarrassed her. That outburst was really meant for her. Willy didn't dare do it to her because she couldn't have taken it. But, boy, she did the scene again and *she* was full of electricity. Willy had all kinds of tricks to get that picture down. But I wouldn't say he was cruel to her. I didn't see it any time."

Heston points out that, contrary to any sense of unhappiness she might have felt, Simmons's performance was "very, very good." He cites one of her scenes—when she decides whether she's going to let Peck buy the Big Muddy from her—as perhaps the single, most unusual moment of the picture. "She has a silent close-up that must run a good forty seconds." Heston says.

Simmons herself has taken note of that scene "in Willy Wyler's favor." She has recalled that "Willy was very agreeable in allowing me to think, and think, and think, and then think some more before I made my reply to Greg's offer. I felt a prompt answer would not serve the moment, and Willy proved most open and agreeable on that count. He could make you worry—order take after take without ever telling you what you were doing to provoke the retakes—but he also could cause you to feel a sense of collaboration."

If anybody on the set had cause to complain of Wyler's treatment, Heston says, it was Carroll Baker. She fell victim to a bruising directorial trick never visited upon Simmons. "I had to fight with Carroll in one of my scenes," Heston recalls. "It's actually one of the best scenes I was in. I've got a grip on her wrists, and she's struggling to get out of it. Willy gave me secret instructions not to let go of her. He told Carroll,

'Break loose, so you can hit him.' Well, I've got a big enough hand I could have held both of her wrists in one. We must have done—I don't know—ten takes, easy, on this shot. She's got sensitive skin and she's getting welts. Between takes they were putting ice and chamois cloths on her wrists. She was weeping with frustration and anger and all kinds of things. Finally she tells Willy, 'Chuck won't let me go.' And he says to her, 'I don't want him to. I want you to get away by yourself.' Christ, I outweighed her by nearly a hundred pounds."

Occasionally Baker and Wyler would clash when, in his view, she wouldn't take direction. One time he stopped everything and gave her a line reading. This offended her Actors Studio training. "Willy, you're not supposed to do that," she told him. Nonplussed, he replied: "Look, I'm the director. They pay me to get you to do the part the way I want you to do it." Robert Belcher, who edited *The Big Country* under Swink's supervision, recalls that the more takes Wyler did with her the less confident she became. "She'd get nervous and upset," he says. "One time, for some reason, she didn't get what he meant at all. So he says to her, 'You know, this isn't television.' Now that was a cutting remark, but he put some butter on it. He said it softly. He didn't say it gruffly. When he said something like that, you never forgot it."

Burl Ives got along with Wyler best, and it showed in his performance. Of all the actors, he was the only one nominated for an Academy Award. His depiction of Rufus Hannassey turned out so well that it eclipsed his other movie role that year: Big Daddy in *Cat on a Hot Tin Roof*, the Tennessee Williams character he'd played on Broadway and reprised for the screen. Ives won the Oscar for best supporting actor as Hannassey and wasn't even nominated for Big Daddy, though he is better remembered for it today because of *Cat*'s success. Wyler had so admired Ives on Broadway he wanted to cast him in *Friendly Persuasion* as Sam Jordan, the role that went to Robert Middleton. Wyler chose not to offer it to Ives only because the actor couldn't have left the play to take it.

"I found Willy delightful," Ives recalled. "I never got annoyed at him. I learned a helluva lot from him. He was enigmatic sometimes, but that's what he did to make me figure things out. There was one scene where I had to ride up to Peck and say somethin' like, 'What you said back there sticks in my craw, and I'm gonna fight it out with Bickford.' I come 'round the corner of this cabin for my close-up and take a ninety degree turn right toward the camera. My horse stops on a dime, just where it should've. But Willy wasn't satisfied with me. After the first take, he says, 'It's gossip.' Nothin' else. I did the scene again and again and again, and each time that's all he says, 'It's gossip.' But he's sayin' it louder and louder. He was really gettin' steamed. I had to think, 'What the hell does he mean?' It finally dawned on me I was playin' the line to Peck because he's the star, when I should've been playin' it to the world because that's stuff I want everybody to know. So I came 'round the corner again and did it like I was talkin' over the back fence. Willy looked up at me from under this big straw hat. He said, 'It's about time.' He just wanted me to find it on my own."

Friction developed on location between Wyler and Peck over the cattle. Although it was not the cause of their falling out, it was an indication that perhaps they couldn't be equal partners. Certainly, it was a symptom of the rift that came between them as director and actor.

Early in the shoot, they planned a panoramic shot of a huge herd of livestock grazing on the Terrill ranch. As originally planned, Peck was supposed to look out toward the horizon and see what he thought of as "a sea of cattle."

Peck says, "What I had in mind was something like ten thousand head. Of course that was out of the question, but I did go for four thousand. We arranged to rent them for the day at ten dollars a head. These cattle were to be driven overnight from neighboring ranches to this place outside of Stockton. It was to be a *big* operation. The next morning I came to the set eager to see if my four thousand head of cattle had made enough of an impression. I looked out and I couldn't find any."

Dumbfounded, Peck called over an assistant director.

"How many head?"

"Four hundred."

Peck went to Wyler. He was angry but reasonable. "You know," he said, "you're not going to get what we had in mind out there."

"Yeah, I cancelled the order," Wyler replied. "Forty thousand dollars a day is too damn much. We can't afford it."

"I didn't feel offended that time," Peck says. "I think perhaps in Willy's mind, more than mine, the lines of authority became crossed at times. The falling out came over another incident. It came much later, the buckboard scene, which appears early in the film. It was a perfectly ridiculous thing, and I think it was because we were under pressure, swimming upstream the whole way.

"In the buckboard scene," Peck continues, "I'm riding across the prairie with Carroll Baker. I've just arrived, and we're riding back to the Terrill ranch. Along the way Chuck Connors and the other Hannasseys try to stop us. They come galloping up, and they make me climb down from the buckboard and tie me up. I'm an effete-looking Easterner and they want to give me a hazing. When I saw the rushes, I felt I had given a very bad, unthinking performance and I knew I could do better. There was one close-up, in which I felt I looked like an idiot. I knew I could do a lot better, and I mentioned it to Willy about four or five times.

"He said, 'Okay, okay, we'll get it before we go home.' We were going back to Los Angeles for interiors."

The day before they were to leave the location, Peck looked at the worksheet and saw his retake wasn't scheduled.

"Willy," he said, "how come?"

"Well, I don't need it," Wyler said. "I'm not gonna do it. I can cut around it."

"It'll only take an hour, two hours," Peck persisted. "We're here. It's the same scenery, the same buckboard, the same actress."

Wyler lost his temper. "I'm sick of hearing about it. I'm not going to do it over. I'm not going to waste my time on it."

"Willy was *not* in a great mood," Peck recounts. "We had script problems. We had physical obstacles. I think Willy sensed this was not going to be one of his great pictures. We were going over schedule and over budget. What we figured would cost two million eight actually cost four million one. For those days, that was a lot. The stress had gotten to both of us. On that particular day I chose to be insulted: 'After all our work together, my friend Willy won't give me a retake. It's for the only close-up I'm really concerned about. He owes me that.' I felt betrayed. I went to my trailer. I took off my costume, got on my clothes and drove all the way to Los Angeles, all the way back to Veronique on Summit Ridge Drive."

By the time Peck got home that night, the phone was ringing off the hook. "My agent was there," he says, "people from my production company. They wanted to know, 'What's the matter? What am I going to do?' I said, 'I'm not going back unless he redoes the buckboard scene.' " Peck *didn't* go back. The following day, Wyler wrapped the shoot near Stockton and returned to Los Angeles to film interiors.

"Willy was offended," Peck says. "An actor walked off his set before the day's work was finished. I can't say that I blame him. What happened was I went to the Goldwyn lot for the remaining scenes. Willy and I didn't speak. He'd be six feet away from me, not looking at me. He'd direct everyone else in the scenes, not me. But I coped. By that time I was so into the character, I didn't need to be directed. I was all revved up, full of adrenaline. I think I did my best acting in those scenes."

When they finished the picture, their friendship was broken off. They did everything through intermediaries. Veronique and Talli kept trying to get them back together. They couldn't understand what was wrong with their husbands. Peck and Wyler didn't see each other or speak to each other for the next three years. "I missed Willy," the actor says. "I don't know whether he missed me. Maybe he did. Because we finally made it up."

Peck recalls they broke the ice in April 1960, at the Pantages Theater in Hollywood for the 1959 Academy Awards. John Wayne had just presented Wyler with the best-directing Oscar—his third—for *Ben-Hur*, which he made immediately after *The Big Country*. As Wyler walked backstage, Peck intercepted him and stuck out his hand.

"Congratulations, Willy, you deserved it," he said.

Wyler looked up at Peck and grinned.

"Thanks," he said, "but I'm still not going to retake the buckboard scene."

Peck laughed. From that moment on, he recalls, "everything was okay. It was like we'd never been alienated at all. I saw him a great deal after that."

WHEN *THE BIG COUNTRY* PREMIERED IN OCTOBER 1958 AT THE Astor in New York, it drew a cool-to-mixed reception from the critics, as might have been predicted by its production troubles. At one end of the spectrum, Bosley Crowther of the *New York Times*, who generally revered Wyler's filmmaking, came to the withering conclusion that for all its ambition and size—*The Big Country* clocked in at two hours and forty-six minutes—the picture was "mighty pretentious" and went only skin deep. At the other end of the spectrum, *Time* termed it "starkly beautiful" (which it is), "carefully written" (which it wasn't), and said it deserved comparison with *Shane*, George Stevens's Western classic (which it doesn't).

The vast landscape also drew considerable attention for its philosophical implications. Critics pointed out that it dwarfed the people, made them seem puny against the immensity of nature. This was said to be in keeping with the picture's anti-macho theme, especially a fight between Peck and Heston that was meant to debunk the old Western cliché about settling scores. What was unusual about the scene was not the fight but how it was filmed.

Wyler had placed his actors in the middle of a bare, sun-parched prairie and set up his camera on a high ridge, looking down at them from a hundred yards away. At the time, Heston couldn't figure out why. He recalls thinking, "I don't know what lens he has on, but we can't be larger than ants in that frame." When Heston tried to spot Wyler and the crew, they were barely distinguishable. "I thought, 'He has to be kidding. He's doing this to be mean. He can't use this footage. Of course, as we see in the picture, he uses those long shots very often to underscore again and again what really was an overriding theme — the futility of violence."

It took a full day to make the sequence, according to Heston, but it showed how exhausting a fistfight could be. He and Peck flail away at each other until they can hardly stand. They're covered with sweat and dust. In medium shots, their blows sound like muffled thumps. In long shots, they can't be heard at all — and the silence was telling. By the end of the fight they're too weak to land any blows. And when they both call it quits, McKay says, "Now, tell me Leech. What did we prove?"

In April, five months before the picture opened, Wyler left Hollywood for Rome without finishing it. He gave Swink "complete authority" over the scoring, dubbing, cutting and editing, with assurances to United Artists that his longtime associate "thoroughly understands my views." He also gave him the option of shooting a new ending because, as Swink remembers, "we didn't have it." To erase any doubt about this transfer of authority, Wyler spelled out in a letter to UA that "after my departure I do not wish to be reached directly either by phone, cable or mail. I will be too heavily involved in my new project."

Wyler's assurances glossed over the fact that he and Swink had agreed to go their separate ways after *The Big Country*. Their own tiffs had come to a head late one night following a long session in the cutting room. Wyler saw that Swink had used a shot he didn't like and began to carp. "When Willy wanted to get on something," Swink recalls, "he could be the worst nag you ever heard in your life." Finally, the forty-year-old editor walked over to his boss's desk and threw in the towel.

"I see I'm not able to satisfy you," he said. "So I guess you'd better get yourself somebody else." Swink turned on his heel and walked to the door. He'd been with Wyler on five pictures since 1950. He'd never been a yes-man. They'd had arguments before, but this time Swink had reached his limit. "When I headed for that door," he recalls, "I didn't know whether I'd ever work with him again." But Wyler got to the door first. "He jumped in front of me and wouldn't let me out," Swink recounts. "Then he let me have all this authority to do with the picture as I pleased."

After Wyler left for Rome, Swink called in Peck and Simmons and took them on location to shoot what became the picture's final scene.

Swink then put together a full-length print of *The Big Country*, and chief cutter Belcher took it to Rome for Wyler's approval. United Artists wanted the picture shortened to two hours for more daily showings. But Wyler backed Swink and wrote him in May from Cinecittà, where he was already at work on *Ben-Hur*.

"I can't begin to tell you how pleased I am with the new ending. . . . The shots [you] made are complete perfection, exactly what was needed. The whole thing has sweep and class and ends the picture with just the right feeling. Am delighted I did not do it myself because I am sure I could not have done it better, and probably not as well. Now for the beefs, which are few and insignificant. . . ."

Moviegoers turned out in force for *The Big Country*, considering that Westerns were more of a television staple than ever. The wide-screen color format of Franz Planer's imposing cinematography, backed by the robust Oscar-nominated score of Jerome Moross, provided the kind of splendor no black-and-white TV picture could match. But while the movie ranked eleventh among the year's top box-office hits, it scarcely broke even. The first-run gross came to five million dollars, and neither Peck nor Wyler ever participated in any profits.

"There were a lot of good things about the movie," Peck says, "but I frankly don't think it was the audience's fault. It was our fault."

37

━━━⟋⟍⟋⟍━━━

Ben-Hur

WYLER HAD MANY REASONS FOR doing *Ben-Hur*. Over the years he would say that he took it on a dare; that he wanted to see if he could out-De Mille De Mille; that it was a chance to return to Rome; that the producer Sam Zimbalist, Jr., kept after him for months to do it; that the picture was MGM's last hope for avoiding bankruptcy.

All were true.

But the deciding factor was none of the above.

"We are told," the British Film Institute noted in 1959, "that Metro has paid Wyler the largest sum ever paid any individual connected with a single film in the history of the medium."

MGM guaranteed him eight percent of the gross revenues or three percent of the net profits—whichever was greater—with an up-front payment of three hundred fifty thousand dollars. *Ben-Hur* would gross roughly seventy-six million worldwide.

Typically, he underplayed the deal: "I felt this picture could make lots of money, and I would get some of it—which I did."

Everything about *Ben-Hur* was colossal.

It turned into the biggest production in movie history and, until then, the biggest money-maker in a first-run release. It had three hundred sets, including the single largest set ever built; it had the most spectacular, most expensive action sequence ever filmed; and it won the most Academy Awards—eleven—a record that still stands nearly four decades later.

Ben-Hur also drew the biggest attack on Wyler's reputation as an artistic filmmaker, earning him "the scorn of the intellectuals." The French auteurists and their American counterparts, then coming into vogue, claimed the picture proved their contention that Wyler was merely a commercial craftsman who didn't deserve the high standing accorded him by André Bazin and others film theorists of the preceding generation.

"*Cahiers du Cinema* never forgave me for the picture," Wyler said, less irked than amused. "I was completely written off as a serious director by the avant-grade, which had considered me a favorite for years. I had prostituted myself."

When Zimbalist approached him in the spring of 1957, Wyler was still preparing to shoot *The Big Country*. The notion that he might be interested in making *Ben-Hur* first struck him as ridiculous. "I thought he was kidding," Wyler said. "But, no, he was serious. He kept after me. I kept turning him down."

MGM's mammoth project, already five years in the planning, had gained such urgency for the studio that Zimbalist begged him to read the script. Along with the aging of MGM's stars and the encroachment of television, Hollywood's most glamorous studio was forced by antitrust regulation to sever its corporate ties to the Loews theater chain in 1952. Cut loose from Loews' deep pockets, MGM was going broke. *Ben-Hur* would either save it or deliver the *coup de grâce*.

Wyler finally agreed to look over the script and concluded that the story wasn't bad but its quality was still out of the question for him. The screenplay, written by Hollywood veteran Karl Tunberg, was "very primitive, elementary"—no better than good hack work. It lacked feeling for character, as well as dramatic nuance.

"Why don't you go after De Mille?" Wyler asked.

Apart from the spectacle, all *Ben-Hur* had were cardboard figures, "villains and heroes," he said. The only material that might interest him, if anything, was the chariot race. One of the best things about the screenplay, he joked, was its brevity on the subject. Tunberg had written just three words—"The Chariot Race"—leaving the rest to the director's imagination.

Zimbalist, who once worked as a cutter on Fred Niblo's 1925 *Ben-Hur*, showed Wyler a storyboard layout for the action sequence. The preliminary drawings brought back Wyler's own memories of working on the chariot race for Niblo. "I could see more time and effort would go into that piece of film than any piece of film ever made," he recalled. "It was the kind of thing you could take your time with and make some absolutely marvelous shots."

Zimbalist told him, "Forget the chariot race. That's just second-unit stuff." He wanted Wyler to give the rest of the picture what it needed—body, depth, intimacy—the sophisticated treatment for which Wyler's work was prized.

Zimbalist did not fail to note that MGM expected to spend as much as ten million dollars on *Ben-Hur*, with the result that Wyler took the script home a second time. By September, he came around. He agreed to make it his next project as soon as he completed filming *The Big Country*. In the meantime, Zimbalist would have to improve the script.

MGM also approached Charlton Heston to play Messala, the Roman heavy, opposite the title character. The actor resisted. "Citron's trying to persuade me into *Ben-Hur*, whether Wyler does it or not," Heston recorded that September in his diary. "Willy telling me what a great part Messala is."

Heston recalls, "Wyler came to me and said, 'You know what would be really great? Why don't we sign a deal? Then later you and I will decide which part you play.' He was notorious for delaying decisions, especially on casting, because he wanted to hold all the options. He wanted to be sure he had me, and he kept telling me villain parts were best and Messala was marvelous.

"But Ben-Hur was better. There was just no question. I said, 'Thanks very much, Willy. If you want me for Ben-Hur, I'm happy to play him.'

"He said, 'You don't want me to give you a choice?'

"I said, 'No. My choice is Ben-Hur, I can tell you that right now.'"

Neither Wyler nor Zimbalist had settled on the actor for the title role. Lots of names came up: Brando, Lancaster, Rock Hudson, Kirk Douglas. According to Catherine Wyler, the studio kept sending her father photo stills of handsome Italian actors. He wondered if they could speak English. "They did have beautiful bodies," she said, "but Dad didn't think that was going to be enough."

The novelist Gore Vidal, then a contract writer for MGM, says Zimbalist asked him to speak to his Malibu neighbor Paul Newman. The handsome actor was a rising Hollywood star, with a couple of acclaimed film roles to his credit. One was Rocky Graziano in the prizefight biopic

Somebody Up There Likes Me, the other was a Korean War veteran accused of treason in *The Rack*. But Newman's screen debut in a disastrous Roman epic called *The Silver Chalice* had put him off the genre for good. Vidal remembers Newman dismissing *Ben-Hur* with a quip: "I will never again act in a movie in a cocktail dress. . . . And besides, I don't have the legs for it."

MGM's deal with Wyler was studio gossip through the fall and winter. In early January 1958 MGM went public. But Heston was still kept dangling. "Willy is proving the champion decision-avoider of the industry," Heston wrote in his diary a week later. "Very damaging to the ego." At last, on January 22, he learned from his agent that Wyler had chosen him for the top role.

Heston's contract guaranteed him two hundred fifty thousand dollars for thirty weeks with a prorated salary after that, plus travel expenses for his family. Toward the end of February, Heston would leave for a grand tour of Europe. Two months later, he would be the first of the cast to arrive in Rome, where the legendary stunt man Yakima Canutt quickly began teaching him how to drive a four-horse team and chariot.

Wyler flew to Rome on April 22 with Zimbalist and Vidal, who'd agreed to rework the script on condition that MGM let him out of the last two years of his long-term contract. On the flight over, Wyler scanned the screenplay. It had been through several changes, including early dialogue rewrites by Broadway dramatists S. N. Behrman and Maxwell Anderson.

Heston greeted the trio at the airport, amid popping flashbulbs and a crowd of reporters who'd shown up despite a cold drizzle. On the drive into the city, Vidal remembers Wyler "looking gray and rather frightened." The thick screenplay lay between them on the backseat of the limo.

"This is awful," Wyler commented, indicating the pages.

"I know," Vidal replied. "What are we going to do?"

"These Romans . . . Do you know anything about them?"

Vidal said he'd done his research.

"Well," Wyler wanted to know, "when a Roman sits down and relaxes, what does he unbuckle?"

It was the first of many such questions.

WYLER EXPECTED TO BE GONE ROUGHLY SIX MONTHS, FROM THE end of May through November. But filming would last into 1959. He and Talli brought their family to Rome, as they had on *Roman Holiday*:

Judy, now a high school junior; Melanie and David, both in grade school. Catherine, who'd finished her freshman year at Stanford, would stay for the summer.

This time they moved into a huge villa on an estate just off the Via Appia Antica, the ancient highway leading to Rome. They lived only ten minutes from Cinecittà and two miles down the road from the Hestons' equally lavish digs. "Everyone got spoiled," Wyler remembered. "We had a flock of servants. Every day they brought in fresh flowers and vegetables from the garden." The villa, leased to them by an Italian marquis, came with a valet and butler. "You could never take off your own coat or light your own cigarette," Wyler said. They had a big black Chrysler—chauffeur-driven, of course. "The driver just honked his way through traffic," Talli said. "You couldn't get him to shut up to save your soul."

Whenever the Chrysler drove out, the chauffeur announced its departure by horn. The gardener's family, who lived in a cottage near the gatehouse, would line up and bow the car through the gate. The ritual changed on the return trip. "The chauffeur would blow that awful horn again," Talli said, "and the butler would appear in his white jacket at the villa door. He would take my packages, while I descended from the car, carrying my purse. This was a far cry from shopping at the market in Beverly Hills, where I came home loaded down with sacks and closed the car door with my behind."

SAM ZIMBALIST KNEW THE SORT OF LENGTHY AND METICULOUS preparations it would take to mount a production as massive and ambitious as *Ben-Hur*. Highly regarded and well liked, Zimbalist was an experienced producer of many popular MGM movies. But he was especially well equipped to deal with large-scale pictures on location. Three of his early fifties productions—*Quo Vadis*, *King Solomon's Mines* and *Mogambo*—testified to that.

To lay the actual groundwork for *Ben-Hur*, Zimbalist turned to MGM production supervisor Henry Henigson, who'd worked for years supervising Wyler's films at Universal. Hard-boiled and efficient but also somewhat intellectual, Henigson put together a technical staff in Rome two years before the picture's start date. He supervised set construction and negotiated all the labor contracts with the fractious Italian unions. Wyler maintained that as expensive as *Ben-Hur* became, it would have been far more so without Henigson.

At the Cinecittà complex in the Roman suburbs, a replica of ancient

Jerusalem went up covering half a square mile. The city's gargantuan entrance, the Joppa Gate, stood more than seven stories high. An artificial lake was dug large. The arena for the chariot race stretched across eighteen back-lot acres. It had fifteen-hundred-foot straightaways and a ten-foot-high central island (the Spina) with four giant statues, each thirty feet high—crouching, no less.

The arena was *Ben-Hur*'s largest set, and the single largest built for a Hollywood picture. MGM trotted out construction figures to dazzle the public: a million pounds of plaster, forty thousand cubic feet of lumber, two hundred and fifty miles of metal tubing, forty thousand tons of white sand from Mediterranean beaches. A track of identical size was built next to the arena to train the eighty-two cart horses brought in from the Yugoslav and Sicilian countrysides. Here, too, the charioteers were taught and the camera shots laid out.

Ben-Hur: A Tale of the Christ had an illustrious history. Lew Wallace, a Civil War general in the Union Army, began writing the novel in Indiana after the war and completed it roughly eight years later in New Mexico, when he was territorial governor. Harper Brothers brought it out in 1880, but sales languished for several years. By 1885, however, the publishers were selling fifty thousand copies a year and had half a million in print by the end of the decade.

Wallace's book would not only become the best-selling American novel of the nineteenth century, it would become a stage sensation. In 1899, Klaw & Erlanger produced *Ben-Hur* at the Broadway Theater in New York. It starred William S. Hart, a Shakespearean actor, as Messala. Later, William Farnum, a vaudeville actor, would take over the role of Ben-Hur. Hart would go on to screen stardom as Hollywood's leading silent cowboy. Farnum, too, would star on the silent screen.

But the chariot race was the *coup de théâtre* that drew the crowds. Ben-Hur and Messala drove a pair of horses and chariots across the stage on a giant treadmill. A painted canvas backdrop rolled in the opposite direction behind them to complete the illusion of laps being run. Many versions of the play toured the country continuously for a total of twenty years, with the producers gradually increasing the number of chariots to eight. Other productions were mounted in London, Paris, Copenhagen and Berlin. At one point, Wallace negotiated a million-dollar deal for the stage rights—a tenth of the play's eventual gross.

In 1907, two years after Wallace died, the Kalem Company brought out the first silent screen version of *Ben-Hur*, a primitive one-reeler featuring costumes from the Metropolitan Opera and a chariot race staged by the Brooklyn Fire Department. The author's heirs sued, contending that Kalem made the film without permission. Kalem had to withdraw its one-reeler and pay the heirs twenty-five thousand dollars. Sam Goldwyn purchased the film rights in 1922. When he was forced out of his failing company with the Metro-Goldwyn-Mayer merger in 1924, MGM took over the rights and produced its lavish *Ben-Hur* silent at a cost of roughly four million dollars.

THE BEGINNING OF WYLER'S *BEN-HUR* SETS THE BIBLICAL SCENE with an ancient map and a stately voice-over: "In the year of Our Lord, Judea for nearly a century has lain under the mastery of Rome. In the seventh year of the reign of Augustus Caesar, an imperial decree ordered every Judean to return to his place of birth to be counted and taxed. . . ." Judah Ben-Hur and Messala don't appear in the Bible, of course, or anywhere else in history. They are Wallace's fictional creations, imagined out of whole cloth. His subtitle, *A Tale of the Christ*, is also misleading, since the screen story revolves around the confrontation between these two boyhood friends—a Roman and a Jew—who find themselves at odds politically, religiously and philosophically.

Messala, who grew up in Judea, has returned as the newly appointed tribune of the Roman province with orders to put down the local rabble-rousers. When he meets Ben-Hur, who has become a wealthy leader of the Jewish ruling class, he asks for his help. Messala wants him to give up the names of the troublemakers and persuade his people that defiance of Rome is futile. Ben-Hur refuses. Their relations turn chilly, then bitter and, in Vidal's words, "vengeance is sworn."

There are many plot twists. Ben-Hur is condemned to life as a galley slave, saves the admiral of the Roman fleet, Quintus Arrius, when their ship goes down, and becomes his adopted son, with all the rights of Roman citizenship and the privileges of power. Eventually, he returns to Jerusalem to reclaim his natural birthright and learn the whereabouts of his mother and sister. He confronts Messala. They duel to the death in a spectacular chariot race. And Ben-Hur discovers his mother and sister, ravaged by leprosy, living in a cave among other lepers.

Jesus Christ comes into the picture early on, but only briefly and anonymously. A Hollywood aura of early Christianity suffuses the picture, however, and Jesus is brought back for the Crucifixion to cap off the tale with miracles.

. . .

"MY FATHER USED TO JOKE THAT IT TOOK A JEW TO MAKE A really good movie about Christ," Catherine Wyler recalls.

Whipping the screenplay into shape would be Wyler's first order of business. Vidal believed the conflict between Ben-Hur and Messala would not be credible unless it were motivated by a deep, perhaps secret, psychological tension. Vidal says he did about ten rewrites of their reunion scene, none to his or Wyler's satisfaction. Then he came up with the idea of giving the scene the subtext of a lover's quarrel.

"If Willy didn't like what you were saying, he would give you his deaf ear," Vidal says. "When I said 'lover's quarrel,' I suddenly got the good ear."

Vidal told him, "Could it be that the two had had some sort of emotional relationship the first time 'round, and now the Roman wants to start up again? Ben-Hur doesn't—and doesn't get the point."

"Gore," Wyler said, "this is *Ben-Hur*. You can't do that."

"If you don't do something like that you won't even have *Ben-Hur*. You'll have a motiveless mess on you hands."

"Well, you can't be overt."

"I'm not going to be overt. There won't be one line. But I can write it in such a way that the audience is going to feel that there is something emotional between these two, which is not stated and which blows the fuse in Messala. He is spurned, so it's a love scene gone wrong."

Vidal has told this version of their conversation many times, and with minor variations in the details—but always with the same basic thrust. There's no reason to doubt it. In subsequent years, however, Wyler said he couldn't recall having this discussion. Vidal has conceded he might have spoken to Zimbalist instead, but didn't think so. Moreover, Wyler liked being cagey and simply may not have wanted to confirm the homoerotic subtext. All he would grant is that Vidal "is a clever fellow and a good writer."

For his part, Heston discounts Vidal's claim. "Obviously, I can't say categorically what he told Willy, because I wasn't present. But I very much doubt he made that suggestion to Willy, and I know he didn't write the scene in the picture. We rehearsed Gore's version, but we never shot it. Willy didn't think he had solved the problem."

Heston also denies that Vidal scripted much of anything Wyler shot, despite Vidal's frequent assertion that he rewrote the entire first half of *Ben-Hur*. According to Heston, Zimbalist persuaded Wyler to hire Vidal, but Wyler preferred the British playwright Christopher Fry.

Everyone seems to agree that once Fry arrived from London in early May, he spent six days a week on the set at Wyler's elbow for the entire shoot, principally as a dialogue doctor but also rewriting scenes on the spot for the next day's filming.

Wyler wanted Fry to elevate the language and give it a certain formality by suggesting an archaic tone without making it sound pompous or stilted. Fry's dialogue rewrites were masterful. He took the colloquial, "How was your dinner?" for example, and changed it to, "Was the food not to your liking?" Heston, who was in just about every scene, maintains that "whatever was good in the dialogue was Fry's. He certainly did not turn in pages and pages, but every change he made was significant. He got us out of the kind of bad period language I would call 'MGM medieval.' You know, 'Yonder lies the castle of my father; surely he will give us shelter.' "

Heston also claims Vidal was on the scene for a couple of weeks at most and couldn't have redone half the screenplay. By Vidal's account, however, he stayed considerably longer. "As agreed, I left in early summer and Christopher Fry wrote the rest of the script," he asserts. If Vidal didn't leave until late June, this would have put him on the picture for at least two months, including the first four weeks of the shoot itself. The dispute over who should or shouldn't have received screenplay credit, and who ultimately did, would turn into an angry public controversy—not unlike what happened with *Friendly Persuasion*, but without the political innuendo.

Andrew Marton, the second-unit director, wanted to film the chariot race in the spring before Wyler began working. He knew once the main production got rolling, their shooting schedules would overlap and Wyler would have priority on the actors. Also, he wanted cool weather for the horses. Roman summers were killers. But despite all the early preparations, Marton recalled, "the arena wasn't ready, the surfacing wasn't right and the horses were not [fully] trained." Heston, who knew how to ride, was proving a quick study as a charioteer. But Stephen Boyd, the actor Wyler cast as Messala, had no experience with horses. Though game, Boyd needed four weeks just to feel comfortable at the reins. Consequently, when Wyler began filming on May 20, Marton hadn't shot any footage of the chariot race. Both of them realized, moreover, that Marton would have to do a lot of close-in shooting on the fly. Otherwise, the audience would not feel the intensity of the race or the actual risk in the stunts. This meant that whatever Marton shot of the arena would be incidental—which left it to Wyler to exploit the grandeur of the setting and the pomp and ceremony of the event.

For the first few days, Wyler warmed up by shooting what were, in effect, locker room scenes: harnessing the horses, moving the chariot teams into position, lining them up outside the stadium, holding them in line. All of this built dramatic tension. Then he moved into the stadium. That day he made a little speech to the crowd of six thousand extras in the stands. He described how he once worked as an assistant on the 1925 chariot race. Indicating the dozens of assistants on the track, he asked through an interpreter, "Which one of these guys is going to direct the next *Ben-Hur*?" The crowd roared.

"It was a fabulous set," Wyler remembered. "Pontius Pilate was supposed to signal the start of the race. But I knew that once the race started there would be no long shots. Without long shots from all angles, the audience would never appreciate that magnificent arena. So I said, 'Let's not get into the race too fast. Let's have a parade of the charioteers go once around the stadium in perfect formation.' This was not the way they did it in ancient times, but I added it anyway. It would be like a ballet. They go around, then come to the starting place, then Pontius Pilate makes his speech, and they're off."

Wyler cast the production to emphasize the difference between the Romans and the Jews. He decided that all the Jews would be played by Americans and all the Romans by non-Americans, principally Englishmen. Since the Romans were in charge, they were the aristocrats. British accents and manners would enhance that perception, particularly for American audiences, who tended to regard anything British as patrician.

Among the other principals were the British actor Jack Hawkins as Ben-Hur's adoptive Roman father Quintus Arrius; actress Cathy O'Donnell as Ben-Hur's sister Tirzah; and the American actor Sam Jaffe as Simonides, who is Esther's father as well as manager of Ben-Hur's estate.

There were exceptions to the rule, of course. Stephen Boyd was Irish, for example. But since Messala was a Roman born in Judea, that would explain his unique accent. Similarly, the lusty Arab sheik, neither Jew nor Roman, would be played by the Welsh actor Hugh Griffith. Wyler also cast Esther, Ben-Hur's love interest, with an Israeli actress, Haya Harareet. And Miriam, Ben-Hur's mother, was played initially by a British actress, Marie Ney. But three weeks into filming, Wyler dismissed Ney and brought in an American for the role.

"Willy called from Rome," Martha Scott recounts. "He said, 'I want you to get on a plane. We've got a wonderful actress, but when it comes to crying, she can't do it. I've got to have an actress whose tears will roll down her cheeks, and this woman just doesn't have it.' I could squeeze out tears."

Scott, who'd gotten along so well with Wyler in *The Desperate Hours*, said she had other plans for a trip with her family. Wyler said to bring her husband and kids over, too, at MGM's expense. When she arrived, he had her whisked to Cinecittà and explained why he hadn't cast her in the first place.

"I didn't want anybody from *The Ten Commandments* in this picture, except Chuck. But I decided to let that rule go."

Scott not only had been in De Mille's biblical epic, she also had played Heston's mother in *Design for Stained Glass Window* on Broadway.

TWO MONTHS INTO THE SHOOT, THE PICTURE'S LOGISTICS BEGAN taking a toll. The company worked six days a week, and for Wyler the working day lasted twelve to fourteen hours. He put in Sundays, too, holding story conferences at home with Fry and Zimbalist. "Everybody thinks we had a glamorous life," Talli said. "But believe me, it was a grueling experience. We may have gone out the first month on Saturday nights, but after that we didn't go out, period. I was not playing hostess, either. I was just trying to keep Willy alive. He didn't have the time or strength to socialize." By midsummer, the heat and humidity wore everyone down. "They had an Italian doctor on the set," Talli said, "and he took care of everybody's health. He began giving people shots that were supposed to make them feel better. He said they were some kind of B-vitamin shots. A lot of people took them." Wyler got them regularly, "maybe twice a week," Talli remembered.

Looking back, she suspected the injections may have been more than vitamins. "Instantly, after we left Rome, Willy got these terrible migraine headaches," she said. "We went for a long-dreamt-of ski vacation, and we had not been in Switzerland two days when these headaches just knocked him for a loop. It got so bad that on the ship home, Willy couldn't leave the cabin for two days. It occurred to me later that the sudden withdrawal of those shots might have been the cause. I've often wondered whether the doctor was giving them speed of some sort. I think everybody who took those shots was 'up' afterward. I know Willy was. I'd bet they were getting a 'Dr. Feelgood' kind of thing."

What made the long days even harder for Wyler was his disappointment with Heston's performance early in the shoot. No matter how spectacular the production might look, none of that would matter unless the star gave a deeply felt portrayal. Heston recalls that Wyler took him aside.

"Chuck, you have to be better in this part."

"Okay. What is it you have in mind?"

"I don't know, but you're not good enough."

"Well, that's kind of hard to deal with, Willy."

"I know, but I thought I should tell you."

Clutching at straws, Heston replied: "You seemed to like what I did in *Big Country*."

"This is a harder part," Wyler said. "It's awfully difficult to make this fella come off plausibly, and you're not doing it yet."

"You can't give me any specific advice on this?"

"Nope, it's just got to be better."

Heston's diary tracked his progress. "I worked my ass off this morning, getting my close-ups in the castle scene with Messala. Sixteen takes for me to say, 'I'm a Jew!'" A week later, he noted a change. "My close-up went like butter today. Either I've actually improved, which is a happy thought, or Willy's given up, which is contrary to nature."

Looking back on his experience, Heston says: "Willy was a very *wise* director, but he didn't empathize with actors as artists—which a lot of actors found irritating. He wasn't a brutish or bullying director. He wasn't loud. He was just not interested in making you feel good. He was only interested in making you *be* good. It was up to you to feel good about yourself if you wanted to. He didn't think that was his job."

Toward the end of shooting they finished up one day close to eight o'clock. "It was raining," Heston remembered, "so they brought the limos up to the sound stage. I just happened to be waiting for mine when Willy was getting into his. I said, 'Good-night, Willy.' He said, 'Good-night, Chuck. You were good today.' I said, 'What?' He said, 'You were good in the scene.' It was the only time in *Ben-Hur* and *The Big Country* that he ever said that."

Wyler's demand for excellence even extended to bit players. He spared no effort and, to MGM's chagrin, no expense to get precisely what he wanted. For example, Wyler took the company to a mountain village, a stand-in for Nazareth, about forty miles outside of Rome to shoot the "centurion scene." In it, Ben-Hur is being marched in chains down to the sea with other prisoners condemned to the galleys. They've been beaten. They are parched from the sun. They're dying of thirst. A carpenter's assistant, whom we see from behind, offers Ben-Hur a drink of water without uttering a word.

Wyler took the scene in long shot to this point, then asked for the centurion — who had one line in the picture, "No water for him!" — to be brought in closer to the camera. As he looked through the lens Wyler was startled.

"That's not the guy I cast!"

"Yeah, but that guy was holding us up for a lot of money," the first assistant director replied. "This is one of the other guys you liked."

"Where's the guy I picked?"

"He's back in Rome, Willy."

"Go get him."

"That's so far away. I don't even know if we can find him."

"We'll wait."

It wasn't the centurion's single line of dialogue that Wyler was concerned about; it was the centurion's reaction shot after delivering the line that interested him. Wyler had decided before production began that he would never show the face of Jesus Christ, but he *would* show the awe that other people felt when they looked at his face. The centurion's reaction was the key to the scene. Wyler lost time waiting for the the right centurion to be brought from Rome. "The wait cost MGM fifteen thousand dollars," Heston recalls.

But the most expensive and time-consuming footage in *Ben-Hur* was the chariot race. For the nine-minute sequence used in the picture, it took five weeks to shoot, over a period of three months, at a cost of a million dollars. Marton, who'd done the Dunkirk sequence for Wyler in *Mrs. Miniver,* turned Tunberg's three little words — "The Chariot Race" — into thirty-eight pages of script, spelling out the details of virtually every crash, every stunt, every shot. Working with Yakima Canutt, who choreographed the stunts, Marton preshot the race with doubles and spliced the footage together to make one continuous sequence. When Zimbalist saw it, he told Marton to show it to Heston and Boyd.

"They were speechless," the second-unit director recalled. "They said, 'What do you want from us? You have the race.' I said, 'Now we want to do everything with you, in close-ups.' They blanched and said, 'You mean, all the dragging?' I said, 'All the dragging, all the falling out, you have to do.'"

Technical problems became evident from the beginning. The race had nine chariots, each with a team of four horses. The track surface had to be hard enough to take a beating from steel-rimmed wheels and pounding hooves but soft enough not to lame the horses. Marton researched the surface composition of ancient Roman circuses and could find nothing definitive. So the engineers laid down a bed of ground rock debris, topped by ground lava and crushed yellow rock. "This lasted only one day when actual shooting began," Marton recounted. "The horses were slowed so much we almost wasted the entire day's work." They removed the yellow rock and all but an inch and a half of the lava.

Now Marton faced the problem of runway distance, horse speed and camera equipment. He had three sixty-five millimeter cameras to shoot with, each worth a quarter of a million dollars. There were only six in existence at the time. Wyler had the other two, and MGM had one on standby in Culver City. These cameras had the largest frame of any wide-screen motion picture camera. By capturing a more panoramic plane of vision with greater detail, they gave viewers the sensation of being inside the scene. But these cameras also were bulky, enormously heavy and awkward to maneuver. "It took an eternity to move them," Wyler said. In addition, the stretched width of the sixty-five millimeter format created a problem for composition in depth.

"Nothing is *out* of the picture, and you can't fill it," Wyler explained of non-action sequences. "You either have a lot of empty space, or you have two people talking and a flock of others surrounding them who have nothing to do with the scene. Your eye wanders just out of curiosity." The result was a paradox, visually and dramatically.

The cameras even presented problems in the action sequences. The lens Marton wanted to use for close-ups of the race had a focal point of no less than fifty feet. This turned out to be too far from the oncoming horses in the turns and even in the straightaways.

The chariot teams took just twenty seconds to cover the straightaway distance. The horses accelerated much faster than Marton's tiny Italian camera car. The combination of their speed and the len's focal length didn't give Marton enough time for his shots. A powerful American camera car solved the problem of speed. The horses still had better pickup, but with a running start the American car could keep pace and stay fifty feet ahead of them. The trouble was even that gave away too much ground. So Marton chose to use a lens with a shorter focal length. He could eke out a few more seconds for his shots if he stayed only a few feet ahead of the chariots. This was extremely risky. If the car stalled, a pileup was certain. But there was no alternative apart from slowing down the horses, which he didn't want to do: They had to be running at nearly top speed for visual impact.

Meanwhile, Heston and Boyd had to drive their chariots not only for close-ups but for many of the stunts. "They did all the driving they seem to be doing," Marton said, "except for two stunts." Canutt devised a scene in which Boyd, doubled by a dummy, is dragged under his chariot. The actor nonetheless had to make part of the shot himself. "We protected him with some steel coverings here and there on his body," Marton said. "He still was bruised and abraded."

The most astonishing stunt of the race showed Heston's double being tossed *out* of his chariot. That was not planned. But once the accident happened, it was Heston who had to climb back in for the close-up with the chariot still running. The stunt, as intended, comes after two chariots pile up. Boyd forces Heston into their path. Heston either has to pull around the pileup and lose the race or jump the pileup and remain in contention. The horses had been trained to jump. But the chariot was so heavy—all of them racing together sounded like the low rumble of thunder—that it had to be launched. Canutt half-buried a telephone pole horizontally across its path in front of the jump. The aboveground half would serve as a rounded curb, much like a springboard.

Heston's double, Joe Canutt, the stunt supervisor's son, managed to take the horses and chariot up and over the pileup. But when the chariot landed, an unexpected bounce flipped Canutt into the air and threw him between the horses. He rescued himself by grabbing a crossbar that harnessed the horses together. Despite being dragged, he came out of the accident with only a gashed chin.

The near-disaster looked so spectacular on film, Marton didn't want to give it up. Zimbalist thought the footage was unuseable, but Marton argued that he could salvage it by picking up the end of the sequence with a shot of Heston climbing back into the chariot. "Later Heston did his shot beautifully," Marton said. "He got in halfway under the chariot, and we had a view of horses going full tilt with nobody in command. Then he fought his way up, got hold of the reins and, of course, won the race."

Wyler did not see Marton's dailies. It was only after they were trimmed to a rough cut with temporary sound effects added that the second-unit director asked Zimbalist to screen it for Wyler.

"Not today," the producer replied. "I don't want him to see it when he is drained. Willy Wyler might tell us to shoot the race over again."

Marton recalls, "I almost fainted. I said to myself, 'What kind of incredible contract must he have that he can tell the producer to shoot the race over?' Willy had okayed me. . . . He had not come around while I was shooting. He trusted me. But, still, as a safety measure he had insisted that the chariot race must meet with his approval."

Several days later, Zimbalist called Marton at home. "I showed it to Willy this morning," he said.

"And? What did he say?"

"That it's one of the greatest cinematic achievements he's seen."

. . .

LATER, MARTON WOULD GET TO ASSESS WYLER'S REACTION firsthand at the first press preview, not long before *Ben-Hur* was released. During the intermission, he ran into Willy and Talli. She wanted to leave.

Talli said, "Come on, let's go home. You've seen this movie ten times."

Wyler said, "I just want to stay for the chariot race. I'm not even going to sit down. I'm just going to watch from here."

"When it was all over," Marton recounted, "he hit me on the shoulder. 'Good job,' he said. *Then* he went home. At that point I knew for myself he loved the race."

Despite the extraordinary demands made on the horses throughout the shoot, none of them were injured. The second-unit director, bowing to the heat, lightened their daily work schedule. People, on the other hand, did not fare as well. Zimbalist learned from Henigson's doctor that the elderly general manager had a heart condition and was likely to collapse. "He is not going to make it through," the doctor told him. "He's going to die if he keeps working day and night."

Henigson was ordered off the production in mid-October. "You're going to Capri for three weeks," Wyler informed him. "We don't want any arguments, no back talk. That's where you're going." Henigson went quietly but returned within days and proved the doctor wrong.

It was Zimbalist who collapsed and died. On November 4, 1958, more than five months into the shoot but with two months still to go, he suffered a massive heart attack. Working in the cutting room that day, he complained of a pain in his jaw and went home about mid-afternoon. A doctor checked on him by phone. Zimbalist said he was feeling better. Shortly afterward, he asked for a drink of water. While it was being brought to him, he gasped and died.

"Sam hadn't been feeling well for weeks," Talli recalled. "He'd gone to a dentist, who couldn't find anything wrong with his teeth. A few days later he had another attack of excruciating pain in his jaw. He went to a neurologist, who found nothing wrong. Today we know that kind of pain can be connected with a heart attack. But nobody thought of it then."

Zimbalist's sudden death shook Wyler, who at fifty-six was only two years older than the producer. He liked him personally, and they'd worked beautifully together. "It was as though the roof had fallen in on me," he said. "I felt alone. I'd never felt alone with Sam around."

Panicked MGM bosses now asked Wyler to take over the producer's job. They offered an additional hundred thousand dollars and promised him the administrative help of an experienced MGM exec. Wyler accepted. There was nothing else to do. The day after Zimbalist's death, he assembled the company and made a short speech. Then he resumed shooting.

ALL THROUGH FILMING, THE *BEN-HUR* PRODUCTION HAD BEEN A major tourist attraction. Not a day went by without MGM feeding promotional tidbits to the press. A steady stream of movie stars and television celebrities visited the set: Bette Davis, Kirk Douglas, Audrey Hepburn, Ed Sullivan, Ava Gardner, Harry Belafonte, Susan Hayward, Alec Guinness and Anna Magnani, among many others. Wyler also began getting weekly visits from the MGM home office, which was increasingly nervous about the picture's rising costs. With Zimbalist gone, the studio chiefs couldn't help worrying about Wyler's prodigal instincts.

But he had things under control, keeping actors on standby for replacement scenes to be shot when scheduled scenes bogged down. Somebody had to pay for his efficiency, though, and it turned out to be Martha Scott and Cathy O'Donnell. "These two poor women spent literally a month wearing leper makeup and rags," Talli recounted. "They were Willy's backup. If something happened and he couldn't shoot what he'd planned, he could always do a leper scene. So Martha and Cathy would go to the studio day after day at five in the morning and put on their makeup. It took hours. That got horribly depressing for them. They looked filthy. They had sores on their hands. They had scabs on their lips. It could not have been pleasant."

Come Thanksgiving, the company arranged a midday dinner with all the trimmings at the Cinecittà restaurant. Cast and crew and all their families were invited. The two actresses did not want to show up in their rags and leper makeup. "But," Scott recalled, "they wouldn't let us take it off. They said we were going to shoot later. So I put on a strand of pearls. Willy hooted. He felt it was a comment on the situation, and he liked that. I knew he'd be amused."

Wyler shot the leper scenes in underground caves just south of Rome. "These were the real thing," Scott said. "Dark and dank. The ancient Romans had kept lions there for the arena. When we were there, a lot of disabled and homeless people were using these awful caves as shelter. It was really depressing. You didn't have to act."

By December, everyone was hoping to get home for Christmas. With production moving slowly, if steadily, Scott went to Wyler and asked if she would be able to get home for Christmas. He laughed and told her not to worry. But as the holiday approached, he took back his assurances. He told Scott he couldn't let her go until he figured out what to do with the Crucifixion.

Wyler recalled, "I spent sleepless nights trying to find a way to deal with the figure of Christ. It was a frightening thing when all the great painters of twenty centuries have painted events you have to deal with, events in the life of the best-known man who ever lived. Everyone already has his own concept of him. I wanted to be reverent, and yet realistic. Crucifixion is a bloody, awful, horrible thing, and a man does not go through it with a benign expression on his face. I had to deal with that. It is a very challenging thing to do that and get no complaints from anybody."

It took Wyler until after New Year's to get to the Crucifixion, and four days to film it. He finished shooting the scene on January 7. "The last setup finally came," Heston noted in his diary, "but it was through in such a flurry of grab shots there was hardly time to mark [the occasion]. For the record, it was a close-up of me watching the descent from the cross."

Calling it a wrap, Wyler turned to Heston and grinned. "Well, Chuck," he said. "Thanks a lot. I'll try to give you a better part next time."

38

~~~WWWW~~~

SECOND TIME AROUND

$$W$$ITH MORE THAN EIGHT GRUEL-
ing months chalked up, *Ben-Hur* still had another six months of post-
production ahead of it. Willy and Talli stayed on in Europe. They
arrived home in March, and Wyler began supervising the editing, dubbing and mixing. The score would be written and conducted by two-
time Oscar winner Miklos Rozsa, whose music enhanced both the
melodrama and grandeur of the picture. Wyler could thank Zimbalist
for hiring him and the cameraman Robert Surtees, who was legendary
for the lushness of his cinematography.

As *Ben-Hur* headed toward its premiere, MGM's final tab reached
nineteen million dollars—just under sixteen million for production and
three million for a promotion campaign that took on the hoopla of a
three-ring circus. Merchandising tie-ins reached new heights, or as
some said, depths. Besides fresh printings of Wallace's novel, there were
Ben-Hur toys, T-shirts, candy bars, jewelry, chariot scooters, perfumes,
neckties, even "Ben-His" and "Ben-Hers" bath towels. The demand created for the picture was so great that exhibitors offered to remodel their
theaters merely to get a booking.

One piece of publicity that MGM had not counted on was a bitter controversy that erupted between Wyler and the Writers Guild. He wanted Christopher Fry to get co-credit for the screenplay and asked Karl Tunberg for his consent. According to Wyler, Tunberg "verbally agreed." But when the matter came before the guild's arbitration committee, Tunberg changed his mind. "He objected," Wyler said.

Vidal maintains that Wyler "wanted Fry to have sole credit." Also according to Vidal, Fry thought Vidal deserved co-credit and told Wyler so. "Wyler said, 'Fine.' Next thing we know . . . this is the sole work of one Karl Tunberg."

When the Guild decided in favor of Tunberg, its former president, Wyler protested and actively campaigned against the solo credit. The Guild then took out a trade ad accusing him of engaging in "a systematic attack" on its integrity. Wyler believed "disgraceful" insider politics were to blame and later wrote off the whole incident as "a sorry episode."

But the controversy lingered, affecting the Academy Awards several months later. When *Ben-Hur* received twelve Oscar nominations, including best screenplay, it swept the prize in all but that category. The Guild was furious. It believed that Wyler had ruined Tunberg's chances. And when Charlton Heston mentioned his gratitude to Christopher Fry while accepting *his* Oscar, the Guild blew its top. The board sent Heston a vituperative letter that stopped just short of threatening legal action for deliberately maligning Tunberg's reputation.

Heston wrote back drily, "I gather I collectively and gravely offended the entire membership of the Writers Guild of America by the use of one of two phrases (or possibly both): 'Thank you' and 'Christopher Fry.'"

When *Ben-Hur* opened November 18, 1959, in New York and the following week in Hollywood, a deluge of raves poured in. The *New York Times* declared that "the artistic quality and taste of Mr. Wyler have prevailed to make this a rich and glowing drama that far transcends the bounds of spectacle." A hyperbolic headline in the *Hollywood Reporter* declared: BEN-HUR EXTRAORDINARY, OF GREATER DIMENSION THAN ANY FILM OF OUR TIME.

The critics endorsed the idea that Wyler had made an intimate epic, in contrast to De Mille's *Ten Commandments*. But it was apparent from all the chariot-race jokes making the rounds that the picture's real drawing card was big action, not intimate melodrama.

Fry himself maintained that the romance between Ben-Hur and Esther was a waste of time. "If I were doing this script from the beginning instead of adapting a semi-classic," he told Heston, "I wouldn't have the girl in it. You're just not interested. You cannot make the audience care about the love story. The only relationship that counts is the one between Ben-Hur and Messala."

Commercially, *Ben-Hur*'s success was so huge that it single-handedly, if only temporarily, saved MGM from financial collapse. Today, *Ben-Hur* does not even rank among the top one hundred all-time money-makers. Movies that do, include *Porky's, Wayne's World, Rambo: First Blood, Part II* and *Lethal Weapon 3*. In fact, only one picture produced before 1960—a Disney animation feature—made the list in 1994. The reasons, of course, are changed economics. Pictures gross in a weekend what used to take years.

For its time, though, *Ben-Hur* revolutionized the industry. Though fifties Bible epics had preceded it—like Howard Hawks's *Land of the Pharoahs* or Henry Koster's *The Robe*—it was *Ben-Hur* that launched a thousand Hollywood mega-ships. In the war to reclaim moviegoers, the studios saw their salvation in more and more blockbusters.

When a reporter asked Wyler whether he thought *Ben-Hur* would ever be shown on television, he replied: "I hope I never live to see the day."

HE CHOSE TO GO HIS OWN WAY WITH HIS NEXT PICTURE. HE wanted to reassert his roots in subject, seriousness and style. He fastened on the idea of doing a black-and-white remake of Lillian Hellman's play *The Children's Hour*, which he had brought to the screen in 1936 as *These Three*.

Wyler had always been irked about sanitizing the original—for the Hays Office, for Goldwyn, for the need to conform to the social climate. Notwithstanding the acclaim he received at the time from the young Graham Greene and others, Wyler felt he could have made a more authentic picture—truer to life and to the play. One irony, as it turned out, was that his attempt to restore *The Children's Hour* backfired because he didn't fully appreciate the new candor or the changing mores of the sixties, at least not yet. Another irony is that the bowdlerized version of the thirties had greater impact in its time for what it accomplished than the genuine remake would have for what it dared to do but was too timid to accomplish.

Wyler had taken several months off following the release of *Ben-Hur*. In March 1960, he told Hellman of his desire to have her adapt the remake. He didn't yet have a deal for financial backing, he said, but he was trying to arrange one and hoped to shoot the picture the following year. Hellman was very receptive. She was, in the words of her agent, "enormously pleased." Wyler told her she would hear more from him in a couple of months. By the end of May, when she hadn't heard, Hellman took for granted that he wasn't able to make the deal, and she accepted a teaching offer from Harvard. He learned of this when he phoned her in August to break the good news that he'd not only found the backing but had offered Audrey Hepburn the principal role. ("Just thrilled," Hepburn wrote back, "and so terribly happy . . . Man, oh, man.")

Wyler wanted to know was it possible for Hellman to postpone the Harvard offer? After all, the teaching job was to begin in February 1961, and would last through spring, just when he expected to be going into production.

"That's settled," Hellman explained, "and there is nothing I can do about it, although I think I might be able to do some work on the side. . . . It's very sad," she added. "I wanted to do the script. But I couldn't guess your plans and I waited to hear from you as long as I could manage. But I have another idea. Would you consider getting somebody else to do the script and then I could do the final editing and polishing? We could arrange preliminary conferences and work out a detailed story outline. . . ."

Wyler knew that not having Hellman on the set during production might present a problem, but he could live with that. He suggested that perhaps she could write the script in the months before going to Harvard. But this, too, wasn't feasible for her. She had a stage production going up in London, with rehearsals to begin probably in late September. She was expected to be there and would not be free again until mid-November. "I can't see that I would have sufficient time for the script," Hellman said, "and I don't want to dash it off or to do it with another job, giving it half the attention it should have."

So they compromised. On October 5, with Hellman already a week overdue, the two of them sailed for Europe on the *Queen Elizabeth*. They would work on the outline during the crossing. In London, moreover, Wyler would get to meet the shy British playwright whom Hellman wanted to write the screenplay. Peter Schaffer, later to become famous for *The Royal Hunt of the Sun*, *Equus* and *Amadeus*, was flattered by Hellman's confidence and impressed with Wyler. But he, too, was caught up in a play. He told Wyler he'd be more than happy to take the job in January, when he expected to be free. But Wyler felt he couldn't wait, nor had he given up the notion that Hellman still could be induced to write the screenplay herself.

They continued drafting the outline, finishing it in Rome when she wanted a break from London. All their expenses were being paid by the Mirisch Company, per the production deal Wyler signed in September. (Harold Mirisch had left Monogram to form the company with his brothers.) Indeed, Hellman, who signed with Mirisch to write the outline, was persuaded to change her mind. On November 17, several days before her return to New York, Mirisch drew up a contract to pay her fifty thousand dollars for a completed screenplay.

But again things went wrong. Hellman arrived in California to discuss what in the outline needed fleshing out. On December 2 she and Wyler had a lengthy story conference. Mirisch became nervous, however, when he learned Hellman would be writing the screenplay in her spare time at Harvard. She wasn't asked to sign the contract. On her way to the airport, Wyler tried to assure her "the assignment was settled." He said he felt certain he could overcome Mirisch's nervousness.

Nevertheless, Wyler would hedge his bet and send the outline to two screenwriters, Ernest Lehman and John Michael Hayes, who came highly recommended. Lehman, the better writer by reputation, withdrew after reading the material. Hayes, the faster writer, was willing to take on the job. But he needed a quick decision because he had other offers. Between the two of them, Wyler preferred Hayes, believing he would be less inclined to depart from the play.

Wyler begged Hellman's forgiveness for failing to persuade Mirisch and then hiring Hayes. She wrote back, "I hope we can work together all our lives, and maybe learn a little from this useless and upsetting mess. And certainly it has nothing to do with the very pure love affair we have had since the first day I met you." But, she wished to be "released from any further work on the script." She felt she had been "twice rejected"—the first time when he hadn't got back to her the previous spring and now.

Wyler replied, "I would carry the most enormous torch should anything happen to our 'love affair' or the prospect of future work together. But, dear Lillian, in fairness to the picture; to Mirisch, who has been most generous to both of us; to United Artists, who is putting up well over two million dollars; and also to myself and the year and a half of work I will have put in, I simply cannot in good conscience release you from the revisions you have agreed to do on the script.

"Of course, I realize that writing is not something which can be squeezed or forced out of any unwilling person. I can only hope that by the time you finish at Harvard you will not feel so strongly about having been 'rejected.' You know that no one else would even remotely have been considered had you been able to do the screenplay under somewhat normal conditions and without interference from other work."

In a note to himself, he would scribble feelings he did not express to her: "No writer has ever been so pursued. I would like to be 'rejected' like that."

These details show how confused, ill-timed and ill-starred the project was from the beginning. It proves, too, that Dashiell Hammett's death in January had nothing to do with Hellman's not writing the screenplay, as some have claimed. After such a wrong-footed start, Wyler might have been better off scrapping the remake.

But he plowed ahead, signing Hayes to write the screenplay for a hundred thousand dollars, payable over four years. Mirisch had paid Goldywn three hundred fifty thousand dollars for screen rights.

Audrey Hepburn signed for a half-million dollars against ten percent of the gross. She played Karen. Shirley MacLaine, who had a three-picture deal with Mirisch, was cast for Martha; James Garner, who'd starred in *Maverick* on television, was cast for Joe; and Fay Bainter, who'd won an Oscar in *Jezebel*, was cast as Mrs. Tilford.

When Hayes delivered the first draft in April, Wyler was not happy with it and sent it to Hellman for her critique. She called it "mostly workable," but added, "the plain fact is that it is not very good, either." She thought it had "a strange flat quality," largely because it borrowed too literally, and not always wisely, from the original play. "Everybody talks too much." The characters did not sound to her like the same people from scene to scene, sometimes within scenes. "Mr. Hayes has a bad ear," she said. She recognized there wasn't time for a major rewrite unless he postponed the picture, and with production already scheduled to begin in May, *that* he couldn't do. "Therefore," she concluded, "do tell me now how best to help you."

Two weeks after production began, Hellman was rewriting scenes at Wyler's request. But she insisted on keeping her distance from the picture. She sent her rewrites from her summer home on Martha's Vineyard. Her revisions were fresh—some scenes were new—but she made clear they were patchwork at best.

If all this were not discouraging enough, Wyler had trouble finding someone to play Mary, the deceitful schoolgirl who tells lies about Karen (Hepburn) and Martha (MacLaine) and sets the tragedy in motion. Less than a month before rehearsals began on May 22, he finally settled on a twelve-year-old actress, Karen Balkin, who'd played the murderous child in a Texas stage production of *The Bad Seed*. As it turned out, her performance in *The Children's Hour* wasn't in the same league as Bonita Granville's in *These Three*.

Wyler made a further complication for himself. The lesbian content of the play—which he hadn't been allowed to explore three decades earlier—was treated with kid gloves. The play was considered bold in its time, merely for bringing up the subject. But in the early sixties, Wyler's depiction of lesbianism as "that kind of love" was coy and dated at best.

"He chickened out," says Shirley MacLaine, who played the lesbian. "He said so himself. He gutted scenes we had in the middle of the picture, which showed that Martha was in love with Karen. He got scared. He said he couldn't do it."

Hellman hated the picture. Later on, Wyler wished he'd never made it. Mirisch and United Artists didn't know what to do with it. Even after its limited release in December 1961, to qualify for the Academy Awards, they were trying to come up with a new title, to replace *The Children's Hour*. Wyler decided against *Infamous*, *With Sinful Knowledge*, *Strange Awareness*, *Whispers in the Dark* and a dozen others like them. In England, though, the picture was renamed *The Loudest Whisper*.

Perhaps the most accurate title was *The Lesbian Said the Better*, a catchy headline over a negative review that reflected the critical consensus. Wyler sent Hellman the clippings. "Here are all the reviews that have so far appeared," he wrote, "so you can form an opinion on the nature of some of the complaints. I don't think you should let them out of your hands, as bad news has a way of traveling fast."

On the bright side, Robert Swink had rejoined Wyler as his editor. Fay Bainter was nominated for an Oscar. MacLaine got fine notices. James Garner made the least of a role that wasn't much to begin with. "If I was taking a part at this moment," he told a reporter after the picture opened, "I doubt that I'd take that on. But I wasn't really looking for the part so much as the association. I wanted to be in good company."

As for Audrey Hepburn, nobody much cared for her performance. It wasn't bad, but it was awfully pricey. Besides her half-million-dollar salary for twelve weeks' work, Hepburn's contract called for a car and chauffeur, a thousand dollars a week for personal expenses, a hundred thousand lira a week for her Italian hairdresser, and travel expenses for her personal secretary.

39

≈≋≋≋≋≋≈

"The Taste of Stamps"

Despite the well-deserved failure of *The Children's Hour*, Wyler's reputation did not suffer greatly. The Hollywood powers-that-be and "the local peasants"—his joking term for the Los Angeles critics—regarded him as one of filmdom's elder statesmen. He had as much prestige as ever, more money, too. The previous summer he'd bought a second home in Malibu.

About to turn sixty, he still was feisty and full of mischief. He had tender eyes in a grizzled face and a head of close-cropped hair going gray. He didn't have a "tough mug," but it looked solid enough to push through a door. When he wasn't working, he was bodysurfing or playing cards—high-stakes poker, low-stakes gin—and, increasingly, traveling.

"He was very lazy, Willy was," Billy Wilder recalls. "Once he started a project, it was his life. He did everything, night and day. But in between? He took it easy."

In May 1962, the Union of Cinema Workers in Moscow invited Wyler to tour its movie studios and meet some of the top Soviet directors. On their way over, Willy and Talli stopped in London and saw old friends, the director Carol Reed and the actress Penelope Ward, his wife. They dined with Peter Ustinov and his wife Suzanne Cloutier, the actress who had been considered for *Roman Holiday*.

After a warm reception in Moscow and Leningrad, where Wyler's reputation preceded him as one of Eisenstein's favorites, they went south to Tbilisi and Erivan and left the Soviet Union by ship from Odessa on the Black Sea. They sailed to Istanbul, then on to the south of France for a yachting holiday on the Riviera. Then it was north to Paris, where they saw Darryl Zanuck. He had just finished producing *The Longest Day*, his World War II epic, and was soon to become president of Twentieth Century–Fox.

Home again in July, Wyler found himself with a ringside seat at the biggest Hollywood showdown in years: the ouster of Spyros Skouras as Twentieth president. Spurred by the runaway cost of *Cleopatra*, which was a forty-million-dollar disaster in the making, the actual showdown took place at corporate headquarters in New York. Wyler's phone jingled like the bell between rounds. Zanuck wanted to put him on the board of directors. So did Skouras and board member Louis Nizer, the famed attorney.

"They said what they needed was a filmmaker, somebody who knew production," Wyler recounted. "I certainly agreed with that. I remember voting in favor of spending two million dollars that Zanuck said he needed to finish *Cleopatra*."

Wyler didn't stay long on the board, though. After two meetings he quietly resigned. Corporate wrangling bored him.

A combination of Zanuck's cost-cutting and the success of *The Longest Day* managed to save Twentieth from sinking. The new president also appointed a new head of production: his Stanford-educated, twenty-seven-year-old son. Richard Zanuck had proved his competence both as a producer and administrator. And he stepped into the job with another, equally important skill: He had a canny feel for popular taste. With Twentieth up and running but not out of danger, the Zanucks asked Wyler to direct a screen version of *The Sound of Music*, the Rodgers and Hammerstein musical then making Broadway history.

Still on the boards after nearly three years, the show was set in Austria in 1938 and had a farfetched story very loosely based on a true-life experience. It revolved around a postulant nun who must leave the convent because her real calling is song. She becomes the governess of a widowed ship captain's seven children, teaches them to sing and marries him. Then she masterminds their escape from the Nazis by taking the family on tour as a troupe of singers.

"I was hard of hearing, a fine fellow to do a musical," Wyler said. But if he didn't have to worry about the music, he might consider it. Twentieth sent him to New York to see the show. He came back slightly mystified. Wyler was mulling things over, when Robert Swink stopped by his house one day.

"Bob," he said, "they want me to make this picture, and I don't know what to do. The people in this musical are playing a scene and all of a sudden somebody starts to sing. Sometimes they're just walking along and somebody starts to sing. Why the hell do they start singing?"

As an old operagoer, Wyler knew why people sang. But the characters in *The Sound of Music* didn't seem to have a reason, except that they just *liked* to sing. He wasn't sure that was a motivation he could hang a movie on.

Ernest Lehman, who signed to do the screen adaptation, pressed Wyler to take the job. Since he'd never tried his hand at a musical, he rationalized that it would at least be a challenge. "I knew it would be a success," Wyler recounted. "The story was made in German, on stage and in film. In some other languages, too. I wrote the producer of the German film. He answered my letter. He said, 'This cannot fail.'"

Wyler told Zanuck to draw up a contract and thought of Julie Andrews for the picture. He'd seen her on Broadway in *My Fair Lady*. She'd already come to Hollywood and was in the process of making *Mary Poppins*, her movie debut, for Walt Disney.

"I went over to the studio and met her on the set," he said. "Walt showed me some rushes, and she was signed."

Wyler then met Maria von Trapp, whose published autobiography provided the story. She came down from Vermont to see him at the St. Regis Hotel in New York. Afterward, he and Talli and Lehman and his wife flew to Austria to scout locations in the Tyrolean Alps. They went to the convent where von Trapp had been a novice. Ushered into its deep underground warrens, Wyler and Lehman were shown to a room with an iron grill. The Mother Superior appeared behind it. Wyler explained to her, in German, that he hoped to make part of his movie there.

The Mother Superior looked at him with disbelieving eyes. Talli nearly broke up with laughter. "It was just hilarious to watch these two Hollywood characters convince this Mother Superior that they weren't mad."

In the Salzburg mayor's office, Wyler began to think that maybe he was crazy. The picture would bring back memories of the Anschluss and how warmly the Austrians welcomed Hitler. He would have to re-create scenes of German soldiers on parade, cheering crowds greeting them with flowers, Nazi banners hanging from the windows.

"You know," he told the mayor, "we have to do it the way it really happened. Maybe some people won't like it."

The mayor took the long view. He said they had lived through it once and survived and they could live through it again.

"We got back," Talli recalled, "and Willy had all but signed. He was already working on the picture. But I would go into his den and he'd be sitting at his desk, staring off into space. He was obviously miserable, just hating every minute of it.

"So finally I said, 'Why do it? If you're going to be this miserable, I don't think I want to live with you while you're doing it. Tell me what's the matter?'

"He said, 'I just can't bear to make a picture about all those nice Nazis.'"

Lehman kept reminding Wyler they weren't making a picture about the Nazis. They were making a musical about a heroic family who'd escaped the Nazis. With Julie Andrews and the Rodgers and Hammerstein score, the picture would be a certain hit.

"Shooting was getting closer," Talli said, "and Willy still felt terribly unhappy about the whole thing. That's when he was saved. Two young men showed up on our doorstep, and they gave Willy a book."

The pair, Judd Kinberg and John Kohn, were former television writers who had left New York for London, where they teamed up to produce movies as Blazer Films. They read *The Collector*, a first novel by British author John Fowles, before publication and purchased the screen rights. Then they pitched the project to the head of Columbia Pictures' overseas productions, Mike Frankovich, who was also based in London. He gave them a go-ahead, and they brought the novel, still in galleys, to British actor Terence Stamp, whom they wanted for the lead.

Meanwhile, Frankovich was called back to Hollywood to take over all Columbia productions as head of the studio. When Kinberg and Kohn told him they wanted Wyler to direct, he sent them to Summit Drive. By this time, the pair had the first draft of a screenplay written by Stanley Mann, which they also left with Wyler.

He didn't look at the screenplay until he digested the novel. "I found I couldn't put the book down," Wyler recalled. "And I'm a man who can put books down very easily." The screenplay was not as riveting, but he liked it enough to tell Frankovich he would do the picture. The studio chief said there was one hitch: Kinberg and Kohn wanted to produce.

"Let them," Wyler replied. "They put this together. But I have the last word." Once that was agreed upon, Wyler asked to be let out of *The Sound of Music*.

FOWLES'S NOVEL BECAME AN IMMEDIATE BEST-SELLER. IT TOLD the story of Freddie Clegg, a repressed, insignificant, lower-class bank clerk who collects butterflies. He wins a national football lottery and uses his winnings to purchase a secluded Tudor mansion with a fortresslike cellar, where he intends to keep the latest addition to his collection—not a butterfly at all. This specimen is a beautiful, virginal, upper-class art student whom he kidnaps off the street.

At first Stamp did not want the role. Freddie sickened him. He also felt intimidated, despite his recent Oscar-nominated film debut in *Billy Budd*. Cast in that film over Warren Beatty, Tony Perkins and Dean Stockwell, the previously unknown, twenty-three-year-old stage actor with the Botticelli face had blazed a sensational media trail since *Billy Budd*—but not always for his acting. It was Stamp's offscreen exploits with some of the most beautiful women in London that kept him in the headlines. "I hadn't gotten any new work in roughly a year," he recounts. "I knew the camera loved me, so I had confidence in that. But I just thought this Freddie character was beyond me. I kept saying, 'Look guys. It's just impossible. You've got to get somebody else.'"

Then Kohn phoned him and said, "Listen, William Wyler has agreed to do the movie. You're not going to turn down William Wyler, are you?'"

Stamp asked if Wyler wanted him.

"That's the point," Kohn said. "He does."

"Who will play the girl?"

That wasn't settled, Kohn told him. Wyler wanted screen tests made of young British actresses. They would be made in London by Robert Parrish. Stamp asked if he could test with some of the actresses. This way, he could try on the role for size. If the director still wanted him after the tests, he said, he would feel better about taking the offer.

Stamp got himself a cheap Bangkok suit, "perfect for an underpaid bank clerk," and a pair of sturdy Oxford shoes. He tested with Sarah Miles and Samantha Eggar. When Wyler flew to London and looked at the test footage, he immediately asked to meet Stamp. The actor arrived at Columbia's offices on Wardour Street. Wyler came out of his office to welcome him at the end of a long corridor.

"This was the big moment," Stamp recounts. "Everybody told me all these gruesome tales about him. He was smaller than I expected. He looked like a big pussycat to me."

Wyler greeted him warmly. The actor detected a slightly foreign American accent. He also noticed the husky sound of the director's voice and the rich scent of leather and French tobacco.

"I've seen the tests," Wyler said.

"Which girl did you like?"

"I haven't looked at the girls yet."

Stamp wondered what he meant.

"I've just been looking at you."

The actor blushed. "Do you think I'm right? In the book—"

Wyler cut him short and put his fingers to his lips. He put his arm around Stamp's shoulder and whispered into his ear, "I'm not going to make the book. I'm going to make a modern love story." Then the director turned the young actor's face to his and looked him directly in the eye. "You're going to be . . . just purrr-fect."

Stamp recalls, "I was immediately a conspirator. Absolutely taken. We had an intuitive rapport." At the back of his mind, though, he couldn't help worrying about all those gruesome tales.

"By the way," he said, "I've heard about you. I hear you really punish actors. You know, forty or fifty takes. I just want to tell you, I like to do one or two."

Wyler gave him "a big monkey smile," Stamp recalls.

"You give me what I want in one," Wyler said, "and we'll get along just fine."

Samantha Eggar would get the role of Miranda, the kidnapped art student, despite having little professional experience. "Frankovich was quite taken with her," says Swink, who edited the picture. "Willy had some rehearsals with her. He wanted to see how she worked. He was afraid she wouldn't be up to the part. Before long, he told me he couldn't do the picture with her. But Frankovich kept after him."

"I got fired three weeks into rehearsals," the actress says. "Terry Stamp's nasty attitude toward me undermined me so much that I just became a sort of squashed balloon and, rightly, I got fired. I went to Mike Frankovich and told him what had happened. He said, 'Well, don't go back to England yet.' They'd conducted a big search to play the girl, and I had come over with all this fanfare.

"But now I was out, and they didn't know what to do with me— whether to shove me back into the hotel and hide me or not. All the press was in the street. It was just unbelievable. So, to cover Columbia's embarrassment, Frankovich sent me down to Palm Springs and hid me away there."

During that time, Wyler offered the role to Natalie Wood. It was just two weeks before shooting was to begin. But she could not accept because of a scheduling conflict. In a handwritten letter she begged Wyler to work with her in the future.

Two days later, Frankovich phoned Eggar and said, "Willy's coming down."

"Sure enough," she remembers, "he did. We read through the entire script. Bob Swink played Terry, and Willy never said a word. He just got up at the end, shook my hand, and said, 'See you on the set Monday.'"

Swink recalls, "Willy made a condition with Frankovich that if there was a coach with her at all times through the picture, he'd use her." Ordinarily, the idea of an actor having a coach on the set was anathema to Wyler. But this time, *he* would pick the coach—Kathleen Freeman, a character actress—and she would work with Eggar according to *his* instructions. If not for the coach, Eggar might not have made it through the filming.

To this day, Stamp says, Eggar has not forgiven him for the way he treated her on the set. He'd told Wyler they had known each other in drama school. "All the guys had crushes on her, she was so beautiful," the actor recalls. "I had a crush on her, too, and I was friendly with her. But when we started the movie, Willy said, 'I don't want you to have anything to do with her.' He wanted me to withdraw my friendship. He didn't want her to have anywhere to go or anyone to talk to, except her coach. He didn't want her to be able to come to me in the evening and say, 'God, it's so awful.'

"He wanted her to live the role. He wouldn't let her off the set during the day. She wasn't allowed to eat with the rest of us. He wanted her in a constant state of terror, and that's really very difficult to act. So he wanted me to conspire with him. He said, 'This is going to look cruel, but we'll get a great performance out of her.' The two of us tortured her. We weren't actually nasty, but I had to be incredibly indifferent. And the fact is, he got her an Academy Award nomination."

From Eggar's point of view, Wyler "had all sorts of ways and methods" to make her feel defenseless. During a rain sequence, she recalls, "I'd come on to the set and he'd sort of click his fingers, and the prop man would come and just throw a bucket of water right in my face. So you say to yourself, 'That's sort of odd.'"

Eggar also had a love scene which made her feel extremely vulnerable. She was to play it nude, while Stamp would be clothed. The actress stalled Wyler with excuses: She couldn't do the scene because she had a cold or a fever or whatever else she thought might work.

"I was able to fool him for about a week and a half," Eggar says. "One day he came into the dressing room and really rapped my knuckles. He pulled me to my senses and embraced me and said, 'Come on. Get on with it.' So we shot that love scene for what seemed like weeks. I kept wondering why I had to stand there with no clothes on when they were only shooting me from the shoulders up. Willy always used to sit, and it was a strange level where his eyes were.

"But anyway, there I stood with Terry Stamp, day after day doing this wretched love scene. And one day some cretin snuck into the studio and was up in the flies with a Hasselblad, of all cameras. You could hear it click. Wyler stood up and had the man literally pulled down from the flies. He was a Swedish photographer. Willy took the camera and ripped out the film and kicked him in the behind out the door. It was the most extraordinary performance."

Wyler's reputation from earlier days — notably having affairs with his leading ladies or being a little bit in love with them — never crossed Eggar's mind. "When I was nude," she remembers, "he said I looked like a little boy. I hardly call that being in love. He said I had a good ass."

THE STARK SUBJECT OF *THE COLLECTOR* LENT ITSELF TO FILMING in black and white, and Wyler scheduled it that way. But when he asked Swink and Bob Surtees, who was again on camera, to do a black-and-white makeup test with Eggar, they made a color test as well.

"Surtees kept saying, 'Look at that red hair. Look at that skin.' She looked like a ripe peach," Swink recalls. "When we ran the tests for Willy, there was no comparison."

Although he opted for color, Wyler wanted subdued hues in this picture. He was careful about the use of color in any case. "A red chair doesn't look unusual in reality," he explained. "But on the screen, you can't take your eyes from it. That's because the frame itself is not natural. It's delimited by the blackness surrounding it. We don't actually see that way with our natural field of vision. I was late in using color partly because I felt color could be phony, exaggerated."

Wyler chose to treat *The Collector* as a psychodrama and filmed the scenes in sequence. This would help Eggar assimilate her role more readily. It also enabled him to build tension, shaping her performance by ratcheting up the pressure. Once rehearsals ended, Wyler filmed for forty-two days, from mid-May to late June, on Columbia sound stages at Sunset and Gower.

Stamp marveled at Wyler's subtle command: "He followed his intuition, which very few directors have the guts to do. He would barely whisper the word 'action.' Sometimes he wouldn't even say it. He would just look at you and roll his hand. He didn't want to jar you out of the scene. He wanted to glide into it. And he had a way of saying the intuitively right thing.

"When we were doing Freddie's paranoid flashback, he sidled up to me and whispered, 'the taste of the stamps.' Nothing else. It was exactly the kind of direction an actor needs. It put me in the right frame of mind without telling me what to do. Freddie licked stamps in the bank, and thinking of that gluey taste gave me an oppressive feeling."

Of course, Wyler's subtlety depended on the actor. When an actor thoroughly displeased him, he could show him no mercy. And this, too, happened on *The Collector*. He had picked the wrong actor for a bit part. Embarrassed by his mistake, Wyler lashed out at him with sarcasm. The actor, Maurice Dallimore, played an older gentleman. He is an English squire who has a small but crucial scene with Freddie.

"This guy turns up on the set," Stamp recounts, "and he's what I call Hollywood English. He looked perfect. But as soon as he said anything, you could hear he wasn't really English or that he'd been in America too long. Well, Dallimore couldn't cut it. Everything this guy did just fell apart. I can't tell you how *green* it was. We did eight or nine takes for him just to open the door, and with every take this poor guy was getting more and more frightened. Willy started calling him 'Barrymore.' He'd say, 'Okay, Barrymore, let's do it again.' He really got sadistic. I drew Wyler aside and told him, 'Willy, it's just not going to work.' And he whispered, 'I hate bad actors.' "

Wyler got along with Stamp so well that he began inviting prominent directors to the set to watch the actor work. "He wanted me to meet them," Stamp says. "It was like he was laying out a career for me, introducing me around. He was very generous to me."

One aspect of the story that Wyler left open to debate was whether Miranda would be rescued at the end of her ordeal or whether she would die, as she did in the novel. He came under pressure to lighten the ending for commercial reasons. "The decision was to go with the book," Wyler said. "If Miranda is trapped in a psycho's basement and the Marines come to the rescue, it would be like any other melodrama. That's not this story."

But that led to another question.

"Willy came up to me," Stamp recalls. "It was the last scene we were going to do before we left for England to shoot the exteriors.

"He said, 'I love the way you've been playing this. It's wonderful and bizarre. She's dead. Staying faithful to your performance, now what do you do?'

"He really trusted me, and I was proud of that. I said, 'The way I've been playing it, Willy, now is my chance to fuck her.'"

Stamp's notion was that Freddie was impotent and that that was his biggest secret. "He can't get a hard-on. Now that she's dead, it's my chance."

Wyler covered his face with his hands and laced his fingers over his eyes. "We can't do that."

"I said, 'Okay, fine. You asked me,' " Stamp recalled. "But here's the interesting thing. We get to London. It's weeks later. On a Saturday night I get a call from him and he asks me to come 'round to the Dorchester, where he's staying. I said I've got this big romance—Jean Shrimpton, the love of my life—do you mind if I bring her? He says, 'No, go ahead.' We get over there. He's very courteous to Jean. He says, 'Would you mind if I talk to Terence alone?' So she sat in the living room and we go into the bedroom.

"As soon as he closes the door, he says, 'Do you remember that conversation we had? Well, Bob Swink has shown me a rough cut, and you were right. I should have had more confidence. If we can do a shot like that, the screenplay is a time bomb. I've made a little studio down in Kent, and I had a piece of the basement wall flown over, just enough for a close-up. Do you think you can give me that look? *Now's my chance to do the thing?*'

"He brought me in on a Sunday morning and we filmed it. They never used it. Too tough. The point, though, is how gracious he was. I'm a young actor and he's a director of enormous stature. And he comes to me and says, 'I was wrong. You were right.'"

Something else occurred on *The Collector* that was rather unusual. Wyler cut an entire performance from the picture. The unlucky actor whose work was sacrificed to shorten the picture was Kenneth More, a top-notch British actor who played Miranda's boyfriend. He was in the film from beginning to end, via her flashbacks.

"When I ran the rough cut for Willy, the pace seemed too slow," Swink recalls. "We also knew it was too long. So we pulled out the first flashback. It ran better. Willy said, 'Why don't we take out the second one?' It ran much better. Eventually we decided to eliminate all of them.

"We were still in the projection booth when Willy picked up the phone, no fussing around, and called Kenneth More. He told him what he had to do. Willy didn't have to make that call personally, but he did. He respected the performance and the actor, and he didn't want him to hear the bad news second or thirdhand."

In London, Wyler made the outdoor sequences in a couple of weeks, with British cinematographer Robert Krasker. Swink also went out with a second-unit crew for added coverage of the film's opening and closing episodes: Freddie stalking Miranda in his van, a wordless prelude to the psychodrama, and the brief but chilling finale in which he prowls the suburban London streets again, stalking his next human butterfly.

With filming finished by mid-July, Wyler was off to Switzerland. He met Talli in Lausanne, city of his high school days, and spent the rest of the summer traveling to Lake Geneva, Zurich, a film festival in Dubrovnik, Venice, back to Switzerland and from there to Paris for meetings with French composer Maurice Jarre, who would score *The Collector*. Also in Paris, they saw Darryl Zanuck, who had another project in mind for Wyler. By mid-September, they were home again.

That fall, Wyler and Swink put the finishing touches on the picture. The winter was a social whirl of dinner parties on Summit Drive with various guests: Trevor Howard, Lillian Hellman, Jarre, the Carol Reeds, Arthur Penn, John Mills, the Hestons, Mike Frankovich, Bryan Forbes and Sy Bartlett.

John Fowles, now enjoying international literary success, saw the finished film in London that February. Wyler had brought him to the Columbia set early in the shoot to critique the script. Fowles had made several suggestions and doctored some dialogue. But basically he'd found the script "a pleasant surprise," telling Wyler he felt that "this might be made into an electrifying film." On seeing Wyler's results now, Fowles wrote from England that he sat through the picture not once but twice: "I enjoyed it just as much the second time as the first—and was a second time astounded with what you managed to extract from Samantha."

Not that Fowles didn't have what he termed "minor" criticisms. He was "least happy" about the music. It went on "too long" and was "too loud." He objected, moreover, that it was "too whimsical" at certain points, especially during Miranda's abduction. "Surely silence would be better." Wyler took the advice, eliminating all the background music in the kidnap sequence, and made other adjustments. But even today Jarre's sound track is egregiously intrusive. It telegraphs rather than evokes, hyping mood and atmosphere with hammy melodrama.

Neither Wyler nor the studio felt any urgency to release the picture right away. In May 1965, Columbia entered *The Collector* at the Cannes Film Festival. Publicity from Cannes was bound to lend it prestige and prepare the ground for a marketing campaign aimed at "mature" audiences. Though the picture did not win the Palme d'Or, Stamp and Eggar won the prizes for best actor and actress. It was the first time in the festival's history that the jury awarded both acting prizes to the same picture.

The Collector opened in New York in June to high praise and some quibbles. Even the leading American auteurist critic Andrew Sarris, who spearheaded the revisionist attack on Wyler in the wake of the French New Wave, had surpisingly good things to say. He began his review in the *Village Voice* by calling it "the most erotic movie ever to come out past the Production Code." He loved "the extraordinary performances," preferring Eggar's to Stamp's. He maintained that the picture offered "conclusive evidence" that all movies should be filmed in color. "There are no black-and-white subjects left anymore."

Sarris also had his reservations, of course. He called Wyler's direction "horridly impersonal," which was the worst accusation an auteurist could make. At the same time he accused Wyler of stealing ideas from the New Wave directors—particularly from François Truffaut, Alain Resnais and Jean-Luc Godard.

Interestingly, Stamp engaged Wyler on the subject of Truffaut one day while waiting for a camera setup on *The Collector*. The actor mentioned that he'd seen Truffaut's *The 400 Blows*. He wondered what Wyler thought of the New Wave.

"Well, in that picture," Wyler said, "he just froze the frame to end it."

"Yeah," said Stamp. "Why do you think he did that?"

"Usually when people freeze the frame, they don't know what else to do. Stills belong in the lobby, not on the screen."

Wyler's general response to the New Wave could be curdling. In 1963 he told Axel Madsen that most of it belonged on the cutting room floor. He said he and Billy Wilder called the New Wave pictures *trouvailles*, that is, "found" material. It was, he said, as dated as "UFA work," a reference to one of Berlin's major studios in the twenties and thirties. Before the New Wave came along, he said, "Max Ophuls had a wild camera in *La Ronde*, and it was already old hat." Too many of the New Wave directors were show-offs, he added. They made films *pour épater les gens*, that is, to amaze their audience with tricks. He took particular exception to Alain Resnais's work: "I forced myself to sit through *Last Year at Marienbad*, because I paid my two dollars. It was the worst form of cinema—*boring* cinema. And Resnais is the biggest bore." Asked about *Hiroshima, Mon Amour*, Resnais's first and more famous picture, Wyler conceded, "Good theme." But Truffaut's *Shoot the Piano Player* and *Jules and Jim* also bored him. As for *The 400 Blows*, he admitted enjoying some of it and said it had "interesting things in it—but it's from the Zola period, for Chrissakes."

Who then, among European directors of the sixties, did Wyler admire? Federico Fellini, Vittorio De Sica and Ingmar Bergman. None of the *nouvelle vague* could stack up against them. Bergman's *The Virgin Spring* was "almost the greatest picture ever made," in Wyler's opinion. And he lauded the "angry young men" of the British "kitchen sink" wave.

Stamp puts Wyler at the top of his list: "The best directors I ever worked with were Fellini and Wyler. What I most wanted to do was work with Wyler again as a mature actor. It would have been a richer experience later in my career. I took what I could from him, but I was young and *The Collector* was really only my second film. I said to him once, 'Maybe one of these days I'm going to direct. Tell me about it.' He said, 'It's eighty percent script and twenty percent you get great actors. There's nothing else to it.'"

40

~~~~~~~

FRENCH SCHEDULE

A N ASPECT OF WYLER'S PERSON-
ality that runs like a motif through his career was the idea of not repeating himself. *The Children's Hour* proved the major exception to the rule.
But Wyler always said to friends from his earliest days, and later to the
press, that one of the challenges for a director was to make as many different kinds of pictures as possible.

This eclecticism tended to hurt his reputation with purists who preferred to think of artists as people obsessed by a lifelong subject or two.
In their view, the artist's entire output may be seen as variations on a
theme. And anyone whose body of work does not conform to that pattern may be regarded as deficient: lacking depth or purpose or—the ultimate deficiency—a true calling.

"My father was a bit hurt toward the end of his life that the variety of
his films was not appreciated," Melanie Wyler says. "Everyone thought
Hitchcock was great because he stuck to the same thing. But my father
used to say, 'He's a prisoner of the medium.' I remember they had a conversation about it. Hitchcock said he was jealous. 'You can do any kind
of film you want. I can't. They won't let me.'"

Wyler's decision to make *Venus Rising*—later retitled *How to Steal a*

Million—played directly into the purists' line of fire. "Willy took that picture at that moment because he didn't have anything better to do," Talli recalls. "It was not a project close to his soul, the way *The Collector* was. He took it because of his longtime friendship with Zanuck and because he felt he *ought* to do another movie."

In Hollywood, the people you work with are often the people you see on the social circuit. It was that way in Wyler's day and it still is. In that respect, Hollywood is no different from any company town. Among the dinner guests at Summit Drive over the winter was Harry Kurnitz, a veteran screenwriter hired by Twentieth Century–Fox to pen a caper comedy called *Venus Rising*. It was his project that Darryl Zanuck had in mind for Wyler when they saw each other the previous summer in Paris.

Wyler had never made a caper comedy and thought it might be fun. In fact, he said many times that the only reason he considered doing *The Sound of Music* was that he'd never done a musical. He wasn't wedded to that notion either, or to any high-minded sense of purity. Having fun, even when it meant working hard, was at the heart of Wyler's personality. What's more, now that he was getting on in years, working hard was becoming less and less fun. His health was beginning to fail. He developed hereditary ulcers. A lifetime of smoking was finally exacting its toll: His lungs were ruined. He almost couldn't breathe without wheezing, which, as it happened, presented a problem for the sound men on his later pictures. They were always reminding him to pipe down during live takes.

Besides the chance to spoof the caper genre, which was then in fashion, Twentieth said it would let him film *Venus Rising* entirely in Paris, where he'd never filmed before. As an added inducement, the picture would be made on "the French schedule." This meant a much easier daily grind than usual.

"It's a miserable life in Hollywood," he told a reporter at the time. "You're up at five or six o'clock in the morning to be ready to start shooting at nine. The working hours aren't arranged to suit the artists and the director; they're for the convenience of the technicians. If you go to a party at night, you'll never find anyone there who's shooting a picture; they're all home in bed." In Paris, on the other hand, "you start at noon. Then you work right through to seven-thirty. It's much less exhausting that way. Anyhow, who can play a love scene at nine o'clock in the morning?"

According to Swink, Twentieth essentially finessed Wyler into doing the picture. When the editor asked Wyler why he was doing "this light little nothing," Wyler told him he'd purposely asked for Audrey Hepburn to star. He didn't think Richard Zanuck could get her, he told Swink. She was more popular than ever, having done a dozen movies after *Roman Holiday*, including *Breakfast at Tiffany's*, *Charade*, *The Nun's Story* and *My Fair Lady*. She'd also been nominated for three Oscars since her Oscar-winning debut. But now that Twentieth had gotten her, that made the offer sweeter.

Also, Wyler liked Twentieth producer Fred Kohlmar's idea of pairing her with Peter O'Toole. A terrific actor, the handsome O'Toole was one of Hollywood's hottest new stars. He had rocketed to international fame in *Lawrence of Arabia* two years earlier and followed up in *Becket*, opposite Richard Burton and John Gielgud. The Hepburn-O'Toole pairing looked like box office magic. And if that weren't enough, O'Toole came from the British stage. Wyler had more respect for British-trained actors than almost anyone.

"We may not have the best script in the world," Wyler told Swink, "but we're going first-class."

The plot complications of *How to Steal a Million* were so outlandish that nobody was expected to believe them. Hepburn and O'Toole pull off a museum heist. They steal a fake masterpiece, which her sculptor grandfather has forged and her father, a dealer in fraudulent masterpieces, has lent the museum for an exhibition. Desperate to save her father from being found out—a certainty, it seems, because the museum intends to authenticate the statue for insurance purposes with the latest scientific tests—Hepburn enlists O'Toole's help, not knowing he is really a private detective suspicious of her father.

The pair not only steal the piece—a twenty-nine-inch replica of Cellini's so-called *Venus*—they fall in love during the caper while stuck for hours in a museum broom closet. Afterward O'Toole dupes Hepburn's wealthy suitor, a dumb American art collector, into smuggling the fake out of the country for his private collection on the condition that he never put it on display and never see Hepburn again.

Since Wyler could not make the picture in an actual museum, he decided to build his own and stock it with paintings by old and modern masters—fakes, naturally, but good enough to look convincing on camera. For this he engaged Alexander Trauner, a Hungarian-born production designer who lived in Paris and who was a legend in Hollywood for his scrupulously detailed sets. Trauner farmed out the work to seven local painters. They produced a collection of Monets, Cezannes, Goyas, Van Goghs, Renoirs, El Grecos, Rembrandts, da Vincis, Tintorettos, Rubenses, Braques and Picassos. Total cost: one hundred thousand dollars. For another fifty thousand, Trauner hung the fakes in authentic frames, some dating to the seventeenth century.

When the Wylers left for Paris in June, two weeks after *The Collector* opened, Trauner's sets were still being built and production was expected to get under way in mid-August. The "French schedule" would allow the Wylers to entertain in the evenings, and they wanted to make the most of it. They took a formal town house, fully staffed, in the city's most elegant neighborhood. They lived on a sedate little street near the Champs Elysées and the Arc de Triomphe. Hepburn took a town house not far away, and O'Toole was put up at the Hotel George V.

Wyler cast Hugh Griffith, the Welsh actor who'd won an Oscar for best-supporting actor in *Ben-Hur*, as Hepburn's father. It was a small but central role that paid fifty thousand dollars for ten weeks' work. Twentieth wanted to cast Walter Matthau in the smaller role of the American art collector. With Hepburn said to be making a million dollars, however, Matthau demanded two hundred thousand—double what the studio offered him. He also wouldn't accept unless he got billing above the title and his name in the same size type as the two stars.

Richard Zanuck dismissed the counteroffer out of hand. "This is ridiculous," he noted, and George C. Scott was cast instead. "Willy was really surprised and delighted when Scott accepted," Talli recalled.

Wyler threw an intimate dinner party for him on August 17 to welcome him to Paris. They got along beautifully. Production had just begun. Except for costume fittings, the actor didn't have to report to the studio for another month. Then the trouble began.

On September 14, the assistant production manager phoned Scott in his suite at the Ritz and asked him to be on the set at noon the next day ready to shoot his first scene. Noon came and went, but he didn't show up. Wyler's personal assistant phoned. He was told Scott hadn't left the hotel. Now the production manager phoned, and Scott's assistant told him the actor had had "a very bad night" and couldn't be awakened. Wyler decided to shoot around him. He canceled the setup, asked for a new one and two hours later began on a different scene.

Meanwhile, Kohlmar sent a doctor to the Ritz. He reported that Scott refused to be examined and threatened to throw him out of the room. "After I introduced myself he became extremely uncivil," the doctor related. "My impression is that he was suffering from the aftereffects of an excessive intake of alcoholic beverages and was still not fully responsible for his actions."

At ten past five, Scott finally arrived at the studio. Kohlmar met him in the director's trailer. Wyler looked in momentarily, greeted him warmly, considering the circumstances, and said he wanted to speak with Scott after he finished shooting. The actor said he'd wait in his dressing room but, without telling anyone, left the studio before Wyler returned at seven-thirty.

"Within the hour," Swink says, "Willy had notices all over that he wanted a new man for the part."

The next morning Wyler held a meeting with Darryl Zanuck and Kohlmar and the production manager in Zanuck's apartment. That afternoon, Scott was fired. Eli Wallach replaced him a few days later.

"Willy told me instantly what happened," Talli recounted. "He said, 'Once George's face is on the screen and we've got a week in the can, *then* what happens when he doesn't show up? Who are they going to replace, me or him?' So he stuck to his guns. He said, 'That's that.'"

Wyler already had to deal with two actors who came to the set hung over: O'Toole and Griffith. "He thanked God for the French schedule," Talli said. "He didn't know what would have happened if they had to get there before noon. But they always managed one way or another, and they came prepared.

"He was very impressed with Peter. Even though he was out carousing every night, Peter was on the set. He knew his lines and knew what he was doing. Willy was even more impressed by his abilities. Sometimes he wouldn't be totally pleased with the way Peter looked. He didn't always look as bright-eyed and bushy-tailed as he ought to have. But Willy was thrilled to have him."

O'Toole's friend and business partner Jules Buck had introduced the two of them for the first time some years earlier. Buck, who knew Wyler from the late thirties, had formed Keep Films, Ltd., with O'Toole. It co-produced *Becket* and *Lord Jim*, among others.

Buck says, "When they knew they would be working together, they both started asking me what the other was like. It was two champs circling before they got in the ring. O'Toole wanted to know, 'Christ, all those takes.' Willy would say, 'Tell me about Pete.' He always called him Pete.

"Anyway, I was back and forth on the set. I forget the sequence, but Peter pulled out his bag of tricks and absolutely stunned Willy. Really stunned him. Willy said, 'Cut.' 'Take.' 'One protection shot.' Then he burst out laughing and went over to him. 'Pete,' he said, 'you did it to me.' They really got along."

·   ·   ·

IN NOVEMBER, WITH THE TWELVE-WEEK SHOOT JUST ABOUT finished, the Cinémathèque Française launched a Wyler retrospective celebrating his career and his place in film history. The De Gaulle government, pushed by its minister of culture, André Malraux, had installed the most comfortable, best-equipped movie auditorium in Paris for the then twenty-nine-year-old film archive. Set inside the Palais de Chaillot, a national monument whose foundations were laid by Napoleon, the Cinémathèque's plush new quarters lent more prestige than ever to what was already regarded as perhaps the world's most famous film archive and certainly one of its greatest. It was, according to Jean Renoir, "the church of movies."

Wyler attended the retrospective's opening film, *The Little Foxes*, but was too busy wrapping his current production to pay much attention to the rest of the homage. The irony could not have escaped him, however, that the foremost directors of the New Wave had all received their film education at the Cinémathèque from its legendary founder, Henri Langlois. Resnais called Langlois "my idol." In Truffaut's words, he taught "by osmosis" and provided "a haven for us, a refuge, our home, everything." *Cahiers du Cinema* editorialized: "Without Langlois there would be no *Cahiers du Cinema* nor New Wave."

And what did Langlois have to say about Wyler? That he "created a new style" in the late thirties and "influenced filmmakers on four continents." The postwar critics erred, Langlois declared, when they credited that style to Orson Welles and *Citizen Kane*. He said Welles "was still groping and being influenced by Wyler." He said Wyler's style "questioned everything by turning filmmaking into an equation, as if it were all a question of proportions, geometric forms and perspectives." At the same time, his "keen perception and moving simplicity" was the touchstone of his art.

Langlois wrote, "Wyler's strength lies in having gone all the way in analyzing the most delicate and impressionistic of human feelings and to have put his art and his science of directing actors at the service of a new concept. This concept was to allow him to go beyond naturalism and, without betraying truth or simplicity in acting, give performances with the intense strength which the masters of the German silent cinema had reached, but without resorting to their artifices and their symbolism."

Langlois's homage was the first of several Wyler tributes over the next six months. The following February in Hollywood, the Directors

Guild of America conferred on him its most coveted prize, the D. W. Griffith Award for "a lifetime of creative achievement," an honor it hadn't bestowed on anyone in five years. Then in April at the Oscar ceremonies, the Academy of Motion Picture Arts and Sciences presented Wyler with its highest accolade, the Irving G. Thalberg Memorial Award, for "consistent high quality of motion picture production." Had Thalberg been alive, he would have had to revise his opinion of Wyler or, at the very least, eaten the words "Worthless Willy."

Honors notwithstanding, Wyler failed to win the best director Oscar that year for *The Collector*. Though he was nominated, the prize went to Robert Wise for — of all pictures — *The Sound of Music*. The nomination would be Wyler's last, capping his career total at fifteen: twelve for directing and three for producing.

When *How to Steal a Million* opened the following July, it received a decidedly mixed reception. *Newsweek* called it entirely "derivative." The *New York Times* said it was "wholly ingratiating." *Newsweek* was closer to the mark. The picture has lost whatever charm it may originally have had, even as a piece of fluff. Hepburn comes off chic as usual, dressed to the nines by Givenchy, bejeweled by Cartier and still girlishly fawnish at age thirty-five. O'Toole fares less well, playing the sort of comic rogue he'd patented in *What's New, Pussycat?*

How to Steal a Million was not the box office blowout Wyler thought it would be. But it grossed almost ten million dollars, nonetheless, and earned the studio a sizable profit. "If every picture that Fox made came out like that," Kohlmar said, "there would never be anything to worry about." Even before the premiere, Darryl and Richard Zanuck asked Wyler to direct *Patton*.

41

~~~VVVV\\\\\~~~

No Pushover

THE FLOSSY ESCAPISM OF *How to Steal a Million* in 1966 could not have been further out of touch with the changing temper of the times. The schizoid sixties, as volatile as any decade since the turn of the century, had wrenched the country out of the naive complacency of the Eisenhower era. The assassination of John F. Kennedy, the civil rights marches, the Vietnam War, the assassinations of Martin Luther King, Jr. and Robert F. Kennedy—all were piped into the nation's living rooms. Television served these realities with dinner.

The war ultimately dealt the biggest blow to the nation's idealized view of itself. By 1967, the war drew hundreds of thousands of protesters into the streets. A mass counterculture—the hippies of the Flower Power generation—defected from the mainstream and turned to psychedelic drugs, New Age gurus, quasi-religious cults. Young men by the hundreds of thousands dodged the draft; some ten thousand fled to Canada; another two hundred thousand declared themselves conscientious objectors.

New Left radicals led campus revolts, organized peace marches, stormed the Pentagon. Urban guerrillas went underground. Armed "liberation movements" sprang up. The prescient words of Mario Savio, a student leader of the Free Speech Movement at Berkeley in 1964, framed the moral issue and portended the outcome: "There is a time when the operation of the machine becomes so odious, makes you so sick at heart, that you can't take part; you can't even passively take part . . . you've got to make it stop."

This was the temper of the times, if not for everybody, certainly for a large portion of America's youth. Inevitably, the trappings of the counterculture would filter into the mainstream: miniskirts and bell bottoms, Indian beads and tie-dyed T-shirts, long hair and marijuana, LSD and acid rock. Just as inevitably, the silent majority would elect Richard M. Nixon to the White House, and the war would grow both in Vietnam and at home. But Hollywood would not make any movies about the war until much later. In the sixties, Hollywood's war pictures looked to the past, for obvious reasons: The conflagration in Vietnam was not only ugly, politically controversial and increasingly unpopular, it was already being televised.

At Twentieth Century–Fox, Richard Zanuck got behind *M*A*S*H*, an absurdist take on war ostensibly about Korea. He also gave the go-ahead to *Patton*, which Darryl Zanuck took under his wing. Like Wyler, he had joined the Army after Pearl Harbor and fought "the good war" making combat documentaries. When Twentieth announced in May 1966 that Wyler was signed to direct *Patton*, it had the ring of an ideal match. The producer would be Frank McCarthy, a retired brigadier general who'd been a top aide to Army Chief of Staff General George C. Marshall. *Patton* was budgeted at more than ten million dollars. Wyler was expected to begin filming in February 1967. The picture would be made on location in Spain, where vast quantities of World War II military equipment were available.

For thirteen years, McCarthy's pet project was to make a picture about General George S. Patton, the military genius whose contradictions fascinated him. It was McCarthy whom Marshall asked to baby-sit the hot-tempered, fiercely opinionated general whenever he got in political hot water. Unfortunately, Twentieth still didn't have a finished screenplay when Wyler's signing was announced. All it had were screen rights to a Patton biography and a first-draft script that McCarthy had commissioned from a recent film school graduate, Francis Ford Coppola.

Coppola had done a poetic job with Patton's "blood and guts" speeches, including what became the picture's brilliant opening. But the script was weak on narrative structure and, in the studio's opinion,

badly in need of a rewrite. Over the next several months Wyler and Mc-
Carthy, who had gone to work for Zanuck after the war, searched for
someone to take on the rewrite. They wanted James Webb, a former
World War II staff officer who was personally familiar with Patton.
Webb was reluctant, partly because he didn't feel sympathetic to the
subject. But Wyler, who'd worked with Webb on *The Big Country*, finally
persuaded him. It didn't hurt, of course, that the studio met Webb's demand for two hundred thousand dollars, after much haggling and a
fruitless, six-month search for another writer.

Patton was scheduled not only as Wyler's next outing but as the first in a
four-picture deal with Twentieth. In September 1966 the studio drew up a
contract calling for two pictures to be directed by Wyler and two to be
produced by him. In addition to an undisclosed percentage of gross revenues, Fox offered Wyler fees of five hundred thousand dollars for the two
pictures he would direct and three hundred thousand for the two he would
produce. Robert Wyler would work on all four pictures at twenty-five
thousand each, and his payment would come out of Willy's fees. The contract was also nonexclusive, allowing Willy to work elsewhere between
pictures.

With the start date for *Patton* eight months away, Wyler had the balance of the year to devote to his family. He would become a grandfather
for the first time in September 1966, with the birth of his eldest daughter Catherine's son Billy. She had married two years earlier, during the
filming of *The Collector*. Wyler also had his hands full at sixty-four as the
father of a rebellious fourteen-year-old son, a daunting experience for
both of them.

"David and my father were very much alike," says Wyler's youngest daughter Melanie. "They butted heads, especially when David got
to be a teenager. It was the sixties. He grew his hair long, and that to
my father was the last straw. David was the only one among the four
of us who would argue back to him. They always loved each other,
but for a while there, they were at daggers drawn. David would sail
right in there. I admired him for that because, even though I was two
years older, I could never do it. I would dissolve in tears in five
minutes."

According to Melanie, her father took a European attitude toward
child-rearing: Children should be seen, not heard.

"He could be very stern in the sense that nothing was ever up for argument, especially not from David or me. If he said something, it had to
be his way. I always felt I knew what some of these actors were talking
about when they said it was hell to work with him. He wasn't the disci-

plinarian in the family. That he left to my mother. But there was no rea-
soning with him if he had something in his head."

She and her brother both wished they had known their father in his
heyday. "Even my older sisters felt that way," Melanie says. "He had a
great wit. He was a really good storyteller. He was always the life of the
party. But as his hearing became worse, he couldn't stand to be around
too many people at a time. When David and I got to be teenagers, his
hearing was really quite bad."

Still, Wyler was hardly cold or aloof; his warmth and impish humor
invariably came to the surface. He was a much-beloved father whom
the entire family wanted to please. Whenever he was not working, they
were always taking trips together. And when he was at the studio but
not in production, he would get home before dinner and perform a daily
ritual called "grenadine time."

"We had this big bar that Fred Astaire built," Melanie recounts. "My
father would always make a drink for my mother and himself. For me
and my brother, he would make 'a drink with grenadine.' He loved
being behind the bar. It was the showman in him. He couldn't boil water
in the kitchen, but behind the bar he could make any kind of drink.
When he learned how to make margaritas, I remember he used to get
my grandmother and mother totally smashed. My eighty-five-year-old
grandmother used to come and visit from Dallas, and she'd say, 'No,
Willy, no more!' "

WHEN THE START DATE FOR *PATTON* ROLLED AROUND, EVERYONE
involved with the production knew it would have to be delayed. Webb
couldn't actually begin rewriting Coppola's script until March 1967, because of prior commitments. With *Patton* stalled, Wyler accepted an
offer from Columbia to direct *Funny Girl*, starring Barbra Streisand in
her Hollywood debut. He was an eleventh-hour replacement for Sidney
Lumet, who left the picture over artistic differences with *Funny Girl* producer Ray Stark and Streisand. Rehearsals were to begin in May. At his
request, Wyler's contract stipulated that he must be finished with *Funny
Girl* by the end of the year, in time to begin filming *Patton* in January
1968. And so, for the rest of 1967, Wyler found himself juggling two of
Hollywood's most important projects.

Streisand reportedly was the world's highest-paid singer. She had
starred in the original *Funny Girl* on Broadway. But movie audiences
didn't know her; she was said to be difficult, not to mention "too Jewish" and unattractive to become a screen star. Columbia wanted Shirley

MacLaine for Streisand's role. Stark wouldn't hear of it. He had considered Carol Burnett and Anne Bancroft as first choices for the Broadway show, which he also produced. But after seeing Streisand's cabaret act and watching her portray the harried Miss Marmelstein, a small Broadway role in *I Can Get It For You Wholesale*, nobody else would do.

Funny Girl was a two-pronged story about Fanny Brice, a Brooklyn-born comedienne who sang like an angel and became famous in vaudeville. First it tells of her discovery by Florenz Ziegfeld and her rise to stardom; then it recounts her rocky marriage to New York gambler Nicky Arnstein. Among Brice's many celebrated songs were "My Man" and "Second Hand Rose," which Streisand reprised in the play.

Stark was a literary agent turned producer, who felt especially possessive about *Funny Girl*. Fanny Brice was his mother-in-law. He had commissioned an authorized biography—based on tape recordings she dictated—but was terribly disappointed with the result. Titled *The Fabulous Fanny*, the biography "captured none of her warmth or vitality," he felt. He tried to halt publication. When he couldn't, he bought back the printer's plates for fifty thousand dollars and commissioned Ben Hecht, one of his former clients, to write a biopic.

Neither Hecht nor other screenwriters were able to satisfy him. The screenplay went through ten different versions before Isobel Lennart penned an eleventh called *My Man*. It not only made Stark happy, it pleased Columbia. The studio offered him four hundred thousand dollars for the property, plus profit participation. But Stark turned the offer down. He decided to produce *Funny Girl* as a stage musical, calling it a "dry run" for the film.

While the show was still on Broadway, Stark asked Wyler to see it "with a view toward directing the film." Streisand early on told her producer that she wanted to have a dramatic director for the screen version. "I thought it should be a dramatic film, with musical numbers," she says. On Wyler's way back from Paris to Hollywood in December 1965—following the wrap of *How to Steal a Million*—he stopped in New York to see one of the Broadway production's final performances. After the curtain, he went backstage to meet Streisand.

"It was like some old-time thing," she recalls. "He wanted to see my profile, my front face, and I thought, 'This is like out of the movies, you know?'"

According to Stark, Wyler claimed he was too hard of hearing to do a musical and, regrettably, turned down the offer. Now, the second time around in February 1967, Wyler decided to reconsider the offer. It was his brother Robert who "pushed him to do that movie," Talli said. "Bob thought it was a terrific property. He just smelled it was going to be really *something*. He was very high on Barbra and the whole project." Willy went back to Stark and told him, "If Beethoven could write his Eroica Symphony stone deaf, then William Wyler can do a musical."

In March, Stark announced that Wyler had agreed to direct. For his part, Wyler moved into a new office at Columbia and told the press: "When I've completed this one, I will be a man who has done everything in the making of all kinds of motion pictures. There will be some new approaches. We're not just going to photograph the play." One approach he had in mind was to avoid the usual Hollywood method of lip-synching a performance on film with prerecorded songs. "It might turn out that the best way to proceed with Barbra," Wyler said, "is to let her sing *while* being photographed."

At the time, Columbia announced that he asked Herbert Ross to stage the picture's musical numbers. Wyler said years later that he told Stark he wouldn't take the job unless he had the assistance of "a first-class musical director and choreographer." But he hadn't stipulated just who that should be. It was Stark who hired Herb Ross. Ross had directed and/or choreographed many Broadway shows, including *I Can Get It For You Wholesale*. Wyler recalled, "I insisted that he should have complete say over the musical numbers because I had the film in the cutting room later if I wanted to change anything."

Streisand flew to Hollywood on May 2, heralded by enormous fanfare and accompanied by her then-husband Elliott Gould and their six-month-old son. She rehearsed on and off until July with Wyler and Ross at Columbia's studio on Gower, taking a short break in June for her free concert in New York's Central Park. On July 10, she and Wyler went east for nine days of location work. They shot their first scene the next day in Jersey City at the New Jersey Central railroad station.

"It was the Ziegfeld girls arriving at the station," Streisand recounts. "I said, 'Willy, I have this idea.' I said, 'Why don't we do a takeoff on Garbo's entrance in *Anna Karenina*. You know, because I had to appear in the train doorway.' I thought, 'Why not like Garbo? The smoke cleared and there was Garbo.' I said, 'Let's put smoke in the shot and I'll appear at the top of the stairs and I'll cough through the smoke and come down the steps.'

"He said, 'No.' "

Streisand got it in anyway at the bottom of the stairs. There was some steam coming up from the train wheels. She remembers, "I sort of ad-libbed the cough. Willy didn't like my idea at the top of the stairs, but now he said, 'That was fine.' I think that's when he got the inkling, the

first day: 'Uh-oh. This girl wants to direct.' I didn't know that was directing, anyway. I thought of it as an idea for an actress. . . .

"He was never threatened by my ideas. After that, I was thrown by
any director who ever was [threatened], because Willy used to get a
kick out of them. He'd use them, not use them, laugh at me, not laugh at
me. I mean, he was a wonderful person to collaborate with."

Wyler was so impressed by Streisand that he let her watch the dailies
with him.

"I was very fortunate to have Willy as my first director," she says.
"What was amazing is that when he showed me the first cut of the
movie, I would say ninety-five percent of the moments I had picked in
my head was in there. It was extraordinary. He just knew when it was
right. He used the right moments all the time."

Despite this, gossip began to circulate that the two couldn't get along.
Columnists had a field day describing rancor on the set. Some wags
claimed Wyler was so intimidated by his star that he agreed to let her
pick the hours they worked. Why else was she always late? Why else
weren't they shooting on the American schedule? Actually, Wyler was
only too happy to arrange a "modified French schedule"—ten to
seven—for himself as well as Streisand.

"I kept hearing reports that Barbra quarreled with me on the picture,"
Wyler said. "But there was never any evidence of it. It's true, she quarreled with Ray Stark. With me she worked desperately hard on her part.
She kept trying to improve herself; she worried about how she looked;
she would come on the set in the morning and ask if we could do a scene
over again. She was totally dedicated. She trusted me, and I trusted her.

"She was very eager to do different things, to try different things," he
added. "She was like Bette Davis used to be. She wants everything to be
the best, the very best. The same as I do. So we were working in perfect
harmony."

Swink, the supervising editor on *Funny Girl*, says he never saw anything like an argument between them. "I would deny that it happened,"
he says. "I felt they got along well. Streisand was easy for Willy to work
with. He had no problem with her. She wasn't what I would call trouble.

"One day Willy called me and said, 'I need a couple of shots out at the
Columbia ranch with Barbra. So I'm getting a camera for you, and I
want you to go out and make a couple of shots of her.' She didn't hesitate a minute. She went right out with me. I took a cameraman and a
few people. That's all we needed. The shot was Streisand running across
the lawn to greet Omar Sharif, who was coming home from one of his
trips. At that point in the story they had a house in the country.

"It was a good half-day's work. The funny thing about that is the first shot I made was kind of a long shot. She's looking at a tree or some flowers and she was to run towards the camera. Well, I saw her breasts bouncing all over the place. So I stopped and got her aside. I said, 'Barbra, can you do anything about that?' She said, 'Bob, I want you to know that's the way they dressed in those days. They didn't wear brassieres.' So I said, 'Well, see if you can run a little, uhm, pleasanter?'"

Sharif landed the role of Nicky Arnstein almost by accident. Wyler caught sight of him in the Columbia cafeteria one day and recommended him for the role. The tall, handsome, debonair actor was easy to spot, of course. He had already played the starring role in *Dr. Zhivago*, following his Oscar-nominated performance as Ali, the fierce but cordial Bedouin sheik in *Lawrence of Arabia*.

Nicky Arnstein was hard to cast with a top leading man because he would not get top billing and wasn't much of a role in any case. Marlon Brando and Gregory Peck turned it down. Frank Sinatra was considered. But, according to songwriter Jule Styne, who wanted him, "Stark said he was too old." David Janssen was named for the role, but Sharif ultimately got the role because he swept Streisand off her feet on their first meeting. Indeed, they would have a four-month affair during the making of *Funny Girl* which contributed to the breakup of her marriage.

Sharif later wrote in his autobiography that "Barbra's villa served as our trysting place." He "fell madly in love with her talent and her personality," not unlike Nicky Arnstein with Fanny Brice.

Wyler, who knew of his stars' off-screen romance, did not hesitate to evoke their feelings for each other in the picture. But he couldn't help being reminded of his own breakup with Maggie Sullavan thirty years earlier. "It was difficult to handle, and I admired Elliott Gould," Wyler said later. "He did it a lot better than I did." They still broke up.

The casting of Sharif also created another problem. If the studio had worried that Streisand looked "too Jewish," now it worried that Sharif was Arabic, an Egyptian of Lebanese descent. Israel had just defeated Egypt in the Six-Day War, and there was an uproar from pro-Israeli groups about the casting of a Jew and an Arab together.

When "some elements at Columbia" broached the subject of removing Sharif from the picture just as shooting got under way, Wyler wouldn't hear of it. "Not hiring an actor because he's Egyptian is outrageous," he declared. "If Omar doesn't make the film, I don't make it either."

Meanwhile, Sharif was suddenly persona non grata in Egypt. American newspapers ran a production shot of Streisand kissing Sharif on the

set. One headline read: OMAR KISSES BARBRA, EGYPT ANGRY. Streisand retorted: "Egypt angry? You should hear what my Aunt Sarah said."

If Wyler didn't get along with anybody on the set, it was the producer, whose excessive need to control the production reminded him of
Goldwyn.

"How can I say this?" Swink says. "Ray Stark wanted to look over
Willy's shoulder and find out what was going on. He ordered this to be
done and that to be done. Willy didn't work that way. Stark would ask
me to do certain things, and if I didn't think I should, I wouldn't. I used
to get notices from the production office with a copy of a letter from
Stark saying to get rid of Bob Swink. He did that a number of times. I
guess he didn't like me."

Another aspect of Stark's style, also reminiscent of Goldwyn, was his
willingness to spend money for quality. "He wasn't cheap," Wyler said.

Swink, however, thought Stark was being profligate.

"Willy," he said, "I don't know anything about budgets. But it looks to
me like they're spending an awful lot of money. They're throwing it away."

"Don't worry about it, Bob," Wyler replied. "I have a percentage of
the gross. I don't worry about it anymore." The picture was budgeted at
roughly eight and a half million dollars and reportedly reached twelve
million.

But Wyler did not forgive Stark for bad publicity and rancor on the
set. "Ray was always giving out stories about how much trouble was
happening on the set," Talli claimed. "It was as if Ray was trying to
make trouble between Willy and Barbra, when there wasn't any."

Wyler was particularly bitter that Swink didn't win the Oscar for
editing *Funny Girl* (he was nominated with the two editors who worked
under him) and blamed the producer. "That goddamned Ray Stark!"
Wyler told Swink. "He's the reason you didn't win. It's because he made
a fuss and created all that ill will."

Talli believed the negative publicity also backfired on Streisand, who
wasn't much loved in Hollywood anyway. "When it came to the Academy Awards," she said, "Barbra had to split the best-actress Oscar with
Katharine Hepburn." Nor did it help Streisand's standing with Academy voters that she was accused of having others in the cast edited out
of the picture. Anne Francis said it was so. Her own case became a *cause
célèbre*. She claimed Streisand had had her role virtually eliminated because of personal and professional jealousy. Streisand denied it. "I
thought, 'What are they talking about?' " she recalls. " 'I have no control over this film.' "

Swink also denied that she had that kind of authority. "I know the

Anne Francis role was cut down terribly," he says. "But Willy only did it for the sake of the picture. He had final cut. Streisand didn't."

There can be no doubt, however, that Streisand could influence Wyler. "I figured out how to charm him," she recalls. "It was a great lesson for me. He was like a father figure. I never had a father. I never knew how to play the charming game, you know, how to get something. But with Willy I could do it. He let me be the little girl to his daddy."

If Wyler didn't want to hear what she had to say, Streisand remembers, he would turn his deaf ear to her. So she would whisper in his good ear. "That's how I would get what I wanted. I could be charming with him. I could win him over."

Still, Wyler was no pushover. He had a formidable ego.

"The only time I ever saw a flaw in Willy's character," she says, "was when Herb [Ross] had to take over one day of dramatic-story shooting because Willy hurt his back. When he saw the dailies, he said, 'We have to reshoot it.' He wanted me to do a line over. He wanted it stronger." Streisand didn't agree, but Wyler dug in his heels. "So I did it for him. I do it my way. I do it his way. He has his choice in the editing room. But I saw his ego there. He didn't want Herb's day of filming in the film, and he had to change my performance a little bit to, you know, justify it."

Wyler also didn't give up complete control of the musical numbers. Ross staged them, but according to first assistant director Ray Gosnell, "Wyler was always there." Though Wyler didn't shoot the big numbers with the Ziegfeld girls, he reserved the right to redo the shots of Streisand's character songs. As it turned out, Wyler ended up shooting the picture's single most remarkable Streisand solo.

His notion of capturing her singing live on film hadn't proved quite as feasible as hoped. Most of the songs had to be prerecorded, after all. But when he saw Ross's close-up shots of Streisand's "My Man" solo, which was to end the picture, he thought they lacked spontaneity and feeling.

"Willy didn't like the shots at all," Swink recounts. "So he went back to film what is now the ending. She's by herself on the stage singing that last sad song. Willy did it very wisely. Very simply. He dreamed it up all of a sudden. He called everybody over to the studio. It was the last day of the shoot; everybody was going home. He got Omar Sharif to stand behind these black curtains—the whole scene was black—and he told him to talk to Streisand between takes. He wanted him around to help build up her sadness. They must've done at least ten takes. Willy shot the thing live and recorded it live. It was pretty emotional for her."

The next day, their affair at an end, Sharif and Streisand went their separate ways.

42

BLACK AND WHITE

WYLER COULD HAVE CAPPED HIS career with *Patton*. While making *Funny Girl*, he advised screenwriter James Webb and producer Frank McCarthy on the rewrite of Coppola's script and approved the first revision. David Brown, head of Twentieth's story department, sent the rewrite to Darryl Zanuck in Paris. Zanuck wired back: WHILE SOME OF COPPOLA'S SCRIPT MAY HAVE SLIGHTLY BETTER DIALOGUE, WEBB'S SCENARIO AND CONTINUITY IS FAR SUPERIOR TO ANYTHING WE HAVE HAD PREVIOUSLY. . . . DOES WYLER AGREE THAT THIS IS AN OUTSTANDING PROJECT?

He did and replied by telegram: I STILL BELIEVE, AS I ALWAYS HAVE, THAT WE HAVE THE MAKINGS OF A MOST UNUSUAL WAR STORY, DIFFERENT FROM MOST THAT HAVE BEEN MADE. IT IS WAR AS FOUGHT BY THE COMMANDING GENERALS WITH A CONFLICT OF PERSONALITIES AND DIFFERING VIEWS ON THE CONDUCT OF THE WAR RATHER THAN BATTLES IN THE FIELD. WHILE PARTS OF SOME BATTLES CAN'T BE AVOIDED, I SHOULD LIKE TO SEE THEM KEPT TO A MINIMUM.

This view meshed exactly with McCarthy's and eased Zanuck's concern about cost. He made clear that he wanted to keep to the projected ten-million-dollar budget. Meanwhile, Burt Lancaster was offered the role of Patton. McCarthy had sounded him out back in February 1967, and Lancaster was "enthusiastic over the idea of doing it with Willy early next year," the producer wrote Zanuck. "Burt will not accept anything for early 1968 without checking with us."

When the New Year rolled around, however the deterioration in Wyler's health had begun to show. Talli strongly resisted the idea of going to Spain for eight months. "I really didn't want him to do that movie," she recalled. "As much as I would have loved for him to do a picture about World War II, and as good as the script was, all I could see ahead was agony. By that time he had stomach ulcers. We had been in Spain before, and he'd gotten very sick on the food." Also, the shoot was pushed back to spring and Lancaster had to drop out. Rod Steiger was offered the role and turned it down because, as he recounts, "I got on my high horse. I thought I was a pacifist." Robert Mitchum reportedly declined. So did Lee Marvin. Next came George C. Scott.

"Willy thought he was right for the role," Swink says. "In a sense he cast Scott. He wanted him. Scott *was* Patton. He was *better* than Patton." But the prospect of working together after their run-in gave Wyler second thoughts and only added fuel to Talli's resistance. "Willy didn't need that aggravation," she said. "It was going to be very unpleasant. I've never regretted that Willy didn't do that movie. Under those circumstances? Absolutely not."

The Wylers were regarded as one of the happiest married couples in Hollywood. At this stage in their lives, that was not about to change. Willy asked to be let out of *Patton*. He made no bones about why. "My wife absolutely refused to spend eight months in Spain. Maybe if I had been younger. The physical work, aside from the intellectual work, just was not worth it."

Franklin J. Schaffner took over *Patton*. It would be a huge hit, opening in January 1970, and would go on to win seven Academy Awards, including the big three: best picture, director and actor. The screenplay also won an Oscar—not for Webb, who ultimately didn't get a credit—but for Coppola and Edmund H. North.

Patton ended up a spectacular glorification of the military, in spite of McCarthy's hope that it "would glorify neither the general nor his profession." The picture became President Nixon's favorite. Before announcing the invasion of Cambodia, he saw it several times, stoking up on its depiction of imperial, red-blooded, superpatriotic monomania. Coincidentally, a nationwide firestorm of antiwar protests broke out. At Kent State University four students were shot and killed by the National Guard, galvanizing the antiwar movement.

Wyler capped his career with another picture instead. It was derided as sociologically inaccurate and out of step, and it died at the box office. But it was a far more provocative choice than *Patton*, and a picture as close to Wyler's soul as any he had made: a militant, hard-edged, uncompromising melodrama about racism that white audiences could not tolerate. It took place in the pre–civil-rights South, but it did not offer the slick overlay of a preachy Hollywood ending, as *In the Heat of the Night* had done. It was merciless, raw and bitter, an indictment of racial injustice that stirred deep fears. One nationally syndicated columnist claimed its angry point of view would incite black youths to violence. Reviewers advised against seeing it.

The picture was adapted from Jesse Hill Ford's 1953 novel, *The Liberation of Lord Byron Jones*. Based on fact and set in rural Tennessee, it told the story of a prosperous black undertaker, Jones, whose sexually provocative wife Emma is sleeping with Willie Joe Worth, a white trash racist from the town's two-bit police force. The undertaker wants an uncontested divorce, but she won't give it to him; nor will she give up her lover. She likes playing a white man's temptress.

Jones persuades the town's wealthiest attorney, Oman Hedgepath, who runs the white power structure, to represent him. Hedgepath would rather not practice what he calls "nigger law," especially since a contested divorce involving a white co-respondent would cause an uproar. So he pressures Willy Joe to "fix things": drop his affair with Jones's wife and get her to agree to an uncontested divorce, otherwise he will face exposure in court.

Willie Joe's method of persuasion is to bully Emma and beat her up. When that doesn't work, he tries to get Jones to drop the divorce. The cuckolded undertaker refuses, sending Willie Joe into a panic. He executes Jones with a bullet to the back of the head, and his partner Bumpas mutilates the body. When Willie Joe confesses to Hedgepath and the mayor, they tell him to take the day off. Meanwhile another black man, Sonny Boy, kills Bumpas to avenge Jones's death by pushing him into a baling machine—one mutilation for another. The last we see of Sonny Boy, he is coolly leaving town on the same train that brought him there just days earlier to settle his own account with Bumpas.

Andrew Sarris, usually Wyler's harshest critic, thought the picture remarkable. He called it "the most provocative brief for Black Power ever to come out of a Hollywood studio." It was, he added, "the first American movie, either black or white, to dramatize the matter-of-fact exploitation of black women by white supremacists. Certainly it is the first American movie to countenance and even condone bloody revenge by the black against his white oppressor."

Talli recalled, "Willy always felt very strongly about bigotry and black segregation. I think he really just wanted to say his piece about all of that. But I didn't think it was a picture that would do well."

Wyler was making up, in part, for a missed opportunity with *The Negro Soldier*, the military training film Capra had offered him in 1942. He'd lost interest in it at the time, not just because he wanted to go overseas; he'd realized he wouldn't be allowed to present the reality of racial segregation as he saw it in the South. After the war, Wyler tried to acquire screen rights to a story about a black physician facing white bigotry in the North. On New Year's Eve, 1948, he urged Paramount to buy it for him:

"I see an opportunity of making a very exciting picture without the preaching usually associated with such social issues. The situation regarding the Negro has changed, as you know, in recent months. First the United States Supreme Court ruled against restrictive covenants in real estate and held that Negroes could not be barred from buying a house because of their color. Then President Truman successfully based a large part of his campaign on a firm stand in support of his Civil Rights program. These are straws in the wind, but they show definitely that the subject in my opinion is just ready for screen treatment."

Paramount didn't buy it.

When Ronald Lubin, an independent producer, brought *The Liberation of L. B. Jones* to him in 1968, Wyler was intrigued by the material. "It seemed a good story. Very powerful. Very blunt. A harsh and shocking story." When he spoke to Ford, he asked if the author was "putting it on a little thick." Ford reminded him that he had merely disguised actual events.

Wyler knew it would be a difficult sell. But he dropped his deal with Twentieth and went to Columbia, which signed him to a contract for six pictures—three to direct and three to produce. *The Liberation of L. B. Jones* would be the first. Columbia paid him six hundred thousand dollars, the largest single expenditure on the three-and-a-half-million dollar picture. The second largest went to Stirling Silliphant, who had written *In the Heat of the Night* and, with Lubin, owned the rights to *Liberation*. Silliphant received two hundred thousand dollars to write the screenplay.

Wyler wanted Henry Fonda for the role of Hedgepath, not just for his box office appeal, but to humanize what is ultimately an unsympathetic character. "Fonda was interested," Talli recalled. "He just couldn't do it when they wanted to shoot it. To get him they would have had to postpone the picture for nearly a year." Instead, the Hollywood veteran Lee J. Cobb took the role and received top billing. The real leads, however, were two black actors—Roscoe Lee Browne as L. B. Jones and Yaphet Kotto as Sonny Boy—as well as Anthony Zerbe as Willie Joe. Lola Falana made her American film debut as Emma. Barbara Hershey and Lee Majors, who were breaking into pictures from television, played a pair of minor roles.

The production was scheduled for a ten-week shoot from May to July of 1969. The first two weeks would be spent on location in and around Humboldt, Tennessee, the rest at Columbia's Gower studios and on nearby Hollywood locations. Again, Wyler's cinematographer was Robert Surtees. Swink played a larger part than ever as second-unit director. He shot the opening and closing sequences and several outdoor scenes with Yaphet Kotto.

"The interesting thing about that picture," Swink says, "is that Willy was getting old, not terribly old but just enough that I don't think he really had a lot of energy. He talked Columbia into letting him have two crews when we went down to Humboldt. That way the production guys couldn't quite figure out what he was doing. He told me he wanted me to shoot about half the film down there."

The Tennessee heat knocked Wyler off his rhythm. "He wasn't breathing very well," Swink recalls. "I'd go over to see him for lunch, and he'd be lying down on a cot." As the dailies came in, Wyler told him, "Bob, you're shooting better film than I am."

Despite the easing of official segregation in the New South, the cast and crew stayed together at a local Holiday Inn to avoid friction in the town. "We only found out later that the black actors didn't go out in the evening," Wyler recalled. "But there was no place to go anyway." Browne, a distinguished stage actor, impressed the locals as somehow "different." According to Wyler, someone approached Browne on the street and asked, "How come you don't talk like other colored folk?" To which he replied, "Because when I was young we had a white maid."

When *The Liberation of L. B. Jones* was released in March, 1970, many reviewers slammed it for drawing a picture of race prejudice that was supposed to have gone out with the Old South. *Saturday Review*'s highbrow critic lambasted it as a "sadistic melodrama" that "fairly pullulates with . . . sickening violence." He took the picture to task for not promoting interracial harmony. "It's a shame," he declared, "that a director of Wyler's stature has seen fit to perpetuate these outdated images of the

South." Apparently, the assassination of Martin Luther King, Jr., two years earlier in Memphis, Tennessee, had escaped the critic's notice.

Charles Champlin perceived the picture more clearly in the *Los Angeles Times*. "There are no punishments, no deathbed repentances," he wrote, "nothing to suggest that anything has changed or will change tomorrow." The picture told of "the ongoing, immutable and settled presumption of white superiority and black inferiority. . . . The argument for the movie is that we can only be served by the truth, unpalatable as it may be." Wyler's last picture was "part of the truth of Memphis motel balconies, the streets of Harlem or Detroit."

Several years after the picture flopped, Wyler believed in it more than ever. "If I had been a black director," he said, "it would have made a big difference. It was one of the first black pictures. It came just before the wave of black films, and black people went to see it. But it was made for white people. The whites stayed away because it made them uncomfortable. It embarrassed them. I saw it recently, and I'm highly prejudiced in its favor."

43

〰〰〰〰

Roasts and Toasts

$\mathbb{N}$OT LONG AFTER *THE LIBERATION of L. B. Jones* came out, Wyler's life changed radically. He kept trolling for new projects, but not with much enthusiasm. He had seen a well-made comedy in Paris, *Forty Carats*, and initially thought of doing it for Columbia as the second in his six-picture deal. In the summer of 1970, he fine-tuned the script, then asked Swink to scout locations for him in Mexico that fall. By then, however, Wyler knew he was bowing out. Still, it took the sudden death of his brother in January 1971 to precipitate his decision.

Robert's wife Cathy O'Donnell had succumbed to cancer eight months earlier, sending Robert into a tailspin. "He was grief-stricken," Talli said. "He never got over it." The day Robert died Willy and Talli were expecting him in Malibu. But he didn't show up. He had a massive heart attack—"alive one moment, dead the next," Talli recalled. "He never even reached the hospital. Willy was absolutely shocked. This was the trigger. He saw how fast his brother went, and he decided no more work."

Several months later Paul Kohner got him out of his contract with Columbia. Willy had confided to his oldest friend, "My doctor tells me that if I don't quit smoking I'll end up just like Bob. And I cannot stop smoking if I go to the studio. So I have the choice, either die very soon or give up pictures."

"I gave him lots of arguments," Kohner said. "But he insisted that he be freed of all commitments. He quit films right then and there."

Wyler didn't tell his associates in so many words, Swink remembers. "He would send me a script or have Kohner call me. 'Willy is trying to get a picture together that you can direct and he'll produce.'" But Wyler's idea of producing was now a form of retirement. "He thought he'd come into the studio at ten," Swink says, "look at the rushes, tell me what was wrong, have some lunch and go home."

With his career at an end, Willy and Talli began a decade of traveling. In late summer 1971, they chartered a hundred-and-twenty-foot sailboat and a crew of six for a tour of the Greek islands. Their entire family — David, Melanie, Judy and her husband, Catherine and hers — met them in Athens. One of the pleasures of the cruise was to be French cuisine. But the French chef quit just before they sailed. The captain hired the first hand he found on the streets of Piraeus, a discovery that came to light with their first meal.

"Trying to hide the food fiasco from my father, who pretended not to notice, made it all very funny," Melanie says.

For the rest of the cruise Wyler's sons-in-law supervised the kitchen. But that was just part of the comedy. Off the Turkish coast the crew refused to enter Turkish waters, claiming they had left their passports at home. The family was deposited on an offshore island with directions to a public ferry that would take them to the mainland. After seeing the ancient ruins of Ephesus, they returned to the boat and sailed back to Piraeus by way of Rhodes and Crete.

From Athens, Talli and Willy flew off by themselves to Beirut and on to Teheran, as invited guests of an international film festival. The real reason for their visit to Teheran, though, was Wyler's taste for fine caviar. "I was so looking forward to it," he said. "But it was such a disappointment. We went to this recommended restaurant and ordered the caviar blini. If it had been served to me in New York or Paris, I would have sent it back."

A little too candidly, Wyler made the comment during an interview on Iranian television. It was printed the next day in the newspapers, which caused an even greater furor. A government minister phoned them at their hotel. "I'm so glad you're still in Teheran," he said. "Are you going to be in your room a bit longer?" The solicitous sound of his voice alarmed Talli. "I thought, 'Oh God. We're going to be shot.'" Instead, a five-pound tub of caviar arrived. "It was fabulous. The best we ever ate." They took their gift with them to Afghanistan and India. "It was like traveling with an infant." Talli said. "We swaddled the tub in ice. We carried it with us everywhere. We never let it out of our sight. It killed Willy that he had to leave it behind when we got to Bangkok. Even he couldn't eat five pounds of caviar."

In subsequent years they satisfied their wanderlust by touring South America from the Amazon to Tierra del Fuego, saw the Gobi Desert in Mongolia and the Himalayas in Nepal, shuttled between Europe and the United States as though it were a brief commute, even tried to book a trip to the South Pole. "They were traveling fools," Melanie, who sometimes hitched a ride with them, says.

On an excursion to Spain to visit Peter Viertel and his wife Deborah Kerr, they were driving along the Costa del Sol when the police pulled Melanie over for speeding. Willy jumped out of the car and started taking pictures of the two officers. "Peter and Deborah were having a heart attack in the car behind us," Melanie remembers. "You didn't take pictures of Franco's police. They demanded the film. My father refused. They said they were going to arrest us. But he wouldn't give in. He was being ornery, a troublemaker to the very end." Typically, Wyler got away with his mischief. The police did not cart them off to jail, and he did not give up his film.

ALONG WITH RETIREMENT AND TRAVEL, THE LAST DECADE OF Wyler's life brought accolades, tributes, retrospectives. In 1971, the Cannes Film Festival feted him and four other directors as its most distinguished filmmakers. What tickled him more than the honor was the company he was in: Ingmar Bergman, Federico Fellini, Luis Buñuel and René Clair. Nevertheless, Wyler felt a growing sense of loss. Despite all the accolades, he believed his work was being forgotten in Hollywood, especially his early pictures from the thirties and forties. Except for a few, they were owned by Sam Goldwyn, who guarded them like family heirlooms. They were not accessible to the public, let alone to young filmmakers. Even when the television networks began leasing movies for broadcast, Goldwyn held out against the practice to maximize the commercial value of his film catalogue. And when he finally signed a deal with CBS in the mid-sixites, he restricted broadcasts to five network-owned stations for a limited number of play dates.

Wyler was delighted, therefore, when the American Film Institute chose him as the fourth recipient of its Lifetime Achievement Award. (The first three were John Ford, James Cagney and Orson Welles.) The AFI ceremony would give him a chance to pick the best clips from his movies and remind the industry of what he had done. He got his old prints out of storage and had his longtime projectionist come to Summit Drive to run them. For almost thirty years, the same projectionist had been in charge of the equipment in the booth behind Wyler's living room. "He smelled like a large cat, and our dog always went after him," Melanie remembers. "But he was the one person in the world who could run our ancient projectors."

Hooked up to the sound system through a hearing aid, Wyler sat at home with Melanie watching movies he hadn't seen in years. Some from the thirties she was seeing for the first time. Her father wanted the tribute to be "a nice evening for his friends," she says. "He just wanted them to see the clips. He didn't really care about the glamour and glory or the rest of the evening."

On March 9, 1976, twelve hundred guests thronged the Los Angeles Ballroom of the Century Plaza Hotel in Beverly Hills. CBS would televise the affair in prime time the following Sunday. Secret Service agents fanned out among the black-tie crowd to provide security for First Lady Betty Ford. Fred Astaire escorted her to Wyler's table, where she joined Talli, Audrey Hepburn, Merle Oberon, Eddie Albert, Myrna Loy, Jessamyn West and Harold Russell.

Mysteriously, Bette Davis canceled at the last moment, claiming to have a cold. But there were plenty of stars to spare. Among the actors and directors who attended were Henry Fonda, Barbra Streisand, Jimmy Stewart, Jennifer Jones, Gregory Peck, Greer Garson, Walter Pidgeon, AFI chairman Charlton Heston, Gene Kelly, Irene Dunne, Groucho Marx, Liza Minnelli, Natalie Wood, Martin Scorsese, Jack Nicholson, Frank Capra, Louis Malle, George Cukor, Milos Forman, Alan Pakula, Brian De Palma and Lee Grant.

Wyler took a lot of kidding that night. He was roasted for his legendary perfectionism and for his reputation as a painstaking taskmaster. Heston quipped that Wyler had not been asked to direct the tribute "because we're supposed to be out of this room by mid-October." He also pointed out that "praise from Willy ran the gamut from faint to nonexistent." Fonda agreed, recalling that Wyler was "damned stingy with compliments." Greer Garson mocked herself and Wyler: "Here we are, Willy, your actors cheerfully standing up in our turn like human milestones. You could call us, more properly, survivors of the Wyler Wars.

Tonight we come to praise our Caesar, not to bury him, although it's a grand opportunity." Walter Pidgeon called him "Hundred-and-Two-Take-Wyler."

Of course, he was not just roasted. The toasts were lavish, too. Fonda praised him as an artist of consummate vision, "the most versatile director ever to grace our industry." Streisand spoke of him with deep admiration, noting that the American Film Institute was honoring "an American film institution." George Stevens, Jr., cited the humanity and self-effacing beauty of Wyler's art, singling out his "ability to conceal the brush-strokes—to put the poem on the pedestal, and not the poet." Audrey Hepburn, who flew in from Rome for the occasion, recited a poem she had written for him. But it was Jessamyn West who brought down the house. The Quaker author said she had little knowledge of movie production when she met Wyler for the first time, and what she knew was chiefly based on the cliché that writers in Hollywood had to prostitute their art. But "in the nine months I worked for and with Mr. Wyler," she remarked, "I was, if prostituted, a very happy hooker."

Wyler made a brief acceptance speech. He claimed not to have understood a word of anything that had been said because he'd turned off his hearing aid. He lauded the writers and cameramen who worked on his pictures; expressed his gratitude to Carl Laemmle for taking a chance on him in the first place; and thanked Samuel Goldwyn, who had died two years earlier, for their "stormy but productive" association. He also noted that since his retirement he had discovered a new passion—making home movies. "It's a case of a professional turned amateur," he said. And "auteur" to boot. He joked that as someone fluent in French, he was "one of the few directors in Hollywood who can pronounce the word correctly." But, he added, his family showed "no appreciation for the out-of-focus and overexposed shots that would make critics jump for joy."

In truth, Wyler was putting on a good face that evening. The AFI's technical planning was so inept that one of the two giant screens flanking the ballroom didn't work at all. Half the crowd couldn't see the clips. What the other half saw on the good screen was mostly out-of-sync. Heston tried to joke about the foul-ups. "One more time," he said from the rostrum, as though asking for another take. But he, too, felt awful. "Unfortunately, this isn't even a joke," he added. Thus, despite all the camaraderie and good-natured ribbing, the evening was a letdown for Wyler. It left him "upset and disappointed," Melanie remembers. "What he cared about most went terribly wrong." Two weeks later the AFI redeemed itself by holding a month-long retrospective of sixteen Wyler films at the Kennedy Center in Washington, D.C. An even longer retro-spective, lasting two months and running to thirty films, was launched in May at the Los Angeles County Museum of Art.

The following year, for Wyler's seventy-fifth birthday, Talli invited everybody who had ever worked on any of his pictures to a huge party. "This was not just for famous stars," she said. "We tracked down whomever we could think of." Invitations, designed to look like a call sheet from Summit Films, were sent out for a picture titled *His First 75 Years*. It would star "Willy Wyler as William the Terrible" and "Talli Wyler as Mother Courage." The production call was for 1:00 P.M. on the Wyler back lot: "Ext. Garden." A mob scene was scheduled. Crowd in-structions noted: "Act as if wishing star 'character' a Happy Birthday — but don't overdo it!" There would be "unlimited takes (at the buffet & bar)." The invitation also noted: "This call-sheet good for 100th year re-takes and added scenes — 2002. Mark date. You are expected to work both calls." More than three hundred extras showed up, this time in-cluding Bette Davis. The party was done up as a county fair. There were tents and amusements, food stands ("Talli's Tamales") and lemon-ade machines filled with margaritas. A royal shrine of sorts paid homage to "William the Terrible," with photos going back to childhood.

The party marked the last phase of Wyler's life. When he wasn't trav-eling, he spent his days at the Hillcrest Country Club and the Friars Club playing gin rummy with Sam Spiegel, Mike Frankovich, Carl Foreman, Paul Kohner and other longtime friends. At night he loved going to drive-in movies. He would get rid of his hearing aid and turn up the volume on the window speaker, blasting the sound track right into his ear. Bruce Lee, the vivid "chop socky" cult hero who outfought and outwitted all opponents, was his favorite drive-in star. Lee's capers entertained him in old age as Feuillade's unbeatable Emperor of Crime had in childhood.

Wyler also found himself in the hospital with increasing frequency. His respiratory system had to be pumped regularly. His bronchial con-dition had turned asthmatic, and he was put on drugs to prevent lung spasms that could suffocate him without treatment. Wyler was diag-nosed with what has come to be called C.O.P.D., Chronic Obstructed Pulmonary Disorder. "He went from feeling not too good some of the time," Melanie recalls, "to feeling lousy all of the time. He would com-plain that he wasn't really living anymore, that he couldn't enjoy any-thing — so what was the point?"

Wyler cared, though, about keeping the record straight. Opening the *Los Angeles Times* one morning in October 1979, he was mortified to read an interview with Merle Oberon filled with self-serving, inaccurate, Goldwyn-glorifying anecdotes about *Wuthering Heights*. What upset him most was that they demeaned his directing and trivialized Olivier's performance.

Oberon was quoted as saying that she had "suffered" under Wyler. "Willy never looked at me," she complained. Directing the death scene, he purportedly said to her that he wanted more tears, specifically from the left eye. She recalled saying to him, "Thank you very much. The first bit of direction you have given me in six weeks is 'a little bit more in the left eye!'" She also claimed he fawned over her co-star. When Olivier reported to the set "made up for the Old Vic," Wyler didn't notice. It was Goldwyn, she maintained, who set things right after seeing the rushes. "Off came the makeup," she said, "out went most of the stage gestures, but not enough to make things easy." At the same time, she implied that Olivier's performance was created by Wyler in the cutting room. "They used to do take after take," she said. "In the end, Willy was cutting little pieces of film together." Which was another way of saying that Olivier had given a histrionic performance and that Wyler had had to salvage it through laboratory cobbling.

Furious at her misrepresentations, Wyler sent Oberon a note: "Belated congratulations for surviving the 'suffering' you endured forty-one years ago — and how you overcame such handicaps as no directing and 'overacting' by your co-star. . . . But that tired old story about 'more tears in the left eye' really needs a face-lift. . . . You used to speak kindly of the people you worked with. What makes you so bitchy now?" He was so angry that he mailed a copy of his note to the *Los Angeles Times* but immediately regretted doing so and asked the editor not to print it.

In all, Wyler drafted five separate letters to Oberon — and the ones he didn't send are even more revealing. He regretted, for instance, that his note had struck a spiteful tone. "I too have become bitchy in my old age," he scribbled. One of the unmailed letters noted: "Larry Olivier needs no defense from me, but the truth is, Merle, that his dynamic performance of Heathcliff is *the* most important contribution to the artistic success of *Wuthering Heights*, far more than yours or mine, and was not made by my 'putting little pieces of film together.'" He also handwrote a list that he chose not to send: "Recipients of Academy awards while 'suffering' under my direction: Bette Davis, Audrey Hepburn, Olivia de Havilland, Barbra Streisand, Greer Garson, Teresa Wright, Fay Bainter, Walter Brennan, Fredric March, Harold Russell, Burl Ives, Charlton Heston, Hugh Griffith. Merle — P. S. Sorry you're not among them."

. . .

TWO MONTHS LATER WYLER HAD AN OPERATION TO REMOVE a cancerous lung tumor. After a lengthy recuperation in the hospital, he came home feeling cheerful. The doctors predicted a vigorous recovery, although he was heavily medicated and still needed round-the-clock nursing. Within days of his release, however, his mood took a mystifying nose dive. "Suddenly he got very strange, very depressed," Talli said. "We called his doctor, but she couldn't find anything physically wrong. Finally, Willy said, 'Maybe it's the house. Let's go to Malibu.' So we moved the whole circus—the nurse, the oxygen machine, the machine to pump his lungs—and he only got worse."

Wyler lay in bed day after day in his Spanish-style bedroom overlooking the beach. He had the curtains drawn, to shut out the panoramic view of azure sky and foaming breakers. He refused to eat. He would not speak to anyone, even to Kohner, who came to see him at Talli's request. He refused all visitors. Finally, he agreed to see John Huston, who made a hurried trip from Mexico.

When Talli ushered him into the upstairs bedroom, Huston was shocked to see Willy looking so gaunt. He could read the despair in Willy's gaze. Talli sat down, facing the bed with her back to the long bank of curtained windows. Willy's hand fumbled with the bed sheet. He said nothing. Huston walked over and asked if there was anything he could do to help. Willy stirred at the question. He took Huston's hand and held it for a long time. Barely above a whisper, he broke the uncomfortable silence.

"Johnny, I don't want any more of this."

"Everyone wants you to get well."

"They won't let me die, and I want to die."

"I think you should give it one more shot. Do what they want for two weeks." Huston paused. "Then if you still feel that way, Willy, I'll help you die."

"You mean it?"

Huston assured him he did.

"That would be criminal, you know."

"Well, there are ways of getting around it."

"Promise me, Johnny."

"You have my word."

Talli was horrified by the conversation. Two days later, she insisted on taking Willy back to the hospital. "I didn't know what else to do. I was just wild to get him there."

Admitted for observation, he was taken off all his drugs and subjected to a battery of tests, including a spinal tap. But the doctors could not diagnose the problem. Meanwhile, his mood suddenly improved without any treatment. Virtually overnight he seemed more like his old self.

"I don't know what made me suspicious," Talli said. "I began to think about all the medication he'd been drenched with." She took all his prescriptions to her pharmacist and asked what they were. One turned out to be a potent tranquilizer for people suffering from epileptic seizures. "Willy was taking three or four of these a day," she said. "It turned out that we'd been given the wrong pills in a bottle labeled with the right prescription."

The hospital apologized. The prospect of having to relive the episode in court kept her from filing a suit. But she always felt that "the whole catastrophe hastened Willy's death."

44

"What an Exit"

Wyler never recovered completely, but he wouldn't give up traveling. He and Talli went to Hong Kong and Shanghai, visiting other ports along the Chinese coast as well. When they flew inland to Beijing, however, he couldn't cope with the city's dust. They had to rush to Tokyo for medical treatment. It was clear to Talli that Willy's condition was deteriorating. He was breathing with greater difficulty than ever.

That winter an invitation arrived from the British Film Institute, asking him to come to London for a retrospective of all his extant films. Sick as he felt, there was no way he would not be there. The retrospective was scheduled for the first week of June. Meanwhile, Catherine Wyler, soon to be working at the Public Broadcasting System as head of cultural and children's programming, wanted to make a feature documentary about her father.

"He didn't like the idea," she says. "Trying to convince him, I said, 'It will be fun.' He sort of looked at me as though I were crazy. He said, 'Fun for you. Work for me.' I never said that again."

Not to be deterred, Catherine went to Sam Goldwyn, Jr., and met her next obstacle—obtaining the rights to clips from her father's Goldwyn pictures. "I told Sam about the project, but he said, 'No,' " she re-members. "He always says no to everybody. So I just couldn't let that stop me." Of course, Goldwyn, Jr.'s, refusal made it much more difficult for her to finance the project. She had planned to sell off foreign rights, raising back-end money to launch the production. But without the rights to any of the Goldwyn clips, that option was dead.

Catherine changed course. She looked for public grants and private donations, a more limited and uncertain process. Goldwyn, Jr.'s, refusal also threw the whole project into doubt in terms of content. It would be ridiculous to make a documentary without showing scenes from *Wuthering Heights*, *The Best Years of Our Lives* or *The Little Foxes*. Eventually, she prevailed upon him to look at whatever she came up with in a rough cut. "Maybe if he liked it, he would give me something," she remembers thinking. At the same time, Talli had managed to soften Willy up. He agreed to be interviewed in New York on his way back from Europe.

In late May, Talli and Willy and his portable breathing machine flew to London for the retrospective. Melanie accompanied them. Before they left, Catherine hired Aviva Slesin to direct and Scott Berg to pre-pare a script. Berg was researching his biography of Goldwyn and had spoken with Wyler about his early career. Slesin was an independent filmmaker with considerable experience as a cutter and a sense of humor. In addition to documentaries, she had made film shorts for *Saturday Night Live*.

"I knew my father would be impossible if I hired a man to direct him," Catherine says. "I knew if it was a woman, he was enough of a gentleman from the old school to be polite, at least. He wouldn't have bothered with a man, which would have made everything impossible."

In London, Willy and Talli checked into the Connaught Hotel, while Melanie stayed with Doreen Hawkins, widow of Jack Hawkins, the British actor who had played Quintus Arrius in *Ben-Hur*. The retrospec-tive at the British Film Institute was a prestigious affair. Talli was "scared stiff" that Willy wouldn't make it through the opening cere-monies. "We watched him on the stage and both of us just prayed that he would last," Melanie recalls. "He was ill and he looked so awful." Among other drugs, Wyler was taking cortisone, which made his face puffy. Yet he still looked "gray, drawn and tired."

They planned to stay a couple of weeks, followed by a Scandinavian cruise. Just before their departure, Wyler went into bronchial spasms. He couldn't breathe. "There was one night I didn't know if he was going to make it," Talli said. Rushed to a specialist, Willy was less concerned about his failing health than missing the fjords. "The bottom line was that he could not be cured and could only get worse," Talli said. "So, according to the doctor, there was no reason not to take the cruise. We got on the ship and it turned out to be lovely." Returning to New York, they stopped in Oslo, Hamburg, Mulhouse and Basel, where he had another attack and was rushed to the hospital. Again they were told there was nothing to be done. As long as they did not go above six thousand feet, they were free to continue their trip. Lugging Willy's breathing machine with them, they spent a couple of weeks soaking up the beauty of the Swiss Alps near Bern.

Back in New York on July 19, they pitched camp on Manhattan's East 57th Street in a cavernous, air-conditioned apartment with a two-story living room and rested for two days. The oppressive summer heat outside rose off the asphalt. Construction workers across the street were putting up a new steel-and-concrete skycraper. Their speed intrigued him. The building was rising at the rate of a floor a day. One morning out of curiosity, he took a cab uptown to see the neighborhood where he'd lived on first coming to America some sixty years before. When the cab let him out at East Ninety-second Street, he didn't recognize the buildings on the street. The old rooming house was gone.

Catherine, Slesin and Berg made final preparations for the interview, which was to begin on Wednesday, July 22. The production crew—a cameraman and a sound man—had arrived to begin setting up. But Wyler changed his mind. "He said he didn't want to do it," Slesin recalls. "He said he never really wanted to do it. Up to the last second he was saying yes. I thought, 'My God! After all our plans he's not going to let us make the film!' "

Catherine got so angry she had to leave. She couldn't have helped anyway. There was nothing she could say to her father that she hadn't already said. Slesin continues, "Now that Willy had said no, he was quite happy. We all had breakfast in the apartment—Talli, Willy, Scott and I—and it was extremely uncomfortable. The cameraman was in the next room, waiting. It was insane."

With Catherine gone—she went to sit in a bar around the corner—Talli went to work on her stubborn husband. She was not someone who would have tried to boss him around. It never would have worked. But she could give him a piece of her mind. "I will deal with this," she said and followed him into his bedroom lair. She opened the door gently, then slammed it shut. The angry sound of muffled voices wafted into the living room. Five minutes later, Talli was back. "Willy will be out in a few moments," she announced—and he was. Talli recorded in her diary: "In the P.M. we did the first hour's shooting and taping. Difficult morning until we got started."

Difficult indeed. Even as he warmed to the task, Wyler tried to sabotage the filming. The next day he parted his hair on the wrong side, but confessed what he'd done before the second interview session began. "You would never have noticed until you got in the cutting room," he informed Slesin. She wasn't amused, but "he thought it was very funny." The second session turned out well, though, and so did the last one on Friday. "He wasn't just happy it was over," Slesin recounts. "He was exhilarated. We all had that sense. He had gotten through it, finished what he'd come to do, and now that it was over he was pleased. There was the feeling of accomplishment."

On Saturday—Catherine's birthday—they went to dinner. Wyler also threw a birthday brunch Sunday morning at the Russian Tea Room, and that afternoon he and Talli flew home to Beverly Hills. She would never forget: "Willy walked in the door, looked around and said, 'Now what'll we do?' I said, 'Come on, Willy, we'll think about that tomorrow.'" The next morning—Monday, July 27, 1981—he went to his study and began opening two months' worth of mail; she unpacked. At lunchtime he ate at his desk; she went to take a nap. She drew the shade in her room. But before lying down, she felt the urge to peek in on him.

When she did, her heart turned over. Willy was slumped in his chair. His face was red. He was gasping for air, couldn't speak. She rushed to him. With one arm she held him up, and with the other she dialed for an ambulance. The paramedics showed up within five minutes. But by then, Willy had stopped breathing. They laid his body on the floor and tried to bring him back. Talli screamed, "Don't be too heroic!" She was terrified that Willy might be revived with brain damage from lack of oxygen. Worse, they might bring him back in a coma, and he'd be trapped in the limbo of life-support machines.

In any case, the paramedics couldn't get his heart beating. Willy was pronounced dead at 2:28 P.M. Years later, recounting his death, Talli was grateful for the way it happened. He had died swiftly, almost instantaneously. "What a great exit," she said. "We'd made the trip, and he died on an upbeat."

There was a private funeral at Forest Lawn—simple and short. Willy was laid to rest next to his infant son Billy, his brother and his brother's wife. The Wyler children made certain their father was not buried in a suit and tie, which he seldom wore, but in the loose-fitting clothes he liked: open at the neck, made of soft fabric and covered with pockets.

A memorial service followed at the Directors Guild of America. The auditorium in the old DGA building on Sunset near Laurel was packed with a large crowd—more than five hundred friends and admirers—that overflowed into the lobby. Catherine and David Wyler spoke for the family. John Huston, clearly broken up, decided to skip his prepared remarks. He spoke briefly, perhaps thirty seconds, and walked sadly away. In the third row from the rear, Bette Davis sat with Roddy McDowall. "This entire town should be at half-mast," she told him. "When the king dies, *all* the flags are at half-mast." After the memorial, Talli held an open house at Summit Drive. It was a warm, sunny day. People were mingling by the pool when Davis made her entrance. "She caused a stir," Berg recounts. "It was a big deal. This was a big display for her. Talli seemed moved. It meant a lot to have Bette Davis there, because it said a lot about Willy."

Davis tugged Talli by the sleeve and they went off to a corner of the dining room by the kitchen, where they had a tête-à-tête for nearly half an hour. When everybody had gone, Catherine asked her mother what they had spoken about. "She told me they talked about my father, what they enjoyed about him. My mother said she and Bette had never really talked to each other. Bette was always the star, and she was always the wife—very different roles." Davis confided later to a friend that she told Talli, "Here we are, the two women who loved him most. I want you to know that after you married him, Willy and I never had anything to do with each other."

It was Philip Dunne's eulogy earlier that afternoon at the Directors Guild, however, that moved Talli most. "Talent," he said, "doesn't care whom it happens to. Sometimes it happens to rather dreadful people. In Willy's case, it happened to the best of us. I remember my daughter, then aged nine, running down the hall to shout to her sisters: 'Willy's coming to dinner! Willy's coming to dinner!' Not Mr. Wyler—Willy."

That, Talli said, told it all.

FILMOGRAPHY

William Wyler directed thirty-two major motion pictures and shared credit on one, in addition to directing twenty-one silent Westerns in Universal Pictures' Mustang series (about twenty-four minutes each), six silent Westerns in its Blue Streak series (about an hour each), two silent Western features (roughly an hour each), three full-length silent features (roughly an hour and a half each, of which two had talking sequences), Universal's first outdoor talkie (also released as a silent), two World War II Air Force documentaries, and one live television drama. Release dates listed.

SILENT WESTERNS

Two-reelers in Universal's Mustang Series

Crook Buster (December 1925), *The Gunless Badman* (March 1926), *Ridin' for Love* (April 1926), *The Fire Barrier* (June 1926), *Don't Shoot* (August 1926), *The Pinnacle Rider* (October 1926), *Martin of the Mounted* (December 1926), *The Two Fister* (January 1927), *Kelcy Gets His Man* (February 1927), *Tenderfoot Courage* (February 1927), *The Silent Partner* (March 1927), *Galloping Justice* (April 1927), *The Haunted Homestead* (April 1927), *The Lone Star* (May 1927), *The Ore Raiders* (May 1927), *The Home Trail* (June 1927), *Gun Justice* (July 1927), *The Phantom Outlaw* (July 1927), *The Square Shooter* (August 1927), *The Horse Trader* (August 1927), *Daze of The West* (September 1927).

Five-reelers in Universal's Blue Streak Series

Lazy Lightning (December 1926), *The Stolen Ranch* (December 1926), *Blazing Days* (March 1927), *Hard Fists* (April 1927), *The Border Cavalier* (September 1927), *Straight Shootin'* (October 1927).

Universal Five-reel Silent Westerns

Desert Dust (December 1927), *Thunder Riders* (April 1928).

SILENT FEATURES

Anybody Here Seen Kelly?
(September 1928, Universal)

Producer: Robert Wyler. Scenario: John B. Clymer. Titles: Walter Anthony and Albert De Mond. Story: Leigh Jason. Photography: Charles Stumar. Editor: George McGuire. Cast: Bessie Love, Tom Moore, Kay Price, Addie McPhail, Bruce Gordon, Alfred Allen, Tom O'Brien.

The Shakedown
(March 1929, Universal)

Also released with talking sequences. Scenario: Charles A. Logue and Clarence Marks. Titles and dialogue: Albert De Mond. Story: Charles A. Logue. Photography: Charles Stumar and Jerome Ash. Editors: Lloyd Nosler and Richard Cahoon. Cast: James Murray, Barbara Kent, Jack Hanlon.

The Love Trap
(August 1929, Universal)

Also with talking sequences. Scenario: John B. Clymer and Clarence Marks. Story: Edward J. Montagne. Titles: Albert De Mond. Dialogue: Clarence Thompson. Photography: Gilbert Warrenton. Editor: Maurice Pivar. Cast: Laura La Plante, Neil Hamilton, Robert Ellis, Jocelyn Lee, Norman Trevor, Clarissa Selwynne, Rita LeRoy.

SOUND FEATURES

Hell's Heroes
(January 1930, Universal)

Also released as a silent. Screenplay and dialogue: Tom Reed, based on the novel *The Three Godfathers* by Peter B. Kyne. Photography: George Robinson. Editor (sound): Harry Marker. Editor (silent): William Boyce and Earl Neville. Cast: Charles Bickford, Raymond Hatton, Fred Kohler, Fritzi Ridgeway, Maria Alba, José de la Cruz, Buck Conners, Walter James.

The Storm
(August 1930, Universal)

Dialogue: Wells Root, based on the play by Langdon McCormick. Adaptation: Charles A. Logue. Photography: Alvin Wyckoff. Cast: Lupe Velez, Paul Cavanagh, William Boyd, Alphonz Ethier, Ernie S. Adams.

A House Divided
(December 1931, Universal)

Producer: Carl Laemmle, Jr. Screenplay: John B. Clymer and Dale Van Every, based on the story "Heart and Hand" by Olive Edens. Dialogue: John Huston. Photography: Charles Stumar. Editor: Ted Kent. Cast: Walter Huston, Kent Douglass, Helen Chandler, Vivian Oakland, Lloyd Ingraham, Charles Middleton, Frank Hagney, Mary Foy.

Tom Brown of Culver
(July 1932, Universal)

Screenplay: George Green and Tom Buckingham. Photography: Charles Stumar. Editor: Ted Kent. Cast: Tom Brown, H. B. Warner, Slim Summerville, Richard Cromwell, Ben Alexander, Sidney Toler, Russell Hopton, Andy Devine, Willard Robertson, Tyrone Power, Jr.

Her First Mate
(August 1933, Universal)

Producer: Carl Laemmle, Jr. Screenplay: Earl Snell and Clarence Marks, based on the play *Salt Water* by Dan Jarrett, Frank Craven, and John Golden. Dialogue: Dan Jarrett. Photography: George Robinson. Editor: Ted Kent. Cast: Slim Summerville, Zasu Pitts, Una Merkel, Warren Hymer, Henry Armetta, Berton Churchill, George Marion.

Counsellor-at-Law
(December 1933, Universal)

Producer: Henry Henigson. Screenplay: Elmer Rice, adapted from his play. Photography: Norbert Brodine. Editor: Daniel Mandell. Art direction: Charles D. Hall. Cast: John Barrymore, Bebe Daniels, Doris Kenyon, Onslow Stevens, Isabel Jewell, Melvyn Douglas, Thelma Todd, Mayo Methot, Marvin Kline, Conway Washburne, John Qualen, Bobby Gordon, John Hammond Dailey, Malka Kornstein, Angela Jacobs, Clara Langsner, T. H. Manning, Elmer Brown, Barbara Perry, Richard Quine, Victor Adams, Frederic Burton, Vincent Sherman.

Glamour
(April 1934, Universal)

Adaptation: Doris Anderson, based on the short story by Edna Ferber. Continuity: Gladys Unger. Photography: George Robinson. Editor: Ted Kent. Art direction: Charles D. Hall. Cast: Paul Lukas, Constance Cummings, Philip Reed, Joseph Cawthorne, Doris Lloyd, Lyman Williams, David Dickinson, Peggy Campbell, Olaf Hytten, Alice Lake, Lita Chevret, Phil Reed, Luis Alberni, Yola D'Avril, Grace Hayle, Wilson Benge.

The Good Fairy
(January 1935, Universal)

Producer: Carl Laemmle, Jr. Screenplay: Preston Sturges, based on the play by Ferenc Molnár. Photography: Norbert Brodine. Editor: Daniel Mandell. Art direction: Charles D. Hall. Cast: Margaret Sullavan, Herbert Marshall, Frank Morgan, Reginald Owen, Alan Hale, Beulah Bondi, Cesar Romero, Eric Blore.

The Gay Deception
(October 1935, Twentieth Century-Fox)

Producer: Jesse L. Lasky. Screenplay: Stephen Avery and Don Hartman. Photography: Joseph Valentine. Art director: Max Parker. Cast: Francis Lederer, Frances Dee, Benita Hume, Alan Mowbray, Paul Hurst, Ferdinand Gottschalk, Richard Carle, Lenita Lane, Lennox Pawle, Adele St. Maur, Lionel Stander, Akim Tamiroff, Barbara Fritchie.

These Three
(March 1936, Samuel Goldwyn)

Producer: Samuel Goldwyn. Screenplay: Lillian Hellman, based on her play *The Children's Hour*. Photography: Gregg Toland. Editor: Daniel Mandell. Art direction: Richard Day. Costumes: Omar Kiam. Music: Alfred Newman. Cast: Miriam Hopkins, Merle Oberon, Joel McCrea, Catherine Doucet, Alma Kruger, Bonita Granville, Marcia Mae Jones, Carmencita Johnson, Margaret Hamilton, Marie Louise Cooper.

Dodsworth
(September 1936, Samuel Goldwyn)

Producer: Samuel Goldwyn. Screenplay: Sidney Howard, based on his play and the novel by Sinclair Lewis. Photography: Rudolph Maté. Editor: Daniel Mandell. Art direction: Richard Day. Costumes: Omar Kiam. Music: Alfred Newman. Cast: Walter Huston, Ruth Chatterton, Paul Lukas, Mary Astor, David Niven, Gregory Gaye, Maria Ouspenskaya, Odette Myrtil, Kathryn Marlowe, John Payne, Spring Byington, Harlan Briggs.

Come and Get It
(November 1936, Samuel Goldwyn)

Shared directing credit: Howard Hawks and William Wyler. Screenplay: Jules Furthman and Jane Murfin, based on the novel by Edna Ferber. Photography: Gregg Toland and Rudolph Maté. Editor: Edward Curtiss. Art direction: Richard Day. Set decoration: Julia Heron. Costumes: Omar Kiam. Music: Alfred Newman. Cast: Edward Arnold, Joel McCrea, Frances Farmer, Walter Brennan, Andrea Leeds, Frank Shields, Mady Christians, Mary Nash, Clem Bevans, Edwin Maxwell, Cecil Cunningham, Rollo Lloyd, Charles Halton.

Dead End
(August 1937, Samuel Goldwyn)

Producer: Samuel Goldwyn. Screenplay: Lillian Hellman, based on the play by Sidney Kingsley. Photography: Gregg Toland. Editor: Daniel Mandell. Art direction: Richard Day. Set decoration: Julia Heron. Costumes: Omar Kiam. Music: Alfred Newman. Cast: Sylvia Sidney, Joel McCrea, Humphrey Bogart, Wendy Barrie, Claire Trevor, Allen Jenkins, Marjorie Main, Billy Halop, Huntz Hall, Bobby Jordan, Leo Gorcey, Gabriel Dell, Bernard Punsly, Charles Peck, Minor Watson, James Burke, Ward Bond, Elizabeth Risdon, Esther Dale, George Humbert, Marcelle Corday, Charles Halton.

Jezebel
(March 1938, Warner Bros.)

Producer: William Wyler. Executive producer: Hal B. Wallis. Associate producer: Henry Blanke. Screenplay: Clements Ripley, Abem Finkel, and John Huston, based on the play by Owen Davis, Sr. Photography: Ernest Haller. Editor: Warren Low. Art direction: Robert Haas. Costumes: Orry-Kelly. Music: Max Steiner. Cast: Bette Davis, Henry Fonda, George Brent, Margaret Lindsay, Donald Crisp, Fay Bainter, Richard Cromwell, Henry O'Neill, Spring Byington, John Litel, Gordon Oliver, Janet Shaw, Theresa Harris, Margaret Early, Irving Pichel, Eddie Anderson, Stymie Beard, Lou Payton.

Wuthering Heights
(April 1939, Samuel Goldwyn)

Producer: Samuel Goldwyn. Screenplay: Ben Hecht and Charles MacArthur, from the novel by Emily Brontë. Photography: Gregg Toland. Editor: Daniel Mandell. Art direction: James Basevi. Set decoration: Julia Heron. Costumes: Omar Kiam. Music: Alfred Newman. Cast: Merle Oberon, Laurence Olivier, David Niven, Flora Robson, Donald Crisp, Hugh Williams, Geraldine Fitzgerald, Leo G. Carroll, Cecil Humphreys, Miles Mander, Cecil Kellaway.
New York Film Critics Award: best picture

The Westerner
(September 1940, Samuel Goldwyn)

Producer: Samuel Goldwyn. Screenplay: Jo Swerling and Niven Busch, based on the story by Stuart N. Lake. Photography: Gregg Toland. Editor: Daniel Mandell. Art direction: James Basevi. Set decoration: Julia Heron. Costumes: Irene Saltern. Music: Dimitri Tiomkin (Alfred Newman, uncredited). Cast: Gary Cooper, Walter Brennan, Doris Davenport, Fred Stone, Forrest Tucker, Lilian Bond, Paul Hurst, Chill Wills, Charles Halton, Tom Tyler, Dana Andrews, Lupita Tovar.

The Letter
(November 1940, Warner Bros./First National)

Executive producer: Hal B. Wallis. Associate producer: Robert Lord. Screenplay: Howard Koch, based on the play by W. Somerset Maugham. Photography: Tony Gaudio. Editors: George Amy and Warren Low. Art direction: Carl Jules Weyl. Costumes: Orry-Kelly. Music:

Max Steiner. Cast: Bette Davis, Herbert Marshall, James Stephenson, Frieda Inescort, Gale Sondergaard, Bruce Lester, Elizabeth Earl, Cecil Kellaway, Sen Yung, Doris Lloyd.

The Little Foxes
(August 1941, Samuel Goldwyn)

Producer: Samuel Goldwyn. Screenplay: Lillian Hellman, based on her play. Photography: Gregg Toland. Editor: Daniel Mandell. Art direction: Stephen Goosson. Set decoration: Howard Bristol. Costumes: Orry-Kelly. Music: Meredith Willson. Cast: Bette Davis, Herbert Marshall, Teresa Wright, Richard Carlson, Patricia Collinge, Dan Duryea, Charles Dingle, Carl Benton Reid, John Marriott, Jessie Grayson, Russell Hicks, Lucien Littlefield, Virginia Brissac.

Mrs. Miniver
(May 1942, Metro-Goldwyn-Mayer)

Producer: Sidney Franklin. Screenplay: Arthur Wimperis, George Froeschel, James Hilton, and Claudine West, based on the book by Jan Struther. Photography: Joseph Ruttenberg. Editor: Harold F. Kress. Art direction: Cedric Gibbons. Set decoration: Edwin B. Willis. Cast: Greer Garson, Walter Pidgeon, Teresa Wright, Dame May Whitty, Reginald Owen, Henry Travers, Richard Ney, Henry Wilcoxon, Christopher Severn, Brenda Forbes, Clare Sandars, Marie de Becker, Helmut Dantine, John Abbott, Connie Leon, Rhys William, Mary Field, Ben Webster.

The Memphis Belle
(A Story of a Flying Fortress)
(April 1944 U.S. 8th Air Force Photographic Section, in cooperation with Army Air Forces First Motion Picture Unit, released by Paramount)

Producer: William Wyler. Photography: William Clothier, Harold Tannenbaum, William Wyler (all uncredited). Editor: Lynn Harrison. Music: Gail Kubik. Narration: Lester Koenig. Narrators: Eugene Kern and John Beal.

Thunderbolt
(July 1947, U.S. Air Force and Carl Krueger Productions, released by Monogram)

Producer: William Wyler. Directing and editing: William Wyler and John Sturges. Script: Lester Koenig. Music: Gail Kubik. Introduced by: James Stewart. Narrators: Eugene Kern and Lloyd Bridges.

The Best Years of Our Lives
(November 1946, Samuel Goldwyn)

Producer: Samuel Goldwyn. Screenplay: Robert E. Sherwood, based on the novel *Glory for Me* by MacKinlay Kantor. Photography: Gregg Toland. Editor: Daniel Mandell. Art direction: George Jenkins and Perry Ferguson. Set decoration: Julia Heron. Costumes: Irene Sharaff. Music: Hugo Friedhofer. Production assistant: Lester Koenig. Cast: Myrna Loy, Fredric March, Dana Andrews, Teresa Wright, Virginia Mayo, Cathy O'Donnell, Hoagy Carmichael, Harold Russell, Gladys George, Roman Bohnen, Ray Collins, Steve Cochran, Minna Gombell, Walter Baldwin, Dorothy Adams, Don Beddoe, Victor Cutler, Erskine Sanford, Marlene Aames, Michael Hall, Charles Halton, Ray Teal, Howland Chamberlin, Dean White, Ralph Sanford.
New York Film Critics Award: best picture

The Heiress
(October 1949, Paramount)

Producer: William Wyler. Associate producers: Lester Koenig and Robert Wyler. Screenplay: Ruth and Augustus Goetz, based on their play suggested by the Henry James novel *Washington Square*. Photography: Leo Tover. Editor: William Hornbeck. Production design: Harry Horner. Art direction: John Meehan. Set decoration: Emile Kuri. Costumes: Edith Head. Men's Wardrobe: Gile Steele. Music: Aaron Copland. Cast: Olivia de Havilland, Ralph Richardson, Montgomery Clift, Miriam Hopkins, Mona Freeman, Vanessa Brown, Selena Royle, Ray Collins, Betty Linley, Paul Lees, Harry Antrim, Russ Conway, Davis Thursby, Harry Pipe.

Detective Story
(November 1951, Paramount)

Producer: William Wyler. Associate producers: Robert Wyler and Lester Koenig. Screenplay: Philip Yordan and Robert Wyler, based on the play by Sidney Kingsley. Photography: Lee Garmes. Editor: Robert Swink. Art direction: Hal Pereira and Earl Hedrick. Set decoration: Emile Kuri. Costumes: Edith Head. Cast: Kirk Douglas, Eleanor Parker, William Bendix, Cathy O'Donnell, Bert Freed, Frank Faylen, William Phillips, Grandon Rhodes, Luis Van Rooten, Craig Hill, Lee Grant, Horace McMahon,

Warner Anderson, George Macready, Joseph Wiseman, Michael Strong, Russell Evans, Howard Joslyn, Gladys George, Burt Mustin, Gerald Mohr, James Maloney, Edmund F. Cobb, Mike Mahoney, Catherine Doucet.

Carrie
(July 1952, Paramount)

Producer: William Wyler. Associate producer: Lester Koenig. Screenplay: Ruth and Augustus Goetz, based on the novel *Sister Carrie* by Theodore Dreiser. Photography: Victor Milner. Editor: Robert Swink. Art direction: Hal Pereira and Roland Anderson. Set decoration: Emile Kuri. Costumes: Edith Head. Music: David Raksin. Cast: Laurence Olivier, Jennifer Jones, Miriam Hopkins, Eddie Albert, Basil Ruysdael, Ray Teal, Barry Kelley, Sara Berner, William Reynolds, Mary Murphy, Harry Hayden.

Roman Holiday
(August 1953, Paramount)

Producer: William Wyler. Associate producer: Robert Wyler. Screenplay: Ian McLellan Hunter and John Dighton, based on the story by Ian McLellan Hunter (Dalton Trumbo, uncredited). Photography: Franz F. Planer and Henri Alekan. Editor: Robert Swink. Art direction: Hal Pereira and Walter Tyler. Costumes: Edith Head. Music score: Georges Auric. Cast: Gregory Peck, Audrey Hepburn, Eddie Albert, Hartley Power, Harcourt Williams, Margaret Rawlings, Tullio Carminati, Paolo Carlini, Claudio Ermelli.
*Directors Guild Award nomination:
best director*

The Desperate Hours
(October 1955, Paramount)

Producer: William Wyler. Associate producer: Robert Wyler. Screenplay: Joseph Hayes, based on his novel and play. Photography: Lee Garmes. Editor: Robert Swink. Art direction: Hal Pereira and Joseph MacMillan Johnson. Costumes: Edith Head. Music: Gail Kubik. Cast: Humphrey Bogart, Fredric March, Arthur Kennedy, Martha Scott, Dewey Martin, Robert Middleton, Richard Eyer, Gig Young, Mary Murphy.

The Letter
(October 1956, "Producer's Showcase," NBC)

A live television remake of the 1940 movie *The Letter.* Cast: Siobhan McKenna, John Mills, Michael Rennie, Anna May Wong.

Friendly Persuasion
(November 1956, Allied Artists)

Producer: William Wyler. Associate producer: Robert Wyler. Screenplay: Jessamyn West, Robert Wyler, and Michael Wilson (all uncredited), based on the collected stories *The Friendly Persuasion*, by Jessamyn West. Photography: Ellsworth Fredricks. Editors: Robert Swink, Edward A. Biery, and Robert A. Belcher. Art direction: Edward S. Haworth. Set decoration: Joe Kish. Costumes: Dorothy Jeakins. Music: Dimitri Tiomkin. Assistant to the producer: Stuart Millar. Cast: Gary Cooper, Dorothy McGuire, Marjorie Main, Anthony Perkins, Richard Eyer, Robert Middleton, Phyllis Love, Mark Richman, Walter Catlett, Joel Fluellen, Richard Hale, Theodore Newton, John Smith.
*Palme d'Or, Cannes Film Festival:
best picture*

*Directors Guild Award nomination:
best director*

The Big Country
(October 1958, Anthony-Worldwide Productions)

Producers: William Wyler and Gregory Peck. Associate producer: Robert Wyler. Screenplay: James R. Webb, Sy Bartlett, and Robert Wilder. Adaptation: Jessamyn West and Robert Wyler, based on the *Saturday Evening Post* serial "Ambush in Blanco Canyon" by Donald Hamilton. Photography: Franz Planer. Supervising editor: Robert Swink. Editors: Robert Belcher and John Faure. Art direction: Frank Hotaling. Set decoration: Edward G. Boyle. Music: Jerome Moross. Cast: Gregory Peck, Jean Simmons, Carroll Baker, Charlton Heston, Burl Ives, Charles Bickford, Alfonso Bedoya, Chuck Connors.
*Directors Guild Award nomination:
best director*

Ben-Hur
(November 1959, Metro-Goldwyn-Mayer)

Producer: Sam Zimbalist. Screenplay: Karl Tunberg (Christopher Fry, uncredited), based on the novel by Lew Wallace. Photography: Robert L. Surtees. Second unit directors: Andrew Marton, Yakima Canutt, and Mario Soldati. Editors: Ralph E. Winters and John D. Dunning. Art direction: William A. Horning and Edward Carfagno. Set decoration: Hugh Hunt. Costumes: Elizabeth Haffenden. Music: Miklos Rozsa. Sound: Franklin Milton. Cast: Charlton Heston, Jack Hawkins, Stephen Boyd, Haya Harareet, Hugh Griffith, Martha Scott, Sam Jaffe, Cathy O'Donnell, Finlay Currie, Frank Thring, Terence Longden, Andre Morell, Marina Berti, George Relph, Adi Berber, Laurence Payne.
New York Film Critics Award: best picture

Directors Guild Award: best director

The Children's Hour
(December 1961, Mirisch–World Wide Productions)

Producer: William Wyler. Associate producer: Robert Wyler. Screenplay: John Michael Hayes. Adaptation: Lillian Hellman, based on her play. Photography: Franz Planer. Editor: Robert Swink. Art direction: Fernando Carrere. Set decoration: Edward G. Boyle. Costumes: Dorothy Jeakins. Music: Alex North. Cast: Audrey Hepburn, Shirley MacLaine, James Garner, Miriam Hopkins, Fay Bainter, Karen Balkin, Veronica Cartwright.
Directors Guild Award nomination: best director

The Collector
(June 1965, Columbia)

Producers: Jud Kinberg and John Kohn. Screenplay: Stanley Mann and John Kohn, based on the novel by John Fowles. Art direction: John Stoll. Editor and second unit director: Robert Swink. Photography: Robert Surtees in Hollywood and Robert Krasker in England.

Music: Maurice Jarre. Cast: Terence Stamp, Samantha Eggar, Mona Washbourne, Maurice Dallimore.

How to Steal a Million
(July 1966, Twentieth Century–Fox)

Producer: Fred Kohlmar. Screenplay: Harry Kurnitz, based on the story "Venus Rising" by George Bradshaw. Photography: Charles Lang. Editor and second unit director: Robert Swink. Production design: Alexander Trauner. Music: Johnny Williams. Cast: Audrey Hepburn, Peter O'Toole, Eli Wallach, Hugh Griffith, Charles Boyer, Fernand Gravey, Marcel Dalio.

Funny Girl
(September 1968, Rastar, Columbia)

Producer: Ray Stark. Screenplay: Isobel Lennart, based on her musical play. Photography: Harry Stradling. Supervising editor: Robert Swink. Editors: Maury Winetrobe and William Sands. Art direction: Robert Luthardt. Set decoration: William Kiernan. Musical numbers directed by Herbert Ross. Music supervisor and conductor: Walter Scharf. Cast: Barbra Streisand, Omar Sharif, Kay Medford, Anne Francis, Walter Pidgeon, Lee Allen, Mae Questel, Gerald Mohr, Frank Faylen, Mittie Lawrence, Gertrude Flynn, Penny Santon.
Directors Guild Award nomination: best director

The Liberation of L. B. Jones
(March 1970, Columbia)

Producer: Ronald Lubin. Screenplay: Stirling Silliphant and Jesse Hill Ford, based on the novel by Jesse Hill Ford. Photography: Robert Surtees. Supervising film editor and second unit director: Robert Swink. Art direction: Kenneth Reid. Set decoration: Frank Tuttle. Music: Elmer Bernstein. Cast: Lee J. Cobb, Anthony Zerbe, Roscoe Lee Browne, Lola Falana, Lee Majors, Barbara Hershey, Yaphet Kotto, Arch Johnson, Chill Wills, Zara Cully, Fayard Nicholas, Lauren Jones, Dub Taylor, Ray Teal, Joseph Attles, Brenda Sykes.

ACADEMY AWARDS

Nominations and Winners

William Wyler won three Academy Awards for directing, on twelve nominations, and received three nominations for producing. His pictures won thirty-eight Academy Awards on one hundred twenty-seven nominations (half in best picture, director and actor categories). These are record numbers, roughly twice what any other director's pictures have earned. He also guided more actors to Academy Awards than anyone by far: thirteen out of thirty-five nominations.

The nominations are listed below, with winners given in boldface type.

1935
The Gay Deception

1. Screenplay (Don Hartman and Stephen Avery)

1936
These Three

1. Supporting actress (Bonita Granville)

Dodsworth

1. Picture
2. Actor (Walter Huston)
3. Supporting actress (Maria Ouspenskaya)
4. Director
5. Screenplay (Sidney Howard)
6. **Art decoration (Richard Day)**
7. Sound recording (Oscar Lagerstrom)

Come and Get It

1. **Supporting actor (Walter Brennan)**
2. Film editing (Edward Curtiss)

1937
Dead End

1. Picture
2. Supporting actress (Claire Trevor)
3. Cinematography (Gregg Toland)
4. Art decoration (Richard Day)

1938
Jezebel

1. Picture
2. **Actress (Bette Davis)**
3. **Supporting actress (Fay Bainter)**
4. Cinematography (Ernest Haller)
5. Musical Score (Max Steiner)

1939
Wuthering Heights

1. Picture
2. Actor (Laurence Olivier)
3. Supporting actress (Geraldine Fitzgerald)
4. Director
5. Screenplay (Ben Hecht and Charles MacArthur)
6. **Cinematography (Gregg Toland)**
7. Art decoration (James Basevi)
8. Original score (Alfred Newman)

1940
The Westerner

1. **Supporting actor (Walter Brennan)**
2. Original story (Stuart N. Lake)
3. Art decoration (James Basevi)

The Letter

1. Picture
2. Actress (Bette Davis)
3. Supporting actor (James Stephenson)
4. Director
5. Cinematography (Tony Gaudio)

6. Original score (Max Steiner)
7. Film editing (Warren Low)

1941
The Little Foxes

1. Picture
2. Actress (Bette Davis)
3. Supporting actress (Teresa Wright)
4. Supporting actress (Patricia Collinge)
5. Director
6. Screenplay (Lillian Hellman)
7. Art decoration (Stephen Goosson, Howard Bristol)
8. Musical scoring (Meredith Willson)
9. Film editing (Daniel Mandell)

1942
Mrs. Miniver

1. **Picture**
2. Actor (Walter Pidgeon)
3. **Actress (Greer Garson)**
4. Supporting actor (Henry Travers)
5. **Supporting actress (Teresa Wright)**
6. Supporting actress (Dame May Whitty)
7. **Director**
8. **Screenplay (George Froeschel, James Hilton, Claudine West, Arthur Wimperis)**
9. **Cinematography (Joseph Ruttenberg)**
10. Sound recording (Douglas Shearer)
11. Film editing (Harold F. Kress)
12. Special effects (A. Arnold Gillespie, Warren Newcombe, Douglas Shearer)

1946
The Best Years of Our Lives

1. **Picture**
2. **Actor (Fredric March)**
3. **Supporting actor (Harold Russell)**
4. **Director**
5. **Screenplay (Robert E. Sherwood)**
6. Sound recording (Gordon Sawyer)
7. **Musical scoring (Hugo Friedhofer)**
8. **Film editing (Daniel Mandell)**

1949
The Heiress

1. Picture
2. **Actress (Olivia de Havilland)**
3. Supporting actor (Ralph Richardson)
4. Director
5. Cinematography (Leo Tover)

6. **Art direction/set decoration (John Meehan and Harry Horner; Emile Kuri)**
7. **Musical scoring (Aaron Copland)**
8. **Costume design (Edith Head and Gile Steele)**

1951
Detective Story

1. Actress (Eleanor Parker)
2. Supporting actress (Lee Grant)
3. Director
4. Screenplay (Philip Yordan and Robert Wyler)

1952
Carrie

1. Art direction/set decoration (Hal Pereira and Roland Anderson; Emil Kuri)
2. Costume design (Edith Head)

1953
Roman Holiday

1. Picture
2. **Actress (Audrey Hepburn)**
3. Supporting actor (Eddie Albert)
4. Director
5. **Writing [story] (Ian McLellan Hunter)**
   Actual author was the blacklisted Dalton Trumbo.
6. Screenplay (Ian McLellan Hunter and John Dighton)
7. Cinematography (Franz F. Planer and Henri Alekan)
8. Art direction/set decoration (Hal Pereira and Walter Tyler)
9. Film editing (Robert Swink)
10. **Costume design (Edith Head)**

1956
Friendly Persuasion

1. Picture
2. Supporting actor (Anthony Perkins)
3. Director
4. Screenplay (Michael Wilson; ineligible for nomination under Academy blacklisting)
5. Sound recording (Gordon R. Glennan and Gordon Sawyer)
6. Song (Music by Dimitri Tiomkin, lyrics by Paul Francis Webster)

1958
The Big Country

1. **Supporting actor (Burl Ives)**
2. Musical scoring (Jerome Moross)

1959
Ben-Hur

1. **Picture**
2. **Actor (Charlton Heston)**
3. **Supporting actor (Hugh Griffith)**
4. **Director**
5. Screenplay based on material from another medium (Karl Tunberg)
6. **Cinematography (Robert L. Surtees)**
7. **Art direction/set direction (William A. Horning and Edward Carfagno; Hugh Hunt)**
8. **Sound (Frank E. Milton)**
9. **Musical scoring (Miklos Rozsa)**
10. **Film editing (Ralph E. Winters and John D. Dunning)**
11. **Costume design (Elizabeth Haffenden)**
12. **Special effects (A. Arnold Gillespie and Robert MacDonald; Milo Lory)**

1961
The Children's Hour

1. Supporting actress (Fay Bainter)
2. Cinematography (Franz F. Planer)
3. Art direction/set direction (Fernando Carrere; Edward G. Boyle)

4. Sound (Gordon Sawyer)
5. Costume design (Dorothy Jeakins)

1965
The Collector

1. Actress (Samantha Eggar)
2. Director
3. Screenplay based on material from another medium (Stanley Mann and John Kohn)

1968
Funny Girl

1. Picture
2. **Actress (Barbra Streisand)**
3. Supporting actress (Kay Medford)
4. Cinematography (Harry Stradling)
5. Sound (Columbia Studio Sound Department)
6. Song (Music by Jule Styne, lyrics by Bob Merrill)
7. Score (Walter Scharf)
8. Film editing (Robert Swink, Maury Winetrobe and William Sands)

NOTES AND SOURCE NOTES

KEY

Note: Catherine Wyler provided transcripts of the interviews filmed for her one-hour 1986 documentary *Directed by William Wyler* (DBWW). Only a fraction of each interview appeared in the film documentary, and some interviews not at all. Quotations from the transcripts are cited with the initials of the person quoted.

All other quotations come from the author's interviews, unless otherwise noted.

PROLOGUE:
SWING GANG

1 "Come on in . . . "Let's talk . . . "He was the best: SSp/DBWW.
2 "the greatest of all American directors: LH/DBWW.
2 "assistant errand boy" WW to AM.
3 All other WW quotes per RP, *Positif Éditions*, Special Issue No. 400, 1994, and RP to JH.

CHAPTER ONE:
THE NAME SHOULD BE WILLI

5 "Instead of 'Camill': Birth certificate No. 1298/1902, Mulhouse archive.
5 "Willy is a perfectly dignified: *Universal Weekly*, 7/27/28.

5 . . . Robert had been born: Birth certificate No. 2257/1900, Mulhouse archive.

6 Theirs was a block-long street: JH visit to Mulhouse.

6 This was a surprising ecumenical: Caron, p. 136.

6 Willy's gender notwithstanding: DP to JH.

6 All the Wyler relatives knew: DP to JH.

6 "We would have dinner first: DP to JH.

6 Leopold Wyler had come to Mulhouse: *Extrait du Registre d'Immatriculation* No. III, 65 (Sept. 24, 1921), Mulhouse archive.

6 He was a small man with: DP to JH.

7 Leopold was born: *Extrait du Registre d'Immatriculation,* Mulhouse archive; also *Familienregister der Heimatgeminde,* Band C, p. 104 (11/30/16), Aargau archive; also AL to JH.

7 His father, Judas Wyler: AL to JH.

7 *Note:* Leopold's grandfather had been the village rabbi. A picture probably from the 1830s shows a prosperous-looking young man gazing intently through Ben Franklin spectacles. His head is covered by the flat-topped beret of a Swiss burgher, not by a rabbi's hat. Only the coiffed prayer locks curling at his temples indicate he is not a Calvinist businessman.

7 Various Wyler families: *Repertoire des noms de famille suisses,* Zurich, 1989, per Lausanne archivist Gilbert Coutaz to JH, 5/21/91.

7 They wed in Stuttgart: *Familienregister,* Aargau archive.

7 "She was a poet": PM to JH.

7 "She was one of the most": RG to JH.

7 Born in Stuttgart: *Familienregister,* Aargau archive, 1916. Other documents give different dates. A French identity card of 1924 lists June 18, 1878; a U.S. immigration form of 1940 gives June 1, 1878.

7 A Spinoza scholar: DP to JH.

7 *Note:* Melanie's father, Ferdinand Auerbach, had been to the United States as a young man. He arrived in July, 1866. Three years later, he declared his "bona fide intention to become a citizen," according to an Ohio court document signed by John Kuhns, Judge of the Probate Court of Putnam County, recorded 5/11/1869. (It was copied and notarized in Mulhouse, 2/13/1919). Ferdinand travelled as far west as Chicago. By the early 1870s, he returned to Stuttgart to marry Helene Laemmle. She did not want to go back to America with him. They remained in Stuttgart, prospering in business. Willy had memories of his grandfather flying an American flag every July Fourth up to the beginning of the First World War. [WW to AM.]

8 "Willy looked like a floozie: DP to JH.

8 "I wasn't consciously: WW to AM.

8 A close childhood friend: WW to AM.

8 When Willy learned to swim: TW to JH.

8 Willy had scaled the outside wall: CW to JH.

8 But his escapades: TW to JH.

8 "The zoo was very important: TW to JH.

9 Within months of: Birth certificate No. 1733/1907, Mulhouse archive.

9 Alsace-Lorraine had more German: Silverman, p. 73.

9 . . . to play "The Marseillaise.": Kitchen, p. 194.

9 to rescind the order: ibid.

9 Its grand salon: *Bulletin de la société industrielle de Mulhouse*

9 The Kaiser's favorite newspaper: Kitchen, p. 195.

10 testy exchanges resulted: ibid, pp. 200–203.

10 *Note:* Besides being vilified as "the dirty Alsatian" traitor, Alfred Dreyfus was reviled as "the dirty Jew." A remark by a fashionable lady in Paris was typical. "I wish that he were innocent. Then he would suffer more." [Snyder, p. xxi]

10 Of the twenty-three hundred: Caron, p. 76.

10 *Note:* The Yiddish-Alsatian term "Aschkeness," meaning German Jew, acquired a disparaging connotation similar to "Boches" the French epithet for the Germans. [Caron, p. 108]

10 Cultural resistance: ibid. pp. 102–4.

11 "We always had detailed letters: DP to JH.

11 German authorities tried: Silverman, p. 88.

11 . . . Melanie prevailed upon Leopold: DP to JH.

11 And on May 20, 1914: Coutaz to JH, 4/5/91.

11 Robert lived there: ibid.

CHAPTER TWO: A KID'S POINT OF VIEW

12 An assault force: Tuchman, pp. 185–87.

12 "I noticed they weren't: WW to AM.

12 A military band played: Tuchman, p. 186.

13 The German Seventh Army: ibid., p. 187.

13 "When the battle broke out": WW to AM; WW/DBWW.

13 Before August ended: Madsen, pp. 11–12.

13 "We'd spend the night: WW/DBWW.

13 "We used to stand": WW to AM.

14 Willy cut a piece: Madsen, pp. 15–16.

14 "Willy is no Eugene Ysaye: AW to JH.

14 Her taste ran to Asta Nielsen: Madsen, p. 8.

14 *Die Arme Jenny:* Shipman, p. 35.

14 Willy's own taste: WW to AM.

14 He invariably outwitted: Shipman, p. 33.

14 He was then forgotten: Roud, pp. 69–72.

15 Alain Resnais, among them,: Robinson, p. 77.

15 "He had no artistic pretensions: ibid.

15 "We had some of the best opera" WW to AM.

15 *Note:* In the fall of 1914, Willy saw Schiller's dramatic trilogy, *Wallenstein,* mounted by the 74th Reserve Infantry Regiment. Programs saved by Melanie Wyler from three dozen professional performances he attended between the winter of 1915 and the summer of 1918 indicate the richness of the offerings in wartime Mulhouse. It is instructive to list some of them if only to appreciate the cultural sophistication he brought to Hollywood, though he never com-

pleted high school. Willy saw Wagner's *Tristan and Isolde, Das Rheingold, Siegfried* and *Gotterdammerung;* Verdi's *Aïda* and *La Traviata;* Rossini's *Il Barbiere di Siviglia;* Humperdinck's *Hansel and Gretel* and Strauss's *Die Fledermaus.*

16 "The troops passed: *Mulhauser Zeitung,* 11/18/18.

16 "After the defeat of the Germans: WW to AM.

17 Of all the soldiers: Paramount Pictures mimeo from 1950s.

CHAPTER THREE:
TROUBLEMAKER

18 the headmaster Benjamin Bloch-Katz: *Feuille d'Avis de Lausanne,* identified in article of 4/24/75 by Louis Polla, per Coutaz to JH.

19 "an absolute charmer: LH/DBWW.

19 The Institut Bloch: Coutaz letter to JH, 5/21/91; also author's visit to Lausanne.

19 "a Jewish institute for boys,": *l'Indicateur vaudois,* per Coutaz to JH.

19 . . . Willy and Melanie arriving in Basel: DP to JH.

19 registered as a boarder: Lausanne city registry, per Coutaz to JH.

19 He had already completed: archives of Lausanne's *École supérieure de commerce,* per Coutaz letter to JH, 5/21/91.

19 . . . on April 28 enrolled: ibid.

19 . . . he did not have to pass: ibid.

19 If the eighty-two-year-old: *La Patrie Suisse,* 6/6/15; description in school literature, 1924; *Nouvelle Revue de Lausanne,* 11/11/69; "l'Histoire de l'Établissement" in *Feuille d'Avis,* 11/7/69; all per Lausanne archive.

20 . . . Robert's scholastic record: Lausanne archive, including school records and city register, per Coutaz.

20 Thus, less than two months: ibid.

20 Robert had become especially close: BT to JH.

20 Also in their immediate circle: MA to JH.

20 Indeed, Willy . . . would become infatuated: BH correspondence with WW, September 1930.

20 For entertainment: MA to JH.

20 "Willy was part of our: MA to JH.

21 "I was kicked out": WW to AM.

21 "He bought a cart": BM to JH.

21 Blanche's mother: BM to JH.

21 *Note:* Willy moved into the Monastery on July 12, 1919.

21 It stood at: JH visit to Lausanne.

21 The Monastery's adolescent: Madsen, p. 22.

21 "The prank worked,": WW to AM.

21 While living at the Monastery: BT to JH.

21 "Manuel did all kinds of stuff: BT to JH.

21 As the largest and most elegant: *Bulletin Technique de la Suisse Romande,* 5/10/11 and 5/10/14; *Nouvelle Revue de Lausanne,* 12/19/87; *Le Bâtiment du Lumen;* all per Lausanne archive.

22 "There were a few of us: WW/DBWW; WW to AM.

22 Only five months after: Lausanne archive, per Coutaz.

22 In letters to his mother: DP to JH.

22 "I had this idea: WW to AM.

22 The prospect of one day: AW to JH.

22 . . . on December 12: Lausanne archive, per Coutaz.

22 After a brief winter holiday: BT to JH; also Coutaz for date of departure.

CHAPTER FOUR:
HIS MOTHER'S SORROW

23 . . . in a neighborhood dotted with parks: JH visit to Mulhouse.

23 . . . he would have to live down: AW to JH.

23 . . . learning how to sell: WW to AM.

23 His habitual misbehavior: PM to JH.

23 Poumy and her mother: PM to JH.

24 Melanie fairly leaped: PM to JH.

24 Willy acquired a certain finesse: AW to JH.

24 "Finally, I got fed up: WW to AM.

24 He had brought his violin: "William Wyler," a profile by Ken Doeckel in *Films in Review,* 10/71, p. 469.

25 His official . . . service record: A comprehensive U.S. Army document of 8/11/45 lists one year at the Conservatory as part of WW's educational history. Many standard reference works mistakenly claim he attended the Conservatoire National de Paris.

25 no trace of Willy: The search included *le Fichier des anciens élèves* and the *Registres d'inscription* at the Conservatory (now named the *Conservatoire national supérieur de musique et de danse de Paris*), per Catherine Rochon 1/9/92; search also included *Les archives anciennes du Conservatoire* at the *Centre d'accueil et de récherche des Archives nationales.*

25 "I couldn't afford: WW to AM.

25 He often sat: AW to JH.

25 He went to the theater: WW to AM.

25 "There were girls all over: WW to AM.

25 "She was kind of pretty: WW to AM.

25 Willy was home little more than a week: DP to JH.

26 . . . Laemmle was in Lucerne: DP to JH.

26 His assistant had: BT to JH.

26 Melanie had a double claim: DP to JH.

26 . . . Laemmle's father needed: Drinkwater, p. 27.

26 Ferdinand Auerbach, had offered: DP to JH.

26 Born in 1867: Drinkwater, p. 11.

26 "The store is full of relatives: Ramsaye, p. 447.

26 . . . he walked by a movie theater: ibid, p. 450; also Florey (1), p. 265.

26 The year was 1906: ibid; also Drinkwater, p. 65.

27 . . . he was soon netting: Drinkwater, p. 68.

27 *Note:* In 1923, Laemmle said in an interview, "It didn't take long to make the business pay. I

showed only Pathé films. Several months later I opened my own film rental agency. I bought seven prints of each film. Pathé reduced my price as long as I bought seven at a time. One of the biggest hits we showed was *The Passion of Christ,* a film in color. I bought thirty prints of that. Two years after I opened my first movie theater my business expenses had climbed to six thousand dollars a week." [Florey (1), p. 265]

27 Within a decade: Laemmle's record is well known and widely described; sources here include Drinkwater, Ramsay and Florey, and both Brownlow and Koszarski (1) for Woolworth characterization.

27 *Note:* Laemmle abandoned the star system by the late teens, preferring to make movies as cheaply as possible, and eventually took pride in Universal's low-end reputation as the Woolworth's of the movie industry. [Brownlow and Koszarski (1)]

27 Willy's first impression: WW to AM; WW/DBWW.

27 "So you're your mother's sorrow: WW to AM.

27 relatives on the payroll: Brownlow, p. 416.

27 As Ogden Nash: Berg, p. 190.

28 He'd hired: Thomas, p. 39.

28 The legendary story: Koszarski (2), p. 35; also Thomas, p. 48.

28 . . . ended up costing ten times: Koszarski (2) p. 37.

28 To Willy's amazement: BT to JH.

28 "How would you like: WW/DBWW.

28 "a trip to the moon": WW to AM; Wyler also told this to many interviewers.

28 "Okay . . . you're on your own": WW/DBWW; Wyler recounted this many times with slight variations.

28 Willy's salary: WW to AM; BT to JH; WW/DBWW; Kohner, p. 17.

29 The embassy's Second Secretary: Letter from U.S. Embassy in Paris to Leopold Wyler, 8/25/20.

CHAPTER FIVE:
like a trip to the moon

30 The *Aquitania* put to sea: *NY Times,* 9/16/20.

30 Among its nearly three: ibid., 9/18/20.

30 . . . newly refitted with: ibid., 7/16/20.

31 Refurbished . . . the dining salon: ibid., 8/25/20.

31 The ship's staff catered: Longstreet, p. 205.

31 On Friday afternoon: *NY Times,* 9/17/20.

31 The blast erupted: ibid.

31 The next thing . . . burst into flame: Ellis, p. 516.

32 "It was all fantastic: WW/DBWW.

32 Coming to America "was something fabulous: WW to AM.

32 . . . the flood of destitute: *NY Times,* 9/25/20.

32 Willy reported to work: WW to AM.

32 . . . occupied the entire third floor: Robert Grau, "The Growth of Universal," in Mac-Cann, pp. 55–56.

32 Another young man: Kohner, p. 23.

32 "If I have taken three hours": ibid., p. 15.

32 Somewhat dismayed: ibid. p. 23.

33 "Are you by any chance": ibid.

33 "Willy didn't like: PK/DBWW.

33 Then one Saturday: PK/DBWW.

33 "They might as well try: Ellis, p. 517.

33 "After half an hour: PK/DBWW.

34 "I'll take care . . . nobody would do it": WW/DBWW.

34 Willy finally went: Kohner, p. 28.

34 "Willy came home: PK/DBWW.

CHAPTER SIX:
NEW YORK

35 Around this time: PK/DBWW; LK to JH.

36 . . . he'd had English grammar: WW/DBWW.

36 . . . evening classes in English: Kohner, p. 24.

36 The idea soon dawned: WW to AM; PK/DBWW; LK to JH.

36 . . . mimeographed sheets: Kohner, p. 24.

36 "The Universal chief": *Motion Picture Weekly,* 1/8/21.

36 "Eddie Polo: ibid.

37 "Youth, animation: ibid.

37 "They have automobiles: ibid., 1/15/21.

37 . . . some notable romances: ibid.

37 *Note:* "Hampton del Ruth was scenario editor at Sennett; he did a bit of directing, but his brother Roy was the director." KB to JH.

37 Laemmle knew nothing: WW to AM; PK/DBWW; LK to JH; also Kohner pp. 24–25.

37 "I received all sorts of papers: PK/DBWW.

37 "Oh boy, you are in: LK to JH; also Madsen, p. 29.

38 "Have you gone mad?": Kohner, p. 25; WW and PK described the entire incident in similar versions to many interviewers, including PK/DBWW and WW to AM.

39 "Willy wanted to know: PK/DBWW.

39 "Willy spoke German and French: PK/DBWW; LK to JH.

39 "Pretty soon papers: PK/DBWW; WW to AM.

39 . . . it whetted his appetite: WW to AM; PK/DBWW.

39 "I don't think: PK/DBWW.

40 Stroheim . . . had begun filming: Koszarski (2), pp. 72–75.

40 . . . Thalberg was unable: ibid.

40 The budget for: *Variety,* 12/23/21.

40 "the first real million-dollar picture.": ibid.

40 official figure: *Motion Picture Weekly,* 7/30/21.

40 "actually cost": *Variety,* 1/27/22.

40 Kohner brainstorm: Kohner, p. 30.

40 The billboard would read: Koszarski (2), p. 75; also described in Curtiss, p. 127.

40 . . . Kohner got a bonus: Kohner, p. 30.

40 *Note:* Kohner's real recompense was to keep von Stroheim company during editing, before the picture's release in January 1922. The director had arrived in New York to

influence the process, which had been taken out of his hands. But Laemmle banned him from the cutting room. Nevertheless, Kohner created such a favorable impression on von Stroheim, giving him new story ideas and finding a composer to write the score for the premiere of *Foolish Wives*, that the director extracted a promise from Laemmle to send Kohner to the West Coast. [Kohner, p. 30]

40 "Willy was a little restless: PK/DBWW.
40 . . . Wyler climbed: PK/DBWW.
40 . . . snapshots . . . tripod and box camera: WW to AM.
40 Instead of writing home: CW/DBWW.
41 "There was Willy: PK/DBWW; WW to AM.
41 . . . he joined the New York State: New York State National Guard Enlistment Paper, 2/7/21.
41 *Note:* Wyler was attached to Battery D of the 1st Field Artillery. It trained one evening a week in an armory at Sixty-Seventh Street and Lexington Avenue, a mile or so uptown from the Mecca Building.
41 "two minor episodes": WW to AM; CW to JH that it was a story often told.
41 "I won the decision,": WW to AM.
41 "We would come in from the field": WW to AM.
42 "all the fun was in California.": CW/DBWW
42 "saved me from being fired,": PK/DBWW.
42 "Do you have any money?": WW to AM.
42 February 1 . . . granted an honorable discharge: New York State National Guard muster sheet.
43 . . . still a buck private: ibid.
43 Uncle Carl was generous but,: WW to AM.
43 Instead of taking: BT to JH.

CHAPTER SEVEN: "WORTHLESS WILLY"

44 . . . Roaring Twenties changed: Levine, p. 293 ("Progress and Nostalgia").
44 . . . gave up corsets, showed their legs: Robinson (2), p. 21.
44 The influx made: WPA Guide, pp. 56–57.
44 Its 1920 population: *First 100 Years*, p. 14.
45 . . . Los Angeles phone directory: Henstell, p. 14.
45 Large industries: McWilliams, p. 43.
45 First came: *Los Angeles*, (WPA guide), pp. 56–57.
45 "No sedate public relations office,": Henstell, p. 19.
45 . . . "midnight revels" and "petting parties": Levine, p. 298.
45 ambivalent feelings . . . general conflict: ibid., p. 294.
45 . . . Arbuckle . . . making thirty-five hundred dollars a week: *Variety*, 9/16/21.
45 "When I was a poor: quoted widely; in *Los Angeles* (WPA guide), p. 76.
46 Production activity: *Variety*, 1/6/22.

46 . . . just three serials: ibid., 2/3/22.
46 Willy moved into: WW/DBWW.
46 When Manuel reached New York: BT to JH.
46 . . . had managed to land occasional: BT to JH.
46 *Robinson Crusoe: Variety*, 2/3/22.
46 Manuel wasn't hired: BT to JH.
46 But Willy remembered watching: WW to KB [*Hollywood*, 1980]; WW to AM.
46 Cradled between sloping hills: Description of Universal City based on WW comments to interviewers; BT to JH; AH to JH; as well as accounts and photos in Kobal, Brownlow, Hirschhorn, I.G. Edmonds, Koszarski, Florey and various newspapers, magazines and trade papers.
47 "Hollywood was like a village: WW to KB.
47 "You took the streetcar: WW to AM.
47 "Bert Roach, who: *Variety*, 10/6/22.
47 He armed himself: Koszarski (2), p. 31.
47 "They'd send me out . . . what it was about": WW to KB.
48 Von Stroheim's next project: *Moving Picture Weekly*, 4/22/22; also ref. in Koszarski (2).
48 "Worthless Willy": WW to KB; WW to AM.
48 "Willy was a cowboy: AH to JH.
48 "electric railway paradise": Henstell, p. 223.
48 "My automobile was out of order: ibid.
48 The Yellow Car trolley: AH to JH.
49 He bought a large: AH to JH; WW to AM.
49 "We'd come up like cops": WW to AM.
49 "My mother wrote back: WW to KB.
49 . . . Wyler often got caught speeding: WW to AM.
49 "Jailbird": WW to KB.
49 The working folk: Florey, p. 9.
49 "That's where Willy ran into: AH to JH.
49 . . . interviewing stars for *Cinemagazine*: Taves, pp. 72–73.
50 Florey tided him over: AH to JH.
50 "Willy got me some jobs: AH to JH.
50 His search ended at 1719 Mariposa Avenue: AH to JH.
50 "Two of us had beds: WW to AM.
50 "On Saturdays: AH to JH.
50 "I'd come home at four or five: WW to AM.
50 "turned an old Maxwell: BT to JH.

CHAPTER EIGHT: SIN CITY

51 . . . Arbuckle had started out: Anger, pp. 27, 30, 33.
51 The party in his twelfth floor: ibid. p. 34; Edmonds, A., pp. 153–284.
52 "did this to me:" Anger, p. 35.
52 The clause required: *NY Times*, 9/22/21.
52 . . . the fan magazine *Photoplay*: Kobal, pp. 188–190.
52 The prominent director: Anger pp. 47, 49, 60; also widely described in general and trade press.
53 "By 1922 Hollywood: Knight, p. 114.

53 "Hollywood is not a nest: *NY Times,* 2/8/22.
53 . . . he rented a cabin: Mast, p. 180 ("The Sins of Hollywood").
53 . . . he did not survive: Anger, p. 74.
53 These revelations: Henstell, p. 80.
53 "We have been plunged: Mast, p. 195. (Ellis Paxson Oberholtzer, "Sex Pictures")
54 "We don't care: *Variety,* 1/13/22.
54 At first he soft-pedaled: ibid., 3/31/22.
54 . . . the film colony got: ibid., 6/9/22.

CHAPTER NINE:
LIGHTS! CAMERA! ACTION!

55 . . . Laemmle sent him a cable: *Variety,* 3/24/22.
55 *Under Two Flags: AFIC,* p. 844; Edmonds, I., p. 110; Hirschhorn, p. 38.
56 . . . a huge explosion: *Variety,* 6/6/22.
56 . . . more than one million: Riley, p. 7.
56 When the summer began: Koszarski (2), pp. 91–92.
56 Filming started . . . spared no expense: ibid., pp. 102, 109; also Curtiss, pp. 145–46.
56 . . . Austrian officers . . . black-and-white movie: Koszarski (2), pp. 102, 104.
56 Thalberg decided: ibid., p. 106; Curtiss, p. 146; Thomas pp. 50–51.
56 Von Stroheim's firing: Brownlow, p. 424.
56 He heard what happened: Curtiss, p. 147.
57 "It was like being an apprentice,": WW to AM.
57 *The Jilt, Paid Back, The Long Chance* and *The Prisoner: AFIC,* pp. 395, 583, 449 and 619, for descriptions.
57 . . . lasted eight months: Riley, p. 18.
57 "How it really was": WW to KB; WW to AM.
57 . . . a melodramatic simplification: *AFIC* p. 369, and Riley, p. 8, for *Hunchback.*
58 . . . the physical production: Riley, pp. 8–11; also *Hunchback* program for New York premiere, Sept. 1923.
58 "The running price: WW to KB.
58 Film stock was so slow: Brownlow, p. 290.
58 "We had every sun arc": WW to AM.
58 . . . Worsley used: Riley, p. 17.
58 "more than an errand boy: WW to KB.
58 . . . public address system: Miller, p. 58.
58 "Willy never stopped running": AH to JH.
59 "I was impressed: Miller, p. 59.
59 "I made my way for the large gates: PK/DBWW.
59 "Kohner stayed over: AH to JH.
59 "Willy couldn't find: AH to JH.
59 . . . Paul had spent the year: Kohner, p. 40.
59 "Never remain in a job: Brownlow, p. 425.
59 Mayer signed him . . . four hundred thousand: Schatz, pp. 31, 39, 45.
60 "You're running too fast: Kohner, p. 40.
61 His only production experience: Curtiss, p. 269.
61 . . . canvassing theater owners: Kohner, p. 41.
61 Thalberg believed . . . ideas for change: Schatz, pp. 20–21.

61 . . . filming of *Hunchback* . . . boat fare: AH to JH.
62 . . . stayed on as Willy's roommate: BT to JH.
62 "always behind in the rent: BT to JH.
62 Wyler wrote Laemmle: CL letter to WW, 7/2/23.
62 "My dear Willy: CL letter to WW, 7/2/23.
62 . . . lost thirty thousand dollars: Gabler, p. 74.
62 . . . he would pay . . . a palatial Beverly Hills mansion: *Variety,* 5/5/25.
63 . . . Robert arrived: BT to JH.
63 "The Walkers were very accommodating: BT to JH.
63 . . . moved into a rented: BT to JH.
63 "He was the one: Miller, p. 59.
63 "Robert's pulchritude": West, pp. 169, 171.
63 "We still had the Maxwell . . . all pretty innocent": BT to JH.
64 "I was just playing the field,": WW to AM.
64 *Fool's Highway, The Rose of Paris, The Gaiety Girl: AFIC* pp. 261, 666, 278.
64 *Note:* Mary Philbin later was engaged to Paul Kohner, but they did not marry.
64 "I decided that directing . . . I felt I could direct": WW to AM.
65 "Exhibitors want bigger pictures: Edmonds, I., p. 135.
65 . . . William Duncan . . . given complete control: ibid., p. 125.
65 A top Western star: Katchmer, p. 256.
65 . . . *Wolves of the North: AFIC,* p. 916, for description.
65 "We shot it in six: WW to AM.
65 "They were all very elementary . . . villain": WW to KB.
66 He booked passage: Cunard and Anchor Lines, Certificate of Identification, 10/7/24.
66 "some of our largest productions . . . first-class Assistant: William Koenig's letter, 9/24/24.
66 "my roots were European: WW to AM.
66 The pair had decided to move: BT to JH.

CHAPTER TEN:
GIVE HIM A TWO-REELER

67 "He'd say to . . . some practice: WW to AM.
68 In June 1925: *Mt. Whitney Observer,* 6/6/25.
68 Wyler worked for: Madsen, p. 48.
68 Hollywood legend has: WW to KB; WW to AM.
69 . . . Wyler wrote Laemmle: WW letter to CL, 7/3/25.
69 "It used to: WW to AM.
69 *Note:* Start dates were: *Ridin' for Love* 7/29/25; *The Fire Barrier* 8/6/25; *Don't Shoot* 8/14/25; *The Pinnacle Rider* 8/24/25. [WW's personal files]
69 "One time they: WW to KB.
70 One of the: WW to AM.
70 . . . Universal had no: *Variety,* 7/15/25.
70 . . . cost very little: WW/DBWW.

70 Between 1925 and 1927: *Classic Images*, No. 138, 12/86.

70 "It was a hell: WW to CLH, *Cinema*, Vol. 3. No. 5, 1967.

70 "trying to think: WW to RD.

70 "We had a circle: WW to KB.

71 . . . Hollywood was facing: *Variety*, 6/23/25 and 6/30/25.

71 A friend of Wyler's: Bruce Humberstone interview with David Shepard, 5/23/83.

71 *Note:* Wyler often recounted that he'd been fired by Universal because of his habitual dalliance in a pool hall near the studio gate. While it is certainly possible he'd once been fired for playing pool and not turning up prepared for work, in the fall of 1925 he simply was laid off with hundreds of other Universal employees.

71–72 . . . stood on a tower . . . playing Messala: *NY Times*, 11/1/25.

72 Estimates varied: *Variety*, 10/7/25; *NY Times*, 11/1/25.

72 "Suddenly I heard: WW to AM.

73 . . . wasn't filmed until: *Variety*, 10/7/25.

73 . . . Laemmle sent word: Isidore Bernstein memo to CL, 11/17/25.

73 "Wyler has not: ibid.

73 *Note:* Bernstein's memo stated: "The last five pictures made with Acord were each done in less than ten days and cost, including overhead, $12,642 – $10,266 – $12,895 – $13,848 – $13,822 – each one of these carrying over two thousand dollars overhead, making the actual money expenditure on each of these pictures from eight to ten thousand."

73 Acord was a: Katchmer, p. 3.

73 "he had a kind: WW to AM.

73 The movie told: *Variety*, 12/29/26.

74 As a teenager: Katz, p. 1249.

74 "sometimes had to: Wray, p. 55.

74 "I had a scene: FW to JH.

74 "I remember he: FW to JH.

74 . . . Wray had been: Wray, p. 56–57.

75 . . . the picture in: *Variety*, 12/29/26.

75 "This would make: Gulick memo to Bernstein, 4/22/26.

75 Again Acord plays: Kern, p. 55.

75 . . . Universal put together: Universal Pictures, exhibitor's advertising campaign.

75 . . . Humes was Universal's: *Variety*, 8/3/27.

76 Humes came from: *Classic Images*, No. 77, 9/81.

76 *Blazing Days* was released 3/27/27.

76 "all business . . . Wyler laughed": EG to JH.

76 "This is a pic-ture: *Variety*, 6/8/27.

77 The scripts he had: WW to KB.

77 . . . it tells the story: Kern, p. 51–52.

77 . . . Willy began making: WW's personal file.

77 *Note:* Start dates were: *The Two Fister* 7/20/26; *Haunted Homestead* 7/28; *Tenderfoot Courage* 8/4; *Galloping Justice* 8/11; *Lone Star* 8/18; *The Ore Raiders* 8/26; *Kelcy Gets His Man* 9/1; *Silent Partner* 9/8; *The Phantom Outlaw* 9/16; *Gun Justice* 9/22; *The Home Trail* 9/30; *Square Shooter* and *The*

Horse Trader, both 10/11; *Daze of the West* 10/21. [WW's personal list]

77 "The only way: WW to KB.

78 "The star, who: WW to AM.

78 "When visitors would: WW to KB.

79 "She always gave: FW to JH.

79 "I dated little: WW to AM.

80 "I left the: WW to AM.

80 "However can you: Lotus Thompson letter, 9/14/28.

81 . . . studio supervisors felt: Universal report on picture, 5/10/27.

81 *Note:* Filming of *The Border Cavalier* began 2/21/27. [WW's personal list]

81 "What a beautiful: Universal daily report, 4/15/27.

81 "a very nice: Universal daily report, 4/27/27.

81 "At last a real: Universal report on picture, 7/28/27.

81 In May 1927: WW/Universal contract.

CHAPTER ELEVEN: LAST OF THE SILENTS

83 . . . an "Irish" program: Kern, p. 4; Madsen, p. 60–61.

83 Invited to the: Hirshhorn, p. 58.

84 He used hidden: Kern, p. 4, Madsen, p. 60.

84 "The story in: Albert De Mond memo to Harry L. Decker, 4/23/28.

84 "I promise to: Henry Henigson memo to WW, 2/3/28.

85 . . . released in two versions: *NY Times*, 4/8/29; *Variety*, 4/10/29.

85 "This is the: Universal report on picture, 11/16/28.

85 "Wouldn't hurt a: Universal report on picture, ibid.

85 "One of the: Universal report on picture, 11/17/28.

85 "purity, directness and: *Nation*, 12/14/46.

85 . . . "meticulous craftsmanship,": Sarris (2), p. 168.

85 "It is fairly: *NY Times*, 4/8/29.

85 "a not bad: *Variety*, 4/10/29.

85 . . . the studios rushed: Knight, p. 123.

85 Of the twenty: ibid.

86 The novelty of: ibid.

86 Universal built four: *Variety*, 7/25/28.

86 . . . the slowest studio: Edmonds, I., pp. 150 and 154.

86 The picture had: WW to AM.

87 The picture was: Hirschhorn, p. 62.

87 The predictable story: Kern, pp. 4–5.

87 "In my heart: CLJr letter to CL, 7/23/29.

87 "Right now the: WW letter to his parents, 7/21/29.

88 The plot of: Hitt, pp. 181–83.

88 Wyler also insisted: WW to AM.

89 To allow moving: WW to AM.

89 Wyler remembered the: WW to AM.

90 Because of that: Madsen, p. 70.
90 "Not enough reflectors: Universal daily report, 11/19/29.
90 "Some censorable stuff: Universal daily report, 9/13/29.
91 "I must ask,": CLJr letter to WW, 10/21/29.
91 "In the most: Universal daily report of the general critic of arts, 9/16/29.
91 But the silent: *Film Spectator*, 8/2/30.
92 . . . was hailed as: *Film Mercury*, 1/24/30.
92 "despite its title: *NY Times*, 12/28/29.
92 . . . incorrectly listing the: *Variety*, 1/1/30.
92 . . . the picture did: Hirschhorn, p. 67; *Variety*, 1/8/30.
92 "Frankly, I think: Peter B. Kyne letter to Tom Reed, not dated.
93 "The success of: WW letter to his parents, 1/30/30.
93 In his first official: Kern, p. 4.
93 "Junior, despite his: WW letter to parents, 7/21/29.
94 . . . was a remake: Hirschhorn, pp. 38, 68.
94 . . . a bonus . . . as great fun: WW to AM.
94 "We had berths: WW to AM.
95 AM CONSIDERING HER: WW night letter to Charles Bickford, not dated.
95 . . . a young Mexican: Katz, p. 1189.
95 "She was quite: WW to AM.
95 "Presumably a yarn: *Motion Picture News*, 8/23/30.
95 "one of the: *LA Times*, 8/15/30.
96 "Mr. Willy Wyler: Waitsfelder letter, 7/18/30.
96 . . . Wyler emptied his: Madsen, p. 73.
96 "I like Willy: BH letter to her mother, 9/4/30.
96 "Dearest Blanche, If: WW postcard to BH, not dated.
97 "When shall we: BH letter to WW, 9/10/30.
97 "Why did you: BH letter to WW, 9/15/30.
97 "All would have: BH letter to WW's mother (MW), 9/23/30.
97 "spoke too quickly,: BH letter to MW, 9/29/30.
97 "My husband is: BH letter to MW, 9/23/30.
97 "Monsieur," Wyler began.: WW letter to Blanche's husband, 9/28/30.
97 *Note*: Blanche fled the Nazis with her two children in the summer of 1940. Wyler sponsored them in the United States and later put her son through college. (BM to JH)
98 "wild, mad city . . . city in Europe": *NY Herald*, 11/23/30.
98 IMMEDIATELY WHETHER [Universal]: WW cable to RW, 10/1/30.
98 DUE ABSENCE OPTION: RW cable to WW, 10/4/30.
98 "Business conditions over: WW letter to RW, 10/4/30.

CHAPTER TWELVE:
DIALOGUE IN SMALL DOSES

99 . . . accept a compromise: WW letter to RW, 12/12/31.

100 "Although there is: WW memo to Henry Henigson, 2/26/31.
100 . . . Universal's Paris office: RW letter to WW, 6/22/31.
100 "There are a: WW letter to RW, 6/14/32.
100 "I think you: WW letter to RW, 10/24/32.
100 . . . running ten days: CLJr memo to WW, 9/15/31.
101 "It was a: WW letter to RW, 10/9/31.
102 "We couldn't shoot: ibid.
102 "working nights, Sundays: WW memo to H. Henigson, 7/13/31.
102 "Understand you are: CLJr memo to WW, 8/19/31.
102 "You do not: CLJr memo to WW, 8/29/31.
102 "For your information: CLJr memo to WW, 9/3/31.
102 The film lost: WW letter to RW, 1/15/32.
102 "Strange as it: *Daily Review Motion Pictures*, 11/18/30.
103 . . . he read his: JoH/DBWW.
103 "Willy was certainly: JoH/DBWW.
103 "There was a: JoH/DBWW.
104 "Willy was not: JoH/DBWW.
104 "Willy used to: JoH/DBWW.
104 "I told him: JoH/DBWW.
104 "Junior seriously said: WW letter to RW, 12/12/31.
105 . . . Mix had agreed: *Toledo Times*, 11/15/31.
105 He would not: *Variety*, 10/30/31.
105 "our New York: Stanley Bergerman memo to WW, 10/6/31.
105 "refused to make: *Variety*, 10/30/31.
105 . . . spent months scouting: *Filmograph*, 9/17/32; *Albany* (NY) *Knickerbocker Press*, 8/28/32.
106 "We anticipate an: CLJr memo to H. Henigson, 6/3/32.
106 But he always: WW letter to RW, 6/14/32.
106 . . . studio spend thirty-five: *LA Times*, 8/26/32.
107 "The picture is: WW letter to RW, 6/14/32.
107 "to make a wholesome: *Culver Alumnus*, 10/32.
107 But the type: *NY Times*, 11/2/92.
107 "rich spoiled kids": FL to JH.
108 "I wanted to: WW to AM.
108 "Mr. Wyler was: Robert Rossow letter to H. Henigson, 5/25/32.
108 "Even with that: FL to JH.
109 "We went on: JoH/DBWW.
109 "I wrote a: JoH/DBWW.

CHAPTER THIRTEEN:
WILD TIMES

110 "I can't be: WW letter to RW, 6/14/32.
110 "he knew how: FL to JH.
111 "She looked like: VS to JH.
111 "Willy was quite: FL to JH.
111 HEREWITH UNREQUESTED BUT: WW telegram to PK and LK, 11/2/32.
111 "were out to: WW letter to PK, 3/22/34.
112 "very good but: ibid.
112 "Naturally knowing my: ibid.

112 "It is not: WW letter to CL, 12/29/32.
113 ... he signed a one-picture: WW/Universal agreement in letter form.
113 "There was no: FL to JH.
113 "It was almost: WW to AM.
113 ... Wyler signed another: WW/Universal contract, 6/1/33.
114 "Robert Wyler, director: *Variety*, 12/19/33.
114 The price tag: Kern, p. 7.
114 "It was a hell: WW to AM.
115 "vacation and work: WW to AM.
115 The studio had: *Cinema*, Vol. 3, No. 5, 1967.
115 But when it: Kern, p. 8.
116 "You and I: WW to AM.
116 "It was a: WW to AM.
117 "My roommate Johnny: VS to JH.
117 "I thought we'd: VS to JH.
117 The star's memory: VS to JH; FL to JH.
117 "But sometimes we: WW to AM.
117 "There was constant: VS to JH.
117 "He was playing: WW to AM.
118 "At times it: FL to JH.
118 "had to tape: VS to JH.
118 "Every day pink slips: FL to JH.
118 "were scared to: FL to JH.
118 "I retained the: WW to CLH, *Cinema*, Vol. 3. No. 5, 1967.
119 "the value of: *Hollywood Reporter*, 11/18/33.
119 "This is one: Kael, p. 124.
120 "A perfectly honorable: WW memo to CLJr, 12/27/33.
121 "a real disappointment: WW to AM.
121 Cummings plays an: Hirschhorn, p. 85.
121 "it was made: WW letter to RW, 4/7/34.
121 "I think it: WW memo to CLJr, 3/28/34.
121 ... "swell as Tchaikovsky: WW memo to CLJr, 3/30/34.
121 "Get me a: CLJr memo to WW, 4/19/34.
122 Junior had great: Curtiss, pp. 97–98.
122 "a genius and: WW to AM.
122 "retained most of: WW letter to RW, 4/7/34.
122 "none of them: WW letter to RW, 5/31/34.
123 "This material is: WW letter to RW, 4/7/34.
123 ... he took the: H. Henigson telegram to WW, 4/23/35.
123 *Note*: Blaise Cendrars was a close friend of Abel Gance and had worked on his films *J'accuse* (1919) and *La Roue* (1922). KB to JH.
124 "I am ready: Cendrars letter to WW, 3/5/34.
124 "who is a: WW letter to Cendrars, 3/23/34.
124 "absolutely gratis: Cendrars letter to WW, 4/25/34.

CHAPTER FOURTEEN:
"THAT BATTY BROAD"

125 "My soul may: WW letter to RW, 7/20/34.
126 ... twelve hundred dollars: Finler, p. 219.
126 "she was an: PD to JH.
126 ... a respectable run: Curtiss, pp. 98–99.
126 ... the general tone: Kern, p. 9.
126 *Note*: Shooting of *The Good Fairy* began 9/14/34.
127 "very cute and: FL to JH.
127 "We fought over: WW to AM.
127 "The girl looks: WW to AM.
128 "Do you think: *NY Post*, no date.
128 "What do you: WW to AM.
128 "There is no: *NY Post*, no date.
128 "What did you: WW to AM.
128 "If I find: WW letter to mother, 1/30/30.
128 "He turned up: FL to JH.
128 "There he was: Hayward, p. 202.
129 "Is she going: ibid.
129 "Miss Sullavan is: *NY Times*, 2/1/35.
130 "I shall try: Maggie Sullavan telegram to in-laws, 2/8/35.
130 "I don't think: WW to AM.
130 "One girl felt: ibid.
130 "One evening in: LK to JH.
131 "It was too: Walter Laemmle to JH, 8/20/90.
132 "I was marched: ibid.
132 "I came back: WW to AM.
133 "The battles started: FL to JH.
133 "pieces of busted: PD to JH.
133 She called him: Quirk (1), pp. 49–51.
133 "You could hear: ibid.
133 Knowing Wyler was: ibid.
133 "She enjoyed making: ibid.
133 "She castrates a: ibid.
133 "She made him: LH/DBWW.
134 "that batty broad: Quirk (1), p. 50.
134 "You have to: WW to AM.
134 "Arrangements practically concluded": Myron Selznick letter to WW, 4/1/35.
135 "Signed one picture: WW telegram to RW, 5/15/35.
135 "With great pride: WW to AM.
135 "It would make: WW letter to Dr. Paul Martin, 8/3/35.
135 "They used to: LK to JH.
136 "He would go: FL to JH.
136 "One day Maggie: LK to JH.
136 "He told me: CW to JH.
136 "The doorbell rang: FL to JH.
137 Dee played Mirabel: Kern, pp. 82–84.
137 "You must receive: WW to CLH, *Cinema*, Vol. 3. No. 5. 1967.
137 "It was a: WW to AM.
138 "Who directed this?": Berg, p. 263.

CHAPTER FIFTEEN:
THE WYLER TOUCH

139 ... he found work: Katz, p. 491.
139 But only months: ibid.
140 "Goldwyn," he said: WW to AM.
141 "It's not about: LH/DBWW.
141 The contract called: WW/Goldwyn contract, 9/19/35.
141 "I always chose: WW to RD; WW to AM.
142 ... three-year contract guaranteeing: Berg, p. 267.
142 "It was I: LH/DBWW.
142 "We had to: Berg, p. 267.

143 "After we'd worked: WW to RD.
143 "I saw he: WW to AM.
143 Modern camera techniques: Baxter, p. 88.
143 "When photographing a: WW to CLH, *Cinema*, Vol. 3. No. 5, 1967.
144 "they differed about: FL to JH.
144 "They got along: FL to JH.
144 The actor knew: Berg. pp. 270–71.
144 "Dozens of girls: "Directed by William Wyler": Life Achievement Award Issue, *American Film*, 4/76.
145 "was a bit: Daniel Mandell transcript/University of California, Los Angeles.
145 "I don't want: ibid.
145 *Note:* Wyler explained to Mandell: "Mary is so unpleasant that if we are not careful about cutting out repetitions of what she says, it may have a nagging influence on the audience. I mean to show just enough of her lies to establish the trouble she is causing and not bore the audience with her." [WW memo]
146 "I had just: WW to RD. This story has been told numerous times by many people. Some also claim it happened on *Dead End* rather than *These Three*.
147 "sensitive, tasteful and moving": *Hollywood Reporter*, 2/22/36.
147 "play has lost: *Variety*, 2/22/36.
147 "I have seldom: *Spectator*, 5/1/36.
147 "are virtually the: Shipman, p. 487.
147 "never knew what: Berg, p. 272.
147 "to make: ibid.
147 "We had a: LH/DBWW.
148 Laemmle was forced: Hirschhorn, p. 55.
148 He'd given the: Kohner, pp. 82–83.
149 "Don't worry," he'd: ibid.
149 But when he: ibid.
149 . . . one-third investment: Mark Cohen letter to Joe Pasternak, 12/8/37.

CHAPTER SIXTEEN: JUST DO IT AGAIN

150 Goldwyn could have: WW/DBWW.
150 "You can't sell: Kanin, p. 311.
150 He snapped up: Marx, pp. 209–10.
151 "I don't understand: ibid.
151 "I don't care: ibid.
151 Goldwyn's first choice: WW to AM.
151 "I was certainly: Grobel, p. 169.
152 Huston's casting in: ibid. p. 177.
152 "We are going: Merritt Hulburd letter to WW, 3/11/36.
152 "I'm not at: WW letter to M. Hulburd, 3/17/36.
153 "He had written: WW to AM.
153 "danger that on: Notes for a motion picture treatment of *Dodsworth*, by Sidney Howard.
153 "exactly what Ruth: Astor, p. 119.
153 "It was like: WW to AM.
153 "She hadn't worked: FL to JH.
153 "I beg you: Felix Young wire to WW, 6/11/36.
154 "She disagreed with: Astor, p. 119.
154 "Her figure was: FL to JH.
154 "Mr. Wyler," she: FL to JH.
154 "Miss Chatterton," he: FL to JH.
154 "When Ruth and Willy: Astor, p. 119; also (with slight variation) *American Film*, 4/76.
154 He described himself: Niven, p. 216–17.
154 "He was not: WW to AM.
155 "When he had: WW to AM.
155 "We got in step: Astor, pp. 118–119.
155 "He was not: WW to AM.
155 "He had played: *Films in Review*, 10/71.
155 She'd had her: Goldstein, p. 238.
155 . . . Astor had agreed: ibid., p. 254.
155 When her attorney: ibid., p. 255.
156 "Almost three pages: ibid.
156 "He fits me: ibid. p. 256.
156 "I had achieved: Astor, p. 126.
156 "Before the story: WW to AM.
156 . . . Goldwyn summoned Astor: Astor, p. 125.
156 "They had heard: ibid. p. 126.
156 "A woman fighting: Berg, p. 285.
157 "In Paris," he: WW notes for scenic shots, 4/18/36.
157 "Don't cut shot: WW memo to Daniel Mandell, 8/21/36.
158 "one entire afternoon: Astor, pp. 120–21.
159 I DO NOT: Berg, p. 285.
160 I CAN ONLY: Madsen, p. 151.
160 "I lost my: Kanin, p. 311–12.
160 "one of the: ibid.

CHAPTER SEVENTEEN: GOLDWYNITIS

161 "I can't just: Berg, p. 283.
162 "We had a: Marx, p. 225.
162 "I ended up: WW to RD.
162 . . . "by actual measurement: Daniel Mandell transcript/UCLA.
162 'Absolutely no!': Marx, p. 225.
163 "as fine in: *NY Times*, 11/12/36.
164 "That would have been disastrous: *NY Times*, 3/21/95, from an interview with Kingsley in *Dramatists Guild Quarterly*, Fall 1984, by Ruth Goetz and John Guare.
164 "a shocking jargon: Atkinson and Hirschfeld, p. 109.
164 "That was the: WW to AM.
165 "just plain stupid,": Berg, p. 289.
165 "It's absolutely hopeless: WW to AM.
165 "the worst language: Berg, p. 289.
165 DEAR MR GOLDWYN: WW telegram to Samuel Goldwyn, 11/10/36.
166 PUBLICITY OUT POTTER: FL wire to WW, 11/27/36.
166 "Willy would go: JoH/DBWW.
166 Wyler captured second: *Daily Manchester*, 2/16/37.
166 "planting tomatoes for: WW to AM.
166 "The cop who: WW to AM.
168 "We would like: Rollyson, p. 102–3.
168 "wanted me to: Berg, p. 290.

168 "We built the: WW to AM.
169 "Goldwyn didn't like: WW/DBWW.
169 "This set is: LH/DBWW.
169 "Wyler was not: SS to JH.
170 "Willy didn't believe: SS to JH.
170 "I found him: SS to JH.
170 "He had a: SS to JH.
171 "took six days: *Detroit News*, 9/27/37.
171 "Bogie was not: FL to JH.
171 "a big mistake: HH to JH.
171 "He rode us: HH to JH.
171 On the first: *Chicago American*, 9/1/37.
171 "He was the: HH to JH.
172 "It started to: HH to JH.
172 "Where are you: HH to JH.
172 "What amazed me: *NY Mirror*, 8/26/37.
172 "The show undoubtedly: *NY Times*, 8/25/37.
172 "a gripping, realistic: *Film Daily*, 8/3/37.

CHAPTER EIGHTEEN:
"I'LL KNOW IT WHEN I SEE IT"

174 . . . had spent more: Stine (2): p. 97.
174 "Despite this morning's: WW memo to CLJr, 12/27/33.
175 . . . was offering Wyler: WW/Warner Bros. agreement, 8/25/37.
175 . . . dropped his option: Davis, p. 214; Shipman, p. 495.
175 . . . for fifty thousand: Shipman, p. 495.
175 . . . fifty-six million: ibid.
175 . . . he paid the: Katz, p. 311.
176 "What do you: Stine (1), p. 14.
176 "Licking my chops: Davis, p. 215.
176 "The first day: BD/DBWW.
176 "What do you: Spada, pp. 131–32.
177 "After about a: BD/DBWW.
177 "She comes in: Higham, p. 107.
177 "Do you want: Davis, p. 216.
177 "Don't wiggle your: Stine (1), p. 16.
177 "No detail, however: ibid.
177 "Her love affair: Wallis, p. 50.
177 "I *adored* Willy,": Spada (1), p. 134.
177 "Willy was *enormously:* Stine (1), p. 19.
178 "Our romance was: ibid.
178 "Do you think: Hal Wallis memo to Henry Blanke, 11/4/37.
178 "In spite of: H. Wallis memo to H. Blanke, 1/8/38; Wallis, p. 192.
178 [Wyler] maintains that: H. Wallis memo to H. Blanke, 10/28/37; Wallis, p. 191.
179 She caught a: Spada (1), pp. 136–37.
179 He had a: ibid. p. 133.
180 "They tried to: BD/DBWW.
180 "after all she: Higham, p. 109.
180 "If you don't: BD/DBWW.
180 "The only thing: Wallis memo to Blanke, 1/6/38.
180 The elaborate scene: BD/DBWW; Stine (1), p. 14.
180 "Willy took five: BD/DBWW.
180 . . . Selznick would hire: Anderegg, pp. 89–90.
180 One story even: Quirk (2), pp. 149–50.
180 "I forget whose: WW to AM.

181 I ADMIRE YOUR: Henry Fonda telegram to WW, 12/21/37.
181 MY DEAR MANY: WW telegram to the Fondas, 12/21/37.
181 "All those close-ups: Stine (1), p. 17.
182 "Looking back, I: ibid., p. 126.
182 "He lost interest: LK to JH.
182 "He made my: Davis, p. 218.
182 "Willy really is: BD/DBWW.
182 Although it had: Spada (1), p. 140.

CHAPTER NINETEEN:
A LITTLE HOOK THAT GETS YOU

183 "I'm here to: WW to AM.
184 "During *Dead End:* WW to AM; WW/DBWW.
184 "Total lie: SS to JH.
185 . . . Hecht had suggested: WW letter to Felix Barker, 11/19/51.
185 He had gone: Cottrell, p. 136.
185 His first experience: Olivier, pp. 176–77.
185 ARE YOU INTERESTED: Holden, p. 136.
186 HAVE BEEN MOTORING: LO wire to WW, 8/3/38.
186 HAVE FOUND HEATHCLIFF: Berg, p. 322.
186 But Goldwyn found Newton: ibid.
186 "I presented what: Cottrell, p. 137.
186 "Only when he: WW letter to Ronald Proyer, 5/8/73.
187 "She immediately rejected: WW to AM.
187 "I went to: Olivier, pp. 178–79.
187 "Would it be: Vivien Leigh letter to WW, 8/31/38.
187 Olivier caught the: Cottrell, p. 138.
187 On an impulse: ibid., p. 142.
187 Goldwyn decided her: Berg, p. 323.
188 "Shhhhh," he memoed: Cottrell, p. 145.
188 He had paid: Berg, p. 329.
188 "I loved doing: WW letter to RW, 10/4/38.
188 "an effect of: *NY Times*, 7/26/39.
189 "Willy was standing: PK/DBWW.
189 "Willy wanted to: LK to JH.
189 "We chatted and: TW to JH.
189 "It happened very: WW to AM.
189 "I didn't know: LK to JH.
190 "Willy never brought: TW to JH.
190 "I've always regretted: TW to JH.
190 "It was a: JoH/DBWW.
190 "Willy was an: LH/DBWW.
191 "I was sent . . . "Of course all . . . "the lowest of . . . "Towards the end . . . "She loaned me . . . "I made a . . . "It was really: TW to JH.
193 "No sooner had: Higham, p. 116.
193 "Bette had great: Howard Gotlieb to JH, 4/18/91.
194 "Anything is always: TW to JH.
194 "a beautiful screenplay: Grobel, p. 201.
194 "There would be: JoH/DBWW; WW to AM.
194 "We had a: WW to AM; WW/DBWW.
195 "she may have . . . "You know, you . . . "I was abominably . . . "It's just lousy: LO to MB, *Sir Laurence—A Life*, South Bank Show, 1982.
196 "For God's sake: BW/DBWW.

196 "I was overacting . . . "I couldn't put: LO to MB.
197 "He's playing a: WW/DBWW.
197 "You despise this: LO to MB.
198 "If any film: Olivier, p. 178.
198 "You're one of: Niven, p. 221.
198 "Willy thrashing around: TW to JH.
199 "He didn't want: WW to AM.
199 . . . one out of: Wiley and Bona, p. 94.
199 "I made it: Madsen, p. 165.
199 "It griped Goldwyn: WW/DBWW.

CHAPTER TWENTY:
GOOD-BYE, SAM

200 "What the hell: FL to JH.
200 "because of all . . . "might have had . . . "he got
    out . . . "My mother was . . . "He didn't like . . . "I
    enjoyed making . . . "Unfortunately": TW to JH.
202 "not more than: Samuel Goldwyn/WW con-
    tract, 6/20/39.
202 "Willy was one: JoH/DBWW.
202 "There must have: BW/DBWW.
202 The producer had: Berg, pp. 337–38.
203 "I'd be playing: WW to AM.
203 "a big argument: Bergman and Burgess. p. 71.
203 "He liked to: WW to AM.
203 "I know this: WW letter to David Selznick, not
    mailed, 11/10/39.
204 "a kindly, excessively: WW's eulogy for CL.
204 "I couldn't figure: Arce, p. 161.
205 "Goldwyn bought a: Meyer, p. 98.
205 . . . threatened to sue: Berg, p. 347.
205 "There was subtle: WW to AM.
206 "If you tell: Meyer, pp. 99–100.
206 "This was one: TW to JH.
206 "She's marvelous in: WW to AM.
206 "Their marriage could: FL to JH.
206 "I had a: TW to JH.
206 "We'd get up: FL to JH.
206 "Willy made it: Jules Buck to JH.
207 . . . and a spectacular: Meyer, p. 105.
207 "There isn't a: ibid., p. 98.
208 "After Jezebel, I: Stine (2), p. 136.
208 "Willy didn't like . . . "We'd heard . . . "We em-
    barked . . . "Nice as it: TW to JH.

CHAPTER TWENTY-ONE:
HE PLEASED HIMSELF

211 "The script said: WW to AM.
211 "Willy was not: HK to JH.
212 "doubled the dramatic: Koch, p. 49.
212 "printing prison stripes: ibid.
212 "Willy never claimed: ibid.
212 "broke the rule: ibid. p. 50; HK to JH.
212 "I criticize and: Films in Review, 10/71.
212 "If she says: WW to AM.
212 "If you try: WW to AM.
212 "It was such: Davis, pp. 250–51.
213 "I came back: ibid.
213 She'd slept with: Spada (1), pp. 143–44, 156,
    158, and 167.

213 . . . just before starting: ibid. p. 174.
213 she took up: ibid. p. 173.
213 "Tony Gaudio, the: Stine (2), p. 126.
213 "an oblique clue: Spada (1), p. 175.
213 "should have married: ibid.
214 "I have a: WW to AM; WW to RD.
214 "he expected really: TW to JH.
214 "I am delighted: Jack Warner memo to WW,
    5/27/40.
214 . . . Jack Warner saw: Warner Bros. camera-
    man's report, 6/26/40.
214 . . . you must discontinue: Jack Warner memo
    to WW, 6/27/40.
215 "Please be assured: draft of letter by WW.
215 "didn't play politics: HK to JH.
215 "had to tag: WW to AM.
215 "less prosaic: Koch, pp. 52–53.
215 "The way Wyler: ibid.
215 "you couldn't leave: WW to CLH, Cinema, Vol.
    3, No. 5, 1967.
216 "the ultimate credit: NY Times, 11/23/40.
216 "Whenever Willy was: TW to JH.
216 "Davis," she wrote: Kael, p. 324.
217 "too caustic for: Marx, p. 270.
217 "a literary masterpiece: WW to AM.
218 Zanuck had bought: Mosley, p. 193.
218 "what had persuaded: Dunne, p. 93.
218 "twice too long: ibid, p. 95.
218 "have a good: ibid.
218 "We'd meet at: PD to JH.
219 "Willy couldn't write: PD to JH.
219 "I wanted an: WW to AM.
219 "You don't want: RMcD to JH.
219 "I have stood: D. Zanuck letter to WW and
    PD, 12/6/40.
220 "As I had: WW memo to D. Zanuck, 12/20/40.
220 WOULD YOU PLEASE: WW wire to D. Zanuck,
    12/28/40.
220 "The New York: PD to JH.
220 "chewing on: Dunne, pp. 97–98.
220 Note: The winners were Sidney Buchman and
    Seton I. Miller for Here Comes Mr. Jordan.

CHAPTER TWENTY-TWO:
DEEP FOCUS

222 "The script doesn't: LH letter to Samuel Gold-
    wyn, 1/27/41.
222 I am carrying: WW letter to LH, 6/11/41.
223 "Oh, Mr. Goldwyn: LH/DBWW.
223 "I wanted Bette: WW to AM.
224 "with scarcely an: Time, 9/1/41.
224 "This was not: ibid.
224 "What's that for?: Spada (1), p. 181.
224 "He hated the: Stine (1), p. 51.
224 "I was a: Stine (2), p. 151.
224 . . . being replaced by: ibid.
224 I am bewildered: LH letter to BD, 5/20/41.
225 "wasn't a quitter: Stine (2), p. 151.
225 "I wasn't pleasing: Stine (1), p. 51.
225 "I don't want: TW to JH.
225 "Bette had it: TeW to JH.

225 "shall not be: *Current Biography*, 1943.
226 "Willy, whatever you: New York *Sunday News*, 8/2/42.
226 "Willy thought Patricia: TW to JH.
227 "You know he: TeW to JH.
227 "motion picture fame: LH/DBWW.
228 "What is interesting: WW to AM.
228 "There is a: Anderegg, p. 106.
228 "A mistake often: WW letter, 5/22/37.
228 "I think most: LH/DBWW.
229 "I'm not knocking: Stine (2), pp. 151–52.
229 "never asked me: ibid.
229 "The war should: BD letter to WW, 4/5/46.
229 "Under my present: WW letter to BD, 1/31/47.
230 "tight, dry performance: Kael, p. 331.

CHAPTER TWENTY-THREE:
VELVET GLOVE

231 "I shopped and: GG/DBWW.
231 "If you handle: *Hartford Courant*, 2/5/43.
232 "Mr. Mayer," Wyler: WW to AM.
232 "Look: said Mayer: WW/DBWW.
232 That might have: Dick, pp. 66–67.
232 . . . a Senate subcommittee: Dick, pp. 89–90.
233 "Willy and I: JoH/DBWW.
233 "I've enlisted in: WW letter to LH, 12/18/41.
233 "I've been thinking: WW/DBWW.
234 "I was a: WW/DBWW.
234 "I jumped at: WW to AM.
234 "I couldn't possibly: TW to JH.
234 "Most of my: GG/DBWW.
235 DEAR MAD WILLIE: David Selznick telegram to WW, 5/3/42.
235 "propaganda worth a: Wiley and Bona, p. 123.
235 . . . Roosevelt was so: De Mille, p. 336. The sermon was reprinted in numerous publications after the release of the movie, including *Time*, *Look*, and *PM*.
236 "Willy felt it: GG/DBWW.
236 "Willy came over: GG/DBWW.
237 "a study in: *Modern Screen*, 7/42.
237 "The finest sermon: WW's BBC transcript, 10/42.
237 "People say we: *NY Daily News*, 8/2/42.
237 it broke foreign: *Hollywood Reporter*, 11/11/42.
237 "only scratched the: WW's BBC transcript, 10/42.

CHAPTER TWENTY-FOUR:
HE DIDN'T WANT TO MISS THE WAR

238 lock of Veronica: *Look*, editors of, p. 204.
238 Theaters held "bond: ibid. p. 211.
238 . . . end of 1942: Revon, p. 60.
238 "He just didn't: TW to JH.
239 WILL ARRIVE IN: WW wire, 2/12/42.
239 "One Darryl Zanuck: Capra, p. 318.
239 "had the charm: ibid.
239 "The next afternoon: Hellman (1), p. 122.
239 "This was unheard: LH/DBWW.

239 "We got, or: Hellman (1), p. 123.
240 "a large part: LH/DBWW.
241 "no vacancy in: War Department letter to WW, 4/16/42.
241 WHEN CAN YOU LEAVE: Capra wire to WW, 4/8/42.
241 . . . DELIGHTED BECAUSE: LH wire to WW, 5/6/42.
242 "In those days: WW to AM.
242 "The timing just: TW to AM.
242 "Everybody was going: WW to AM.
242 . . . it had six: Parton, p. 155.
243 "General," he said,: WW to AM; WW/DBWW.

CHAPTER TWENTY-FIVE:
IT COULD BRING YOU BACK ALIVE

244 AFTER SOBER REFLECTION: Irwin Shaw wire to WW, 7/10/42.
245 "I have seldom: WW letter to TW, 7/6/42.
245 "Better than any: WW army memo, 6/23/42.
245 And here is: WW postcard to TW, 8/8/42.
246 The Eighth Air: Duerksen, p. 17.
246 "kids would stop: WW to AM.
246 "The trouble with: WW letter to TW, 10/4/42.
246 "for public morale: WW army memo, 9/5/42.
248 It wasn't long: Duerksen, p. 27.
248 "Things are progressing: WW letter to TW, 9/28/42.
248 "My equipment had: Madsen, p. 231.
248 "Willy didn't know: TW to JH.
249 "I was supposed: Beirne Lay to AM.
250 "identifying aircraft in: Madsen, p. 231.
250 "narrowly escaped serious: *NY Times*, 2/4/43.
250 "I hope that: WW letter to TW, 2/10/43.
251 "this over-age major: *Collier's*, 2/4/50.
252 ". . . assignment to hell: *Sunday Dispatch*, London, 2/28/43.
252 "Aerial warfare takes: *LA Herald and Express*, 2/15/43.
252 "for all the: Beirne Lay to AM.
253 "Heard about Garson: WW letter to TW, 12/17/42.
253 "If some of: WW letter to TW, 1/9/43.
253 "I've seen Larry: WW letter to TW, 11/15/42.
253 "I'm not your: WW to AM.
254 "I am practically: Wiley and Bona, pp. 129–30.
254 "I could have: WW letter to TW, 4/9/43.
255 "He never once: Robert Hanson to JH.
255 ". . . great Hollywood director: Charles Leighton to JH.
255 "We lost over: Robert Morgan to JH.
255 "You wouldn't have: Bill Clothier to JH.
256 "We were always: Robert Morgan to JH.
256 "While I knew: WW letter to TW, 5/16/43.
256 ". . . words of comfort: WW letter to Mrs. Harold Tannenbaum, 5/5/43.
256 "Wyler kept shouldering: Clarence Winchell to JH.
256 "General Eaker became: Beirne Lay to AM.

CHAPTER TWENTY-SIX:
A BATTLEFRONT LIKE NO OTHER

258 "Suddenly it was: Bill Clothier to JH.
259 "They lined: Clarence Winchell to JH.
259 "The fifth was: WW to AM.
259 . . . dubbed them "Flak: *Stars and Stripes*, 5/31/43.
259 SUGGEST BRUSHING UP: WW wire to TW, 6/4/43.
260 ". . . no matter how: WW letter to TW, 11/3/42.
260 "Each day, no: WW letter to TW, 5/11/43.
261 "You're strangers but: TW to JH.
261 "I got the: WW/DBWW transcript. (Wyler remembered the Hampshire House as the Plaza Hotel.)
261 He not only: Duerksen, pp. 236–40.
261 POSSIBILITIES OF THIS: WW letter to Beirne Lay, 7/27/43.
261 "an ineffective presentation: WW letter to T. McCrary, 11/12/43.
261 "A picture cut: WW letter to T. McCrary, 11/6/43.
262 "He had all: Casimir Nastal to JH.
262 "I said, 'Anyone?': Bob Hanson to JH.
262 "I didn't get: Robert Morgan to JH.
263 "I couldn't get: WW to AM.
263 *Note:* Wyler's promotion to lieutenant colonel came through 10/20/43.
263 "in large measure: WW army memo, no date
263 "It looks like: WW letter to T. McCrary, 11/27/43.
264 "I don't consider: WW letter to T. McCrary, 12/22/43.
264 "The success of: WW letter to T. McCrary, 11/27/43.
264 ". . . a terrific reception: WW to AM.
266 DEAR MOSS, TERRIBLY: WW wire, 2/20/44.
266 DEAR DARRYL, I: WW wire, 2/22/44.
267 "He was arrested: JP to JH.
268 "as vivid and: *NY Times*, 4/1/44.
268 "They'd heard about: WW to AM.

CHAPTER TWENTY-SEVEN:
ITALIAN ASSIGNMENT

269 "Wyler was recording: JS to JH.
269 "tactical air operations: 5/18/44 military orders.
270 "With so many: WW military memo, no date.
270 . . . roam virtually at will: JS to JH. ("We had orders from General Arnold personally," John Sturges recalled. "That enabled us to do about anything.")
271 ". . . a most holy: TW letter to WW, 11/9/44.
271 "We were together: JS to JH.
272 "Willy thought they: TW to JH.
272 "we'd always get: JP to JH.
273 ". . . a walk-through: JS to JH.
273 "Willy was dying: JP to JH.
273 "As I seem: WW letter to T. McCrary, 10/12/44.
274 "The kid brother: WW to AM.
274 *Note:* Nothing could have prepared Wyler for Henriette Helm's gift. She pressed a wad of

money into his hand. "It belongs to you," she told him. The amount came to slightly more than two hundred thousand French francs. It was his family's share of the shop's earnings during the war. "She had buried it at the risk of her life," Wyler recalled. When he got back to Paris, he sent the money home. It was the equivalent of four thousand fifty-eight dollars.

275 "I usually flew: WW/DBWW.
275 "Instead of a: TW to JH.
275 "I'd never seen: LH/DBWW.
276 "He was terribly: TW to JH.
276 "We went through: JS to JH.

CHAPTER TWENTY-EIGHT:
NOT HOLLYWOOD-AS-USUAL

278 "No one could: *Theater Arts*, 2/47.
278 "The war had: Marx, p. 307.
279 "Like it or: McBride, pp. 503–8.
279 "It would have: WW to AM.
279 "changed his plans: WW letter, 7/11/45.
279 ". . . ten thousand wasted: Marx, p. 308.
279 "This is what: WW to AM.
280 "the ordinary GI: Marx, p. 308.
280 "I've come home: *NY Times*, 11/17/46.
280 . . . the equivalent of: Center for Economic Research at Chapman University.
280 "it was no problem: *Theater Arts*, 2/47.
281 "imposed a responsibility . . . His first night home . . . pity for him": WW manuscript, published as "No Magic Wand" in *Screen Writer*, 2/47.
282 "I realized: *NY Times*, 11/17/46.
282 "So you're gonna . . . put claws on.": HR to JH; Russell, p. 38.
282 "We're the ones: *NY Times*, 11/17/46.
282 "I flew out: HR to JH.
283 "it's very important: WW letter to Fredric March, 2/15/46.
283 "We had to . . . appraisal of himself . . . : "No Magic Wand."
286 "We are having: WW letter to LH, 2/5/46.
286 "Any day now: WW letter to LH, 3/25/46.
286 "Mr. Goldwyn arranged: HR to JH.
286 "the breakup of: Gardner, pp. 163–64.
287 "The family was: TW to JH.
287 "Pretty clever, no?: Russell, p. 41.
287 "He adored Freddie . . . I had ever seen: TeW to JH.
288 "When I say: HR to JH: Russell, p. 44.
288 "Willy just stalled: TeW to JH.
288 "Wyler came late: HR to JH.
289 "We decided to . . . scene is about: "No Magic Wand."
290 "is not to provoke: Madsen, p. 274.
290 "It is through: ibid., p. 275.
290 "By working this: No Magic Wand.
290 "quite a bit: Mandell transcript/UCLA.
291 "After a euphoric: TW to JH.
291 . . . nearly half a million: Berg, p. 418.
291 "not only as: *NY Times*, 11/22/46.

291 "William Wyler has: *Nation*, 12/7/46.
292 . . . highest grossing picture: *NY Herald-Tribune*, 12/27/53.
292 . . . had a huge success: Marx, p. 116.
292 "What you have: TeW to JH.
292 "Willy Wyler, a very: *Hollywood Reporter*, 7/11/58.
293 "I don't much: WW letter, 6/6/58.
293 . . . when Wyler agreed: Bergman letter, 10/12/62.

CHAPTER TWENTY-NINE:
ARE YOU NOW, OR HAVE YOU
EVER BEEN?

295 Wyler borrowed on: *Collier's*, 2/4/50.
295 . . . slightly different amounts: Capra, p. 373.
295 LAST ONE IN: McBride, p. 526.
295 All-time high: Shipman, p. 683.
295 "I can't begin: Capra, p. 378.
296 "They assured us: Madsen, p. 288.
296 "to be smart: WW to AM.
296 "This is the: WW letter, 8/19/48.
297 "I was so excited: TW to JH.
297 "There wasn't a: WW to AM.
297 "The summer was: TW to JH.
298 "alleged subversive influence: Kahn, p. 5.
298 "Our first meeting: PD to JH.
298 "Share and share . . . propaganda films: Goodman, p. 203.
299 "We the undersigned: Kahn, p. 138.
299 "had no interest: *Washington Daily News*, 11/6/47.
299 "Originally Huston was: PD to JH.
300 "If anyone aboard: Dunne, p. 194.
300 "Wyler told us: Bacall, p. 212.
300 "I told them: Cogley, p. 7.
300 "We had two: Dunne, pp. 197–99.
300 "It caused heated: PD to JH.
300 "finally agreed: Dunne, pp. 197–99.
301 "I didn't like: PD to JH.
301 "counted on to foul things: PD to JH.
301 "grand old man: Goodman, p. 207–11.
302 "stool pigeons, neurotics: Cogley, p. 19.
302 "their tactics: PD to JH.
302 "We phoned Willy: PD to JH.
303 "I wouldn't be: Kahn, pp. 221–22.
303 "swayed, intimated: Goodman, pp. 220–21.
304 "under oath that . . . from any source: Cogley, p. 22.
304 "In the aftermath: PD to JH.
304 "have been and: WW letter to LH, 11/14/47.
304 "seen as spineless: PD to JH.
305 "Willy excused himself: RP to JH.

CHAPTER THIRTY:
EATING ACTORS ALIVE

307 "We came down . . . was first-rate: RG to JH.
308 . . . two hundred and: *NY Times*, 8/15/47.
308 . . . an open-ended salary: RG to JH.
308 Four hundred thousand: *NY Times*, 8/15/47.
308 drove big fast: Clough, p. 234.

308 "Morris," he replied: Errol Flynn letter to WW, dated "Sunday 26th."
309 ". . . any actor would: *Collier's*, 2/4/50.
309 "I don't bawl: La Guardia, p. 70.
309 "This annoyed Willy: TW to JH.
309 "Monty was brand-new: RG to JH.
309 "She memorizes her: Bosworth, p. 140.
310 "I had a sense: La Guardia, p. 71.
310 "Can't that man: Bosworth, p. 140.
310 "in the first: WW/DBWW transcript.
310 "a display laying: Madsen, p. 293.
310 "She got a lot: RG to JH.
311 "Willy called me: RG to JH.
312 "The emotion and: *NY Herald-Tribune*, 10/2/49.
312 "In my opinion: Copland, p. 98.
312 "I feel that . . . but do *something*: ibid., p. 100–103.
313 At Grauman's Chinese: Bosworth, p. 178.
313 "We didn't really: TW to JH.
314 "I expected it: *Variety*, 5/26/50.
314 "sloughed off by: WW letter, 11/29/51.
314 "Wyler's version was: *LA Times*, 11/22/93.

CHAPTER THIRTY-ONE:
HE DIDN'T WANT A YES-MAN

316 . . . got along badly: JK to JH.
316 "at the low point: WW to AM.
316 "Willy loved the: TW to JH.
316 "Every time Oona: KP to JH.
317 "I made the decision: WW to AM.
317 "I remember the: TW to JH.
318 POSITIVE WOULD LIKE: LH wire to WW, 6/17/47.
318 "in case you: RW letter to WW, 1/22/48.
318 MILLER BUSY ON: LH wire to WW, 3/17/49.
318 FEEL THAT MAILER: WW wire to LH, 3/24/49.
319 "weakness of . . . the gas jet": WW letter, 6/7/49.
320 WITH VERY MUCH: LO wire to WW, 1/25/50.
321 WILL GLADLY POSTPONE: WW wire to LO, 2/1/50.
321 "My schedule of: WW letter to LO, 2/11/50.
321 ANY REPORT YOU: WW wire to LO, 6/14/50.
322 "The character of: WW to AM.
322 "I'm genuinely eager: David Selznick memo to WW, 11/14/49.
322 I MUST NOW ASK: David Selznick wire to WW, 6/14/50.
323 "this desperate and: WW letter, 6/19/50.
324 . . . hundred fifty-four: Thomson, p. 558.
324 ". . . in seventh heaven . . . what he wanted: RS to JH.
325 ". . . very useful thing: WW letter to LO, 7/24/50.
326 "check my accent: LO wire to WW, 8/5/50.
326 "Almost nightly: TW to JH.
326 Speed was essential: RS to JH.
327 "Willy replaced her: RS to JH.
327 "This was serious: EA to JH.
327 "He told me: TW to JH.
328 "we tore up: David Selznick memo to WW, 11/15/50.

328 hundred thirty thousand: Thomson, p. 558.
328 "Jennifer tells me: David Selznick memo to Briskin, 11/15/50.
328 "I really don't: EA to JH.
329 "Why are we: WW to AM.
329 "The thing that: *NY Post* (Archer Winsten), 2/11/52.
330 . . . Martin Berkeley, named: Goodman, p. 302.
330 "I was in Rome: WW to AM.
331 "mawkish reworking: *NY Times,* 7/17/52.
331 "Jennifer was much: RG to JH.
331 "Wyler, whatever his: Shipman, p. 684.

CHAPTER THIRTY-TWO:
DUPE, IDIOT OR COMMUNIST

332 "decided to step: WW to AM.
332 "It gives me: WW wire to Sidney Kingsley, 12/21/48.
332 "it was something: WW to AM.
333 "categoric disapproval: *NY Times,* 7/23/50.
333 "Certain subjects can't: ibid.
334 "The nature of: WW letter to LO, 3/5/51.
335 "We just sailed: WW to AM.
335 "They were delighted: WW to AM.
335 "After doing the: Douglas, p. 163.
335 "Ain't you Kirk: ibid. p. 164.
335 "Kirk swept me: TW to JH.
336 "a bit of an: *American Film,* 4/76.
336 "I never knew: ibid.
336 "He would watch: ibid.
336 "Willy, watch your: MacCann's, "Hollywood Letter," no date.
336 "Willy was legendary: *American Film,* 4/76.
336 "We moved easily: WW to AM.
337 "I didn't do: RS to JH.
337 "I wanted you: Kirk Douglas letter to WW, not dated.
337 "slam-bang melodrama": *New Yorker,* 11/17/51.
337 "On the whole: *NY Times,* 11/17/51.
338 "He was definitely: TW to JH.
338 "If anybody doubts: Madsen, p. 304.
338 "kept Willy safe: PD to JH.
338 "He's no Commie: WW to AM, TW to JH.
339 "In my own case: LH/DBWW.
339 "I like Dash: LH/DBWW.
340 ". . . to hurt innocent: Hellman (3), p. 98; Goodman, p. 305; Cogley, p. 101.
340 "Why cite her: Rollyson, p. 328.

CHAPTER THIRTY-THREE:
ROMAN HOLIDAY

341 "It was very: TW to JH.
341 "Charlie was hounded: TW to JH.
341 "I AM NOT: Katz, p. 226.
342 "That's why we: TW to JH.
342 "No, No . . . I won't make it: WW to AM.
342 "They passed it: WW to AM.
343 "Our new romantic: WW letter to LO, 11/12/51.
343 "Black-and-white film: SS to JH.

343 "I could not: *American Weekly,* 3/23/52.
344 "He told me: AHe/DBWW.
344 "She impressed me: WW to UCLA/USC film students, 2/24/54.
344 "I'd never really: AHe/DBWW.
344 "very intrigued by: TW to JH.
344 "The Hepburn test: WW letter, 11/12/51.
345 "I remember him: AHe/DBWW.
345 "He said he: GP to JH.
345 "He said, 'Well,: WW to AM.
345 "I have no: GP to JH.
346 "We wanted to: JK to JH.
346 "He asked me . . . but Communist stuff: IMH to JH.
347 "We had Dighton: RS to JH.
347 "Filming in Rome: WW to AM.
348 "We'd only been: TW to JH.
348 "working for Willy: EA to JH.
348 "What I remember: AHe/DBWW.
349 "In spite of: GP to JH.
349 "What I think . . . like a game: GP to JH.
350 "It scared them: WW to UCLA/USC film students, 2/24/54.
350 "Willy said to: GP to JH.
350 "He didn't hesitate: RS to JH.
350 "There was one: AHe/DBWW.
350 "We all knew: GP to JH.
350 "There was a: AHe/DBWW.
351 'Let's go get: RS to JH.
351 "Leaping on and: TW to JH.
352 "He made his music: BB to JH.
352 "It was leading: GP to JH.
353 "But," Swink recounted: RS to JH.
354 "All we need: *Hollywood Reporter,* 9/9/54.
354 "When someone directs: IMH to JH.
354 "I have gone: WW letter, 11/30/53.
355 "Thirty thousand Muscovites: *NY Times,* 3/22/60.
355 "Here is where: WW to AM.
356 HUAC wanted Koenig's . . . up for renewal: Navasky, p. 148.
356 "If people saw: JuK to JH.
356 "My father was . . . of each other: JK to JH.

CHAPTER THIRTY-FOUR:
THE MAN YOU HATE TO LOVE

358 "You really want . . . about the gangster: WW to AM.
358 . . . was such a hot: *Louisville Courier Journal,* 10/2/55.
358 "Tracy liked it: WW to AM.
359 Hayes signed with: *New York Sunday News,* 10/16/55.
359 "I cannot imagine: Joseph Hayes wire to WW, 5/2/54.
359 "Without any desire: Joseph Hayes letter to WW, 5/29/54.
359 "The audience loved: Don Hartman memo to WW, 8/2/54.
360 . . . a sheaf of clippings: *New York Sunday News,* 10/16/55.

360 "typical midwestern setting: Joseph Hayes letter to WW, 5/24/54.
360 "pleasant and very . . . deepened and intensified: Production notes 30
361 "We had a: MS to JH.
362 "He wanted to: RoS to JH.
362 "He was afraid: RS to JH.
362 "If Erich von: *American Film*, 4/76.
362 "One time and . . . in the ass: MS to JH.
363 "Willy's hearing must: SM to JH.
363 "Show gets off: *Daily Variety*, 1/6/55.
363 "Hollywood producers may: *Weekly Variety*, 1/6/55.
364 "Pardon my understandable: WW letter, 8/25/55.
364 "This is a: *Boston Herald*, 9/19/55.
365 "Six this season: *Cue*, 10/6/55.

CHAPTER THIRTY-FIVE: PACIFIST'S DILEMMA

367 "Willy stopped me . . . a seamless whole: SM to JH.
367 "a major rewrite . . . old she is?: SM to JH.
368 "Somebody called from . . . strong man refraining: West, pp. 4, 7, 8, 25, 33, 89, 92–94.
372 "Everybody had an: RS to JH.
372 "excellent raw material: SM affidavit.
372 "covert action not: *American Film*, 4/76.
372 URGE YOU TO: WW wire to Vivien Leigh, 6/16/55.
372 DREADFULLY SORRY. QUITE: Vivien Leigh wire to WW, 6/22/55.
372 HOW I WOULD: Ingrid Bergman wire to WW, 8/1/55.
373 "Every woman between: SM to JH.
373 "What do you: West, p. 186.
373 "He had me: DM to JH.
373 "Jimmy and Willy: SM to JH.
373 "I was just: AP/DBWW.
374 "everybody was raving: SM to JH.
374 "In those days: AP/DBWW.
375 "was motivated very: SM to JH.
375 "Pull it down: West, p. 213.
376 "Willy just wasn't: RS to JH.
376 "Coop is a: *LA Times* (Hedda Hopper), 1960.
376 "like a nice: BB to JH.
377 "this disgraceful bullshit: WW to AM.
378 "We must have: RS to JH.
378 "it was a really: SM to JH.
378 "They didn't know: SM to JH.
379 "The film has: *NY Times*, 5/30/88.
379 "They needlessly lambasted: SM to JH.

CHAPTER THIRTY-SIX: BIG MUDDY

380 "The big difference: *Time*, 10/29/56.
381 "a one-shot experiment . . . always there: ibid.
381 "This thing didn't . . . at the time: GP to JH.
382 "I had a: GP to JH.

383 "How are you: WW to AM.
383 "I'll pass. There . . . I'll do it: CH to JH.
383 "Willy didn't want: RS to JH.
384 "Charlie Bickford was: CH to JH.
385 "Willy liked all: GP to JH.
385 "very, very cruel: JB to JH.
385 "very dodgy—the: *The Big Country*, Screen Classics, laser disc, p. 15.
385 "I thought Willy: GP to JH.
386 "We were shooting: BI to JH.
386 "very, very good: CH to JH.
386 "in Willy Wyler's: *The Big Country*, Screen Classics, laser disc, p. 17.
386 "I had to: CH to JH.
387 "Willy, you're not: CH to JH.
387 "She'd get nervous: BB to JH.
387 "I found Willy: BI to JH.
388 "What I had: GP to JH.
390 "I don't know: CH/DBWW.
391 "complete authority" over: WW letter, 4/16/58.
391 "we didn't have: RS to JH.
391 "after my departure: WW letter, 4/16/58.
391 "When Willy wanted: RS to JH.
392 "I can't begin: WW letter, 5/16/58.
392 "There were a: GP to JH.

CHAPTER THIRTY-SEVEN: BEN-HUR

393 "I felt this: WW/DBWW.
394 "the scorn of: *Action 8*, Sept./Oct. 1973.
394 "I thought he: WW to AM.
394 "Why don't you: WW to AM.
395 "Forget the chariot: WW to AM.
395 "Citron's trying to: Heston, p. 31.
395 "They did have: CW, *Ben-Hur: The Making of an Epic*, MGM–UA Home Video Entertainment, 1993; also CW to JH.
396 "I will never: Gore Vidal, *Making . . .*
396 "looking gray . . . does he unbuckle?": Vidal, pp. 143–44.
397 "Everybody got spoiled: WW to AM.
397 "The driver just: TW to JH.
398 Harper Brothers brought: MGM's *Facts About Ben-Hur.*
398 Wallace's book would: ibid.
399 "vengeance is sworn: Vidal, p. 144.
400 "My father used: CW, *Making . . .*; also CW to JH.
400 "If Willy didn't: Vidal, *Making . . .*; also Vidal p. 144.
400 "is a clever fellow: WW to AM.
400 "Obviously, I can't: CH to JH.
401 "whatever was good: CH to JH.
401 "the arena wasn't: *American Cinematographer*, 2/60.
402 "It was a fabulous: WW to AM.
402 "Willy called from: MS to JH.
403 "Everybody thinks we: TW to JH.
403 "Chuck, you have: CH/DBWW.
404 "I worked my: Heston, p. 51.
404 "Willy was a: CH to JH.

405 "That's not the: CH to JH.
405 "The wait cost: Heston, p. 54.
406 "It took an: WW to AM.
406 "They did all: *American Cinematographer*, 2/60.
406 The most astonishing: D'Antonio, p. 284.
407 He rescued himself: ibid. p. 285.
407 "Later Heston did: ibid. p. 286.
407 "Not today . . . loved the race: ibid. p. 312–313.
408 "He is not: WW to AM.
408 "Sam hadn't been: TW to JH.
408 "It was as: *LA Examiner*, 11/15/59.
409 A steady stream: *MGM's* The story of the making of Ben-Hur.
409 "These two poor: TW to JH.
409 "they wouldn't let: MS to JH.
410 "I spent sleepless: WW to CLH, *Cinema*, Vol. 3, No. 5, 1967.
410 "The last setup: Heston, p. 64.
410 "Well, Chuck: CH to JH.

CHAPTER THIRTY-EIGHT:
SECOND TIME AROUND

412 . . . Tunberg, "verbally agreed: WW to AM.
412 "wanted Fry to: Vidal on Turner documentary.
412 "I gather I collectively: CH letter to Writers Guild of America, 4/15/60.
412 "The artistic quality: *NY Times*, 11/19/59.
412 "If I were: CH to JH.
413 "I hope I: *Film Daily*, 3/16/60.
414 "Just thrilled: AHe letter to WW, 8/5/60.
414 "That's settled: LH letter to WW, 8/5/60.
414 "I can't see: ibid.
415 "the assignment was: Kay Brown letter to WW, 3/17/61.
415 could overcome Mirisch's nervousness: WW letter to LH, 2/1/61.
415 "I hope we: LH letter to WW, 2/22/61.
415 "I would carry: WW letter to LH, 3/7/61.
416 "mostly workable: LH letter to WW, dated end of 4/61.
417 "He chickened out: ShM to JH.
417 "Here are all: WW letter to LH, 12/29/61.
417 "If I was: *Newsweek*, 3/12/62.

CHAPTER THIRTY-NINE:
"THE TASTE OF STAMPS"

418 "He was very: BW/DBWW transcript.
419 "They said what: Madsen, p. 364.
419 "I was hard: WW/DBWW.
420 "Bob, he said: RS to JH.
420 "I knew it: WW to AM.
420 "It was just: TW to JH.
421 "You know," he: WW to AM.
421 "We had a: TW to JH.
421 "I found I: *Time*, 6/18/65.
422 "I hadn't gotten: TS to JH.
423 "This was the: Stamp, p. 110–11.
423 "Frankovich was quite: RS to JH.
423 "I got fired: SE/DBWW.

424 "Willy's coming down: SE/DBWW.
424 "Willy made a: RS to JH.
424 "All the guys: TS to JH.
424 "had all sorts: SE/DBWW.
425 "Surtees kept saying: TS to JH.
425 "A red chair: WW to AM.
426 "He followed his . . . "This guy turns . . . "Willy came up: TS to JH.
428 "When I ran: RS to JH.
428 "a pleasant surprise: John Fowles letter, 3/2/64.
428 "I enjoyed it: John Fowles letter, 2/15/65.
429 "the most erotic: *Village Voice*, 6/24/65.
429 "Well, in that: TS to JH.
429 "Max Ophuls had: WW to AM.
430 "The best directors: TS to JH.

CHAPTER FORTY:
FRENCH SCHEDULE

431 "My father was: MW to JH.
432 "Willy took that: TW to JH.
432 "It's a miserable: *Saturday Review*, 12/25/65.
433 "We may not: RS to JH.
433 They produced a: *Life*, 11/12/65.
434 "After I introduced: Dr. Jean Dax memo, 9/15/65.
435 "Within the hour: RS to JH.
435 "Willy told me: TW to JH.
435 "He thanked God: TW to JH.
435 "When they knew: Jules Buck to JH.
436 Resnais called Langlois: Roud, pp. xxiv–xxvi, 65.
437 "derivative: *Newsweek*, 7/25/66.
437 "wholly ingratiating: *NY Times*, 7/15/66.
437 "If every picture: RS to JH.

CHAPTER FORTY-ONE:
NO PUSHOVER

439 "There is a: Gitlin, p. 291.
440 "David and my: MW to JH.
442 "captured none of: *LA Herald-Examiner*, 10/6/68.
442 a "dry run: ibid.
442 "with a view: ibid.
442 "It was like: BS/DBWW.
442 "pushed him to: TW to JH.
443 "If Beethoven could: *LA Herald-Examiner*, 10/6/68.
443 "When I've completed: *Variety*, 3/31/67.
443 "I insisted that: WW/DBWW.
443 "It was the: BS/DBWW.
444 "I was very: BS/DBWW.
444 "I kept hearing: WW/DBWW.
444 "She was very: *Action*, April-May 1968.
444 "I would deny . . . uhm, pleasanter?: RS to JH.
445 Wyler caught sight: Riese, p. 259.
445 "Stark said he: Spada (2), p. 98.
445 "Barbra's villa served: Sharif, pp. 106–9.
445 "It was difficult: WW to AM.
445 "Not hiring an: Riese, p. 260.
446 OMAR KISSES BARBRA: WW to AM.
446 "How can I: RS to JH.

446 "Ray was always: TW to JH.
446 "That goddamned Ray: RS to JH.
446 "When it came: TW to JH.
446 "I thought, 'What: BS/DBWW.
446 "I know the: RS to JH.
447 "I figured out: BS/DBWW.
447 "Wyler was always: Spada (2), p. 96.
447 "Willy didn't like: RS to JH.

CHAPTER FORTY-TWO:
BLACK AND WHITE

448 WHILE SOME OF: D. Zanuck wire, 9/15/67.
448 I STILL BELIEVE: WW wire, 9/19/67.
449 "enthusiastic over the: Frank McCarthy memo, 2/1/67.
449 "I really didn't: TW to JH.
449 "I got on: RoS to JH.
449 "Willy thought he: RS to JH.
449 "Willy didn't need: TW to JH.
449 "My wife absolutely: WW to AM.
450 "the most provocative: *Show*, 3/70.
451 "Willy always felt: TW to JH.
451 "I see an opportunity: WW letter to Paramount, 12/31/48.
451 "It seemed a: WW to AM.
451 "Fonda was interested: TW to JH.
452 "The interesting thing: RS to JH.
452 "We only found: WW to AM.
452 "sadistic melodrama: *Saturday Review*, 3/28/70.
453 "There are no: *LA Times*, 3/15/70.
453 "If I had: WW to AM.

CHAPTER FORTY-THREE:
ROASTS AND TOASTS

454 "He was grief-stricken: TW to JH.
454 "My doctor tells...then and there: PK/DBWW transcript.
455 "He would send: RS to JH.
455 "Trying to hide: MW to JH.
455 "I was so looking..."I'm so glad: TW to JH.
456 "They were traveling fools: MW to JH.
456 ...Goldwyn held out: SB to JH; Berg, p. 496.

457 "because we're supposed: *Hollywood Reporter*, 3/11/76; also reported in newspapers around the country.
457 "damned stingy: ibid.
457 "Here we are: *Variety*, 3/17/76.
458 "the most versatile: ibid.
458 "an American film: ibid.
458 "in the nine months: *American Film*, 4/76.
458 "It's a case: *Variety*, 3/17/76; also reported in newspapers around the country.
458 "One more time...not even a joke: ibid.
458 "upset and disappointed: MW to JH.
459 "This was not: TW to JH.
459 ...he loved going...Bruce Lee: DW to JH.
459 "He went from: MW to JH.
460 "Willy never looked...pieces of film together: *LA Times*, 10/2/77.
460 "Belated congratulations...not among them: WW's personal files.
461 "Suddenly he got: TW to JH.
461 "Johnny, I don't...You have my word: JoH/DBWW.
462 "I don't know..."the whole catastrophe: TW to JH.

CHAPTER FORTY-FOUR:
"WHAT AN EXIT"

463 "He didn't like..."I told Sam..."maybe if he..."I knew my: CW to JH.
464 "We watched him...gray, drawn and tired: MW to JH.
464 "There was one...turned out to be lovely: TW to JH.
465 Construction workers...a cab uptown: SB to JH.
465 "I will deal..."Willy will be out...: TW to JH.
466 "You would never: AS to JH.
466 "Willy walked in..."Don't be too..."What a great exit: TW to JH.
467 "This entire town: RMcD to JH.
467 "She caused a: SB to JH.
467 "She told me: CW to JH.
467 "Here we are: Stine (1), p. 215.
467 "Talent," he said...Not Mr. Wyler—Willy.": Philip Dunne eulogy.

BIBLIOGRAPHY

AFIC (*American Film Institute Catalog of Motion Pictures Produced in the United States*). R. R. Bowker. New York. 1988.

Anderegg, Michael A. *William Wyler.* Twayne's Theatrical Arts Series. Twayne Publishers. Boston. 1979.

Anger, Kenneth. *Hollywood Babylon.* Dell Publishing Co., Inc. New York. 1975.

Arce, Hector. *Gary Cooper.* William Morrow and Company, Inc. New York. 1979.

Astor, Mary. *A Life in Film.* Delacorte Press. New York. 1967.

Atkinson, Brooks, and Hirschfeld, Al. *The Lively Years 1920–1973.* Da Capo Paperback. New York. 1985.

Bacall, Lauren. *By Myself.* Ballantine Books. New York. 1980.

Berg, A. Scott. *Goldwyn.* Alfred A. Knopf. New York. 1989.

Bergman, Ingrid, and Burgess, Alan. *Ingrid Bergman.* Delacorte Press, New York. 1980.

Brownlow, Kevin. *The Parade's Gone By . . .* Alfred A. Knopf. New York. 1969.

Baxter, John. *Sixty Years of Hollywood.* A. S. Barnes and Co. New York. 1973.

Bosworth, Patricia. *Montgomery Clift.* Harcourt Brace Jovanovich. New York. 1978.

Bulletin de la société industrielle de Mulhouse, numéro special, 1975.

Capra, Frank. *The Name Above the Title.* Vintage Books. New York. 1985.

Caron, Vicki. *Between France and Germany: The Jews of Alsace-Lorraine 1871–1918.* Stanford University Press. Stanford, CA. 1988.

Clough, Valerie. *Sir Ralph Richardson.* Churchman Publishing. Sussex, Great Britain. 1989.

Cogley, John. *Report on Blacklisting.* Arno Press and *New York Times.* New York. 1972.

Copland, Aaron and Perlis, Vivian. *Copland Since 1943.* St. Martin's Press. New York. 1989.

Cottrell, John. *Laurence Olivier.* Prentice-Hall, Inc. Englewood Cliffs, NJ. 1975.

Curtis, James. *Between Flops.* Harcourt Brace Jovanovich. New York. 1982.

Curtiss, Thomas Quinn. *Von Stroheim.* Farrar, Straus and Giroux. New York. 1971.

D'Antonio, Joanne. *Andrew Marton.* The Scarecrow Press. Metuchen, NJ, and London. 1991.

Davis, Bette. *The Lonely Life.* G. P. Putnam's Sons. New York. 1962.

De Mille, Cecil B. *The Autobiography of Cecil B. De Mille.* Prentice-Hall, Inc. Englewood Cliffs, NJ. 1959.

Dick, Bernard F. *The Star-Spangled Screen.* University Press of Kentucky. Lexington, KY. 1985.

Douglas, Kirk. *The Ragman's Son.* Pocket Books. New York. 1988.

Drinkwater, John. *The Life and Adventures of Carl Laemmle.* G. P. Putnam's Sons. New York. 1931.

Duerksen, Menno. *The Memphis Belle.* Castle Books, Inc. Memphis, TN. 1987.

Dunne, Philip. *Take Two.* McGraw-Hill Book Co. New York. 1980.

Durahm, Lowell. *Abravanel!* University of Utah Press. Salt Lake City, UT. 1989.

Edmonds, Andy. *Frame-Up!* William Morrow and Co. New York. 1991.

Edmonds, I. G. *Big U: Universal in the Silent Days.* A. S. Barnes and Co. London. 1977.

Ellis, Edward Robb. *The Epic of New York City.* Coward-McCann. New York. 1966.

Everson, William K. *American Silent Film.* Oxford University Press. New York. 1978.

The First 100 Years: 1850–1950. The City of Los Angeles Yearbook, 1949.

Fenin, George N. and Everson, William K. *The Western.* Grossman Publishers. New York. 1973.

Finler, Joel W. *The Hollywood Story.* Crown Publishers, Inc. New York. 1988.

Florey, Robert. (1) *Deux ans dans les studios américains.* Editions d'Aujourd'hui. Paris. 1984. (Reprint of 1926 edition.)

———. (2) *Filmland — Los Angeles et Hollywood, les capitales du cinéma.* Editions de Cinémagazine. Paris. 1923.

Gabler, Neal. *An Empire of Their Own: How the Jews Invented Hollywood.* Crown Publishers. New York. 1988.

Gardner, Gerald. *The Censorship Papers.* Dodd, Mead and Company. New York. 1987.

Garfield, Brian. *Western Films.* Rawson Associates. New York. 1982.

Gitlin, Todd. *The Sixties.* Bantam Books. New York. 1987.

Goldstein, Malcolm. *George S. Kaufman.* Oxford University Press. New York. 1979.

Goodman, Walter. *The Committee.* Farrar, Straus and Giroux. New York. 1968.

Grobel, Lawrence. *The Hustons.* Charles Scribner's Sons. New York. 1989.

Hayward, Brooke. *Haywire.* Bantam Books, New York, 1978.

Hellman, Lillian. (1) *An Unfinished Woman.* Little, Brown and Co. Boston. 1969.

———. (2) *Pentimento.* Little, Brown and Co. Boston. 1973.

———. (3) *Scoundrel Time.* Little, Brown and Co. Boston. 1976.

Henstell, Bruce. *Sunshine and Wealth: Los Angeles in the Twenties and Thirties.* Chronicle Books. San Francisco. 1984.

Heston, Charlton. *The Actor's Life.* E. P. Dutton. New York. 1978.

Higham, Charles. *Bette.* Macmillan Publishing Co., Inc. New York. 1981.

Hirschhorn, Clive. *The Universal Story.* Crown Publishers. New York. 1983.

Hitt, Jim. *The American West from Fiction into Film.* McFarland and Company, Inc. Jefferson, NC. 1990.

Holden, Anthony. *Laurence Olivier.* Atheneum. New York. 1988.

Kael, Pauline. *5001 Nights at the Movies.* Holt, Rinehart and Winston. New York. 1984.

Kahn, Gordon. *Hollywood on Trial.* Boni and Gaer. New York. 1948.

Kanin, Garson. *Hollywood.* Limelight Editions. New York. 1984.

Katchmer, George. *Eighty Silent Film Stars.* McFarland and Co. Jefferson, NC. 1991.

Katz, Ephraim. *The Film Encyclopedia.* Harper and Row. New York. 1979.

Kern, Sharon. *William Wyler: A Guide to References and Resources.* G. K. Hall and Co. Boston. 1984.

Kitchen, Martin. *The German Officer Corps 1890–1914.* Clarendon Press. Oxford. 1968.

Knight, Arthur. *The Liveliest Art.* Macmillan Co. New York. 1957.

Kobal, John. *Hollywood: The Years of Innocence.* Thames and Hudson. London. 1985.

Koch, Howard. *As Time Goes By.* Harcourt Brace Jovanovich. New York. 1979.

Kohner, Fred. *The Magician of Sunset Boulevard.* Morgan Press. Palos Verdes, CA. 1977.

Koszarski, Richard. (1) *An Evening's Entertainment: The Age of the Silent Feature Picture 1915–1928.* Charles Scribner's Sons. New York. 1990.

———. (2) *The Man You Loved to Hate: Erich Von Stroheim and Hollywood.* Oxford University Press. Oxford. 1983.

La Guardia, Robert. *Monty.* Arbor House. New York. 1977.

Levine, Lawrence W., and Middlekauff, Robert, eds. *The National Temper: Readings in American Culture and Society.* Harcourt Brace Jovanovich. New York. 1972.

Longstreet, Stephen. *City on Two Rivers.* Hawthorn Books. New York. 1975.

Look, editors of. *Movie Lot to Beachhead.* Doubleday, Doran and Co., Inc. Garden City, NY. 1945.

Madsen, Axel. *William Wyler.* Thomas Y. Crowell Co. New York. 1973.

MacCann, Richard Dyer. *The First Tycoons.* Scarecrow Press. Metuchen, NJ. 1987.

Marx, Arthur. *Goldwyn.* W. W. Norton and Co., Inc. New York. 1976.

Mast, Gerald, ed. *The Movies in Our Midst.* University of Chicago Press. Chicago. 1982.

McBride, Joseph. *Frank Capra.* Simon and Schuster. New York. 1992.

McWilliams, Carey. *The Education of Carey McWilliams.* Simon and Schuster. New York. 1978.

Meyer, William R. *The Making of the Great Westerns.*

Arlington House Publishers. New Rochelle, NY. 1979.

Miller, Patsy Ruth. *My Hollywood.* O'Raghailligh Ltd., 1988.

Mosley, Leonard. *Zanuck.* Little, Brown and Co. Boston. 1984.

Nadeau, Remi. *Los Angeles: From Mission to Modern City.* Longmans, Green and Co. New York. 1960.

Navasky, Victor S. *Naming Names.* Viking Press. New York. 1980.

Niven, David. *The Moon's a Balloon.* G. P. Putnam's Sons. New York. 1972.

Olivier, Laurence. *On Acting.* Weidenfeld and Nicolson. London. 1986.

Parish, James Robert and Pitts, Michael. *The Great Western Pictures.* Scarecrow Press. Metuchen, NJ. 1976.

Parton, James. *Air Force Spoken Here.* Adler and Adler. Bethesda, MD. 1986.

Quirk, Lawrence J. (1) *Child of Fate.* St. Martin's Press. New York. 1986.

———. (2) *Fasten Your Seat Belts.* William Morrow and Co., Inc. New York. 1990.

Ramsaye, Terry. *A Million and One Nights.* Frank Cass and Co., Ltd. London. 1926.

Revon, Michael. *Hollywood's Wartime Women.* U.M.I. Research Press. Ann Arbor, MI. 1988.

Riese, Randall. *Her Name Is Barbra.* Birch Lane Press. New York. 1993.

Riley, Philip J. *The Hunchback of Notre Dame.* Magic Image Filmbooks. Atlantic City, NJ. 1988.

Robinson, David. (1) *World Cinema: A Short History.* Eyre Methuen, Ltd. London. 1973.

———. (2) *Hollywood in the Twenties.* Paperback Library. New York. 1970.

Rollyson, Carl. *Lillian Hellman.* St. Martin's Press. New York. 1988.

Roud, Richard. *A Passion for Films: Henri Langlois and the Cinémathèque Francaise.* Viking Press. New York. 1983.

Russell, Harold. *The Best Years of My Life.* Paul S. Eriksson. Middlebury, VT. 1981.

Sarris, Andrew. (1) *Confessions of a Cultist.* Simon and Schuster. New York. 1970.

———. (2) *The American Cinema.* Octagon Books. New York. 1982.

Schatz, Thomas. *The Genius of the System.* Pantheon Books. New York. 1988.

Sharif, Omar. *l'Éternel Masculin.* Editions Stock. 1976.

Shipman, David. *The Story of Cinema.* St. Martin's Press. New York. 1982.

Silverman, Dan P. *Reluctant Union.* Pennsylvania State University Press. University Park, PA, and London. 1972.

Snyder, Louis L. *The Dreyfus Case: A Documentary History.* Rutgers University Press. New Brunswick, NJ. 1973.

Spada, James. (1) *More Than A Woman.* Bantam Books. New York. 1993.

———. (2) *Streisand.* Doubleday and Co., Inc. Garden City, NY. 1981.

Stamp, Terence. *Double Feature.* Bloomsbury. London. 1989.

Stine, Whitney. (1) *I'd Love to Kiss You.* Pocket Books. New York. 1990.

———. (2) *Mother Goddam.* Hawthorne Books, Inc. New York. 1974.

Taves, Brian. *Robert Florey: The French Expressionist.* Scarecrow Press. Metuchen, NJ. 1987.

Thomas, Bob. *Thalberg: Life and Legend.* Doubleday and Co. Garden City, NY. 1969.

Thomson, David. *Showman.* Alfred A. Knopf. New York. 1992.

Tuchman, Barbara. *The Guns of August.* Macmillan Co. New York. 1962.

Wallis, Hal. *Starmaker.* Macmillan Co., Inc. New York. 1980.

West, Jessamyn. *To See the Dream.* Harcourt Brace and Co. New York. 1957.

Wiley, Mason, and Bona, Damien. *Inside Oscar.* Ballantine Books. New York. 1986.

WPA (Works Progress Administration, U.S.). *Los Angeles: A Guide to the City and Its Environs.* Compiled by workers of the Writers' Program of the Works Projects Administration in Southern California. American Guide Series. Hastings House. New York. 1941.

Wray, Fay. *On the Other Hand.* St. Martin's Press. New York. 1989.

INDEX

ACKNOWLEDGMENTS

I could not have begun this book without the generosity of the Wyler family or completed it without the bounty of Janet Leong Herman, my wife, who was instrumental in every aspect of its creation and who is my closest, warmest, and wisest friend.

To Talli Wyler I owe an immense debt for consenting to many hours of interviews at Summit Drive and speaking about her husband with what I believe to have been complete frankness. She also gave me access to his private, previously unavailable papers, which were an indispensable source for this book.

To the Wyler children—Catherine, Judy, Melanie, and David—I am deeply grateful for their unfailing kindness and hospitality. With enthusiasm and restraint, practical assistance and patience, they offered the same kind of support their mother had offered before she died, so unexpectedly, in 1991. It was David Wyler who discovered a filing cabinet of his father's papers that had gone unopened for fifty years. I should make clear, however, that the family did not have approval of the manuscript and is not responsible for what I have written. Any errors are my own.

I am especially indebted to Catherine Wyler. I can still remember her fielding my tactless questions in our first meeting on the veranda of a Sunset Boulevard restaurant. She was not only gracious but unflappable and made this project possible in myriad ways. Among other forms of assistance, she offered me unedited, unpublished transcripts of interviews with various people who knew or worked with her father. Small excerpts from a handful of these interviews, filmed between 1981 and 1985, were part of a documentary she produced, *Directed by William Wyler*, for the "American Masters" series on PBS. For the use of those transcripts, I am grateful to her and to Barbra Streisand, Billy Wilder, John Huston, Bette Davis, Audrey Hepburn, Lillian Hellman, Ralph Richardson, Charlton Heston, Gregory Peck, Terence Stamp, Greer Garson, Tony Perkins, Samantha Eggar, Paul Kohner, and Steven Spielberg.

Between 1989 and 1995, I interviewed many of William Wyler's friends, associates, and relatives, who offered insights I could not have obtained otherwise. They not only gave me a vivid sense of Wyler's personality but helped put the thousands of documents I examined into a useful context. Chief among them were his longtime film editor, Bob Swink, whose generosity was unending; the author and screenwriter Philip Dunne; the director and author Robert Parrish, and Wyler's script girl–cum–personal assistant of many years, Freda Rosenblatt Lerch.

Others who consented to interviews and shared their impressions of Wyler with me were Charlton Heston, Gregory Peck, Terence Stamp, Ruth Goetz, Lupita Kohner, Teresa Wright, Sylvia Sidney, John Sturges, Burl Ives, Eddie Albert, Howard Koch, Harold Russell, Stuart Millar, Huntz Hall, Vincent Sherman, Dora Picard, Armand Wyler, Bruno Traveletti, Arthur Hurni, Maurice Abravanel, Blanche Marso, and Walter Laemmle. I owe each of them thanks.

Also deepening my perception of Wyler were Fay Wray, Rod Steiger, Shirley MacLaine, Fred Zinnemann, Dorothy McGuire, Roddy McDowall, Peter Viertel, Amanda Dunne, Jules Buck, James Parton, Tex McCrary, Peter Mark Richman, Ian McLellan Hunter, Robert Belcher, Kathleen Parrish, Poumy Moreuil, Ena

Gregory, Robert Morgan, Robert Hanson, Clarence Winchell, Charles Leighton, Casimer Nastal, Joseph Josephson, William Clothier, Steve Banks, Aviva Slesin, and A. Scott Berg. I am grateful to each of them.

I wish to acknowledge a singular debt to Axel Madsen. He was kind enough to give me the transcripts of the interviews he did with Wyler largely between May and December of 1972 for his biography, *William Wyler*. Because his subject had a hand in the creation of that book, Madsen had to leave certain aspects of Wyler's life unexplored. I have disregarded that sense of delicacy and, with Madsen's blessings, quote from all portions of the original interviews.

I wish to thank Irv Letofsky, who suggested me for this book in the first place; Alice Martell, my literary agent, who hatched the idea, nurtured it, and kept the faith; Neil Nyren, my publisher at Putnam, who took the chance and gave me the title; David Highfill, my editor, and his assistant, Lorraine Martindale, who shepherded the manuscript into print; Julie Duquet, whoever you are, for the book design; and Tony Lioce, the keeper of the light at the *Los Angeles Times*.

For sustenance of all kinds I am grateful to Jean Adelsman, Carl Weissner, Steve and Helene Deutch, Genevieve Dishotsky, Jess Bravin, Henry Kisor, Allan Jalon, John A. Gallagher, Gisela Freisinger, Pierre-Louis Cereja, Carole Hollrigel, Jeffrey Glass, Olivia Herman, Janice Page, Marisa Archer, Jonathan Bliss, Gary Ambrose, Irv and Sylvia Glasser, Viviane and Ellis Wayne, Pat Broeske, Mike Spencer, and for reading the unedited manuscript, Cecilia Fannon.

In the course of my research, I also received assistance from archivists, curators, and librarians whom I would like to thank: Linda Mehr, Margaret Herrick Library, Academy of Motion Picture Arts and Sciences, Los Angeles; Brigitte J. Kueppers, University of California, Los Angeles, Theater Arts Library, William Wyler Collection; Ned Comstock, University of Southern California Cinema-Television Library and Archives of Performing Arts, Universal Collection; Leith Adams, Warner Bros. Archive, School of Cinema-Television Library, USC; Kay Bost, curator of manuscripts, DeGolyer Library, Southern Methodist University, Dallas; Brian Taves, Library of Congress, Washington, D.C.; Howard Gotlieb, curator, Special Collections, Boston University; Paul Gray, assistant director, Military Personnel Records, National Personnel Center, St. Louis; the staff of the Federal Bureau of Investigation, Freedom of Information–Privacy Acts Section, Records Management Division, Washington, D.C.; Chris Karpiak, New York State Archives, Cultural Education Center, New York State Education Department, Albany; Harold L. Miller, Wisconsin Center for Film and Theater Research, State Historical Society of Wisconsin, Madison; Adele Field, Oral Histories editor, Directors Guild of America, Special Projects, Los Angeles.

Also, Jean-Claude Genoud, Musée Historique de Lausanne; Gilbert Coutaz, Archives de la Ville de Lausanne; and the staffs at Archives du Département du Haut-Rhin, Affaires Démographique Etat Civil, Ville de Mulhouse; Archives Département du Haut-Rhin, Commune de Mulhouse; Centre d'accueil et de recherches des Archives nationales, Paris; Archives anciennes du Conservatoire national supérieur de musique et de danse de Paris; Collections de l'Association du Vieux-Lausanne; Schweizerissche Eidgenssenschaft, Kanton Aargau, Switzerland.